W9-AVI-333

HARCOURT SCHOOL PUBLISHERS
STORYtown

Blast Off!

TEACHER EDITION

Senior Authors
Isabel L. Beck • Roger C. Farr • Dorothy S. Strickland

Authors
Alma Flor Ada • Roxanne F. Hudson • Margaret G. McKeown
Robin C. Scarcella • Julie A. Washington

Consultants
F. Isabel Campoy • Tyrone C. Howard • David A. Monti

Harcourt
SCHOOL PUBLISHERS

www.harcourtschool.com

4

ISBN 10 0-15-372128-6
ISBN 13 978-0-15-372128-1

1 2 3 4 5 6 7 8 9 10   030   17 16 15 14 13 12 11 10 09 08

Program Authors

SENIOR AUTHORS

Isabel L. Beck
Professor of Education and Senior Scientist at the Learning Research and Development Center, *University of Pittsburgh*

RESEARCH CONTRIBUTIONS:
Reading Comprehension, Vocabulary, Beginning Reading, Phonics

Roger C. Farr
Chancellor's Professor Emeritus of Education and Former Director for the Center for Innovation in Assessment, *Indiana University, Bloomington*

RESEARCH CONTRIBUTIONS:
Instructional Assessment, Reading Strategies, Reading in the Content Areas

Dorothy S. Strickland
Samuel DeWitt Proctor Professor of Education and The State of New Jersey Professor of Reading, *Rutgers University, The State University of New Jersey*

RESEARCH CONTRIBUTIONS:
Early Literacy, Elementary Reading/ Language Arts, Writing, Intervention

AUTHORS

Alma Flor Ada
Professor Emerita, *University of San Francisco*

RESEARCH CONTRIBUTIONS:
Literacy, Biliteracy, Multicultural Children's Literature, Home-School Interaction, First and Second Language Acquisition

Roxanne F. Hudson
Assistant Professor, Area of Special Education *University of Washington*

RESEARCH CONTRIBUTIONS:
Reading Fluency, Learning Disabilities, Interventions

Margaret G. McKeown
Senior Scientist at the Learning Research and Development Center, *University of Pittsburgh*

RESEARCH CONTRIBUTIONS:
Vocabulary, Reading Comprehension

Robin C. Scarcella
Professor, Director of Academic English and ESL, *University of California, Irvine*

RESEARCH CONTRIBUTIONS:
English as a Second Language

Julie A. Washington
Professor, College of Letters and Sciences, *University of Wisconsin*

RESEARCH CONTRIBUTIONS:
Understanding of Cultural Dialect with an emphasis on Language Assessment, Specific Language Impairment and Academic Performance; Early Childhood Language and Early Literacy of African American Children

CONSULTANTS

F. Isabel Campoy
President, Transformative Educational Services

RESEARCH CONTRIBUTIONS:
English as a Second Language, Applied Linguistics, Writing in the Curriculum, Family Involvement

Tyrone C. Howard
Associate Professor Urban Schooling, *University of California, Los Angeles*

RESEARCH CONTRIBUTIONS:
Multicultural Education, The Social and Political Context of Schools, Urban Education

David A. Monti
Professor Emeritus Department of Reading and Language Arts, *Central Connecticut State University*

RESEARCH CONTRIBUTIONS:
Reading Comprehension, Alternative Assessments, Flexible Grouping

Theme 4: Dream Big

Lesson 16   T16

Mr. Putter and Tabby Write the Book T46

by Cynthia Rylant • illustrated by Arthur Howard • REALISTIC FICTION

Paired Selections

Interview with Author Loreen Leedy T71

INTERVIEW

Connections T72

Theme Writing   **Reading-Writing Connection** T104

Student Writing Model: Story

Lesson 17   T116

SOCIAL STUDIES

Annie's Gifts T146

by Angela Shelf Medearis • illustrated by Anna Rich •
REALISTIC FICTION

Paired Selections

Sarah Enters a Painting T174

by Susan Katz • illustrated by R. W. Alley • POETRY

ART

Connections T176

Additional Resources

Data-Driven Instruction

① ASSESS

Use assessments to track student progress.

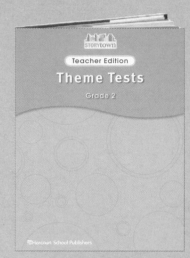

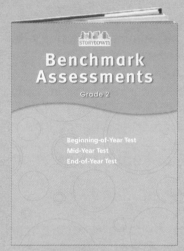

▲ Weekly Lesson Tests (grades 1–6)

▲ Theme Tests

▲ Benchmark Assessments
- Beginning-of-Year
- Mid-Year
- End-of-Year

 Online Assessment, *StoryTown*

② TEACH

Provide instruction in key areas of reading.

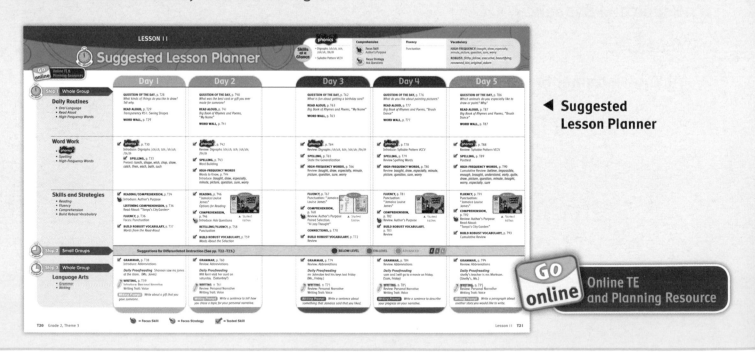

◀ Suggested Lesson Planner

Online TE and Planning Resource

③ DIFFERENTIATE INSTRUCTION

Use daily Monitor Progress notes to inform instruction.

✓ MONITOR PROGRESS

Partner Reading

IF students need more support in fluency-building and in using appropriate pace,	THEN have them echo-read with you, paying close attention to punctuation marks to direct their pace.

Small-Group Instruction, p. S105:

- ● BELOW-LEVEL: Reteach
- ● ON-LEVEL: Reinforce
- ● ADVANCED: Extend

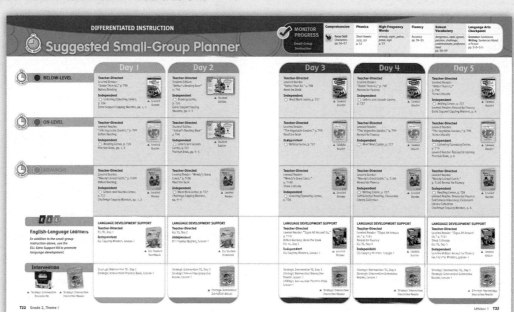

▲ **Suggested Small-Group Planner**

④ ASSESS, REMEDIATE, AND EXTEND

Use assessment results to remediate instruction.

INTENSIVE INTERVENTION PROGRAM

▲ **Strategic Intervention Resource Kit**

▲ **Challenge Resource Kit**

▲ **Intervention Station, Primary**

- • Phonemic Awareness
- • Phonics
- • Comprehension
- • Vocabulary
- • Fluency

Overview of a Theme

FIRST FOUR LESSONS

- **Explicit Systematic Instruction**

- **Spiraled Review of Key Skills**

- **Abundant Practice and Application**

- **Point-of-Use Progress-Monitoring**

- **Support for *Leveled Readers***

- **Digital Support for Teachers and Students**

FIFTH LESSON THEME REVIEW

- **Review Skills and Strategies**

- **Build and Review Vocabulary**

- **Celebrate with Readers' Theater**

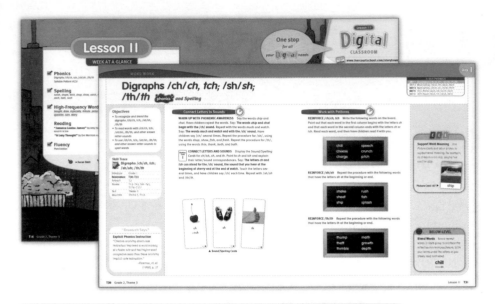

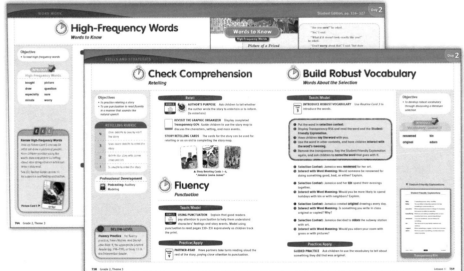

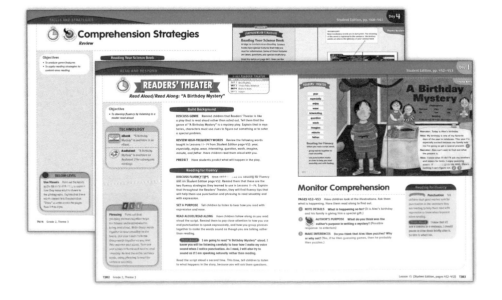

READING-WRITING CONNECTION

- **Reading-Writing Connection in *Student Edition***

- **Instruction in *Teacher Edition***

- **Focus on the Six Traits of Good Writing:**
  - Organization
  - Ideas
  - Sentence Fluency
  - Word Choice
  - Voice
  - Conventions

- **Develop a Variety of Writing Strategies**

- **Develop One Major Form Through the Writing Process:**
  - Personal Narrative
  - Respond to a Story
  - Friendly Letter
  - Story
  - Description
  - Research Report

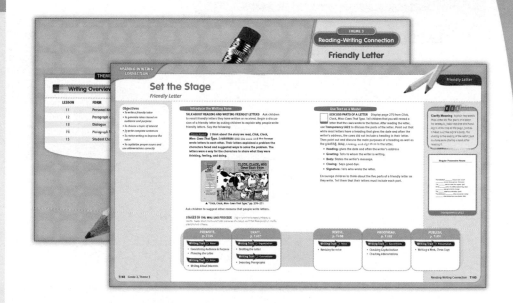

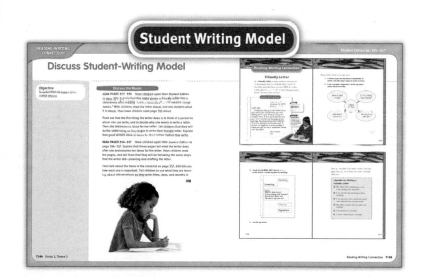

Overview of a Lesson

- **Lesson Resources**

- **Suggested Lesson Planner**

- **Suggested Small-Group Planner**

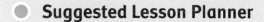

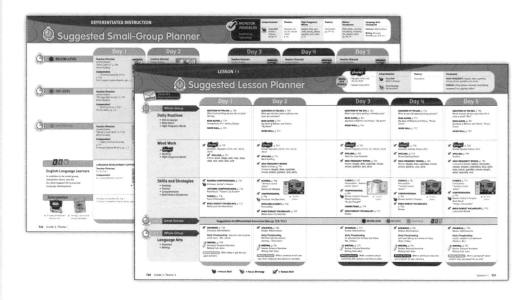

- *Leveled Readers* and **Leveled Practice**

ROUTINES

- Oral Language

- Read Aloud

- Word Wall

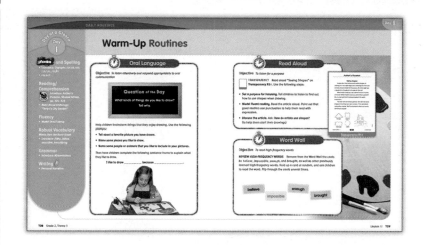

PHONICS/SPELLING

- Connect Letter and Sound

- Word Building

- Work with Patterns

- Spelling Pretest and Posttest

- Introduce and Review Structural Elements

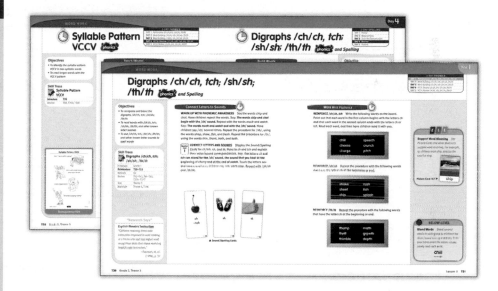

Overview of a Lesson (continued)

READING

- **Main Selections**

- **Paired Selections**

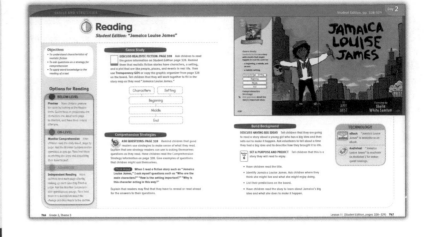

FLUENCY

- **Explicit Instruction in Rate, Accuracy, and Prosody**

- **Repeated Readings**

- **Readers' Theater**

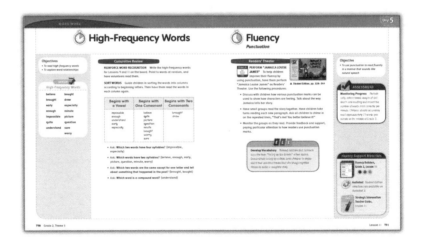

COMPREHENSION

- **Focus Skills**

- **Focus Strategies**

- **Listening Comprehension**

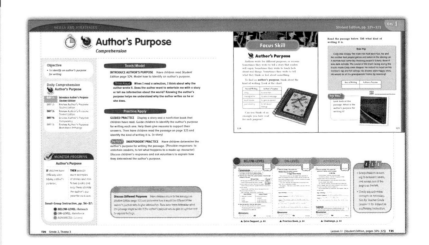

ROBUST VOCABULARY

- **Robust Vocabulary**
  - Tier Two Words

- **Instructional Routines**

- **Student-Friendly Explanations**

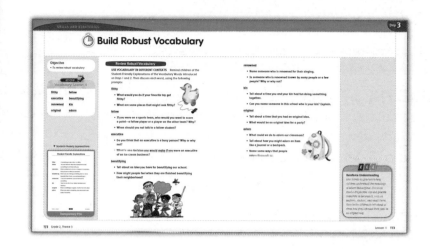

LANGUAGE ARTS

- **Grammar**

- **Writing**

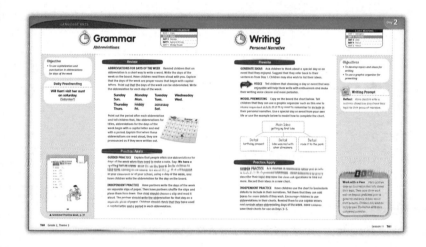

LEVELED READERS

- **Reinforce Skills and Strategies**

- **Review Vocabulary**

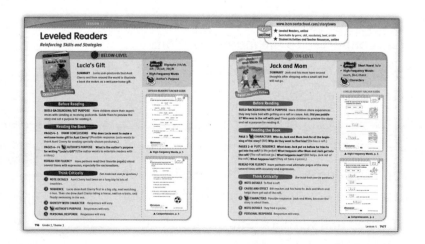

Introducing the Book

Discuss the Book's Organization

EXAMINE THE *STUDENT EDITION* Have children turn to each of the following features in the *Student Edition*. Briefly discuss how each part helps readers use the book and understand the stories.

- **Contents** Shows titles, authors, and page numbers.

- **Comprehension Strategies** Describes tools readers can use to read well.

- **Theme Overview** Lists literature, skills, and strategies in that theme.

- **Lesson Overview** Lists literature, focus skill, and focus strategy in that lesson.

- **Focus/Phonics Skill** Provides instruction in skills related to the literature.

- **Words to Know/Vocabulary** Introduces new high-frequency words or robust vocabulary words from the selection.

- **Genre Study** Describes the characteristic of the selection's genre.

- **Focus Strategy** Tells how to use strategies during reading.

- **Paired Selection** Presents poetry and other selections connected to the main selection.

- **Connections** Provides questions and activities related to both selections.

- **Reading-Writing Connection** Connects the literature to a good model of student writing.

- **Glossary** Provides student-friendly explanations for robust vocabulary words from each selection.

- **Index of Titles and Authors** Shows titles and authors in alphabetical order.

Introduce Strategies

USING *STUDENT EDITION* PAGES 10–13 Have children open their *Student Editions* to page 10, and explain to them that these pages will help them think about ways to better understand what they read. Tell them that these ways are called "strategies," and that they can use strategies before they read, while they read, and after they read.

BEFORE YOU READ Tell children that before they read, they can think about what they already know about a topic to help them understand. They can also set a purpose for reading.

> **Think Aloud** If I was going to read a book about dogs, I could think about what I already know about dogs. I could also think about why I'm reading. These would help me understand the book better.

WHILE YOU READ Model strategies children can use while they read as follows:

> **Think Aloud** Asking questions about what I'm reading helps me know if I'm understanding it. If I'm not understanding, I can go back and reread parts of the book. When I answer questions about a book, I can be sure that I understood it.

AFTER YOU READ Explain how retelling and making connections can help children understand what they read. Say:

> **Think Aloud** After I read something, I tell myself what I just read. This helps me remember and understand. I also think about other things I have read, heard, or learned. Sometimes I can make connections between two different books.

Comprehension Strategies

Before You Read

Think about what you
already know.
Look over the words and pictures
before you read.

Set a purpose.
Decide why you are reading.

I want to enjoy reading a story.

10

While You Read

Use story structure.
Think about a story's characters, setting, and plot.

Use graphic organizers.
Use a story map, web, or chart to help you read.

Monitor your reading.
Use fix-up strategies such as reading ahead or rereading.

11

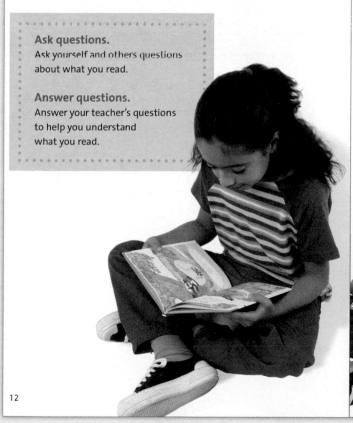

Ask questions.
Ask yourself and others questions about what you read.

Answer questions.
Answer your teacher's questions to help you understand what you read.

12

After You Read

Summarize.
Think about the main ideas of what you read.

Make connections.
Think about how what you read is like something else.

13

Dream Big

Theme Resources

 Go online eBook STUDENT EDITION

STUDENT EDITION LITERATURE

Lesson 16

PAIRED SELECTIONS

"Mr. Putter and Tabby Write the Book," pp. 22–43
REALISTIC FICTION

"Interview with Author Loreen Leedy,"
pp. 44–45
INTERVIEW

Lesson 19

PAIRED SELECTIONS

"The Life of George Washington Carver,"
pp. 122–135
BIOGRAPHY

"Nutty Facts About Peanuts," pp. 136–137
MAGAZINE ARTICLE

Lesson 17

PAIRED SELECTIONS

"Annie's Gifts,"
pp. 58–87
REALISTIC FICTION

"Sarah Enters a Painting,"pp. 88–89
POETRY

Lesson 20   Theme Review

READERS' THEATER

"What's My Job?,"
pp. 142–153
GAME SHOW

Lesson 18

PAIRED SELECTIONS

"Ah, Music!,"
pp. 98–111
NONFICTION

"Come, My Little Children, Here are Songs for You,"
pp. 112–113
POETRY

COMPREHENSION STRATEGIES

"North America,"
pp. 154–157
SOCIAL STUDIES TEXTBOOK

 Literature selections are available on Audiotext Grade 2, CD 4.

THEME 4 CLASSROOM LIBRARY

For Self-Selected Reading

▲ **The Dot,** *by Peter H. Reynolds*

One little dot marks the beginning of Vashti's journey of surprise and self-discovery.

▲ **Billy's Bucket,** *by Kes Gray*

Despite his parents' protest, Billy wants nothing for his birthday but a very special bucket and all goes well until the bucket is borrowed without permission.

▲ **Classroom Library Books Teacher Guide**

ADDITIONAL RESOURCES

▲ **Writer's Companion**

▲ **Grammar Practice Book**

▲ **Spelling Practice Book**

▲ **Literacy Center Kit**

▲ **Reading Transparencies**

▲ **Language Arts Transparencies**

▲ **Fluency Builders**

▲ **Picture Card Collection**

PROFESSIONAL DEVELOPMENT

• **Professional Development Book**

• 📱 **Videos for Podcasting**

Leveled Resources

BELOW-LEVEL

- phonics
- Vocabulary
- Focus Skills

ON-LEVEL

- phonics
- Vocabulary
-  Focus Skills

ADVANCED

- phonics
- Vocabulary
- Focus Skills

E L L

- Build Background
- Concept Vocabulary
- Scaffolded Language Development

Teaching suggestions for the Leveled Readers can be found on pp. T100–T103, T202–T205, T286–T289, T368–T371, T442–T445

Leveled Readers System

■ **Leveled Readers**

■ **Leveled Readers CD**

■ **Leveled Readers Teacher Guides**
- Vocabulary
- Comprehension
- Oral Reading Fluency Assessment

■ **Response Activities**

■ **Leveled Readers Assessment**

TECHNOLOGY

 GO online www.harcourtschool.com/storytown

✔ **Leveled Readers Online Database** *Searchable by Genre, Skill, Vocabulary, Level, or Title*

✔ **Student Activities and Teacher Resources,** *online*

Strategic Intervention Resource Kit,
Lessons 16–20

Strategic Intervention Interactive Reader: *Balancing Act*

- "The Art Hound"
- "The Band"
- "Keep the Beat"
- "His Land Is Our Land"
- "What Am I?"

Also available:

- Strategic Intervention Teacher Guide
- Strategic Intervention Practice Book
- Audiotext CD
- Skill Cards
- Teacher Resource Book
- Strategic Intervention Assessment Book

 Strategic Intervention Interactive Reader eBook

ELL Extra Support Kit,
Lessons 16–20

- ELL Student Handbook
- ELL Teacher Guide
- ELL Copying Masters

Challenge Resource Kit,
Theme 4

- Challenge Book Packs
- Challenge Teacher Guide
- Challenge Student Activities

Leveled Practice

- ⬤ **BELOW-LEVEL**
  Extra Support Copying Masters

- ⬤ **ON-LEVEL**
  Practice Book

- ⬤ **ADVANCED**
  Challenge Copying Masters

INTENSIVE INTERVENTION PROGRAM

Intervention Station, Primary

GRADES K–3 Sets of intervention material providing targeted instruction in:

- Phonemic Awareness
- Phonics
- Comprehension
- Vocabulary
- Fluency

Digital Classroom

to go along with your Print Program

 www.harcourtschool.com/storytown

FOR THE TEACHER

Prepare

GO online Professional Development

in the Online TE

PROFESSIONAL DEVELOPMENT

📱 Videos for Podcasting

Plan & Organize

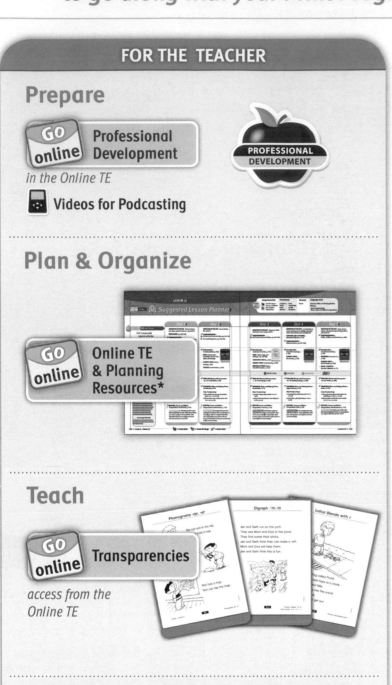

GO online Online TE & Planning Resources*

Teach

GO online Transparencies

access from the Online TE

Assess

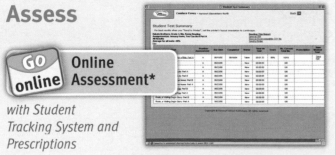

GO online Online Assessment*

with Student Tracking System and Prescriptions

FOR THE STUDENT

Read

GO online Student eBook*

GO online Strategic Intervention Interactive Reader

GO online Leveled Readers

⬤ BELOW-LEVEL
⬤ ON-LEVEL
⬤ ADVANCED

E L L

Practice & Apply

Splash into Phonics CD-ROM

 Also available on CD-ROM

Monitor Progress

Plan Ahead

to inform instruction for Theme 4

MONITOR PROGRESS

Looking Back to Theme 3

IF performance was	THEN, in addition to core instruction, use these resources:
● **BELOW-LEVEL Reteach**	• Below-Level Leveled Readers • Leveled Readers System • Extra Support Copying Masters • Strategic Intervention Resource Kit • Intervention Station, Primary
● **ON-LEVEL Reinforce**	• On-Level Leveled Readers • Leveled Readers System • Practice Book
● **ADVANCED Extend**	• Advanced-Leveled Readers • Leveled Readers System • Challenge Copying Masters • Challenge Resource Kit

ONLINE ASSESSMENT

✔ Prescriptions for Reteaching

✔ Weekly Lesson Tests

✔ Theme Test

✔ Student Profile System to track student growth

 www.harcourtschool.com/storytown

Tested
THEME 4 TESTED SKILLS

Domain	Skills
PHONICS/SPELLING	• Digraphs /n/*kn*; /r/*wr*; /f/*gh, ph* • Short Vowel /e/*ea* • Vowel Diphthong /oi/*oi,oy* • *r*-Controlled Vowel /ir/*ear, eer*
COMPREHENSION	• Comprehension of Grade-level Text 🔖 Setting 🔖 Locate Information
VOCABULARY	• Robust Vocabulary
FLUENCY	• Oral Reading Fluency 📱 Podcasting: Assessing Fluency
GRAMMAR	• Adjectives • Adjectives for Senses • Number Words • Words That Compare
WRITING	• Story
WRITING TRAITS	• Organization • Word Choice

Theme at a Glance

	LESSON 16 pp. T16–T103 	LESSON 17 pp. T116–T205 	LESSON 18 pp. T206–T289 
• **Phonics/ Spelling**	☑ **DIGRAPHS** /n/kn; /r/wr; /f/gh, ph ☑ **SUFFIXES** -ly, -ness	☑ **SHORT VOWEL** /e/ea **SYLLABLE PATTERN** V/CV	☑ **VOWEL DIPHTHONG** /oi/oi,oy ☑ **SUFFIXES** -ful, -less
• **Reading**	**PAIRED SELECTIONS** "Mr. Putter and Tabby Write the Book" REALISTIC FICTION "Interview with Author Loreen Leedy" INTERVIEW	**PAIRED SELECTIONS** "Annie's Gifts" REALISTIC FICTION "Sarah Enters a Painting" POETRY	**PAIRED SELECTIONS** "Ah, Music!" NONFICTION "Come, My Little Children, Here Are Songs for You" POETRY
• **Comprehension**	☑ ⊚ Setting ⊚ Monitor Comprehension: Read Ahead	☑ ⊚ Setting ⊚ Monitor Comprehension: Read Ahead	☑ ⊚ Locate Information ⊚ Answer Questions
• **Robust Vocabulary**	☑ **ROBUST VOCABULARY** *disturb, underneath, cozy, enchanting, instead, thrilled, review, celebrate, procrastinate, diversion*	☑ **ROBUST VOCABULARY** *journeyed, frail, stomped, sipped, entertain, except, carefree, screeching, horrendous, melodious*	☑ **ROBUST VOCABULARY** *attract, territory, volume, expression, creative, performance, concentrate, relieved, universal, audible*
• **Fluency**	☑ **FLUENCY:** Intonation	☑ **FLUENCY:** Intonation	☑ **FLUENCY:** Accuracy

Theme Writing ▸ **Reading-Writing Connection** ▸ Story pp. T104–T115

• **Grammar**	☑ **GRAMMAR:** Adjectives	☑ **GRAMMAR:** Adjectives for Senses	☑ **GRAMMAR:** Number Words
• **Writing**	✎ **WRITING FORM:** How-to Paragraph ✎ **WRITING TRAIT:** Organization	✎ **WRITING FORM:** Description ✎ **WRITING TRAIT:** Organization	✎ **WRITING FORM:** Poem ✎ **WRITING TRAIT:** Word Choice

✎ **THEME 4**
Theme Project: Musical Creations

⊚ = Focus Skill   ⊚ = Focus Strategy   ☑ = Tested Skill

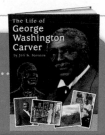

LESSON 19
pp. T290–T371

 r-CONTROLLED VOWEL
/ir/ear, eer

SYLLABLE PATTERN VC/V

PAIRED SELECTIONS
"The Life of George Washington Carver" BIOGRAPHY
"Nutty Facts About Peanuts" MAGAZINE ARTICLE

 Locate Information
 Ask Questions

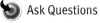 **ROBUST VOCABULARY**
brew, snug, supplies, crop, provide, earn, committee, experiments, innovation, edible

 FLUENCY: Accuracy

Writing Traits Organization, Word Choice

 GRAMMAR: Words that Compare

 WRITING FORM: Narrative

 WRITING TRAIT: Word Choice

READERS' THEATER

"What's My Job?"

- **Build Fluency**

- **Review and Build Vocabulary**

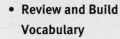

COMPREHENSION STRATEGIES

"North America"

REVIEW FOCUS STRATEGIES
 Monitor Comprehension: Read Ahead

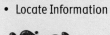 Answer Questions

ADDITIONAL REVIEW
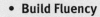 **Focus Skills**
- Setting
- Locate Information

 and Spelling

Grammar

Writing: Revise and Publish

Planning for Reading Success

Tested Skill	Teach/Model	✓ Monitor Progress	Additional Support
PHONICS/SPELLING • Digraphs /n/*kn*; /r/*wr*; /f/*gh, ph*	Lesson 16, pp. T30–T33	Lesson 16, p. T43	Small-Group Instruction, pp. S2–S3
• Short Vowel /e/*ea*	Lesson 17, pp. T130–T133	Lesson 17, p. T143	Small-Group Instruction, pp. S14–S15
• Vowel Diphthong /oi/*oi, oy*	Lesson 18, pp. T220–T223	Lesson 18, p. T233	Small-Group Instruction, pp. S26–S27
• *r*-Controlled Vowel /ir/*ear, eer*	Lesson 19, pp. T304–T307	Lesson 19, p. T317	Small-Group Instruction, pp. S38–S39
ROBUST VOCABULARY	Lessons 16–20, pp. T37, T44, T59, T137, T144, T163, T227, T234, T245, T311, T318, T329, T390, T399, T409	Lessons 16–20, pp. T96, T198, T282, T364	Small-Group Instruction, pp. S10–S11, S22–S23, S34–S35, S46–S47
COMPREHENSION 🌀 Setting	Lesson 16, pp. T34–T35	Lesson 16, p. T34	Small-Group Instruction, pp. S6–S7, S18–S19
🌀 Locate Information	Lesson 18, pp. T224–T225	Lesson 18, p. T224	Small-Group Instruction, pp. S30–S31, S42–S43
FOLLOW DIRECTIONS	Lesson 16, pp. T68–T69	Lesson 16, p. T68	Small-Group Instruction, pp. S8–S9, S20–S21
USE REFERENCE SOURCES	Lesson 18, pp. T254–T255	Lesson 18, p. T254	Small-Group Instruction, pp. S32–S33, S44–S45
DIBELS **FLUENCY** • Intonation • Accuracy	Lesson 16, p. T58 Lesson 18, p. T244	Lesson 16, p. T82 Lesson 18, p. T268	Small-Group Instruction, pp. S4–S5, S16–S17 Small-Group Instruction, pp. S28–S29, S40–S41
WRITING CONVENTIONS **Grammar**	Lesson 16-19, pp. T38, T60, T76, T138, T164, T180, T228, T246, T262, T312, T330, T346,	Lesson 16-19, pp. T98, T200, T284, T366	Small-Group Instruction, pp. S12–S13, S24–S25, S36–S37, S48–S49
WRITING	Lesson 16, p. T39 Reading-Writing Connection, pp. T104–T115 Lesson 17, p. T139 Lesson 18, p. T229 Lesson 19, p. T313	Scoring Rubric, p. T99 Scoring Rubric, p. T113 Scoring Rubric, p. T201 Scoring Rubric, p. T285 Scoring Rubric, p. T367	Small-Group Instruction, pp. S12–S13, S24–S25, S36–S37, S48–S49

 = Focus Skill

Review	 Assess
Lesson 16, pp. T42–T43, T64–T65 Lesson 17, pp. T142–T143, T168–T169 Lesson 18, pp. T232–T233, T250–T251 Lesson 19, pp. T316–T317, T334–T335	Weekly Lesson Tests 16, 17, 18, 19 Theme 4 Test
Lessons 16–19, Cumulative Review, T96–T97, T198–T199, T282–T283, T364–T365	Weekly Lesson Tests 16–20 Theme 4 Test
Lesson 16, pp. T67, T83, T95 Lesson 17, pp. T134–T135, T171, T187, T197	Weekly Lesson Tests 16, 17 Theme 4 Test
Lesson 18, pp. T253, T269, T281 Lesson 19, pp. T308–T309, T337, T353, T363	Weekly Lesson Tests 18, 19 Theme 4 Test
Lesson 17, pp. T172–T173	Weekly Lesson Tests 16, 17
Lesson 19, pp. T338–T339	Weekly Lesson Tests 18, 19
Lesson 17, p. T162 Lesson 19, p. T328	Oral Reading Fluency Tests
Lesson 20, pp. T400, T420, T432, T440	Weekly Lesson Tests 16–19 Theme 4 Test
Lesson 20, pp. T401, T421, T433, T441	Theme 4 Test

☑ INTEGRATED TEST PREP

- 4-Point Rubric, p. R8
- Daily Writing Prompts, pp. T20–T21, T120–T121, T210–T211, T294–T295, T376–T377
- Writing on Demand, pp. T114–T115
- Short Response, pp. T57, T243, T327
- Extended Response, p. T161

TEST PREP SYSTEM

- Practice Workbook: Reading and Writing

☑ TEST PREP MINUTES

For early finishers, beginning of class, or anytime:

- **WORDS THAT COMPARE** Write a few sentences that use comparing words. (Possible answer: The teacher's desk is bigger than my desk.)

- **WRITING/SETTING** Brainstorm a list of different settings you could use in stories that you might write. (Answers will vary but should be ideas for where a story could take place.)

- **ROBUST VOCABULARY** Draw pictures of some of your favorite edible things. Write a sentence that tells which one is your favorite. (Possible answer: My favorite edible item is a chocolate chip cookie.)

- **WRITING** Think about a time that you solved a problem by using your imagination or being creative. Write a few sentences about it.

Theme Project
Musical Creations

Objectives
- *To research information and instructions*
- *To follow written instructions*
- *To organize a presentation that combines speaking and performance*

Materials
- metal and plastic containers
- cardboard tubes
- everyday materials that can be used to make musical sounds (rubber bands for plucking, beans for rattles, bottle caps for jingling, and so on)
- scissors, glue, tape

See **Project Ideas from The Bag Ladies,** pp. 8–9

Getting Started

Use a ruler to tap out a rhythm on an empty container. Tell children that you have just created a musical instrument. Explain that your simple drum is an example of a *percussion* instrument—it makes its sounds by being tapped or beaten. Follow children's suggestions for making your percussion instrument sound loud or soft, and for making the sounds higher or lower or different in other ways. Tell children that they will do research to learn about homemade instruments, and they will combine their learning and imagination to create instruments of their own.

Along the Way

1 **Brainstorm** Ask children to describe simple instruments that they might tap, shake, pluck, scrape, or blow to make music. Organize children into groups that will make several instruments. Tell each group that they will form a band with their instruments and play music together.

2 **Research** Have each band work together to find books and online resources with information about simple musical instruments. Help them to use the diagrams, the lists of materials, and the step-by-step instructions to choose the instruments they will make.

3 **Plan** Help the band members gather the needed materials or make appropriate substitutions. Encourage them to help one another with the construction of the instruments. Tell them to choose or make up a song to play together and to start rehearsing.

4 **Complete the Project** Have the members of each band give a talk about each instrument and how it makes music before playing their song together.

LISTENING AND SPEAKING

Children can develop listening and speaking skills as they work in small groups to plan and make their instruments and to plan and practice their song. Emphasize the rules of effective listening and speaking:

- **Contribute to group discussions.**
- **Ask and answer relevant questions.**
- **Wait for a speaker to finish before making comments.**
- **Paraphrase what a speaker has said to show that you were listening and understanding.**

SUGGESTIONS FOR INQUIRY

The theme project can be a springboard for inquiry into a variety of topics and ideas. Help children formulate questions about music instruments, such as:

- **What are some different kinds of drums?**
- **Where can we hear the sounds of different musical instruments?**

Guide children in locating answers to some of their questions. Invite them to present their findings to the class.

Clarify Terms Use your voice or an instrument to demonstrate terms used in discussions of music—*loud, soft, high, low, rhythm, melody, pitch.* Encourage children to use the words as they describe how to play their instrument.

 BELOW-LEVEL

Support Concepts Help children to understand how musical sounds are created. Use pictures of familiar instruments to guide children in describing how sound is made.

Instrument	How Played
drum	hit with hand or sticks
harmonica	blow through holes
guitar	pluck or strum strings

 ### School-Home Connection

Children may be able to ask family members for help in finding materials and using tools.

Build Theme Connections

Dream Big

Relate to Personal Experience

Discuss Creative Expression Tell children that certain kinds of activities are considered *creative*—people use imagination and skill to create music, art, plays, poetry, stories, and more. Encourage children to name forms of creative expression that they are familiar with. Explain that sometimes creative forms are combined: An artist might create a painting of a poem, for example, or a poet might create a poem about music. Then read aloud a poem about singing.

Sing Me a Song

Rhythm and rhyme
aren't worth a dime
if your voice don't swing
and make hearts climb.

Belt out a tune
bounce to the beat,
make me clap loud
and jump out my seat.

Tempo and time
aren't worth a dime,
if your notes are flat
and your words don't
shine.

Spin 'em around
toss 'em up high
let your notes soar
make the song fly.

It makes no difference
if you're big or small,
just inhale deeply
and
give it your alllllll.

It don't
really matter
if your high notes
can make glass shatter
just ...

Belt out a tune
bounce to the beat,
make me clap loud
and jump out my seat.

Yeah!

—CHARLES R. SMITH, JR.

Talk About the Theme

DISCUSS THE THEME TITLE   Have children read the theme title, "Dream Big," and tell what it has to do with imagination and creativity. Tell children that the artwork shows what an artist imagined music would look like if it could be seen. Ask children what the picture helps them imagine.

PREVIEW THE THEME   Have children page through the selections in this theme. Tell them to read the story and article titles and to look at the illustrations. Ask for ideas about how imagination and creativity will be shown in the selections in this theme.

Talk About Fine Art

DISCUSS THE ARTWORK   Have children look closely at the painting *Music* by the Cuban-American artist Xavier Cortada. Ask: **Why do you think the artist chose bright colors? What instruments can you see in the painting? If this painting could make sounds, do you think they would be quiet or loud?**

Lesson 16

WEEK AT A GLANCE

✔ Phonics
Digraphs /n/*kn*; /r/*wr*; /f/*gh, ph*
Suffixes *–ly, –ness*

✔ Spelling
knot, wrong, know, wreck, graph, wrap, knife, tough, phone, laugh

Reading
"Mr. Putter and Tabby Write the Book"
by Cynthia Rylant REALISTIC FICTION

"Interview with Author Loreen Leedy"
INTERVIEW

✔ Fluency
Intonation

✔ Comprehension
🌀 Setting
Follow Directions

🌀 Monitor Comprehension: Read Ahead

✔ Robust Vocabulary
disturb, underneath, cozy, enchanting, instead, thrilled, review, celebrate, procrastinate, diversion

✔ Grammar [Quick Write]
Adjectives

Writing
Form: How-to Paragraph
Trait: Organization

Weekly Lesson Test

🌀 = Focus Skill   🌀 = Focus Strategy   ✔ = Tested Skill

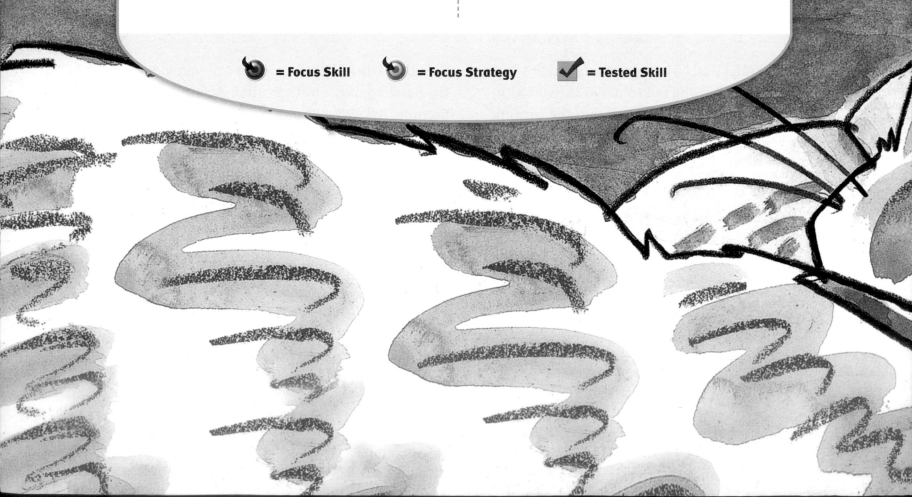

One stop
for all
your **Digital** *needs*

Digital
CLASSROOM

 www.harcourtschool.com/storytown
To go along with your print program

FOR THE TEACHER

Prepare Professional Development

 Videos for Podcasting

Plan & Organize Online TE & Planning Resources*

Teach  Transparencies

access from Online TE

Assess Online Assessment*

with Student Tracking System and Prescriptions

FOR THE STUDENT

Read Student eBook*

 Strategic Intervention Interactive Reader

 Leveled Readers

Practice & Apply  Splash into Phonics CD-ROM

 Also available on CD-ROM

Literature Resources

STUDENT EDITION

 **GO online** eBook STUDENT EDITION

Genre: Realistic Fiction

Genre: Interview

 ◀ **Audiotext** *Student Edition selections are available on Audiotext Grade 2, CD 4.*

 ◀ *Practice Quizzes for the Selection*

THEME CONNECTION: DREAM BIG
Comparing Realistic Fiction and an Interview

....

Paired Selections

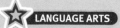 **LANGUAGE ARTS**   **Mr. Putter and Tabby Write the Book, pp. 22–43**

SUMMARY   Mr. Putter decides to write a great mystery novel, but runs into several distractions along the way.

LANGUAGE ARTS   **Interview with Author Loreen Leedy, pp. 44–45**

SUMMARY   Author Loreen Leedy answers questions about being a writer.

Support for Differentiated Instruction

Go online **LEVELED READERS**

● **BELOW-LEVEL**   ● **ON-LEVEL**   ● **ADVANCED**

E L L

LEVELED PRACTICE

◀ **Strategic Intervention Resource Kit, Lesson 16**

◀ **Strategic Intervention Interactive Reader, Lesson 16**
Strategic Intervention Interactive Reader Online

◀ **ELL Extra Support Kit, Lesson 16**

◀ **Challenge Resource Kit, Lesson 16**

● **BELOW-LEVEL**
Extra Support Copying Masters, pp. 118, 120–124

● **ON-LEVEL**
Practice Book, pp. 118–125

● **ADVANCED**
Challenge Copying Masters, pp. 118, 120–124

ADDITIONAL RESOURCES

- Decodable Book 13
- Spelling Practice Book, pp. 51–53
- Grammar Practice Book, pp. 55–58
- Reading Transparencies R76–R82
- Language Arts Transparencies LA31–LA32
- Test Prep System
- ◀ **Literacy Center Kit, Cards 76–80**
- Sound/Spelling Card
- ◀ **Fluency Builders**
- ◀ **Picture Card Collection**
- Read-Aloud Anthology, pp. 60–63

ASSESSMENT

✔ **Monitor Progress**

✔ **Weekly Lesson Tests, Lesson 16**

- Comprehension
- Phonics and Spelling
- Focus Skill
- Robust Vocabulary
- Grammar
- Follow Directions

 www.harcourtschool.com/storytown
Online Assessment
Also available on CD-ROM—Exam View®

Suggested Lesson Planner

 GO online Online TE & Planning Resources

 Step 1 | Whole Group

Daily Routines

- Oral Language
- Read Aloud
- High-Frequency Words

Word Work

- phonics
- Spelling

Skills and Strategies

- Reading
- Fluency
- Comprehension
- Build Robust Vocabulary

 Step 2 | Small Groups

 Step 3 | Whole Group

Language Arts

- Grammar
- Writing

Day 1

QUESTION OF THE DAY, p. T28
What makes it fun to read a story that could not happen in real life?

READ ALOUD, p. T29
Transparency R76: The Blue and Green Cat

WORD WALL, p. T29

---

  phonics, p. T30
Introduce: Digraphs /n/kn; /r/wr; /f/gh, ph

SPELLING, p. T33
Pretest: *knot, wrong, know, wreck, graph, wrap, knife, tough, phone, laugh*

READING/COMPREHENSION, p. T34
 Introduce: Setting

LISTENING COMPREHENSION, p. T36
Read-Aloud: "The Best Story Ever"

FLUENCY, p. T36
Focus: Intonation

BUILD ROBUST VOCABULARY, p. T37
Words from the Read-Aloud

GRAMMAR, p. T38
Introduce: Adjectives

Daily Proofreading
The Little bird sang in its cage (little, cage.)

 WRITING, p. T39
Introduce: How-to Paragraph
Writing Trait: Organization

Writing Prompt *Draw and write about something you know how to make.*

Day 2

QUESTION OF THE DAY, p. T40
Which do you like better, cats or dogs? Tell why.

READ ALOUD, p. T41
Big Book of Rhymes and Poems, "My Cat and I"

WORD WALL, p. T41

---

 phonics, p. T42
Review: Digraphs /n/kn; /r/wr; /f/gh, ph

SPELLING, p. T42
Word Building

BUILD ROBUST VOCABULARY, p. T44
Words from the Selection
Word Detective, p. T45

READING, p. T46
"Mr. Putter and Tabby Write the Book"
Options for Reading

COMPREHENSION, p. T46
 Introduce: Monitor Comprehension: Read Ahead

RETELLING/FLUENCY, p. T58 Intonation

BUILD ROBUST VOCABULARY, p. T59
Words About the Selection

▲ Student Edition

GRAMMAR, p. T60
Review: Adjectives

Daily Proofreading
gary saw a frog green. (Gary, green frog)

 WRITING, p. T61
Review: How-to Paragraph
Writing Trait: Organization

Writing Prompt *Tell what you learned from a how-to paragraph that you have read recently.*

Suggestions for Differentiated Instruction (See pp. T22–T23.)

 = Focus Skill   = Focus Strategy    = Tested Skill

Skills at a Glance

phonics
- Digraphs /n/kn; /r/wr; /f/gh, ph
- Suffixes –ly, –ness

Comprehension

 Focus Skill: Setting

 Focus Strategy: Monitor Comprehension: Read Ahead

Fluency

Intonation

Vocabulary

ROBUST: *disturb, underneath, cozy, enchanting, instead, thrilled, review, celebrate, procrastinate, diversion*

Day 3

QUESTION OF THE DAY, p. T62
Imagine that you are a cat. Why do you like your owner?

READ ALOUD, p. T63
Big Book of Rhymes and Poems, "My Cat and I"

WORD WALL, p. T63

 phonics, p. T64
Review: Digraphs /n/kn; /r/wr; /f/gh, ph

☑ **SPELLING,** p. T65
State the Generalization

FLUENCY, p. T66
Intonation:
"Mr. Putter and Tabby Write the Book"

☑ **COMPREHENSION,** p. T67
Review: Setting
Introduce: Follow Directions
Paired Selection: "Interview with Author Loreen Leedy"

▲ **Student Edition**

CONNECTIONS, p. T72

☑ **BUILD ROBUST VOCABULARY,** p. T74
Review

Day 4

QUESTION OF THE DAY, p. T78
What are your favorite quiet activities or places?

READ ALOUD, p. T79
Big Book of Rhymes and Poems, "First Snow"

WORD WALL, p. T79

 phonics, p. T80
Introduce: Suffixes –ly, –ness

☑ **SPELLING,** p. T81
Review Spelling Words

FLUENCY, p. T82
Intonation:
"Mr. Putter and Tabby Write the Book"

☑ **COMPREHENSION,** p. T83
Review: Setting
Maintain: Character
Maintain: Plot

▲ **Student Edition**

☑ **BUILD ROBUST VOCABULARY,** p. T86
Review

Day 5

QUESTION OF THE DAY, p. T90
Think of what it might be like when it snows. What do you like or dislike about snow?

READ ALOUD, p. T91
Big Book of Rhymes and Poems, "First Snow"

WORD WALL, p. T91

 phonics, p. T92
Review: Suffixes –ly, –ness

☑ **SPELLING,** p. T93
Posttest

FLUENCY, p. T94
Intonation:
"Mr. Putter and Tabby Write the Book"

☑ **COMPREHENSION,** p. T95
Review: Setting
Read-Aloud: "The Best Story Ever"

▲ **Student Edition**

☑ **BUILD ROBUST VOCABULARY,** p. T96
Cumulative Review

● **BELOW-LEVEL**   ● **ON-LEVEL**   ○ **ADVANCED**   **E L L**

☑ **GRAMMAR,** p. T76
Review: Adjectives

Daily Proofreading
did you cook the rice brown
(Did, brown rice?)

✏ **WRITING,** p. T77
Review: How-to Paragraph
Writing Trait: Organization

Writing Prompt *Write about what is easy or difficult about writing how-to paragraphs.*

☑ **GRAMMAR,** p. T88
Review: Adjectives

Daily Proofreading
put the blue vase on the tabel.
(Put, table)

✏ **WRITING,** p. T89
Review: How-to Paragraph
Writing Trait: Organization

Writing Prompt *Write what you like about your partner's how-to paragraph.*

☑ **GRAMMAR,** p. T98
Review: Adjectives

Daily Proofreading
The rabbit white hopped in the snow?
(white rabbit, snow.)

✏ **WRITING,** p. T99
Review: How-to Paragraph
Writing Trait: Organization

Writing Prompt *Make a list of ideas for other how-to paragraphs.*

Suggested Small-Group Planner

45-60+ Minutes

	Day 1	Day 2

BELOW-LEVEL

15-20+ Minutes

Day 1

Teacher-Directed
Leveled Reader:
"A New Painting," p. T100
Before Reading

Independent
⭐ Listening/Speaking Center,
p. T26
Extra Support Copying Masters,
pp. 118, 120

▲ Leveled Reader

Day 2

Teacher-Directed
Student Edition:
"Mr. Putter and Tabby
Write the Book," p. T46

Independent
⭐ Reading Center,
p. T26
Extra Support Copying
Masters, pp. 121–123

▲ Student Edition

ON-LEVEL

15-20+ Minutes

Day 1

Teacher-Directed
Leveled Reader:
"The Best Birthday," p. T101
Before Reading

Independent
⭐ Reading Center, p. T26
Practice Book, pp. 118, 120

▲ Leveled Reader

Day 2

Teacher-Directed
Student Edition:
"Mr. Putter and Tabby
Write the Book," p. T46

Independent
⭐ Letters and Sounds
Center, p. T27
Practice Book, pp. 121–122

▲ Student Edition

ADVANCED

15-20+ Minutes

Day 1

Teacher-Directed
Leveled Reader:
"First Prize," p. T102
Before Reading

Independent
⭐ Letters and Sounds Center,
p. T27
Challenge Copying Masters, pp. 118, 120

▲ Leveled Reader

Day 2

Teacher-Directed
Leveled Reader:
"First Prize," p. T102
Read the Book

Independent
⭐ Word Work Center, p. T27
Challenge Copying Masters,
pp. 121–122

▲ Leveled Reader

E L L

English-Language Learners

*In addition to the small-group
instruction above, use the
ELL Extra Support Kit to promote
language development.*

LANGUAGE DEVELOPMENT SUPPORT

Teacher-Directed
ELL TG, Day 1

Independent
ELL Copying Masters, Lesson 16

▲ ELL Student
Handbook

LANGUAGE DEVELOPMENT SUPPORT

Teacher-Directed
ELL TG, Day 2

Independent
ELL Copying Masters, Lesson 16

▲ ELL Student
Handbook

Intervention

▲ Strategic Intervention   ▲ Strategic Intervention
Resource Kit   Interactive Reader

Strategic Intervention TG, Day 1
Strategic Intervention Practice Book, Lesson 16

Strategic Intervention TG, Day 2
Strategic Intervention Interactive
Reader, Lesson 16

▲ Strategic Intervention
Interactive Reader

MONITOR PROGRESS

Small-Group Instruction

Comprehension	Phonics	Comprehension	Fluency	Robust Vocabulary	Language Arts Checkpoint
 **Focus Skill** Setting pp. S6–S7	Digraphs/n/kn; /r/wr; /f/gh, ph pp. S2–S3	Follow Directions pp. S8–S9	Intonation pp. S4–S5	*disturb, underneath, cozy, enchanting, instead, thrilled, review, celebrate, procrastinate, diversion* pp. S10–S11	**Grammar:** Adjectives **Writing:** How-to Paragraph pp. S12–S13

Day 3

Teacher-Directed
Leveled Reader:
"A New Painting," p. T100
Read the Book

Independent
⭐ Word Work Center, p. T27
Extra Support Copying Masters, p. 123

▲ Leveled Reader

Teacher-Directed
Leveled Reader:
"The Best Birthday,"
p. T101
Read the Book

Independent
⭐ Writing Center, p. T27
Practice Book, p. 123

▲ Leveled Reader

Teacher-Directed
Leveled Reader:
"First Prize," p. T102
Think Critically

Independent
⭐ Listening/Speaking Center, p. T26
Challenge Copying Masters, p. 123

▲ Leveled Reader

LANGUAGE DEVELOPMENT SUPPORT

Teacher-Directed
Leveled Reader: "Katie's Book," p. T103
Before Reading; Read the Book
ELL TG, Day 3

Independent
ELL Copying Masters, Lesson 16

▲ Leveled Reader

Strategic Intervention TG, Day 3
Strategic Intervention Interactive Reader, Lesson 16
Strategic Intervention Practice Book, Lesson 16

▲ Strategic Intervention Interactive Reader

Day 4

Teacher-Directed
Leveled Reader:
"A New Painting," p. T100
Reread for Fluency

Independent
⭐ Letters and Sounds Center, p. T27

▲ Leveled Reader

Teacher-Directed
Leveled Reader:
"The Best Birthday," p. T101
Reread for Fluency

Independent
⭐ Word Work Center, p. T27

▲ Leveled Reader

Teacher-Directed
Leveled Reader:
"First Prize," p. T102
Reread for Fluency

Independent
⭐ Writing Center, p. T27
Self-Selected Reading:
Classroom Library Collection

▲ Leveled Reader

LANGUAGE DEVELOPMENT SUPPORT

Teacher-Directed
Leveled Reader: "Katie's Book," p. T103
Reread for Fluency
ELL TG, Day 4

Independent
ELL Copying Masters, Lesson 16

▲ Leveled Reader

Strategic Intervention TG, Day 4
Strategic Intervention Interactive Reader, Lesson 16

▲ Strategic Intervention Interactive Reader

Day 5

Teacher-Directed
Leveled Reader:
"A New Painting," p. T100
Think Critically

Independent
⭐ Writing Center, p. T27
Leveled Reader: Reread for Fluency
Extra Support Copying Masters, p. 124

▲ Leveled Reader

Teacher-Directed
Leveled Reader:
"The Best Birthday," p. T101
Think Critically

Independent
⭐ Listening/Speaking Center, p. T26
Leveled Reader: Reread for Fluency
Practice Book, p. 124

▲ Leveled Reader

Teacher-Directed
Leveled Reader:
"First Prize," p. T102
Reread for Fluency

Independent
⭐ Reading Center, p. T26
Leveled Reader: Reread for Fluency
Self-Selected Reading:
Classroom Library Collection
Challenge Copying Masters, p. 124

▲ Leveled Reader

LANGUAGE DEVELOPMENT SUPPORT

Teacher-Directed
Leveled Reader: "Katie's Book," p. T103
Think Critically
ELL TG, Day 5

Independent
Leveled Reader: Reread for Fluency
ELL Copying Masters, Lesson 16

▲ Leveled Reader

Strategic Intervention TG, Day 5
Strategic Intervention Interactive Reader, Lesson 16

▲ Strategic Intervention Interactive Reader

Leveled Readers & Leveled Practice
Reinforcing Skills and Strategies

LEVELED READERS SYSTEM

- **Leveled Readers**
- **Leveled Readers, CD**
- **Leveled Readers Teacher Guides**
  - *Comprehension*
  - *Vocabulary*
  - *Oral Reading Fluency Assessment*
- **Response Activities**
- **Leveled Readers Assessment**

See pages T100–T103 for lesson plans.

BELOW-LEVEL

A New Painting
by Lynne Coulter • illustrated by Susy Boyer

- **phonics** Digraphs /n/kn; /r/wr; /f/gh, ph
- **Robust Vocabulary**
- **Setting**

LEVELED READERS TEACHER GUIDE

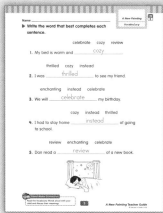

▲ Vocabulary, p. 5

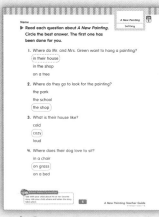

▲ Comprehension, p. 6

ON-LEVEL

The Best BIRTHDAY
by Lynne Coulter
illustrated by Debbie Mourtzios

- **phonics** Digraphs /n/kn; /r/wr; /f/gh, ph
- **Robust Vocabulary**
- **Setting**

LEVELED READERS TEACHER GUIDE

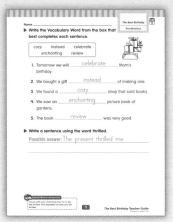

▲ Vocabulary, p. 5

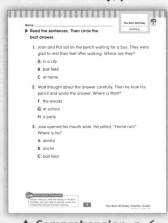

▲ Comprehension, p. 6

ADVANCED

☆ Language Arts

First Prize
by Lynne Coulter
illustrated by Clive Taylor

Harcourt

- **phonics** Digraphs /n/kn; /r/wr; /f/gh, ph
- **Robust Vocabulary**
- **Setting**

LEVELED READERS TEACHER GUIDE

▲ **Vocabulary, p. 5**

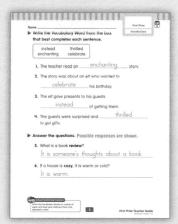

▲ **Comprehension, p. 6**

ELL

 *Note: title image*

☆ Language Arts

Katie's Book
by Lynne Coulter
illustrated by Liz Alger

Harcourt

- **Build Background**
- **Concept Vocabulary**
- **Scaffolded Language Development**

LEVELED READERS TEACHER GUIDE

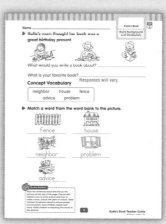

▲ **Build Background, p. 5**

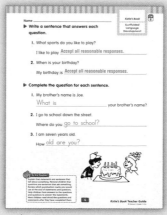

▲ **Scaffolded Language Development, p. 6**

CLASSROOM LIBRARY
for Self-Selected Reading

EASY
▲ *The Dot* by Peter H. Reynolds. **FICTION**

AVERAGE
▲ *Billy's Bucket* by Kes Gray. **FICTION**

CHALLENGE
▲ *Mae Jemison* by Thomas Streissguth. **NONFICTION**

▲ **Classroom Library Books Teacher Guide, Lesson 16**

LESSON 16

Literacy Centers
15 Min. each

Management Support
While you provide direct instruction to individuals or small groups, other children can work on literacy center activities.

▲ Literacy Center Pocket Chart

My Activities
✓ Put a check mark next to the activities you complete.

Literacy Activities
- Listening/Speaking Read with a Recording
- Reading Read with a Recording
- Writing Write a How-to Paragraph
- Word Work Read and Write Words
- Letters and Sounds Complete Words

Leveled Readers
- Rereading for Fluency
- Activities (See inside back cover.)

Practice Pages
- pages 118–125

Lesson 16   49   Teacher Resource Book

▲ Teacher Resource Book, p. 49

Homework for the Week

TEACHER RESOURCE BOOK, PAGE 19
The *Homework Copying Master* provides activities to complete for each day of the week.

 GO online www.harcourtschool.com/ storytown

LISTENING/SPEAKING
Read with a Recording

Objective
To develop fluency by listening to familiar selections and reading them aloud

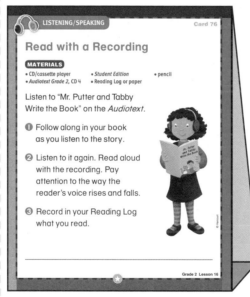

LISTENING/SPEAKING   Card 76

Read with a Recording

MATERIALS
- CD/cassette player
- Audiotext Grade 2, CD 4
- Student Edition
- Reading Log or paper
- pencil

Listen to "Mr. Putter and Tabby Write the Book" on the *Audiotext*.

❶ Follow along in your book as you listen to the story.

❷ Listen to it again. Read aloud with the recording. Pay attention to the way the reader's voice rises and falls.

❸ Record in your Reading Log what you read.

Grade 2 Lesson 16

⭐ **Literacy Center Kit • Card 76**

READING
Read and Respond

Objective
To develop comprehension by reading nonfiction selections and responding to them

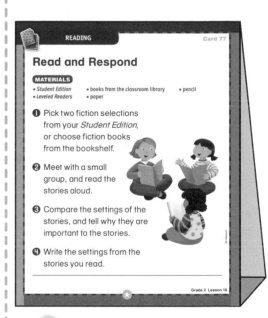

READING   Card 77

Read and Respond

MATERIALS
- Student Edition
- Leveled Readers
- books from the classroom library
- paper
- pencil

❶ Pick two fiction selections from your *Student Edition*, or choose fiction books from the bookshelf.

❷ Meet with a small group, and read the stories aloud.

❸ Compare the settings of the stories, and tell why they are important to the stories.

❹ Write the settings from the stories you read.

Grade 2 Lesson 16

⭐ **Literacy Center Kit • Card 77**

T26   Grade 2, Theme 4

WRITING

Write a How-to Paragraph

Objective
To practice writing a how-to paragraph

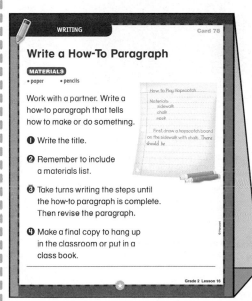

Literacy Center Kit • Card 78

WORD WORK

Read and Write Words

Objective
To practice using Vocabulary Words

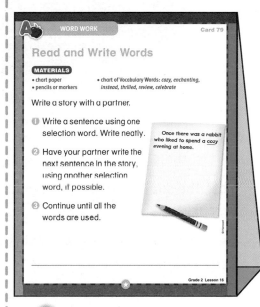

Literacy Center Kit • Card 79

LETTERS AND SOUNDS

Complete Words

Objective
To read and write words using known letter/sound correspondences

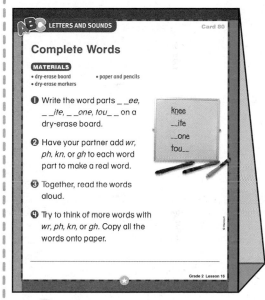

Literacy Center Kit • Card 80

knife

write

phone

graph

touch

wrong

Day at a Glance

Day 1

 phonics and Spelling

- Introduce: Digraphs /n/*kn;* /r/*wr;* /f/*gh, ph*
- Pretest

Reading/ Comprehension

 Introduce: Setting
Student Edition, pp. 18–19

- *Read-Aloud Anthology:* "The Best Story Ever"

Fluency

- Model Oral Fluency

Robust Vocabulary

Words from the Read-Aloud

- Introduce: *disturb, underneath*

Grammar Quick Write

- Introduce: Adjectives

Writing ✏️

- How-to Paragraph

Warm-Up Routines

 Oral Language

Objective *To listen attentively and respond appropriately to oral communication*

Question of the Day

What makes it fun to read a story that could not happen in real life?

Invite children to share ideas about what makes fantasy stories fun to read. List their ideas on the board. Use the following prompts:

- **Describe some things that animals can do in stories that they can't do in real life.**

- **Describe some things that people can do in stories that they can't do in real life.**

- **Name places you have read about in stories that you could never visit in real life.**

Read Aloud

Objective *To listen for enjoyment*

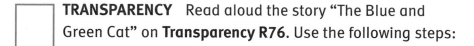

TRANSPARENCY Read aloud the story "The Blue and Green Cat" on **Transparency R76**. Use the following steps:

- **Set a purpose for listening.** Tell children that they are going to hear a story. Help children set a purpose for listening. If necessary, suggest that they listen for enjoyment.

- **Model fluent reading.** Read the passage aloud. Remind children that good readers let their voices rise and fall so their reading sounds like natural speech.

- **Discuss the story.** Ask: **Where does the story take place?** (in a kitchen) **When does the story take place?** (one afternoon)

> ### The Blue and Green Cat
>
> One afternoon, Ahmed sat in his kitchen and drew a cat. He drew a small circle for the head and two triangles for the ears. Then he drew the body, four legs, and a long tail. He was happy with his picture, and he went outside to play.
>
> His little sister came in for a snack and saw the drawing. She took a blue crayon and colored the body blue. She took a green crayon and colored the tail green. Then she got an apple and went outside to play.
>
> When Ahmed came in, he looked at his drawing and was sad. "Mom," he said. "My drawing is ruined!"
>
> "I'm sorry," his mother said. "Your sister didn't know better. Let's make up a story about how a cat became blue and green." Then she gave him a hug.
>
> Grade 2, Lesson 16   R76   Comprehension

Transparency R76

Word Wall

Objective *To read high-frequency words*

REVIEW HIGH-FREQUENCY WORDS Point to and read the following words on the Word Wall: *everything, idea, brought, minute, though,* and *enough.* Crumple a piece of paper into a ball and toss it to a child. Point to one of the words again and have that child read the word. Have the child toss the paper back to you. Continue until all children have had a chance to read a word at least once.

everything	idea	brought
minute	though	enough

Digraphs /n/ kn; /r/ wr; /f/ gh, ph
phonics *and Spelling*

Objectives

- *To recognize and blend the digraphs /n/kn; /r/wr; /f/gh, ph*
- *To read words with the digraphs /n/kn; /r/wr; /f/gh, ph and other known letter-sounds*
- *To use the digraphs /n/kn; /r/wr; /f/gh, ph and other known letter-sounds to spell words*

Skill Trace

 Tested Digraphs /n/ *kn;* /r/ *wr;* /f/ *gh, ph*

Introduce	T30–T33
Reteach	S2–S3
Review	T42–T43, T64–T65, T386–T387
Test	Theme 4
Maintain	Theme 5, T274

 Refer to *Sounds of Letters CD* Track 13 for pronunciation of /n/, /r/, and /f/.

"Research Says"

Decoding Skills "Poor decoding skill leads to little reading and little opportunity to increase one's basic vocabulary and knowledge through reading, leaving a shaky foundation for later reading comprehension."

—Juel (1988)

Connect Letters to Sounds

WARM UP WITH PHONEMIC AWARENESS Say the words *knife* and *know*. Have children say the words. Say: **The words *knife* and *know* begin with the /n/ sound.** Have children say /n/ several times. Repeat for /r/ using the words *wrench* and *wrong,* and for /f/ using the words *phone* and *photo.*

Routine Card 1 **CONNECT LETTERS AND SOUNDS** Display the *Sound/Spelling Card* for *Nn.* Point to the letters *kn* and introduce their letter/sound correspondence. Say: **The letters *kn* can stand for the /n/ sound, the sound at the beginning of *knife.* The letter *k* does not stand for /k/ when it comes before the letter *n.*** Touch the letters several times, and have children say /n/ each time. Repeat with the *Sound/Spelling Card* for *Rr,* using the word *wrong.* Point out that the letter *w* is silent. Then repeat with the *Sound/Spelling Card* for *Ff,* using the words *enough* and *phone.*

▲ **Sound/Spelling Cards**

Day 1

5-DAY PHONICS

DAY 1	Introduce /n/*kn*; /r/*wr*; /f/*gh, ph*
DAY 2	Word Building with /n/*kn*; /r/*wr*; /f/*gh, ph*
DAY 3	Word Building with /n/*kn*; /r/*wr*; /f/*gh, ph*
DAY 4	Suffixes -*ly*, -*ness*; Review /n/*kn*; /r/*wr*; /f/*gh, ph*
DAY 5	Suffixes -*ly*, -*ness*; Review /n/*kn*; /r/*wr*; /f/*gh, ph*

Work with Patterns

INTRODUCE CVC PATTERN WITH /n/*kn*; /r/*wr* Write the word *knit* on the board. Introduce the consonant-vowel-consonant pattern in which *kn* stands for /n/. Elicit from children that the *k* is silent and the letter *i* stands for the short *i* sound.

Tell children that other words with *kn* also have the CVC pattern, including *knot, knock,* and *knack*. Help children extend the pattern to CVC words in which *wr* stands for /r/, including *wrap, wrist,* and *wren*. Remind children that many words with the CVC pattern have additional consonants at the end.

Digraphs /n/kn; /r/wr; /f/gh, ph
phonics and Spelling

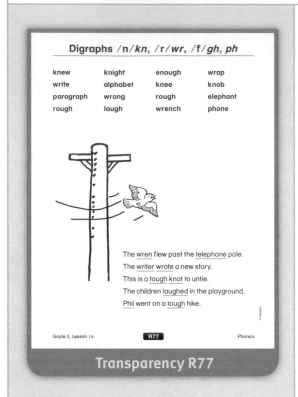

Digraphs /n/kn, /r/wr, /f/gh, ph

knew	knight	enough	wrap
write	alphabet	knee	knob
paragraph	wrong	rough	elephant
rough	laugh	wrench	phone

The wren flew past the telephone pole.
The writer wrote a new story.
This is a tough knot to untie.
The children laughed in the playground.
Phil went on a tough hike.

Grade 2, Lesson 16   **R77**   Phonics

Transparency R77

Reading Words

GUIDED PRACTICE Display **Transparency R77** or write the words and sentences on the board. Point to the word *knew*. Read the word. Have children read the word with you.

INDEPENDENT PRACTICE Point to the remaining words in the top portion and have children read them. Then have children read aloud the sentences and identify words with the digraphs *kn*, *wr*, *gh*, and *ph*.

Decodable Books

Additional Decoding Practice

- **Phonics**
  Digraphs /n/*kn*, /r/*wr*, /f/*gh*, *ph*
- **Decodable Words**
- **High-Frequency Words**
  See lists in *Decodable Book 13*.

  See also *Decodable Books*, online (Take-Home Version).

▲ **Decodable Book 13**
"The Gentle Knight," "Wrap It Up!,"
"Dolphins"

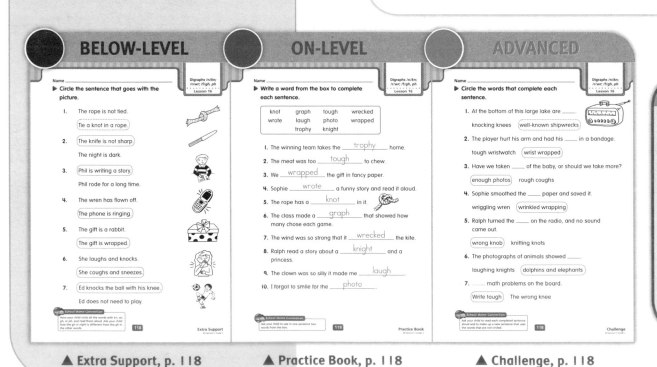

BELOW-LEVEL

▲ **Extra Support, p. 118**

ON-LEVEL

▲ **Practice Book, p. 118**

ADVANCED

▲ **Challenge, p. 118**

ELL

- Group children according to academic levels, and assign one of the pages on the left.

- Clarify any unfamiliar concepts as necessary. See *ELL Teacher Guide* Lesson 16 for support in scaffolding instruction.

5-DAY SPELLING

DAY 1	Pretest
DAY 2	Word Building
DAY 3	State the Generalization
DAY 4	Review
DAY 5	Posttest

Introduce Spelling Words

PRETEST Say the first word and read the dictation sentence. Repeat the word as children write it. Write the word on the board and have children check their spelling. Tell them to circle the word if they spelled it correctly or write it correctly if they did not. Repeat for words 2–10

Words with /n/kn; /r/wr; /f/gh, ph

1.	knot	That **knot** is hard to untie.
2.	wrong	He dialed the **wrong** number.
3.	know	Do you **know** how to speak Spanish?
4.	wreck	Be careful not to **wreck** the flowers.
5.	graph	Jaime made a **graph** in math class.
6.	wrap	Lucy will **wrap** a scarf around her neck.
7.	knife	Use the **knife** to slice the bread.
8.	tough	Is the bike route **tough** or easy?
9.	phone	The **phone** rang in the kitchen.
10.	laugh	My sisters and I **laugh** at the puppy all the time.

ADVANCED

Challenge Words Use the challenge words in these dictation sentences.

11.	elephant	The **elephant** sprayed water from its trunk.
12.	photograph	I took a **photograph** with my new camera.
13.	handwriting	Ted used his best **handwriting** on the postcard.
14.	knuckle	You can use your **knuckle** to knock.
15.	enough	The kitten got **enough** milk to drink.

Spelling Words

1.	knot	6.	wrap
2.	wrong	7.	knife
3.	know	8.	tough
4.	wreck	9.	phone
5.	graph	10.	laugh

Challenge Words

11.	elephant	14.	knuckle
12.	photograph	15.	enough
13.	handwriting		

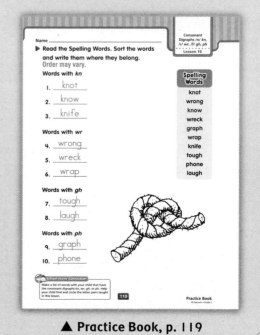

▲ Practice Book, p. 119

Lesson 16 **T33**

Setting
Comprehension

Objective

• *To identify the setting of a story*

Daily Comprehension
Setting

DAY 1:	Introduce Setting, *Student Edition*
DAY 2:	Review Setting, *Student Edition*
DAY 3:	Review Setting, *Student Edition*
DAY 4:	Review Setting, *Transparency*
DAY 5:	Review Setting, *Read-Aloud Anthology*

✓ MONITOR PROGRESS

Setting

IF children have difficulty identifying the setting,	**THEN** have them recall a familiar story and tell when and where it takes place.

Small-Group Instruction, pp. S6–S7:

● **BELOW-LEVEL:** Reteach
● **ON-LEVEL:** Reinforce
● **ADVANCED:** Extend

Teach/Model

INTRODUCE SETTING Have children read *Student Edition* page 18. Model how to determine the setting of a story.

> **Think Aloud** As I read the beginning of the story about Daniel and his dog, I look for story details that tell where and when the story takes place. The words *in the winter* tell *when*; the words *in the backyard* tell *where*. This helps me picture the setting in my mind.

Practice/Apply

GUIDED PRACTICE Draw a two-column chart such as the one on *Student Edition* page 19. Then read "Mia's Snowman" with children. Guide them to identify when the story takes place. (Saturday; winter) Add the information to the chart. Ask: **Why is the setting important to the story?** (Possible response: Because it is winter, Mia can make a snowman outside.)

Try This! **INDEPENDENT PRACTICE** Ask children to look back at the story and tell where the story takes place. (the family's farm) Add their responses to the chart. Then discuss how the story might be different if it took place in the summer or in the city.

When	Where
Saturday in winter	the family's farm

E L L

Model Vocabulary To clarify unknown vocabulary from "Mia's Snowstorm," you may want to model some of the words. For example, model *stomped* by stomping your feet as you walk through the classroom. Say: **I stomped my feet just as Mia did when she stomped through the snow.**

Focus Skill

Setting

Every story has characters, a setting, and a plot. The **setting** is when and where the story takes place.

Read this story beginning. Look for words that tell about the setting.

In the winter, Daniel and his dog, Duke, liked to play in the backyard.

The words *in the winter* tell when. The words *in the backyard* tell where.

Setting	
When	Where
in the winter	in the backyard

Read this story. Look for clue words that tell when the story takes place.

Mia's Snowman

It was Saturday, and Mia had made a snowman near the barn on her family's farm. It had taken her most of the day to build him.

Now it was time for dinner, and she had one more thing to add. Mia reached into her pocket and pulled out a scarf. "Now you won't get cold tonight," she said.

Setting	
When	Where
• Saturday	•
•	•
•	

online www.harcourtschool.com/storytown

Try This!

Look back at the story above. What words tell where the story happens?

18   19

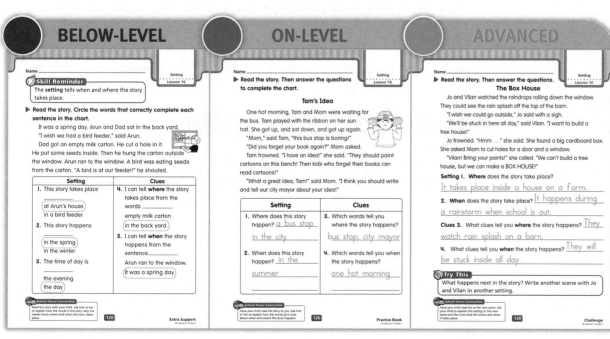

▲ Extra Support, p. 120   **▲ Practice Book, p. 120**   **▲ Challenge, p. 120**

ELL

• Group children according to academic levels, and assign one of the pages on the left.

• Clarify any unfamiliar concepts as necessary. See ELL Teacher Guide Lesson 16 for support in scaffolding instruction.

Listening Comprehension
Read Aloud

Objectives

- *To set a purpose for listening*
- *To identify the setting of a story*

Build Fluency

Focus: Intonation   Tell children that good readers let their voices rise and fall naturally, as they do when they are speaking. For example, they raise their voices at the end of a question and when they read a word in slanted type.

Figurative Language   Explain that the *door flew open* means that the door was opened quickly. Show this action using your classroom door.

Before Reading

CONNECT TO PRIOR KNOWLEDGE   Tell children that they will listen to the fiction story "The Best Story Ever." Explain that the story is about a girl who wants to write the best story ever written. Ask children to share experiences that they have had with writing stories.

▲ **Read-Aloud Anthology, "The Best Story Ever," p. 60**

Routine Card 2   **GENRE STUDY: REALISTIC FICTION**   Tell children that realistic fiction has characters and events that seem real and a setting that could be a real place. Explain that when they listen to realistic fiction, they should listen to enjoy the story.

Focus Skill   **REVIEW SETTING**   Remind children that the setting is when and where a story takes place. Read aloud the first paragraph of "The Best Story Ever." Model identifying the setting of the story.

> **Think Aloud**   I look for details about when and where the story takes place because that may be important to understanding what happens in the story. After reading the first sentence, I learn that this story takes place in Meg's home and begins on a Friday after school.

Read aloud the story "The Best Story Ever" to children.

After Reading

RESPOND   Have children summarize the story by recalling the setting, the characters, the problem, and the solution. Write a group summary on the board.

Build Robust Vocabulary

Words from the Read-Aloud

Teach/Model

Routine Card 3 **INTRODUCE ROBUST VOCABULARY** Use *Routine Card 3* to introduce the words.

❶ Put the word in **selection context**.
Display Transparency R81, and read the word and the **Student-Friendly Explanation**.
❸ Have children **say the word** with you.
❹ Use the word in other contexts, and have children **interact with the word's meaning**.
Remove the transparency. Say the Student-Friendly Explanation again, and ask children to **name the word** that goes with it.

❶ **Selection Context:** Meg wrote a "Do not **disturb**" sign so she would be left alone.
❹ **Interact with Word Meaning:** A loud noise can disturb my quiet time. Which would disturb you, a chiming clock or a siren? Why?

❶ **Selection Context:** A piece of paper was **underneath** Meg's bed.
❹ **Interact with Word Meaning:** Worms live underneath the ground. Which would you be more likely to find underneath your desk—a book bag or a lamp?

Practice/Apply

GUIDED PRACTICE Ask children to do the following:

• Imagine that you are helping a grown-up care for a baby. What might *disturb* the baby's nap?

• Imagine that you are playing hide-and-seek. Name some things you could hide *underneath*.

Objective

• *To develop robust vocabulary through discussing a literature selection*

INTRODUCE Tested ✓

Vocabulary: Lesson 16

| disturb | underneath |

▼ **Student-Friendly Explanations**

Student-Friendly Explanations

disturb	If you disturb someone, you make a noise that bothers him or her.
underneath	If something is underneath you, it is below you.
procrastinate	If you procrastinate, you delay or avoid doing something you need to do.
diversion	A diversion is something that takes you away from what you are doing or thinking about.

Grade 2, Lesson 16   R81   Vocabulary

Transparency R81

Grammar
Adjectives

Quick Write

5-DAY GRAMMAR

DAY 1	Introduce Adjectives
DAY 2	Identify Adjectives
DAY 3	Using Adjectives in Sentences
DAY 4	Apply to Writing
DAY 5	Weekly Review

Objective

- *To recognize that adjectives describe nouns*

Daily Proofreading

The Little bird sang in its cage
(little, cage.)

Writing Trait

Strengthening Conventions

Parts of Speech Use this short lesson with children's own writing to build a foundation for revising/editing longer connected text on Day 5. See also *Writer's Companion*, Lesson 16.

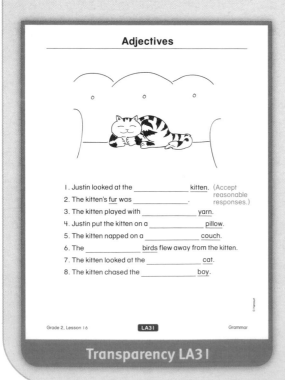

Adjectives

1. Justin looked at the _____ kitten. (Accept reasonable responses.)
2. The kitten's fur was _____.
3. The kitten played with _____ yarn.
4. Justin put the kitten on a _____ pillow.
5. The kitten napped on a _____ couch.
6. The _____ birds flew away from the kitten.
7. The kitten looked at the _____ cat.
8. The kitten chased the _____ boy.

Grade 2, Lesson 16   **LA31**   Grammar

Transparency LA31

Teach/Model

INTRODUCE ADJECTIVES   Explain that an **adjective** is a describing word that tells about a noun. Some adjectives tell about color. Some adjectives tell about size or shape.

Write on the board this phrase from "The Best Story Ever" (*Read-Aloud Anthology*, p. 60):

green fangs

Read the phrase aloud. Then point out that the word *green* is an adjective that describes the noun *fangs*. It tells what color the fangs are. Write these nouns as examples, then work with children to think of an adjective to tell about each:

apple   **box**   **building**

Guided Practice

COMPLETE SENTENCES   Display **Transparency LA31**. Explain that children will help you think of adjectives to tell about the underlined nouns. Read the first sentence and work with children to think of an adjective, such as *little* or *gray*. Complete the remaining items together, eliciting responses from volunteers.

Practice/Apply

WRITE COMPLETE SENTENCES   Write these sentences on the board. Have children rewrite the sentences by adding an adjective to each one. Have partners read aloud their sentences to each other.

The puppy has a dish.

The puppy slept on a blanket.

The puppy played on the grass.

Carol wrote a story about her pup.

Writing
How-to Paragraph

5-DAY WRITING	
DAY 1	Introduce
DAY 2	Prewrite
DAY 3	Draft
DAY 4	Revise
DAY 5	Revise

Teach/Model

INTRODUCE A HOW-TO PARAGRAPH Display **Transparency LA32** or write the sentences on the board. Explain that this paragraph was written by a child to tell how to make a sandwich. Read the paragraph aloud to children, and discuss its organization. Work together to develop a list of characteristics for a how-to paragraph.

How-to Paragraph

- A how-to paragraph tells how to do or make something.
- The title explains what the paragraph is about.
- Materials are listed first.
- Each sentence tells a step to follow, in order.
- The sentences are written as commands.

WRITING TRAIT **ORGANIZATION** Discuss with children how the directions for making the sandwich flow together in the right order, or sequence. Explain that this helps the reader know what to do *first*, *next*, and *last*.

Guided Practice

DRAFT A HOW-TO PARAGRAPH Model writing a title and a list of materials for a how-to paragraph, such as, "How to Sharpen a Pencil." Have children generate ideas to help you complete the paragraph.

Practice/Apply

SHARE IDEAS FOR HOW-TO PARAGRAPHS Have children make word webs with the words "How to _____ " in the center. Tell them to fill their webs with ideas for a how-to paragraph. Have them share their webs with a partner and save for use on Days 2–5.

Objectives

- *To read and respond to a how-to paragraph as a model for writing*
- *To develop ideas and topics for writing*

Writing Prompt

Independent Writing Have children draw and write about something they know how to make.

Student Model: How-to Paragraph

How to Make a Peanut Butter and Jelly Sandwich

You need two slices of bread, peanut butter, jelly, and a knife to make a peanut butter and jelly sandwich. First, use the knife to spread peanut butter on one slice of bread. Then, spread jelly on the other slice of bread. Last, put the two slices of bread together, with the peanut butter and jelly facing each other. Now you are ready to eat and enjoy!

Grade 2, Lesson 16   **LA32**   Writing

Transparency LA32

Day at a Glance

Day 2

  phonics and Spelling

- Review: Digraphs /n/*kn*; /r/*wr*; /f/*gh, ph*
- Build Words

Robust Vocabulary

- Introduce: *cozy, enchanting, instead, thrilled, review, celebrate*

Comprehension

Monitor Comprehension: Read Ahead

Setting

Reading

- "Mr. Putter and Tabby Write the Book," *Student Edition,* pp. 22–43

Fluency

- Intonation

Robust Vocabulary

Words About the Selection

- Introduce: *procrastinate, diversion*

Grammar Quick Write

- Review: Adjectives

Writing ✏

- How-to Paragraph

Warm-Up Routines

 ## Oral Language

Objective *To listen attentively and respond appropriately to oral communication*

Question of the Day

Which do you like better, cats or dogs?
Tell why.

Organize children into two groups. Have one group give reasons why cats are the best pets and have the other group give reasons why dogs are the best pets. Use the following prompts:

- **What do you like to do with cats or dogs?**

- **How do cats or dogs like to play?**

- **How do cats or dogs show how they are feeling?**

- **How do cats or dogs learn new tricks?**

Then have children complete the following sentence frame.

I like _____ better because _____ .

Read Aloud

Objective *To listen for enjoyment*

BIG BOOK OF RHYMES AND POEMS Display the poem "My Cat and I" on page 29 and read the title aloud. Ask children to listen for enjoyment. Then track the print as you read the poem aloud. Reread the poem, asking children to join in. Model how to slow down and pause at the end of the line "with her paws." Invite children to say what they enjoyed most about the poem.

▲ **Big Book of Rhymes and Poems, p. 29**

Word Wall

Objective *To read high-frequency words*

REVIEW HIGH-FREQUENCY WORDS Point to the following words on the Word Wall: *sugar*, *different*, *sign*, *police*, *special*, and *children*. For each word, have children read it, spell it, and use it in a sentence.

sugar	different	sign
police	special	children

Digraphs /n/*kn*; /r/*wr*; /f/*gh, ph*

 phonics *and Spelling*

Objectives

- *To blend sounds into words*
- *To spell words with digraphs /n/kn; /r/wr; /f/gh, ph*

Skill Trace

Tested ✓ **Digraphs /n/*kn*; /r/*wr*; /f/*gh, ph***

Introduce	T30–T33
Reteach	S2–S3
Review	**T42–T43, T64–T65, T386–T387**
Test	Theme 4
Maintain	Theme 5, T274

Spelling Words

1. **knot**	6. **wrap**
2. **wrong**	7. **knife**
3. **know**	8. **tough**
4. **wreck**	9. **phone**
5. **graph**	10. **laugh**

Challenge Words

11. **elephant**	14. **knuckle**
12. **photograph**	15. **enough**
13. **handwriting**	

Word Building

READ A SPELLING WORD Write the word *knot* on the board. Ask children to identify the letters that stand for the /n/ sound. Remind them that the letter *k* is silent when it is next to letter *n* in a word.

BUILD SPELLING WORDS Ask children which letter you should change to make *knot* become *know*. (Change *t* to *w*.) Write the word *know* on the board. Point to the word, and have children read it. Continue building spelling words in this manner. Say:

- **Which letters do I have to change to make the word *knife*?** (Change *ow* to *ife*.)

Then write the word *wrong* on the board and repeat the procedure to have children identify the digraph *wr* and read the word. Say:

- **Which letters do I have to change to make the word *wreck*?** (Change *ong* to *eck*.)

- **Which letters do I have to change to make the word *wrap*?** (Change *eck* to *ap*.)

- **Which letters do I have to change to make the word *graph*?** (Change *wr* to *gr*. Add *h* after the *p*.)

> knot
> know
> knife
> wrong
> wreck
> wrap
> graph

Continue building the remaining spelling words in this manner.

BELOW-LEVEL

Focus on Digraphs Write the spelling words in four columns on the board according to their digraphs *(kn, wr, ph, gh)*. Ask volunteers to circle the letters that stand for each digraph and say the sound. Help children read each word aloud.

ADVANCED

Word Roots Write the words *photograph* and *graph* on the board. Point out that the word *photograph* has the word *graph* in it. Have children think of other words related to the spelling words, such as *know* and *knowledge*, and list them on the board.

5-DAY PHONICS/SPELLING

DAY 1	Pretest
DAY 2	Word Building
DAY 3	State the Generalization
DAY 4	Review
DAY 5	Posttest

Read Words in Context

APPLY PHONICS   Write the following sentences on the board or on chart paper. Have children read each sentence silently. Then track the print as children read the sentence aloud.

The mother will <u>wrap</u> her baby in a blanket.

Dad used the <u>knife</u> to slice the turkey.

The waves will <u>wreck</u> the sand castle.

Phil solved a <u>tough</u> puzzle.

Do you <u>know</u> how to add three numbers?

WRITE   Dictate several spelling words. Have children write the words in their notebook or on a dry-erase board.

phonics Resources

Phonics Practice Book, pp. 97–102

MONITOR PROGRESS

Digraphs /n/kn; /r/wr; /f/gh, ph

IF children have difficulty building and reading words with the digraphs /n/kn; /r/wr; /f/gh, ph,	**THEN** have them cover the *k* and *w* in the digraphs and read the words *knot* and *wrong*. For *laugh* and *phone*, have children emphasize the /f/ sound in the words.

Small-Group Instruction, pp. S2–S3:

● **BELOW-LEVEL:** Reteach

● **ON-LEVEL:** Reinforce

● **ADVANCED:** Extend

BELOW-LEVEL   ON-LEVEL   ADVANCED

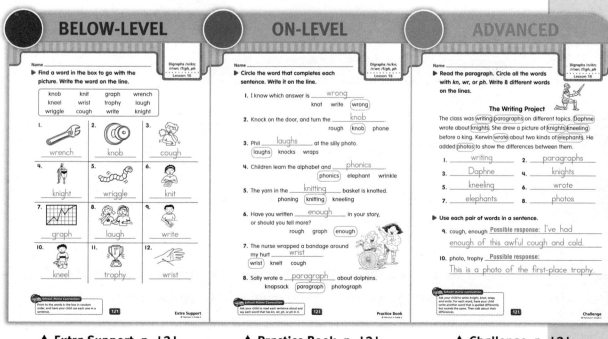

▲ Extra Support, p. 121   ▲ Practice Book, p. 121   ▲ Challenge, p. 121

E L L

- Group children according to academic levels, and assign one of the pages on the left.

- Clarify any unfamiliar concepts as necessary. See *ELL Teacher Guide* Lesson 16 for support in scaffolding instruction.

Build Robust Vocabulary
Words from the Selection

Objective
- *To build robust vocabulary*

INTRODUCE ✓ Tested
Vocabulary: Lesson 16

cozy	thrilled
enchanting	review
instead	celebrate

Student-Friendly Explanations

cozy	If a place is cozy, it makes you feel warm, happy, and comfortable.
enchanting	If you think someone or something is enchanting, you think that person or thing is likeable and enjoyable.
instead	When you do one thing instead of a second thing, you do it in place of the second thing.
thrilled	If something thrilled you, it made you feel excited and happy.
review	If you say or write what you think about a play, a book, or a movie, you are giving a review.
celebrate	If you are happy about something, you may have a party to celebrate.

Grade 2, Lesson 16   R82   Vocabulary

Transparency R82

Word Detective

Magazine Search Have children look for two Vocabulary Words in a children's magazine. HOMEWORK/INDEPENDENT PRACTICE

Teach/Model

 INTRODUCE ROBUST VOCABULARY Use *Routine Card 4* to introduce the words.

❶ Display Transparency R82, and read the word and the **Student-Friendly Explanation**.
❷ Have children **say the word** with you.
❸ Have children **interact with the word's meaning** by asking them the appropriate question below.

- I feel **cozy** when I'm in my bed. Where do you feel **cozy**?

- The garden was **enchanting**. Is a forest **enchanting**? Explain.

- I read a book **instead** of watching TV. What can you do **instead** of watching TV?

- I was **thrilled** when I won a race. When were you **thrilled**?

- I gave the boring movie a bad **review**. What movie would you give a good **review**?

- I **celebrate** on the Fourth of July. When do you **celebrate**?

Develop Deeper Meaning

EXPAND WORD MEANINGS: PAGES 20–21 Have children read the passage. Then read the passage aloud, pausing at the end of page 20 to ask children questions 1–2. Read page 21 and then discuss children's answers to questions 3–6.

1. What makes a poem **enchanting**?
2. What types of furniture are **cozy**?
3. What did the girl see **instead** of a rabbit?
4. How do the parents show they are **thrilled** with the poem?
5. Did the girl get a good **review**? How can you tell?
6. How did the girl and her parents **celebrate**?

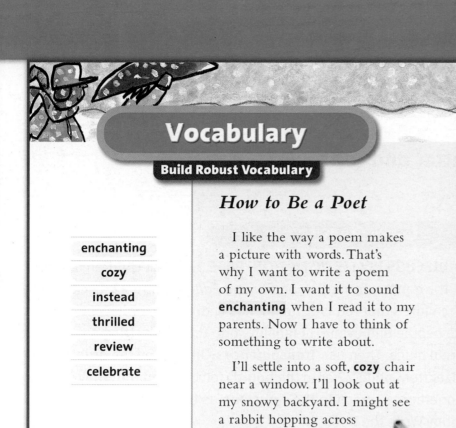

Vocabulary

Build Robust Vocabulary

How to Be a Poet

enchanting

cozy

instead

thrilled

review

celebrate

I like the way a poem makes a picture with words. That's why I want to write a poem of my own. I want it to sound **enchanting** when I read it to my parents. Now I have to think of something to write about.

I'll settle into a soft, **cozy** chair near a window. I'll look out at my snowy backyard. I might see a rabbit hopping across the snow. I'll write a word picture of what I see.

When I look out, I see my dog, Lulu, **instead** of a rabbit. She's playing in the snow. I grab my pencil and write as fast as I can.

My parents are **thrilled** with my poem. They clap and tell me they can see the picture I made with words. That's the best **review** I could ask for! They even want to **celebrate** by taking me skating. I'm going to like being a poet!

 www.harcourtschool.com/storytown

Word Detective

Where else can you find the Vocabulary Words? Look in your favorite magazine. Listen for the words on your favorite TV show. When you see or hear one of the words, write it in your vocabulary journal and tell where you found it. Happy word hunting!

20

21

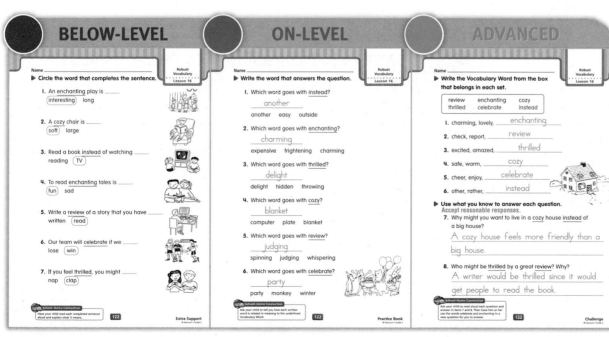

▲ Extra Support, p. 122   ▲ Practice Book, p. 122   ▲ Challenge, p. 122

ELL

- Group children according to academic levels, and assign one of the pages on the left.

- Clarify any unfamiliar concepts as necessary. See *ELL Teacher Guide* Lesson 16 for support in scaffolding.

 Reading

Student Edition: "Mr. Putter and Tabby Write the Book"

Objectives

- *To recognize features of realistic fiction*
- *To read ahead as a strategy for comprehension*
- *To represent information in charts*
- *To apply word knowledge to the reading of a text*

Options for Reading

 BELOW-LEVEL

Preview Have children preview the story by looking at the illustrations. Guide them to predict what the setting will be. Then read each page of the story to children, and have them read it after you.

 ON-LEVEL

Monitor Comprehension Have children read the story aloud, page by page. Ask the Monitor Comprehension questions as you go.

 ADVANCED

Independent Reading Have children read each page silently, looking up when they finish a page. Ask the Monitor Comprehension questions as you go.

Genre Study

DISCUSS REALISTIC FICTION: PAGE 22 Ask children to read the genre information on *Student Edition* page 22. Elicit from children that realistic fiction has characters and events that are like people and events in real life, and that the setting seems like a real place. Then use **Transparency GO4** or copy the graphic organizer from page 22 onto the board. Tell children that they will work together to complete the story map as they read "Mr. Putter and Tabby Write the Book."

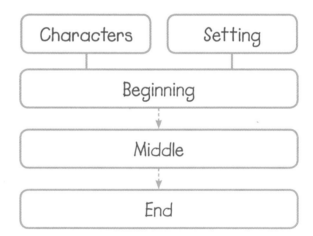

Comprehension Strategies

MONITOR COMPREHENSION—READ AHEAD: PAGE 22 Remind children that good readers monitor how well they understand what they read. Have children read aloud the Comprehension Strategy information on page 22. Point out that if they do not understand something about the story, they can read ahead to gather more information.

Award-Winning Author

Mr. Putter & Tabby Write the Book

Realistic Fiction

Genre Study
Realistic fiction is a story that could really happen. Look for

- characters who do things that real people do.
- a realistic setting.

Characters → Setting
↓
Beginning
↓
Middle
↓
End

Comprehension Strategy
Monitor comprehension—Read ahead if you do not understand something.

22

Mr. Putter and Tabby Write the Book

by CYNTHIA RYLANT

illustrated by ARTHUR HOWARD

23

Build Background

DISCUSS WRITING STORIES   Tell children that they are going to read a realistic fiction story about a man who wants to write a book. Ask them to share places where they like to write and to describe things that help them write. Write their responses on the board.

Routine Card **6**   **SET A PURPOSE AND PREDICT**   Tell children that this is a realistic fiction story that they will read for enjoyment.

- Have children read the title and the names of the author and illustrator.

- Discuss what they see in the picture.

- Have them predict what might happen in the story. List their predictions on the board.

- Invite children to read the story to find out how Mr. Putter and Tabby write the book.

TECHNOLOGY

 eBook   "Mr. Putter and Tabby Write the Book" is available in an eBook.

 Audiotext   "Mr. Putter and Tabby Write the Book" is available on *Audiotext Grade 2,* CD 4 for subsequent readings.

1

An Idea

In the winter a big snow always came to Mr. Putter's house. Mr. Putter and his fine cat, Tabby, liked big snows. But they couldn't go out in them. They were too old. Mr. Putter ❷ might slip and break something. Tabby might catch a bad cold. ❶ ❸

24

25

Monitor Comprehension

PAGES 24–25 Say: **I see snow falling and Mr. Putter and Tabby looking out the window. I also see the heading "An Idea." What will this chapter be about? Read to find out.**

❶ **MAKE PREDICTIONS** **What might the "idea" be? Why do you think this?** (Possible response: The idea might be finding something to do inside when it is snowing.)

❷ **CAUSE-EFFECT** **Why can't Mr. Putter and Tabby go out in big snows?** (They are too old.)

❸ **MAKE INFERENCES** **Might Mr. Putter and Tabby like to go out in the snow? Why do you think this?** (Possible response: They might like to go out. From their window, they watch the children. They both look a little sad that they can't join the children.)

They didn't mind staying in, though, because Mr. Putter's house was so cozy. It had nice soft chairs. It had velvet pillows. It had a fireplace. Staying in was all right when everything was so soft and velvety and warm. **1**

One day when Mr. Putter and Tabby were inside for a big snow, Mr. Putter got an idea. His idea was to write a book. **2**

He had everything a writer needed: a soft chair, a warm fire, and a good cat. *And* he had a pen and plenty of paper.

"I have always wanted to write a mystery novel," Mr. Putter said to Tabby. **3** **4**

26   27

Monitor Comprehension

PAGES 26–27 Say: **Look at the illustration. How do you think Mr. Putter is feeling? Read to find out.**

1 **NOTE DETAILS** **How does Mr. Putter feel about staying inside?** (Possible response: He doesn't mind because he has a warm, cozy house.)

2 **SETTING** **Why is the winter setting important to the story?** (Because it is snowing, Mr. Putter decides to stay inside and write a book.)

3 **EXPRESS PERSONAL OPINIONS** **What would you do if a big snow kept you inside?** (Possible responses: play games, read books)

4 **CONFIRM PREDICTIONS** **Were your predictions about the idea correct?** (Responses will vary.)

Apply
Comprehension Strategies

Monitor Comprehension: Read Ahead Explain to children how they can read ahead to answer questions they may have about the characters, setting, or events.

Think Aloud On page 26, I learn that Mr. Putter has an idea to write a book. Since he won't go outside, I wonder if he has a pen and enough paper to write a book. I also wonder what kind of book he will write. When I read ahead to page 27, I find out that he does have paper and a pen and that he wants to write a mystery story.

So he brought out lots of paper, lit the fire, plumped his chair, and got ready to begin.

First he had to think of a title. He thought and thought and thought. **①**

28

Finally he told Tabby, "I shall call my book *The Mystery of Lighthouse Cove*."

It was a very good title. It was full of mystery. As a boy he had read lots of books with titles like that. **②**

29

Monitor Comprehension

PAGES 28–29   Say: **I see a picture of Mr. Putter and a picture of a boy reading. I wonder if this is Mr. Putter as a boy. Read to find out.**

① **SEQUENCE**   **What does Mr. Putter do first? Can you point to the word that helped you figure out the answer?** (He thinks of a title. Children should point to the word *first*.)

② **DRAW CONCLUSIONS**   **Why does Mr. Putter think he has a title that readers will like?** (Possible response: He read books with titles like that when he was a boy.)

E L L

Idiomatic Expressions   Explain that *full of mystery* means that the story has many clues that the reader has to solve.

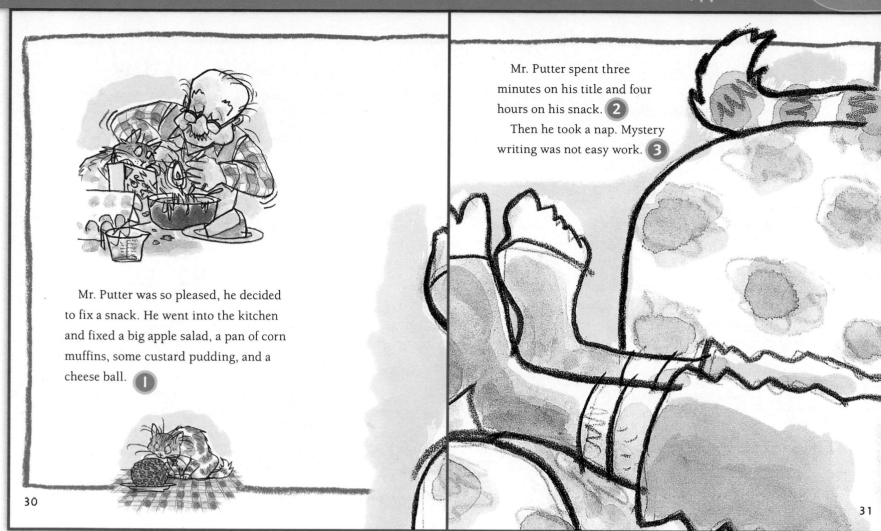

Mr. Putter was so pleased, he decided to fix a snack. He went into the kitchen and fixed a big apple salad, a pan of corn muffins, some custard pudding, and a cheese ball. **1**

30

Mr. Putter spent three minutes on his title and four hours on his snack. **2**

Then he took a nap. Mystery writing was not easy work. **3**

31

Monitor Comprehension

PAGES 30–31 Say: **Where is Mr. Putter now? Read to find out.**

1 🎯 *Focus Skill* **SETTING Why is the kitchen important to the story?** (It's where Mr. Putter makes a big snack instead of writing some of his story.)

2 **NOTE DETAILS How much time does Mr. Putter spend writing his title? Making his snack?** (He spends three minutes on his title and four hours on his snack.)

3 **EXPRESS PERSONAL OPINIONS Do you think it's funny that the author says that mystery writing is not easy work?** (Possible response: Yes; Mr. Putter spends more time making a snack than writing.)

Use Multiple Strategies

Use Graphic Organizers Demonstrate how to use a story map to comprehend the characters, setting, and plot to this point.

Characters	Setting
Mr. Putter, Tabby	Mr. Putter's house; a snowy winter day

Beginning
Mr. Putter wants to write a book.

Middle
He spends more time cooking and taking naps than writing.

End

Lesson 16 (*Student Edition*, pages 30–31) **T51**

2

Chapter One

On the second day that he was a mystery writer, Mr. Putter had a nice long breakfast with Tabby of oatmeal and tea. Then he settled down to write again. But first he had to stoke the fire.

32

Then he had to clean Tabby's ears.

Then he had to find a sweater.

Then he had to move his chair closer to the window. Then he had to move it back.

Then he settled down again. He was ready to write. Mr. Putter looked at the walls and he thought. He thought and thought and thought.

33

Monitor Comprehension

PAGES 32–33 Say: **The heading says *Chapter One*. I wonder what Mr. Putter will write about in the first chapter of his book. Read to find out.**

1 SEQUENCE **What does Mr. Putter do on the second day of writing?** (He has a breakfast, stokes the fire, cleans Tabby's ears, finds a sweater, moves his chair, and thinks.)

2 MAKE PREDICTIONS **Is this what you thought he would do? Explain.** (Possible response: no; I thought he'd start writing right away because he didn't get much writing done the day before. The heading says *Chapter One*, so I thought he would write the first chapter.)

Finally he wrote: CHAPTER ONE.

He began to think some more. As he was thinking, he looked out the window.

He decided to fix a snack. He went into the kitchen and fixed twenty boiled eggs and a vegetable stew. Mr. Putter spent one minute on CHAPTER ONE and three hours on eggs and stew. **1**

Then he took a bath. Then he took a nap. Mystery writing wore him out. **2**

34

35

Monitor Comprehension

PAGES 34–35 Say: **I see Tabby with a paper that says *Chapter One*. Then I see Mr. Putter napping. I wonder if Mr. Putter will ever write his book. Read to find out.**

1 **NOTE DETAILS** **How much time does Mr. Putter spend writing? Cooking?** (He spends one minute on Chapter One and three hours on eggs and stew.)

2 **CHARACTERS' TRAITS** **Is Mr. Putter a hard-working writer? Why do you think this?** (Possible response: no, because he thinks of ways not to write.)

3

Good Things

The third day that he was a mystery writer, Mr. Putter woke up ready to write again. He liked being a writer ready to write.

First he and Tabby had cinnamon toast and tea. Then Mr. Putter petted Tabby and began to think. He looked out of his window, thinking. He looked at his fire, thinking. He looked at Tabby, thinking.

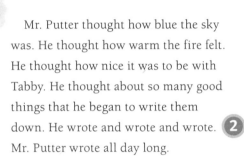

Mr. Putter thought how blue the sky was. He thought how warm the fire felt. He thought how nice it was to be with Tabby. He thought about so many good things that he began to write them down. He wrote and wrote and wrote. ② Mr. Putter wrote all day long.

36

37

Monitor Comprehension

PAGES 36–37 Say: **I see Mr. Putter writing a list called "Good Things." Why is he writing about good things? Read to find out.**

① CHARACTERS' EMOTIONS **Why does Mr. Putter like being a writer ready to write?** (Possible response: He gets ready to write by doing things that make him happy.)

② CAUSE/EFFECT **Why does Mr. Putter begin writing? Can you show where you found your answer?** (Possible response: He thinks about so many good things that he begins to write them down. Perhaps he doesn't want to forget any good things.)

Apply
Comprehension Strategies

Monitor Comprehension: Read Ahead Explain to children that if they're not sure if their predictions are correct, they can read ahead to get more information.

Think Aloud I predict that Mr. Putter will start to write about good things in his mystery story. As I read page 37, I find out that he is thinking again. I wonder if he will think more than he will write. I read ahead and find out that he does start to write a lot, but about good things, not things in a mystery.

When he finally stopped writing, the big snow had melted. Mr. Putter went next door with Tabby to visit Mrs. Teaberry and her good dog, Zeke. They had some french-fried butternut squash for supper. **1**

Then Mr. Putter read *Good Things.* When he finished, Mrs. Teaberry said it was "enchanting." She said Mr. Putter was a wonderful writer. She said she could listen forever. **2**

"I wanted to write *The Mystery of Lighthouse Cove,*" Mr. Putter said sadly. "But I wrote *Good Things* instead. And I ate too much and took too many naps."

Mrs. Teaberry told him not to worry. She said the world is full of mystery writers. But writers of good things are few and far between. **3**

38

39

Monitor Comprehension

PAGES 38–39   Say: **I see Mr. Putter reading to someone. I wonder if she will like what he wrote. Read to find out.**

1 **SETTING   What happens outside that allows Mr. Putter to visit Mrs. Teaberry?** (The big snow melts.)

2 **CHARACTERS' TRAITS   How is Mrs. Teaberry a good friend to Mr. Putter?** (She gives him dinner and tells him he is a wonderful writer.)

3 **THEME   Is Mr. Putter happy to hear Mrs. Teaberry's comments? Why do you think so?** (Possible response: Yes. He feels badly that he didn't write a mystery. She helps him see that writers of good things are rare.)

SUPPORTING STANDARDS

Forms of Water   Explain that the sun's heat melts snow into water. Invite children to share what they have observed about forms of water and to describe tests they can do to identify, predict, and test the use of heat on water.

Mr. Putter did not feel so sad then. He did not feel sad at all. In fact, he was thrilled. (Every writer loves a good review.) **1**

To celebrate good reviews and good neighbors, Mr. Putter took Mrs. Teaberry and Tabby and Zeke out for vanilla malts. **2**

40

And Mr. Putter had so much fun and thought of so many good things that he could not wait for the next big snow . . .

. . . so he could be a writer again.

41

Monitor Comprehension

PAGES 40–41   Say: **I see Mr. Putter and Mrs. Teaberry at a café or restaurant. How is Mr. Putter feeling? Read to find out.**

1 **CHARACTERS' EMOTIONS**   **How do Mr. Putter's feelings change on these pages? Why do they change?** (Possible response: At first, he is sad because he didn't write a mystery, ate too much, and took too many naps. Then he is happy because he wrote *Good Things* and Mrs. Teaberry liked it.)

2 **Focus Skill** **SETTING**   **Why does the story end at the café?** (Possible response: Mr. Putter enjoys food as a treat. He wants a treat to celebrate his good review.)

ANALYZE AUTHOR'S PURPOSE

Author's Purpose   Remind children that authors have a purpose, or reason, for writing. After children have finished reading the story, ask:

Why did the author write "Mr. Putter and Tabby Write the Book"?

- to persuade readers to write a mystery story
- to inform readers about the steps to follow to write a book
- to entertain readers with a story about Mr. Putter and Tabby

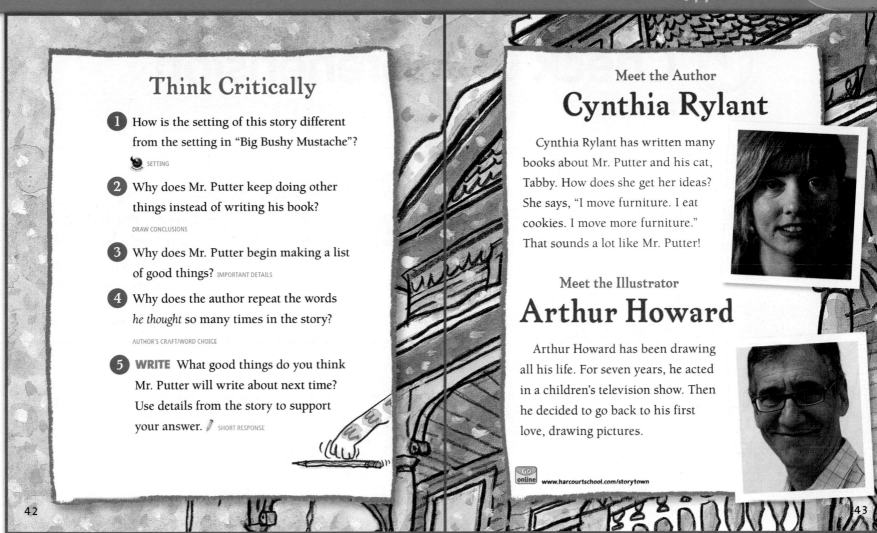

Think Critically

Respond to the Literature

1. Possible response: This story is set in winter and takes place over three days. *Big Bushy Mustache* is set in spring and happens over one day and night. **SETTING**

2. Possible response: He is having trouble deciding what to write. **DRAW CONCLUSIONS**

3. Accept reasonable responses. **IMPORTANT DETAILS**

4. Possible response: to show that writing takes a lot of thinking. **AUTHOR'S CRAFT/WORD CHOICE**

5. **WRITE** Possible response: Mr. Putter might write about good things on a warm, sunny day. **SHORT RESPONSE**

Meet the Author and the Illustrator

PAGE 43 Ask children whether it would be more fun to write a story or illustrate a story another person has written. Point to Cynthia Rylant and Arthur Howard on page 43. Tell children that they have worked together on many books about Mr. Putter and Tabby, including *Mr. Putter and Tabby Pour the Tea* and *Mr. Putter and Tabby Feed the Fish*. Ask children to read page 43. Discuss why the same illustrator draws the pictures for all the books about Mr. Putter and Tabby.

RUBRIC For additional support in scoring the WRITE item, see the rubric on p. R6.

Check Comprehension
Retelling

Objectives

- *To practice retelling a story*
- *To read accurately and fluently with intonation that sounds like natural speech*

RETELLING RUBRIC

4	Uses details to clearly retell the story
3	Uses some details to retell the story
2	Retells the story with some inaccuracies
1	Is unable to retell the story

Professional Development

 Podcasting: Auditory Modeling

BELOW-LEVEL

Fluency Practice   For fluency practice, have children read *Decodable Book 13*, the appropriate *Leveled Readers* (pp. 100–103), or Story 16 in the *Strategic Intervention Interactive Reader.*

Retell

 DIBELS Oral Reading Fluency **ORF** — Focus Skill

SETTING   Ask children to name the settings in the story and to tell why they are important. (wintertime; Mr. Putter's house, Mrs. Teaberry's house, a café; Mr. Putter decides to write a book because it snows.)

REVISIT THE GRAPHIC ORGANIZER   Display completed **Transparency GO4**. Guide children to identify the story elements.

STORY RETELLING CARDS   The cards for the story can be used for retelling or as an aid to completing the graphic organizer.

▲ **Story Retelling Cards 1–6,** "Mr. Putter and Tabby Write the Book"

 # Fluency
Intonation

Teach/Model

 DIBELS Oral Reading Fluency **ORF**

INTONATION   Explain that good readers let their voices rise and fall so their reading sounds like natural speech. Read pages 24–25, modeling correct intonation.

Practice/Apply

Routine Card 8 **ECHO-READ**   Read aloud the rest of the story, one page at a time, modeling intonation. Have children echo-read each page after you.

Build Robust Vocabulary

Words About the Selection

Teach/Model

 Routine Card 3

INTRODUCE THE WORDS Use *Routine Card 3* to introduce the words.

❶ Put the word in **selection context**.

❷ Display Transparency R81 and read the word and the **Student-Friendly Explanation**.

❸ Have children **say the word** with you.

❹ Use the word in other contexts, and have children **interact with the word's meaning**.

❺ Remove the transparency. Say the Student-Friendly Explanation again, and ask children to **name the word** that goes with it.

❶ **Selection Context:** Mr. Putter can **procrastinate** by napping instead of writing.

❹ **Interact with Word Meaning:** I procrastinate when I read a magazine instead of weeding the garden. Which might be an example of procrastinating—doing your homework right away so that you can play outside or watching TV when you have to study for a spelling test?

❶ **Selection Context:** For a **diversion**, Mr. Putter made stew.

❹ **Interact with Word Meaning:** For a diversion, I listen to music. Would you rather listen to music or play a game as a diversion?

Practice/Apply

GUIDED PRACTICE Ask children to do the following:

- Imagine you have to study for a spelling test. Is it better to *procrastinate* or to study first? Why?

- Imagine that it is raining outside and you want an indoor *diversion*. What could you do?

Objective

- *To develop robust vocabulary through discussing a literature selection*

INTRODUCE ✓ **Tested**

Vocabulary: Lesson 16

procrastinate   **diversion**

▼ **Student-Friendly Explanations**

Student-Friendly Explanations	
disturb	If you disturb someone, you make a noise that bothers him or her.
underneath	If something is underneath you, it is below you.
procrastinate	If you procrastinate, you delay or avoid doing something you need to do.
diversion	A diversion is something that takes you away from what you are doing or thinking about.

Grade 2, Lesson 16   R81   Vocabulary

Transparency R81

Grammar
Quick Write

Adjectives

5-DAY GRAMMAR	
DAY 1	Introduce Adjectives
DAY 2	Identify Adjectives
DAY 3	Using Adjectives in Sentences
DAY 4	Apply to Writing
DAY 5	Weekly Review

Objective
- *To identify and use adjectives*

Daily Proofreading

gary saw a frog green.
(Gary; green frog)

Word Order If children have difficulty using nouns and adjectives in the correct order in sentences, make word cards with nouns and adjectives, such as *red* and *cat*. Have children choose a noun and adjective and draw a picture to match. Then have them label the picture, using correct word order.

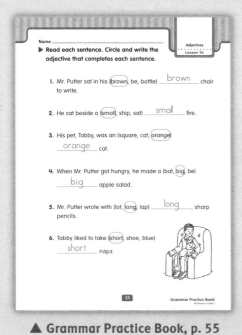

▲ Grammar Practice Book, p. 55

Review

IDENTIFY ADJECTIVES Write these phrases on the board, omitting the answers in parentheses.

the red book (red; color)

a big desk (big; size)

the long scarf (long; shape)

an orange marble (orange; color)

Have children read the phrases aloud. Explain that each phrase has an adjective. Remind them that an adjective can tell the color, size, or shape of a noun. Ask children to identify the adjective and then tell whether it describes the noun's color, size, or shape.

Practice/Apply

GUIDED PRACTICE Write the following incomplete sentences on the board. Have volunteers read them aloud. Then tell children that one of the words in parentheses is an adjective and one is not. Model how to identify the adjective that belongs in the first sentence. Work with children to rewrite the remaining sentences with the correct adjective in parentheses.

A _____ storm went through town. (today, big)

We saw the _____ snow. (white, fall)

My sister wore her _____ boots. (coat, blue)

I made a _____ snowball. (round, skates)

INDEPENDENT PRACTICE Have children write sentences describing what they are wearing today using adjectives.

Writing
How-to Paragraph

5-DAY WRITING	
DAY 1	Introduce
DAY 2	Prewrite
DAY 3	Draft
DAY 4	Revise
DAY 5	Revise

Prewrite

GENERATE IDEAS Tell children to look again at the word webs they made on Day 1 (page T39). Ask them to think of sentences that might give more information about one of their ideas.

WRITING TRAIT **ORGANIZATION** Tell children that they can number their steps to make sure they are in the correct order.

MODEL PREWRITING Copy the chart below. Tell children that using a chart is a good way to organize their ideas for their how-to paragraphs. Model filling in the sequence chart to prepare for writing.

How to Make a Paper-Bag Puppet

Materials: paper bag, markers, yarn, and glue

> **Step 1**
> Turn the bag upside-down and draw eyes, a mouth, and a nose by the fold.

↓

> **Step 2**
> Glue on yarn for hair.

↓

> **Step 3**
> Put your hand in the bag and make your puppet "talk."

Practice/Apply

GUIDED PRACTICE Ask children to brainstorm several ideas for their how-to paragraphs. List their ideas on the board.

INDEPENDENT PRACTICE Tell children to use their word webs and sequence charts to brainstorm ideas for writing their paragraphs. Tell children to save their webs and charts to use on Days 3–5.

Objectives

- *To develop ideas and topics for writing*
- *To use a graphic organizer for prewriting*

 ## Writing Prompt

Independent Writing Have children recall a how-to paragraph they have recently read and write about what they have learned from it.

 ### BELOW-LEVEL

Use Props If children have difficulty completing their sequence charts, work with them to choose a familiar topic, such as how to draw a car. Then use props to have them orally describe the materials and the steps.

DAILY ROUTINES

Day at a Glance

Day 3

 phonics and Spelling

- Review: Digraphs /n/*kn*; /r/*wr*; /f/*gh, ph*
- State the Generalization

Fluency

- Intonation
- "Mr. Putter and Tabby Write the Book," *Student Edition*, pp. 22–43

Comprehension

 Focus Skill   Review: Setting

- Introduce: Follow Directions

Reading

- "Interview with Author Loreen Leedy," *Student Edition*, pp. 44–45   **Read!**

Robust Vocabulary

- Review: *disturb, underneath, procrastinate, diversion, cozy, enchanting, instead, thrilled, review, celebrate*

Grammar [Quick Write]

- Review: Adjectives

Writing

- How-to Paragraph

Warm-Up Routines

Oral Language

Objective *To listen attentively and respond appropriately to oral communication*

> ### Question of the Day
>
> Imagine that you are a cat.
>
> Why do you like your owner?

Ask children to imagine that they are cats. Have them picture in their minds what their owner would be like. Encourage them to think of describing words such as *fun* or *kind*. Use the following prompts.

- **How do you play with your owner?**
- **How does your owner care for you?**
- **What does your owner remind you of?**

Have children complete the following sentence frame to tell about their reasons.

I like my owner because _____ .

Read Aloud

Objective *To identify rhymes in poetry*

BIG BOOK OF RHYMES AND POEMS Display the poem "My Cat and I" on page 29 and read the title aloud. Invite children to recall what the poem is about. Then read the poem aloud with children several times. Invite children to identify the pairs of rhyming words. *(rest, chest; paws, claws; away, play)*

▲ **Big Book of Rhymes and Poems, p. 29**

Word Wall

Objective *To read high-frequency words*

REVIEW HIGH-FREQUENCY WORDS Point to the following words on the Word Wall: *draw, enjoy, expensive, thumb,* and *care*. Call on pairs of children to read each word, spell it, and then use it in a sentence. Continue until all children have had a chance to participate.

Digraphs /n/kn; /r/ wr; /f/gh, ph phonics and Spelling

	5-DAY PHONICS
DAY 1	Introduce /n/kn; /r/wr; /f/gh, ph
DAY 2	Word Building with /n/kn; /r/wr; /f/gh, ph
DAY 3	**Word Building with /n/kn; /r/wr; /f/gh, ph**
DAY 4	Suffixes -ly, -ness; Review /n/kn; /r/wr; /f/gh, ph
DAY 5	Suffixes -ly, -ness; Review /n/kn; /r/wr; /f/gh, ph

Objectives

- *To read phonetically regular and irregular words*
- *To read and write common word families*
- *To recognize spelling patterns*

Skill Trace

 Tested **Digraphs /n/kn; /r/wr; /f/gh, ph**

Introduce	T30–T33
Reteach	S2–S3
Review	**T42–T43, T64–T65, T386–T387**
Test	Theme 4
Maintain	Theme 5, T274

Digraphs /n/kn; /r/wr; /f/gh, ph

Phyllis had enough practice for the concert.

She knew she had chosen a tough song.

She felt a knot in her stomach as she stepped onstage.

She smiled as Mom snapped a photo.

She did not sing any wrong notes.

She bowed as she wrapped up her song.

Grade 2, Lesson 16   R78   Phonics

Transparency R78

Work with Patterns

INTRODUCE PHONOGRAMS Write the following phonograms at the top of six columns.

-ap	-ing	-ot	-ife	-ough	-one

Tell children that these are the endings of some words. Slide your hand under the letters as you read each phonogram. Repeat, having children read the phonograms with you.

BUILD AND READ WORDS Write the letters *wr* in front of *-ap* and *-ing*. Guide children to read each word: /r/-*ap*, *wrap*; /r/-*ing*, *wring*. Continue in the same manner with *kn* in front of *-ot* and *-ife*, *r* in front of *-ough*, and *ph* in front of *-one*. Have them identify the digraphs in the words.

Then have children name other words that end with *-ap*, *-ing*, *-ot*, *-ife*, *-ough*, and *-one*. Have them tell which letter or letters to add to build each word, and write their ideas on the board under the appropriate column. Have children read each column of words. Then point to words at random and have children read them.

Read Words in Context

READ SENTENCES Display **Transparency R78** or write the sentences on the board or on chart paper. Have children echo-read the sentences as you track the print. Then ask volunteers to read each sentence aloud and to underline words with the phonograms *-ap*, *-ing*, *-ot*, *-ife*, *-ough*, or *-one*. (*enough, tough, knot, snapped, wrapped*) Then have them name the words with the digraphs *kn, wr, gh,* and *ph*. (*Phyllis, knew, photo, wrong*)

Day 3

5-DAY SPELLING
DAY 1 Pretest
DAY 2 Word Building
DAY 3 State the Generalization
DAY 4 Review
DAY 5 Posttest

Review Spelling Words

STATE THE GENERALIZATION FOR DIGRAPHS /n/kn; /r/wr; /f/gh, ph List spelling words 1–10 on chart paper or on the board. Circle the words in which the letters *kn* stand for the /n/ sound, and have children read them. Ask: **What is the same in each word?** (In each word, the letters *kn* stand for the /n/ sound.) Then, using a different color, circle the words in which the letters *wr* stand for the /r/ sound, and repeat the procedure. Continue for the digraph /f/gh, ph.

WRITE Have children write the spelling words in their notebooks. Remind them to use their best handwriting and to use the chart to check their spelling.

Handwriting

PENCIL GRIP Remind children to make sure they are holding their pencils correctly.

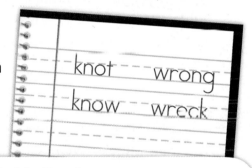

Spelling Words

1. knot
2. wrong
3. know
4. wreck
5. graph
6. wrap
7. knife
8. tough
9. phone
10. laugh

Challenge Words

11. elephant
12. photograph
13. handwriting
14. knuckle
15. enough

Decodable Books

Additional Decoding Practice

- **Phonics**
  Digraphs /n/kn; /r/wr; /f/gh, ph
- **Decodable Words**
- **High-Frequency Words**
  See the lists in *Decodable Book 13.*
  See also *Decodable Books,* online (Take-Home Version).

▲ Decodable Book 13
"Fun with Tricky Knots,"
"The Twice-Wrapped Gifts,"
"A Fun Day for Phil"

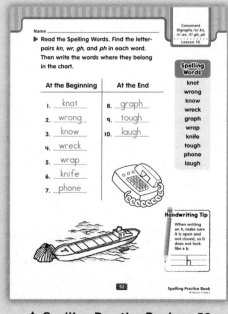

▲ Spelling Practice Book, p. 52

Fluency
Intonation

Objective

- *To read accurately and fluently with intonation that sounds like natural speech*

BELOW-LEVEL

Fluency Practice   Have children reread using *Decodable Book 13*, Story 16 in the *Strategic Intervention Interactive Reader,* or the appropriate *Leveled Reader.* (See pp. T100–T103.) Have them practice reading the text several times.

Additional Related Reading

- ***Thesaurus Rex*** by Laya Steinberg. Barefoot, 2003. **EASY**

- ***Arthur Writes a Story*** by Marc Brown. Little, Brown, 1998. **AVERAGE**

- ***Look at My Book: How Kids Can Write & Illustrate Terrific Books*** by Loreen Leedy. Holiday House, 2005. **CHALLENGE**

Review

DIBELS
Oral
Reading
Fluency
ORF

MODEL INTONATION
Remind children that good readers let their voices rise and fall naturally as they read. Tell children to:

▲ **Student Edition, pp. 22–43**

- use punctuation such as question marks and periods to know when to let their voice rise or fall.

- use key words such as action words to know when to raise their voices.

Think Aloud   **I'm going to read aloud part of "Mr. Putter and Tabby Write the Book." I'll skim ahead to see what punctuation is at the end of a group of words or the sentence. Then I'll change my voice to read the words as if I'm speaking naturally.**

Practice/Apply

GUIDED PRACTICE   Read pages 32–33 aloud. Then have children practice reading the same pages several times with a partner. Circulate among children, monitoring their intonation as they read.

Routine Card 10   **INDEPENDENT PRACTICE**   Have partners reread "Mr. Putter and Tabby Write the Book" aloud. Remind them to pay attention to the punctuation and key words so that their reading sounds like natural speech. Have children offer feedback on their partner's reading.

Setting
Comprehension

Review

DISCUSS SETTING Elicit from children that the setting is when and where a story takes place. Remind them that they can use word and picture clues to figure out the setting. Explain that paying attention to the setting can help them figure out why things are happening in the story.

Think Aloud When I read a story, I picture in my mind when and where the events are taking place. I notice how the setting causes the characters to do or say certain things.

Practice/Apply

GUIDED PRACTICE Have children read pages 36–37 of "Mr. Putter and Tabby Write the Book." Ask children to look for word and picture clues that help them figure out when and where the events on these pages take place. Copy the chart below on the board and work with children to fill it in.

When	Where
winter	the living room of Mr. Putter's house

Then ask children why the setting is important to the events in this part of the story. (Mr. Putter is inside because it is winter, and there is a big snow. He looks out the window of his living room and around his living room and thinks about good things. He gets the idea to write them down.)

INDEPENDENT PRACTICE Have children meet with partners to read pages 38–39 of "Mr. Putter and Tabby Write the Book." Have children complete a setting chart with their partners. (Setting: winter; Mrs. Teaberry's house) Then have partners share their charts. Discuss why the setting is important to this part of the story. (Mr. Putter is able to have supper and share his story with his friend at her house.)

Objectives

- *To identify the setting of a story*
- *To identify the importance of the setting to the story*

Skill Trace

Tested **Setting**

Introduce	T34–T35
Reteach	S6–S7
Review	**T67, T83, T95, T134–T135, T171, T187, T197, T389, T406**
Test	Theme 4
Maintain	Theme 5, T87

Follow Directions
Comprehension

Objective

- *To follow simple multi-step written directions*

Skill Trace

 Tested **Follow Directions**

Introduce	T68–T69
Reteach	S8–S9
Review	T172–T173, T407, T417
Test	Theme 4
Maintain	Theme 6, T87

Follow Directions

BROAD St.

MAPLE St.

Directions from the Restaurant to Mr. Putter's House

· First, walk down Main Street to Maple Street.

· Next, turn left onto Maple Street.

· Then, take a right on Broad Street.

· Finally, walk to 412 Broad Street.

Grade 2, Lesson 16   R79   Comprehension

Transparency R79

Teach/Model

INTRODUCE FOLLOW DIRECTIONS   Ask children to tell about times when they have to follow directions, such as completing a school assignment or traveling to a place for the first time. Then discuss what problems they may face if they don't follow directions carefully. (Possible responses: having to re-do an assignment or getting lost)

Tell children that good readers understand how to follow directions. Explain that when they follow directions, they should always:

- Read the directions all the way through before beginning.

- Gather all the materials they need to begin.

- Look at any photographs or illustrations.

- Look for clue words such as *first, next, then,* and *finally.*

- Follow the steps in order.

Display **Transparency R79** or write the sentences on the board. Read the sentences aloud to children and elicit what the directions are for. (to travel from one place to another) Model how to use time-order words as clues to determine the order of steps.

Think Aloud   The word *first* is a time-order word. It gives me a clue that lets me know that the first thing I need to do is walk down Main Street to Maple Street. The word *next* tells me that the second direction is to turn left onto Maple Street.

Practice/Apply

GUIDED PRACTICE Reread the directions on **Transparency R79** aloud to children. Guide children to think about why it is important to follow directions carefully. Ask:

• **How do you know the order to follow to do the steps?** (Possible response: I look at the time-order, or clue, words *first*, *next*, *then*, and *finally*. They tell me the order to follow.)

• **What would happen if you did step 2 before you did step 1?** (Possible response: You might get lost or confused.)

• **What is the last step?** (Walk to 412 Broad Street.)

INDEPENDENT PRACTICE Ask children to write directions from one part of the classroom to another, using the words *left* and *right*. Have them create a map that matches the directions. Then have partners follow each other's directions.

MONITOR PROGRESS

Follow Directions

| **IF** children have difficulty reading and following directions, | **THEN** ask them to act out each step as you read the directions to them. |

Small-Group Instruction, pp. S8–S9:

● **BELOW-LEVEL:** Reteach
● **ON-LEVEL:** Reinforce
● **ADVANCED:** Extend

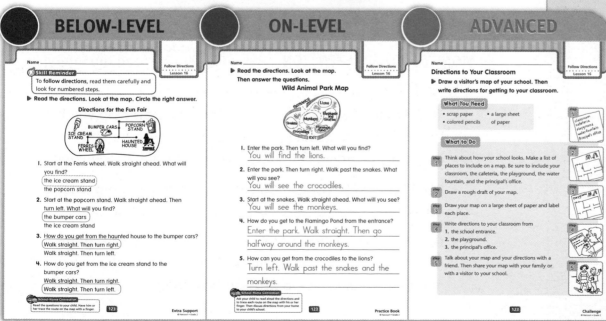

BELOW-LEVEL

▲ Extra Support, p. 123

ON-LEVEL

▲ Practice Book, p. 123

ADVANCED

▲ Challenge, p. 123

ELL

• Group children according to academic levels, and assign one of the pages on the left.

• Clarify any unfamiliar concepts as necessary. See *ELL Teacher Guide* Lesson 16 for support in scaffolding instruction.

Reading

Student Edition: Paired Selection

Objectives

- *To understand characteristics of interviews*
- *To apply word knowledge to the reading of a text*

Genre Study

DISCUSS INTERVIEWS   Explain to children that "Interview with Author Loreen Leedy" is a nonfiction interview. Point out that it contains questions and answers between two real people—the interviewer and the person being interviewed.

TEXT FEATURES   Tell children that most interviews have certain features that can help them understand and enjoy what they read. These features may include:

- photographs and captions

- questions about a person's life or work, beginning with the word *Interviewer* and a colon

- answers that help the reader get to know the person being interviewed, beginning with the person's name and a colon

USE PRIOR KNOWLEDGE/SET A PURPOSE   Read aloud the title of the interview. Point out the photographs. Guide children to use prior knowledge and set a purpose for listening. Then have two children read the interview aloud, one taking the role of the interviewer and the other taking the role of Loreen Leedy.

Respond to the Article

MONITOR COMPREHENSION   Ask children to reread the interview silently. Ask:

- **TEXT FEATURES   What words in the interview help you keep track of who is speaking?** (The word *Interviewer* and the author's last name help me keep track of who is speaking.)

- **PERSONAL RESPONSE   Do you ask friends for help when you are writing? Why or why not?** (Responses will vary.)

- **GENRE   Do you like reading about real authors? Explain.** (Possible response: Yes; I like knowing why and how they write stories because I like to write stories, too.)

Social Studies

Interview

Interview with Author
Loreen Leedy

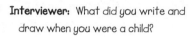

Many children who read "Mr. Putter and Tabby Write the Book" want to know more about being a writer. Our interviewer spoke with Florida author Loreen Leedy to find out more.

Interviewer: What did you write and draw when you were a child?

Leedy: I wrote stories about real things that happened. I also made up stories. I liked to draw animals, especially horses.

Interviewer: In "Mr. Putter and Tabby Write the Book," Mr. Putter has trouble thinking of something to write. What do you do if that happens to you?

Leedy: I don't usually get "writer's block." If I ever do get stuck, I might show a friend what I'm working on. My friend might help me think of some new ideas.

44

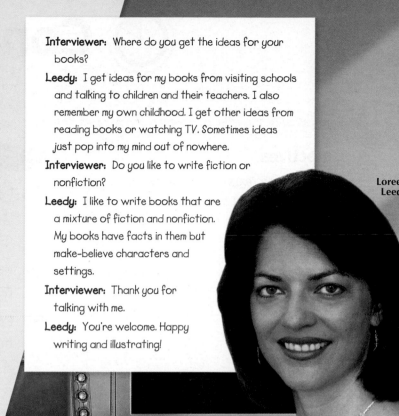

Interviewer: Where do you get the ideas for your books?

Leedy: I get ideas for my books from visiting schools and talking to children and their teachers. I also remember my own childhood. I get other ideas from reading books or watching TV. Sometimes ideas just pop into my mind out of nowhere.

Interviewer: Do you like to write fiction or nonfiction?

Leedy: I like to write books that are a mixture of fiction and nonfiction. My books have facts in them but make-believe characters and settings.

Interviewer: Thank you for talking with me.

Leedy: You're welcome. Happy writing and illustrating!

Loreen Leedy

45

🌐 **SOCIAL STUDIES**

SUPPORTING STANDARDS

Publishing and Transportation Explain that a publishing company is in the business of publishing books. Together with shipping companies, publishers move their books from warehouses to bookstores and libraries. The books might be transported on trucks, planes, or trains. Today, some books are also available online, for people to print from their computer. Discuss the advantages and disadvantages of the ways people are able to get books.

E L L

Use Realia Display examples of fiction books and nonfiction books. Work with children to identify the characteristics of each. If possible, display books by Loreen Leedy, and ask children yes/no questions about them, based on the content of the interview.

 Connections

Objectives

- *To compare texts*
- *To connect texts to personal experiences*

Comparing Texts

1. Possible response: They are alike because they both describe ways that authors write. They are different because one is a fiction story and one is a nonfiction interview. **TEXT TO TEXT**

2. Responses will vary, but may include poems, letters, reports, how-to paragraphs, and stories. **TEXT TO SELF**

3. Possible response: They can read their stories, publish them in a book, or publish them online. **TEXT TO WORLD**

Connections

Comparing Texts

❶ Think about the story of Mr. Putter and the interview with Loreen Leedy. How are they alike? How are they different?

❷ What kinds of writing have you tried?

❸ How can writers share their work?

Phonics

Make a Chart

Write _knee_, _write_, _cough_, and _graph_ in a chart.
Below each word, write two more words that have the same spelling and sound as the underlined letters.
Read your words to a partner.

knee	write	cough	graph
know			

46

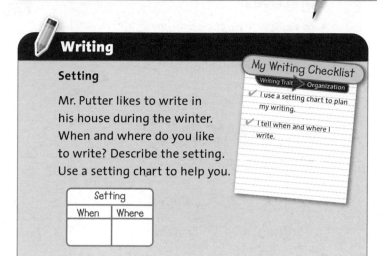

Fluency Practice

Read with Feeling

Read the story again with a partner. Take turns reading one or two pages at a time. Make your voices go up and down to show how Mr. Putter is feeling.

Writing

Setting

Mr. Putter likes to write in his house during the winter. When and where do you like to write? Describe the setting. Use a setting chart to help you.

Setting	
When	Where

My Writing Checklist

Writing Trait ▶ Organization

✓ I use a setting chart to plan my writing.

✓ I tell when and where I write.

47

 PHONICS

Make a Chart Draw a four-column chart on the board. Read the words in each column aloud, and have children repeat. Model identifying another word with the letters _kn_ that has the /n/ sound. (_know_) Write _know_ in the correct column of the chart. Do the same for _write_. (_wrong_) Then have children copy the chart and work with a partner to complete it.

knee	write	cough	graph
know	wrong	laugh	phone
knight	wren	tough	para-graph

 FLUENCY

Read with Feeling Model how to read with feeling. Suggest that children choose one or two of their favorite pages to read aloud. Ask partners to give feedback and encouragement for how well their partners read with feeling.

WRITING

Setting Help children create and give suggestions for a setting chart, telling when and where they like to write. Then remind them to write their paragraph with a main idea and supporting details. Invite children to share their finished writing.

When	Where
at night	kitchen table

Portfolio Opportunity
Children may choose to place their writing in their portfolios.

Build Robust Vocabulary

Objectives

- *To review robust vocabulary*
- *To determine a word's meaning based on context*

REVIEW

Vocabulary: Lesson 16

disturb	instead
underneath	review
procrastinate	enchanting
diversion	thrilled
cozy	celebrate

Review Robust Vocabulary

USE VOCABULARY IN DIFFERENT CONTEXTS   Remind children of the Student-Friendly Explanations of the Vocabulary Words introduced on Days 1 and 2. Then discuss each word in a new context using the following prompts:

disturb

- If you disturb your sister while she is resting, will she be happy or angry? Why?

- If you made a "Do Not Disturb" sign, where would you put it? Why?

underneath

- Would you like to explore underneath the ocean's surface? Why or why not?

- If you looked underneath a rock, what might you find?

procrastinate

- When it's time to get ready for school, do you procrastinate, or do you hurry to get ready? Why?

- When is a time when you would not want to procrastinate? Explain.

diversion

- What would you do for a diversion during a long car trip?

- Is a diversion for a baby the same as a diversion for someone your age? Explain.

cozy

- Which would make a cozy pet, a cat or a snake? Explain.

- Who would you give a cozy blanket to? Why?

enchanting

- Which is more enchanting, a rainbow or a puddle? Why?
- What would you draw in an enchanting picture?

instead

- Would you want to go to the zoo instead of to a movie theater? Explain.
- If you couldn't go outside for recess, what would you do instead?

thrilled

- What makes you feel thrilled? Why?
- How would you show that you are thrilled to win an award?

review

- Which word would you use in a good review: *excellent* or *terrible*? Explain.
- How would you cheer up a friend whose story got a bad review?

celebrate

- How do you like to celebrate your birthday?
- Would you celebrate if you lost your jacket? Why or why not?

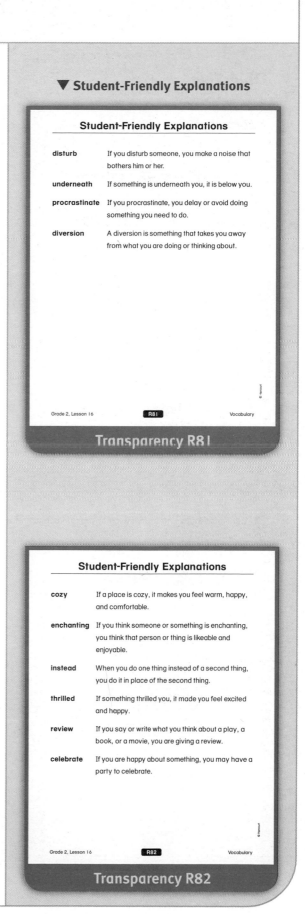

▼ **Student-Friendly Explanations**

Student-Friendly Explanations

disturb	If you disturb someone, you make a noise that bothers him or her.
underneath	If something is underneath you, it is below you.
procrastinate	If you procrastinate, you delay or avoid doing something you need to do.
diversion	A diversion is something that takes you away from what you are doing or thinking about.

Grade 2, Lesson 16   R81   Vocabulary

Transparency R81

Student-Friendly Explanations

cozy	If a place is cozy, it makes you feel warm, happy, and comfortable.
enchanting	If you think someone or something is enchanting, you think that person or thing is likeable and enjoyable.
instead	When you do one thing instead of a second thing, you do it in place of the second thing.
thrilled	If something thrilled you, it made you feel excited and happy.
review	If you say or write what you think about a play, a book, or a movie, you are giving a review.
celebrate	If you are happy about something, you may have a party to celebrate.

Grade 2, Lesson 16   R82   Vocabulary

Transparency R82

Grammar *Quick Write*

Adjectives

5-DAY GRAMMAR	
DAY 1	Introduce Adjectives
DAY 2	Identify Adjectives
DAY 3	Using Adjectives in Sentencs
DAY 4	Apply to Writing
DAY 5	Weekly Review

Objective

• *To form sentences with adjectives correctly*

Daily Proofreading

did you cook the rice brown

(Did; brown rice?)

TECHNOLOGY

 www.harcourtschool.com/storytown
Grammar Glossary

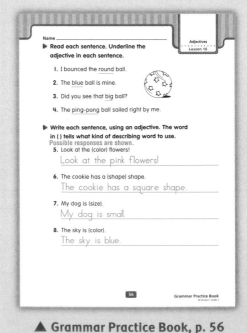
▲ Grammar Practice Book, p. 56

Review

FORMING SENTENCES WITH ADJECTIVES   Review that adjectives describe the size, color, or shape of a noun. Write and read aloud these sentences.

Simon cut _____ beans for the stew.

We ate a _____ bowl of stew.

Explain to children that they can tell more about the nouns in these sentences by adding adjectives. Underline the word *beans*. **Ask: What word can we add to describe the color of the beans?** (green) Then rewrite the sentence by adding *green* in front of *beans*. Underline the word *bowl* in the second sentence. Ask: **What word can we add to describe the size of the bowl?** (Possible responses: *big, little*) Then rewrite the sentence by adding an adjective in front of *bowl*.

Practice/Apply

GUIDED PRACTICE   Write these sentences on the board. For the first sentence, model how to add an adjective to tell more about the underlined noun. Then work together to revise the remaining sentences.

Miguel peeled the _____ <u>apples</u>.

Lily stirred the _____ <u>pot</u>.

Jin set the _____ <u>table</u>.

Cameron washed the _____ <u>dishes</u>.

 INDEPENDENT PRACTICE   Have children rewrite the following sentences by adding adjectives.

Ben ate the cheese.

Sarah poured milk into the cup.

Jimmy folded the napkin.

Annie sat on the chair.

Writing
How-to Paragraph

5-DAY WRITING	
DAY 1	Introduce
DAY 2	Prewrite
DAY 3	**Draft**
DAY 4	Revise
DAY 5	Revise

Draft a How-to Paragraph

REVIEW A LITERATURE MODEL   Have children open their *Student Edition* to "Mr. Putter and Tabby Write the Book," page 37. Read aloud the first sentence: *First he and Tabby had cinnamon toast and tea.* Invite children to explain how to make cinnamon toast as if they were planning to write a how-to paragraph. Then point out the following:

- A how-to paragraph tells how to do or make something.
- The title explains what the paragraph is about.
- Materials are listed first.
- Each sentence tells a step to follow, in order.
- The sentences are written as commands.

DRAFT A HOW-TO PARAGRAPH   Have children use their word webs and filled-in sequence charts to write a how-to paragraph that tells how to do or make something that they enjoy.

WRITING TRAIT ▶ **ORGANIZATION**   As children write their sentences, remind them to use time order or clue words to keep track of the order, or flow, of steps.

CONFER WITH CHILDREN   Meet with individual children and help them draft their how-to paragraphs. Encourage them for what they are doing well, and make constructive suggestions for improving an aspect of the writing, as needed.

Objectives
- *To read and discuss a writing model*
- *To draft a how-to-paragraph*

Writing Prompt

List   Have children jot down what they find easy or difficult about writing how-to paragraphs.

▲ **Writer's Companion, Lesson 16**

BELOW-LEVEL

Use Commands   Remind children to write the sentences as commands, or sentences that make a request or demand something. Provide a model of a command, such as *Hold the pencil.* Work with children to identify commands in their writing and to revise any other types of sentences.

Day at a Glance

Day 4

phonics  and Spelling

- Introduce: Suffixes *-ly, -ness*
- Review: Digraphs /n/*kn*; /r/*wr*; /f/*gh, ph*

Fluency

- Intonation
- "Mr. Putter and Tabby Write the Book," *Student Edition*, pp. 22–43

 Read!

Comprehension

 Review: Setting
Focus Skill

- Maintain: Characters
- Maintain: Plot

Robust Vocabulary

- Review: *disturb, underneath, procrastinate, diversion, cozy, enchanting, instead, thrilled, review, celebrate*

Grammar [Quick Write]

- Review: Adjectives

Writing

- How-to Paragraph

Warm-Up Routines

 Oral Language

Objective *To listen attentively and respond appropriately to oral communication*

Question of the Day

What are your favorite quiet activities or places?

Ask children to close their eyes and listen to the quiet sounds in the classroom. Have them think about things they like to do that are quiet, and about how they feel when they are in quiet places. Use the following prompts.

- **What did you hear in the classroom?**
- **What times of day or night are quiet for you?**
- **What places do you go to that are especially quiet?**
- **What are some of your favorite quiet things to do?**

Read Aloud

Objective *To identify rhymes in poetry*

BIG BOOK OF RHYMES AND POEMS Display the poem "First Snow" on page 30 and read the title aloud. Ask children what they picture in their minds when they think about what the first snowfall of a winter might be like. Then read the poem aloud. Tell children that *household* is another word for *house* or *home*. Reread the poem, asking children to join in. Have children identify the pair of rhyming words at the ends of lines 2 and 4. *(knows, snows)*

▲ **Big Book of Rhymes and Poems, p. 30**

Word Wall

Objective *To read high-frequency words*

REVIEW HIGH-FREQUENCY WORDS Remove the following words from the Word Wall: *sure*, *picture*, *wash*, *board*, *woods*, and *eight*. Call on children to take turns choosing a card. Have them hand the card to another child to read and spell. Then that child can choose a card for another child to read and spell. Continue until all children have had a chance to participate.

Suffixes -ly, -ness

phonics

5-DAY PHONICS	
DAY 1	Introduce /n/kn; /r/wr; /f/gh, ph
DAY 2	Word Building with /n/kn; /r/wr; /f/gh, ph
DAY 3	Word Building with /n/kn; /r/wr; /f/gh, ph
DAY 4	Suffixes -ly, -ness; Review Digraphs
DAY 5	Suffixes -ly, -ness; Review /n/kn; /r/wr; /f/gh, ph

Objectives

- *To use the suffixes* -ly *and* -ness *to determine the meanings of two-syllable words*
- *To read longer words with the suffixes* -ly *and* -ness

Skill Trace

Tested ✔ **Suffixes -ly, -ness**

Introduce	T80
Review	T92
Test	Theme 4

Suffixes -ly, -ness

Philip played baseball badly.

The wrens sleep in the darkness.

Shortly, Meg will finish the tough puzzle.

Write the words slowly so that you don't make a mistake.

The knitted hat fit Ana's head tightly.

Grade 2, Lesson 16   R80   Phonics

Transparency R80

Teach/Model

INTRODUCE THE SUFFIXES -*ly*, -*ness* Write the words *wrongly* and *roughness* on the board, and have children read them with you. Cover the suffixes and ask children to identify the root words and their meanings. Tell children that a suffix is a word part added to the end of a root word that changes the word's meaning. Underline and provide the meanings for each suffix. (*ly*—"in a way that is"; *ness*—"state of") Then help children figure out the meanings of *wrongly* and *roughness*. Repeat the procedure with the words *kindly* and *kindness*.

MODEL DECODING WORDS WITH THE SUFFIXES -*ly*, -*ness* Model how to blend the syllables to read *kindness*.

- Cover the second syllable and have children read /kīnd/.
- Cover the first syllable and have children read /nes/.
- Have children read the word, *kindness*.

Distribute Syllabication Card 10 (*Teacher Resource Book*, p. 92), and read it aloud. Write the example *gladly* on the board and have children divide and read the word.

Guided Practice

MAINTAIN LONG VOWEL /ī/ie, igh Write the following words on the board: *nightly*, *highness*, and *tightness*. Guide children to identify each suffix. Then have them read and provide the meaning for each word.

Practice/Apply

READ SENTENCES Display **Transparency R80** or write the sentences on the board. Have children read the sentences aloud and discuss the meaning of each word with a suffix.

Digraphs /n/kn; /r/wr; /f/gh, ph phonics and Spelling

5-DAY SPELLING

DAY 1	Pretest
DAY 2	Word Building
DAY 3	State the Generalization
DAY 4	**Review**
DAY 5	Posttest

Build Words

REVIEW THE WORDS Have children open their notebooks to the spelling words that they wrote on Day 3. Have them read the words several times and then close their notebooks.

MAP LETTERS TO SOUNDS Have children follow your directions to change one or more letters in each of the following words to spell a spelling word. Have them write the word on a sheet of paper. Then have a volunteer change the spelling of the word on the board so that children can self-check their spelling.

- Write *slot* on the board. Ask: **Which spelling word can you make by changing the first two letters?** *(knot)*

- Write *touch* on the board. Ask: **Which spelling word can you make by changing the next to the last letter?** *(tough)*

- Write *grape* on the board. Ask: **Which spelling word can you make by changing the last letter?** *(graph)*

Follow a similar procedure with the following words: *along (wrong), snow (know), deck (wreck), trap (wrap), wife (knife), alone (phone), launch (laugh)*.

CHALLENGE WORDS Write the first syllable of each challenge word on the board. Ask volunteers to spell each word in its entirety and write the missing letters.

Objective

- *To use digraphs /n/kn; /r/wr; /f/gh, ph and other known letter-sounds to spell and write words*

Spelling Words

1.	knot	6.	wrap
2.	wrong	7.	knife
3.	know	8.	tough
4.	wreck	9.	phone
5.	graph	10.	laugh

Challenge Words

11.	elephant	14.	knuckle
12.	photograph	15.	enough
13.	handwriting		

BELOW-LEVEL

Focus on Digraphs Write the spelling words on the board, with a blank where the digraphs should be. Then prompt children to complete each word by asking questions such as, "What letters can you add to *gra___* to make *graph*?" Have children spell each completed word.

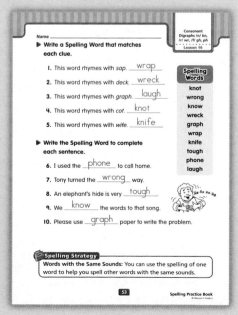

▲ Spelling Practice Book, p. 53

Fluency
Intonation

Objective

- *To read accurately and fluently with intonation that sounds like natural speech*

BELOW-LEVEL

Tape-Record Reading Provide children with a tape recorder so they can tape-record their reading of page 36 of "Mr. Putter and Tabby Write the Book." Before recording, tell children to practice reading with proper intonation. After reading, have them listen to their recording to make sure they read all the words with proper intonation.

 MONITOR PROGRESS

Fluency

IF children have difficulty reading accurately, with intonation that sounds like natural speech,	THEN model reading with appropriate intonation as you have children echo-read with you.

Small-Group Instruction, pp. S4–S5:

- ● **BELOW-LEVEL:** Reteach
- ● **ON-LEVEL:** Reinforce
- ● **ADVANCED:** Extend

Review

DIBELS
Oral Reading Fluency
ORF

MODEL USING INTONATION Remind children that when good readers read, it sounds like natural speech. Tell children that as they read they should:

▲ **Student Edition, pp. 22–43**

- let their voice rise and fall to emphasize important parts.
- pay attention to ending punctuation.

Read aloud page 36 of "Mr. Putter and Tabby Write the Book." Point out the word *liked* in the sentence *He liked being a writer ready to write.*

Think Aloud **When I read a word such as *liked*, I raise my voice a little. I want readers to pay attention to this word because it is important to the story.**

Practice/Apply

GUIDED PRACTICE Guide children to read pages 36–37 with you, matching your expression and intonation.

Routine Card 7 **INDEPENDENT PRACTICE** Have children read along with "Mr. Putter and Tabby Write the Book" on *Audiotext 4*. Have them practice reading the selection several times until they can read it in "one voice." You may wish to divide the class into groups and assign chapters to each group to read.

Setting
Comprehension

Review

DESCRIBE SETTING   Ask children to tell how they figure out the setting of a story. (Look for details about where and when the story takes place; use word and picture clues.) Remind children that the setting is important because it affects what the characters do.

Practice /Apply

GUIDED PRACTICE   Display **Transparency R76**. Have children read the passage and identify when and where the story takes place. Guide children to think about how the setting is important. Ask:

- **When does the story take place?** (an afternoon)

- **Where does the story take place?** (at Ahmed's kitchen)

- **How would the story change if it were set in Ahmed's classroom in the morning?** (Possible response: His sister wouldn't be there to draw on his picture.)

INDEPENDENT PRACTICE   Ask children to reread the beginning of "Mr. Putter and Tabby Write the Book." Ask them to identify the opening setting and then to describe how they figured out the setting. (Possible response: the winter; Mr. Putter's house; used story and picture clues)

Objectives

- *To identify the setting of a story*
- *To analyze the importance of the setting of a story*

Skill Trace

 Setting

Introduce	T34–T35
Reteach	S6–S7
Review	**T67, T83, T95, T134–T135, T171, T187, T197, T389, T406**
Test	Theme 4
Maintain	Theme 5, T87

The Blue and Green Cat

One afternoon, Ahmed sat in his kitchen and drew a cat. He drew a small circle for the head and two triangles for the ears. Then he drew the body, four legs, and a long tail. He was happy with his picture, and he went outside to play.

His little sister came in for a snack and saw the drawing. She took a blue crayon and colored the body blue. She took a green crayon and colored the tail green. Then she got an apple and went outside to play.

When Ahmed came in, he looked at his drawing and was sad. "Mom," he said. "My drawing is ruined!"

"I'm sorry," his mother said. "Your sister didn't know better. Let's make up a story about how a cat became blue and green." Then she gave him a hug.

Grade 2, Lesson 16   R76   Comprehension

Transparency R76

Characters
Comprehension

Objectives

- *To identify the characters in a story*
- *To analyze characters, including their traits*

Skill Trace

Tested **Characters**

Introduce	Theme 1, T34–T35
Reteach	Theme 1, S16–S17
Review	Theme 1, T70, T84, T94, T132–T133, T164, T180, T190, T377, T394
Test	Theme 1
Maintain	**Theme 4, T84**

Reinforce the Skill

REVIEW CHARACTERS Remind children that every story has characters, or the people and animals who do and say things in the story. Reread pages 38–39 of "Mr. Putter and Tabby Write the Book." Model identifying the characters.

> **Think Aloud** **I know that Mr. Putter is a character. As I read, I think about what he says and does. Mrs. Teaberry is a character, too. I think about what makes these characters alike and different.**

Practice/Apply

GUIDED PRACTICE On the board, draw a character chart like the one below. Guide children to add what they know about Mr. Putter to the chart. Ask: **What does this information tell you about Mr. Putter?** (Possible responses: He is a nice person.)

Mr. Putter	Mrs. Teaberry
• wants to write a mystery. • likes good things. • writes about good things. • is friends with Mrs. Teaberry.	• is friends with Mr. Putter. • likes Mr. Putter's story. • comforts Mr. Putter.

INDEPENDENT PRACTICE Have children work with a partner to tell what they know about Mrs. Teaberry. Then have volunteers share their responses with the class. Add them to the chart.

Plot

Comprehension

Reinforce the Skill

REVIEW PLOT Remind children that every story has a plot, or events that happen in the story. Elicit from children that a plot has three parts: the beginning, the middle, and the end.

Think Aloud **As I read, I think about events and whether they happen before or after other events. This helps me keep track of what is happening in the beginning, middle, and end of the story.**

Practice/Apply

GUIDED PRACTICE Draw a story map on the board. Then work with children to identify the important events in the beginning, middle, and end of "Mr. Putter and Tabby Write the Book." Add the information to the chart. Ask: **Does the story have a happy ending? Explain.** (Possible response: Yes; Mr. Putter finds good things to write about.)

> **Beginning**
> Mr. Putter wants to write a mystery.

> **Middle**
> He naps, makes snacks, and thinks a lot.
> He does not get much writing done on his mystery.
> He thinks of good things and writes a book about them.

> **End**
> Mrs. Teaberry likes his book, and Mr. Putter is happy.

INDEPENDENT PRACTICE Have children complete a story map about another story they have read recently. Meet with children to compare the plots.

Objectives

- *To identify the plot of a story*
- *To compare plots of stories by different authors*

Skill Trace

 Plot

Introduce	Theme 2, T218–T219
Reteach	Theme 2, S36–S37
Review	Theme 2, T252, T266, T276, T302–T303, T338–T339, T354, T364, T416, T437
Test	Theme 2
Maintain	**Theme 4, T85**

⏱ Build Robust Vocabulary

Objectives

- *To review robust vocabulary*
- *To understand vocabulary in new contexts*

REVIEW ✓ Tested

Vocabulary: Lesson 16

disturb	instead
underneath	review
procrastinate	enchanting
diversion	thrilled
cozy	celebrate

Extend Word Meanings

USE VOCABULARY IN DIFFERENT CONTEXTS Remind children of the Student-Friendly Explanations of the Vocabulary Words. Then discuss each word using the following activities:

disturb Tell children that you will name someone's activities. If they think the activity would disturb them while they are resting, they should cover their ears. If not, they should show the "OK" sign.

> **playing a drum**   **reading a book**
> **drawing a picture**

procrastinate Tell children that you will make some statements a person might make before doing a chore. If they think the person wants to procrastinate, they should stand up. If not, they should stay seated.

> I want to play first.   I'll start now.
> I want to begin right away.

instead Tell children that you will name some summer activities. If they think the activities are good for summer, they should say, "Summer fun!" If not, they should remain silent.

> **swim**   **make a snowman**
> **ice-skate**   **play tag**

review Tell children that you will say some adjectives. If they think the words describe a good review, they should smile. If they think the words describe a bad review, they should frown.

> **awful**   **boring**
> **funny**   **terrific**

celebrate Tell children that you will name some things. If they think these things are used to celebrate, have them clap. If not, they should do nothing.

> party hats   a birthday cake
> a hammer   a rug

Word Relationships

ANTONYMS Explain to children that an antonym is a word that is the opposite of another word. Write these sentences on the board, underlining the words as shown.

I looked for my shoe <u>above</u> the table. (underneath)

Denise sat on the <u>uncomfortable</u> chair. (cozy)

The fairy tale has an <u>unpleasant</u> ending. (enchanting)

We were <u>unhappy</u> to win the championship. (thrilled)

As a <u>job</u>, the mother played catch with her son.
(diversion)

Ask children to read the sentences aloud and replace each underlined word with a Vocabulary Word that is an antonym. Provide help as needed.

▼ **Student-Friendly Explanations**

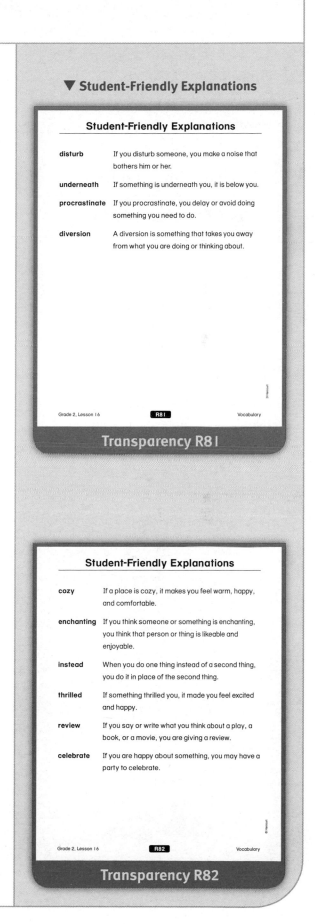

Student-Friendly Explanations

disturb	If you disturb someone, you make a noise that bothers him or her.
underneath	If something is underneath you, it is below you.
procrastinate	If you procrastinate, you delay or avoid doing something you need to do.
diversion	A diversion is something that takes you away from what you are doing or thinking about.

Grade 2, Lesson 16   R81   Vocabulary

Transparency R81

Student-Friendly Explanations

cozy	If a place is cozy, it makes you feel warm, happy, and comfortable.
enchanting	If you think someone or something is enchanting, you think that person or thing is likeable and enjoyable.
instead	When you do one thing instead of a second thing, you do it in place of the second thing.
thrilled	If something thrilled you, it made you feel excited and happy.
review	If you say or write what you think about a play, a book, or a movie, you are giving a review.
celebrate	If you are happy about something, you may have a party to celebrate.

Grade 2, Lesson 16   R82   Vocabulary

Transparency R82

Grammar *Quick Write*

Adjectives

5-DAY GRAMMAR

DAY 1	Introduce Adjectives
DAY 2	Identify Adjectives
DAY 3	Using Adjectives in Sentences
DAY 4	Apply to Writing
DAY 5	Weekly Review

Objective

- *To write adjectives correctly in sentences*

Daily Proofreading

put the blue vase on the tabel.

(Put; table)

Writing Trait ▶

Strengthening Conventions

Adjectives   Use this short lesson with children's own writing to build a foundation for revising/editing longer connected text on Day 5. See also *Writer's Companion*, Lesson 16.

▲ Grammar Practice Book, p. 57

Review

DISCUSS ADJECTIVES   Review with children that an adjective can tell the color, size, or shape of a noun. Write the following on the board:

chair	**fireplace**
table	**window**

Tell children that an adjective can be added to each noun to tell about its color, size, or shape. Point to and read aloud the word *chair*. Write the word *red* before the word *chair*. Discuss how the word *red* tells the color of the chair.

USE EDITOR'S MARKS   Add adjectives describing the color, size, or shape of each remaining noun. Model using basic Editor's Marks to add a word.

Editor's Marks

∧	Add
⌀	Take out
⌐	Change
⊙	Add a period
≡	Capitalize

Practice/Apply

GUIDED PRACTICE   Tell children that you are going to write three sentences about a house. Explain that you will use adjectives to describe the house. Model writing the first sentence. Ask volunteers to suggest additional sentences. After you write each sentence, have children check that each is complete, uses adjectives correctly, begins with a capital letter, and ends with a period. Use Editor's Marks as necessary.

INDEPENDENT PRACTICE   Ask children to write three complete sentences that tell about their home. Remind them to include adjectives. Have partners exchange sentences and check that their sentences are complete thoughts, use adjectives correctly, begin with a capital letter, and have end punctuation.

5-DAY WRITING	
DAY 1	Introduce
DAY 2	Prewrite
DAY 3	Draft
DAY 4	Revise
DAY 5	Proofread and Share

Writing
How-to Paragraph

Revise How-to Paragraphs

WRITE Have children continue writing their how-to paragraph. Remind them that the sentences in their paragraph should tell how to do or make something and the steps should be in the correct order.

WRITING TRAIT **ORGANIZATION** Have children make sure their details flow in sequence so the reader can follow the directions more easily.

REVISE Have children read their how-to paragraphs to a partner. Guide them to evaluate their paragraphs for logical thinking by making sure the steps are described in order and give all the necessary information. Remind them that they can include adjectives that tell more about the nouns. Suggest that children use this list of criteria to improve their paragraphs.

How-to Paragraph

- The how-to paragraph tells how to do or make something.
- The title explains what the paragraph is about.
- Materials are listed first.
- Each sentence tells a step to follow, in order.
- The sentences are written as commands.

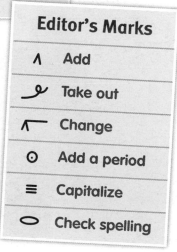

Have children revise their paragraphs. Let them work together to make sure each sentence is a step in the correct order and is written as a command. Remind them to check that adjectives are used correctly. Remind children that they can use Editor's Marks to revise their writing. Save children's paragraphs to revise further on Day 5.

Editor's Marks

∧	Add
℘	Take out
⌐	Change
⊙	Add a period
≡	Capitalize
⬯	Check spelling

Objectives
- *To revise a how-to paragraph*
- *To use adjectives correctly in writing*

 ## Writing Prompt

Evaluate Have children jot down what they like about their partner's how-to paragraph.

Dictate Steps Suggest that children draw pictures in numbered boxes and dictate the steps. Help them work through the revision process by reading back their steps and asking simple questions about any changes they would like to make.

Day at a Glance

Day 5

 **and Spelling**

- Review: Suffixes *-ly, -ness*
- Posttest: Digraphs /n/*kn*; /r/*wr*; /f/*gh, ph*

Fluency

- Intonation
- "Mr. Putter and Tabby Write the Book," *Student Edition*, pp. 22–43

 Read!

Comprehension

Focus Skill Review: Setting

- *Read-Aloud Anthology:* "The Best Story Ever"

Robust Vocabulary

- Cumulative Review

Grammar Quick Write

- Review: Adjectives

Writing

- How-to Paragraph

Warm-Up Routines

Oral Language

Objective *To listen attentively and respond appropriately to oral communication*

> ### Question of the Day
>
> Think of what it might be like when it snows. What do you like or dislike about snow?

Have children think about how they feel about snow. Use the following prompts.

- **What are some things you can't do when it is snowing?**
- **What kinds of things are you able to do in the snow?**
- **Is it hot or cold outside when it snows?**
- **Would you rather live in a place where it snows or where it doesn't snow?**

Read Aloud

Objective *To listen for enjoyment*

BIG BOOK OF RHYMES AND POEMS Display the poem "First Snow" on page 30 and read the title aloud. Ask children to recall what the poem was about. Then read the poem aloud, inviting children to join in. Read the poem several times, with feeling. Then discuss what children like about the poem, such as how it makes them feel or what it makes them picture in their mind.

First Snow

There is a special kind of quiet
every household knows
we hear it in our sleep
the first night it snows.

Charlotte Zolotow

▲ Big Book of Rhymes and Poems, p. 30

Word Wall

Objective *To read high-frequency words*

REVIEW HIGH-FREQUENCY WORDS Point to the following words on the Word Wall: *guess, sometimes, finally, hundred, touch,* and *minute*. Call on a volunteer to read a word and spell it. Continue until all children have had a chance to participate.

guess	sometimes	finally
hundred	touch	minute

Suffixes -ly, -ness

phonics

5-DAY PHONICS	
DAY 1	Introduce /n/kn; /r/wr; /f/gh, ph
DAY 2	Word Building with /n/kn; /r/wr; /f/gh, ph
DAY 3	Word Building with /n/kn; /r/wr; /f/gh, ph
DAY 4	Suffixes -ly, -ness; Review /n/kn; /r/wr; /f/gh, ph
DAY 5	Suffixes -ly, -ness; Review Digraphs

Objectives

• *To use the suffixes -ly and -ness to determine the meaning of two-syllable words*

• *To read longer words with the suffixes -ly and -ness*

Skill Trace

 Suffixes -ly, -ness

Introduce	T80
Review	**T92**
Test	Theme 4

Review

READ WORDS WITH -ly, -ness Write the word *slowly* on the board. Ask children to identify the suffix and read the word. Remind them that good readers look for word parts and root words to help them read unfamiliar words. Review the meanings for -ly ("in a way that is") and *ness* ("state of being").

Practice/Apply

GUIDED PRACTICE Make a chart as shown. Ask volunteers to read each word and tell its meaning. Have children add more words to the chart.

Words with -*ly*	Words with -*ness*
quietly	sadness

INDEPENDENT PRACTICE Have children think of other -*ly* and -*ness* words and write sentences using them. Point out that -*ly* words such as *slowly* and *quietly* are adverbs and that they tell the way in which something is done.

BELOW-LEVEL · **ON-LEVEL** · **ADVANCED**

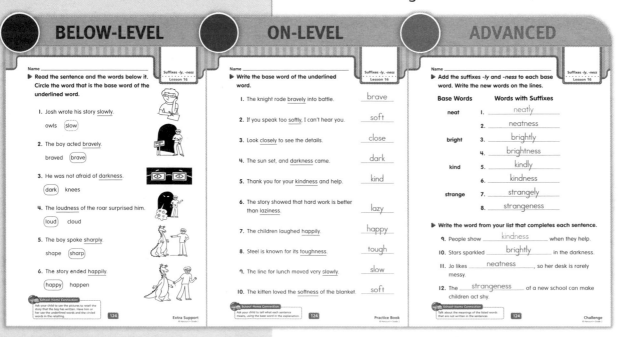

▲ Extra Support, p. 124   ▲ Practice Book, p. 124   ▲ Challenge, p. 124

• Group children according to academic levels, and assign one of the pages on the left.

• Clarify any unfamiliar concepts as necessary. See *ELL Teacher Guide* Lesson 16 for support in scaffolding instruction.

Digraphs /n/kn; /r/wr; /f/gh, ph phonics and Spelling

5-DAY SPELLING
DAY 1   Pretest
DAY 2   Word Building
DAY 3   State the Generalization
DAY 4   Review
DAY 5   Posttest

Assess

POSTTEST   Assess children's progress. Use the dictation sentences from Day 1.

Words with /n/kn; /r/wr; /f/gh, ph

1. knot	That **knot** is hard to untie.
2. wrong	He dialed the **wrong** number.
3. know	Do you **know** how to speak Spanish?
4. wreck	Be careful not to **wreck** the flowers.
5. graph	Jaime made a **graph** in math class.
6. wrap	Lucy will **wrap** a scarf around her neck.
7. knife	Use the **knife** to slice the bread.
8. tough	Is the bike route **tough** or easy?
9. phone	The **phone** rang in the kitchen.
10. laugh	My sisters and I **laugh** at the puppy all the time.

ADVANCED

Challenge Words   Use the challenge words in these dictation sentences.

11. elephant	The **elephant** sprayed water from its trunk.
12. photograph	I took a **photograph** with my new camera.
13. handwriting	Ted used his best **handwriting** on the postcard.
14. knuckle	You can use your **knuckle** to knock.
15. enough	The kitten got **enough** milk to drink.

WRITING APPLICATION   Have children write a conversation between themselves and a friend, using two or more of the spelling words.

"Did you get any wrong answers?" I asked.
"Yes, it was a tough test," Jasmine said.
"I know you'll do better next time," I said.

Objective

- *To use the digraphs /n/kn; /r/wr; /f/gh, ph and other known letter-sounds to spell and write words*

Spelling Words

1.	**knot**	6.	**wrap**
2.	**wrong**	7.	**knife**
3.	**know**	8.	**tough**
4.	**wreck**	9.	**phone**
5.	**graph**	10.	**laugh**

Challenge Words

11.	**elephant**	14.	**knuckle**
12.	**photograph**	15.	**enough**
13.	**handwriting**		

Fluency
Intonation

Objective

- *To read fluently with intonation that sounds like natural speech*

✓ ASSESSMENT

Monitoring Progress

Periodically, take a timed sample of children's oral reading and measure the number of words read correctly per minute. Children should accurately read approximately 72 words per minute in the middle of Grade 2.

Fluency Support Materials

Fluency Builders, Grade 2, Lesson 16

Audiotext *Student Edition* selections are available on *Audiotext Grade 2*, CD 4.

Strategic Intervention Teacher Guide, Lesson 16

Readers' Theater

DIBELS
Oral Reading Fluency
ORF

PERFORM "MR. PUTTER AND TABBY WRITE THE BOOK" To help children improve their intonation, have them perform "Mr. Putter and Tabby Write the Book" as Readers' Theater. Use the following procedures:

▲ **Student Edition, pp. 22–43**

- Discuss with children how they can use punctuation and key words to know when to raise or lower their voice to make their reading sound like natural speech.

- Have groups of three children read the selection together. Children should alternate sections or pages.

- Listen to the groups read. Provide feedback and support.

- Invite the groups to read a section of the story to classmates. Remind them to focus on raising and lowering their voices as they read to make their words sound like natural speech.

ELL

Total Physical Response As you discuss how to use key words to read the story with the appropriate intonation, also focus on action words such as *clean, find,* and *move* on page 33. Ask children to point to the words in the picture and act them out. Model reading the words in context. Then have children match your intonation.

Setting
Comprehension

Review

REVIEW SETTING   Remind children that good readers try to figure out a story's setting, or when and where the story takes place. They look for clues in the words and in the pictures. Point out that understanding the setting can help them figure out why things are happening a certain way in the story.

▲ Read-Aloud Anthology, "The Best Story Ever," p. 60

SET A PURPOSE FOR LISTENING   Guide children to set a purpose for listening that includes:

- listening to enjoy the story.

- listening to find out when and where the story takes place.

Practice/Apply

GUIDED PRACTICE   As you read aloud "The Best Story Ever," have children help you record in a chart information about the setting.

When	Where
after school on Friday, Saturday, Sunday, and Monday	Meg's house

INDEPENDENT PRACTICE   Have children review what they know about the setting of a story by looking at the chart. Then have them tell how knowing the setting helps them understand what is happening in the story. (Possible response: Figuring out where and when a story takes place helps me understand the events that are happening and why characters act the way they do.)

Objectives

- *To identify the setting of a story*
- *To identify the importance of the setting to a story's meaning*

Skill Trace

 Tested   **Setting**

Introduce	T34–T35
Reteach	S6–S7
Review	**T67, T83, T95, T134–T135, T171, T187, T197, T389, T406**
Test	Theme 4
Maintain	Theme 5, T87

Use Picture Cards   If children have difficulty figuring out the setting of "The Best Story Ever," ask yes/no questions using *Picture Card 68* (house) and *Picture Card 28* (clock).

Build Robust Vocabulary

Objectives

- *To review robust vocabulary*
- *To demonstrate knowledge of word meanings*

REVIEW ✓ Tested

Vocabulary

Lesson 14	Lesson 16
dappled	disturb
entranced	underneath
trooped	procrastinate
circling	diversion
adorable	cozy
assortment	enchanting
habitat	instead
immense	thrilled
	review
	celebrate

Cumulative Review

REINFORCE MEANINGS   Ask children the following questions.

- If your *habitat* is *cozy*, would you rather live somewhere else *instead* of your home?

- If you had an *assortment* of toys and books, would they make a good *diversion* from something that was boring?

CONNOTATIONS CHART   Guide children in completing a chart that lists words based on whether they make children think of good feelings or bad feelings. Display **Transparency GO1** or draw a two-column chart on the board. In the left-hand column, write *Good Feelings*. In the right-hand column, write *Bad Feelings*. Then read the following words aloud: *entranced, adorable, cozy, disturb, enchanting, thrilled, procrastinate, celebrate*. After each one, pause to ask children in which column the word belongs. Encourage children to share their reasoning.

Good Feelings	Bad Feelings
entranced	disturb
adorable	procrastinate
cozy	
enchanting	
thrilled	
celebrate	

TRUE/FALSE Ask children the following true/false questions. Then discuss children's answers.

1. There is an **immense habitat underneath** the ocean. True or false? (True; Underneath the ocean is a large habitat for many kinds of living things.)

2. It is better for a movie **review** to tell how a movie ends **instead** of just telling whether the movie is good or bad. True or false? (False; a movie review that tells the end ruins the movie for others.)

3. A good **diversion** for a rancher is to watch horses **circling** the corral. True or false? (False; a diversion is something you do for amusement. This would be work for a rancher.)

4. An **assortment** of **dappled** animals would be interesting to see. True or false? (True; the dappled patterns would make the animals look interesting.)

5. If several classes **trooped** into the library at the same time, it would be hard for the library to stay quiet. True or false? (True; trooped means to move along or gather as a crowd.)

MONITOR PROGRESS

Build Robust Vocabulary

| **IF** children do not demonstrate understanding of the words and have difficulty using them, | **THEN** model using each word in several sentences, and have children repeat each sentence. |

Small-Group Instruction, pp. S10–S11:

● **BELOW-LEVEL:** Reteach
● **ON-LEVEL:** Reinforce
● **ADVANCED:** Extend

Grammar
Quick Write

Adjectives

5-DAY GRAMMAR	
DAY 1	Introduce Adjectives
DAY 2	Identify Adjectives
DAY 3	Using Adjectives in Sentences
DAY 4	Apply to Writing
DAY 5	Weekly Review

Objectives

- *To write adjectives correctly in sentences*
- *To speak in complete, coherent sentences*

Daily Proofreading

The rabbit white hopped in the snow?

(white rabbit, snow.)

Language Arts Checkpoint

If children have difficulty with the concepts, see page S12–S13 to reteach adjectives.

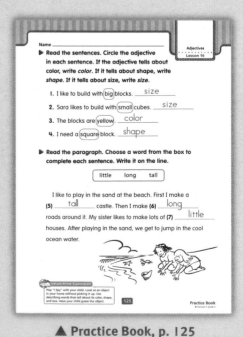

▲ Practice Book, p. 125

Review

REVIEW ADJECTIVES Review with children the following rules for identifying and using adjectives in sentences.

- An adjective describes a noun.
- Some adjectives tell about color.
- Some adjectives tell about size or shape.

Practice/Apply

GUIDED PRACTICE Model adding an adjective to tell the shape of the following noun.

table (square table)

Write the following sentences on the board. Ask volunteers to help you add adjectives to tell about the underlined nouns.

The <u>walls</u> are _____ .

The _____ <u>door</u> is open.

The _____ <u>pencil</u> is mine.

INDEPENDENT PRACTICE Have children write sentences using adjectives that tell about the color, size, or shape of an object in the classroom. Have volunteers read aloud their sentences.

Writing
How-to Paragraph

5-DAY WRITING

DAY 1	Introduce
DAY 2	Prewrite
DAY 3	Draft
DAY 4	Revise
DAY 5	Revise

Revise

REVISE HOW-TO PARAGRAPHS Ask children to check that their writing meets the criteria for a how-to paragraph and that adjectives are used correctly. Children should also make sure that their hand-writing is neat.

PROOFREADING Encourage children to use these Editor's Marks to mark any missing or incorrect words.

Editor's Marks	
∧	Add
℘	Take out

WRITING TRAIT **ORGANIZATION** Use examples from children's para-graphs to identify writing that shows a clear organization. Discuss how making the details flow together in the right order helps readers understand the steps.

NOTE: A 4-point rubric appears on page R8.

SCORING RUBRIC

	6	5	4	3	2	1
FOCUS	Completely focused, purposeful.	Focused on topic and purpose.	Generally focused on topic and purpose.	Somewhat focused on topic and purpose.	Related to topic but does not maintain focus.	Lacks focus and purpose.
ORGANIZATION	Ideas progress logically; how-to paragraph conveys sense of completeness.	Organization mostly clear, how-to paragraph gives sense of completeness.	Organization mostly clear, but some lapses occur; may seem unfinished.	Some sense of organization; seems unfinished.	Little sense of organization.	Little or no sense of organization.
SUPPORT	Strong, specific details; clear, exact language; freshness of expression.	Mostly strong de-tails; mostly clear, exact language.	Adequate support and word choice.	Limited supporting details; limited word choice.	Few supporting details; limited word choice.	Little develop-ment; limited or unclear word choice.
CONVENTIONS	Varied sentences; few, if any, errors.	Varied sentences; few errors.	Some sentence variety; few errors.	Simple sentence structures; some errors.	Simple sentence structures; many errors.	Unclear sentence structures; many errors.

REPRODUCIBLE RUBRICS for specific writing purposes and presentations are available on pages R2–R8.

Objective
• *To revise how-to paragraphs*

Writing Prompt

Independent Writing Have children generate a list of ideas for other how-to paragraphs.

WEEKLY LESSON TEST

▲ **Weekly Lesson Tests, pp. 164–175**

• Selection Comprehension with Short Response
• Phonics and Spelling
• Focus Skill
• Follow Directions
• Robust Vocabulary
• Grammar
• Fluency Passage  **FRESH READS**

GO online For prescriptions, see pp. A2–A6. Also available electronically on StoryTown Online Assessment and Exam View®.

 Podcasting: Assessing Fluency

Leveled Readers
Reinforcing Skills and Strategies

BELOW-LEVEL

A New Painting

SUMMARY   Mr. and Mrs. Green cannot find a painting that looks like their dog, so they paint the dog's portrait themselves.

Genre: Realistic Fiction

- **phonics** Digraphs /n/ *kn*; /r/ *wr*; /f/, *gh, ph*
- **Vocabulary**

  Setting

  Focus Skill

LEVELED READERS TEACHER GUIDE

▲ Vocabulary, p. 5

Before Reading

BUILD BACKGROUND/SET PURPOSE   Discuss why people like to display photographs or paintings of family and friends. Then guide children to preview the story and set a purpose for reading it.

Reading the Book

PAGES 11–12   PROBLEM/SOLUTION   What problem do the Greens have, and how do they solve it? (Possible response: None of the paintings in the shop look enough like their dog, so they make their own painting.)

PAGE 14   SETTING   How is the setting at the end of the story different from the setting at the beginning? (Possible response: It is days later, and there is a finished painting on the wall.)

REREAD FOR FLUENCY   Have groups of three take the parts of the narrator, Mr. Green, and Mrs. Green to read the story as Readers' Theater.

Think Critically   *(See inside back cover for questions.)*

1 **NOTE DETAILS**   The Greens wanted the dog in the painting to look like their dog and they wanted the dog to be sitting on grass.

2 **SETTING**   the Greens' cozy house and a shop

3 **DRAW CONCLUSIONS**   The paintings contained dogs the wrong size and dogs not sitting on grass.

4 **SEQUENCE**   They wrote a review of the pictures they had seen. Then they decided to paint their own picture.

5 **EXPRESS PERSONAL OPINION**   Answers will vary.

▲ Comprehension, p. 6

www.harcourtschool.com/storytown

★ **Leveled Readers Online Database**
Searchable by Genre, Skill, Vocabulary, Level, or Title
★ **Student Activities and Teacher Resources, online**

Genre: Realistic Fiction

ON-LEVEL

The Best Birthday

SUMMARY   Dad, Jasmine, Todd, and Tay decide that the birthday present Mom would like best is a funny play they perform themselves, and they are right.

 **phonics** Digraphs /n/*kn*; /r/*wr*; /f/*gh, ph*

• **Vocabulary**

Setting

Focus Skill

Before Reading

BUILD BACKGROUND/SET PURPOSE   Talk about the kinds of things children do to celebrate a parent's birthday. Then guide children to preview the story and set a purpose for reading it.

Reading the Book

PAGES 3–7   SUMMARIZE   Why does the family decide not to take Mom to the theater to see a play? (Possible response: One play is frightening, and another is too sad. Mom likes funny plays.)

PAGE 9 **SETTING   What does the family do to create the setting for the play?** (Possible response: They paint and paste.)

REREAD FOR FLUENCY   Have partners take turns reading. Remind them to express the characters' feelings by making their voice rise and fall naturally.

Think Critically   *(See inside back cover for questions.)*

① **IDENTIFY WITH CHARACTERS**   Possible response: happy, thrilled

② **DRAW CONCLUSIONS**   Possible response: Mom liked funny plays best, and there were no funny plays to see at the theater.

③ **SEQUENCE**   Three days before Mom's birthday, the family wrote the script. Two days before, they painted and pasted. One day before, they dressed up in funny costumes and practiced the play.

④ **SETTING**   the family's home

⑤ **EXPRESS PERSONAL OPINION**   Responses will vary.

LEVELED READERS TEACHER GUIDE

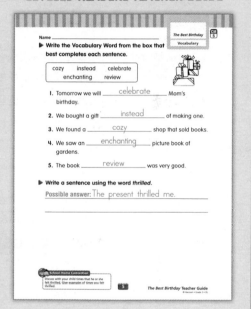

▲ Vocabulary, p. 5

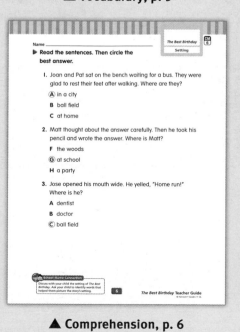

▲ Comprehension, p. 6

Leveled Readers
Reinforcing Skills and Strategies

 **ADVANCED**

by Lynne Coulter
illustrated by Clive Taylor

Genre: Realistic Fiction

First Prize

SUMMARY Joe is disappointed when his review of the book *The Biggest Cake* does not win first prize. His mood lifts when he meets Mr. Mack, the chef/author.

- **phonics** Digraphs /n/*kn*; /r/*wr*; /f/*gh, ph*
- **Vocabulary**

 Setting

Focus Skill

Before Reading

BUILD BACKGROUND/SET PURPOSE Ask children what the purpose of a book review is. Have them imagine that they have just finished reading the best book they have ever read. What might they say in a book review? Then guide children to preview the story and set a purpose for reading it.

Reading the Book

PAGES 6–8 DRAW CONCLUSIONS Why does reading the book make Joe want to meet the author? (Possible responses: Joe is curious about how someone could make such a big cake. He wants to ask the author questions.)

PAGE 14 **SETTING What is the setting at the ending of this story?** (The setting is a classroom after the prize is delivered.)

REREAD FOR FLUENCY Have partners take turns reading the story a page at a time. Remind children to make their voices rise and fall to match the mood and meaning.

Think Critically
(See inside back cover for questions.)

1. **CAUSE AND EFFECT** He baked it for his mom's sixtieth birthday.

2. **CONTEXT CLUES** Possible responses: delightful, lovely

3. **EXPRESS PERSONAL OPINION** Responses will vary.

4. **SETTING** The two settings are Joe's house and Joe's school.

5. **DRAW CONCLUSIONS** Possible response: when Joe read until he finished the book and went to tell his mom about it

LEVELED READERS TEACHER GUIDE

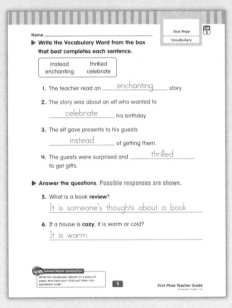

▲ Vocabulary, p. 5

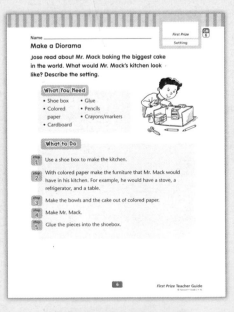

▲ Comprehension, p. 6

E L L

Genre: Realistic Fiction

Katie's Book

SUMMARY   Katie needs a topic for a book she is writing as a birthday gift for her mother. Katie follows the advice of her neighbor, a writer, and writes successfully on a topic she knows well—herself.

- Build Background
- Concept Vocabulary
- Scaffolded Language Development

Before Reading

BUILD BACKGROUND/SET PURPOSE   Ask children to name topics of books they can find in the library. List their suggestions. Talk about what an author needs to know to write on the topics, and ask children whether they think they could write on any of the topics. Then guide children to preview the story and set a purpose for reading it.

Reading the Book

PAGES 5–8   PROBLEM/SOLUTION   On page 7, Mr. Phillips asks, **"What's the problem?" What is Katie's problem?** (Possible response: She thought she knew about hamsters and cats, but she doesn't know enough to write about them. She wants to write about something she knows.)

PAGE 11 🔁 SETTING   **Where and when does Katie write her book?** (Possible response: She writes for a week, in the morning and in the afternoon. Sometimes she writes indoors and sometimes outdoors.)

REREAD FOR FLUENCY   Have partners take turns reading the story a page at a time. Remind children to pay attention to question marks and to make their voices go up at the end of a question.

Scaffolded Language Development

(See inside back cover for teacher-led activity.)

Provide additional examples and explanation as needed.

LEVELED READERS TEACHER GUIDE

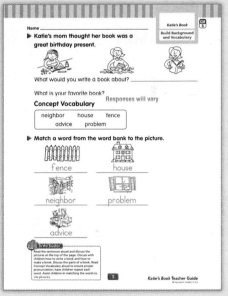

▲ Build Background and Vocabulary, p. 5

▲ Scaffolded Language Development, p. 6

Reading Writing Connection → Story

LESSON	FORM	TRAIT
16	How-to Paragraph	Organization
17	Description	Organization
18	Poem	Word Choice
19	Narrative: Biography	Word Choice
20	Student Choice: Revise and Publish	Organization and Word Choice

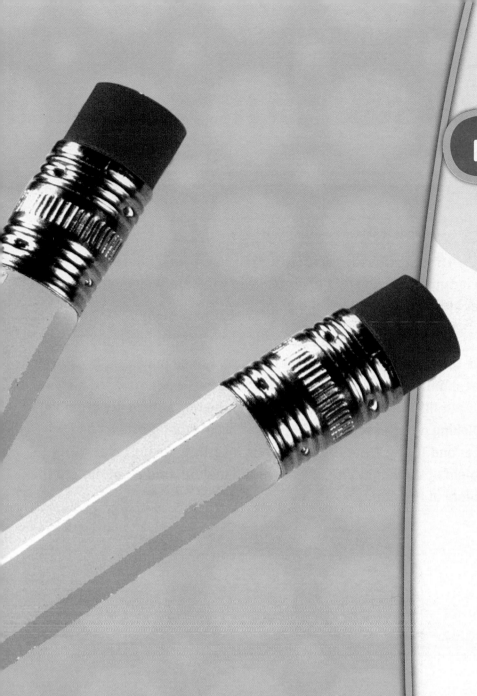

Focus on

Organization and Word Choice

Children will

- Use a literature model to generate ideas

- Select a topic

- Plan and draft a story

- Organize the story to include a beginning, middle, and end with a problem and solution

- Revise the story for word choice by replacing vague adjectives with sharp, colorful adjectives

- Publish a final version of the story

Set the Stage

Story

Objectives

- *To write a story*
- *To understand the elements of a story*
- *To generate and select ideas for writing*
- *To understand how events in stories are organized*
- *To learn how to revise writing to improve word choice*
- *To use quotation marks in dialogue*

Introduce the Writing Form

TALK ABOUT READING AND WRITING STORIES Tell children that they will be learning how to write a story. Review the story elements in a familiar story by saying the following:

Think Aloud We just read the fiction story "Mr. Putter and Tabby Write the Book." The story is set in a cozy house in winter. Mr. Putter is the main character. He wants to write a mystery story, but he can't put his ideas on paper. By the end, he has solved his problem by picking a better topic to write about. Like most stories, "Mr. Putter and Tabby Write the Book" has a setting, a character with a problem at the beginning, events in the middle, and a solution to the problem at the end.

▲ Student Edition, pp. 22–23

STAGES OF THE WRITING PROCESS Adjust pacing to meet children's needs. Guide them back and forth between the stages until the final product meets established criteria.

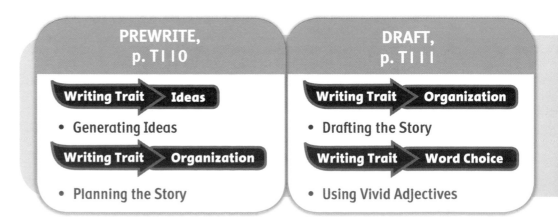

PREWRITE, p. T110	**DRAFT, p. T111**
Writing Trait ▸ Ideas	**Writing Trait** ▸ Organization
• Generating Ideas	• Drafting the Story
Writing Trait ▸ Organization	**Writing Trait** ▸ Word Choice
• Planning the Story	• Using Vivid Adjectives

Use Text as a Model

DISCUSS STORY ELEMENTS Tell children you will reread to them "The Best Story Ever" (*Read-Aloud Anthology*, page 60). Ask them to listen for the parts of a story: a setting, characters, a problem at the beginning, events in the middle, and a solved problem at the end. After reading the story, use **Transparency GO4** as you guide children to identify the story elements.

▲ Read-Aloud Anthology,
p. 60

Characters	Setting
Meg, Nick, Mom, Dad	Meg's house from Friday night to Monday night

Beginning
Meg wants to write the best story ever, but she can't finish any of the stories she begins.

Middle
Meg keeps starting different stories but still can't finish any and feels discouraged.

End
Meg tries her first story idea again and succeeds.

Tell children that when they plan their own stories, they should think about where and when it takes place, who the characters will be, and what will happen at the beginning, middle, and end.

E L L

Clarify Meaning Have children name a familiar story. Ask: **Who are the characters in the story?** Help them begin their replies with "The characters are..." Ask: **What is the setting?** Remind children that the setting is when and where the story happens. Help them begin their replies with "The setting is..."

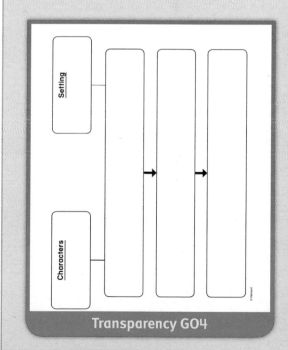

Transparency GO4

REVISE, p. T112	PROOFREAD, p. T112	PUBLISH, p. T113
Writing Trait ▶ Word Choice	**Writing Trait** ▶ Conventions	**Writing Trait** ▶ Presentation
• Revising for Word Choice	• Checking for Quotation Marks with Dialogue • Checking for Paragraph Indents	• Making a Clean Copy • Sharing the Story

Student Writing Model

Objective
To understand the stages of the writing process

Discuss the Model

READ PAGES 48–49   Have children turn to page 48 in the *Student Edition*. Explain that this page shows a story that a child wrote. Have children read the story. Ask them why the writer used the story title "The Shiny Red Pencil." Then have them read page 49.

Point out that the first thing the writer did was to think of different story ideas. Then the writer chose one that could lead to an interesting story. Tell children that they will do the same thing before they write their stories. Explain that good writers think about ideas for their stories before they write.

READ PAGES 50–51   Have children turn to pages 50–51. Explain that these pages tell what the writer does after choosing a story idea. Have children read the pages, and tell them that they will be following the same steps that the writer did—making a plan with a story map, writing a draft, and revising the draft. Emphasize that good writers go through these steps to make sure the final story is as good as it can be.

Then talk about the items in the checklist on page 51, and discuss why each one is important. Tell children to keep the checklist in mind as they write.

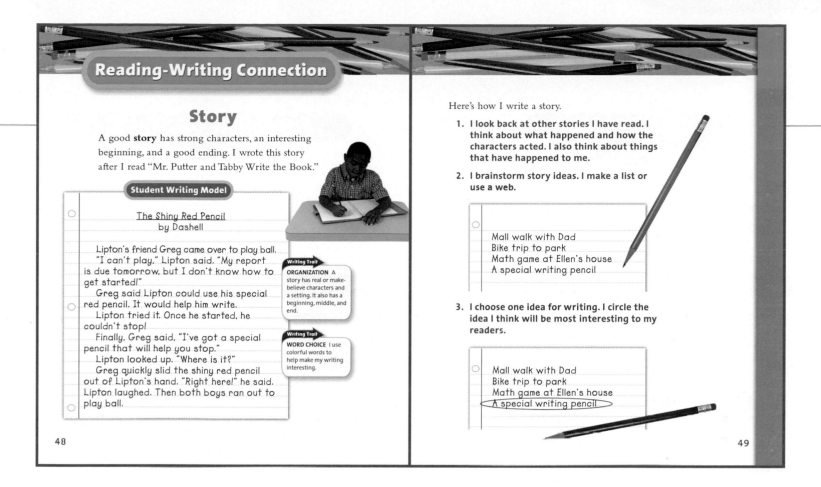

Reading-Writing Connection

Story

A good **story** has strong characters, an interesting beginning, and a good ending. I wrote this story after I read "Mr. Putter and Tabby Write the Book."

Student Writing Model

The Shiny Red Pencil
by Dashell

Lipton's friend Greg came over to play ball. "I can't play," Lipton said. "My report is due tomorrow, but I don't know how to get started!"

Greg said Lipton could use his special red pencil. It would help him write.

Lipton tried it. Once he started, he couldn't stop!

Finally, Greg said, "I've got a special pencil that will help you stop."

Lipton looked up. "Where is it?"

Greg quickly slid the shiny red pencil out of Lipton's hand. "Right here!" he said. Lipton laughed. Then both boys ran out to play ball.

Writing Trait
ORGANIZATION A story has real or make-believe characters and a setting. It also has a beginning, middle, and end.

Writing Trait
WORD CHOICE I use colorful words to help make my writing interesting.

48

Here's how I write a story.

1. I look back at other stories I have read. I think about what happened and how the characters acted. I also think about things that have happened to me.

2. I brainstorm story ideas. I make a list or use a web.

Mall walk with Dad
Bike trip to park
Math game at Ellen's house
A special writing pencil

3. I choose one idea for writing. I circle the idea I think will be most interesting to my readers.

Mall walk with Dad
Bike trip to park
Math game at Ellen's house
A special writing pencil

49

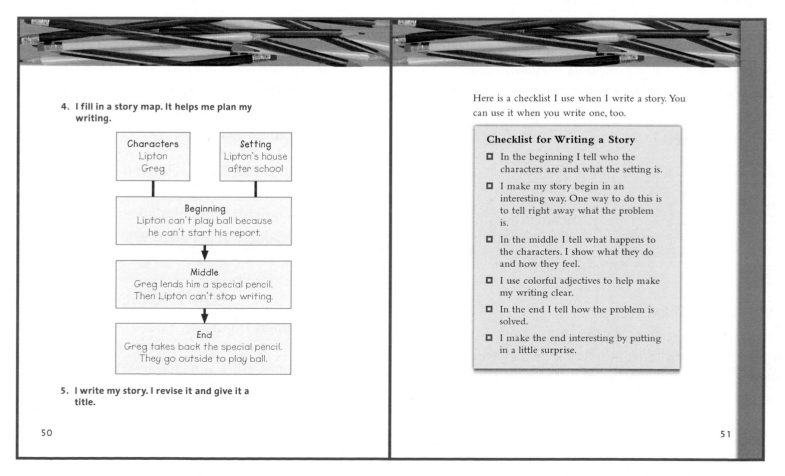

4. I fill in a story map. It helps me plan my writing.

Characters	Setting
Lipton Greg	Lipton's house after school

Beginning
Lipton can't play ball because he can't start his report.

↓

Middle
Greg lends him a special pencil. Then Lipton can't stop writing.

↓

End
Greg takes back the special pencil. They go outside to play ball.

5. I write my story. I revise it and give it a title.

50

Here is a checklist I use when I write a story. You can use it when you write one, too.

Checklist for Writing a Story

☐ In the beginning I tell who the characters are and what the setting is.

☐ I make my story begin in an interesting way. One way to do this is to tell right away what the problem is.

☐ In the middle I tell what happens to the characters. I show what they do and how they feel.

☐ I use colorful adjectives to help make my writing clear.

☐ In the end I tell how the problem is solved.

☐ I make the end interesting by putting in a little surprise.

51

Prewrite

GENERATING IDEAS
Writing Trait ▸ Ideas

Objective
To generate and select ideas for writing

Teach/Model

DISCUSS PLOT IDEAS   Display and read aloud the first two pages of "Mr. Putter and Tabby Write the Book," *Student Edition* pages 24–25. Then say:

> **Think Aloud**   The author gave her character Mr. Putter a goal right at the start. Mr. Putter's goal is to write a story. Many stories begin with a character who wants to reach a goal or solve a problem.

Apply to Writing

GUIDED PRACTICE   Encourage children to think of what characters want or need to do in other stories. They should also think of goals they have wanted to reach. Record children's ideas in a chart like this one.

Character	Goal
Jamaica Louise James	to give her grandmother an art surprise
Gus	to learn to ride a two-wheeled bike
a new student	to make friends

INDEPENDENT PRACTICE   Guide children in choosing an idea for their own story that seems especially interesting. Children should include a character and a goal.

PLANNING THE STORY
Writing Trait ▸ Organization

Objective
To plan a story that includes character, setting, and plot

Teach/Model

PLAN STORY ELEMENTS   Tell children that imagining a story character who wants to reach a goal or solve a problem will help them plan a story. To finish their plan, they should think about story elements. Say:

> **Think Aloud**   I will think about where and when the events will take place. I have to think about what my character will do at the beginning, and what will happen after that and at the end.

Apply to Writing

GUIDED PRACTICE   Have children turn to page 50 in their *Student Editions*. Ask them to tell you a goal or a problem in the beginning (Lipton can't play ball until he finishes the report) and to note how Lipton and Greg have solved the problem. (Greg takes back the pencil, and they go out to play.)

INDEPENDENT PRACTICE   Remind children of the character and goal they chose to write about. Guide them to complete their planning by using a story map (*Teacher Resource Book*, page 97).

CONFERENCE

Use a Graphic Organizer   Check that children understand that a story map will help them identify the setting and characters and what will happen throughout the story. Tell them to use clear descriptions in their maps. Model for children, as necessary.

Draft

DRAFTING THE STORY
Writing Trait ▶ Organization

> **Objective**
> *To draft a story*

Teach/Model

WRITING WITH A PLAN   Show children how to draft a story using their story maps. Revisit the Student Writing Model on *Student Edition* page 48. Compare the model story map on page 50 with the beginning of the story:

> **Think Aloud** The writer introduces the main character, the setting, and the character's problem or goal right away. The story map helped the writer stay focused on what was important to the story.

Apply to Writing

GUIDED PRACTICE   Have children read the problem in the Beginning box of the story map on page 50. Then have them reread the first three sentences of the story on page 48. Ask: **Did the writer use the story map's beginning to help him stay focused?** (Yes) **How do you know?** (The story's beginning follows the plan.)

INDEPENDENT PRACTICE   Have children use their completed story maps to start their drafts. Remind them that they should try to write a beginning that introduces readers to the setting, character, and problem and makes the readers want to find out more. As children draft, encourage them to refer to their story maps to stay focused on the story organization. Remind them that they can always revise their writing later.

DRAFTING THE STORY
Writing Trait ▶ Word Choice

> **Objective**
> *To use vivid adjectives*

Teach/Model

USE VIVID ADJECTIVES   Explain that sharp, colorful adjectives help readers picture what the writer is telling them. Write the following sentence on the board: *Ed's dog was nice.* Model replacing *nice* with a vivid adjective. Say:

> **Think Aloud** The adjective *nice* does not really help the reader picture the dog. I'll replace *nice* with *gentle*.

Apply to Writing

GUIDED PRACTICE   Have children suggest other possible replacements for *nice*, such as *friendly*, *playful*, or *obedient*.

INDEPENDENT PRACTICE   Tell children to choose adjectives as they write that will help their readers picture people, animals, and places clearly.

E L L

Support Drafting Encourage children to sketch the events in their story. Talk about each scene, and guide children to use vivid adjectives in their writing.

CONFERENCE

Drafting Check that children understand that vivid adjectives create a picture in their readers' minds. Guide them to incorporate descriptions from the graphic organizer into their stories. Model, as nessessary.

Revise/Proofread

REVISING A DRAFT
Writing Trait ▶ Word Choice

Objective
To revise a story for effective word choice

Teach/Model

CHOOSING EFFECTIVE WORDS   Tell children to imagine the scene as you read aloud *Student Edition* page 26. Talk about what they visualized. Draw attention to the phrase *everything was so soft and velvety and warm*. Emphasize that authors try to choose the best words to help readers "see" a scene.

Revise

Sammy had a great time at the beach. He did many things that were a lot of fun.

Sammy splashed in the cool ocean water. He learned to float on his back. He dug a deep tunnel in the golden sand. He wished he could stay at the beach forever.

Grade 2, Theme 4   **LA33**   Reading-Writing Connection

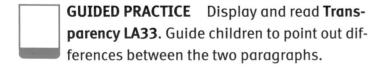

Transparency LA33

Apply to Writing

GUIDED PRACTICE   Display and read **Transparency LA33**. Guide children to point out differences between the two paragraphs.

INDEPENDENT PRACTICE   Have children reread their drafts to look for descriptions that could be made livelier. Confer with them, encouraging them to change or add words to help a reader imagine the scene.

CHECKING FOR QUOTATION MARKS
Writing Trait ▶ Conventions

Objective
To use quotation marks with dialogue

Review

REVIEWING QUOTATION MARKS   Tell children to proofread their characters' dialogue, for two things: quotation marks around the spoken words, and a new paragraph for each new speaker. Demonstrate how to show corrections.

"Thank you," said Marla.

 "You're welcome," answered Vic.

Apply to Writing

GUIDED PRACTICE   Have children check to make sure they correctly used quotation marks and indents to show dialogue. Tell them to proofread their drafts, mark corrections, and share their corrections with partners. Circulate and guide them, as needed.

Common Editing Marks

℘	delete text
∧	insert text
⋀	replace text
⁊	new paragraph

CONFERENCE

Editing Marks Check that children understand what mark to use for inserting quotation marks and where to insert them. Refer them to the list of editing marks. (See *Teacher Resource Book,* page 152.)

Evaluate/Publish

Objective
To use available technology to publish a story

Share the Writing

MAKING A CLEAN COPY Have children make clean copies of their stories, including any revision. Invite them to read their stories to each other.

The Strange Lunch

LaShawn Jeffries

 ## TECHNOLOGY

Use a Computer Encourage children to create covers for their stories using a computer. Guide them in selecting fonts and in inserting clip art.

PORTFOLIO OPPORTUNITY Place children's stories in their portfolios.

CONFERENCE

Evaluate Final Product Use the Writing Conference guide on *Teacher Resource Book* page 158 to help children evaluate their stories.

 ## ASSESSMENT

SELF-ASSESSMENT CHECKLIST Talk about the checklist children used to write their stories. Then have them self-assess their own writing in small groups and discuss with each other how they met each of the points. Discuss how each of these points supports the traits of writing and appears on rubrics.

Observation Checklist

☐ Includes a beginning that introduces the characters and setting and prepares readers for the story problem.

☐ Shows characters' feelings as events develop.

☐ Includes a resolution of the problem at the end.

☐ Includes colorful adjectives.

☐ Uses quotation marks with dialogue correctly.

NOTE: *A 4-point rubric appears on p. R8.*

SCORING RUBRIC

	6	5	4	3	2	1
FOCUS	Completely focused, purposeful.	Focused on topic and purpose.	Generally focused on topic and purpose.	Somewhat focused on topic and purpose.	Related to topic but does not maintain focus.	Lacks focus and purpose.
ORGANIZATION	Ideas progress logically; paper conveys sense of completeness.	Organization; mostly clear, paper gives sense of completeness.	Organization mostly clear, but some lapses occur; may seem unfinished.	Some sense of organization; seems unfinished.	Little sense of organization.	Little or no sense of organization.
SUPPORT	Strong, specific details; clear, exact language; freshness of expression.	Strong, specific details; clear, exact language.	Adequate support and word choice.	Limited supporting details; limited word choice.	Few supporting details; limited word choice.	Little development; limited or unclear word choice.
CONVENTIONS	Varied sentences; few, if any, errors.	Varied sentences; few errors.	Some sentence variety; few errors.	Simple sentence structures; some errors.	Simple sentence structures; many errors.	Unclear sentence structures; many errors.

REPRODUCIBLE STUDENT RUBRICS for specific writing purposes and presentations are available on pp. R2–R8.

Writing on Demand

PREPARATION

Objectives
- *To write in response to a narrative prompt*
- *To organize ideas using graphic organizers*
- *To revise and proofread for grammar, punctuation, capitalization, and spelling*

Prepare to Write

DISCUSS TIMED WRITING   Tell children that in this theme, they have written or are writing a story in which a character wants to reach a goal or solve a problem. Tell children that on a writing test, however, they may have only 30 minutes to write a story. Explain that the test will have a prompt that will tell them what their story should be about. Tell children that they will now practice writing a timed story.

ANALYZE THE PROMPT   Display **Transparency LA34.** Read the prompt with children. Explain that the prompt asks them to write a story about a character who has to solve a problem.

Point out that the first part of this prompt helps them think about characters in stories they know. The second and third parts ask them to use their knowledge of stories to make up their own.

DISCUSS ORGANIZATION Tell children that to do well on a timed writing test such as this one, they must remember the features of good narrative writing.

- The story is told in an order that makes sense.
- The story has a beginning, a middle, and an ending.
- The story shows what characters say and do, and how characters feel.

DISCUSS STAYING ON TOPIC   Tell children that in a timed test, they will not be expected to write a long and complicated story. Instead, they should focus on the main elements of a fictional story and stick to their plan:

- Start with the character's goal or problem.
- Show what the character does first, next, and after that.
- At the end, show how the goal is met or the problem is solved.

DISCUSS BUDGETING TIME   Remind children that they have 30 minutes to write, so it is important to plan their time and stay on task. Point out the suggested time allotment on Transparency LA34. Explain that some children will need more or less time for each step and that you will let them know how much time is left while they are writing.

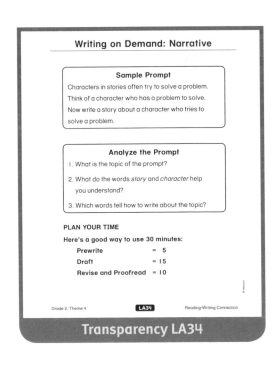

Writing on Demand: Narrative

Sample Prompt

Characters in stories often try to solve a problem. Think of a character who has a problem to solve. Now write a story about a character who tries to solve a problem.

Analyze the Prompt

1. What is the topic of the prompt?
2. What do the words *story* and *character* help you understand?
3. Which words tell how to write about the topic?

PLAN YOUR TIME

Here's a good way to use 30 minutes:

Prewrite	= 5
Draft	= 15
Revise and Proofread	= 10

Grade 2, Theme 4   **LA34**   Reading-Writing Connection

Transparency LA34

NARRATIVE WRITING

Write the Narrative

RESPOND TO A PROMPT Provide each child with a color pencil. Write the following prompt on the board and have children begin writing with lead pencils. Tell them when the first 5 minutes have passed. At the end of 30 minutes, ask children to stop writing. Then tell them to use the color pencil to complete their narratives.

> *Characters in stories may try to do something for the first time.*
>
> *Think of a character who tries to do something for the first time.*
>
> *Now write a story to tell about a character who tries to do something for the first time.*

DISCUSS TIMED WRITING Ask children to discuss their experiences during the timed writing assignment. Ask questions such as the following:

- How much of your story did you write using the color pencil? What could you do differently in order to finish on time?

- Does your writing do all the things the prompt asked you to do?

- In what ways was your prewriting helpful as you wrote your draft?

- What changes did you make in the beginning, middle, and end of your story as you revised it?

- Did you have time to proofread and correct errors?

- What could you do better the next time you write a timed story?

EVALUATE Display the rubric on page R7 and discuss what is necessary for receiving a score of 6. Provide copies of the rubric for children who may have misplaced theirs, and have them work independently or in pairs to evaluate their papers.

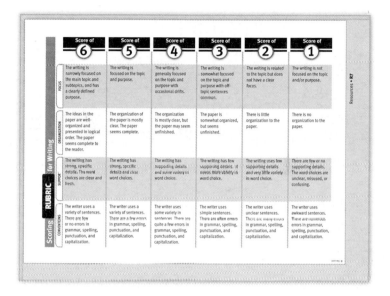

PORTFOLIO OPPORTUNITY
Children may keep their compositions in portfolios and compare them with earlier narrative writing to assess their progress.

Lesson 17

WEEK AT A GLANCE

 **Phonics**
Short Vowel /e/ea
Syllable Pattern V/CV

 **Spelling**
heavy, steady, bread, sweat, head, thread, breath, ready, meant, health

Reading
"Annie's Gifts" by Angela Shelf Medearis
REALISTIC FICTION

"Sarah Enters a Painting" by Susan Katz
POETRY

 **Fluency**
Intonation

 **Comprehension**
Setting
Follow Directions

Monitor Comprehension: Read Ahead

 **Robust Vocabulary**
journeyed, frail, stomped, sipped, entertain, except, carefree, screeching, horrendous, melodious

 **Grammar** Quick Write
Adjectives for Senses

Writing
Form: Description
Trait: Organization

Weekly Lesson Test

 = Focus Skill   = Focus Strategy   = Tested Skill

One stop *for all* *your* **Digital** *needs*

Digital
CLASSROOM

 www.harcourtschool.com/storytown
To go along with your print program

FOR THE TEACHER

Prepare Professional Development

 Videos for Podcasting

Plan & Organize Online TE & Planning Resources*

Teach Transparencies

access from Online TE

Assess  Online Assessment*

with Student Tracking System and Prescriptions

FOR THE STUDENT

Read  Student eBook*

 Strategic Intervention Interactive Reader

 Leveled Readers

Practice & Apply Splash into Phonics CD-ROM

 Also available on CD-ROM

Literature Resources

STUDENT EDITION

eBook STUDENT EDITION

ANNIE'S GIFTS
by Angela Shelf Medearis

Illustrated by Anna Rich

Genre: Realistic Fiction

Sarah Enters a Painting

Genre: Poetry

 ◀ **Audiotext** *Student Edition selections are available on Audiotext Grade 2, CD 4.*

 ◀ *Practice Quizzes for the Selection*

THEME CONNECTION: DREAM BIG
Comparing Realistic Fiction and Poetry

 Paired Selections

SOCIAL STUDIES **Annie's Gifts, pp. 58–87**

SUMMARY Annie struggles to find her own unique and special gift in a family of talented musicians.

ART **Sarah Enters a Painting, pp. 88–89**

SUMMARY A girl imagines what she would do if she could become part of the painting that she is viewing.

Support for Differentiated Instruction

   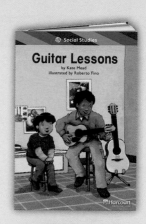

● **BELOW-LEVEL**　　● **ON-LEVEL**　　● **ADVANCED**

E L L

LEVELED PRACTICE

◀ **Strategic Intervention Resource Kit,**
Lesson 17

◀ **Strategic Intervention Interactive**
Reader, Lesson 17
Strategic Intervention Interactive Reader
Online

◀ **ELL Extra Support Kit, Lesson 17**

◀ **Challenge Resource Kit, Lesson 17**

● **BELOW-LEVEL**
Extra Support Copying Masters,
pp. 126, 128–132

● **ON-LEVEL**
Practice Book, pp. 126–133

● **ADVANCED**
Challenge Copying Masters,
pp. 126, 128–132

ADDITIONAL RESOURCES

- Decodable Book 14
- Spelling Practice Book, pp. 54–56
- Grammar Practice Book, pp. 59–62
- Reading Transparencies R83–R89
- Language Arts Transparencies LA35–LA36
- Test Prep System
◀ **Literacy Center Kit, Cards 81–85**
- Sound/Spelling Cards
◀ **Fluency Builders**
◀ **Picture Card Collection**
- Read-Aloud Anthology, pp. 64–67

ASSESSMENT

✔ **Monitor Progress**

✔ **Weekly Lesson Tests, Lesson 17**
- Comprehension　　• Robust Vocabulary
- Phonics and Spelling　• Grammar
- Focus Skill　　　　• Follow Directions

 www.harcourtschool.com/
storytown
Online Assessment
Also available on CD-ROM—Exam View®

Suggested Lesson Planner

Online TE &
Planning Resources

	Day 1	Day 2
Step 1 **Whole Group** **Daily Routines** • Oral Language • Read Aloud • High-Frequency Words	**QUESTION OF THE DAY,** p. T128 *What activities do you enjoy and do well?* **READ ALOUD,** p. T129 *Transparency R83: Cole's Collection* **WORD WALL,** p. T129	**QUESTION OF THE DAY,** p. T140 *If you could sound like a musical instrument, which one would it be? Why?* **READ ALOUD,** p. T141 *Big Book of Rhymes and Poems, "The Drum"* **WORD WALL,** p. T141
Word Work • phonics • Spelling	✔ phonics, p. T130 Introduce: Short Vowel /e/ea ✔ **SPELLING,** p. T133 Pretest: *heavy, steady, bread, sweat, head, thread, breath, ready, meant, health*	✔ phonics, p. T142 Review: Short Vowel /e/ea ✔ **SPELLING,** p. T143 Word Building
Skills and Strategies • Reading • Fluency • Comprehension • Build Robust Vocabulary	✔ **READING/COMPREHENSION,** p. T134 Introduce: Setting **LISTENING COMPREHENSION,** p. T136 Read-Aloud: "Sophie's Masterpiece" **FLUENCY,** p. T136 Focus: Intonation ✔ **BUILD ROBUST VOCABULARY,** p. T137 *Words from the Read-Aloud*	✔ **BUILD ROBUST VOCABULARY,** p. T144 *Words from the Selection* Word Champion, p. T145 ✔ **READING,** p. T146 "Annie's Gifts" *Options for Reading* ✔ **COMPREHENSION,** p. T146 Introduce: Monitor Comprehension: Read Ahead **RETELLING/FLUENCY,** p. T162 Intonation ✔ **BUILD ROBUST VOCABULARY,** p. T163 *Words About the Selection*

▲ Student Edition

Step 2 **Small Groups**	**Suggestions for Differentiated Instruction (See pp. T122–T123.)**	

| **Step 3** **Whole Group**

Language Arts
• Grammar Quick Write
• Writing | ✔ **GRAMMAR,** p. T138
Introduce: Adjectives for Senses

Daily Proofreading
i played with Andys train (I, Andy's, train.)

✏ **WRITING,** p. T139
Introduce: Description
Writing Trait: Organization

Writing Prompt Describe a classroom object by using all of your senses. | ✔ **GRAMMAR,** p. T164
Review: Adjectives for Senses

Daily Proofreading
On monday, I put away the dishs clean.
(Monday, clean dishes.)

✏ **WRITING,** p. T165
Review: Description
Writing Trait: Organization

Writing Prompt Write about an experience that you have had visiting a special place with family or friends. |

 = Focus Skill   = Focus Strategy   ✔ = Tested Skill

Skills at a Glance

phonics	Comprehension	Fluency	Vocabulary
• Short Vowel /e/ea • Syllable Pattern V/CV	**Focus Skill** Setting **Focus Strategy** Monitor Comprehension: Read Ahead	Intonation	**ROBUST:** *journeyed, frail, stomped, sipped, entertain, except, carefree, screeching, horrendous, melodious*

Day 3

QUESTION OF THE DAY, p. T166
What do you think of when you hear the beat of a drum?

READ ALOUD, p. T167
Big Book of Rhymes and Poems, "The Drum"

WORD WALL, p. T167

 phonics, p. T168
Review: Short Vowel /e/ea

✔ **SPELLING,** p. T169
State the Generalization

FLUENCY, p. T170
Intonation:
"Annie's Gifts"

✔ **COMPREHENSION,** p. T171
Review: Setting
Introduce: Follow Directions
Paired Selection:
"Sarah Enters a Painting"

CONNECTIONS, p. T176

 ✔ **BUILD ROBUST VOCABULARY,** p. T178
Review

 ▲ Student Edition

Day 4

QUESTION OF THE DAY, p. T182
Picture a clean sheet of lined paper. What words describe the paper?

READ ALOUD, p. T183
Big Book of Rhymes and Poems, "New Notebook"

WORD WALL, p. T183

 phonics, p. T184
Introduce: Syllable Pattern V/CV

✔ **SPELLING,** p. T185
Review Spelling Words

FLUENCY, p. T186
Intonation:
"Annie's Gifts"

✔ **COMPREHENSION,** p. T187
Review: Setting

✔ **BUILD ROBUST VOCABULARY,** p. T188
Review

 ▲ Student Edition

Day 5

QUESTION OF THE DAY, p. T192
Which would you rather have—a notebook or separate sheets of paper? Why?

READ ALOUD, p. T193
Big Book of Rhymes and Poems, "New Notebook"

WORD WALL, p. T193

  phonics, p. T194
Review: Syllable Pattern V/CV

✔ **SPELLING,** p. T195
Posttest

FLUENCY, p. T196
Intonation:
"Annie's Gifts"

✔ **COMPREHENSION,** p. T197
Review: Setting
Read-Aloud:
"Sophie's Masterpiece"

✔ **BUILD ROBUST VOCABULARY,** p. T198
Cumulative Review

 ▲ Student Edition

● **BELOW-LEVEL** ● **ON-LEVEL** ● **ADVANCED** **E L L**

✔ **GRAMMAR,** p. T180
Review: Adjectives for Senses

Daily Proofreading
the noisy gooses flew overhead.
(The, geese)

  WRITING, p. T181
Review: Description
Writing Trait: Organization

Writing Prompt *Write a sentence describing Annie in "Annie's Gifts."*

✔ **GRAMMAR,** p. T190
Review: Adjectives for Senses

Daily Proofreading
did you make a mess that was sticky
(Did, sticky? or Did, a sticky mess?)

  WRITING, p. T191
Review: Description
Writing Trait: Organization

Writing Prompt *Compare writing a description of a place to drawing it. Which would you like more? Why?*

✔ **GRAMMAR,** p. T200
Review: Adjectives for Senses

Daily Proofreading
Aunt lucy gave Me a fluffy bunny.
(Lucy, me)

 WRITING, p. T201
Review: Description
Writing Trait: Organization

Writing Prompt *Make a list of ideas about a new topic of your choice for writing.*

Suggested Small-Group Planner

 45-60+ Minutes

	Day 1	Day 2
15-20+ Minutes **BELOW-LEVEL**	**Teacher-Directed** Leveled Reader: "Hannah's Dance," p. T202 Before Reading **Independent** ⭐ Listening/Speaking Center, p. T126 Extra Support Copying Masters, pp. 126, 128 ▲ Leveled Reader	**Teacher-Directed** Student Edition: "Annie's Gifts," p. T146 **Independent** ⭐ Reading Center, p. T126 Extra Support Copying Masters, p. 130 ▲ Student Edition
15-20+ Minutes **ON-LEVEL**	**Teacher-Directed** Leveled Reader: "Joshua and the Tigers," p. T203 Before Reading **Independent** ⭐ Reading Center, p. T126 Practice Book, pp. 126, 128 ▲ Leveled Reader	**Teacher-Directed** Student Edition: "Annie's Gifts," p. T146 **Independent** ⭐ Letters and Sounds Center, p. T127 Practice Book, p. 130 ▲ Student Edition
15-20+ Minutes **ADVANCED**	**Teacher-Directed** Leveled Reader: "Hunter's Secret," p. T204 Before Reading **Independent** ⭐ Letters and Sounds Center, p. T127 Challenge Copying Masters, pp. 126, 128 ▲ Leveled Reader	**Teacher-Directed** Leveled Reader: "Hunter's Secret," p. T204 Read the Book **Independent** ⭐ Word Work Center, p. T127 Challenge Copying Masters, p. 130 ▲ Leveled Reader
 **English-Language Learners** *In addition to the small-group instruction above, use the ELL Extra Support Kit to promote language development.*	**LANGUAGE DEVELOPMENT SUPPORT** **Teacher-Directed** ELL TG, Day 1 **Independent** ELL Copying Masters, Lesson 17 ▲ ELL Student Handbook	**LANGUAGE DEVELOPMENT SUPPORT** **Teacher-Directed** ELL TG, Day 2 **Independent** ELL Copying Masters, Lesson 17 ▲ ELL Student Handbook
Intervention ▲ Strategic Intervention Resource Kit ▲ Strategic Intervention Interactive Reader	Strategic Intervention TG, Day 1 Strategic Intervention Practice Book, Lesson 17	Strategic Intervention TG, Day 2 Strategic Intervention Interactive Reader, Lesson 17 ▲ Strategic Intervention Interactive Reader

MONITOR PROGRESS
Small-Group Instruction

Comprehension	Phonics	Comprehension	Fluency	Robust Vocabulary	Language Arts Checkpoint
Focus Skill Setting pp. S18–S19	Short Vowel /e/ea pp. S14–S15	Follow Directions pp. S20–S21	Intonation pp. S16–S17	*journeyed, frail, stomped, sipped, entertain, except, carefree, screeching, horrendous, melodious,* pp. S22–S23	**Grammar:** Adjectives for Senses **Writing:** Description pp. S24–S25

Day 3

Teacher-Directed
Leveled Reader:
"Hannah's Dance," p. T202
Read the Book

Independent
⭐ Word Work Center, p. T127
Extra Support Copying Masters,
p. 131

▲ Leveled Reader

Teacher-Directed
Leveled Reader:
"Joshua and the Tigers," p. T203
Read the Book

Independent
⭐ Writing Center, p. T127
Practice Book, p. 131

▲ Leveled Reader

Teacher-Directed
Leveled Reader:
"Hunter's Secret," p. T204
Think Critically

Independent
⭐ Listening/Speaking Center,
p. T126
Challenge Copying Masters, p. 131

▲ Leveled Reader

LANGUAGE DEVELOPMENT SUPPORT

Teacher-Directed
Leveled Reader: "Guitar Lessons,"
p. T205
Before Reading; Read the Book
ELL TG, Day 3

Independent
ELL Copying Masters, Lesson 17

▲ Leveled Reader

Strategic Intervention TG, Day 3
Strategic Intervention Interactive
Reader, Lesson 17
Strategic Intervention Practice Book,
Lesson 17

▲ Strategic Intervention Interactive Reader

Day 4

Teacher-Directed
Leveled Reader:
"Hannah's Dance," p. T202
Reread for Fluency

Independent
⭐ Letters and Sounds Center,
p. T127

▲ Leveled Reader

Teacher-Directed
Leveled Reader:
"Joshua and the Tigers," p. T203
Reread for Fluency

Independent
⭐ Word Work Center, p. T127

▲ Leveled Reader

Teacher-Directed
Leveled Reader:
"Hunter's Secret," p. T204
Reread for Fluency

Independent
⭐ Writing Center, p. T127
Self-Selected Reading:
Classroom Library Collection

▲ Leveled Reader

LANGUAGE DEVELOPMENT SUPPORT

Teacher-Directed
Leveled Reader: "Guitar Lessons,"
p. T205
Reread for Fluency
ELL TG, Day 4

Independent
ELL Copying Masters, Lesson 17

▲ Leveled Reader

Strategic Intervention TG, Day 4
Strategic Intervention Interactive
Reader, Lesson 17

▲ Strategic Intervention Interactive Reader

Day 5

Teacher-Directed
Leveled Reader:
"Hannah's Dance," p. T202
Think Critically

Independent
⭐ Writing Center, p. T127
Leveled Reader: Reread for Fluency
Extra Support Copying Masters,
p. 132

▲ Leveled Reader

Teacher-Directed
Leveled Reader:
"Joshua and the Tigers," p. T203
Think Critically

Independent
⭐ Listening/Speaking Center,
p. T126
Leveled Reader: Reread for Fluency
Practice Book, p. 132

▲ Leveled Reader

Teacher-Directed
Leveled Reader:
"Hunter's Secret," p. T204
Reread for Fluency

Independent
⭐ Reading Center, p. T126
Leveled Reader: Reread for Fluency
Self-Selected Reading:
Classroom Library Collection
Challenge Copying Masters, p. 132

▲ Leveled Reader

LANGUAGE DEVELOPMENT SUPPORT

Teacher-Directed
Leveled Reader: "Guitar Lessons,"
p. T205
Think Critically
ELL TG, Day 5

Independent
Leveled Reader: Reread for Fluency
ELL Copying Masters, Lesson 17

▲ Leveled Reader

Strategic Intervention TG, Day 5
Strategic Intervention Interactive
Reader, Lesson 17

▲ Strategic Intervention Interactive Reader

Leveled Readers & Leveled Practice
Reinforcing Skills and Strategies

LEVELED READERS SYSTEM

- **Leveled Readers**
- **Leveled Readers, CD**
- **Leveled Readers Teacher Guides**
  - *Comprehension*
  - *Vocabulary*
  - *Oral Reading Fluency Assessment*
- **Response Activities**
- **Leveled Readers Assessment**

See pages T202–T205 for lesson plans.

BELOW-LEVEL

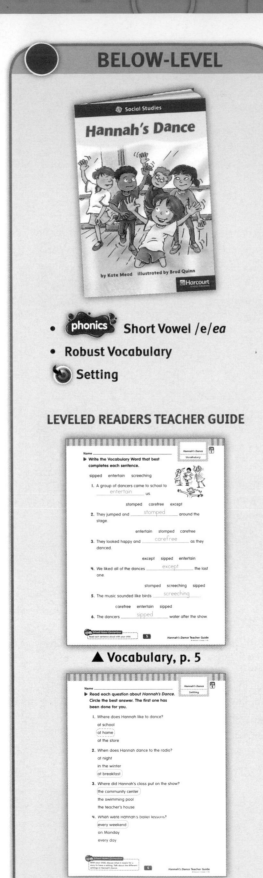

- **phonics** Short Vowel /e/*ea*
- **Robust Vocabulary**
- **Setting**

LEVELED READERS TEACHER GUIDE

▲ Vocabulary, p. 5

▲ Comprehension, p. 6

ON-LEVEL

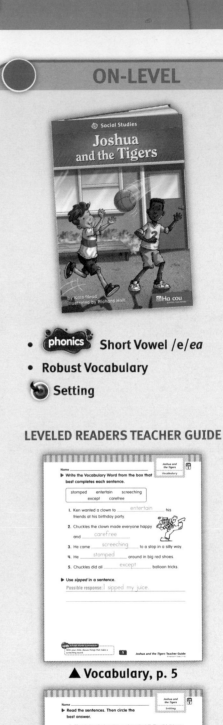

- **phonics** Short Vowel /e/*ea*
- **Robust Vocabulary**
- **Setting**

LEVELED READERS TEACHER GUIDE

▲ Vocabulary, p. 5

▲ Comprehension, p. 6

www.harcourtschool.com/storytown

GO online

★ **Leveled Readers, Online Database**
Searchable by Genre, Skill, Vocabulary, Level, or Title

★ **Student Activities and Teacher Resources, online**

ADVANCED

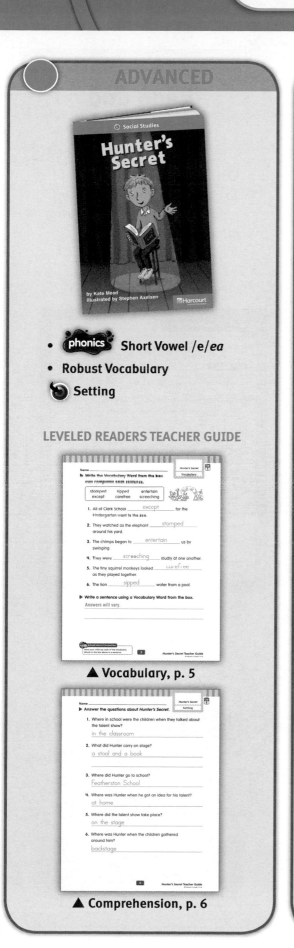

Social Studies

Hunter's Secret
by Kate Mead
illustrated by Stephen Axelsen
Harcourt

- **phonics** Short Vowel /e/*ea*
- **Robust Vocabulary**
- **Setting**

LEVELED READERS TEACHER GUIDE

▲ Vocabulary, p. 5

▲ Comprehension, p. 6

E L L

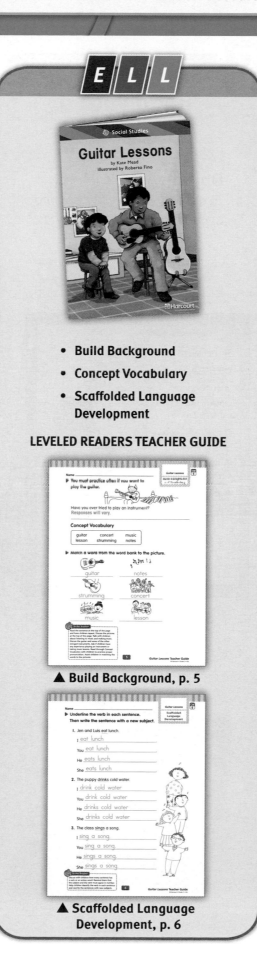

Social Studies

Guitar Lessons
by Kate Mead
illustrated by Roberto Fino
Harcourt

- **Build Background**
- **Concept Vocabulary**
- **Scaffolded Language Development**

LEVELED READERS TEACHER GUIDE

▲ Build Background, p. 5

▲ Scaffolded Language Development, p. 6

CLASSROOM LIBRARY

for Self-Selected Reading

EASY

▲ *The Dot* by Peter H. Reynolds.
FICTION

AVERAGE

▲ *Billy's Bucket* by Kes Gray.
FICTION

CHALLENGE

▲ *Mae Jemison* by Thomas Streissguth.
NONFICTION

Classroom Library Books
Teacher Guide

▲ Classroom Library Books
Teacher Guide, Lesson 17

Literacy Centers

15 Min. each

Management Support

While you provide direct instruction to individuals or small groups, other children can work on literacy center activities.

▲ **Literacy Center Pocket Chart**

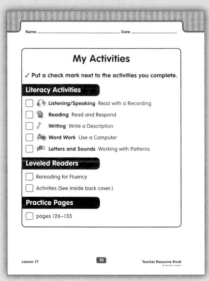

Name _____ Date _____

My Activities

✓ Put a check mark next to the activities you complete.

Literacy Activities

☐ **Listening/Speaking** Read with a Recording

☐ **Reading** Read and Respond

☐ **Writing** Write a Description

☐ **Word Work** Use a Computer

☐ **Letters and Sounds** Working with Patterns

Leveled Readers

☐ Rereading for Fluency

☐ Activities (See inside back cover.)

Practice Pages

☐ pages 126–133

Lesson 17   50   Teacher Resource Book

▲ **Teacher Resource Book, p. 50**

Homework for the Week

TEACHER RESOURCE BOOK, PAGE 20

The *Homework Copying Master* provides activities to complete for each day of the week.

GO online **www.harcourtschool.com/ storytown**

LISTENING/SPEAKING

Read with a Recording

Objective
To develop fluency by listening to and reading familiar stories

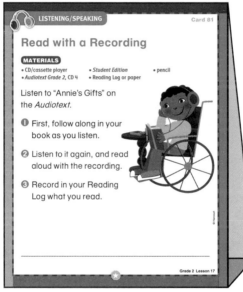

LISTENING/SPEAKING   Card 81

Read with a Recording

MATERIALS
- CD/cassette player
- Audiotext Grade 2, CD 4
- Student Edition
- Reading Log or paper
- pencil

Listen to "Annie's Gifts" on the *Audiotext*.

❶ First, follow along in your book as you listen.

❷ Listen to it again, and read aloud with the recording.

❸ Record in your Reading Log what you read.

Grade 2 • Lesson 17

⭐ **Literacy Center Kit • Card 81**

ANNIE'S GIFTS
by Angela Shelf Medearis

Illustrated

READING

Read and Respond

Objective
To develop comprehension by reading silently and comparing familiar stories

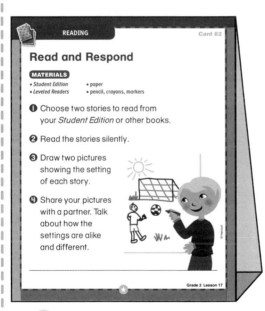

READING   Card 82

Read and Respond

MATERIALS
- Student Edition
- Leveled Readers
- paper
- pencil, crayons, markers

❶ Choose two stories to read from your *Student Edition* or other books.

❷ Read the stories silently.

❸ Draw two pictures showing the setting of each story.

❹ Share your pictures with a partner. Talk about how the settings are alike and different.

Grade 2 • Lesson 17

⭐ **Literacy Center Kit • Card 82**

Mae Jemison

STORYTOWN

BILL

WRITING

Write a Description

Objective
To practice writing a description

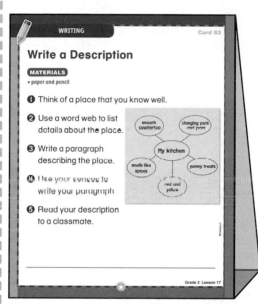

WRITING   Card 83

Write a Description

MATERIALS
• paper and pencil

❶ Think of a place that you know well.

❷ Use a word web to list details about the place.

❸ Write a paragraph describing the place.

❹ Use your sentences to write your paragraph.

❺ Read your description to a classmate.

smooth countertop / clanging pots and pans / My kitchen / smells like spices / yummy treats / red and yellow

Grade 2 Lesson 17

⭐ **Literacy Center Kit** • Card 83

red and yellow / smells like spices / My Kitchen / yummy treats / smooth countertop

WORD WORK

Use a Computer

Objective
To practice using Vocabulary Words

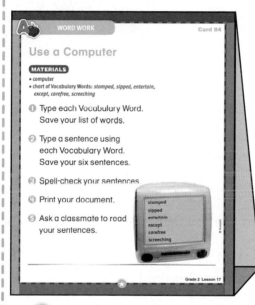

WORD WORK   Card 84

Use a Computer

MATERIALS
• computer
• chart of Vocabulary Words: *stomped, sipped, entertain, except, carefree, screeching*

❶ Type each Vocabulary Word. Save your list of words.

❷ Type a sentence using each Vocabulary Word. Save your six sentences.

❸ Spell-check your sentences.

❹ Print your document.

❺ Ask a classmate to read your sentences.

stomped / sipped / entertain / except / carefree / screeching

Grade 2 Lesson 17

⭐ **Literacy Center Kit** • Card 84

I stomped to my room. The butterfly looked carefree.

LETTERS AND SOUNDS

Working with Patterns

Objective
To use common spelling patterns to read, write, and sort words

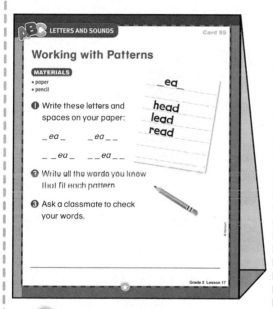

LETTERS AND SOUNDS   Card 85

Working with Patterns

MATERIALS
• paper
• pencil

❶ Write these letters and spaces on your paper:

_ea_   _ea_ _

_ _ea_   _ _ea_ _

_ea_ / head / lead / read

❷ Write all the words you know that fit each pattern.

❸ Ask a classmate to check your words.

Grade 2 Lesson 17

⭐ **Literacy Center Kit** • Card 85

Day at a Glance

Day 1

 **phonics** and Spelling

- Introduce: Short Vowel /e/*ea*
- Pretest

Reading/ Comprehension

 Introduce: Setting, *Student Edition,* pp. 54–55

- *Read-Aloud Anthology:* "Sophie's Masterpiece"

Fluency

- Model Oral Fluency

Robust Vocabulary

Words from the Read-Aloud
- Introduce: *journeyed, frail*

Grammar Quick Write

- Introduce: Adjectives for Senses

Writing

- Description

Warm-Up Routines

 Oral Language

Objective *To listen attentively and respond appropriately to oral communication*

> ## Question of the Day
>
> **What activities do you enjoy and do well?**

Help children brainstorm activities that they do well. Remind children to respond courteously to each question. Use the following prompts:

- **What activity do you like to do for fun? What makes you good at this activity?**

- **Do you play any sports? If so, what makes you a good player?**

- **Do you sing, dance, or play a musical instrument? Which one do you do?**

Then have children complete the following sentence frame to explain the reasons for their choice.

I am good at _____

because _____.

Read Aloud

Objective *To listen for a purpose*

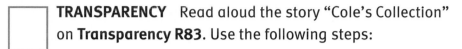

TRANSPARENCY Read aloud the story "Cole's Collection" on **Transparency R83**. Use the following steps:

- **Set a purpose for listening.** Tell children to listen to find out what Cole collects.

- **Model fluent reading.** Read the story aloud. Point out that good readers read with feeling. They change the tone and pitch, or intonation, of their voice to show the mood and meaning of words in the story.

- **Discuss the story.** Ask: **Where and when does this story take place?** (a hot day in July; on a basketball court at the playground, and at Cole's home)

Setting

Cole's Collection

It was a hot day in July. Cole wanted to play basketball in the park with his older brothers.

"You're not tall enough yet," said Jared.

"Sorry, but you can't dribble fast enough," said Tyrone as Cole headed off the court.

Back at home, Cole poked his head into his sister's room. Shana was working on her scrapbook. "Can I help?" asked Cole.

"Thanks, Cole, but you're too young to cut this special paper," Shana told him. "This cutting takes a steady hand."

Cole shuffled to his room. Everyone thought he was too young to do anything well. Then Cole remembered his collection. He pulled it off its special place on his shelf. Cole looked at the pictures he had drawn of insects and spiders that he'd seen in his yard. Butterflies, spiders, ants, grasshoppers—his drawings showed every small detail.

"I will draw some more bugs," said Cole. "I know I can do that!"

Grade 2, Lesson 17   R83   Comprehension

Transparency R83

Word Wall

Objective *To read high-frequency words*

REVIEW HIGH-FREQUENCY WORDS Review the words *children, ears, special, sometimes,* and *brother.* Randomly point to a word and ask children to read it. Point to each word—in order and randomly—several times.

children   ears   special

sometimes   brother

Short Vowel /e/ea

 phonics *and Spelling*

Objectives

- *To recognize and blend the short vowel sound of /e/ea*
- *To read words with /e/ea and other known letter-sounds*
- *To use /e/ea and other known letter-sounds to spell words*

Skill Trace

 Tested **Short Vowel /e/ea**

Introduce	T130–T133
Reteach	S14–S15
Review	T142–T143, T168–T169, T404
Text	Theme 4
Maintain	Theme 6, T82

Refer to *Sounds of Letters CD* Track 14 for pronunciation of /e/.

Connect Letters to Sounds

WARM UP WITH PHONEMIC AWARENESS Say the words *head* and *thread*. Have children say the words. Say: **The words *head and thread* have the /e/ sound in the middle.** Have children say /e/ several times. Then have children substitute the /e/ sound for other sounds to create new words. Say:

- **Say the word *study*. Change the /u/ sound to /e/. What's the new word?** (steady)

- **Say the word *wither*. Change the /i/ sound to /e/. What's the new word?** (weather)

- **Say the word *braid*. Change the /ā/ sound to /e/. What's the new word?** (bread)

Routine Card 1 **CONNECT LETTERS AND SOUNDS** Display the *Sound/Spelling Card* for *e*. Point to the letters *ea* and review their letter/sound correspondence. Say: **The letters *ea* can stand for the /e/ sound, the sound in *bread*.** Touch the vowel pair several times, and have children say the /e/ sound each time.

▲ **Sound/Spelling Card**

5-DAY PHONICS	
DAY 1	Introduce /e/ea
DAY 2	Word Building with /e/ea
DAY 3	Word Building with /e/ea
DAY 4	Syllable Pattern V/CV; Review /e/ea
DAY 5	Syllable Pattern V/CV; Review /e/ea

Work with Patterns

REINFORCE /e/ea Write the words *head, weather,* and *team* on the board and have children read them with you. Underline *ea* in each word.

Tell children that in the words *head* and *weather*, the letters *ea* stand for the /e/ sound. Remind them that *ea* can also stand for the /ē/ sound, as in *team*.

Explain that good readers use the sound that makes sense in the sentence they are reading. Write the following sentences on the board and discuss the correct pronunciation of the underlined words in each one.

> May I <u>please</u> have some <u>bread</u>?
>
> I was covered with <u>sweat</u> after my <u>team</u> won the game.
>
> She <u>read</u> a wonderful book last week.
>
> The <u>weather</u> was perfect for the game.

Short Vowel /e/ea

phonics *and Spelling*

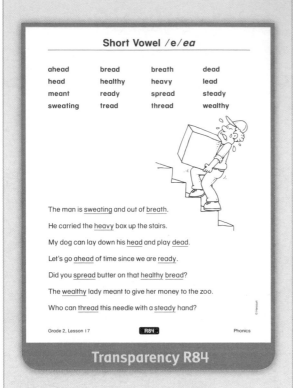

Short Vowel /e/ea

ahead	bread	breath	dead
head	healthy	heavy	lead
meant	ready	spread	steady
sweating	tread	thread	wealthy

The man is sweating and out of breath.

He carried the heavy box up the stairs.

My dog can lay down his head and play dead.

Let's go ahead of time since we are ready.

Did you spread butter on that healthy bread?

The wealthy lady meant to give her money to the zoo.

Who can thread this needle with a steady hand?

Grade 2, Lesson 17   **R84**   Phonics

Transparency R84

Reading Words

GUIDED PRACTICE Display **Transparency R84** or write the words and sentences on the board. Point to the word *ahead*. Read the word, and then have children read the word with you.

INDEPENDENT PRACTICE Point to the remaining words in the top portion and have children read them. Then have children read aloud the sentences and identify the words that have the short vowel pair *ea*.

Decodable Books

Additional Decoding Practice

- **Phonics**
  Short Vowel /e/ea
- **Decodable Words**
- **High-Frequency Words**
  See lists in *Decodable Book 14*.

  See also *Decodable Books*, online (Take-Home Version).

▲ **Decodable Book 14**
"Get Ready, Get Fit, Go!"

BELOW-LEVEL   **ON-LEVEL**   **ADVANCED**

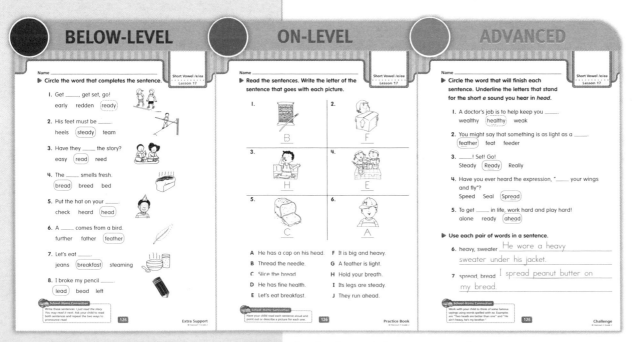

▲ **Extra Support, p. 126**   ▲ **Practice Book, p. 126**   ▲ **Challenge, p. 126**

ELL

- Group children according to academic levels, and assign one of the pages on the left.

- Clarify any unfamiliar concepts as necessary. See *ELL Teacher Guide* Lesson 17 for support in scaffolding instruction.

5-DAY SPELLING

DAY 1	Pretest
DAY 2	Word Building
DAY 3	State the Generalization
DAY 4	Review
DAY 5	Posttest

Introduce Spelling Words

PRETEST Say the first word and read the dictation sentence. Repeat the word as children write it. Write the word on the board and have children check their spelling. Tell them to circle the word if they spelled it correctly or write it correctly if they did not. Repeat for words 2–10.

Words with /e/*ea*

1.	heavy	The box is too **heavy** to lift.
2.	steady	The drummer plays with a **steady** beat.
3.	bread	Jan ate a slice of **bread**.
4.	sweat	Hard work can make you **sweat**.
5.	head	Cover your **head** with a hat.
6.	thread	Matt used blue **thread** to sew on his button.
7.	breath	Catch your **breath** after the mile run.
8.	ready	Are you **ready** to go to school?
9.	meant	The teacher **meant** to give everyone a sticker.
10.	health	Daily exercise can help you have good **health**.

ADVANCED

Challenge Words Use the challenge words in these dictation sentences.

11.	meadow	The lark sings in the **meadow**.
12.	instead	I'll eat an apple **instead** of chips.
13.	breakfast	Lisa ate toast for **breakfast**.
14.	treasure	Divers found the **treasure** chest.
15.	feather	The man wears a **feather** in his hat.

Spelling Words

1.	heavy	6.	thread
2.	steady	7.	breath
3.	bread	8.	ready
4.	sweat	9.	meant
5.	head	10.	health

Challenge Words

11.	meadow	14.	treasure
12.	instead	15.	feather
13.	breakfast		

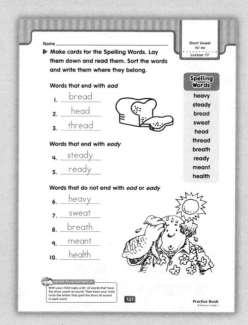

▲ Practice Book, p. 127

Setting
Comprehension

Objectives

- *To identify the setting of a story*
- *To analyze setting elements*

Daily Comprehension
Setting

DAY 1:	Introduce Setting *Student Edition*
DAY 2:	Review Setting *Student Edition*
DAY 3:	Review Setting *Student Edition*
DAY 4:	Review Setting *Transparency*
DAY 5:	Review Setting *Read-Aloud Anthology*

✓ MONITOR PROGRESS

Setting

IF children have difficulty identifying when and where the story takes place,	**THEN** have them suggest a favorite story and help them tell when and where that story takes place.

Small-Group Instruction, pp. S18–S19:

- ● **BELOW-LEVEL:** Reteach
- ● **ON-LEVEL:** Reinforce
- ● **ADVANCED:** Extend

Teach/Model

DISCUSS SETTING   Have children read *Student Edition* page 54. Model how to determine the setting of a story.

> **Think Aloud**   As I read a story, I think about when and where it takes place. I look for clues that tell me the time of day. I also look for clues that tell me where the main character is. Sometimes, knowing where and when the story takes place helps me understand what happens to the characters in the story.

Practice/Apply

GUIDED PRACTICE   Draw a setting chart like the one on *Student Edition* page 55. Then read "Mr. Joseph's Jingle" with children. Guide them to tell when the story takes place. (one whole day) Add the information to the chart. Ask: **Which words tell you that the story takes place during one whole day?** (morning, at lunch, dinner, at the end of the day)

Try This!   INDEPENDENT PRACTICE   Ask children to tell where the story takes place. (the city) Add their response to the chart.

Setting	
When	**Where**
• one whole day	• city

Focus Skill

Setting

The **setting** is the time and place in which a story happens. A story can happen over any length of time. It can happen in one or more places.

As you read, look for details that tell the exact time and place of the story. This chart shows some setting details to watch for.

Setting	
When	**Where**
Season	City
Day of week	Street
Time of day	Kind of home

Think about why the setting is important in a story. Ask yourself how the story would be different if its setting were changed.

54

Read the story. Which words tell you when the story takes place?

Mr. Joseph's Jingle

Mr. Joseph jingles when he walks. That's because he always carries a lot of coins in his pockets. He doesn't go anywhere in the city without his pennies, nickels, dimes, and quarters.

Mr. Joseph needs quarters for the bus in the morning. He uses dimes to buy a newspaper at lunch. He gives the baker nickels for fresh bread for dinner. At the end of the day, he puts his pennies into a jar. When the jar is full, he gives it to the city's animal shelter.

Setting	
When	**Where**

Try This!

Look back at the story. What words tell where the story takes place?

www.harcourtschool.com/storytown

55

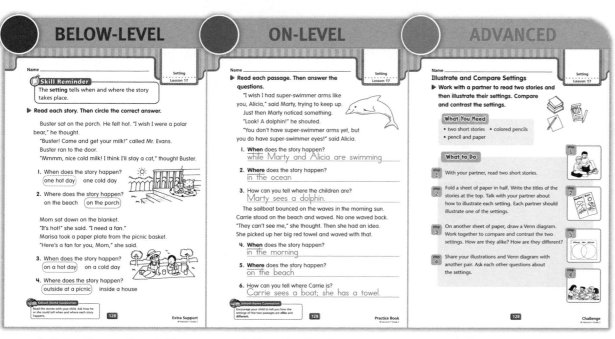

BELOW-LEVEL

▲ Extra Support, p. 128

ON-LEVEL

▲ Practice Book, p. 128

ADVANCED

▲ Challenge, p. 128

ELL

- Group children according to academic levels, and assign one of the pages on the left.

- Clarify any unfamiliar concepts as necessary. See *ELL Teacher Guide* Lesson 17 for support in scaffolding instruction.

Listening Comprehension
Read Aloud

Objectives
- *To discuss the genre of tales*
- *To identify the setting of a tale*

Build Fluency

Focus: Intonation Tell children that good readers try to read every sentence with feeling. Feeling can come from changing the tone (low, medium, or high pitch) of your voice when reading aloud.

"Research Says"

Fluency "Fluency represents a level of expertise beyond word recognition accuracy, and reading comprehension may be aided by fluency. Skilled readers read words accurately, rapidly and efficiently."

—National Reading Panel (2000)

Connect to Prior Knowledge
Draw a spider on the board. Then show children both sides of *Picture Card 69*. Explain that spiders have eight legs, a body in two segments, and no wings. Remind children that real spiders catch insects in their webs for food.

Before Reading

CONNECT TO PRIOR KNOWLEDGE Tell children that they will listen to a tale called "Sophie's Masterpiece." Explain that the story is about the life of a spider whose special gift is spinning beautiful webs. Ask children to describe spider webs they have seen.

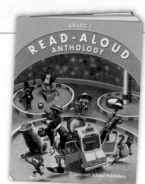

▲ Read-Aloud Anthology, "Sophie's Masterpiece," p. 64

Routine Card 2

GENRE STUDY: FICTION Remind children that fiction is a made up story that has characters, a setting, a problem, and a solution. Tell children that when they listen to a fiction story they should listen for enjoyment. Read aloud the first several sentences of "Sophie's Masterpiece" and guide children to think about the setting.

> **Think Aloud** The first sentence says that Sophie is a house spider. This means that the story will probably take place inside a house. I will read on to see if this is correct.

Read the story "Sophie's Masterpiece" to children.

After Reading

RESPOND Discuss the ending of "Sophie's Masterpiece" with children. Have them tell why the baby's blanket was Sophie's masterpiece. Ask them why it was so important to Sophie that she finish the baby's blanket. Then have children identify the different settings in "Sophie's Masterpiece." List the settings on the board. (Beekman's Boardinghouse, front parlor, tugboat captain's closet, the cook's bedroom, a young woman's third-floor room)

 REVIEW SETTING Remind children that every story has a setting.

Build Robust Vocabulary

Words from the Read-Aloud

Teach/Model

Routine Card 3

INTRODUCE ROBUST VOCABULARY Use **Transparency R88** to introduce the first two words. Cover the bottom two words, as they will be introduced on Day 2.

❶ Put the word in **selection context**.

❷ Display Transparency R88 and read the word and the **Student-Friendly Explanation**.

❸ Have children **say the word** with you.

❹ Use the word in other contexts, and have children **interact with the word's meaning**.

❺ Remove the transparency. Say the Student-Friendly Explanation again, and ask children to **name the word** that goes with it.

❶ **Selection Context:** Sophie **journeyed** across the rug and under Cook's door.

❹ **Interact with Word Meaning:** Would you have journeyed a long distance if you drove across the state or if you drove across town?

❶ **Selection Context:** Sophie grows **frail.**

❹ **Interact with Word Meaning:** Would you feel frail after having the flu or after a night's sleep? Why?

Practice/Apply

GUIDED PRACTICE Guide children in naming places to which they have *journeyed*. Write their suggestions on the board.

Objective

- *To develop robust vocabulary through discussing a literature selection*

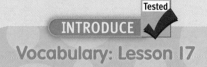

Tested

INTRODUCE ✔

Vocabulary: Lesson 17

journeyed   **frail**

▼ **Student-Friendly Explanations**

Student-Friendly Explanations	
journeyed	If you have traveled on a long trip, you have journeyed.
frail	When you feel very weak, you are frail.
horrendous	When you see or hear something horrible or frightening, it is horrendous.
melodious	If you hear musical sounds that are pleasant to listen to, you are hearing something melodious.

Grade 2, Lesson 17   R88   Vocabulary

Transparency R88

Grammar
Quick Write

Adjectives for Senses

5-DAY GRAMMAR	
DAY 1	Introduce Sense Adjectives
DAY 2	Identify Sense Adjectives
DAY 3	Choose Colorful Adjectives
DAY 4	Apply to Writing
DAY 5	Weekly Review

Objective

- *To identify adjectives that tell how something looks, sounds, feels, tastes, or smells*

Daily Proofreading

i played with Andys train

(I, Andy's, train.)

Writing Trait

Strengthening Conventions

Parts of Speech Use this short lesson with children's own writing to build a foundation for revising/editing longer connected text on Day 5. See also *Writer's Companion*, Lesson 17.

Sense Adjectives

1. Cam climbed onto the noisy train. (noun: train)
2. The train car felt hot and stuffy. (noun: car)
3. Cam sat on a soft, bouncy seat. (noun: seat)
4. A conductor with a blue hat punched Cam's ticket. (noun: hat)
5. The hole puncher made a sharp, snapping sound. (noun: sound)
6. Cam tore open a shiny bag of popcorn. (noun: bag)
7. The train suddenly blew its very loud whistle. (noun: whistle)
8. A small child next to Cam let out a cry. (noun: child)
9. Cam shared his salty popcorn with the child. (noun: popcorn)
10. The child wiped off his wet cheeks and smiled. (noun: cheeks)

Grade 2, Lesson 17   **LA35**   Grammar

Transparency LA35

Teach/Model

INTRODUCE SENSE ADJECTIVES Explain that some adjectives describe how something looks, smells, tastes, sounds, or feels.

Write on the board these sentences from "Sophie's Masterpiece" (*Read-Aloud Anthology*, p. 67):

Sophie had seen that quilt. It was scratchy and drab.

Read the sentences aloud. Then underline *scratchy* and *drab*. Draw an arrow from each adjective to *quilt*. Tell children: **Scratchy tells how the quilt feels, and *drab* tells how the quilt looks. Both *scratchy* and *drab* are sense adjectives**. Then write this sentence on the board:

Sophie had seen the scratchy, drab quilt.

Underline *scratchy* and *drab* and draw an arrow from each adjective to *quilt*. Explain that sense adjectives can come before or after the word they describe.

Guided Practice

LOCATE ADJECTIVES Display **Transparency LA35**. Read the first sentence aloud. Point to *noisy* and explain that it is an adjective that tells how the train sounds. Then draw an arrow to the word it describes. Continue for the rest of the sentences having volunteers underline the sense adjective or adjectives in each sentence and draw an arrow to the word each adjective describes.

Practice/Apply

COMPLETE SENTENCES Have children write sentences with one or more sense adjectives. Have pairs read aloud their sentences to each other.

Writing
Description

5-DAY WRITING	
DAY 1	Introduce
DAY 2	Prewrite
DAY 3	Draft
DAY 4	Revise
DAY 5	Revise

Teach/Model

INTRODUCE DESCRIPTION Display **Transparency LA36,** and explain that this paragraph describes a favorite place. Read the paragraph aloud, and discuss the information in it. Point out the sense adjectives in the paragraph. Elicit that sense adjectives tell how things look, sound, smell, taste, and feel. Together, develop a list of characteristics for a paragraph of description.

Description

- The first sentence tells what will be described.
- Each sentence gives details that create a picture.
- Sense adjectives are used throughout the paragraph.

WRITING TRAIT **ORGANIZATION** Tell children that a well-written descriptive paragraph will often end in a satisfying, funny, or clever way. Use the last sentence of the student model as a guide.

Guided Practice

WRITE A DESCRIPTIVE SENTENCE Show children a picture of an exciting place. Then write a sentence describing this place such as, "The roaring waves crashed on the white sand." Read the sentence to children. Talk about how the sentence includes sense adjectives that tell how the waves sound and the sand looks. (roaring, white)

Practice/Apply

SHARE DESCRIPTIVE SENTENCES Have children draw a picture of a favorite place to visit. Ask them to write a sentence describing the place using one or two sense adjectives. Invite partners to take turns sharing their pictures and sentences. Children should save their pictures and sentences for use on Days 2–5.

Objectives

- *To read and respond to a paragraph of description as a model for writing*
- *To identify elements of a descriptive paragraph*
- *To practice writing sentences with sense adjectives*

Writing Prompt

Describe an Object Have children describe a classroom object by using all five of their senses.

Student Model: Description

The Seashore

My favorite place is the seashore. I love to smell the salty ocean breeze. I like to listen to the screeching seagulls as they search for food. I run through the soft, warm sand and find a place to put my things. I spread out my striped beach towel. Then I take out my red bucket, a sharp shovel, and a short rake. I'll use all these tools to make a huge sandcastle after I go for a swim. As I step into the cool water, I feel the sticky seaweed cling to my legs. I knock it off and plunge into the blue water. Ohhhh, it feels salty good!

Grade 2, Lesson 17   **LA36**   Writing

Transparency LA36

Day at a Glance

Day 2

 phonics and Spelling

- Review: Short Vowel /e/*ea*
- Build Words

Robust Vocabulary

Words from the Selection

- Introduce: *stomped, sipped, entertain, except, carefree, screeching*

Comprehension

Monitor Comprehension: Read Ahead

Focus Strategy

Setting

Focus Skill

Reading

- "Annie's Gifts," *Student Edition,* pp. 58–87

 Read!

Fluency

- Intonation

Robust Vocabulary

Words About the Selection

- Introduce: *horrendous, melodious*

Grammar Quick Write

- Review: Adjectives for Senses

Writing

- Description

Warm-Up Routines

Oral Language

Objective *To listen attentively and respond appropriately to oral communication*

Question of the Day

If you could sound like a musical instrument, which one would it be? Why?

Help children think about musical instruments that they are familiar with and that they like. Use the following prompts:

- **When you play, what musical instrument do you sound like? Why?**

- **When you are angry, what musical instrument do you sound like? Why?**

- **When you are sleeping, what musical instrument do you sound like? Why?**

Then have children complete the following sentence frame to explain the reasons for their choice.

If I could sound like a musical instrument, I would sound like a _____ because _____.

Read Aloud

Objective *To listen for a purpose*

BIG BOOK OF RHYMES AND POEMS   Display the poem "The Drum" on page 31 and read the title aloud. Ask children to listen for details that tell about the drum as a musical instrument. Then read the poem aloud. Invite children to name details about the drum. (tight and hard; can beat out rhythm) Explain to children that, like a drum, the child in the poem plans to have his or her own unique "sound" in the world.

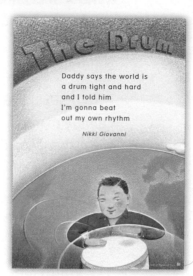

▲ **Big Book of Rhymes and Poems, p. 31**

 ## Word Wall

Objective *To read and spell high-frequency words*

REVIEW HIGH-FREQUENCY WORDS   Review the words *learn*, *laughed*, *draw*, *picture*, and *father* as well as any other previously learned words from the Word Wall. Have children begin snapping their fingers to keep time. Point to each word and have children spell and read the word to the beat of the snaps. Repeat until all words have been read several times.

Short Vowel /e/ea

 phonics *and Spelling*

Objectives

- *To blend sounds into words*
- *To spell four-, five-, and six- letter short vowel words*

Skill Trace

 Tested **Short Vowel/e/*ea***

Introduce	T130–T133
Reteach	S14–S15
Review	T142–T143, T168–T169, T404
Test	Theme 4
Maintain	Theme 6, T82

Spelling Words

1.	heavy	6.	thread
2.	steady	7.	breath
3.	bread	8.	ready
4.	sweat	9.	meant
5.	head	10.	health

Challenge Words

11.	meadow	14.	treasure
12.	Instead	15.	feather
13.	breakfast		

Word Building

READ A SPELLING WORD   Write the word *ready* on the board. Ask children to identify the vowel pair in the word. Remind children that *ea* can stand for /e/, the short *e* sound. Then read the word and have children repeat.

BUILD SPELLING WORDS   Ask children which letter you should change to make *ready* become *steady*. (Change *r* to *st*.) Write the word *steady* on the board, and have children read it. Continue building spelling words in this manner. Say:

- **Which letters do I have to change to make the word *head*?** (Change *st* to *h* and drop *y*.)
- **Which letter do I have to change to make the word *bread*?** (Change *h* to *br*.)
- **Which letter do I have to change to make the word *breath*?** (Change *d* to *th*.)
- **Which letters do I have to change to make the word *thread*?** (Change *b* to *th* and *th* to *d*.)

ready
steady
head
bread
breath
thread

Continue building the remaining spelling words in this manner.

BELOW-LEVEL

Build Spelling Words   List the spelling words on the board. Point to the words one at a time and read each word aloud. Have children repeat and trace each word on the palm of one hand with their index finger for kinesthetic reinforcement.

ADVANCED

Word Constructions   Have children combine the beginning, middle, and ending letters below to make all the spelling words.

Beginning	Middle	Ending
br, h, m, r, st, sw, thr	ea	d, dy, lth, nt, t, th, vy

5-DAY PHONICS/SPELLING	
DAY 1	Pretest
DAY 2	Word Building
DAY 3	State the Generalization
DAY 4	Review
DAY 5	Posttest

Read Words in Context

APPLY PHONICS Write the following sentences on the board or on chart paper. Have children read each sentence silently. Then track the print as children read each sentence aloud.

> Jenny held her <u>breath</u> to swim under water.
>
> Tate bumped his <u>head</u> at the playground.
>
> Is everyone <u>ready</u> for the trip?
>
> The baker sold a loaf of <u>bread</u>.

 WRITE Dictate several spelling words. Have children write the words in their notebook or on a dry-erase board.

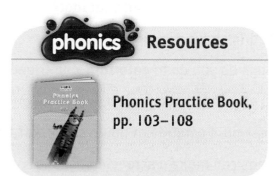

phonics Resources

Phonics Practice Book, pp. 103–108

 MONITOR PROGRESS

Short Vowel /e/ea

IF children have difficulty building and reading words with short vowel /e/ea,	**THEN** help them identify the part of each word that is the same and then say the beginning and middle of each word, the middle and ending of each word, and finally the whole word.

Small-Group Instruction, pp. S14–S15:

● **BELOW-LEVEL:** Reteach
● **ON-LEVEL:** Reinforce
○ **ADVANCED:** Extend

BELOW-LEVEL **ON-LEVEL** **ADVANCED**

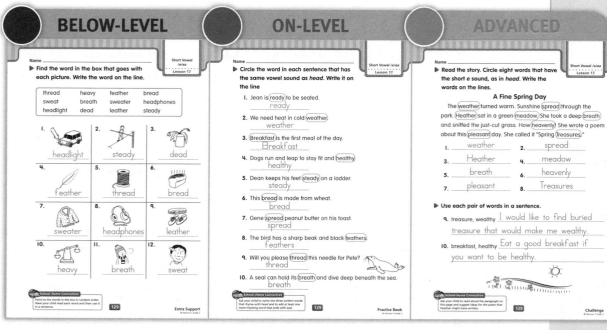

▲ Extra Support, p. 129   ▲ Practice Book, p. 129   ▲ Challenge, p. 129

E L L

- Group children according to academic levels, and assign one of the pages on the left.

- Clarify any unfamiliar concepts as necessary. See *ELL Teacher Guide* Lesson 17 for support in scaffolding instruction.

Build Robust Vocabulary

Words from the Selection

Objectives

- *To build robust vocabulary*
- *To build and expand word meanings*

Tested ✓

INTRODUCE

Vocabulary: Lesson 17

stomped	**except**
sipped	**carefree**
entertain	**screeching**

Student-Friendly Explanations

stomped	If you stomped, you used your feet to make heavy, pounding steps.
sipped	If you sipped, you took a very small drink of something.
entertain	When you entertain an audience, you do something, such as acting or singing, that you think people will enjoy.
except	When you talk about every thing except one, you mean all but that one.
carefree	A carefree person does not worry about problems.
screeching	If you hear a screeching noise, you hear a loud, high sound that can hurt your ears.

Grade 2, Lesson 17   **R89**   Vocabulary

Transparency R89

Word Champion

Talk to Others Encourage children to use one Vocabulary Word each day in speech. HOMEWORK/ INDEPENDENT PRACTICE

Teach/Model

Routine Card 4

INTRODUCE ROBUST VOCABULARY Introduce the words, using the following steps.

❶ Display Transparency R89 and have children read the word and the **Student-Friendly Explanation.**

❷ Have children **say the word** with you.

❸ Have children **interact with the word's meaning** by asking them the appropriate question below.

- When have you ever **stomped** your foot?
- What hot drink have you **sipped** lately?
- What things do you do to **entertain** your friends? Explain.
- Have you ever finished a project **except** for one thing? Explain.
- Do you feel more **carefree** at home or school? Explain.
- What things can make a **screeching** sound?

Develop Deeper Meaning

EXPAND WORD MEANINGS: PAGES 56–57 Have children read the passage. Then read the passage aloud, pausing at the end of page 56 to ask children questions 1–4. Read page 57 and then discuss children's answers to questions 5–6.

1. Cora's family plays every instrument **except** which one? (violin)
2. Why did Cora's violin make **screeching** sounds at first? (because Cora was just beginning to learn how to play it)
3. Who **stomped** away from practicing? (Cora)
4. How does Cora **entertain** her family and friends? (She plays her violin for them.)
5. Who does Cora play **carefree** music with? (Mr. Miles)
6. What does Cora tell Mr. Miles as he **sipped** his coffee? (She likes to play the violin because it surprises her sometimes.)

Vocabulary

Build Robust Vocabulary

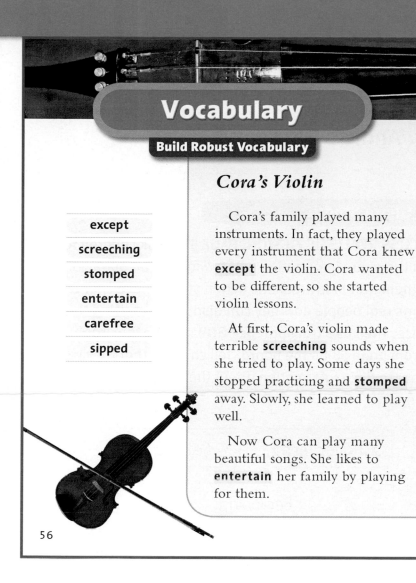

except

screeching

stomped

entertain

carefree

sipped

Cora's Violin

Cora's family played many instruments. In fact, they played every instrument that Cora knew **except** the violin. Cora wanted to be different, so she started violin lessons.

At first, Cora's violin made terrible **screeching** sounds when she tried to play. Some days she stopped practicing and **stomped** away. Slowly, she learned to play well.

Now Cora can play many beautiful songs. She likes to **entertain** her family by playing for them.

One day, Cora and her teacher, Mr. Miles, were playing some lively, **carefree** music. Suddenly, Cora's violin squawked. They soon saw the cause—a broken string.

Later, as Mr. Miles **sipped** his drink, Cora laughed. "You never know what surprises your violin has for you!" she said.

Word Champion

Your challenge this week is to use the Vocabulary Words while talking to others. For example, tell a classmate about something you do to <u>entertain</u> your family. Each day, write in your vocabulary journal the sentences you spoke.

 www.harcourtschool.com/storytown

56

57

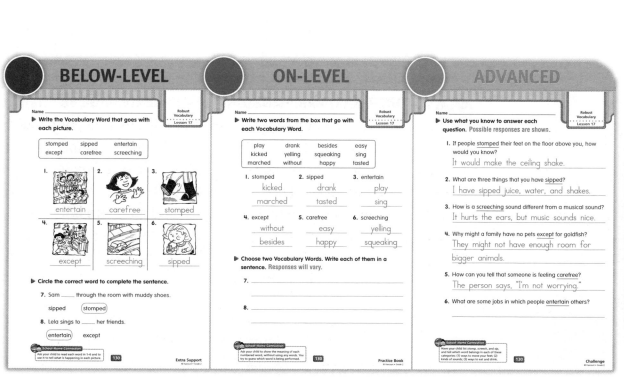

▲ Extra Support, p. 130 ▲ Practice Book, p. 130 ▲ Challenge, p. 130

ELL

• Group children according to academic levels, and assign one of the pages on the left.

• Clarify any unfamiliar concepts as necessary. See *ELL Teacher Guide* Lesson 17 for support in scaffolding instruction.

Reading

Student Edition: **Annie's Gifts**

Objectives

- *To recognize features of realistic fiction*
- *To read ahead as a strategy for comprehension*
- *To represent information in charts*
- *To apply word knowledge to the reading of a text*

Options for Reading

BELOW-LEVEL

Preview Have children preview the story by looking at the illustrations. Guide them to predict what the setting will be. Read each page to children, and have them read it after you.

ON-LEVEL

Monitor Comprehension Have children read the story aloud, page by page. Ask the Monitor Comprehension questions as you go.

ADVANCED

Independent Reading Have children read each page silently, looking up when they finish a page. Ask the Monitor Comprehension questions as you go.

Genre Study

DISCUSS REALISTIC FICTION: PAGE 58 Ask children to read the genre information on *Student Edition* page 58. Tell them that many realistic fiction stories have characters that do things real people do. They can also have a setting that is a real place. Then use **Transparency GO4** or copy the graphic organizer from page 58 on the board. Tell children that they will work together to fill in information about the story as they read "Annie's Gifts."

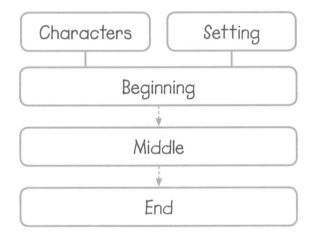

Comprehension Strategies

MONITOR COMPREHENSION—READ AHEAD: PAGE 58 Tell children that good readers use strategies to help them make sense of what they read. Have children read aloud the Comprehension Strategy information on page 58. Explain that one way readers can better understand what they read is to read ahead. Point out that sometimes readers read ahead in a story to find out more about a character, the setting, or story events. Tell children that they should use the read ahead strategy when they do not understand something they have read and need clarification.

Genre Study
Realistic fiction is a story that could really happen.
Look for
• characters who do things real people do.
• a realistic setting.

Characters → Setting
Beginning
Middle
End

Comprehension Strategy

 Monitor Comprehension— Read ahead to find out more if something does not make sense.

58

Award-Winning Author

ANNIE'S GIFTS
by Angela Shelf Medearis

Realistic Fiction

Annie's Gifts

by Angela Shelf Medearis
illustrated by Anna Rich

59

Build Background

DISCUSS TALENT   Tell children that they are going to read a story about a girl who discovers that she doesn't quite have the same type of talent that her brother and sister have. Explain that talent is the ability to do something well. Ask children to think about their own talents, and invite volunteers to name things that they know they do well.

Routine Card 6

SET A PURPOSE AND PREDICT   Tell children that this is a story they will read to enjoy.

• Read the title to children.

• Identify Annie. Ask what they think Annie might be trying to do.

• List their predictions on the board.

• Invite children to read the story to find out about Annie and her gifts.

TECHNOLOGY

GO online **eBook**   "Annie's Gifts" is available in an eBook.

Audiotext   "Annie's Gifts" is available on *Audiotext Grade 2,* CD 4 for subsequent readings.

Once there lived a family that loved music. Every morning the children, **3** Lee, Patty, and Annie, turned on some music. The floors trembled as they stomped their feet to the loud bass **1** **2** beat. Soon they were moving down the street to catch the school bus.

After the children left for school, Momma would turn on the radio. Momma swayed with the sweet rhythm as she sipped her coffee.

60

61

Monitor Comprehension

PAGES 60–61 Say: **The children look as if they're having fun. Read to find out what they are doing.**

1 **NOTE DETAILS** **What does the family do in the morning?** (They listen to music and stomp their feet.)

2 **CAUSE/EFFECT** **What causes the floors to tremble?** (The floors tremble because the children are stomping their feet to the music.)

3 **SETTING** **Where is Annie? What time of day is it?** (She is at home; it is morning.)

Apply
Comprehension Strategies

Monitor Comprehension: Read Ahead Demonstrate how to read ahead to confirm the setting of the story.

Think Aloud I want to know more about the setting. I'll read ahead to see if the story mostly takes place in Annie's home or if it switches to another place and time.

T148 Grade 2, Theme 4 (*Student Edition*, pages 60–61)

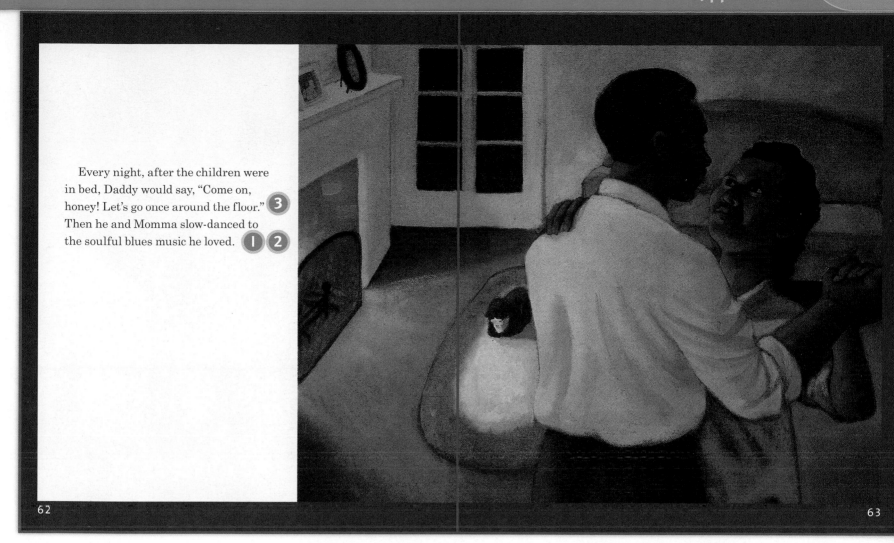

62   63

Monitor Comprehension

PAGES 62–63   Say: **I see Annie's parents dancing. I wonder what kind of music they like to listen to. Read to find out.**

1 **NOTE DETAILS**   What type of music are they listening to? (soulful blues music)

2 **DRAW CONCLUSIONS**   What do you think "soulful blues music" might sound like? (Possible response: Blues music sounds sad and slow and expresses deep feeling.)

3 **UNDERSTAND FIGURATIVE LANGUAGE**   What do you think Daddy means when he says, "Let's go once around the floor"? (Possible response: He probably means, "Let's dance together.")

SUPPORTING STANDARDS

Daily Lives   Have children compare and contrast their daily lives with those of their parents, grandparents, or guardians. Help them brainstorm topics and formulate questions to ask that will show how daily lives are alike and different. Encourage children to include a question about tastes in music. Model how to record and analyze results.

Me
I go to school.

Both
We like show music—music from movies and plays.

Grandma
She volunteers at a hospital.

Lesson 17 (*Student Edition*, pages 62–63)   **T149**

Lee loved music so much that he joined his school band. Annie thought Lee looked wonderful in his uniform with the shiny brass buttons. Lee's music sounded like the circus. When ②️ he swung into a song on the trumpet, Annie tapped her feet and clapped her hands. ①️ ③️

64

65

Monitor Comprehension

PAGES 64–65 Say: **I see Annie dancing. She is with some children who are dressed in uniforms. Read to find out who they are.**

①️ **DRAW CONCLUSIONS Why is Annie dancing?** (because she loves Lee's music)

②️ **AUTHOR'S CRAFT Why might the author compare Lee's music to the sound of a circus?** (because circus music is loud and lively and full of brassy sounds like the music a school band makes)

③️ **CHARACTERS' EMOTIONS How does Annie feel about her brother, Lee? How can you tell?** (Possible response: Annie admires Lee. She likes the way he looks in his uniform and she dances to his music.)

E L L

Word Meanings Use the illustrations to clarify the meanings of *school band*, *uniform*, *brass buttons*, *trumpet*, *feet*, and *hands*. Read each sentence aloud and point to the corresponding object in the illustration. Then have children point to the correct object in the illustration as you say each sentence. Ask clarifying questions such as *Is Lee playing a piano or a trumpet in the band?*

Patty was a wonderful musician, too. When Patty played the piano, it made Annie think of pretty colors, soft rain, and springtime flowers. Patty **2** also had a lovely singing voice. When company came, she would entertain **1** the guests.

"Wonderful, just wonderful," the guests would sigh and clap their hands after Patty's performance. Annie **3** decided that she wanted to play an instrument, too.

66   67

Monitor Comprehension

PAGES 66–67   Say: **I see some women holding cups and chatting. Read to find out why Patty is playing the piano for them.**

1 **DRAW CONCLUSIONS**   **Why does Patty play the piano and sing for company?** (to entertain them)

2 **MAKE INFERENCES**   **How can you tell that Annie enjoys music?** (Annie thinks of pretty colors, soft rain, and springtime flowers when she hears Patty's music. Annie taps and claps when she hears Lee's music.)

3 **NOTE DETAILS**   **How do the guests feel about Patty's music? How can you tell?** (The guests enjoy Patty's music. They say her music is wonderful, sigh, and clap their hands in appreciation.)

One day, Annie's school music teacher, Mrs. Mason, passed out instruments to the class. She gave Annie a recorder.

The class practiced a group song for months. Everyone played their part perfectly, everyone except Annie. When Annie played, the recorder squeaked and squawked like chickens at feeding time. **2**

"I don't think the recorder is the instrument for you," Mrs. Mason said.

"I guess you're right," Annie said. "Maybe I can play the cello."

"Let's give it a try," Mrs. Mason said. "I'll show you how to play it."

68

69

Monitor Comprehension

PAGES 68–69   Say: **I see a woman and lots of chickens. Let's read to find out what these chickens have to do with Annie.**

1 **NOTE DETAILS**   **What instrument does Annie practice for months at school?** (a recorder)

2 **AUTHOR'S CRAFT**   **To what sound does the author compare Annie's recorder playing? Why?** (The squeaking and squawking of chickens at feeding time. The author wants to show how loud and unpleasant Annie's playing sounds.)

3 **MAKE PREDICTIONS**   **Will Annie sound better when she plays the cello? Why do you think that?** (Answers will vary.)

BELOW-LEVEL

Reinforce Meaning   If possible, make or play a recording of the sounds chickens make. Discuss whether it is a compliment to compare Annie's music to the sounds of chickens at feeding time. Ask children to suggest some examples of more positive comparisons, as well as additional negative ones.

ADVANCED

Extend Meaning   Show children real examples or pictures of wind and string instruments. Ask them to identify the key differences between the two kinds of instruments and how they are played.

When Mrs. Mason played the cello, it sounded warm and carefree, like carousel music. Annie tried and tried, but when she played the cello, it always sounded like a chorus of screeching alley cats.

"Oh," Mrs. Mason sighed and rubbed her ears. "Annie, darling, I just don't think this is the instrument for you. How would you like to make a banner and some posters announcing our program?"

"Okay," said Annie. She was disappointed, but she did love to draw. Annie drew while everyone else practiced.

70   71

Monitor Comprehension

PAGES 70–71   Say: **I see Annie playing the cello and I see lots of noisy, unhappy-looking cats. Read to find out why the cats are there.**

1 **UNDERSTAND FIGURATIVE LANGUAGE   To what does the author compare Mrs. Mason's and Annie's cello playing?** (Mrs. Mason's playing sounds like carousel music; Annie's playing sounds like a chorus of screeching alley cats.)

2 **MAKE JUDGMENTS   Would you rather listen to Mrs. Mason or Annie play the cello? Why?** (Possible response: Mrs. Mason, because her playing has a pleasant sound.)

3 **THEME   Why does Mrs. Mason ask Annie to make a banner and some posters?** (Possible response: She wants to give Annie a chance to show off her talent as an artist.)

ELL

Reinforce Meaning   As you read sentences aloud to children, use facial expressions and intonation to show emotions such as *warm*, *carefree*, *sighed*, and *disappointed*. Use body movements and gestures to reinforce the meanings of actions such as *played the cello*, *tried and tried*, *rubbed her ears*, and *drew*.

That evening, Annie picked up Lee's trumpet and tried to play it. Her playing sounded like an elephant with a bad cold. Lee begged her to stop. Annie's feelings were hurt, but she put the trumpet away.

"I wish I could find an instrument to play," Annie told her mother.

"Cheer up!" Momma said. "We're going to get a new piano and everyone is going to take piano lessons!"

73

Monitor Comprehension

PAGES 72–73 Say: **I see Annie playing the trumpet and I see an angry-looking elephant. Read to find out why an elephant is in Annie's living room.**

① **FIGURATIVE LANGUAGE** **To what does the author compare Annie's trumpet playing? Why?** (to an elephant with a bad cold because her playing sounded bad)

② **SETTING** **What do the illustration and text tell you about the setting at this point in the story?** (Annie is in her living room at home, and it is evening.)

③ **CHARACTERS' EMOTIONS** **Why does Annie feel hurt that Lee begs her to stop playing the trumpet?** (Possible response: She admires Lee and wants to play as well as he does.)

Monitor Comprehension: Read Ahead Tell children that they can read ahead if something in the story confuses them.

Think Aloud The illustration on page 72 shows an elephant in Annie's living room. I know that this is a realistic fiction story, so I know there isn't really an elephant in the room. I'll read ahead to page 73 to find out why it's there. When I read ahead to page 73, I find out that the author compares the sound of Annie's playing to the sound an elephant with a bad cold would make.

Soon, a beautiful, new piano was delivered to Annie's house. The piano was made of shiny, brown mahogany. Annie peeked under the piano lid while Patty played a song. "Melody Maker" was written in beautiful gold letters. **1**

That week, all three children started piano lessons with Mrs. Kelly. After every lesson, Mrs. Kelly gave them new sheet music to practice.

Patty and Lee did very well. Mrs. Kelly always told them how talented they were. **2**

74   75

Monitor Comprehension

PAGES 74–75   Say: **I see the children and a teacher around a piano. Maybe Annie will find that the piano is a better instrument for her to play than the cello or the trumpet. Read to find out about the piano.**

1 **AUTHOR'S PURPOSE**   **What details does the author give about the piano? Why does she give so many?** (The piano is beautiful, new, shiny, and made of brown mahogany. It has gold letters that spell "Melody Maker." The author may have included the details to show how valuable the piano is.)

2 **MAKE PREDICTIONS**   **Will Annie play as well on the piano as her sister and brother? Why do you think that?** (Possible response: no, because she has not done very well with any of the other instruments)

SPECIAL NEEDS

Use Multisensory Methods
Build in visual, oral, and tactile learning opportunities as children read and discuss the selection. For example, as the group discusses the details of the new piano, invite children to stand briefly and pretend to play the keys on the piano, going up and down the keyboard. Compliment positive behaviors and self-monitoring techniques.

we left off here. Need to read this page.

Oh, but when Annie played the piano, Mrs. Kelly's smile turned into a frown. The low notes sounded like a diesel truck honking its horn and the middle ones like croaking frogs. The high notes sobbed like a crying baby. **1**

Once, Annie tried to sing and play the piano for her parents' guests. Her performance made everyone squirm in their chairs. Annie was so embarrassed that she went up to her room and cried. She couldn't play the recorder or the cello. She couldn't play the piano or sing or play the trumpet. Annie had never felt so sad in her life. **3** **4**

2

76

77

Monitor Comprehension

PAGES 76–77 Say: **I see Annie singing and playing the piano. I wonder why there are frogs all around. Read to find out.**

1 **UNDERSTAND FIGURATIVE LANGUAGE** **What three things does Annie's piano playing sound like?** (a honking truck, croaking frogs, and a crying baby)

2 **CHARACTERS' EMOTIONS** **How does Annie feel after her piano performance?** (She feels embarrassed and very sad.)

3 **SUMMARIZE** **What instruments has Annie tried, but failed, to play?** (the recorder, cello, trumpet, piano, and voice)

4 **CONFIRM PREDICTIONS** **Were your predictions about Annie's playing correct?** (Responses will vary.)

E L L

Visualize Use *Picture Cards* to reinforce the meanings of words such as *truck* (123), *frog* (56), *baby* (7), *chairs* (24), and *sad* (101). Use other visual aids from magazines or books to reinforce the words *piano*, *trumpet*, *recorder*, and *cello*.

Sometimes when Annie was sad, she liked to write poetry to make herself feel better. She decided to write a poem about music. **1**

I love to hear music play.
I practice hard every day.
But even though I try and try,
the sounds I play
make people laugh and cry. **2**

That night, Annie put her poem on Daddy's pillow. Then she went to sleep. **3**

78

79

Monitor Comprehension

PAGES 78–79   Say: **I see Annie working on something. She seems to be concentrating on what she is doing. Read to find out what she is working on.**

1 **MAKE INFERENCES**   **What does Annie write? Why?** (Possible response: She wrote a poem about music because she feels sad about her musical experiences and writing makes her feel better.)

2 **AUTHOR'S CRAFT**   **What words rhyme in Annie's poem?** (*play and day; try and cry*)

3 **CHARACTERS' MOTIVATIONS**   **Why does Annie give her poem to Daddy?** (Possible response: because she wants to let her parents know how she is feeling)

Author's Craft   Guide children to clap or tap out the rhythm of Annie's poem. Invite children to read the poem aloud, emphasizing the words that rhyme, and the rhythm.

In the morning, Daddy and Momma had a long talk with Annie.

"I just can't seem to do anything right," Annie sighed.

"Yes, you can," Daddy said. "There are lots of things you can do."

"Really, Daddy?" Annie asked.

"Of course," Momma said. "Not everyone can play the piano and sing like Patty. Not everyone can play the trumpet like Lee. That's his special gift. And not everyone can write poetry and draw beautiful pictures the way you can." **1**

"I didn't think about it that way," Annie said. "I can't sing or play an instrument well, but I can do *a lot* of other things." **2**

80

81

Monitor Comprehension

PAGES 80–81 Say: **I see Annie with her parents. They look as if they might be worried about something. Read to find out what the problem is.**

1 **PROBLEM/SOLUTION** **What is Annie's problem? How do her parents help her solve it?** (Annie's problem is that she feels bad that she can't make wonderful music like Lee and Patty. Her parents help her solve her problem by reminding her of the things she *can* do well, such as write poetry and draw pictures.)

2 **IDENTIFY WITH CHARACTERS** **If you were Annie's friend, what could you tell her to make her feel better?** (Answers will vary.)

Use Multiple Strategies

Use Graphic Organizers Model how to complete the story map.

Think Aloud The story map helps me keep track of what is happening.

Characters	Setting
Annie, Momma, Daddy, Lee, Patty	Annie's house

Beginning
Annie tries to play different instruments.

↓

Middle
Annie can't play or sing well.

↓

End
Annie's parents help her see that she can do other things well.

Now, if you should pass by Annie's house, you ① ② might hear Patty singing and playing on the piano. Perhaps you'll hear Lee playing his trumpet. And sometimes, if you stop and listen very, very closely, ③ you might hear Annie playing . . .

82

83

Monitor Comprehension

PAGES 82–83   Say: **I see the outside of a house. Read to find out whose house this is.**

① **SETTING**   **What is the setting at this point in the story?** (outside Annie's house in the evening)

② **AUTHOR'S PURPOSE**   **Why does the author talk to readers directly by using the pronoun _you_?** (Possible response: She wants to draw readers into the story, as if they are friends or neighbors.)

③ **MAKE PREDICTIONS**   **What do you think Annie is playing?** (Answers will vary.)

her radio!

Annie plays loud, finger-popping music when she feels like laughing and drawing pictures. She plays soft, sweet music when she writes her poems. She can play any kind of music she likes on her radio.

She still can't play the piano or sing like Patty, and she still can't play the trumpet like Lee. **2**

But now Annie has found she's happiest when drawing her pictures and writing poetry. Because art and writing are Annie's gifts. **3**

84

85

Monitor Comprehension

PAGES 84–85 Say: **I see Annie at her easel. She looks happy. Read to find out what she's doing.**

1 **DRAW CONCLUSIONS** **Is the radio a good solution for Annie's problem? Why or why not?** (Possible response: Yes. Annie can listen to different kinds of music while she writes poetry and draws pictures.)

2 **EXPRESS PERSONAL OPINIONS** **Could Annie have become a musician with more practice? Why do you think that?** (Answers will vary.)

3 **AUTHOR'S CRAFT** **Why does the author end the story with the words *Annie's gifts*?** (Possible responses: to help readers remember the title of the story; to remind readers that Annie had to discover her gifts)

ANALYZE AUTHOR'S PURPOSE

Author's Purpose Remind children that authors have a purpose, or reason, for writing. After children have finished reading "Annie's Gifts," ask which of these three purposes fits best.

- to persuade readers that not everyone has the same talent and to find what he or she does best
- to inform readers about the steps to play a musical instrument
- to entertain readers with a story in which everyone in a family plays beautiful music

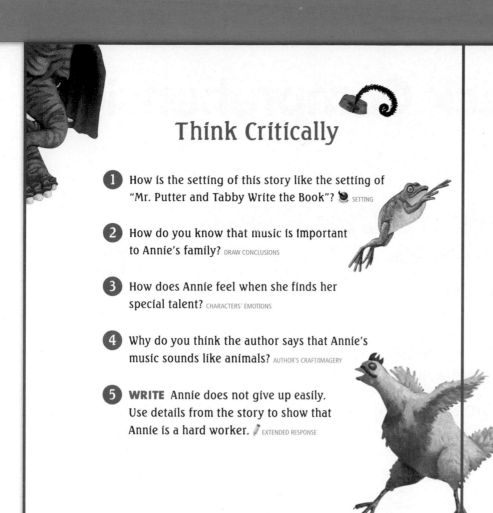

Think Critically

1. How is the setting of this story like the setting of "Mr. Putter and Tabby Write the Book"? SETTING

2. How do you know that music is important to Annie's family? DRAW CONCLUSIONS

3. How does Annie feel when she finds her special talent? CHARACTERS' EMOTIONS

4. Why do you think the author says that Annie's music sounds like animals? AUTHOR'S CRAFT/IMAGERY

5. **WRITE** Annie does not give up easily. Use details from the story to show that Annie is a hard worker. EXTENDED RESPONSE

Meet the Author
Angela Shelf Medearis

"Annie's Gifts" is based on Angela Shelf Medearis's life. Now that she has discovered her talent, she writes all the time.

Angela Shelf Medearis likes to make children laugh. What parts of the story do you think are funny?

Meet the Illustrator
Anna Rich

Anna Rich began to draw when she was young, and she has never stopped. She has illustrated many children's books, including two others by Angela Shelf Medearis.

Anna Rich likes to knit, sew, and, of course, paint. She says that when she reads a story, pictures appear in her brain.

www.harcourtschool.com/storytown

86

87

Think Critically

Respond to the Literature

1. Both take place mostly in and around the main character's home. **SETTING**

2. There is always music. Lee plays the trumpet and Patty plays the piano and sings. **DRAW CONCLUSIONS**

3. Possible response: She feels very happy. **CHARACTERS' EMOTIONS**

4. Possible response: She wants readers to imagine the sounds and to think of noises that sound terrible. **AUTHOR'S CRAFT/IMAGERY**

5. **WRITE** Annie practices the recorder. She tries to play the cello, the trumpet, and the piano. She works hard to write a poem and draw pictures. **EXTENDED RESPONSE**

Meet the Author and the Illustrator

PAGE 87 Have children read about the author and respond to the question "What parts of the story do you think are funny?" Record their responses. Then have children read about the illustrator and review the story illustrations. Ask them to name their favorite pictures and tell why. Record their responses. Then take a class vote to see which story part children think is the funniest and which illustrations are their favorites.

RUBRIC For additional support in scoring the WRITE item, see the rubrics on pp. R6–R8.

Lesson 17 (*Student Edition*, pages 86–

Check Comprehension

Retelling

Objectives

- *To practice retelling a story*
- *To read with intonation in a manner that sounds like natural speech*

RETELLING RUBRIC

4	Uses details to clearly retell the story
3	Uses some details to retell the story
2	Retells the story with some inaccuracies
1	Is unable to retell the story

Professional Development

 Podcasting: Auditory Modeling

 **E L L**

Fluency Practice   For fluency practice, select several colorful sentences from "Annie's Gifts" for children to reread. Model reading each sentence with intonation, adding gestures when appropriate. Then have children repeat the reading, matching your intonation.

Retell

 SETTING   Ask children to name the setting in "Annie's Gifts." (Annie's home during the school year)

REVISIT THE GRAPHIC ORGANIZER   Display completed **Transparency GO4**. Guide children to identify the characters, setting, and plot of the story.

STORY RETELLING CARDS   The cards for "Annie's Gifts" can be used for retelling or as an aid to completing the graphic organizer.

▲ Story Retelling Cards 1–6, "Annie's Gifts"

 # Fluency

Intonation

Teach/Model

 READ WITH INTONATION   Explain that good readers change the tone or pitch of their voice to match the meaning of certain words, phrases, and punctuation as they read. Model reading *Student Edition* pages 60–61 with intonation.

Practice/Apply

 **CHORAL-READ**   Organize children into groups and assign them alternating pages to read with you. Remind children to match your intonation when it is their turn to choral-read.

Build Robust Vocabulary
Words About the Selection

Objectives
- *To build robust vocabulary through discussing a literature selection*
- *To understand and use vocabulary in new contexts*

Tested

INTRODUCE ✓

Vocabulary: Lesson 17

horrendous   **melodious**

Teach/Model

Routine Card 3   **INTRODUCE THE WORDS**   Use *Routine Card 3* to introduce the last two words.

❶ Put the word in **selection context**.

❷ Display Transparency R88 and read the word and the **Student-Friendly Explanation**.

❸ Have children **say the word** with you.

❹ Use the word in other contexts, and have children **interact with the word's meaning**.

❺ Remove the transparency. Say the Student-Friendly Explanation again, and ask children to **name the word** that goes with it.

❶ **Selection Context:** Annie makes **horrendous** sounds on the cello and trumpet.

❹ **Interact with Word Meaning:** Would you cover your ears or hum along if you heard a horrendous sound? Why?

❶ **Selection Context:** Annie's sister makes **melodious** sounds on the piano.

❹ **Interact with Word Meaning:** When you hear melodious music do you frown or do you smile?

Practice/Apply

GUIDED PRACTICE   Lead children to practice and apply their knowledge of the Vocabulary Words. Ask them to do the following with you:

- Draw a picture of an instrument—real or pretend—that can make a *horrendous* sound.
- Imagine a sound that is *melodious*. Act out how you would behave if you heard that sound.

▼ **Student-Friendly Explanations**

Student-Friendly Explanations	
journeyed	If you have traveled on a long trip, you have journeyed.
frail	When you feel very weak, you are frail.
horrendous	When you see or hear something horrible or frightening, it is horrendous.
melodious	If you hear musical sounds that are pleasant to listen to, you are hearing something melodious.

Grade 2, Lesson 17   R88   Vocabulary

Transparency R88

Grammar *Quick Write*

Adjectives for Senses

5-DAY GRAMMAR

DAY 1	Introduce Sense Adjectives
DAY 2	**Identify Sense Adjectives**
DAY 3	Choose Colorful Adjectives
DAY 4	Apply to Writing
DAY 5	Weekly Review

Objective

- *To identify sense adjectives*

Daily Proofreading

On monday, I put away the dishs clean.

(Monday, clean dishes)

Word Order Word order in children's home language may differ from English. Model and reinforce that, in English, an adjective may come before the noun it describes. *Annie draws pretty pictures.*

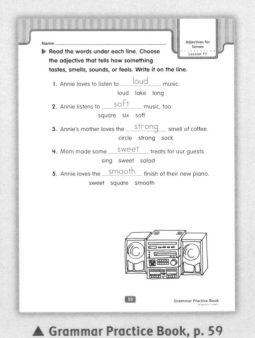

▲ Grammar Practice Book, p. 59

Review

IDENTIFY SENSE ADJECTIVES Remind children that sense adjectives describe the way something looks, sounds, smells, feels, or tastes. Write these sentences on the board:

June's squeaky violin needs new strings.

Does that rose smell sweet?

Mark's bike is red.

Read the first sentence aloud. Tell children that the word *squeaky* is a sense adjective because it describes how the violin sounds. Then have children read aloud the rest of the sentences one at a time. Ask volunteers to identify the sense adjective in each sentence and tell whether each adjective describes how something looks, tastes, smells, sounds, or feels.

Practice/Apply

GUIDED PRACTICE Write these sentences on the board. Model how to underline the sense adjective in the first sentence. Elicit responses from children to identify the sense adjectives in the remaining sentences.

Josh's shirt had a fresh smell. (fresh)

The lemon tasted sour. (sour)

The cat let out a loud meow. (loud)

 INDEPENDENT PRACTICE Have children write four sentences. Have partners underline the sense adjectives in each sentence.

Writing

Description

5-DAY WRITING	
DAY 1	Introduce
DAY 2	Prewrite
DAY 3	Draft
DAY 4	Revise
DAY 5	Revise

Prewrite

GENERATE IDEAS Have children look again at the picture they drew and the descriptive sentence they wrote on Day 1 (page T139). Ask them to think of details that tell more about the place they described.

WRITING TRAIT ➤ ORGANIZATION Tell children that good writers create a good ending for each paragraph or story they write. An ending should leave the reader satisfied and eager to read more by the same author. Encourage children to think of stories they think have a good ending. Have them tell what makes them good endings.

MODEL PREWRITING Copy the chart below. Tell children that using this kind of chart or other graphic organizer is a good way to think of details for writing a description. Model filling out the first column of the chart below with sensory details about the "look" of a place you have visited.

Place: Park

Look	Feel	Sound	Taste	Smell
green, shaded, trees	cool and refreshing, peaceful	noisy, windy, quiet	fresh	fragrant, flowery

Practice/Apply

GUIDED PRACTICE Have children help you brainstorm the rest of the sensory details about a place. Have volunteers share details covering the remaining senses about the place you have chosen. Add their responses to the chart.

 **INDEPENDENT PRACTICE** Have children brainstorm sensory details for a descriptive paragraph about their favorite place to visit. Have them copy the chart. Tell them to fill in details for each sense. Invite them to look carefully at their drawing from Day 1 to help them think of more details for their chart. Have children save their five-senses chart to use on Days 3–5.

Objectives

- *To develop ideas and details for a description*
- *To use a graphic organizer for prewriting*

 ### Writing Prompt

Independent Writing Have children record their reflections on experiences they have had visiting a special place with their family or friends.

E L L

Reinforce Sensory Details If children have difficulty filling out the five-senses chart, use gestures and pictures to help them comprehend each sense. Point to the sense organ as you help them generate details for that sense. Show picture cards of places to visit, colors, sounds, tastes, and textures to reinforce and expand vocabulary.

Day at a Glance
Day 3

phonics and Spelling
- Review: Short Vowel /e/*ea*
- State the Generalization

Fluency
- Intonation
- "Annie's Gifts," *Student Edition*, pp. 58–87

Comprehension

Focus Skill Review: Setting

Reading
- "Sarah Enters a Painting," *Student Edition*, pp. 88–89

 Read!

Robust Vocabulary
- Review: *journeyed, frail, stomped, sipped, entertain, except, carefree, screeching, horrendous, melodious*

Grammar [Quick Write]
- Review: Adjectives for Senses

Writing ✏
- Description

Warm-Up Routines

Oral Language

Objective *To listen attentively and respond appropriately to oral communication*

Question of the Day

What do you think of when you hear the beat of a drum?

Use the following prompts to help children think about the sound of a drum.

- **At what events do you hear the sound of a drum?**
- **What things in nature can make drum-like sounds?**
- **How do your hands feel when you beat on a drum?**
- **Is a drumbeat always loud? Why or why not?**

Have children complete the following sentence frame to explain the reasons for their choice.

When I hear a drum beat,

I think about _____

because _____.

Read Aloud

Objective *To identify the use of rhythm in poetry*

BIG BOOK OF RHYMES AND POEMS Display "The Drum" on page 31, and ask children to tell what they remember about it. Read the poem aloud, emphasizing the rhythm by clapping or snapping your fingers. Then ask children to join in, imitating the rhythmic pattern with their voices and by clapping.

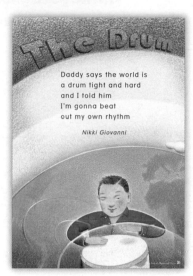

▲ **Big Book of Rhymes and Poems, p. 31**

Word Wall

Objective *To read high-frequency words*

REVIEW HIGH-FREQUENCY WORDS Point to the following words on the Word Wall and ask children to read them aloud in unison: *sign, finally, bicycle, million,* and *quite.* Then invite children to play the game "Bounce and Throw." Point to a word and have children read it aloud. Ask one child to pretend to "bounce" a ball as he or she spells the word. Then the child "throws" the ball to a classmate as he or she says the word. Repeat the procedure for all of the words.

Short Vowel /e/ea

phonics *and Spelling*

5-DAY PHONICS	
DAY 1	Reintroduce /e/ea
DAY 2	Word Building with /e/ea
DAY 3	**Word Building with /e/ea**
DAY 4	Syllable Pattern V/CV; Review /e/ea
DAY 5	Syllable Pattern V/CV; Review /e/ea

Objectives

- *To read phonetically regular words*
- *To read and write common word families*
- *To recognize spelling patterns*

Skill Trace

 Tested **Short Vowel /e/ea**

Introduce	T130–T133
Reteach	S14–S15
Review	**T142–T143, T168–T169, T404**
Test	Theme 4
Maintain	Theme 6, T82

Short Vowel /e/ea

Dan wants to bake bread today instead of a cake.

He'll make whole wheat bread because it's good for his health.

Dan plans ahead and gets ready to make bread.

He mixes the heavy dough with a steady hand.

Dan sweats and stops to catch his breath as he works.

Dan's head tells him that making bread is hard work.

Grade 2, Lesson 17   R85   Phonics

Transparency R85

Work with Patterns

INTRODUCE PHONOGRAMS   Write the following phonograms at the top of three columns.

-ead	-ealth	-eady

Tell children that these are the endings of some words. Slide your hand under the letters as you read each phonogram. Repeat, having children read the phonograms with you.

BUILD AND READ WORDS   Write the letter *h* in front of the first phonogram. Guide children to read the word: /h/-*ead, head*. Have them identify the vowel pair *ea* in the word. Repeat the procedure with the second and third phonograms, adding *w* in front of *-ealth,* to form the word *wealth*, and adding *r* in front of *-eady,* to form the word *ready*.

Have children name other words that end with *-ead, -ealth,* and *-eady*. Have them tell which letter or letters to add to build each word, and write it on the board under the appropriate column. Have children read each column of words. Then point to words at random and have children read them.

Read Words in Context

READ SENTENCES   Display **Transparency R85** or write the sentences on the board. Have children choral-read the sentences as you track the print. Then ask volunteers to read each sentence aloud and underline words with short /e/*ea*. Invite volunteers to add words to the appropriate column of phonograms.

MAINTAIN /ē/ey, y   Remind children that the *y* in *ready* makes the /ē/ sound. Have them read words from the *-eady* column again, stressing the final /ē/ sound.

5-DAY SPELLING

DAY 1	Pretest
DAY 2	Word Building
DAY 3	**State the Generalization**
DAY 4	Review
DAY 5	Posttest

Review Spelling Words

STATE THE GENERALIZATION FOR /e/ea List Spelling Words 1–10 on chart paper or on the board. Have children read the words. Ask: **What is the same in each word?** (Each word has the short *e* sound and the vowel pair *ea*.) Have volunteers read each word and underline the letters that stand for the short *e* sound.

WRITE Have children write the spelling words in their notebooks. Remind them to use their best handwriting and to use the chart to check their spelling.

Handwriting

LETTER SHAPE Remind children to close circle letters *(a, d, o)*, connect lines *(k, t, y)*, and make retrace lines smooth *(h, m, p)*.

Spelling Words

1.	**heavy**	6.	**thread**
2.	**steady**	7.	**breath**
3.	**bread**	8.	**ready**
4.	**sweat**	9.	**meant**
5.	**head**	10.	**health**

Challenge Words

11.	**meadow**	14.	**treasure**
12.	**instead**	15.	**feather**
13.	**breakfast**		

Decodable Books

Additional Decoding Practice

- **Phonics**
  Short Vowel /e/*ea*
- **Decodable Words**
- **High-Frequency Words**
  See lists in *Decodable Book 14.*

  See also *Decodable Books,* online (Take-Home Version).

▲ **Decodable Book 14:** "Monkey and the Wealthy Cat"

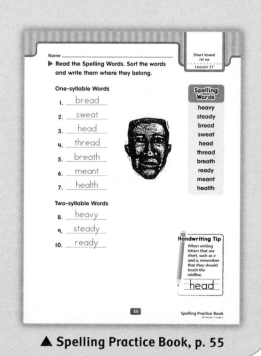

▲ Spelling Practice Book, p. 55

Fluency
Intonation

Objectives

- *To build fluency through rereading*
- *To read with intonation in a manner that sounds like natural speech*

BELOW-LEVEL

Fluency Practice   Have children reread *Decodable Book 14,* Story 17 in the *Strategic Intervention Interactive Reader*, or the appropriate *Leveled Reader* (pp. T202–T205). Have them practice reading the text several times.

Additional Related Reading

- *What Do You Like?* by Michael Grejniec. North-South, 1995. **EASY**

- *What Can You Do?: A Book About Discovering What You Do Well* by Shelley Rotner and Sheila M. Kelly, Ed.D. Millbrook, 2001. **AVERAGE**

- *This Jazz Man* by Karen Ehrhardt. Harcourt, 2006. **CHALLENGE**

Review

DIBELS
Oral Reading Fluency
ORF

MODEL READING WITH INTONATION   Remind children that good readers change the tone or pitch of their voices to match the meanings of the words, phrases, and punctuation in the story.

▲ **Student Edition, pp. 58–87**

They look for clues in the text to help them determine the mood of the characters. Tell children to:

- think about the meanings of the words as they read.

- raise or lower the pitch of their voice to match the meanings.

Think Aloud   **I'm going to read part of "Annie's Gifts" aloud. I'll lower the pitch of my voice when I come to a word that makes me think of something serious, dark, or sad. I'll make my voice higher when I come to a word that makes me think of something light, silly, or carefree.**

Practice/Apply

GUIDED PRACTICE   Read pages 64–65 aloud. Then have children read aloud these pages several times with a partner. Circulate among the pairs of children, encouraging them to change the tone or pitch of their voices to match the vibrancy of words and phrases.

INDEPENDENT PRACTICE   Have partners read two new pages of "Annie's Gifts" to practice their intonation. Have them focus on changing their tone to match meaning.

Setting
Comprehension

Objectives

- *To identify the setting of a story*
- *To analyze elements of setting*

Skill Trace

Tested **Setting**

Introduce	T34–T35
Reteach	S18–S19
Review	T67, T83, T95, T134–T135, T171, T187, T197, T389, T406
Test	Theme 4
Maintain	Theme 5, T89

Review

DISCUSS SETTING   Review with children that the setting tells when and where a story happens. On the board, write setting elements to look for when reading a story.

- When: season, day of week, time of day

- Where: region, city or country, street, type of home

Then model how to determine the setting of a story.

Think Aloud   **As I read a story, I look for text and picture clues that tell me about the setting. I try to find out what time of day it is and what season. I pay attention to where the characters live and play so I can tell where the story is happening.**

Practice/Apply

GUIDED PRACTICE   Draw on the board a setting chart like the one on *Student Edition* page 55. Then invite children to tell what they know about the setting of the first several pages of "Annie's Gifts." Guide them to identify details about when and where the story takes place. Add the information to the chart.

When	Where
p. 60–morning	home, neighborhood, school bus
p. 62–night	home, living room
p. 64–daytime	school

INDEPENDENT PRACTICE   Ask children to draw their own setting chart. Have them add to the chart details about the setting for pages 67, 68, and 73 of "Annie's Gifts."

Follow Directions

Comprehension

Objective

• *To read and follow multistep directions*

Skill Trace

 Follow Directions

Introduce	T68–T69
Reteach	S12–S13
Review	**T172–T173, T407, T417**
Test	Theme 4
Maintain	Theme 6, T87

✓ MONITOR PROGRESS

Follow Directions

IF children have difficulty reading and following directions,	**THEN** ask them to act out each step as you read the directions to them.

Small-Group Instruction, pp. S20–S21:

⬤ **BELOW-LEVEL:** Reteach

⬤ **ON-LEVEL:** Reinforce

⬤ **ADVANCED:** Extend

Teach/Model

REVIEW FOLLOWING DIRECTIONS   Invite children to think about times when they need to read and follow directions. Write their suggestions on the board. (Possible responses: playing a game, taking a test, cooking, putting something together) Then elicit that the following tips will help them read and understand directions:

• Read the directions all the way through before beginning.

• Gather all the materials you need to begin.

• Look at any photographs or illustrations.

• Look for numbered steps or clue words, such as *first, next, then,* and *finally.*

• Follow the steps in order.

Then model how to read and follow directions:

> **Think Aloud**   **As I read directions, I look for numbered steps or words such as *first, next, then,* and *finally.* These words help me know what to do and when to do it.**

Practice/Apply

GUIDED PRACTICE   Display **Transparency R86.** Read aloud to children the directions for *How to Make a Paper Tambourine.* Then have children read the directions aloud with you. Ask questions like these: **Should you place the paper plates together before or after stapling around the edges?** (before) **How do you know the last step to follow?** (by the word *finally*) Then lead children in acting out the steps, reading aloud the directions as you pantomime the procedure.

INDEPENDENT PRACTICE   Pair children. Ask them to partner-read the second set of directions, *How to Make a Drum,* on **Transparency R86.** Then have children name the clue words. Children can take turns acting out the steps as the partner reads aloud the directions.

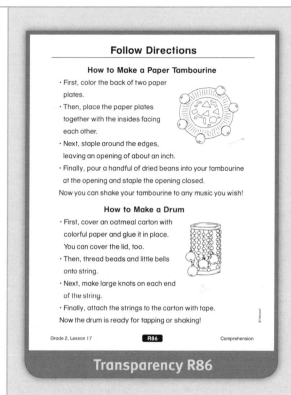

Follow Directions

How to Make a Paper Tambourine
- First, color the back of two paper plates.
- Then, place the paper plates together with the insides facing each other.
- Next, staple around the edges, leaving an opening of about an inch.
- Finally, pour a handful of dried beans into your tambourine at the opening and staple the opening closed.

Now you can shake your tambourine to any music you wish!

How to Make a Drum
- First, cover an oatmeal carton with colorful paper and glue it in place. You can cover the lid, too.
- Then, thread beads and little bells onto string.
- Next, make large knots on each end of the string.
- Finally, attach the strings to the carton with tape.

Now the drum is ready for tapping or shaking!

Grade 2, Lesson 17   R86   Comprehension

Transparency R86

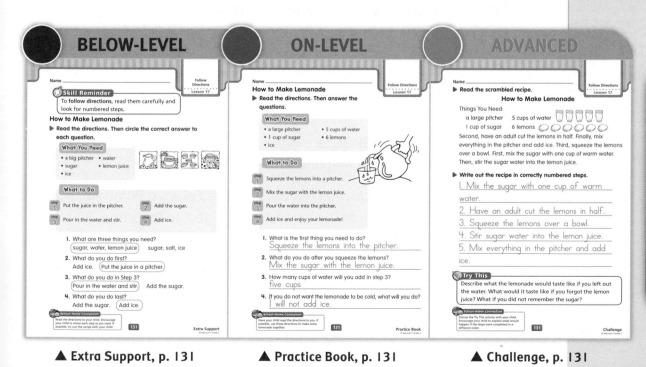

▲ **Extra Support, p. 131**   ▲ **Practice Book, p. 131**   ▲ **Challenge, p. 131**

E L L

- Group children according to academic levels, and assign one of the pages on the left.

- Clarify any unfamiliar concepts as necessary. See *ELL Teacher Guide* Lesson 17 for support in scaffolding instruction.

 Reading
Student Edition: Paired Selection

Objectives

- *To understand characteristics of poetry*
- *To apply word knowledge to the reading of a poem*

Writing Prompt

Reflect Have children write their own poem about "stepping into" a physical object. Encourage them to use sense adjectives that tell how things look, sound, smell, taste, and feel.

Genre Study

INTRODUCE THE POEM Remind children that one of Annie's gifts was writing poetry. Explain to children that "Sarah Enters a Painting" is a poem that someone like Annie might have written.

TEXT FEATURES Tell children that most poems have certain features that help them better understand and enjoy what they read. These features may include:

- rhyming words
- rhythm, which is a strong, regular beat that holds the poem together
- sense adjectives, words with the same beginning sounds, and words that imitate sounds

SHARE THE POEM Point out the illustration of the girl, Sarah, looking at the painting. Read the poem aloud to children, emphasizing its rhythm. Then reread the poem, asking children to read aloud with you.

Respond to the Poem

MONITOR COMPREHENSION Ask children to reread the poem silently. Ask:

- **SETTING Where is Sarah in this poem?** (She is in an art museum.)
- **PERSONAL RESPONSE What kind of painting would you like to "step into"?** (Responses will vary.)
- **GENRE How can you tell that "Sarah Enters a Painting" is a poem?** (The words are carefully arranged on the page, it uses the sense adjectives *curved* and *brown* to express ideas, and the subject is very imaginative.)

Art

Poetry

Sarah Enters a Painting

by Susan Katz
picture by R. W. Alley

If I stepped
into this painting,
I'd hurry past the grown-ups
dozing in their chairs
and rush up to the table
where that boy is reaching
for something I can't see from here.
A toy house? A train? A set of paints?
Maybe I'd stop
to play with him awhile.
And then I'd climb
that curved brown stair
to find out what
the painter hid way up there.

88

89

SCIENCE

SUPPORTING STANDARDS

Compare and Sort Common Objects

Have children list the common objects named in the poem. (chairs, table, toy house, train, set of paints, stair) Have them compare and sort the objects according to two or more physical attributes, such as size and weight. Children can make predictions about size and weight based on their personal experience as well as comparable objects available for them to lift and measure in the classroom. Encourage them to show the results of their investigation in a simple graph or chart.

Reinforce Meaning Help children understand the culture and vocabulary of the poem by showing relevant *Picture Cards* to them as you read the poem aloud. Show *Picture Cards 5* (artist), *24* (chair), *34* (crayons), *68* (house), *86* (paint), *121* (train).

cha   house   ain

Connections

Objectives

- *To make connections between texts*
- *To make connections between texts and personal experiences*
- *To respond to text through writing*

Comparing Texts

1. They are alike because they both have to do with finding things. Annie finds her gifts of writing poems and making art. Sarah finds meaning in the painting. Also, the poem itself is illustrated with art in the same way that Annie might write and illustrate a poem. They are different because one is a realistic fiction story and one is a poem. **TEXT TO TEXT**

2. Responses will vary. **TEXT TO SELF**

3. Responses will vary. **TEXT TO WORLD**

Connections

Comparing Texts

❶ How are "Annie's Gifts" and "Sarah Enters a Painting" alike? How are they different?

❷ What gift, or talent, would you most like to have? Why?

❸ What do you think your classmates enjoy the most—music, art, or writing? Explain.

Phonics

Guess the Word

With a group, think of short *e* words that have the letters *ea*. Write each word on a card. Then mix the cards, and place them face down. Take turns drawing a card and giving clues about the word. The person who guesses the word must spell it aloud.

bread

90

Fluency Practice

Read with a Partner

Work with a partner to perform a section of "Annie's Gifts" as Readers' Theater. Think about the most important words in each sentence. Read them in a clear, strong way.

 ### Writing

Write About Setting

On a chart, list details about the setting of "Annie's Gifts." Then use your chart to help you write a description of the setting. Share your writing with a partner.

 My Writing Checklist
Writing Trait ▶ Organization
✓ My description is in an order that makes sense.
✓ I use a setting chart to plan my writing.

Setting	
When	Where

91

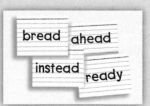 **PHONICS**

Guess the Word Help children generate a list of short *e* words with the letters *ea*. Suggest that they use the spelling words from this lesson as well as any other short *e* words with the letters *ed* that they can think of. Model how to give clues about a word by using facial and body gestures.

bread ahead
instead ready

 **FLUENCY**

Read with a Partner Pair children and help them select a section of "Annie's Gifts" to perform. Guide them in identifying the most important words in each sentence. Model how to raise and lower the pitch of your voice to show children how to vary their intonation while reading aloud.

WRITING

Writing About Setting Have children copy the chart with the headings *When* and *Where*. Help them find setting details in "Annie's Gifts" by prompting them with questions such as "Where are the characters now? and "What time of day is it?

Portfolio Opportunity Children may choose to place their description in their portfolios.

Build Robust Vocabulary

Objectives

- *To review robust vocabulary*
- *To figure out a word's meaning based on the context*

REVIEW

Vocabulary: Lesson 17

journeyed	sipped
frail	entertain
horrendous	except
melodious	carefree
stomped	screeching

Review Robust Vocabulary

USE VOCABULARY IN DIFFERENT CONTEXTS   Remind children of the Student-Friendly Explanations of the Vocabulary Words introduced on Days I and 2. Then discuss each word, using the following examples:

journeyed

- Name some places you have journeyed to.
- What experiences might a spider have if she journeyed through a school?

frail

- Name some activities frail people might do.
- Are you frail If you can ride a bike up a steep hill? Why or why not?
- Tell about a time when you felt frail.

horrendous

- Name some sounds that are horrendous.
- What would you do if a small child was frightened by a horrendous sound? Why?

melodious

- Name some classroom sounds that are melodious.
- What creatures make melodious sounds?
- Name some songs that sound melodious to you.

stomped

- Name some times when you have stomped your feet.
- If you had wanted to be really quiet, would you have tiptoed or would you have stomped your feet?

sipped

- If you had been really thirsty, would you have sipped some water or would you have gulped it? Why?
- Could you have sipped some cake at your last school party? Why or why not?
- If someone sipped from your cup, what would you do?

entertain

- How do you entertain your friends when they visit? How is it different from how your parents entertain their friends?
- What would you do to entertain a two-year-old?
- What could you do to entertain yourself if you had to be silent?

except

- Where might you live if you never ate any food except fish?
- What might you wear if everything except your feet felt cold?

carefree

- Would you do homework on a carefree day? Why or why not?
- What time at school makes you feel the most carefree? Why?
- Would you be carefree if you were too late to catch the bus to school? Why or why not?

screeching

- When does a screeching noise signal danger?
- What animals make a screeching sound?
- Would a screeching noise help you fall asleep? Why or why not?

▼ Student-Friendly Explanations

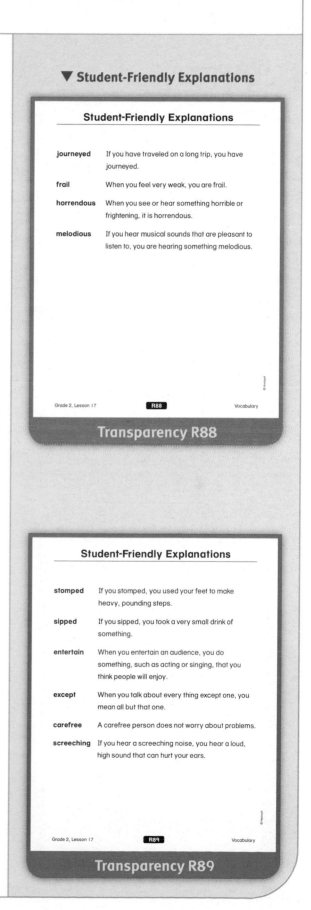

Student-Friendly Explanations

journeyed	If you have traveled on a long trip, you have journeyed.
frail	When you feel very weak, you are frail.
horrendous	When you see or hear something horrible or frightening, it is horrendous.
melodious	If you hear musical sounds that are pleasant to listen to, you are hearing something melodious.

Grade 2, Lesson 17   R88   Vocabulary

Transparency R88

Student-Friendly Explanations

stomped	If you stomped, you used your feet to make heavy, pounding steps.
sipped	If you sipped, you took a very small drink of something.
entertain	When you entertain an audience, you do something, such as acting or singing, that you think people will enjoy.
except	When you talk about every thing except one, you mean all but that one.
carefree	A carefree person does not worry about problems.
screeching	If you hear a screeching noise, you hear a loud, high sound that can hurt your ears.

Grade 2, Lesson 17   R89   Vocabulary

Transparency R89

Grammar Quick Write

Adjectives for Senses

5-DAY GRAMMAR	
DAY 1	Introduce Sense Adjectives
DAY 2	Identify Sense Adjectives
DAY 3	**Choose Colorful Adjectives**
DAY 4	Apply to Writing
DAY 5	Weekly Review

Objectives

- *To identify sense adjectives*
- *To choose colorful adjectives*

Daily Proofreading

the noisy gooses flew overhead.

(The, geese)

TECHNOLOGY

 www.harcourtschool.com/storytown
Grammar Glossary

▲ Grammar Practice Book, p. 60

Review

CHOOSING COLORFUL ADJECTIVES Write and read aloud these phrases from "Annie's Gifts":

loud bass beat	screeching alley cats
soft rain	croaking frogs
shiny brass buttons	loud finger-popping music

Tell children that the author chose sense adjectives to make her writing colorful and fun to read. Point to each colorful adjective and draw an arrow to the word that it describes.

Practice/Apply

GUIDED PRACTICE Write and read aloud these adjectives from "Annie's Gifts": *sweet, soft, gold.*

Then write these sentences on the board. Model how to add one of the colorful adjectives above to the first sentence. Work with children to add a colorful adjective to each of the remaining sentences.

Momma swayed to the rhythm.
(sweet rhythm)

The piano had letters written on it.
(gold letters)

Patty's piano music sounded like rain.
(soft rain)

INDEPENDENT PRACTICE Have children write sentences, using one of these colorful adjectives, or others of your choice: *croaking, faded, musty.* Have children share their sentences with a partner.

Writing
Description

5-DAY WRITING	
DAY 1	Introduce
DAY 2	Prewrite
DAY 3	Draft
DAY 4	Revise
DAY 5	Revise

Draft Description

REVIEW WITH A LITERATURE MODEL Have children open their *Student Edition* to "Annie's Gifts," page 76. Read aloud the first paragraph, which uses sense adjectives to describe the music Annie makes on the piano. Point out the following:

- The first sentence tells what will be described.
- Each sentence gives details that create a picture.
- Sense adjectives are used throughout the paragraph.

 DRAFT DESCRIPTIONS Have children use their filled-in graphic organizers, pictures, and what they now know to write a paragraph describing their favorite place to visit.

WRITING TRAIT **ORGANIZATION** As children write their descriptions, remind them to include sensory adjectives in their ending to make it powerful and satisfying.

CONFER WITH CHILDREN Meet with individual children, helping them as they write their descriptive paragraph. Offer encouragement for what they are doing well, as well as make constructive suggestions for improving an aspect of the writing, as needed.

Objectives

- *To read and discuss a writing model*
- *To draft a descriptive paragraph*

 Writing Prompt

Describe a Character Have children write a sentence describing Annie in "Annie's Gifts."

▲ Writer's Companion, Lesson 17

ADVANCED

Organization Encourage children to create a clear and dominant impression of their favorite place (for example, "My favorite place is noisy and full of life.") that they establish in the beginning, develop in the middle, and reinforce at the end of their paragraph.

Warm-Up Routines

Day at a Glance

Day 4

phonics and Spelling

- Introduce: Syllable Pattern V/CV
- Review: Short Vowel /e/*ea*

Fluency

- Intonation
- "Annie's Gifts," *Student Edition*, pp. 58–87

Read!

Comprehension

Review: Setting

Robust Vocabulary

- Review: *journeyed, frail, stomped, sipped, entertain, except, carefree, screeching, horrendous, melodious*

Grammar [Quick Write]

- Review: Adjectives for Senses

Writing ✏

- Description

Oral Language

Objective *To listen attentively and respond appropriately to oral communication*

Question of the Day

Picture a clean sheet of lined paper.

What words describe the paper?

Help children brainstorm adjectives and comparisons that describe a clean sheet of paper, and record their ideas in a web. Use the following prompts.

- **What colors do you see on the paper?**
- **What does the paper smell like?**
- **What does the paper feel like?**
- **How is the paper like the pages of a book? How is it different?**

Display the web for children to revisit throughout the lesson.

Read Aloud

Objective *To listen for enjoyment*

BIG BOOK OF RHYMES AND POEMS Display the poem "New Notebook" on page 32, and read the title. If possible, show children a notebook similar to the one described in the poem. Tell children to listen to the poem for enjoyment. Then read the poem aloud. Be sure that children understand that "fine" refers to something very thin or delicate, like a fine strand of hair. Explain that "wet, black strokes" are pen markings and "a flock" is a large number or group. Discuss what children liked about the poem.

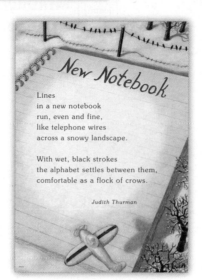

New Notebook

Lines
in a new notebook
run, even and fine,
like telephone wires
across a snowy landscape.

With wet, black strokes
the alphabet settles between them,
comfortable as a flock of crows.

Judith Thurman

▲ **Big Book of Rhymes and Poems, p. 32**

Word Wall

Objective *To read high-frequency words*

REVIEW HIGH-FREQUENCY WORDS Review each of the following words from the Word Wall: *sweat, bought, touch, knee,* and *clear,* and any other previously learned words. Give clues for each word, such as *Which word ends with a vowel sound and is a body part?* Have children say and spell the correct word. Continue until all words have been guessed.

sweat   bought   touch   knee   clear

Syllable Pattern V/CV  phonics

5-DAY PHONICS	
DAY 1	Reintroduce /e/ea
DAY 2	Word Building with /e/ea
DAY 3	Word Building with /e/ea
DAY 4	**Syllable Pattern V/CV; Review /e/ea**
DAY 5	Syllable Pattern V/CV; Review /e/ea

Objectives

- *To identify words with syllable pattern V/CV*
- *To read words with syllable pattern V/CV*

Skill Trace

 Tested **Syllable Pattern V/CV**

Introduce	T184
Review	T194

Syllable Pattern V/CV

The toy robot belongs to Macon.

Jolene gave her final student report today.

Mrs. Linus stayed in a cozy room at the hotel.

The bicycle the police found belongs to Cody Casen.

Have you chosen which motel you want to stay in when you visit?

Grade 2, Lesson 17   R87   Phonics

Transparency R87

Teach/Model

Routine Card 11   **INTRODUCE SYLLABLE PATTERN V/CV**   Write the word *chosen* on the board and guide children to help you label the vowel/consonant/vowel pattern. Explain that in words with the V/CV pattern, the vowel sound before the syllable break is usually long.

c h o s e n

V / C V

Model how to blend the syllables to read *chosen*.

- Cover the second syllable and have children read /chō/.
- Cover the first syllable and have children read /zen/.
- Then have children read the word, *chosen*.

Repeat the procedure with *final, hotel, student, behave,* and *favor*.

Guided Practice

IDENTIFY V/CV PATTERN   Make a chart as shown on the board. Identify the vowel-consonant-vowel pattern of the word *polar* by writing each letter in the appropriate column. Say: ***Polar* has two syllables. The vowel *o*, before the syllable break, is a long vowel.** Then blend and read the word. Follow a similar procedure with the words *music* and *moment*.

Word	V	C	V
polar	o	l	a

Practice/Apply

READ SENTENCES   Display **Transparency R87** or write the sentences on the board. Have children read the sentences aloud. Remind them to use what they have learned about the syllable pattern V/CV to help them read accurately.

Short Vowel /e/ea
phonics and Spelling

5-DAY SPELLING	
DAY 1	Pretest
DAY 2	Word Building
DAY 3	State the Generalization
DAY 4	Review
DAY 5	Posttest

Build Words

REVIEW THE WORDS Have children open their notebooks to the spelling words that they wrote on Day 3. Have them read the words several times and then close their notebooks.

MAP LETTERS TO SOUNDS Have children follow your directions to change, add, or take off one or two letters in each of the following words to spell a spelling word. Have them write the word on a sheet of paper or in their journals. Then have a volunteer change the spelling of the word on the board so that children can self-check their spelling.

- Write *sweet* on the board. Ask: **Which spelling word can you make by changing a letter?** *(sweat)*

- Write *read* on the board. Ask: **Which spelling word can you make by changing the first letter?** *(head)*

- Write *wealth* on the board. Ask: **Which spelling word can you make by changing the first letter?** *(health)*

Follow a similar procedure with the following words: *leave (heavy), unsteady (steady), lead (bread), spread (thread), break (breath), read (ready), mean (meant).*

CHALLENGE WORDS Write the first or second syllable of each challenge word on the board. Ask volunteers to spell each word in its entirety by providing the missing letters.

BELOW-LEVEL

Focus on Vowel Pairs Write the spelling words on the board, with a blank where the vowel pair *ea* should be. Then prompt children to complete each word by asking questions such as "What letters can you add to *st__dy* to make *steady*?" Have children spell each completed word.

Objective
- *To use /e/ea and other known letter-sounds to spell and write words*

Spelling Words
1. heavy
2. steady
3. bread
4. sweat
5. head
6. thread
7. breath
8. ready
9. meant
10. health

Challenge Words
11. meadow
12. instead
13. breakfast
14. treasure
15. feather

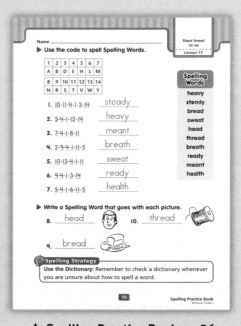

▲ Spelling Practice Book, p. 56

Fluency
Intonation

Objectives

- *To build fluency through rereading a story*
- *To read with intonation in a manner that sounds like natural speech*

BELOW-LEVEL

Echo-Read   On the board, write sentences from the story that children have trouble reading fluently. Read each sentence aloud and have children repeat, matching your speed, phrasing, and intonation. Repeat until children can read each sentence effortlessly.

MONITOR PROGRESS

Fluency

IF children have difficulty reading accurately, with intonation that sounds like natural speech,	**THEN** model reading with appropriate intonation as you have children echo-read with you.

Small-Group Instruction, pp. S16–S17:

- ● **BELOW-LEVEL:** Reteach
- ● **ON-LEVEL:** Reinforce
- ● **ADVANCED:** Extend

Review

DIBELS
Oral Reading Fluency
ORF

MODEL READING WITH INTONATION   Read aloud pages 82–84 of the *Student Edition*. Point out the sentence, "And sometimes, if you stop and listen very, very closely, you might hear Annie playing . . . her radio!"

▲ Student Edition, pp. 58–87

Think Aloud   This sentence has many intonation clues for me to pay attention to. I will lower my pitch and volume when I read "very, very closely." The exclamation point at the end of the sentence tells me to make my voice louder and higher when I read, ". . . her radio!"

Practice /Apply

Routine Card 8

GUIDED PRACTICE   Have children echo-read pages 82–84 with you, matching your intonation. Give them feedback after the first reading. Point out the words *singing* and *playing*. Model how to vary your pitch for these words to avoid dull repetition. Then have them read with you again. Repeat several times until they read the pages fluently.

INDEPENDENT PRACTICE   Have children read along with "Annie's Gifts" on *Audiotext Grade 2,* CD 4. Have them practice reading the story several times until they can read it with proper intonation. Give feedback after their reading. Point out what differences in intonation you heard.

Setting
Comprehension

Review

EXPLAIN SETTING   Ask children to explain what the setting of a story is. (when and where the story happens) Explain that the setting can happen over any length of time and in more than one place.

Practice/Apply

GUIDED PRACTICE   Display **Transparency R83**. Reread the story aloud to children and ask them to identify the setting at the beginning. (a hot day in July, the park) Guide children to think about the setting of the rest of the story. Ask:

- **How does the setting change?** (the day continues, Cole goes home)

- **Where does Cole go once he's home?** (to his sister's room and then to his own room)

- **Why is it important that Cole is at home at the end of the story?** (Home is where he keeps his collection of pictures.)

INDEPENDENT PRACTICE   Ask children to compare the setting of "Annie's Gifts" to the setting of "Cole's Collection." (Possible response: Both take place in and around a home over a period of time.)

Objectives

- *To identify the setting of a story*
- *To identify details that create the setting*

Skill Trace

 Setting

Introduce	T34–T35
Reteach	S18–S19
Review	**T67, T83, T95, T134–T135, T171, T187, T197, T389, T406**
Test	Theme 4
Maintain	Theme 5, T87

Setting

Cole's Collection

It was a hot day in July. Cole wanted to play basketball in the park with his older brothers.

"You're not tall enough yet," said Jared.

"Sorry, but you can't dribble fast enough," said Tyrone as Cole headed off the court.

Back at home, Cole poked his head into his sister's room. Shana was working on her scrapbook. "Can I help?" asked Cole.

"Thanks, Cole, but you're too young to cut this special paper," Shana told him. "This cutting takes a steady hand."

Cole shuffled to his room. Everyone thought he was too young to do anything well. Then Cole remembered his collection. He pulled it off its special place on his shelf. Cole looked at the pictures he had drawn of insects and spiders that he'd seen in his yard. Butterflies, spiders, ants, grasshoppers—his drawings showed every small detail.

"I will draw some more bugs," said Cole. "I know I can do that!"

Grade 2, Lesson 17   R83   Comprehension

Transparency R83

 Build Robust Vocabulary

Objectives

- *To review robust vocabulary*
- *To understand vocabulary in new contexts*

REVIEW Tested ✓

Vocabulary: Lesson 17

journeyed	**sipped**
frail	**entertain**
horrendous	**except**
melodious	**carefree**
stomped	**screeching**

Extend Word Meanings

USE VOCABULARY IN DIFFERENT CONTEXTS Remind children of the Student-Friendly Explanations of the Vocabulary Words. Then discuss the words using the following activities:

sipped Tell children that you will name some drinks that they may have sipped. Tell them that if they have sipped and liked the drink, they should rub their stomach. If they have sipped the drink and didn't like it, they should stick out their tongue. If they have not sipped the drink, they should do nothing.

lemonade   hot chocolate
tomato juice   prune juice
chicken broth   milk

screeching, melodious Tell children that you will name some sounds. If the sound is screeching, they should cover their ears. If it is melodious, they should do nothing.

fire alarm   nails on a chalkboard
birds chirping   a parent singing a lullaby
alarm clock   a choir giving a concert

journeyed Tell children that you will name some activities. If the activity involves someone who journeyed, they should stand up and march in place. If the activity does not involve someone who journeyed, they should remain seated.

bicycling across the country
visiting a museum
walking to school
traveling to the North Pole
visiting a neighbor
sailing across the ocean

Word Relationships

SYNONYMS   Tell children that a synonym is a word that means the same as another word. Write these sentences on the board, underlining the words as shown. Ask children to read the sentences aloud and replace each underlined word with its Vocabulary Word synonym.

Gina feels <u>weak</u> after her long illness. (frail)

Mrs. Spinelli <u>traveled</u> for many days to get home. (journeyed)

Lucky barked at the <u>awful</u> noise. (horrendous)

Bill wanted everything <u>but</u> onions on his burger. (except)

ANTONYMS   Tell children that an antonym is a word that means the opposite of another word. Write these sentences on the board, underlining the words as shown. Ask children to read the sentences aloud and replace each underlined word with its Vocabulary Word antonym.

Tana <u>gulped</u> her glass of milk. (sipped)

Sammy <u>tiptoed</u> through the house. (stomped)

Andy walked to the park in a <u>careful</u> way. (carefree)

▼ **Student-Friendly Explanations**

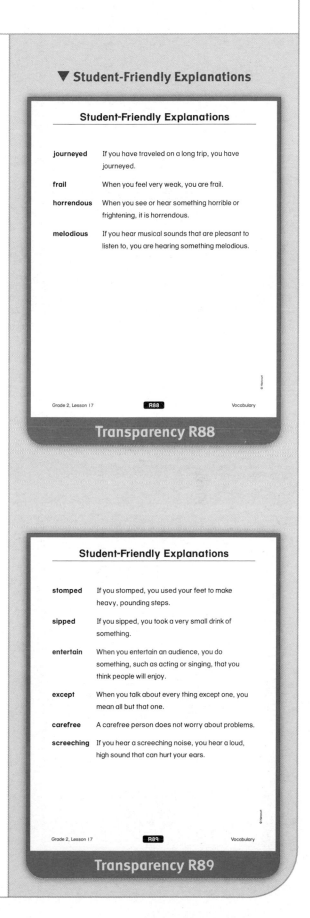

Student-Friendly Explanations

journeyed	If you have traveled on a long trip, you have journeyed.
frail	When you feel very weak, you are frail.
horrendous	When you see or hear something horrible or frightening, it is horrendous.
melodious	If you hear musical sounds that are pleasant to listen to, you are hearing something melodious.

Grade 2, Lesson 17   **R88**   Vocabulary

Transparency R88

Student-Friendly Explanations

stomped	If you stomped, you used your feet to make heavy, pounding steps.
sipped	If you sipped, you took a very small drink of something.
entertain	When you entertain an audience, you do something, such as acting or singing, that you think people will enjoy.
except	When you talk about every thing except one, you mean all but that one.
carefree	A carefree person does not worry about problems.
screeching	If you hear a screeching noise, you hear a loud, high sound that can hurt your ears.

Grade 2, Lesson 17   **R89**   Vocabulary

Transparency R89

Grammar   *Quick* Write

Adjectives for Senses

5-DAY GRAMMAR

DAY 1	Introduce Sense Adjectives
DAY 2	Identify Sense Adjectives
DAY 3	Choose Colorful Adjectives
DAY 4	**Apply to Writing**
DAY 5	Weekly Review

Objective

• *To write using sense adjectives*

Daily Proofreading

did you make a mess that was sticky.

(Did, sticky? or Did, a sticky mess?)

Writing Trait ▶

Strengthening Conventions

Parts of Speech   Use this short lesson with children's own writing to build a foundation for revising/ editing longer connected text on Day 5. See also *Writer's Companion*, Lesson 17.

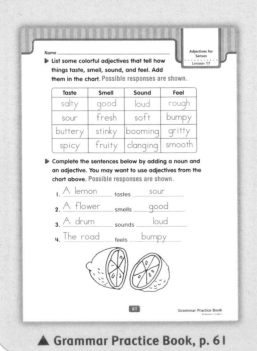

▲ Grammar Practice Book, p. 61

Review

DISCUSS SENSE ADJECTIVES   Review with children that sense adjectives describe how something looks, smells, tastes, sounds, or feels. Write the following sentence on the board:

Annie's piano music sounded like stomping elephants.

Read the sentence aloud and tell children that the words *stomping elephants* describe the sound of Annie's playing. Then ask volunteers to dictate several sentences that include at least one sense adjective in each. Write their suggested sentences on the board, underlining the sense adjective(s).

Practice/Apply

GUIDED PRACTICE   Tell children that you are going to write three sentences about things you see, smell, taste, hear, or feel in the classroom. Explain that you are going to include at least one sense adjective in each sentence. Model writing the first sentence. Elicit additional sentence ideas from children. After you write each sentence, ask a volunteer to underline the sense adjective.

INDEPENDENT PRACTICE   Ask children to write three sentences about their bedroom or another room in their home. Have them include one or more sense adjectives in each sentence. Have partners exchange sentences and check that sentences include a sense adjective. Children can also practice using editor's marks to proofread and correct, if necessary, their partner's spelling, capitalization, and punctuation.

Writing
Description

5-DAY WRITING	
DAY 1	Introduce
DAY 2	Prewrite
DAY 3	Draft
DAY 4	**Revise**
DAY 5	Revise

Revise Descriptions

WRITE Have children continue writing their descriptive paragraphs. Remind them to include sense adjectives to create a vivid word picture of their favorite place to visit.

WRITING TRAIT ▶ **ORGANIZATION** Tell children that an interesting closing sentence will make their readers feel that they have "seen" the special place and now know it well.

REVISE Have children read their descriptive paragraphs to a partner. Ask partners to check that the paragraphs create a picture and include sense adjectives. Children can use the list of criteria for a descriptive paragraph to improve their writing.

Description

- The first sentence tells what will be described.
- Each sentence gives details that create a picture.
- Sense adjectives are used throughout the paragraph.

Have children revise their paragraphs. Let them work together to make sure that their paragraphs include a main idea sentence and detail sentences. Have them check to make sure they include adjectives that cover all five senses, if possible. Encourage children to use editor's marks to revise their writing. Save children's paragraphs to revise further on Day 5.

Editor's Marks

∧	Add
℘	Take out
⌢	Change

Objective

- *To revise descriptions*

Writing Prompt

Compare Writing to Illustrating
Have children compare writing a description of a place to drawing it. Which one would they enjoy doing more? Why?

BELOW-LEVEL

Revise If children are unsure of how to revise their paragraphs, go over each point on the list of criteria with them. Suggest that they use the checklist to make sure their paragraphs follow the correct format.

Day at a Glance

Day 5

phonics and Spelling
- Review: Syllable Pattern V/CV
- Posttest: Short Vowel /e/ea

Fluency
- Intonation
- "Annie's Gifts,"
  Student Edition, pp. 58–87

Read!

Comprehension

 Focus Skill Review: Setting

- *Read-Aloud Anthology:* "Sophie's Masterpiece"

Robust Vocabulary
- Cumulative Review

Grammar [Quick Write]
- Review: Adjectives for Senses

Writing ✏
- Description

Warm-Up Routines

 Oral Language

Objective *To listen attentively and respond appropriately to oral communication*

Question of the Day

Which would you rather have — a note-book or separate sheets of paper? Why?

Invite children to consider the advantages and disadvantages of a notebook and of separate sheets of paper. Use the following prompts.

- **Is it easier to carry a notebook or separate sheets of paper? Tell why.**

- **Which would you use if you were writing something important? Tell why.**

- **Which would make it easier to save your writing for a long time? Tell why.**

Have children complete the following sentence frame to explain the reasons for their choice.

> **I would rather have _____**
>
> **because _____.**

Read Aloud

Objective *To identify imagery in poetry*

BIG BOOK OF RHYMES AND POEMS
Display the poem "New Notebook" on page 32. Ask children to listen for words that paint pictures in their minds. Then read the poem aloud. Guide children to identify the images in the poem. (lines on a white page are like telephone wires across a snowy landscape; writing on a page is like crows sitting on the telephone wires) Then read the poem again, encouraging children to join in. Invite children to draw a picture of the poet's idea of what a new notebook looks like.

New Notebook

Lines
in a new notebook
run, even and fine,
like telephone wires
across a snowy landscape.

With wet, black strokes
the alphabet settles between them,
comfortable as a flock of crows.

Judith Thurman

▲ **Big Book of Rhymes and Poems, p. 32**

Word Wall

Objective *To read high-frequency words*

REVIEW HIGH-FREQUENCY WORDS Review the following words in random order and have children read the words quickly: *everything, prove, exercise, ago, enough,* and *year.* Then point to the words again and have volunteers use each word in a sentence.

everything	prove	exercise
ago	**enough**	year

Syllable Pattern V/CV

phonics

5-DAY PHONICS	
DAY 1	Reintroduce /e/*ea*
DAY 2	Word Building with /e/*ea*
DAY 3	Word Building with /e/*ea*
DAY 4	Syllable Pattern V/CV; Review /e/*ea*
DAY 5	Syllable Pattern V/CV; Review /e/*ea*

Objectives

- *To identify the syllable pattern V/CV in words*
- *To read words with the syllable pattern V/CV*

Skill Trace

Tested **Syllable Pattern V/CV**

Introduce	T184
Review	T194

Review

READ V/CV WORDS   Write the word *student* on the board. Guide children to label the V/CV pattern and read the word aloud. Point out that the word has two syllables and the first vowel has a long sound. Have children blend the syllables to read the word.

Practice/Apply

GUIDED PRACTICE   Write the following words on the board: *motel, label, recent, silent, begin, taken, hotel,* and *robot*. Then make a chart as shown. Guide children in sorting the words by the vowel sound in the first syllable. Add them to the chart.

Long *a*	Long *e*	Long *i*	Long *o*	Long *u*

INDEPENDENT PRACTICE   Have children read aloud the words in the chart above.

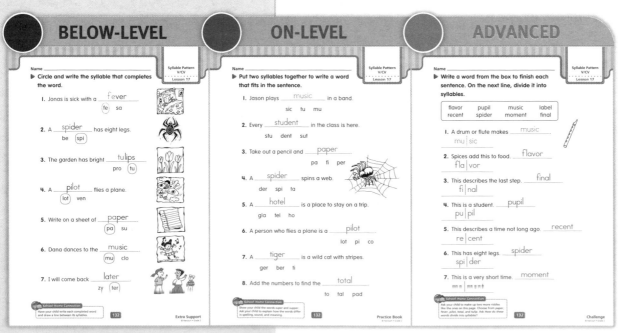

BELOW-LEVEL	**ON-LEVEL**	**ADVANCED**

▲ Extra Support, p. 132   ▲ Practice Book, p. 132   ▲ Challenge, p. 132

ELL

- Group children according to academic levels, and assign one of the pages on the left.

- Clarify any unfamiliar concepts as necessary. See *ELL Teacher Guide* Lesson 17 for support in scaffolding instruction.

Short Vowel /e/ea
phonics and Spelling

5-DAY SPELLING

DAY 1	Pretest
DAY 2	Word Building
DAY 3	State the Generalization
DAY 4	Review
DAY 5	Posttest

Assess

POSTTEST Assess children's progress. Use the dictation sentences from Day 1.

Words with /e/ea

1.	heavy	The box is too **heavy** to lift.
2.	steady	The drummer plays with a **steady** beat.
3.	bread	Jan ate a slice of **bread**.
4.	sweat	Hard work can make you **sweat**.
5.	head	Cover your **head** with a hat.
6.	thread	Matt used blue **thread** to sew on his button.
7.	breath	Catch your **breath** after the mile run.
8.	ready	Are you **ready** to go to school?
9.	meant	The teacher **meant** to give everyone a sticker.
10.	health	Daily exercise can help you have good **health**.

ADVANCED

Challenge Words Use the challenge words in these dictation sentences.

11.	meadow	The lark sings in the **meadow**.
12.	instead	I'll eat an apple **instead** of chips.
13.	breakfast	Lisa ate toast for **breakfast**.
14.	treasure	Divers found the **treasure** chest.
15.	feather	The man wears a **feather** in his hat.

WRITING APPLICATION Have children write a note to a classmate, using one or more of the spelling words. Remind them to write neatly.

Objective

- *To use short vowel /e/ea and other known letter-sounds to spell and write words*

Spelling Words

1.	**heavy**	6.	**thread**
2.	**steady**	7.	**breath**
3.	**bread**	8.	**ready**
4.	**sweat**	9.	**meant**
5.	**head**	10.	**health**

Challenge Words

11.	**meadow**	14.	**treasure**
12.	**instead**	15.	**feather**
13.	**breakfast**		

Dear Chris,

I <u>meant</u> to tell you about the race. I ran at a <u>steady</u> pace and didn't run out of <u>breath</u> or <u>sweat</u> very much. My dad says I'm in very good <u>health</u>.

Your friend,
Kyle

Fluency
Intonation

Objective

- *To read fluently with appropriate intonation*

ASSESSMENT

Monitoring Progress Periodically, take a timed sample of children's oral reading and record the number of words read correctly per minute. Children should accurately read approximately 72 words per minute in the middle of Grade 2.

Fluency Support Materials

 Fluency Builders, Grade 2, Lesson 17

 Audiotext *Student Edition* selections are available on *Audiotext Grade 2,* CD 4.

 Strategic Intervention Teacher Guide, Lesson 17

Readers' Theater

DIBELS Oral Reading Fluency **ORF** **PERFORM "ANNIE'S GIFTS"** To help children improve their fluency, have them perform "Annie's Gifts" as Readers' Theater. Use the following procedures:

▲ **Student Edition, pp. 58–87**

- Discuss with children how the characters might feel and sound throughout the story.

- Have groups of five children read the story together. One child should take the part of the narrator, one child should read Annie's lines, one child should read Daddy's lines, one child should read Momma's lines, and one child should read the lines for the guests and Mrs. Mason.

- Listen to the groups read. Provide feedback and support.

- Invite the groups to read the story to classmates. Remind them to focus on reading with proper intonation.

E L L

Build Fluency As you discuss how characters in the story might feel, focus on words and punctuation that indicate emotion or attitude. For example, model expressing encouragement and excitement when Momma says, "Cheer up! We're going to get a new piano and everyone is going to take piano lessons!" Have children imitate your expression and intonation as they say the words. Provide feedback and support.

Setting
Comprehension

▲ Read-Aloud Anthology, "Sophie's Masterpiece," p. 64

Review

REVIEW THE SKILL   Remind children that good readers pay attention to when and where a story takes place. Point out that a story can happen over any length of time and in more than one place. Explain that setting details are important because they create the "world" in which the story characters live.

SET A PURPOSE FOR LISTENING   Guide children to set a purpose for listening that includes

- listening for details about when Sophie spins her webs.

- listening for details that tell where Sophie does her spinning.

Practice/Apply

GUIDED PRACTICE   As you read aloud "Sophie's Masterpiece," record in a chart information about when and where the story takes place.

When	Where
The lifetime of a spider: When Sophie is a baby spider, a young spider, an adult spider, and an elderly spider	Beekman's Boardinghouse: front parlor, tugboat captain's closet, Cook's bedroom slipper, a knitting basket in a third-floor bedroom

INDEPENDENT PRACTICE   Have children review what they know about the setting of the tale by looking at the chart. Then have them tell why this setting is important to the story. (Possible response: The setting is important because each change provides a different home for Sophie and a new challenge.)

Objectives

- *To review identifying the setting of a story*
- *To review finding details that tell where and when the story takes place*

Skill Trace

Tested **Setting**

Introduce	T34–T35
Reteach	S18–S19
Review	**T67, T83, T95, T134–T135, T171, T187, T197, T389, T406**
Test	Theme 4
Maintain	Theme 5, T89

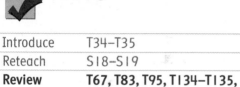

Understand Setting   If children have difficulty understanding the setting, draw the boardinghouse on chart paper. Have children help you label the different places named in the story: front parlor, tugboat captain's closet, Cook's bedroom, and the third-floor bedroom. Ask volunteers to use two fingers and move like Sophie through the boardinghouse to the places named as you read the story aloud.

 Build Robust Vocabulary

Objectives

- *To review robust vocabulary*
- *To demonstrate knowledge of word meaning*
- *To organize word meanings in order to understand word relationships*

REVIEW ✓ Tested

Vocabulary

Lesson 16	Lesson 17
disturb	journeyed
underneath	frail
cozy	stomped
enchanting	sipped
instead	entertain
thrilled	except
review	carefree
celebrate	screeching
procrastinate	horrendous
diversion	melodious

Cumulative Review

RELATING WORDS   Ask children the following questions:

- **Would you be thrilled if you heard a screeching noise in the middle of the night? Why or why not?**

- **Would it disturb or entertain you if someone flew a toy plane in your bedroom? Why?**

- **Would you rather write a review about a melodious song or a horrendous song? Why?**

- **What might travelers on camels have sipped as they journeyed through the desert?**

- **If you were frail, why would you choose a cozy chair instead of a hard one?**

MAKE WORD WEBS   Using **Transparency GO9**, guide children to complete word webs to enrich their understanding of *procrastinate, horrendous, carefree,* and *journeyed.* Write *procrastinate* in the center circle and have children name familiar words and phrases that are related to it. Write their responses in the outer circles.

Repeat the procedure for *horrendous, carefree,* and *journeyed.*

REINFORCE MEANINGS Discuss children's answers to these questions.

1. **Is an injured kitten frail or healthy? Why?**

2. **How would you feel if everyone in the class except you forgot his or her homework?**

3. **Why might you procrastinate about finishing a book that you are not enjoying?**

4. **What game would you play if you wanted a diversion from cleaning your room?**

5. **How would you like to celebrate your next birthday?**

6. **What kind of book would you find enchanting?**

7. **Would you like to spend time exploring underneath the sea? Why?**

 MONITOR PROGRESS

Build Robust Vocabulary

IF children do not demonstrate understanding of the words and have difficulty using them,	**THEN** model using each word in several sentences, and have children repeat each sentence.

Small-Group Instruction, pp. S22–S23:

● **BELOW-LEVEL:** Reteach
● **ON-LEVEL:** Reinforce
● **ADVANCED:** Extend

Grammar Quick Write

Adjectives for Senses

5-DAY GRAMMAR

DAY 1 Introduce Sense Adjectives
DAY 2 Identify Sense Adjectives
DAY 3 Choose Colorful Adjectives
DAY 4 Apply to Writing
DAY 5 Weekly Review

Objectives

- *To recognize that sense adjectives describe how something looks, smells, tastes, sounds, or feels*
- *To recognize that sense adjectives make writing more colorful*

Daily Proofreading

Aunt lucy gave Me a fluffy bunny.

(Lucy, me)

 Language Arts Checkpoint

If children have difficulty with the concepts, see pages S24–S25 to reteach.

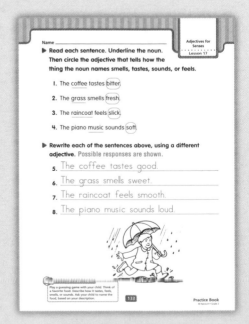

▲ **Practice Book, p. 133**

Review

REVIEW SENSE ADJECTIVES   Review the following points with children:

- **Sense adjectives are words that describe how something looks, smells, tastes, sounds, or feels.**
- **Sense adjectives can come before or after the words they describe.**
- **Sense adjectives make writing more colorful and fun to read.**

Practice/Apply

GUIDED PRACTICE   Model revising the following sentence to include one or more sense adjectives.

I saw a butterfly fly over a flower. (I saw a butterfly with soft blue wings fly over a bright red flower.)

Write the following sentences on the board. Ask volunteers to help you add sense adjectives to each one.

Connie gave me a present.

The fans cheered for their team.

Mr. Grant sipped a cup of tea.

INDEPENDENT PRACTICE   Have partners work together to choose sense adjectives to add to sentences. Have volunteers read aloud their colorful sentences.

Writing
Description

5-DAY WRITING	
DAY 1	Introduce
DAY 2	Prewrite
DAY 3	Draft
DAY 4	Revise
DAY 5	Revise

Revise

REVISE DESCRIPTIONS Have children check one last time that their paragraph meets the guidelines for a descriptive paragraph. Children should also check for correct spelling and legible handwriting.

EXCHANGE DESCRIPTIONS Allow children to exchange descriptions of a favorite place to visit and read them. Encourage them to discuss their descriptions.

WRITING TRAIT ▶ **ORGANIZATION** After children share their descriptions, discuss as a class the different ways children ordered their descriptions.

Editor's Marks
∧	Add
ℐ	Take out
⌒	Change
⊙	Add a period
≡	Capitalize
○	Check spelling

Objective
• *To revise descriptions*

Writing Prompt

Independent Writing Have children generate a list of ideas about a new topic of their choice for writing.

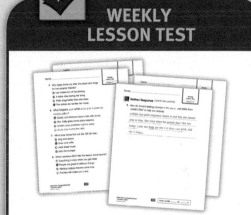

WEEKLY LESSON TEST

▲ **Weekly Lesson Tests, pp. 177–187**

• Selection Comprehension with Short Response
• Phonics and Spelling
• Focus Skill
• Follow Directions
• Robust Vocabulary
• Grammar
• Fluency Passage **FRESH READS**

 For prescriptions, see pp. A2–A6. Also available electronically on StoryTown Online Assessment and Exam View®.

Podcasting: Assessing Fluency

NOTE: A 4-point rubric appears on page R8.

		6	5	4	3	2	1
	FOCUS	Completely focused, purposeful.	Focused on topic and purpose.	Generally focused on topic and purpose.	Somewhat focused on topic and purpose.	Related to topic but does not maintain focus.	Lacks focus and purpose.
	ORGANIZATION	Ideas progress logically; paper conveys sense of completeness.	Organization mostly clear; paper gives sense of completeness.	Organization mostly clear, but some lapses occur; may seem unfinished.	Some sense of organization; seems unfinished.	Little sense of organization.	Little or no sense of organization.
	SUPPORT	Strong, specific details; clear, exact language; freshness of expression.	Strong, specific details; clear, exact language.	Adequate support and word choice.	Limited supporting details; limited word choice.	Few supporting details; limited word choice.	Little development; limited or unclear word choice.
	CONVENTIONS	Varied sentences; few, if any, errors.	Varied sentences; few errors.	Some sentence variety; few errors.	Simple sentence structures; some errors.	Simple sentence structures; many errors.	Unclear sentence structures; many errors.

SCORING RUBRIC

REPRODUCIBLE STUDENT RUBRICS for specific writing purposes and presentations are available on pages R2–R8.

Leveled Readers
Reinforcing Skills and Strategies

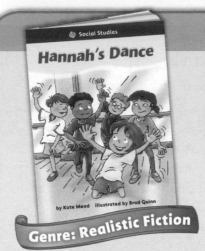

Genre: Realistic Fiction

BELOW-LEVEL

Hannah's Dance

SUMMARY Hannah loves to dance but does not enjoy her ballet lessons until she learns a new, carefree way to move to music.

• **phonics** Short Vowel /e/ *ea*
• **Vocabulary**
 Setting
Focus Skill

Before Reading

BUILD BACKGROUND/SET PURPOSE Have children share their experiences with dancing, watching dance performances, or performing themselves. Ask what is easy and hard about dancing. Then guide children to preview the story and set a purpose for reading it.

Reading the Book

PAGES 10–12 DRAW CONCLUSIONS Why does Hannah dance so well at the performance? (Possible responses: She likes this carefree kind of dancing better than ballet. She enjoys matching her moves to the music.)

PAGE 3–14 SETTING What is the setting in the beginning, middle, and end of the story? (Possible responses: It begins at home. Then story events happen at ballet school. After that, Hannah performs at a community center. The story ends back at home.)

REREAD FOR FLUENCY Have partners take turns reading the story again. Tell them to make their voices go up and down to show Hannah's feelings.

Think Critically   *(See inside back cover for questions.)*

1 **SETTING** Hannah's home, dance school, community center.

2 **COMPARE/CONTRAST** Hannah did not like ballet. She loved the carefree dancing.

3 **CONTEXT CLUES** Possible responses: relaxed, happy

4 **NOTE DETAILS** Mom said Hannah danced like a bird.

5 **PERSONAL RESPONSE** Answers will vary.

LEVELED READERS TEACHER GUIDE

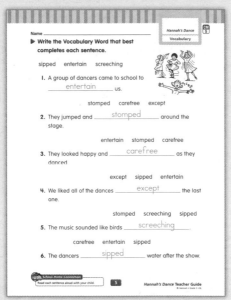

▲ Vocabulary, p. 5

▲ Comprehension, p. 6

www.harcourtschool.com/storytown

Go online

★ Leveled Readers Online Database
Searchable by Genre, Skill, Vocabulary, Level, or Title
★ Student Activities and Teacher Resources, online

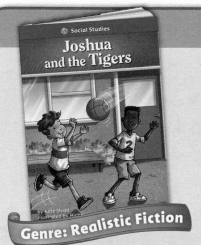

Social Studies

Joshua and the Tigers

Genre: Realistic Fiction

ON-LEVEL

Joshua and the Tigers

SUMMARY Joshua cannot play the violin as well as his sister and cannot dance as well as his brother. Then he discovers his talent for basketball and looks forward to joining the school team, the Tigers.

- **phonics** Short Vowel /e/*ea*
- **Vocabulary**

Focus Skill **Setting**

Before Reading

BUILD BACKGROUND/SET PURPOSE Talk about why the youngest child in a family might try to do the things older brothers and sisters do. Then guide children to preview the story and set a purpose for reading it.

Reading the Book

PAGES 3–7 DRAW CONCLUSIONS How does Joshua probably feel on page 7? Why do you think that? (Possible response: He probably feels bad about himself when he can't play the violin or dance. Everybody wants to be good at something.)

PAGES 12–13 ◉ **SETTING Where and when does Mrs. Diaz tell Joshua's parents about his special ability?** (Possible response: At school in the evening, after she sees Joshua playing basketball.)

REREAD FOR FLUENCY Have partners take turns reading pages of the story. Remind them that voices go up and down to match the feelings.

Think Critically *(See inside back cover for questions.)*

① ◉ **SETTING** Joshua's home, the park, Joshua's school

② **NOTE DETAILS** Joshua's sister was good at playing the violin. His brother was good at dancing.

③ **CHARACTER'S EMOTIONS** sad, miserable, disappointed, unhappy

④ **DRAW CONCLUSIONS** Possible responses: She noticed Joshua was good at sports; she suggested he could join the basketball team.

⑤ **PERSONAL RESPONSE** Answers will vary.

LEVELED READERS TEACHER GUIDE

Name _____

▶ Write the Vocabulary Word from the box that best completes each sentence.

| stomped | entertain | screeching |
| except | carefree | |

1. Ken wanted a clown to ___entertain___ his friends at his birthday party.
2. Chuckles the clown made everyone happy and ___carefree___.
3. He came ___screeching___ to a stop in a silly way.
4. He ___stomped___ around in big red shoes.
5. Chuckles did all ___except___ balloon tricks.

▶ Use *sipped* in a sentence.
Possible response: I sipped my juice.

School-Home Connection
With your child, discuss things that make a screeching sound.

5 *Joshua and the Tigers Teacher Guide*

▲ Vocabulary, p. 5

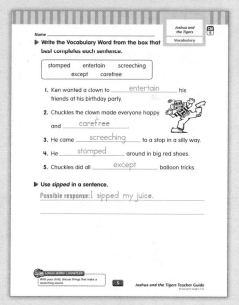

Name _____

▶ Read the sentences. Then circle the best answer.

1. Maggie laughed as she ran down the hill. She didn't have school because it was Saturday. Her family was having a picnic. Where is Maggie?
   A at school
   B a park
   C a library
2. Jonah said, "Look at the lions." Bill said, "Wow! They're real!" Jonah said, "Look at the tigers!" Where are they?
   F factory
   G playground
   H zoo
3. Su's mom taught her how to cook. They make meals together. Today she made spring rolls. Where is she?
   A a kitchen
   B a store
   C an airplane

School-Home Connection
Discuss with your child where he or she would set a story.

6 *Joshua and the Tigers Teacher Guide*

▲ Comprehension, p. 6

Leveled Readers
Reinforcing Skills and Strategies

ADVANCED

by Kate Mead
illustrated by Stephen Axelsen

Genre: Realistic Fiction

Hunter's Secret

SUMMARY Hunter isn't sure he can find anything to do for the talent show—until he thinks about what he is good at. His storytelling performance is a big hit.

 **phonics** Short Vowel /e/ea
- **Vocabulary**

Focus Skill Setting

Before Reading

BUILD BACKGROUND/SET PURPOSE Have students suggest types of performances for a talent show. List their ideas and ask if they would want to give any of the performances. Then guide children to preview the story and set a purpose for reading it.

Reading the Book

PAGE 3 CHARACTERS' EMOTIONS What is a "glum" look, and why does Hunter have it? (Possible response: He is a little sad and worried because he is unhopeful that he'll be in the show.)

PAGE 3–4 SETTING Why is the setting important to this story? (Possible response: The talent show will raise money for the school library, so the school is where most of the events occur.)

REREAD FOR FLUENCY Have partners take turns reading the story. Remind children to change their voice to match the story's mood.

Think Critically   *(See inside back cover for questions.)*

1. **NOTE DETAILS** to raise money for the school library
2. **SETTING** He was at home.
3. **COMPARE/CONTRAST** At the end, Hunter felt happy. At the beginning, Hunter felt worried.
4. **DESCRIBE CHARACTERS** Possible responses: caring, kind, helpful
5. **PERSONAL RESPONSE** Answers will vary.

LEVELED READERS TEACHER GUIDE

Name _____

▶ Write the Vocabulary Word from the box that completes each sentence.

| stomped | sipped | entertain |
| except | carefree | screeching |

1. All of Clark School _____except_____ for the kindergarten went to the zoo.
2. They watched as the elephant _____stomped_____ around his yard.
3. The chimps began to _____entertain_____ us by swinging.
4. They were _____screeching_____ loudly at one another.
5. The tiny squirrel monkeys looked _____carefree_____ as they played together.
6. The lion _____sipped_____ water from a pool.

▶ Write a sentence using a Vocabulary Word from the box.
Answers will vary.

▲ **Vocabulary, p. 5**

Name _____

▶ Answer the questions about *Hunter's Secret.*

1. Where in school were the children when they talked about the talent show?
in the classroom

2. What did Hunter carry on stage?
a stool and a book

3. Where did Hunter go to school?
Featherston School

4. Where was Hunter when he got an idea for his talent?
at home

5. Where did the talent show take place?
on the stage

6. Where was Hunter when the children gathered around him?
backstage

▲ **Comprehension, p. 6**

www.harcourtschool.com/storytown

GO online

★ **Leveled Readers Online Database**
Searchable by Genre, Skill, Vocabulary, Level, or Title
★ **Student Activities and Teacher Resources, online**

E L L

Genre: Realistic Fiction

Guitar Lessons

SUMMARY Miguel learns to play the guitar, and readers learn along with him.

- **Build Background**
- **Concept Vocabulary**
- **Scaffolded Language Development**

Before Reading

BUILD BACKGROUND/SET PURPOSE Have children pantomime playing a guitar. Ask how they might learn to play a guitar and how they might become good at guitar playing. Then guide children to preview the story and set a purpose for reading it.

Reading the Book

PAGE 3 ⏺ **SETTING** Where and when does Miguel take guitar lessons? (He takes guitar lessons at a music school once a week.)

PAGES 9–10 COMPARE AND CONTRAST Show the two actions Miguel learns to make on the guitar. How are the actions different? (Possible response: He strums with the thumb of his right hand, and he uses the fingers of his left hand to make chords.)

REREAD FOR FLUENCY Have partners prepare a reading of the book so that as one child reads, the other pantomimes the action described. They may split the book into two parts and exchange roles. Model expressive intonation as a reminder.

Scaffolded Language Development

(See inside back cover for teacher-led activity.)

Provide additional examples and explanation as needed.

LEVELED READERS TEACHER GUIDE

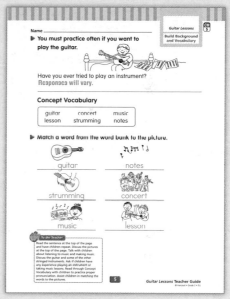

▲ **Build Background and Vocabulary, p. 5**

▲ **Scaffolded Language Development, p. 6**

Lesson 18

Phonics
Vowel Diphthong /oi/*oi, oy*
Suffixes *–ful, –less*

Spelling
join, boil, joy, soil, noise, boy, voice, point, toy, coin

Reading
"Ah, Music!" by Aliki NONFICTION

"Come, My Little Children, Here Are Songs for You" by Robert Louis Stevenson POETRY

Fluency
Accuracy

Comprehension
 Locate Information
Use Reference Sources

 Answer Questions

Robust Vocabulary
attract, territory, volume, expression, creative, performance, concentrate, relieved, universal, audible

Grammar
Number Words

Writing
Form: Poem
Trait: Word Choice

Weekly Lesson Test

 = Focus Skill   = Focus Strategy   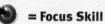 = Tested Skill

One stop *for all* *your* **Digital** *needs*

Digital
CLASSROOM

 GO online www.harcourtschool.com/storytown
To go along with your print program

FOR THE TEACHER

Prepare **GO online** Professional Development

 Videos for Podcasting

Plan & Organize **GO online** Online TE & Planning Resources*

Teach **GO online** Transparencies

access from Online TE

Assess **GO online** Online Assessment^

with Student Tracking System and Prescriptions

FOR THE STUDENT

Read  **GO online** Student eBook*

 GO online Strategic Intervention Interactive Reader

 **GO online** Leveled Readers

Practice & Apply Splash into Phonics CD-ROM

 Also available on CD-ROM

Literature Resources

Genre: Nonfiction

BY ROBERT LOUIS STEVENSON

Genre: Poetry

 ◀ **Audiotext** *Student Edition selections are available on Audiotext Grade 2, CD 4.*

 ◀ *Practice Quizzes for the Selection*

THEME CONNECTION: DREAM BIG
Comparing Nonfiction and Poetry

Paired Selections

🎵 **MUSIC** **Ah, Music!, pp. 98–111**

SUMMARY Children will discover a broad overview of music from basic definitions to composing and performing.

⭐ **LANGUAGE ARTS** **Come, My Little Children, Here Are Songs For You, pp. 112–113**

SUMMARY This classic poem encourages children to learn and appreciate music.

Support for Differentiated Instruction

BELOW-LEVEL **ON-LEVEL** **ADVANCED**

E L L

LEVELED PRACTICE

◀ **Strategic Intervention Resource Kit, Lesson 18**

◀ **Strategic Intervention Interactive Reader, Lesson 18**
Strategic Intervention Interactive Reader Online

◀ **ELL Extra Support Kit, Lesson 18**

◀ **Challenge Resource Kit, Lesson 18**

● **BELOW-LEVEL**
Extra Support Copying Masters, pp. 134, 136–140

● **ON-LEVEL**
Practice Book, pp. 134–141

● **ADVANCED**
Challenge Copying Masters, pp. 134, 136–140

ADDITIONAL RESOURCES

- Decodable Book 15
- Spelling Practice Book, pp. 57–59
- Grammar Practice Book, pp. 63–66
- Reading Transparencies R90–R96
- Language Arts Transparencies LA37–LA38
- Test Prep System
◀ **Literacy Center Kit, Cards 86–90**
- Sound/Spelling Cards
◀ **Fluency Builders**
◀ **Picture Card Collection**
- Read-Aloud Anthology, pp. 68–71

ASSESSMENT

✔ **Monitor Progress**

✔ **Weekly Lesson Tests, Lesson 18**

- Comprehension
- Phonics and Spelling
- Focus Skill
- Robust Vocabulary
- Grammar
- Use Reference Sources

GO online **www.harcourtschool.com/storytown**
Online Assessment
Also available on CD-ROM—Exam View®

Suggested Lesson Planner

 GO online Online TE & Planning Resources

	Day 1	**Day 2**
Step 1 Whole Group **Daily Routines** • *Oral Language* • *Read Aloud* • *High-Frequency Words*	**QUESTION OF THE DAY,** p. T218 *What do you like about music?* **READ ALOUD,** p. T219 *Transparency R90: The Flute* **WORD WALL,** p. T219	**QUESTION OF THE DAY,** p. T230 *What do you like best about the music you hear at a parade? Tell why.* **READ ALOUD,** p. T231 *Big Book of Rhymes and Poems,* "Here Comes the Band" **WORD WALL,** p. T231

Word Work

• phonics
• *Spelling*

Skills and Strategies

• *Reading*
• *Fluency*
• *Comprehension*
• *Build Robust Vocabulary*

Day 1

☑ **phonics**, p. T220
Introduce: Vowel Diphthong /oi/*oi,oy*

☑ **SPELLING,** p. T223
Pretest: *join, boil, joy, soil, noise, boy, voice, point, toy, coin*

☑ **READING,** Words with *oi* and *oy*, T221
COMPREHENSION, p. T224
 Introduce: Locate Information

LISTENING COMPREHENSION, p. T226
Read-Aloud: "Sounds All Around"

FLUENCY, p. T226
Focus: Accuracy

☑ **BUILD ROBUST VOCABULARY,** p. T227
Words from the Read-Aloud

Day 2

☑ **phonics**, p. T232
Review: Vowel Diphthong /oi/*oi,oy*

☑ **SPELLING,** p. T233
Word Building

☑ **BUILD ROBUST VOCABULARY,** p. T234
Words from the Selection,
Word Scribe, p. T235

☑ **READING,** p. T236
"Ah, Music!"
Options for Reading

☑ **COMPREHENSION,**
p. T236

Introduce: Answer
Questions

▲ Student Edition

RETELLING/FLUENCY, p. T244
Accuracy

☑ **BUILD ROBUST VOCABULARY,** p. T244
Words About the Selection

 Step 2 Small Groups

Suggestions for Differentiated Instruction (See pp. T212–T213.)

 Step 3 Whole Group

Language Arts

• *Grammar* Quick Write
• *Writing*

Day 1

☑ **GRAMMAR,** p. T228
Introduce: Number Words

Daily Proofreading
kyle ate three oranges
(Kyle, oranges.)

 WRITING, p. T229
Introduce: Poem
Writing Trait: Word Choice

Writing Prompt *Write about a noisy sound and a quiet sound that you like.*

Day 2

☑ **GRAMMAR,** p. T246
Review: Number Words

Daily Proofreading
does Mr James play the trumpet.
(Does, Mr., trumpet?)

 WRITING, p. T247
Review: Poem
Writing Trait: Word Choice

Writing Prompt *Record ideas about sounds you don't like to hear.*

 = Focus Skill   = Focus Strategy    = Tested Skill

phonics

Skills at a Glance

Comprehension

Fluency

Vocabulary

- Vowel Diphthong /oi/*oi*, *oy*
- Suffixes *–ful*, *–less*

Focus Skill
Locate Information

Focus Strategy
Answer Questions

Accuracy

ROBUST: *attract, territory, volume, expression, creative, performance, concentrate, relieved, universal, audible*

Day 3

QUESTION OF THE DAY, p. T248
What instrument in a marching band do you think sounds the most interesting?

READ ALOUD, p. T249
Big Book of Rhymes and Poems, "Here Comes the Band"

WORD WALL, p. T249

  phonics, p. T250
Review: Vowel Diphthong /oi/*oi, oy*

 SPELLING, p. T251
State the Generalization

FLUENCY, p. T252
Accuracy: "Ah, Music!"

 **COMPREHENSION,**
p. T253
 Review: Locate Information
Paired Selection: "Come, My Little Children, Here Are Songs for You"

RESEARCH/STUDY SKILL,
Introduce: Use Reference Sources

CONNECTIONS, p. T258

 **BUILD ROBUST VOCABULARY,** p. T260
Review

Day 4

QUESTION OF THE DAY, p. T264
Why is it important for a musician to listen closely when he or she is playing an instrument or singing?

READ ALOUD, p. T265
Big Book of Rhymes and Poems, "Benita Beane"

  phonics, p. T266
Introduce: Suffixes *–ful, –less*

SPELLING, p. T267
Review Spelling Words

FLUENCY, p. T268
Accuracy: "Ah, Music!"

 COMPREHENSION,
p. T269
Review: Locate Information
Maintain: Main Idea and Details
Maintain: Fiction and Nonfiction

 **BUILD ROBUST VOCABULARY,** p. T272
Review

▲ Student Edition

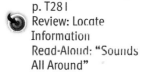

Day 5

QUESTION OF THE DAY, p. T276
Which musical instrument would you like to learn to play? Why?

READ ALOUD, p. T277
Big Book of Rhymes and Poems, "Benita Beane"

WORD WALL, p. T277

 phonics, p. T278
Review: Suffixes *–ful, –less*

SPELLING, p. T279
Posttest

FLUENCY, p. T280
Accuracy: "Ah, Music!"

COMPREHENSION,
p. T281
Review: Locate Information
Read-Aloud: "Sounds All Around"

 **BUILD ROBUST VOCABULARY,** p. T282
Cumulative Review

▲ Student Edition

● **BELOW-LEVEL**   ● **ON-LEVEL**   ○ ADVANCED   [E][L][L]

 GRAMMAR, p. T262
Review: Number Words

Daily Proofreading
I need to more pennys
(two, pennies.)

 WRITING, p. T263
Review: Poem
Writing Trait: Word Choice

Writing Prompt *Write about words that you enjoyed hearing in "Here Comes the Band."*

 GRAMMAR, p. T274
Review: Number Words

Daily Proofreading
May i have two apples on friday?
(I, Friday)

 WRITING, p. T275
Review: Poem
Writing Trait: Word Choice

Writing Prompt *Write whether you think writing a poem is hard fun. Explain your response.*

GRAMMAR, p. T284
Review: Number Words

Daily Proofreading
Dans birthday is in february.
(Dan's, February)

WRITING, p. T285
Review: Poem
Writing Trait: Word Choice

Writing Prompt *Write a list of ideas about a new topic of your choice for writing.*

Suggested Small-Group Planner

45-60+ Minutes

	Day 1	**Day 2**

BELOW-LEVEL
15-20+ Minutes

Day 1

Teacher-Directed
Leveled Reader:
"Music Is About Sounds," p. T286
Before Reading

Independent
⭐ Listening/Speaking Center,
p. T216
Extra Support Copying Masters,
pp. 134, 136

▲ Leveled Reader

Day 2

Teacher-Directed
Student Edition:
"At, Music!," p. T236

Independent
⭐ Reading Center,
p. T216
Extra Support Copying
Masters, pp. 137–138

▲ Student Edition

ON-LEVEL
15-20+ Minutes

Day 1

Teacher-Directed
Leveled Reader:
"Playing in an Orchestra," p. T287
Before Reading

Independent
⭐ Reading Center, p. T216
Practice Book, pp. 134, 136

▲ Leveled Reader

Day 2

Teacher-Directed
Student Edition:
"At Music!," p. T236

Independent
⭐ Letters and Sounds
Center, p. T217
Practice Book, pp. 137–138

▲ Student Edition

ADVANCED
15-20+ Minutes

Day 1

Teacher-Directed
Leveled Reader:
"Music for Everyone," p. T288
Before Reading

Independent
⭐ Letters and Sounds Center,
p. T217
Challenge Copying Masters,
pp. 134, 136

▲ Leveled Reader

Day 2

Teacher-Directed
Leveled Reader: "Music for
Everyone," p. T288
Read the Book

Independent
⭐ Word Work Center, p. T217
Challenge Copying Masters,
pp. 137–138

▲ Leveled Reader

ELL

English-Language Learners

In addition to the small-group instruction above, use the ELL Extra Support Kit to promote language development.

Day 1

LANGUAGE DEVELOPMENT SUPPORT
Teacher-Directed
ELL TG, Day 1
Independent
ELL Copying Masters, Lesson 18

▲ ELL Student Handbook

Day 2

LANGUAGE DEVELOPMENT SUPPORT
Teacher-Directed
ELL TG, Day 2
Independent
ELL Copying Masters, Lesson 18

▲ ELL Student Handbook

Intervention

▲ Strategic Intervention Resource Kit   ▲ Strategic Intervention Interactive Reader

Day 1

Strategic Intervention TG, Day 1
Strategic Intervention Practice Book, Lesson 18

Day 2

Strategic Intervention TG, Day 2
Strategic Intervention Interactive
Reader, Lesson 18

▲ Strategic Intervention Interactive Reader

MONITOR PROGRESS

Small-Group Instruction

Comprehension	Phonics	Comprehension	Fluency	Robust Vocabulary	Language Arts Checkpoint
Focus Skill Locate Information pp. S30–S31	Vowel Diphthong /oi/*oi, oy* pp. S26–S27	Use Reference Sources pp. S32–S33	Accuracy pp. S28–S29	*attract, territory, volume, expression, creative, performance, concentrate, relieved, universal, audible,* pp. S34–S35	**Grammar:** Number Words **Writing:** Poem pp. S36–S37

Day 3

Teacher-Directed
Leveled Reader:
"Music Is About Sounds," p. T286
Read the Book

Independent
⭐ Word Work Center, p. T217
Extra Support Copying Masters, p. 139

 ▲ Leveled Reader

Teacher-Directed
Leveled Reader:
"Playing in an Orchestra," p. T287
Read the Book

Independent
⭐ Writing Center, p. T217
Practice Book, p. 139

 ▲ Leveled Reader

Teacher-Directed
Leveled Reader:
"Music for Everyone," p. T288
Think Critically

Independent
⭐ Listening/Speaking Center, p. T216
Challenge Copying Masters, p. 139

 ▲ Leveled Reader

LANGUAGE DEVELOPMENT SUPPORT

Teacher-Directed
Leveled Reader: "It's Fun to Dance," p. T289
Before Reading; Read the Book
ELL TG, Day 3

Independent
ELL Copying Masters, Lesson 18

 ▲ Leveled Reader

Strategic Intervention TG, Day 3
Strategic Intervention Interactive Reader, Lesson 18
Strategic Intervention Practice Book, Lesson 18

  ▲ Strategic Intervention Interactive Reader

Day 4

Teacher-Directed
Leveled Reader:
"Music Is About Sounds," p. T286
Reread for Fluency

Independent
⭐ Letters and Sounds Center, p. T217

 ▲ Leveled Reader

Teacher-Directed
Leveled Reader:
"Playing in an Orchestra," p. T287
Reread for Fluency

Independent
⭐ Word Work Center, p. T217

 ▲ Leveled Reader

Teacher-Directed
Leveled Reader:
"Music for Everyone," p. T288
Reread for Fluency

Independent
⭐ Writing Center, p. T217
Self-Selected Reading:
Classroom Library Collection

 ▲ Leveled Reader

LANGUAGE DEVELOPMENT SUPPORT

Teacher-Directed
Leveled Reader: "It's Fun to Dance," p. T289
Reread for Fluency
ELL TG, Day 4

Independent
ELL Copying Masters, Lesson 18

 ▲ Leveled Reader

Strategic Intervention TG, Day 4
Strategic Intervention Interactive Reader, Lesson 18

 ▲ Strategic Intervention Interactive Reader

Day 5

Teacher-Directed
Leveled Reader:
"Music Is About Sounds," p. T286
Think Critically

Independent
⭐ Writing Center, p. T217
Leveled Reader: Reread for Fluency
Extra Support Copying Masters, p. 140

 ▲ Leveled Reader

Teacher-Directed
Leveled Reader:
"Playing in an Orchestra," p. T287
Think Critically

Independent
⭐ Listening/Speaking Center, p. T216
Leveled Reader: Reread for Fluency
Practice Book, p. 140

 ▲ Leveled Reader

Teacher-Directed
Leveled Reader:
"Music for Everyone," p. T288
Reread for Fluency

Independent
⭐ Reading Center, p. T216
Leveled Reader: Reread for Fluency
Self-Selected Reading:
Classroom Library Collection
Challenge Copying Masters, p. 140

 ▲ Leveled Reader

LANGUAGE DEVELOPMENT SUPPORT

Teacher-Directed
Leveled Reader: "It's Fun to Dance," p. T289
Think Critically
ELL TG, Day 5

Independent
Leveled Reader: Reread for Fluency
ELL Copying Masters, Lesson 18

 ▲ Leveled Reader

Strategic Intervention TG, Day 5
Strategic Intervention Interactive Reader, Lesson 18

  ▲ Strategic Intervention Interactive Reader

Leveled Readers & Leveled Practice
Reinforcing Skills and Strategies

LEVELED READERS SYSTEM

- **Leveled Readers**
- **Leveled Readers, CD**
- **Leveled Readers Teacher Guides**
  - *Comprehension*
  - *Vocabulary*
  - *Oral Reading Fluency Assessment*
- **Response Activities**
- **Leveled Readers Assessment**

See pages T286–T289 for lesson plans.

BELOW-LEVEL

Music

Music Is About Sounds

by Lauris Shaw
Illustrated by Kate Ashforth

Harcourt

- **phonics** Vowel Diphthong /oi/*oi*, *oy*
- **Robust Vocabulary**
- **Locate Information**

LEVELED READERS TEACHER GUIDE

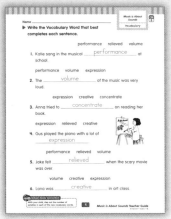

▲ Vocabulary, p. 5

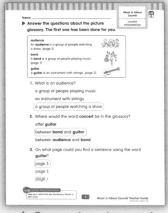

▲ Comprehension, p. 6

ON-LEVEL

Music

Playing in an Orchestra

by Lauris Shaw
illustrated by Christina Miesen

Harcourt

- **phonics** Vowel Diphthong /oi/*oi*, *oy*
- **Robust Vocabulary**
- **Locate Information**

LEVELED READERS TEACHER GUIDE

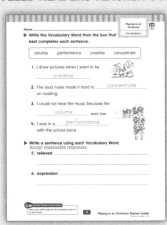

▲ Vocabulary, p. 5

▲ Comprehension, p. 6

ADVANCED

by Dianne Irving
Illustrated by Ben O'Hagan

- **phonics** Vowel Diphthong /oi/*oi*, *oy*
- **Robust Vocabulary**
- **Locate Information**

LEVELED READERS TEACHER GUIDE

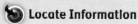

▲ **Vocabulary, p. 5**

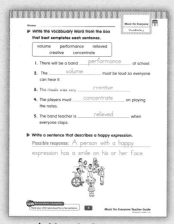

▲ **Comprehension, p. 6**

ELL

- **Build Background**
- **Concept Vocabulary**
- **Scaffolded Language Development**

LEVELED READERS TEACHER GUIDE

▲ **Build Background, p. 5**

▲ **Scaffolded Language Development, p. 6**

CLASSROOM LIBRARY
for Self-Selected Reading

EASY
▲ *The Dot* by Peter H. Reynolds.
FICTION

AVERAGE
▲ *Billy's Bucket* by Kes Gray.
FICTION

CHALLENGE
▲ *Mae Jemison* by Thomas Streissguth.
NONFICTION

▲ **Classroom Library Books Teacher Guide, Lesson 18**

Literacy Centers

15 Min. each

Management Support

While you provide direct instruction to individuals or small groups, other children can work on literacy center activities.

▲ **Literacy Center Pocket Chart**

Name _____ Date _____

My Activities

✓ Put a check mark next to the activities you complete.

Literacy Activities
- [ ] **Listening/Speaking** Read with a Recording
- [ ] **Reading** Read and Respond
- [ ] **Writing** Write a Poem
- [ ] **Word Work** Use Words in Sentences
- [ ] **Letters and Sounds** Create Word Lists

Leveled Readers
- [ ] Rereading for Fluency
- [ ] Activities (See inside back cover.)

Practice Pages
- [ ] pages 134–141

Lesson 18   51   Teacher Resource Book

▲ **Teacher Resource Book, p. 51**

Homework for the Week

TEACHER RESOURCE BOOK, PAGE 21

The *Homework Copying Master* provides activities to complete for each day of the week.

GO online www.harcourtschool.com/storytown

LISTENING/SPEAKING

Read with a Recording

Objective
To develop fluency by reading and recording a familiar story

LISTENING/SPEAKING   Card 86

Read with a Recording

MATERIALS
- CD/cassette player
- *Audiotext Grade 2*, CD 4
- *Student Edition*
- *Reading Log* or paper
- pencil

Listen to "Ah, Music!" on the *Audiotext*.

1. First, follow along in your book as you listen.

2. Listen to it again, and read aloud with the recording.

3. Record in your Reading Log what you read.

Grade 2 Lesson 18

⭐ **Literacy Center Kit • Card 86**

READING

Read and Respond

Objective
To develop comprehension by rereading familiar stories and responding to them

---

READING   Card 87

Read and Respond

MATERIALS
- *Student Edition*
- library books
- pencil
- paper

1. Choose a story to read from your *Student Edition* or other books. You can work alone or read aloud with a partner.

2. After reading the story, write the title and tell about the story.

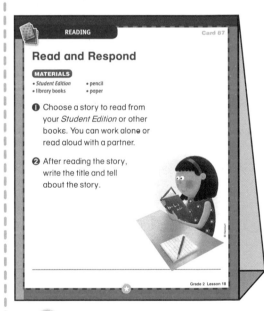

Grade 2 Lesson 18

⭐ **Literacy Center Kit • Card 87**

✏️ WRITING

Write a Poem

Objective
To practice writing a poem

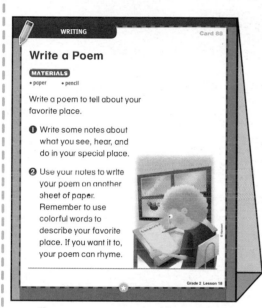

WRITING — Card 88

Write a Poem

MATERIALS
• paper • pencil

Write a poem to tell about your favorite place.

❶ Write some notes about what you see, hear, and do in your special place.

❷ Use your notes to write your poem on another sheet of paper. Remember to use colorful words to describe your favorite place. If you want it to, your poem can rhyme.

Grade 2 Lesson 18

⭐ **Literacy Center Kit • Card 88**

🅰️ WORD WORK

Use Words in Sentences

Objective
To practice using Vocabulary Words

WORD WORK — Card 89

Use Words in Sentences

MATERIALS
• Word Cards for *volume, expression, creative, performance, concentrate, relieved*   • paper • pencils

❶ With a partner, create sentences that include at least two of the words on the Word Cards.

❷ Take turns writing your sentences on a sheet of paper.

To the Teacher: TK
TK

Grade 2 Lesson 18

⭐ **Literacy Center Kit • Card 89**

My performance at the concert was very creative.

🔤 LETTERS AND SOUNDS

Create Word Lists

Objective
To write words using known letter/sound correspondences

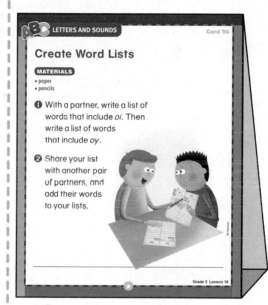

LETTERS AND SOUNDS — Card 90

Create Word Lists

MATERIALS
• paper
• pencils

❶ With a partner, write a list of words that include *oi*. Then write a list of words that include *oy*.

❷ Share your list with another pair of partners, and add their words to your lists.

Grade 2 Lesson 18

⭐ **Literacy Center Kit • Card 90**

oi	oy
coin	boy
point	toy
oil	loyal

Day at a Glance

Day 1

 phonics and Spelling
- Introduce: Vowel Diphthong /oi/, *oi, oy*
- Pretest

Reading
- Words with *oi* and *oy*, *Student Edition*, pp. 94–95

Comprehension
 Introduce: Locate Information
- *Read-Aloud Anthology*: "Sounds All Around"

Fluency
- Model Oral Fluency

Robust Vocabulary
Words from the Read-Aloud
- Introduce: *attract, territory*

Grammar [Quick Write]
- Introduce: Number Words

Writing
- Poem

Warm-Up Routines

 ## Oral Language

Objective *To listen attentively and respond appropriately to oral communication*

Question of the Day

What do you like about music?

Help children brainstorm the ways that music is a part of their lives. Use the following prompts:

- **Name some places you hear or play music.**
- **What kinds of songs or music do you enjoy?**
- **What are some ways that music can make you feel?**

Then have children complete the following sentence frame.

> **What I like best about music is _____ because _____.**

Read Aloud

Objective *To listen for a purpose*

TRANSPARENCY Read aloud the nonfiction passage "The Flute" on **Transparency R90**. Use the following steps:

- **Set a purpose for listening.** Tell children to listen to find out what a flute is.

- **Model fluent reading.** Read the passage aloud. Tell children that good readers go back and reread when they make a mistake.

- **Discuss the passage.** Ask: **Is this passage an article in a magazine or is it part of a book? Why do you think that?** (Possible response: It is part of a book, because it has a chapter number and title.)

Transparency R90

Locate Information

Chapter 4

The Flute

The flute is an instrument that can be heard in a band or an orchestra. The flute is played by blowing air across a hole near one end of a long metal tube and pressing keys that **produce** sounds.

Kinds of Flutes

Flutes are best known for their high, sweet tones. However, flutes can produce both high *and* low notes. There are at least twelve different kinds of flutes that may be played in concerts. Each kind of flute has a special group of notes that can be played on it.

Flutes are different in different parts of the world, but all flutes can make great music. One thing is certain: people enjoy playing and hearing flutes!

−48−

Grade 2, Lesson 18 · **R90** · Comprehension

Transparency R90

Word Wall

Objective *To read high-frequency words*

REVIEW HIGH-FREQUENCY WORDS Point to the following words on the Word Wall: *learn, curve, accept, understand, imagine,* and *touch*. Have children read each word. Then point to each word again and have volunteers read and spell the word.

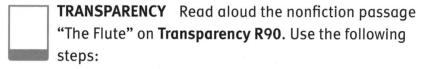

learn   curve   accept

understand   imagine   touch

Vowel Diphthong /oi/ *oi, oy*

 phonics *and Spelling*

Objectives

- *To recognize and blend the vowel diphthong /oi/oi, oy*
- *To read words with /oi/oi, oy and other known letter/sounds*
- *To use /oi/oi, oy and other known letter/sounds to spell words*

Skill Trace

Tested ✓ **Vowel Diphthong /oi/ oi, oy**

Introduce	T220–T223
Reteach	S26–S27
Review	T232–T233, T250–T251, T414
Test	Theme 4
Maintain	Theme 5, T184

 Refer to *Sounds of Letters CD* Track 15 for pronunciation of /oi/.

Connect Letters to Sounds

WARM UP WITH PHONEMIC AWARENESS   Say the word *join* and have children repeat it. Say: **The word *join* has the /oi/ sound in the middle of the word.** Then say the words *joy* and *boy* and have children repeat. Say: **The words *joy* and *boy* end with the /oi/ sound.** Have children say /oi/ several times.

[Routine Card 1] **CONNECT LETTERS AND SOUNDS**   Display the *Sound/Spelling Card* for /oi/oi, oy. Point to *oi* and review the letter/sound correspondence. Say: **The letters *oi* can stand for the /oi/ sound, the sound in the middle of *join*.** Touch *oi* several times, and have children say /oi/ each time. Repeat with /oi/*oy*.

▲ **Sound/Spelling Card**

Phonics Skill

Words with *oi* and *oy*

The letters *oi* and *oy* stand for the sound at the end of *boy*. Read these words. Do they all have that sound?

noise   toy   soil   joy

Now read these longer words.

boiling   **enjoy**   **pointer**

Point to the letters in each word that stand for the vowel sound you hear in *boy*.

94

Read each word on the left. Tell which word on the right has the same sound.

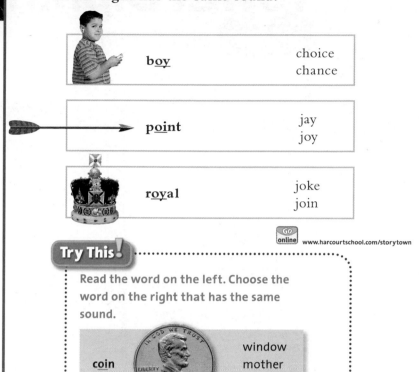

| b<u>oy</u> | choice |
| | chance |

| p<u>oi</u>nt | jay |
| | joy |

| r<u>oy</u>al | joke |
| | join |

online www.harcourtschool.com/storytown

Try This!

Read the word on the left. Choose the word on the right that has the same sound.

coin   window / mother / boyhood

95

Reading Words

GUIDED PRACTICE Have children read *Student Edition* page 94. Ask volunteers to read aloud the words below the pictures and the longer words, and have children repeat. Then read aloud the word *boy* and the first set of words on the top of *Student Edition* page 95, as children follow along. Then have children read the words with you. Elicit from them that the word *choice* has the same /oi/ sound that they hear in *boy*. Repeat the procedure for the remaining words.

Try This! Have children use what they have learned to identify the word with the same sound as *coin*. (*boyhood*)

Vowel Diphthong /oi/ *oi, oy*

phonics *and Spelling*

Transparency R91

Vowel Diphthong /oi/*oi, oy*

royal	moist	spoil
cowboy	enjoy	poison
noisy	coil	toy

That baby's drum is a noisy toy!
Put the milk in the refrigerator so it won't spoil.
The ground was moist after the light rain.
The queen looked royal when she wore her crown.
Did you enjoy the book about colors?

Grade 2, Lesson 18   R91   Phonics

Reading Words

INDEPENDENT PRACTICE   Display **Transparency R91** or write the words and sentences on the board. Point to the words in the top portion and have children read them. Then have children read aloud the sentences and identify the words in which *oi* or *oy* stand for /oi/.

Decodable Books

Additional Decoding Practice

- **Phonics**
  Vowel Diphthong /oi/*oi, oy*
- **Decodable Words**
- **High-Frequency Words**
  See lists in *Decodable Book 15*.

  See also *Decodable Books*, online (Take-Home Version).

▲ Decodable Book 15
"The Best Toy"

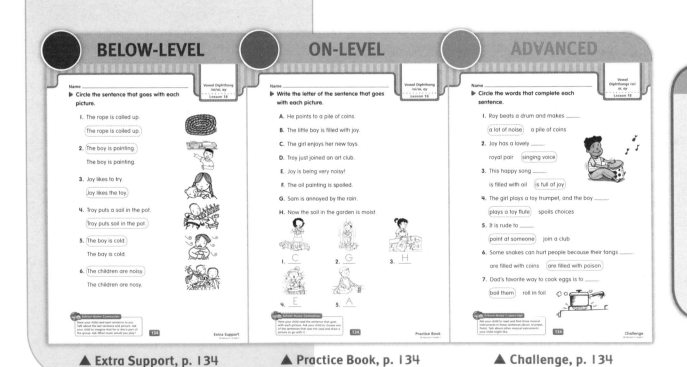

BELOW-LEVEL   **ON-LEVEL**   **ADVANCED**

▲ Extra Support, p. 134   ▲ Practice Book, p. 134   ▲ Challenge, p. 134

E L L

- Group children according to academic levels, and assign one of the pages on the left.

- Clarify any unfamiliar concepts as necessary. See *ELL Teacher Guide* Lesson 18 for support in scaffolding instruction.

5-DAY SPELLING

DAY 1	Pretest
DAY 2	Word Building
DAY 3	State the Generalization
DAY 4	Review
DAY 5	Posttest

Introduce Spelling Words

PRETEST   Say the first word and read the dictation sentence. Repeat the word as children write it. Write the word on the board and have children check their spelling. Tell them to circle the word if they spelled it correctly or write it correctly if they did not. Repeat for words 2–10.

Words with /oi/*oi, oy*

1.	join	Alisa will **join** us at the beach this afternoon.
2.	boil	We need to **boil** water to cook the pasta.
3.	joy	Seeing a rainbow filled me with **joy**.
4.	soil	Let's rake the **soil** before we plant our seeds.
5.	noise	I can't hear you because of all the **noise**!
6.	boy	My little brother is a very loud **boy**!
7.	voice	Esteban has a deep speaking **voice**.
8.	point	Could you **point** out the way to the nearest exit?
9.	toy	Monica got a **toy** cash register for her birthday.
10.	coin	The shiny **coin** under that chair could be a quarter.

Spelling Words

1.	join	6.	boy
2.	boil	7.	voice*
3.	joy	8.	point
4.	soil	9.	toy
5.	noise	10.	coin

Challenge Words

11.	destroy	14.	loyal
12.	avoid	15.	enjoy*
13.	annoy		

* Words from "Ah, Music!"

ADVANCED

Challenge Words   Use the challenge words in these dictation sentences.

11.	destroy	Flooding may **destroy** the farmer's crops.
12.	avoid	Please try to **avoid** stepping in those puddles!
13.	annoy	Our cat likes to **annoy** the neighbor's dog.
14.	loyal	The knight was always **loyal** to the king.
15.	enjoy	Did you **enjoy** seeing the parade?

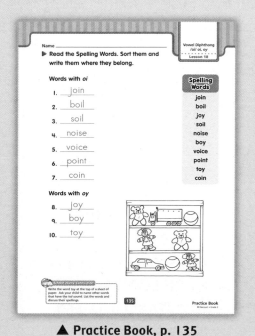

▲ Practice Book, p. 135

Locate Information

Comprehension

Objective

• *To use the parts of a book to locate information*

Daily Comprehension

Locate Information

DAY 1:	Introduce Locate Information, *Student Edition*
DAY 2:	Review Locate Information, *Student Edition*
DAY 3:	Review Locate Information, *Student Edition*
DAY 4:	Review Locate Information, *Transparency*
DAY 5:	Review Locate Information, *Read-Aloud Anthology*

✓ MONITOR PROGRESS

Locate Information

IF children have difficulty understanding guide words,	**THEN** have partners work together to look for specific words in a classroom dictionary. Have them write the guide words they find for each word.

Small-Group Instruction, p. S30–S31:

● **BELOW-LEVEL:** Reteach
● **ON-LEVEL:** Reinforce
● **ADVANCED:** Extend

Teach/Model

INTRODUCE LOCATE INFORMATION   Tell children that good readers understand the parts of a book. Explain that most nonfiction books are organized so that it is easy for readers to find information.

• Ask children to find the title of their *Student Edition* by looking at the cover. Elicit that the title is the name of a book, a unit, a chapter, or a story.

• Have children open their *Student Edition* to pages 4–9 to view the Table of Contents. Explain that the table of contents is a list of selection titles with the page numbers.

• Ask children to turn to page 100 in their *Student Edition* and view the heading "Music Is Sound." Explain that a heading is the title that comes before each new part of a selection.

• Have children turn to the Glossary beginning on page 486. Tell them that a glossary is a dictionary of important words found in a book. Like a regular dictionary, the words are arranged in alphabetical order. Point out the guide words on page 486, and explain how they can help a reader find where the definition for a word is located.

• Have children locate the Index of Titles and Authors on pages 498–499. Point out that an index is a list of subjects, arranged in alphabetical order, with page numbers. Explain that it is usually at the back of a book.

E L L

Clarify Terms   Help students understand terms that tell about parts of books. Explain that a *table*, like a chart, is a way to show information so that it can be read more easily. If necessary, point out that *table* is a multiple-meaning word. Tell them that a *heading* is at the top, or head, of a section. Point out that the word *guide* means to "show the way."

Practice/Apply

GUIDED PRACTICE   Have children practice locating information in different parts of a book by asking the following questions about the *Student Edition*:

1. **Where would I find on what page number Theme 5 starts?** (in the table of contents)

2. **On what page does "The Bee" start?** (page 244)

3. **On what page does the Glossary begin?** (page 486) **What are the guide words on the page where you can find the word *crop*?** (committee and crumpled)

4. **Look at the Index of Titles and Authors. On what pages can a story by Cynthia Rylant be found?** (pages 22–43)

INDEPENDENT PRACTICE   Have partners use a classroom dictionary to locate the words *join*, *noise*, and *toy*. Have partners find and write down the guide words that appear on the pages for the words.

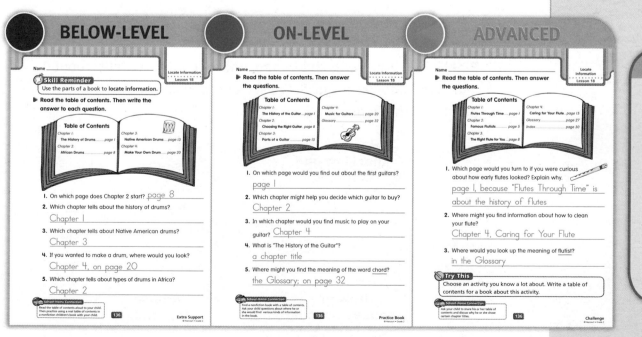

▲ Extra Support, p. 136   ▲ Practice Book, p. 136   ▲ Challenge, p. 136

ELL

- Group children according to academic levels, and assign one of the pages on the left.

- Clarify any unfamiliar concepts as necessary. See *ELL Teacher Guide* Lesson 18 for support in scaffolding instruction.

Listening Comprehension
Read Aloud

Objectives
- *To set a purpose for listening*
- *To identify main idea and details*

Build Fluency

Focus: Accuracy Tell children that good readers read each word correctly. If they make a mistake, they go back and reread so that the sentence makes sense.

▲ Read-Aloud Anthology, "Sounds All Around," p. 68

Before Reading

CONNECT TO PRIOR KNOWLEDGE Tell children that they will listen to a selection called "Sounds All Around." Explain that the selection tells about the many types of sounds in the world.

Routine Card 2 **GENRE STUDY: NONFICTION** Remind children that nonfiction gives facts and details about a particular topic.

 REVIEW LOCATE INFORMATION Remind children that they can use parts of a book to help them find information. Have children explain how you might use a table of contents or an index to find this selection or its author.

Think Aloud If I wanted to find this selection in a book, I could look at the table of contents to find the title and the page number on which the selection begins. I could also use the index and look for the selection title or for the author's name.

Read the selection "Sounds All Around" to children.

After Reading

RESPOND Work with children to make a chart that tells about a main idea and details from the selection. Record the main idea and details on the board.

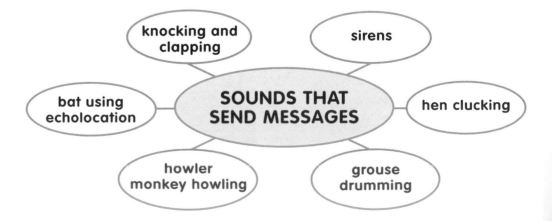

ELL

Support Comprehension
As you read "Sounds All Around" aloud, emphasize onomatopoeic words such as *crinkle-crunch* and *knock, knock* to support meaning. Use gestures and body movements to illustrate verbs that tell about sounds.

Build Robust Vocabulary

Words from the Read-Aloud

Teach/Model

Routine Card 3

INTRODUCE ROBUST VOCABULARY Use *Routine Card 3* to introduce the words.

❶ Put the word in **selection context**.

❷ Display Transparency R95 and read the word and the **Student-Friendly Explanation**.

❸ Have children **say the word** with you.

❹ Use the word in other contexts, and have children **interact with the word's meaning**.

❺ Remove the transparency. Say the Student-Friendly Explanation again, and ask children to **name the word** that goes with it.

❶ **Selection Context:** Hoping to **attract** a mate, a grouse makes a sound like a drum.

❹ **Interact with Word Meaning:** A bird called a manakin vibrates its wings very quickly to attract a female with its sound. What type of weather might attract you to play outside, warm and sunny or cold and rainy?

❶ **Selection Context:** A howler monkey uses its loud howl to protect its **territory**.

❹ **Interact with Word Meaning:** Our dog protects its territory by barking whenever someone comes to our door. Would a lion protect its territory by roaring loudly or sleeping quietly?

Practice/Apply

GUIDED PRACTICE Guide children to name other types of animals that protect their *territory*. Write their suggestions on the board.

Objective

• *To develop robust vocabulary through discussing a literature selection*

Tested

INTRODUCE ✓

Vocabulary: Lesson 18

attract	territory

▼ **Student-Friendly Explanations**

Student-Friendly Explanations

attract	If you attract someone, you make that person want to come to you.
territory	An animal's territory is an area of land that it sees as its home.
universal	If something is universal, everyone in the world knows or experiences it.
audible	If you can hear something, it is audible.

Grade 2, Lesson 18   R95   Vocabulary

Transparency R95

Grammar *Quick Write*
Number Words

5-DAY GRAMMAR	
DAY 1	Introduce Number Words
DAY 2	Identify Number Words
DAY 3	Use Number Words in Sentences
DAY 4	Apply to Writing
DAY 5	Weekly Review

Objective

- *To understand the use of exact and inexact number words*

Daily Proofreading

kyle ate three oranges

(Kyle, oranges.)

➤ **Writing Trait**

Strengthening Conventions

Parts of Speech   Use this short lesson with children's own writing to build a foundation for revising/editing longer connected text on Day 5. See also *Writer's Companion*, Lesson 18.

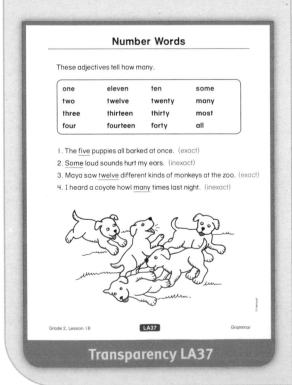

Number Words

These adjectives tell how many.

one	eleven	ten	some
two	twelve	twenty	many
three	thirteen	thirty	most
four	fourteen	forty	all

1. The <u>five</u> puppies all barked at once. (exact)
2. <u>Some</u> loud sounds hurt my ears. (inexact)
3. Maya saw <u>twelve</u> different kinds of monkeys at the zoo. (exact)
4. I heard a coyote howl <u>many</u> times last night. (inexact)

Grade 2, Lesson 18   **LA37**   Grammar

Transparency LA37

Teach/Model

INTRODUCE NUMBER WORDS   Have children count off to find out how many are present. Say: **There are (number) of us here right now**. Write the number word on the board. Then say: **Most of us are here**. Write *most* on the board. Explain that words that tell how many are adjectives.

Write these sentences on the board from "Sounds All Around" (*Read-Aloud Anthology*, p. 68):

> **Whispering measures only about twenty decibels.
> Clatter some pans.**

Read aloud the sentences. Point to *twenty*. Explain that *twenty* is a number word that tells how many. Then point to *some*. Explain that *some* also tells about how many. Say: **Twenty and some are words that tell how many. Twenty is a number word. A number word tells exactly how many. Some tells how many, but it does not tell an exact number.**

Guided Practice

COMPLETE SENTENCES   Display **Transparency LA37**. Read aloud the list of number words. Point out that the number words in the first three columns tell exactly how many. Explain that the number words in the last column, *some*, *many*, *most*, and *all*, do not tell an exact number. Read aloud the first item. Explain that *five* is an exact number word. Read aloud the remaining sentences. Ask children to identify the number word in each sentence and tell if it is exact or inexact.

Practice/Apply

WRITE COMPLETE SENTENCES   Have children write new sentences that use number words from the transparency. Invite volunteers to read sentences aloud. Have listeners tell whether each sentence uses a number word that is exact or a number word that is not exact.

Writing

Poem

5-DAY WRITING	
DAY 1	Introduce
DAY 2	Prewrite
DAY 3	Draft
DAY 4	Revise
DAY 5	Revise

Teach/Model

INTRODUCE POEM Display **Transparency LA38**, and explain that these two poems were written by children to tell about sounds they like to hear. Read aloud the poems, and discuss the similarities and differences between the two. Together, develop a list of characteristics for a poem.

Poem

- A poem tells a writer's feelings about a topic.
- A poem may be rhymed or unrhymed.
- A poem uses colorful words and details to help the reader see, feel, or hear what the writer is telling about.
- A poem may use comparisons.
- A poem includes a title.

WRITING TRAIT **WORD CHOICE** Point out that each poem includes colorful words that tell about sounds, such as *zip*, *zoom*, *crash*, *gurgles*, *bubbles*, *bang*, and *boom*. Explain that these words help the reader "hear" the sounds.

Guided Practice

DRAFT A POEM Explain that a poet may make a list of rhyming words that he or she can use when writing a poem. Make a list of rhyming words that tell about sounds and write them on the board, such as *crash*, *smash*; *clink*, *plink*; *rumble*, *grumble*. Model using the rhyming words to begin a draft of a poem.

Practice/Apply

INDEPENDENT PRACTICE Invite children to generate more rhyming words and record them. Children should save their lists for use on Days 2–5.

Objectives

- *To read and respond to poems as a model for writing*
- *To develop an understanding of writing poetry*
- *To generate a list of rhyming words*

Writing Prompt

Write to Tell Have children write to tell about a noisy sound and a quiet sound that they like.

Student Model: Poem

Sounds Like FUN!
I leap into the pool.
I make a big SPLASH!
Toy cars on a track
go zip, zoom, CRASH!

I drop coins in my bank
with a clink, clank, CLANG!
Fireworks at night
go pop, boom, BANG!

Quiet Sounds, Noisy Sounds
I like to hear quiet sounds—
how the water in a stream gurgles and bubbles,
how a bird chirps its lovely song,
how a lullaby soothes a baby to sleep.

I like to hear noisy sounds
when we yell and scream playing tag,
when a hammer hits a nail—BANG!
when a drum BOOMS its steady beat.

Grade 2, Lesson 18   LA38   Writing

Transparency LA38

Day at a Glance

Day 2

 **and Spelling**

- Review: Vowel Diphthong /oi/ *oi, oy*
- Build Words

Robust Vocabulary

Words from the Selection

- Introduce: *volume, expression, creative, performance, concentrate, relieved*

Comprehension

 Answer Questions

 Locate Information

Reading

- "Ah, Music!," *Student Edition*, pp. 98–111

 Read!

Fluency

- Accuracy

Robust Vocabulary

Words About the Selection

- Introduce: *universal, audible*

Grammar Quick Write

- Review: Number Words

Writing ✏

- Poem

Warm-Up Routines

 ## Oral Language

Objective *To listen attentively and respond appropriately to oral communication*

Question of the Day

What do you like best about the music you hear at a parade? Tell why.

Help children think about the music they hear at parades and what they like about it. Use the following prompts:

- **Tell about a time you have seen marching bands play at a parade.**

- **What words would you use to describe the music that you hear at a parade?**

- **How do you feel when you hear a marching band play?**

Read Aloud

Objective *To identify the use of rhyme*

BIG BOOK OF RHYMES AND POEMS Display the poem "Here Comes the Band" on page 33. Tell children to listen for rhyming words as you read the poem aloud. Ask children to name the rhyming words. Point to them as they are named. (*street, tweet; blare, air; clapping, tapping*) Then read the poem again and have children join in.

▲ **Big Book of Rhymes and Poems, p. 33**

Word Wall

Objective *To read high-frequency words*

REVIEW HIGH-FREQUENCY WORDS Point to and read the following words on the Word Wall: *different, hundred, woods, eight, woman,* and *enjoy.* Then point to each word again and have children read it. Then ask children to clap for the number of syllables in each word.

Vowel Diphthong /oi/ *oi, oy*

 phonics *and Spelling*

Objectives

- *To blend sounds into words*
- *To spell words that include the vowel diphthong /oi/oi, oy*

Skill Trace

Tested ✓ **Vowel Diphthong /oi/ oi, oy**

Introduce	T220–T223
Reteach	S26–S27
Review	**T232–T233, T250–T251, T414**
Test	Theme 4
Maintain	Theme 5, T134

Spelling Words

1.	join	6.	boy
2.	boil	7.	voice*
3.	joy	8.	point
4.	soil	9.	toy
5.	noise	10.	coin

Challenge Words

11.	destroy	14.	loyal
12.	avoid	15.	enjoy*
13.	annoy		

* Words from "Ah, Music!"

Word Building

READ A SPELLING WORD Write the word *joy* on the board. Ask children to identify the letters that stand for the /oi/ sound. Then have them read the word. Remind children that both *oi* and *oy* stand for the /oi/ sound.

BUILD SPELLING WORDS Ask children which letter you should change to make *joy* become *toy*. (Change the *j* to *t*.) Write the word *toy* on the board. Point to the word, and have children read it. Continue building spelling words in this manner. Say:

- **Which letter do I have to change to make the word *boy*?** (Change *t* to *b*.)

- **Which letters do I have to change to make the word *boil*?** (Change *oy* to *oi* and add *l*.)

- **Which letters do I have to change to make the word *coin*?** (Change *b* to *c*, and the *l* to *n*.)

- **Which letter do I have to change to make the word *join*?** (Change *c* to *j*.)

- **Which letters do I have to change to make the word *point*?** (Change *j* to *p* and add *t*.)

Continue building the remaining spelling words in this manner.

joy
toy
boy
boil
coin
join
point

BELOW-LEVEL

Chart Words Make a two-column chart with the headings *oi* and *oy*. Point to each spelling word on the board, and have a volunteer write the word in the appropriate column. Have children say and spell each word aloud.

ADVANCED

Build Longer Words Have partners work together to list longer words they could form from the spelling words, such as *joined, boiling, cowboy,* and *voices.* Then have partners share lists with another pair.

Day 2

5-DAY PHONICS/SPELLING
DAY 1 Pretest
DAY 2 Word Building
DAY 3 State the Generalization
DAY 4 Review
DAY 5 Posttest

Read Words in Context

APPLY PHONICS Write the following sentences on the board or on chart paper. Have children read each sentence silently. Then track the print as children read the sentence aloud.

> I heard my mother's <u>voice</u> calling for me.
>
> I like the <u>noise</u> a <u>coin</u> makes when I drop it in my bank.
>
> Will you be able to <u>join</u> us at the party on Saturday?
>
> Mom asked Kara to <u>point</u> to the <u>toy</u> she wanted.

WRITE Dictate several spelling words. Have children write the words in their notebook or on a dry-erase board.

phonics Resources

Phonics Practice Book, pp. 109–114

MONITOR PROGRESS

Vowel Diphthong /oi/ oi, oy

| IF children have difficulty building and reading words with *oi* and *oy*, | THEN help them blend and read the words *joy, join, boy, boil, soil,* and *coin*. |

Small-Group Instruction, pp. S26–S27:

● **BELOW-LEVEL:** Reteach
● **ON-LEVEL:** Reinforce
○ **ADVANCED:** Extend

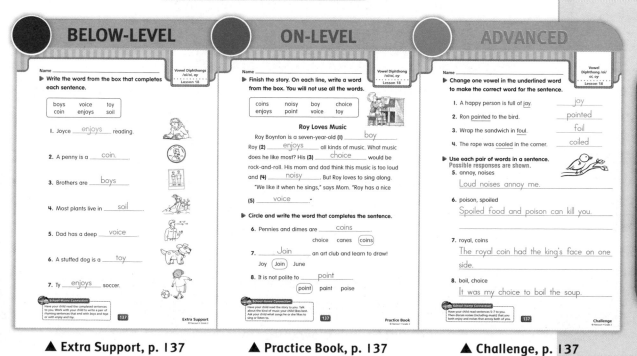

▲ Extra Support, p. 137   ▲ Practice Book, p. 137   ▲ Challenge, p. 137

ELL

- Group children according to academic levels, and assign one of the pages on the left.

- Clarify any unfamiliar concepts as necessary. See *ELL Teacher Guide* Lesson 18 for support in scaffolding instruction.

Build Robust Vocabulary

Words from the Selection

Objective

• *To build robust vocabulary*

INTRODUCE ✓ Tested

Vocabulary: Lesson 18

volume	performance
expression	concentrate
creative	relieved

▼ **Student-Friendly Explanations**

Student-Friendly Explanations

volume	When you change the volume on a TV or a radio, you change how loud or soft the sound is.
expression	If you use expression when you speak, you use your voice, your face, or your body to add meaning to what you say.
creative	If you are creative, you use new or different ideas to make or do something.
performance	When you sing, dance, or act in front of an audience, you are giving a performance.
concentrate	When you concentrate, you put all of your attention on one thing.
relieved	If you are relieved, you feel happy because some kind of worry is gone.

Grade 2, Lesson 18   R96   Vocabulary

Transparency R96

Word Scribe

Use a Partner Have children check with a partner each day to tell which word they used in their writing and to share their sentences.

HOMEWORK/INDEPENDENT PRACTICE

Teach/Model

Routine Card 4

INTRODUCE ROBUST VOCABULARY Use *Routine Card 4* to introduce the words.

❶ Display Transparency R96 and read the word and the **Student-Friendly Explanation.**
❷ Have children **say the word** with you.
❸ Have children **interact with the word's meaning** by asking them the appropriate question below.

• If you wanted to play music at a softer **volume,** would you turn the sound up or down? Explain.

• How does your facial **expression** help show your feelings?

• Why is making a gift for someone more **creative** than buying one?

• Would you rather see a **performance** by dancers or by acrobats?

• Would a quiet crowd or a noisy crowd help a singer **concentrate**?

• Would you be more **relieved** to find a favorite toy or to lose it?

Develop Deeper Meaning

EXPAND WORD MEANINGS: PAGES 96–97 Have children read the passage. Then read it aloud, pausing at the end of page 96 to ask questions 1–3. Read page 97 and then ask questions 4–6.

1. Does Grandpa feel **relieved** when his grandson turns off his pop music? Why do you think that?

2. Why does Grandpa leave the room when his grandson turns up the **volume** on his pop music?

3. How does wearing headphones help someone **concentrate**?

4. How might an opera **performance** be like a pop concert?

5. Was Mom's idea **creative**? Tell why or why not.

6. What did Grandpa's **expression** look like?

Vocabulary

Build Robust Vocabulary

The Sounds of Music

- relieved
- volume
- concentrate
- performance
- creative
- expression

Grandpa and I both love to listen to music, but we have a problem. We don't like the same kind of music. I'm always **relieved** when Grandpa turns his music off. I don't like opera music.

Grandpa feels the same way about my pop music. When I turn the **volume** up, he snorts and walks out of the room. Then Mom tells me to use my headphones. I don't mind. I can **concentrate** better when I'm wearing them.

One day, Mom surprised us. She had tickets for a **performance** of an opera. She also had tickets to a pop concert. She wanted Grandpa and me to see how **creative** both kinds of music can be.

I had to laugh when I saw the **expression** on Grandpa's face. I couldn't tell whether he was about to laugh or cry!

www.harcourtschool.com/storytown

Word Scribe

This week your task is to use the Vocabulary Words in your writing. For example, you might write a note that says "I'm **relieved** that we don't have a test today." At the end of each day, write in your vocabulary journal the sentences that had Vocabulary Words.

96

97

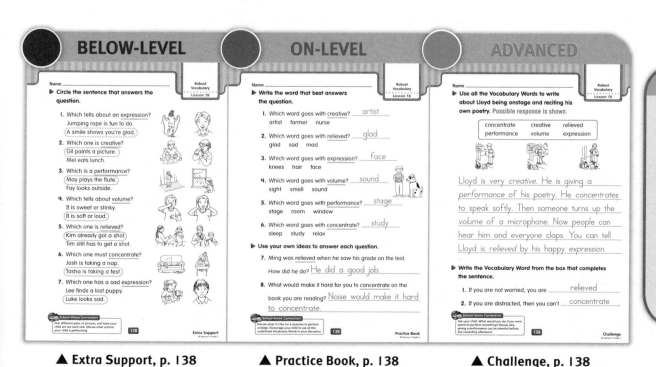

▲ Extra Support, p. 138   ▲ Practice Book, p. 138   ▲ Challenge, p. 138

E L L

- Group children according to academic levels, and assign one of the pages on the left.

- Clarify any unfamiliar concepts as necessary. See *ELL Teacher Guide* Lesson 18 for support in scaffolding instruction.

Reading

Student Edition: **"Ah, Music!"**

Objectives

- *To understand characteristics and features of nonfiction*
- *To use graphic organizers as a strategy for comprehension*
- *To apply knowledge of how to answer questions to the reading and understanding of a text*

Options for Reading

BELOW-LEVEL

Preview Have children preview the selection by looking at the headings and illustrations. Guide them to predict what the selection will be about. Read each page of the story to children, and have them read it after you.

ON-LEVEL

Monitor Comprehension Have children read the selection aloud, page by page. Ask the Monitor Comprehension questions as you go.

ADVANCED

Independent Reading Have children read each page silently, looking up when they finish a page. Ask the Monitor Comprehension questions as you go.

Genre Study

DISCUSS NONFICTION: PAGE 98 Ask children to read the genre information on *Student Edition* page 98. Remind children that nonfiction gives facts about a specific topic. Explain that many nonfiction selections have headings that tell about each section. Tell children that each section that follows a heading will include a main idea and details that support it. Then use **Transparency GO6** or copy on the board the graphic organizer from page 98. Tell children that they will work together to fill in the headings and details as they read the nonfiction selection "Ah, Music!"

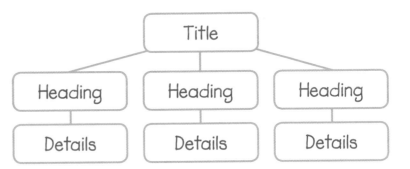

Comprehension Strategies

ANSWER QUESTIONS: PAGE 98 Read aloud the Comprehension Strategy information on page 98. Tell children that there are several ways to find answers to questions during and after reading. The answers to some questions about a topic are easily found because they are "right there" in a nonfiction selection. Other questions may require them to look in more than one place in the selection for an answer. For some other questions, they will need to think about what they already know. They can then put together their own knowledge with what they learn from the nonfiction selection to answer the question.

Genre Study

Nonfiction gives facts about a topic. Look for

- main ideas and details.
- headings that tell what each section is about.

Title
Heading	Heading	Heading
Details	Details	Details

Comprehension Strategy

Answer questions by looking back at information in different parts of the selection.

98

Ah, Music!

written and illustrated by

Aliki

99

Build Background

DISCUSS MUSIC   Tell children that they are going to read a nonfiction selection about music. Ask them to recall a time when music was part of a special day. Invite volunteers to share their experiences.

[Routine Card 6] **SET A PURPOSE AND PREDICT**   Tell children that this is a selection they will read to be informed about music. Have them turn to pages 98–99 in the *Student Edition*, and follow these steps.

- Have children read the title and the name of the author.

- Preview the selection, and read the section headings aloud. Ask children to predict what information they might learn from this selection.

- List their predictions on the board.

- Invite children to read the selection to find out the many elements that are a part of music.

TECHNOLOGY

[GO online] **eBook**   "Ah, Music!" is available in an eBook.

Audiotext   "Ah, Music!" is available on *Audiotext Grade 2*, CD 4 for subsequent readings.

Music Is Sound

If you hum a tune,

play an instrument,

or clap out a rhythm,

you are making music.
You are listening to it, too. **1**

100

Music Is Rhythm

That is the beat I can clap.

Rhythm is a marching-band beat, a puffing-train beat,

a beating-the-eggs beat, a heart beat.
Some rhythm beats are stronger than others.
You can count the accents. **2**

A person who cannot hear
can feel the vibration of the beat. **3**

101

Monitor Comprehension

PAGES 100–101 Say: **I see illustrations that show people making music. I also see a train. I wonder what these pictures have to do with each other. Read to find out.**

1 **NOTE DETAILS** What words does the author use to tell about ways to make sounds and music? *(hum, play, clap)*

2 **MAKE COMPARISONS** How are a marching band beat and a train beat alike? (Possible responses: They both have rhythm. Some of the beats are strong or accented; others are weak.)

3 **SYNTHESIZE** How can music be both sound and rhythm? (Possible response: Music usually has a sound and a beat at the same time. Sound and rhythm are two important parts of music.)

Apply
Comprehension Strategies

Answer Questions Remind children that good readers answer questions as they read. Explain that sometimes the answers come from the selection, and sometimes they come from the reader. Elicit that the answers to questions 1 and 2 are "right there" in the selection. Explain that for question 3, they will need to use their own ideas with what they are learning.

Think Aloud Question 3 asks how music can be both sound and rhythm. This is called an "On My Own" question. You won't find the answer in the selection. You think about what you hear in music to answer the question.

Music Is Melody

That is the tune I can hum,

or the song that is sung
if words are set to music.
Often the words are poetry.

Music Is Volume

That is the loudness or the softness of the sound. ① ②

Shhh.

102

103

Monitor Comprehension

PAGES 102–103   Say: **What are the headings on these pages? Read to find out what else we can learn about music.**

①   TEXT FEATURES   Why does the author follow explanations in the text with illustrations that look like comic strips? (Possible response: The illustrations help make her ideas clearer and give more information. They are fun to read and look at.)

②   LOCATE INFORMATION   Under which heading would you look to find information about loudness and softness? Why? (Possible response: I would look under the heading Music Is Volume because *volume* means how loud or soft a sound is.)

SCIENCE

SUPPORTING STANDARDS

Volume and Pitch   Clarify for children that *volume* tells only about a sound's loudness or softness, while *pitch* tells how high or low a sound is. Explain that sounds can have different pitches and volumes. For example, a siren has a high volume and a high pitch; a foghorn also has a high volume, but its pitch is low.

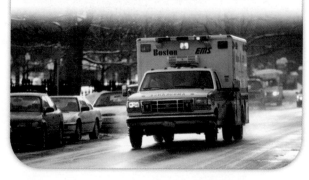

Music Is Feeling

It sets a mood.

Music speaks not with words, as in a song.
It speaks with expression.
Everyone can understand music, because
everyone has feelings.
Music can make you feel happy or sad or scared.
It can make you want to dance, to march, to sing,
or to be quiet, to listen, and to dream.

Ah, music!

Here will we sit
and let the sounds of music
creep in our ears.

*Shakespeare
said that.*

104

I listen to music,
and I can see pictures
in my head.

I imagine I hear
twittering birds.

I hear a cool waterfall.

I see a brilliant sunrise.

I see a scary dark forest.

I hear a noisy city.

105

Monitor Comprehension

PAGES 104–105 Say: **I see pictures of people with different expressions on their faces. Read to find out what they have to do with music.**

1 CONTEXT CLUES **What clues help you understand what the phrase "sets a mood" means?** (*feeling, happy, sad, scared;* that music makes you feel a certain way without using words)

2 THEME **How does music help you see pictures in your head?** (Possible response: Music reminds you of certain sounds and feelings, and it helps you imagine the places where you might hear those sounds or feel those feelings.)

Use Multiple Strategies

Use Prior Knowledge Lead children in a discussion of how music affects thoughts and feelings. Say: **The author says that music can make you feel different ways. I know that songs that have a lively beat and melody make me feel happy when I sing them. I also know that hearing quiet songs at bedtime makes me feel peaceful and sleepy. This helps me understand what the author means.**

Music Is a Creative Art

Just as a writer uses words, *Words, words*

or an artist uses paint,

a composer uses music
to create images and feelings.
He or she writes it down in notes, symbols,
and numbers on lines and spaces.
The notations describe the rhythm, tone, pitch,
feeling, and even the silences of the piece. ❶

Wolfgang Amadeus Mozart wrote his first composition when he was five years old.

I'd better get busy!

106

Practice Makes Perfect

We make music.
Making music is hard fun.
It takes lots of practice to learn
to play an instrument. *But when you do, it is forever.*

 *That's the hard part.* *Here's the fun part.*

As you practice and learn,
you begin to make
beautiful sounds.
Practice becomes fun. ❷

You learn new pieces to play.
You feel proud.
Your music teacher says
you will play in a recital.
You will play for an audience.

A metronome
helps keep time.

107

Monitor Comprehension

PAGES 106–107   Say: **I see a drawing of a writer and a painter. Read to find out how they are connected to music.**

❶ *Focus Skill*   **LOCATE INFORMATION   Under which heading would you look to find information about how a composer creates music? What is the page number on which you would find this information? How do the illustrations help you know this is the correct heading to locate the information?** ("Music Is a Creative Art"; page 106; There is an illustration of a man writing at a piano. He must be a composer.)

❷ **SPECULATE   Why does the author say that "practice becomes fun"?** (Possible response: As you get more comfortable with the music and your instrument, you get better at playing and you enjoy it more.)

ANALYZE AUTHOR'S PURPOSE

Author's Purpose   Remind children that authors have a purpose, or reason, for writing. After children have finished reading the story, ask:

Why did the author write "Ah, Music!"?

- to persuade readers that composers are more creative than writers and artists
- to inform readers that music involves many things and is for everyone to enjoy
- to entertain readers with a story about children who sing in a school chorus

The Performance

At your recital it is your turn to play.
Everyone is looking at you.

You concentrate.
You do the best you can.

When you finish, everyone claps.
It sounds like waves breaking.
It feels good. You take a bow.
You feel relieved and very proud. **2**

You celebrate.
Everyone says you did well.
Next time it will be even
better, because you are
learning more every day.
Practice makes perfect. **1**

108

Music Is for Everybody

It is for anyone who wants to
hear the sound,
dance to the rhythm,
clap to the beat,
sing along,
or be still to imagine....

I love music.
Me too.
Ruff!

109

Monitor Comprehension

PAGES 108–109 Say: **Look at the headings and illustrations. What will these pages be about? Read to find out.**

1 **AUTHOR'S CRAFT** **Why does the author seem to talk directly to "you" in the section called "The Performance"?** (Possible response: The author wants the reader to understand what it is like to prepare for and give a performance. It makes the reader feel like it is he or she who is playing.)

2 **CAUSE/EFFECT** **Why does the author say that when you have finished a recital, "you feel relieved and very proud"?** (Possible response: because you are glad that it is over, and because you have done a good job)

Apply
Comprehension Strategies

Answer Questions Guide children to see that the answer to question 2 comes from the selection and also from the reader. Explain that answers can come from a combination of what the reader knows and information the author gives.

Think Aloud I have been in performances, and I have seen some, too. I was really nervous to perform, and I was very glad when I did just what I had practiced. So I know that you feel proud, but you're also happy that it is over. The author wants me to understand that these are the feelings that many people have.

Think Critically

1 Under what heading would you look to find examples of rhythm? 🌀 LOCATE INFORMATION

2 What are some ways music can make you feel? IMPORTANT DETAILS

3 What do you think the author means when she says that making music is "hard fun"? DRAW CONCLUSIONS

4 Why might it be important to play in a recital? DRAW CONCLUSIONS

5 WRITE How are a composer, a writer, and an artist alike? Use details from the selection to support your answer. SHORT RESPONSE

110

Meet the Author and Illustrator

Aliki

Ever since she was a young girl, Aliki has been writing down her feelings. She thinks that doing this was good practice for when she became an author.

"Ah, Music!" took over three years for Aliki to write and draw. She had to do a lot of studying to find out about music and what different instruments looked like.

GO online www.harcourtschool.com/storytown

111

Think Critically

Respond to the Literature

 1 Music Is Rhythm **LOCATE INFORMATION**

2 Possible responses: happy, sad, scared **IMPORTANT DETAILS**

3 Possible response: Making music is a challenge, but it is enjoyable to do it. **DRAW CONCLUSIONS**

4 Possible response: It gives musicians a chance to show how well they can play. When the audience claps, it is a reward for hard work. **DRAW CONCLUSIONS**

5 WRITE All are creative people. They use different ways to make images and feelings. **SHORT RESPONSE**

Meet the Author and Illustrator

PAGE 111 Explain that Aliki is both the author and the illustrator for "Ah, Music!" Invite children to tell whether her writing and drawings work well together in this selection. Encourage them to explain their responses.

Point out that Aliki has written about her feelings since she was a young girl. Discuss how children can tell that knowing about feelings is important in "Ah, Music!"

RUBRIC For additional support in scoring the WRITE item, see the rubric on p. R6.

Lesson 18 (*Student Edition*, pages 110–111) **T243**

Check Comprehension

Summarizing

Objectives

- *To practice summarizing a nonfiction selection*
- *To read accurately in a manner that sounds like natural speech*

RETELLING RUBRIC

4	Uses details to clearly summarize the selection
3	Uses some details to summarize the selection
2	Summarizes the selection with some inaccuracies
1	Is unable to summarize the selection

Professional Development

 Podcasting: Auditory Modeling

BELOW-LEVEL

Fluency Practice For fluency practice, have children read *Decodable Book 15*, the appropriate *Leveled Readers* (pp. 286–289), or Story 18 in the *Strategic Intervention Interactive Reader*.

Summarize

  LOCATE INFORMATION Ask children to tell what part of the text they would use if they wanted to find information about music. (the headings)

REVISIT THE GRAPHIC ORGANIZER Display completed **Transparency GO6.** Guide children to use the headings to identify the selection's main ideas and details.

STORY RETELLING CARDS The cards can be used for retelling or as an aid to completing the graphic organizer.

▲ Story Retelling Cards 1–6, "Ah, Music!"

Fluency

Accuracy

Teach/Model

READING WITH ACCURACY Explain that good readers are careful to read words accurately. Have children turn to page 101 and track the print as you read aloud. Explain that if you make a mistake, you go back and reread the word.

Practice/Apply

 ECHO-READ Read aloud pages 104–105, modeling accuracy. Have children echo-read each page.

Routine Card 8

Build Robust Vocabulary

Words About the Selection

Teach/Model

 Routine Card 3

INTRODUCE THE WORDS Use *Routine Card 3* to introduce the words.

---

❶ Put the word in **selection context**.

❷ Display Transparency R95 and read the word and the **Student-Friendly Explanation**.

❸ Have children **say the word** with you.

❹ Use the word in other contexts, and have children **interact with the word's meaning**.

❺ Remove the transparency. Say the Student-Friendly Explanation again, and ask children to **name the word** that goes with it.

---

❶ **Selection Context:** Music is **universal** because everyone can understand it.

❹ **Interact with Word Meaning:** I think that feelings are universal because everyone in the world has them. Which do you think is a universal need—having enough food or having new restaurants?

❶ **Selection Context:** Sounds that are very, very quiet are still **audible**.

❹ **Interact with Word Meaning:** Even on a noisy playground, the principal's voice is audible when she calls everyone inside. Which would be more audible at a party—a telephone ringing or a clock ticking?

Practice/Apply

GUIDED PRACTICE Ask children to respond to the following prompts:

• What are some needs that are *universal* to all people? Why is each of these things needed by people all over the world?

• What is something that you wish was not *audible* in the morning? Why?

Objective

• *To develop robust vocabulary through discussing a literature selection*

INTRODUCE ✔ Tested

Vocabulary: Lesson 18

universal **audible**

▼ **Student-Friendly Explanations**

Student-Friendly Explanations

attract	If you attract someone, you make that person want to come to you.
territory	An animal's territory is an area of land that it sees as its home.
universal	If something is universal, everyone in the world knows or experiences it.
audible	If you can hear something, it is audible.

Grade 2, Lesson 18   R95   Vocabulary

Transparency R95

Grammar Quick Write

Number Words

5-DAY GRAMMAR	
DAY 1	Introduce Number Words
DAY 2	**Identify Number Words**
DAY 3	Use Number Words in Sentences
DAY 4	Apply to Writing
DAY 5	Weekly Review

Objective

- *To identify exact and inexact number words*

Daily Proofreading

does Mr James play the trumpet.

(Does, Mr., trumpet?)

Words for Numbers Tell children that numbers may appear as numerals or as words. Numerals and number words are pronounced the same.

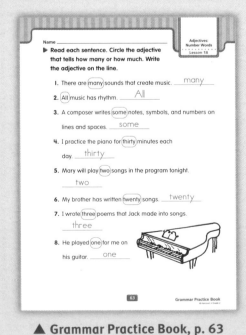

▲ Grammar Practice Book, p. 63

Review

IDENTIFY NUMBER WORDS Remind children that words such as *six* or *fourteen* tell exactly how many, while other words, such as *most, some, many,* and *few* do not tell exactly how many. Write the following sentences on the board.

Some children played in the band.
Two children played trombone.
There were five clarinet players.

Underline *Some*. Explain that it describes how many, but it is not exact. Underline *Two* and *five*. Explain that they are number words that tell exactly how many.

Practice/Apply

GUIDED PRACTICE Work with children to compile a list of information about items they are wearing. Ask questions like the following: *How many children are wearing gym shoes? How many children have on something that is red?* Guide children to use the information to create statements that use number words, such as *Three children are wearing yellow today. A few children are wearing red today.* Write the statements on the board and have children identify the number words. Have children tell whether they are exact or inexact.

INDEPENDENT PRACTICE Display an assortment of classroom items, such as crayons or markers. Ask children to write two statements about the items that use exact number words and two statements about the items that use inexact number words. Then invite volunteers to read one of their statements. Have children identify the number word used in the statement.

Writing

Poem

5-DAY WRITING	
DAY 1	Introduce
DAY 2	Prewrite
DAY 3	Draft
DAY 4	Revise
DAY 5	Revise

Prewrite

GENERATE IDEAS   Tell children that they will work on writing a poem about sounds they like to hear. Explain that their poems may be rhymed or unrhymed. Ask children to make a list of sounds they enjoy hearing.

 WORD CHOICE   Explain to children that using colorful words will help the reader "hear" the sounds. Some colorful words, such as *slam, hiss, crackle,* and *drip,* sound like the ideas they name. Discuss other ways to use colorful words. For example, saying *I screeched* or *I whispered* are colorful ways to say *I said.*

MODEL PREWRITING   Copy the chart below. Tell children that using a graphic organizer is a good way to get ideas for writing a poem. Model using the chart to record ideas about sounds. Point out that this chart can also help them record colorful words.

Sound	What It Sounds Like		
shaking sleigh bells	jingle	jangle	ching
thunder	crash	boom	bang
throwing rocks in a pond	plop	sploosh	

Practice/Apply

GUIDED PRACTICE   Tell children to brainstorm several ideas about sounds they might include in their poems. Encourage volunteers to share their ideas, and add them to the chart.

INDEPENDENT PRACTICE   Have children use their ideas and the chart to think about ideas for sounds to tell about in their poems. Have children save their charts and ideas to use on Days 3–5.

Objectives

- *To develop topics and ideas for writing*
- *To use a graphic organizer for prewriting*

 Writing Prompt

Independent Writing   Have children record ideas about sounds they do not like to hear.

BELOW-LEVEL

Generate Sound Words   Some children may find it helpful to think of onomatopoeic words first and then think of what creates the sounds, such as *buzz* (bees) or *tweet* (a whistle). Tell children that they should concentrate on generating ideas and not worry about spelling at this point. Children may check their spelling on future days.

Day at a Glance

Day 3

phonics and Spelling

- Review: Vowel Diphthong /oi/*oi*, *oy*

Fluency

- Accuracy
- "Ah, Music!," *Student Edition*, pp. 98–111

Comprehension

 **Review: Locate Information**

- Research/Study Skill: Introduce— Use Reference Sources

Reading

- "Come, My Little Children, Here Are Songs for You," *Student Edition*, pp. 112–113 Read!

Robust Vocabulary

- Review: *attract, territory, volume, expression, creative, performance, concentrate, relieved, universal, audible*

Grammar [Quick Write]

- Review: Number Words

Writing

- Poem

Warm-Up Routines

 Oral Language

Objective *To listen attentively and respond appropriately to oral communication*

Question of the Day

What instrument in a marching band do you think sounds the most interesting?

Help children think about the music that marching bands play, and the sounds that different instruments make. Use the following prompts:

- **What are some instruments you might hear in a marching band at a parade?**

- **What does a flute sound like? A tuba? A trumpet? A bass drum?**

- **Which instrument in a marching band do you like best? Why?**

Read Aloud

Objective *To listen for and identify onomatopoeia in poetry*

BIG BOOK OF RHYMES AND POEMS Display "Here Comes the Band" on page 33 and read it aloud. Emphasize onomatopoeic words such as *booming*, *oomphs*, and *tweet*. Explain to children that these words sound like what they name. Invite children to suggest more examples of onomatopoeia. The examples do not have to come from the poem. *(ooh's, ahs, buzz, hiss)* Then read the poem again, asking children to join in.

▲ **Big Book of Rhymes and Poems, p. 33**

Word Wall

Objective *To read high-frequency words*

REVIEW HIGH-FREQUENCY WORDS Point to the following words on the Word Wall: *thumb*, *million*, *early*, *world*, and *care*. Assign each child a partner. Point to a word, and have children repeat it with you. Then have one child spell the word to his or her partner, and have the partner spell it back. Repeat the process until each word has been spelled several times.

Vowel Diphthong /oi/
oi, oy  phonics and Spelling

5-DAY PHONICS	
DAY 1	Reintroduce /oi/*oi*, *oy*
DAY 2	Word Building with /oi/*oi*, *oy*
DAY 3	**Word Building with /oi/*oi*, *oy***
DAY 4	Suffixes -*ful*, -*less*; Review /oi/*oi*, *oy*
DAY 5	Suffixes -*ful*, -*less*; Review /oi/*oi*, *oy*

Objectives

- *To read and write common word families*
- *To recognize spelling patterns*

Skill Trace

 Tested **Vowel Diphthong /oi/ *oi*, *oy***

Introduce	T220–T223
Reteach	S26–S27
Review	**T232–T233, T250–T251, T414**
Test	Theme 4
Maintain	Theme 5, T134

Vowel Diphthong /oi/*oi, oy*

Let's wrap the muffins in <u>foil</u> so we can <u>enjoy</u> them later.
The little <u>boy</u> tried to <u>annoy</u> his older sister.
His first <u>choice</u> for a new <u>toy</u> is a model race car.
A loud <u>voice</u> boomed, "Do not <u>destroy</u> that!"
Come <u>join</u> us and have a piece of this <u>moist</u> fudge cake!
Be careful not to <u>spoil</u> your dinner.
A snake curled up in a <u>coil</u> on the warm, sunny <u>soil</u>.

Grade 2, Lesson 18   R92   Phonics

Transparency R92

Work with Patterns

INTRODUCE PHONOGRAMS   Write the following phonograms at the top of four columns.

-oy	-oil	-oice	-oist

Tell children that these are the endings of some words. Slide your hand under the letters as you read each phonogram. Repeat, and have children read the phonograms with you.

BUILD AND READ WORDS   Write the letter *b* in front of the first two phonograms. Guide children to read the words aloud: /b/-*oy, boy;* /b/-*oil, boil. Follow a similar procedure by adding ch to -oice, and m to -oist.*

Then have children name other words that end with -*oy*, -*oil*, -*oice*, and -*oist*. Have them tell which letter or letters to add to build each word, and write it on the board under the appropriate column. Have children read each column of words. Then point to words at random and have children read them.

Read Words in Context

READ SENTENCES   Display **Transparency R92** or write the sentences on the board or on chart paper. Have children choral-read the sentences as you track the print. Then have volunteers read each sentence aloud and underline words with *oi or oy*. Invite volunteers to identify words that end with the phonograms -*oy*, -*oil*, -*oice*, or -*oist* and add them to the appropriate columns of the chart.

MAINTAIN /s/*c*, /j/*g*, *dge*   Remind children that words that end with -*oice* also have the *c* that sounds like /s/. Ask children to find two more words that have a *c* with an /s/ sound (race, piece). Ask if they see a word ending with a *dge* consonant combination that sounds like /j/ (fudge).

5-DAY SPELLING

DAY 1	Pretest
DAY 2	Word Building
DAY 3	**State the Generalization**
DAY 4	Review
DAY 5	Posttest

Review Spelling Words

STATE THE GENERALIZATION FOR /oi/ *oi, oy* List spelling words 1–10 on chart paper or on the board. Circle the words *join* and *boil*, and have children read them. Ask: **What is the same in each word?** (Each word has the /oi/ sound spelled *oi*.) Have children circle the other words in which /oi/ is spelled *oi*. Then, using a different color pen, repeat the procedure for words with /oi/ spelled *oy*. Finally, ask: **What is the same about all of the words?** (They all have the /oi/ sound.)

WRITE Have children write the spelling words in their notebooks. Remind them to use their best handwriting and to use the chart to check their spelling.

Handwriting

APPROPRIATE LETTER SIZE Remind children to make sure they use an appropriate letter size when they write tall letters and short letters.

Decodable Books

Additional Decoding Practice

- **Phonics**
  Vowel Diphthong /oi/ *oi, oy*
- **Decodable Words**
- **High-Frequency Words**
  See lists in *Decodable Book 15.*
  See also *Decodable Books,* online (Take-Home Version).

▲ Decodable Book 15
"Coins, Coins, Coins"

Spelling Words

1.	**join**	6.	**boy**
2.	**boil**	7.	**voice***
3.	**joy**	8.	**point**
4.	**soil**	9.	**toy**
5.	**noise**	10.	**coin**

Challenge Words

11.	**destroy**	14.	**loyal**
12.	**avoid**	15.	**enjoy***
13.	**annoy**		

* Words from "Ah, Music!"

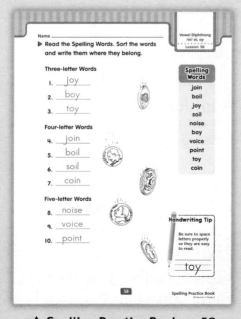

▲ Spelling Practice Book, p. 58

Fluency
Accuracy

Objective

- *To read accurately and fluently in a manner that sounds like natural speech*

 ### BELOW-LEVEL

Fluency Practice   Have children reread *Decodable Book 15*, Story 18 in the *Strategic Intervention Interactive Reader*, or the appropriate *Leveled Reader* (pp. T286–T289). Have them practice reading the text several times.

"Research Says"

Fluency Instruction   "The major conclusion of this study was that repeated reading worked."
　　　　　　　　　—Dowhower (1987)

Additional Related Reading

- *Plucking (Making Music)* by Angela Aylmore. Steck-Vaughn, 2006. **EASY**

- *My Family Plays Music* by Judy Cox. Holiday-House, 2003. **AVERAGE**

- *Lentil* by Robert McCloskey. Puffin, 1978. **CHALLENGE**

Review

DIBELS
Oral Reading Fluency
ORF

MODEL ACCURACY   Remind children that good readers make sure that they read every word correctly. Tell children to:

- read slowly so that they can pronounce each word correctly.
- go back and reread if they make a mistake.

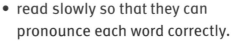 ▲ Student Edition, pp. 98–111

Think Aloud   **I'm going to read aloud part of "Ah, Music!" I'll read very carefully so that I don't make mistakes. If I make a mistake, I'll go back and try that word again.**

Practice/Apply

GUIDED PRACTICE   Read page 106 aloud. Then have children practice reading the same page aloud several times with a partner. Circulate among children, giving feedback as needed.

Routine Card 10   **INDEPENDENT PRACTICE**   Have members of small groups take turns reading aloud a page of "Ah, Music!" Remind children to read carefully and to accurately pronounce each word. Have listeners follow along in their *Student Edition* and alert the reader when a word is misread. When this happens, have all members of the group reread the sentence aloud together.

Locate Information
Comprehension

Review

DISCUSS LOCATE INFORMATION   Remind children that most nonfiction books are organized so that readers can find information easily. Have children use their *Student Edition* to locate and discuss how to use the table of contents, the index, and the glossary.

Practice/Apply

GUIDED PRACTICE   Use children's science or social studies textbook to practice locating information. Guide children to locate the following:

- the table of contents

- chapter titles

- headings within a chapter

- the index

- the glossary

- guide words

Then ask the following questions:

- **In which part of the book would you look to find out the meaning of a word used in this book?** (glossary) **What would help you locate the word in that part?** (guide words)

- **In which part of the book would you look to find out on what page a certain chapter begins?** (table of contents)

- **In which part or parts of the book would you look to find out where information on a certain topic is located?** (table of contents, index)

INDEPENDENT PRACTICE   Provide children with topics to look for in their science or social studies textbook's index. Have them write down the page numbers they find for each topic. Then have them compare their answers with a partner.

Objective

- *To use the parts of a book to locate information*

Skill Trace
 Tested Locate Information

Introduce	T224–T225
Reteach	S30–S31
Review	**T253, T268, T281, T308–T309, T337, T353, T363, T416, T437**
Test	Theme 4
Maintain	Theme 5, T279

Use Reference Sources

Research/Study Skill

Objectives

- *To understand the purposes of various reference sources*
- *To identify which reference source to use to accomplish a task*
- *To practice using a dictionary, thesaurus, encyclopedia, and atlas*

Skill Trace

Tested	Use Reference Sources

Introduce	T254–T255
Reteach	S32–S33
Review	T338–T339, T429, T438
Test	Theme 4
Maintain	Theme 6, T273

✓ MONITOR PROGRESS

Use Reference Sources

IF children have difficulty distinguishing among reference sources,	**THEN** guide children to create a chart to tell about each reference source.

Small-Group Instruction, pp. S32–S33:

- ● **BELOW-LEVEL:** Reteach
- ● **ON-LEVEL:** Reinforce
- ● **ADVANCED:** Extend

Teach/Model

INTRODUCE USE REFERENCE SOURCES   Tell children that good readers use reference sources to help them find information. Explain that there are print resources such as a dictionary, a thesaurus, an atlas, and encyclopedias. Mention that there are technology resources such as the Internet, CDs, and DVDs. Provide children with the following information:

- Use a **dictionary** to find a word's meaning, spelling, part of speech, and pronunciation. Dictionaries are organized in alphabetical order with guide words at the top of each page.

- Use a **thesaurus** to find synonyms. A thesaurus is set up like a dictionary.

- Use an **atlas** to find a map of a state, country, or part of the world.

- Use an **encyclopedia**, which is a set of books, to find information on a topic. Topics are arranged in alphabetical order.

- Use the **Internet** to find many kinds of information. You can read documents, see pictures and artwork, listen to music, and take a virtual tour of many places. Some websites might have mistakes, so be careful to use sites that are trusted. Model how to use the Internet to find information.

Think Aloud   Since the Internet has a lot of information, I can use a search engine to find what I need to know about a topic. First, I enter a keyword or group of words in the search engine field on the screen. Then I click SEARCH or GO. A list of websites about my topic appears on the screen. I click on the site or sites that I think will have the information I need. I can take notes or print out a paper copy.

Guided Practice

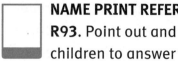

NAME PRINT REFERENCE SOURCES Display **Transparency R93.** Point out and name each reference source. Guide children to answer these questions:

- **Which reference source would you use to find a word that means about the same as *burning*?** (thesaurus)

- **Which reference source would you use to find out about the history of Florida?** (encyclopedia)

- **Would you find the meaning of the word *float* on this page of the dictionary? Tell why or why not.** (No. *Float* does not come between *flower* and *fold* alphabetically.)

Practice/Apply

WRITE QUESTIONS Have children work with a partner to write two questions that could be answered using the reference sources shown on the transparency. Then have partners exchange their questions with another pair, and work together to answer the questions.

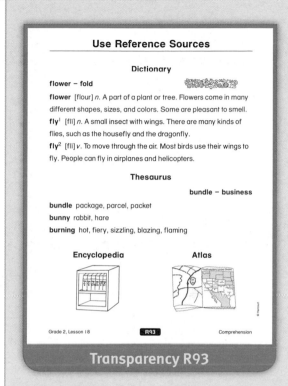

Use Reference Sources

Dictionary

flower – fold

flower [flour] *n.* A part of a plant or tree. Flowers come in many different shapes, sizes, and colors. Some are pleasant to smell.

fly[1] [fli] *n.* A small insect with wings. There are many kinds of flies, such as the housefly and the dragonfly.

fly[2] [fli] *v.* To move through the air. Most birds use their wings to fly. People can fly in airplanes and helicopters.

Thesaurus

bundle – business

bundle package, parcel, packet
bunny rabbit, hare
burning hot, fiery, sizzling, blazing, flaming

Encyclopedia   **Atlas**

Grade 2, Lesson 18   R93   Comprehension

Transparency R93

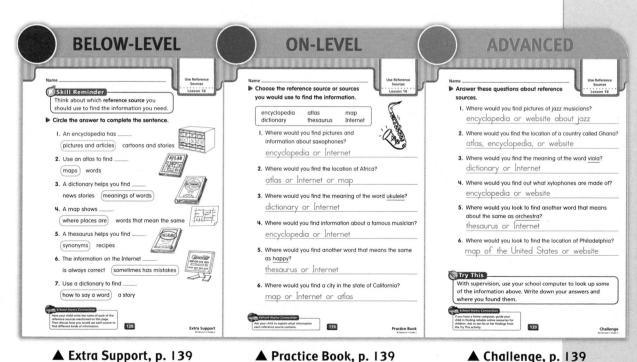

▲ **Extra Support, p. 139**   ▲ **Practice Book, p. 139**   ▲ **Challenge, p. 139**

E L L

- Group children according to academic levels, and assign one of the pages on the left.

- Clarify any unfamiliar concepts as necessary. See *ELL Teacher Guide* Lesson 18 for support in scaffolding instruction.

Reading
Student Edition: Paired Selection

Objective

- *To understand characteristics of poetry*

INTRODUCE THE POEM   Remind children that when they read "Ah, Music!," they learned that music can create feelings. Tell children they will read a poem called "Come, My Little Children, Here Are Songs for You," written by Robert Louis Stevenson.

TEXT FEATURES   Tell children that poems have certain features that are different from other types of writing. These features may include:

- rhyming words that can help create a mood or feeling

- repeated words that add rhythm

USE PRIOR KNOWLEDGE/SET A PURPOSE   Guide children to think about what they know about learning new songs, and have them listen for rhymes and repeated words as they listen to the poem.

SHARE THE POEM   Read the poem aloud, using repeated words to emphasize the rhythm. Then have children choral-read the poem with you.

Respond to the Poem

MONITOR COMPREHENSION   Have children reread the poem silently. Ask:

- **GENRE   What are some words that the poet repeats? Why do you think he repeats them?** (*Some, very, mark, all*; they add rhythm.)

- **PERSONAL RESPONSE   How does the poem make you feel?** (Accept reasonable responses.) **How is it like a lullaby?** (It makes you feel quiet and peaceful, as when you are getting ready to sleep.)

Writing Prompt

Write a Poem   Invite children to write a short poem about a time when they felt like singing. Tell children their poems can be rhymed or unrhymed. Invite volunteers to share their poems with the class.

About the Author

ROBERT LOUIS STEVENSON Born in Scotland in 1850, Robert Louis Stevenson was the son of a lighthouse keeper. He was often very ill as a child, but he loved adventure and exploring. As he grew older, he followed those passions and traveled widely, over lands, mountains, and oceans. His first major literary success, *Treasure Island*, told the rollicking tale of pirates on the high seas. A remarkably talented and popular writer in many genres, Stevenson also wrote the short novel *The Strange Case of Dr. Jekyll and Mr. Hyde*, and his collection of poetry, *A Child's Garden of Verses*, is still loved by many today. Stevenson was also an amateur composer and enjoyed writing songs for himself and his family. Stevenson's life and work has influenced many other writers, and he remains one of the world's most widely read authors.

E L L

Clarify Verb Meanings Direct children's attention to the second stanza. Explain that the verb *mark* can have several meanings, but that here it means "to notice" or "to study." Point out that the verbs in the first line on page 113, *rises* and *fall*, refer to pitch. Demonstrate rising and falling notes by singing or humming. Have children "sing" the words *rising* and *falling* with you using a corresponding pitch for each word.

 Connections

Objectives

- *To compare texts*
- *To connect texts to personal experiences*

Comparing Texts

1 Possible response: Both have to do with music. "Ah, Music!" is nonfiction; "Come, My Little Children, Here Are Songs for You" is poetry. **TEXT TO TEXT**

2 Accept reasonable responses. Children should include reasons to support their ideas. **TEXT TO SELF**

3 Accept reasonable responses. Possible responses: learning to play a new sport or game, reading, writing, or learning to dance or sing **TEXT TO WORLD**

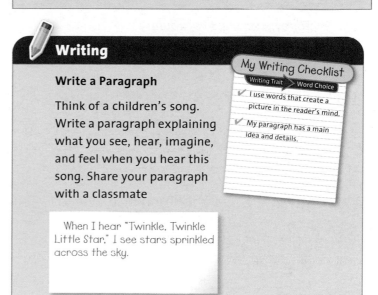

Connections

Comparing Texts

❶ How are "Ah, Music!" and "Come, My Little Children, Here Are Songs for You" alike? How are they different?

❷ What instrument and what song would you like to play at a recital? Why?

❸ What other activities are both hard and fun?

Phonics

Reading Words

Think of eight words that have the letters *oi* and *oy*. Write each word on a card. Trade cards with a partner. Who can read the words the fastest without mistakes?

soil
toy

114

Fluency Practice

Read Naturally

Choose a section of "Ah, Music!" to read aloud. Read the phrases in the section the way you would say them if you were talking to a friend. Practice reading the section several times.

Writing

Write a Paragraph

Think of a children's song. Write a paragraph explaining what you see, hear, imagine, and feel when you hear this song. Share your paragraph with a classmate

My Writing Checklist
Writing Trait ▸ Word Choice
✔ I use words that create a picture in the reader's mind.
✔ My paragraph has a main idea and details.

When I hear "Twinkle, Twinkle Little Star," I see stars sprinkled across the sky.

115

 PHONICS

Reading Words Children may use spelling words as a starting point for their eight words, but they should think of additional words with *oi* and *oy* to include on their cards. After partners have exchanged cards and read all the words, they should exchange them with other pairs.

boil   enjoy
choice   loyal
annoy   noise
point   employ

FLUENCY

Read Naturally Have children use headings to choose one section to read. After children have practiced on their own several times, have them read the section aloud to a partner.

WRITING

Write a Paragraph
Children may wish to use sentence beginnings such as "I see," "I hear," and "I feel" in their paragraphs. Encourage children to use colorful details and sensory words. Invite children to make a drawing to illustrate one of the sentences in their paragraphs.

📁 **Portfolio Opportunity**
Children may choose to place their paragraph in their portfolios.

 Build Robust Vocabulary

Objectives

- *To review robust vocabulary*
- *To demonstrate knowledge of word meaning*

REVIEW ✓ Tested

Vocabulary: Lesson 18

attract	performance
territory	concentrate
volume	relieved
expression	universal
creative	audible

Review Robust Vocabulary

USE VOCABULARY IN DIFFERENT CONTEXTS Remind children of the Student-Friendly Explanations of the Vocabulary Words introduced on Days 1 and 2. Then discuss each word in a new context using the following prompts.

attract

- **What are some objects that magnets attract?**
- **What kind of music might attract a large crowd? Why do you think this?**

territory

- **Describe the territory that belongs to our school.**
- **Name some kinds of animals that have their own territory.**

volume

- **Does a fire alarm have a low or high volume? How do you feel when you hear it?**
- **What are some machines on which you can change the volume?**

expression

- **How do your body movements show expression when you are angry at someone?**
- **Tell about a time when you tried to change your expression.**

creative

- **Tell about someone you admire because he or she is creative.**
- **Tell about a time when you did something in a creative way. How was it creative?**

performance

- If you could choose one type of performance to attend, what would it be? Tell why.
- Would you rather give a performance for people you know or for strangers? Why?

concentrate

- Do you have to concentrate more when you take a spelling test or when you walk a dog? Why?
- How can you tell when someone is really trying to concentrate?

relieved

- Do you usually feel more relieved before you take a test or after? Tell why.
- Tell about a time when you felt relieved because something *didn't* happen.

universal

- What would it be like if everyone spoke a universal language?
- Is laughter universal? Why do you think that?

audible

- What should you do if someone says your voice is not audible during a phone call? Why?
- Tell about a time when it was difficult to make your voice audible. Why was it difficult?

▼ **Student-Friendly Explanations**

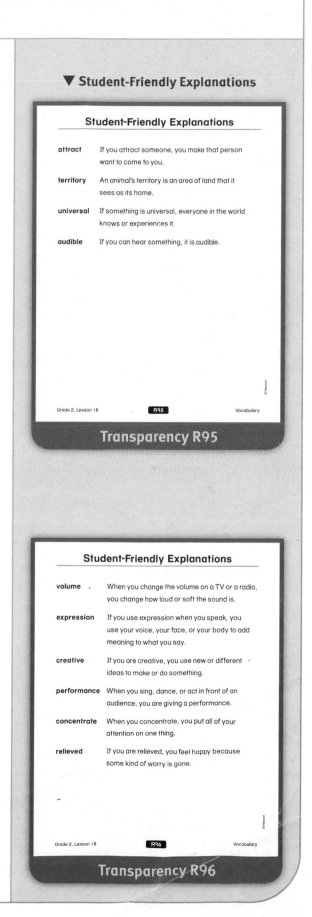

Student-Friendly Explanations

attract	If you attract someone, you make that person want to come to you.
territory	An animal's territory is an area of land that it sees as its home.
universal	If something is universal, everyone in the world knows or experiences it.
audible	If you can hear something, it is audible.

Grade 2, Lesson 18   R95   Vocabulary

Transparency R95

Student-Friendly Explanations

volume	When you change the volume on a TV or a radio, you change how loud or soft the sound is.
expression	If you use expression when you speak, you use your voice, your face, or your body to add meaning to what you say.
creative	If you are creative, you use new or different ideas to make or do something.
performance	When you sing, dance, or act in front of an audience, you are giving a performance.
concentrate	When you concentrate, you put all of your attention on one thing.
relieved	If you are relieved, you feel happy because some kind of worry is gone.

Grade 2, Lesson 18   R96   Vocabulary

Transparency R96

Grammar
Number Words

5-DAY GRAMMAR

DAY 1	Introduce Number Words
DAY 2	Identify Number Words
DAY 3	**Use Number Words in Sentences**
DAY 4	Apply to Writing
DAY 5	Weekly Review

Objective

• *To use exact and inexact number words in sentences*

Daily Proofreading

I need to more pennys

(two, pennies.)

Review

USE NUMBER WORDS IN SENTENCES Write the following number words on the board: *most, six, forty, few, some, eleven*. Have children identify which words are exact and which are inexact. Ask children to name other number words and add them to the list on the board.

Write the following sentences on the board:

Bring one towel to the beach.

I will pack some bottles of sunscreen.

Many of us could bring buckets.

Work with children to identify the number words in each sentence, and label each as exact or inexact. *(one, some, many)*

Practice/Apply

GUIDED PRACTICE Display a number of different classroom items such as pencils, erasers, and books. Then have one child ask for some of the items using a number word in the question, such as *May I have one pencil*? Continue in this manner until all children have had a chance to participate.

INDEPENDENT PRACTICE Have partners use number words in sentences. Have each child tell a partner what to draw, such as "Draw two rabbits." Each child should draw the picture and then write a sentence about the picture that includes a number word.

Name _____

Adjectives:
Number Words
Lesson 18

▶ Read each sentence. Complete each sentence with an adjective that tells how many. Possible responses are shown.

1. There are ___five___ second-grade classes in my school.

2. There are ___twenty___ children in my class.

3. I am ___eight___ years old.

4. There are ___ten___ boys in our class.

5. There are ___ten___ girls in our class.

6. My teacher plays ___three___ different drums.

7. My brother can play ___some___ guitars very well.

8. ___All___ the students enjoy listening to the band.

64

Grammar Practice Book

▲ **Grammar Practice Book, p. 64**

Writing

Poem

5-DAY WRITING	
DAY 1	Introduce
DAY 2	Prewrite
DAY 3	**Draft**
DAY 4	Revise
DAY 5	Revise

Draft a Poem

REVIEW A LITERATURE MODEL   Display "Here Comes the Band" on page 33 of the *Big Book of Rhymes and Poems*. Read the poem aloud. Point out the following:

> • The poet tells about the sounds you can hear in a marching band.
>
> • The poem uses rhyming words.
>
> • The poet uses colorful words to describe the sounds different instruments make, so that the reader can "hear" them, too.

DRAFT A POEM   Have children use the ideas from their charts to draft of a poem about sounds they like to hear. Children may also wish to use their list of rhyming words from Day 1, but remind them that their poems do not have to rhyme.

 WORD CHOICE   As children write their poems, remind them that they should use colorful words to bring their poems to life.

CONFER WITH CHILDREN   Meet with individual children to help them write their poems. Offer encouragement for what they are doing well, as well as make constructive suggestions for improving an aspect of the writing, as needed.

Objectives

- *To write a draft of a poem*
- *To include effective word choice in writing*

Writing Prompt

Write About Words   Have children write about words they enjoyed hearing in "Here Comes the Band" in the *Big Book of Rhymes and Poems*, p. 33.

▲ Writer's Companion, Lesson 18

Share Writing with a Partner
Partner children with English-proficient peers, and invite them to read each other's writing. Encourage partners to ask questions and clarify ideas and meanings.

Warm-Up Routines

Day at a Glance

Day 4

phonics and Spelling
- Introduce: Suffixes *-ful*, *-less*
- Review: Vowel Diphthong /oi/*oi*, *oy*

Fluency
- Accuracy
- "Ah, Music!," *Student Edition*, pp. 98–111

Comprehension

Review: Locate Information

- **Maintain: Main Idea and Details**
- **Maintain: Fiction and Nonfiction**

Robust Vocabulary
- Review: *attract, territory, volume, expression, creative, performance, concentrate, relieved, universal, audible*

Grammar [Quick Write]
- Review: Number Words

Writing
- Poem

 ## Oral Language

Objective *To listen attentively and respond appropriately to oral communication*

> ### Question of the Day
>
> **Why is it important for a musician to listen closely when he or she is playing an instrument or singing?**

Guide children to discuss why listening is important for a musician. List their ideas on the board. Use the following prompts:

- **What might happen if musicians in an orchestra or band did not listen closely to their playing?**

- **How can a musician tell if the sound coming from his or her instrument is good music?**

- **What might a song sound like if a singer covered his or her ears? Why?**

Read Aloud

Objective *To listen for enjoyment*

BIG BOOK OF RHYMES AND POEMS   Before
you display the poem "Benita Beane" on page
34, say: **Sometimes poems are meant to be
funny. As I read this poem, see if you can
find the joke the poet is making.** Then read
the poem aloud. Guide children to use the
illustration to find the joke about playing a
trumpet by ear. Read the poem aloud again,
and have children use gestures on the last
line to illustrate the joke.

▲ **Big Book of Rhymes
and Poems, p. 34**

Word Wall

Objective *To read high-frequency words*

REVIEW HIGH-FREQUENCY WORDS   Point to and read the following words
on the Word Wall: *already*, *special*, *ago*, *caught*, *clear* and *straight*. Point to
the words again and have children choral read the words, snapping their
fingers to keep time. Then ask volunteers to use each word in a sentence.

Suffixes -*ful*, -*less* phonics

5-DAY PHONICS	
DAY 1	Reintroduce /oi/*oi*, *oy*
DAY 2	Word Building with /oi/*oi*, *oy*
DAY 3	Word Building with /oi/*oi*, *oy*
DAY 4	Suffixes -*ful*, -*less*; Review /oi/*oi*, *oy*
DAY 5	Suffixes -*ful*, -*less*; Review /oi/*oi*, *oy*

Objectives

- *To identify the suffixes* -ful, -less
- *To read longer words with the suffixes* -ful, -less

Skill Trace

Tested ✓ Suffixes -*ful*, -*less*

Introduce	T266
Review	T278
Test	Theme 4

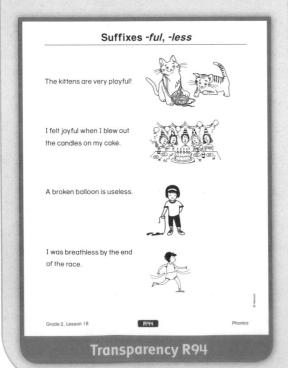

Transparency R94

Teach/Model

INTRODUCE SUFFIXES -*ful*, -*less*   Write the following on the board:

joy	Our family party was a time of great *joy*.
joyful	I felt *joyful* on my birthday.
joyless	The rainy day felt *joyless*.

Read aloud the first word and sentence. Remind children that *joy* means "the feeling you have when you are very happy." Next, point to *joyful* and read it aloud. Underline *ful*, and explain that the suffix -*ful* means "full of." Read the sentence aloud. Repeat the procedure for *joyless*. Explain that the suffix -*less* means "without."

MODEL DECODING WORDS WITH SUFFIXES -*ful*, -*less*   Model how to read the word *joyful*.

- Cover *ful* in *joyful*. Point out the root word *joy*. Have children read the word aloud. Uncover *ful* and have children read *joyful* aloud with you.

Distribute Syllabication Card 10 (*Teacher Resource Book*, p. 92) and read it aloud. Write the words *fearless* and *fearful* on the board and have children divide and read each word.

Guided Practice

READ WORDS   Write the following words on the board: *helpless*, *careful, sleepless,* and *thankful*. Guide children to identify the suffixes -*ful* and -*less* and blend the syllables to read each word.

Practice/Apply

READ SENTENCES   Display **Transparency R94** or write the sentences on the board. Have children read the sentences aloud. Remind them to use what they have learned about suffixes to help them read accurately.

Vowel Diphthong /oi/ oi, oy  and Spelling

5-DAY SPELLING

DAY 1	Pretest
DAY 2	Word Building
DAY 3	State the Generalization
DAY 4	Review
DAY 5	Posttest

Word Building

REVIEW THE WORDS   Have children open their notebooks to the spelling words that they wrote on Day 3. Have them read the words several times and then close their notebooks.

MAP LETTERS TO SOUNDS   Have children follow your directions to change one or more letters in each of the following words to make a spelling word. Have them write the word on a sheet of paper or in their notebooks. Then have a volunteer change the spelling of the word on the board so that children can self-check their spelling.

- Write *buy* on the board. Ask: **Which spelling word can you make by changing the second letter?** *(boy)*

- Write *sail* on the board. Ask: **Which spelling word can you make by changing the second letter?** *(soil)*

- Write *choice* on the board. Ask: **Which spelling word can you make by changing the first two letters to a single letter?** *(voice)*

Follow a similar procedure with the following words: *joint (join), bail (boil), jay (joy), nose (noise), paint (point), try (toy), corn (coin).*

CHALLENGE WORDS   In a column on the board, write the first syllable of each challenge word: *de, an, en, loy,* and *a.* Create another column for the second syllables: *void, joy, stroy, al,* and *noy.* Ask volunteers to match the syllables and write the complete word.

Objective

- *To use /oi/oi, oy and other known letter-sounds to spell and write words*

Spelling Words

1.	**join**	6.	**boy**
2.	**boil**	7.	**voice***
3.	**joy**	8.	**point**
4.	**soil**	9.	**toy**
5.	**noise**	10.	**coin**

Challenge Words

11.	**destroy**	14.	**loyal**
12.	**avoid**	15.	**enjoy***
13.	**annoy**		

* Words from "Ah, Music!"

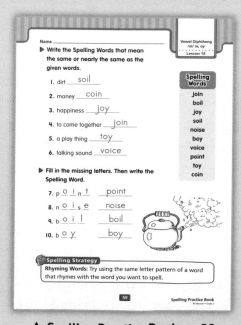

▲ Spelling Practice Book, p. 59

BELOW-LEVEL

Focus on Vowels   Write each spelling word on the board, with a blank where the /oi/ sound should be. Then invite children to add *oi* or *oy* to correctly spell each word.

Fluency

Accuracy

Objectives

- *To build fluency through rereading*
- *To read with accuracy*

⬤ BELOW-LEVEL

Echo-Read Identify sentences or words that children are having difficulty reading accurately. If a full sentence is difficult, discuss what the sentence means. Then read it aloud, and have children echo-read it with you. If a word is difficult, discuss its meaning and have children repeat the word after you several times.

✓ MONITOR PROGRESS

Fluency

IF children have difficulty reading accurately and in a manner that sounds like natural speech,	**THEN** have them write words that are difficult and practice reading the words out of context.

Small-Group Instruction, pp. S28–S29:

- ⬤ **BELOW-LEVEL:** Reteach
- ⬤ **ON-LEVEL:** Reinforce
- ⬤ **ADVANCED:** Extend

Review

DIBELS Oral Reading Fluency **ORF**

MODEL USING ACCURACY
Have children turn to page 108 of "Ah, Music!" Point out that most of the sentences are short.

▲ **Student Edition, pp. 98–111**

Think Aloud Since most of the sentences on page 108 are short, I can tell what each sentence is about. I can pronounce each word with care. Only the second-to-last sentence on the page is long, so I will read that sentence a little more carefully to be as accurate as I can.

Practice /Apply

GUIDED PRACTICE Guide children to read page 108 with you. Remind children to use a natural voice, as though they were speaking to a friend.

INDEPENDENT PRACTICE Have children listen to "Ah, Music!" on *Audiotext Grade 2,* CD 4. Have them listen to one page at a time and then read the page aloud on their own. Continue until children have completed reading the selection aloud.

Locate Information
Comprehension

Review

EXPLAIN LOCATING INFORMATION   Ask children to name some of the parts of a book that can help them locate information. (table of contents, chapter titles, headings, index, glossary, guide words) Remind children that nonfiction books often include these parts to help readers locate information.

Practice/Apply

GUIDED PRACTICE   Display **Transparency R90**. Explain to children that this passage might be in a nonfiction book about musical instruments. Guide children to determine how to locate information. Ask:

- **What is the chapter title?** ("The Flute") **What is the heading?** ("Kinds of Flutes") **On what page does this chapter begin?** (48)

- **Where would you look to find out if the book contains information on the saxophone?** (table of contents, index)

- **Where would you look to find the meaning of the word *produce*?** (glossary)

INDEPENDENT PRACTICE   Have children list the headings the author uses in "Ah, Music!" Then have them use the glossary in their *Student Edition* to locate the Selection Vocabulary Words. Children should list the guide words they used to find each word.

Objective

- *To use the parts of a book to locate information*

Skill Trace
 Locate Information

Tested	
Introduce	T224–T225
Reteach	S30–S31
Review	T253, T269, T281, T308–T309, T337, T353, T363, T416, T437
Test	Theme 4
Maintain	Theme 5, T279

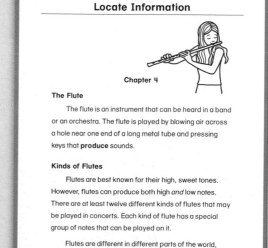

Locate Information

Chapter 4

The Flute

The flute is an instrument that can be heard in a band or an orchestra. The flute is played by blowing air across a hole near one end of a long metal tube and pressing keys that **produce** sounds.

Kinds of Flutes

Flutes are best known for their high, sweet tones. However, flutes can produce both high *and* low notes. There are at least twelve different kinds of flutes that may be played in concerts. Each kind of flute has a special group of notes that can be played on it.

Flutes are different in different parts of the world, but all flutes can make great music. One thing is certain: people enjoy playing and hearing flutes!

–48–

Grade 2, Lesson 18   R90   Comprehension

Transparency R90

Main Idea and Details
Comprehension

Objectives

- *To identify the main idea of informational text and its supporting details*
- *To use a graphic organizer to restate main idea and details*

Skill Trace

 Main Idea and Details [Tested]

Introduce	Theme 1, T216–T217
Reteach	Theme 1, S26–S27
Review	Theme 1, T246, T260, T270, T296–T297, T328, T342, T352, T404, T425
Test	Theme 1
Maintain	**T270**

Reinforce the Skill

REVIEW MAIN IDEA AND DETAILS   Review with children that the main idea of a selection is the most important idea that the author wants the reader to know about a topic. The author gives details that tell more about the main idea. Have children turn to page 101 of "Ah, Music!"

> **Think Aloud**   **The heading usually tells the main idea of a section. The heading "Music Is Rhythm" tells me that this section is about rhythm.**

Draw the following graphic organizer on the board, and fill in the main idea. Read aloud page 101 and add the details that support the main idea to the chart.

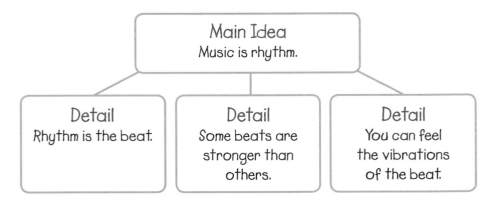

Practice /Apply

GUIDED PRACTICE   Work together to create a similar graphic organizer to show the main idea and details of the section "Music Is Feeling" on pages 104–105 of "Ah, Music!" Explain to children that they can add boxes to the organizer to list additional details, if necessary.

INDEPENDENT PRACTICE   Have children work independently to create and complete a graphic organizer of the main idea and details for the section "Practice Makes Perfect" on page 107. After they have finished, ask partners to share their organizers and discuss how they decided which details to include.

Fiction and Nonfiction

Comprehension

Reinforce the Skill

REVIEW FICTION AND NONFICTION   Remind children of what they have learned about the characteristics of fiction and nonfiction. Work together to create a chart like the following that shows the differences between fiction and nonfiction.

Fiction	Nonfiction
• tells a made-up story • has a beginning, a middle, and an end • has characters, a setting, and a plot • is usually written to entertain	• gives facts and details about a topic • may include headings and graphic aids such as charts and diagrams • is usually written to inform

Practice/Apply

GUIDED PRACTICE   Read aloud the titles of the selections from Theme 4. Work together with children to identify each selection as fiction or nonfiction. Have children explain their responses.

INDEPENDENT PRACTICE   Have children look at the table of contents for Theme 3 to help them recall selections they have already read. Ask children to record whether each selection is fiction or nonfiction. Then have partners share lists and discuss the reasons for their responses. As an alternate activity, provide children with an assortment of books from the classroom library. Have children list them as fiction or nonfiction.

Objectives

• *To understand the elements of fiction and nonfiction*

• *To distinguish fiction from nonfiction*

Skill Trace

 Fiction and Nonfiction

Introduce	Theme 3, T212–T213
Reteach	Theme 3, S26–S27
Review	Theme 3, T248, T262, T272, T298–T299, T330, T344, T354, T404, T425
Test	Theme 3
Maintain	**T271**

Build Robust Vocabulary

Objectives

- *To review robust vocabulary*
- *To demonstrate knowledge of word meaning*

REVIEW Tested

Vocabulary: Lesson 18

attract	universal
territory	audible
volume	performance
expression	concentrate
creative	relieved

Extend Word Meanings

USE VOCABULARY IN DIFFERENT CONTEXTS   Remind children of the Student-Friendly Explanations of the Vocabulary Words. Then discuss the words using the following activities.

universal   Tell children that you will name some things that children might want. If they think all children would want the thing, they should say, "That's universal!" If they think that it is something that not everyone would want, they should remain silent.

a cozy place to sleep	**ice cream every day**
a fancy dollhouse	**a friend to play with**

volume, audible   Tell children that you will describe some animal sounds. If children believe the sound could interrupt people who are talking, children should say, "Turn down the volume!" If the sound would not be audible when people are talking, children should say, "Turn up the volume!"

a mouse snoring	**an elephant trumpeting**
a squirrel chattering	**a dog barking**

relieved   Explain that you will describe some situations. If children think they would feel relieved about the situation, they should say, "Whew!" If not, they should shudder.

leaving your lunch at home

breaking a mirror

getting to a movie just before it begins

finding a misplaced library book

Word Relationships

SYNONYMS Tell children that a synonym is a word that means the same as another word. Write these sentences on the board, underlining the words *focus, imaginative, look, interest,* and *area.* Read the sentences aloud and have children replace each underlined word with the Vocabulary Word that is its synonym.

I have to <u>focus</u> on my homework.
(*concentrate*)

Krista's art work is <u>imaginative</u>.
(*creative*)

Marcus had a puzzled <u>look</u> on his face. (*expression*)

The store owners tried to <u>interest</u> customers so they would visit the new mall. (*attract*)

The field beyond the shed is our cat's special <u>area</u>. (*territory*)

ROOT WORDS Explain to children that they can look for a root word, or smaller word, in some longer words. Write the following Vocabulary Words on the board. Guide children to find the root word in each.

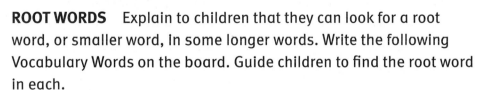

expression (*express*)   **creative** (*create*)

performance (*perform*)   **universal** (*universe*)

Discuss the meaning of each root word. Invite children to use each root word in a sentence.

▼ **Student-Friendly Explanations**

Student-Friendly Explanations

attract	If you attract someone, you make that person want to come to you.
territory	An animal's territory is an area of land that it sees as its home.
universal	If something is universal, everyone in the world knows or experiences it.
audible	If you can hear something, it is audible.

Grade 2, Lesson 18   R95   Vocabulary

Transparency R95

Student-Friendly Explanations

volume	When you change the volume on a TV or a radio, you change how loud or soft the sound is.
expression	If you use expression when you speak, you use your voice, your face, or your body to add meaning to what you say.
creative	If you are creative, you use new or different ideas to make or do something.
performance	When you sing, dance, or act in front of an audience, you are giving a performance.
concentrate	When you concentrate, you put all of your attention on one thing.
relieved	If you are relieved, you feel happy because some kind of worry is gone.

Grade 2, Lesson 18   R96   Vocabulary

Transparency R96

Grammar Quick Write
Number Words

5-DAY GRAMMAR

DAY 1	Introduce Number Words
DAY 2	Identify Number Words
DAY 3	Using Number Words in Sentences
DAY 4	**Apply to Writing**
DAY 5	Weekly Review

Objective

- *To use exact and inexact number words in writing*

Daily Proofreading

May i have two apples on friday?

(I, Friday)

Writing Trait ▶

Strengthening Conventions

Adjectives Use this short lesson with children's own writing to build a foundation for revising/editing longer connected text on Day 5. See also *Writer's Companion*, Lesson 18.

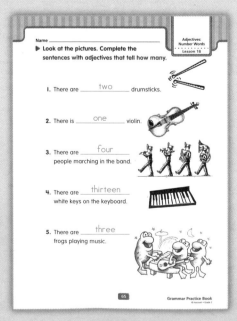

▲ Grammar Practice Book, p. 65

Review

DISCUSS NUMBER WORDS Write the following number words on the board: *five, twelve, some, twenty, few, many*. Ask children to name other number words, and add them to the list on the board. Have children identify which words are exact and which are inexact. Then write the following sentences on the board:

> **I need to buy some lettuce, two tomatoes, and a few carrots.**
>
> **I have one cucumber and some olives already.**

Work with children to identify the exact and inexact number words in each sentence. *(some, two, few, one, some)*

Practice/Apply

GUIDED PRACTICE Tell children that you are going to write sentences about ingredients that could be used to make a giant pizza. Model by writing this sentence on the board: *We will need one bag of flour to make the crust.* Identify that *one* is an exact number word. Have volunteers list more sentences on the board. Guide children to identify the number words in each sentence and tell whether they are exact or inexact.

INDEPENDENT PRACTICE Have children use number words to write three sentences about the ingredients they use to make a favorite snack. Ask children to underline the number words they use in each sentence.

5-DAY WRITING

DAY 1	Introduce
DAY 2	Prewrite
DAY 3	Draft
DAY 4	**Revise**
DAY 5	Revise

Writing
Poem

Write Poems

✏️ **WRITE** Have children continue writing their poems. Remind them that poets say things in a creative way in order to help the reader understand their ideas.

WRITING TRAIT ➤ **WORD CHOICE** Tell children that poets often express their ideas by using a few words, so it is important that the words are strong and colorful.

REVISE Explain to children that many poems are written to be read aloud because of the ways the words sound. Have children read their poem to a partner. Children can use the list of criteria for a poem to check and improve their writing.

Poem

- A poem tells a writer's feelings about a topic.

- A poem may be rhymed or unrhymed.

- A poem uses colorful words and details to help the reader see, feel, or hear what the writer is telling about.

- A poem may use comparisons.

- A poem usually includes a title.

Have partners discuss whether the sounds they discuss are clearly identified and described. Encourage children to use Editor's Marks to make revisions. Have children continue to work on revising their drafts. Tell them that they will complete a final revision on Day 5.

Editor's Marks

∧	Add
ℐ	Take out
⌐	Change
⊙	Add a period
≡	Capitalize
◯	Check spelling

Objectives

- *To revise a draft of a poem*
- *To edit a draft for appropriate grammar, spelling, and punctuation*

Writing Prompt

Respond and Explain Remind children that in "Ah, Music!," Aliki described making music as "hard fun." Have children write about whether they think writing a poem is hard fun, too. Have children explain their response.

ADVANCED

Check Rhythm Have children review their poems and listen for rhythm, or a regular beat. Children can tap the beat as they read their poems aloud. Encourage children to revise their poems toward producing a more consistent or identifiable rhythm.

Warm-Up Routines

 **and Spelling**

- Review: Suffixes *-ful, -less*
- Posttest: Vowel Diphthong /oi/*oi, oy*

Fluency

- Accuracy
- "Ah, Music!," *Student Edition,* pp. 98–111

 Read!

Comprehension

 Review: Locate Information

- *Read-Aloud Anthology:* "Sounds All Around"

Robust Vocabulary

- Cumulative Review

Grammar [Quick Write]

- Review: Number Words

Writing

- Poem

 Oral Language

Objective *To listen attentively and respond appropriately to oral communication*

Question of the Day

Which musical instrument would you like to learn to play? Why?

Invite children to tell about musical instruments they might want to learn to play. Use the following prompts:

- **Name some musical instruments you know.**

- **What do you like about some of these instruments?**

- **Would any of these instruments be easy or hard to learn to play? Tell why you think that.**

Write the following sentence frame on the board, and have children complete it to explain what musical instrument they would like to learn to play.

I would like to learn to play _____

because _____.

Read Aloud

Objective *To identify rhymes in poetry*

BIG BOOK OF RHYMES AND POEMS Display the poem "Benita Beane" on page 34. Ask children to listen for words that rhyme as you read the poem aloud. Guide children to identify the rhyming words *Beane, queen*; *play, way*; and *cheer, ear*. Then read the poem aloud again, inviting children to join in.

▲ **Big Book of Rhymes and Poems, p. 34**

Word Wall

Objective *To read high-frequency words*

REVIEW HIGH-FREQUENCY WORDS Point to and have children read the following words on the Word Wall: *believe, half, enough, learn, enjoy,* and *draw.* Next, assign each child a partner. Point to one word at a time and have one child use the word to ask his or her partner a question. Have the partner use the same word to answer the question.

Suffixes -ful, -less phonics

5-DAY PHONICS	
DAY 1	Reintroduce /oi/*oi*, *oy*
DAY 2	Word Building with /oi/*oi*, *oy*
DAY 3	Word Building with /oi/*oi*, *oy*
DAY 4	Suffixes -*ful*, -*less*; Review /oi/*oi*, *oy*
DAY 5	Suffixes -*ful*, -*less*; Review /oi/*oi*, *oy*

Objectives

- *To identify suffixes* -ful, -less
- *To read longer words with the suffixes* -ful, -less

Skill Trace

 Tested **Suffixes -*ful*, -*less***

Introduce	T266
Review	**T278**
Test	Theme 4

Review

READ WORDS WITH SUFFIXES -*ful*, -*less* Write the word *peaceful* on the board. Underline -*ful*, and remind children that the suffix -*ful* means "full of." Ask children what they think *peaceful* means. ("full of peace") Repeat the procedure with the word *toothless*, reminding children that the suffix -*less* means "without."

Practice/Apply

GUIDED PRACTICE Write the following words on the board and have children read them: *harmful*, *shoeless*, *playful*, and *sleepless*. Then make a chart as shown. Guide children to add each word to the chart.

-ful	-less
harmful	shoeless
playful	sleepless

INDEPENDENT PRACTICE Have children add more words to the chart and tell the meaning of each.

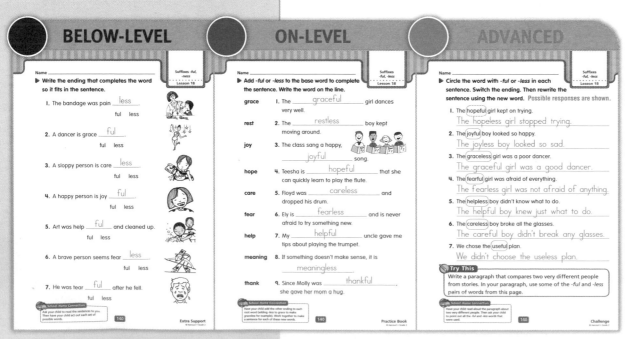

▲ **Extra Support, p. 140**   ▲ **Practice Book, p. 140**   ▲ **Challenge, p. 140**

E L L

- Group children according to academic levels, and assign one of the pages on the left.
- Clarify any unfamiliar concepts as necessary. See *ELL Teacher Guide* Lesson 18 for support in scaffolding instruction.

5-DAY SPELLING

DAY 1 Pretest
DAY 2 Word Building
DAY 3 State the Generalization
DAY 4 Review
DAY 5 Posttest

Vowel Diphthong /oi/ oi, oy  and Spelling

Assess

POSTTEST Assess children's progress. Use the dictation sentences from Day 1.

Words with /oi/ *oi, oy*

1.	join	Alisa will **join** us at the beach this afternoon.
2.	boil	We need to **boil** water to cook the pasta.
3.	joy	Seeing a rainbow filled me with **joy**.
4.	soil	Let's rake the **soil** before we plant our seeds.
5.	noise	I can't hear you because of all the **noise**!
6.	boy	My little brother is a very loud **boy**!
7.	voice	Esteban has a deep speaking **voice**.
8.	point	Could you **point** out the way to the nearest exit?
9.	toy	Monica got a **toy** cash register for her birthday.
10.	coin	The shiny **coin** under that chair could be a quarter.

ADVANCED

Challenge Words Use the challenge words in these dictation sentences.

11.	destroy	Flooding may **destroy** the farmer's crops.
12.	avoid	Please try to **avoid** stepping in those puddles!
13.	annoy	Our cat likes to **annoy** the neighbor's dog.
14.	loyal	The knight was always **loyal** to the king.
15.	enjoy	Did you **enjoy** seeing the parade?

WRITING APPLICATION Have children write and illustrate a question using one or more of the spelling words.

What was that loud noise?

Objective

• *To use /oi/ oi, oy and other known letter-sounds to spell and write words*

Spelling Words

1.	**join**	6.	**boy**
2.	**boil**	7.	**voice***
3.	**joy**	8.	**point**
4.	**soil**	9.	**toy**
5.	**noise**	10.	**coin**

Challenge Words

11.	**destroy**	14.	**loyal**
12.	**avoid**	15.	**enjoy***
13.	**annoy**		

* Words from "Ah, Music!"

Fluency

Accuracy

Objective

• *To read fluently with accuracy and appropriate expression*

✓ ASSESSMENT

Monitoring Progress   Periodically, take a timed sample of children's oral reading and record the number of words read correctly per minute. Children should accurately read approximately 72 words per minute in the middle of Grade 2.

Fluency Support Materials

Fluency Builders, Grade 2, Lesson 18

 Audiotext *Student Edition* selections are available on *Audiotext Grade 2,* CD 4.

 Strategic Intervention Teacher Guide, Lesson 18

Readers' Theater

DIBELS Oral Reading Fluency **ORF**

PERFORM "AH, MUSIC!"
Have children perform "Ah, Music!" as Readers' Theater to help them improve their fluency. Use the following procedures:

▲ **Student Edition, pp. 98–111**

• Assign a different child to read each page or section. Assign other children to play the parts of the characters and animals who, in speech balloons, remark upon the text throughout the selection.

• Have each group involved in reading a page or section practice reading it aloud together. Circulate among the groups as they practice and provide feedback and support. Encourage children who are playing characters to use lively vocal and body expressions, as though they were in a play.

• Invite children to read the selection to another class. Remind them to concentrate on reading accurately and with expression.

E L L

Develop Vocabulary   Point out that the mood, or feeling, of some sections is quiet and that the mood of other sections is noisier. Help children identify words that help create the mood. (*hum, poetry; marching-band beat, stronger*) Read aloud the sentences with these words and have children echo-read them with you.

Locate Information
Comprehension

Review

REVIEW THE SKILL Remind children that good readers use the parts of a book to help them locate information that they need. Have volunteers name the parts of a book that can help them locate information. (table of contents, chapter titles, headings, index, glossary, and guide words)

Practice/Apply

GUIDED PRACTICE Draw the following chart on the board. Have children use their *Student Edition, Volume I,* to locate information about the selection "Rain Forest Babies." Guide children to complete the first two rows of the chart.

Information You Need	Part of the Book to Find It	Page Numbers
Where can you find the selection "Rain Forest Babies"?	table of contents	428–445
Where can you find the meanings of the highlighted words?	glossary	464–471
What are the selection headings?	Tropical Rain Forests of the World	430–431
	Elephant	432–433
	Tiger	434–435
	Macaw	436–437
	Frog	438–439
	Kangaroo	440–441
	Sugar Glider	442–443

INDEPENDENT PRACTICE Have children work independently to complete the last row of the chart. Have them check their answers with a partner when finished.

Objective

• *To use the parts of a book to locate information*

Skill Trace

 Tested **Locate Information**

Introduce	T224–T225
Reteach	S30–S31
Review	**T253, T268, T281, T308– T309, T337, T353, T363, T416, T437**
Test	Theme 4
Maintain	Theme 5, T279

Work with Partners Have children work with a proficient English partner to complete the chart. Have children locate and point to information, say it aloud, and record the information.

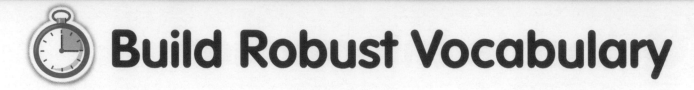

Build Robust Vocabulary

Objectives

- *To review robust vocabulary*
- *To demonstrate knowledge of word meanings*

REVIEW Tested ✓

Vocabulary

Lesson 17	Lesson 18
journeyed	attract
frail	territory
stomped	volume
sipped	expression
entertain	creative
except	performance
carefree	concentrate
screeching	relieved
horrendous	universal
melodious	audible

Cumulative Review

SORT WORDS Guide children in sorting Vocabulary Words into three groups. Draw on the board a chart like the following. Have children complete the chart by writing the Vocabulary Words in the appropriate column.

Action Words	Naming Words	Adjectives
journeyed	territory	carefree
attract	(volume)	audible
(stomped)	(expression)	(frail)
(sipped)	(performance)	(horrendous)
(entertain)		(melodious)
(screeching)		(creative)
(concentrate)		(universal)
(relieved)		

Have partners use the chart to play a game. Have them write Action Word on one index card, Naming Word on a second card, and Adjective on a third card. Then have children place the cards facedown. Have partners take turns choosing one of the cards and choosing a Vocabulary Word from that category to use in a sentence.

REVIEW VOCABULARY Discuss children's answers to these questions.

1. **Would you entertain a baby by taking him or her to a ballet performance? Why or why not?** (Possible response: No, because a baby would probably not enjoy or be able to appreciate a ballet.)

2. **What might a lion do if another lion journeyed into its territory?** (Possible response: The first lion might roar at the second lion and possibly fight with it to make it leave.)

3. **If someone stomped out of a room, would you say he or she was relieved? Why or why not?** (Possible response: no, because a person who felt relieved probably wouldn't stomp)

4. **What kind of body expression would you use to show that you felt carefree?** (Accept reasonable responses.)

5. **Think about the following sounds: a bird singing, a child humming, a car horn beeping, and a band playing. Why are all these sounds melodious except the car horn beeping?** (Possible response: The others are pleasant sounding.)

6. **If the volume on a radio was audible, would you raise or lower it if you suddenly heard horrendous screeching sounds?** (Possible response: I would lower it.)

 MONITOR PROGRESS

Build Robust Vocabulary

IF children do not demonstrate understanding of the words and have difficulty using them,	**THEN** model using each word in several sentences, and have children repeat each sentence.

Small-Group Instruction, pp. S34–S35:

● **BELOW-LEVEL:** Reteach
● **ON-LEVEL:** Reinforce
○ **ADVANCED:** Extend

Grammar Quick Write

Number Words

5-DAY WRITING	
DAY 1	Introduce Number Words
DAY 2	Identify Number Words
DAY 3	Using Number Words in Sentences
DAY 4	Apply to Writing
DAY 5	Weekly Reveiw

Objectives

- *To identify exact and inexact number words*
- *To use exact and inexact number words in writing*

Daily Proofreading

Dans birthday is in february.

(Dan's, February)

 Language Arts Checkpoint

If children have difficulty with the concepts, see pages S36–S37 to reteach.

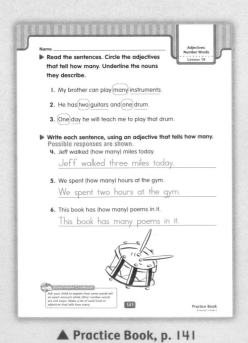

▲ **Practice Book, p. 141**

Review

REVIEW NUMBER WORDS   Use the following questions to review what children have learned about number words.

- **What are some exact number words?** (Possible responses: *eight, thirteen, thirty*)

- **What are some inexact number words?** (Possible responses: *some, few, all, many*)

Practice/Apply

GUIDED PRACTICE   Write the following sentences on the board:

> There are twenty bushes in the park.
> Twelve of them have red roses.
> Five of them have pink roses.
> Three of them have white roses.

Model identifying the number word in the first sentence. Then work with children to revise the last three sentences by replacing the exact number words with inexact words. (Possible responses: *Most, Some, Few*)

INDEPENDENT PRACTICE   Have children fold a sheet of paper into three sections. Tell children to draw three pictures that show things they might see in a park. Each picture should show more than one of the same thing. Have children write a sentence about each picture using a number word to tell how many. Tell children that the number word can be exact or inexact.

Writing

Poem

5-DAY WRITING	
DAY 1	Introduce
DAY 2	Prewrite
DAY 3	Draft
DAY 4	Revise
DAY 5	**Revise**

Revise

REVISE POEMS Tell children that when they reread their poems, they should ask themselves questions such as the following:

- Are the sounds I tell about described clearly?

- Have I used colorful words that help the reader "hear" the sounds?

Encourage children to revise their poems to clarify descriptions and revise and strengthen their word choices.

PROOFREADING Explain to children that while poems do not necessarily have to follow all standard grammatical conventions, children should include punctuation so that the reader can follow their ideas clearly. Children should also check for correct spelling and legible handwriting.

WRITING TRAIT **WORD CHOICE** Invite volunteers to share how they added or changed words to make their language more vivid. Discuss how using colorful words helps writers express their ideas more clearly.

NOTE: A 4-point rubric appears on page R8.

SCORING RUBRIC					
6	**5**	**4**	**3**	**2**	**1**
FOCUS Completely focused, purposeful.	Focused on topic and purpose.	Generally focused on topic and purpose.	Somewhat focused on topic, purpose.	Related to topic but does not maintain focus.	Lacks focus and purpose.
ORGANIZATION Ideas progress logically; poem conveys sense of completeness.	Organization mostly clear, poem gives sense of completeness.	Organization mostly clear, but some lapses occur; may seem unfinished.	Some sense of organization; seems unfinished.	Little sense of organization.	Little or no sense of organization
SUPPORT Strong, specific details; clear, exact language; freshness of expression.	Strong, specific details; clear, exact language.	Adequate support and word choice.	Limited supporting details; limited word choice.	Few supporting details; limited word choice.	Little development, limited or unclear word choice.
CONVENTIONS Conventions appropriate to poem; few, if any, errors.	Conventions appropriate to poem; few errors.	Most conventions appropriate to poem; few errors.	Most conventions appropriate to poem; some errors.	Some conventions appropriate to poem; many errors.	Conventions not appropriate to poem; many errors.

REPRODUCIBLE RUBRICS for specific writing purposes and presentations are available on pages R2–R8.

Objective

- *To revise a poem*

Writing Prompt

Independent Writing Have children generate ideas for a new writing topic.

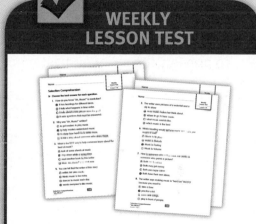

WEEKLY LESSON TEST

▲ **Weekly Lesson Tests, pp. 188–199**

- Selection Comprehension with Short Response
- Phonics and Spelling
- Focus Skill
- Use Reference Sources
- Robust Vocabulary
- Grammar
- Fluency Passage  **FRESH READS**

 GO online For prescriptions, see pp. A2–A6. Also available electronically on StoryTown Online Assessment and Exam View®.

 Podcasting: Assessing Oral Fluency

Leveled Readers
Reinforcing Skills and Strategies

Genre: Nonfiction

BELOW-LEVEL

Music Is About Sounds

SUMMARY   Different musical instruments produce sounds in different ways. Hitting, blowing, plucking, and pressing are four ways to make musical sounds.

- **phonics** Vowel Diphthong /oi/*oi, óy*
- **Vocabulary**

  Focus Skill Locate Information

Before Reading

BUILD BACKGROUND/SET PURPOSE   Have children name musical instruments and pantomime playing each instrument. Then guide them to preview the story and set a purpose for reading it.

Reading the Book

PAGE 4   MAIN IDEA   What is the most important idea on page 4? (Possible response: Music is made in many different creative ways.)

PAGE 9 LOCATE INFORMATION   Which heading in this book would lead you to information about instruments that are plucked? ("Listen to the Guitar")

REREAD FOR FLUENCY   Have partners take turns pointing to a picture and reading the sentences that go with it. Remind children to practice until they read every word correctly.

Think Critically   *(See inside back cover for questions.)*

1 **NOTE DETAILS**   expression, beat, volume

2 **LOCATE INFORMATION**   drum: page 5, horn: page 7, guitar: page 9, piano: page 11

3 **CAUSE/EFFECT**   You have to blow the horn to produce sound.

4 **AUTHOR'S PURPOSE**   Possible response: so you can learn different facts about each instrument

5 **EXPRESS PERSONAL OPINION**   Responses will vary.

LEVELED READERS TEACHER GUIDE

▲ Vocabulary, p. 5

▲ Comprehension, p. 6

GO online

★ **Leveled Readers Online Database**
Searchable by Genre, Skill, Vocabulary, Level, or Title
★ **Student Activities and Teacher Resources, online**

ON-LEVEL

Genre: Nonfiction

Playing in an Orchestra

SUMMARY   A narrator describes the experience of hearing an orchestra. She tells about the four families of instruments—string, woodwind, brass, and percussion—and the role of the conductor.

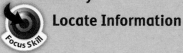

• **phonics** Vowel Diphthong
/oi/*oi, oy*

• **Vocabulary**

Focus Skill Locate Information

Before Reading

BUILD BACKGROUND/SET PURPOSE   Have children share what they know about an orchestra. Then guide them to preview the story and set a purpose for reading it.

Reading the Book

PAGES 6–7 🎯 **LOCATE INFORMATION**   If you wanted to learn about woodwind instruments, why would the heading on page 6 help you? (It is "Instrument Families," and woodwinds are a family.)

PAGES 9–10   IMPORTANT DETAILS   What is the conductor doing when he waves the baton? (Possible response: He is directing the playing to be loud, soft, fast, slow, or otherwise.)

REREAD FOR FLUENCY   Have partners take turns reading the book, a page or a section at a time. Remind children to say the words and sentences correctly and smoothly.

Think Critically   *(See inside back cover for questions.)*

1. **NOTE DETAILS**   They play together using different instruments.

2. **SEQUENCE**   string, woodwind, brass, percussion

3. 🎯 **LOCATE INFORMATION**   Composer: p. 11; Conductor: pp. 9–10.

4. **DRAW CONCLUSIONS**   Possible responses: the music would get all mixed up; it wouldn't sound right.

5. **PERSONAL RESPONSE**   Answers will vary.

LEVELED READERS TEACHER GUIDE

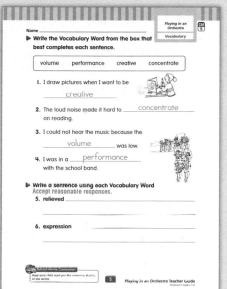

▲ Vocabulary, p. 5

▲ Comprehension, p. 6

Leveled Readers
Reinforcing Skills and Strategies

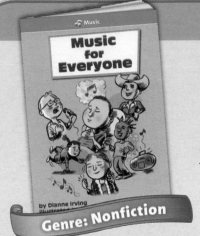

by Dianne Irving
Illustrated

Genre: Nonfiction

Music for Everyone

SUMMARY   Young narrators present a variety of musical styles they enjoy listening to, including jazz, classical, reggae, country, and rock. A choir and a piano recital are also shown.

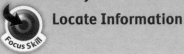

- **phonics** Vowel Diphthong /oi/*oi, oy*
- **Vocabulary**

  Focus Skill **Locate Information**

Before Reading

BUILD BACKGROUND/SET PURPOSE   Talk with children about the kinds of music they listen to and the kinds that family members listen to. How is one kind of music different from another? Then guide children to preview the story and set a purpose for reading it.

Reading the Book

PAGES 4–5 **LOCATE INFORMATION**   **Under what heading would you find information about swing music?** (under the heading "Jazz")

PAGE 6   DRAW CONCLUSIONS   Why is one kind of music called the blues? (Possible response: One way of saying you feel sad is that you feel blue. Music called the blues is full of sad feeling.)

REREAD FOR FLUENCY   Have small groups read this book as a radio play, with pauses for sound effects. Help them find appropriate recordings. Remind children that their reading should sound smooth and correct.

Think Critically   *(See inside back cover for questions.)*

1. **NOTE DETAILS**   sound that has rhythm, melody, or harmony

2. **CAUSE/EFFECT**   Members of a choir blend their voices, with some singing high notes and some singing low notes to produce music.

3. **LOCATE INFORMATION**   Reggae music is found on page 8.

4. **CONTEXT CLUES**   Possible responses: clever, talented, musical

5. **EXPRESS PERSONAL OPINION**   Answers will vary.

LEVELED READERS TEACHER GUIDE

▲ Vocabulary, p. 5

▲ Comprehension, p. 6

www.harcourtschool.com/storytown

★ **Leveled Readers Online Database**
Searchable by Genre, Skill, Vocabulary, Level, or Title
★ **Student Activities and Teacher Resources, online**

E L L

It's Fun to Dance

SUMMARY Traditional dances from around the world are shown and described.

Genre: Nonfiction

- **Build Background**
- **Concept Vocabulary**
- **Scaffolded Language Development**

Before Reading

BUILD BACKGROUND/SET PURPOSE Tell children that all over the world, people dance. Ask for their ideas about why dancing is a part of people's lives almost everywhere. Then guide children to preview the story and set a purpose for reading it.

Reading the Book

PAGE 2 LOCATE INFORMATION How does the title help you know what information will be in the book? (Possible response: The word *dance* in the title tells the topic.)

PAGE 14 MAIN IDEA What is the most important idea on page 14? (There are many different ways of dancing.)

REREAD FOR FLUENCY Have partners take turns choosing a favorite picture and reading the accompanying text aloud. Remind children to practice until they can read all words correctly and all sentences smoothly.

Scaffolded Language Development

(See inside back cover for teacher-led activity.)

Provide additional examples and explanation as needed.

LEVELED READERS TEACHER GUIDE

▲ Build Background and Vocabulary, p. 5

▲ Scaffolded Language Development, p. 6

Lesson 19

 **Phonics**
r-Controlled Vowel /ir/*ear*, *eer*
Syllable Pattern VC/V

 **Spelling**
gear, deer, fear, year, cheer, near, hear, clear, steer, rear

Reading
"The Life of George Washington Carver"
by Joli K. Stevens BIOGRAPHY

"Nutty Facts About Peanuts" from *Ranger Rick* by Gail Skroback Hennessey MAGAZINE ARTICLE

 Fluency
Accuracy

 Comprehension
 Locate Information
Use Reference Resources
 Ask Questions

Robust Vocabulary
brew, snug, supplies, crop, provide, earn, committee, experiments, innovation, edible

Grammar [Quick Write]
Words that Compare

Writing
Form: Narrative
Trait: Word Choice

Weekly Lesson Test

 = Focus Skill   = Focus Strategy   ✔ = Tested Skill

One stop *for all*
your Digital *needs*

Lesson 19

Digital
CLASSROOM

 www.harcourtschool.com/storytown
To go along with your print program

FOR THE TEACHER

Prepare Professional Development

 Videos for Podcasting

Plan & Organize Online TE & Planning Resources*

Teach Transparencies

access from Online TE

Assess  Online Assessment*

with Student Tracking System and Prescriptions

FOR THE STUDENT

Read Student eBook*

 Strategic Intervention Interactive Reader

Leveled Readers

Practice & Apply Splash into Phonics CD-ROM

 Also available on CD-ROM

Literature Resources

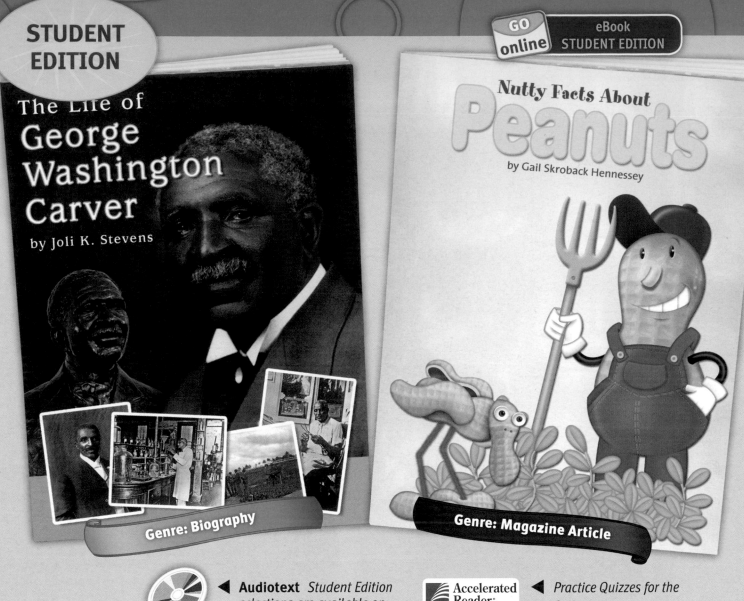

STUDENT EDITION

The Life of
**George
Washington
Carver**
by Joli K. Stevens

Genre: Biography

GO online · eBook STUDENT EDITION

Nutty Facts About
Peanuts
by Gail Skroback Hennessey

Genre: Magazine Article

 ◀ **Audiotext** *Student Edition selections are available on Audiotext Grade 2, CD 4.*

Accelerated Reader ◀ *Practice Quizzes for the Selection*

THEME CONNECTION: DREAM BIG
Comparing a Biography and a Magazine Article

....

Paired Selections

 **SOCIAL STUDIES**   **The Life of George Washington Carver, pp. 122–135**

SUMMARY   This biography follows the life and accomplishments of George Washington Carver from childhood through adulthood.

 SCIENCE   **Nutty Facts About Peanuts, pp. 136–137**

SUMMARY   Children will learn facts and statistics about peanuts.

Support for Differentiated Instruction

GO online **LEVELED READERS**

Thomas Alva Edison
A Great Inventor
by Jordan Maxwell

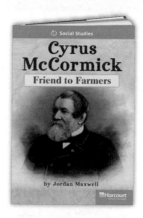

Madam C. J. Walker
Making Dreams Happen
by Jordan Maxwell

Cyrus McCormick
Friend to Farmers
by Jordan Maxwell

Peanuts
by Jordan Maxwell

● **BELOW-LEVEL**   ● **ON-LEVEL**   ● **ADVANCED**

E L L

LEVELED PRACTICE

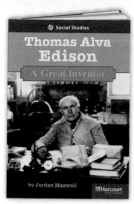

◀ **Strategic Intervention Resource Kit, Lesson 19**

◀ **Strategic Intervention Interactive Reader, Lesson 19**
Strategic Intervention Interactive Reader Online

◀ **ELL Extra Support Kit, Lesson 19**

◀ **Challenge Resource Kit, Lesson 19**

● **BELOW-LEVEL**
Extra Support Copying Masters, pp. 142, 144–148

● **ON-LEVEL**
Practice Book, pp. 142–149

● **ADVANCED**
Challenge Copying Masters, pp. 142, 144–148

ADDITIONAL RESOURCES

farmer   scientist

- Decodable Book 16
- Spelling Practice Book, pp. 60–62
- Grammar Practice Book, pp. 67–70
- Reading Transparencies R97–R103
- Language Arts Transparencies LA39–LA40
- Test Prep System
◀ **Literacy Center Kit, Cards 91–95**
- Sound/Spelling Card
◀ **Fluency Builders**
◀ **Picture Card Collection**
- Read-Aloud Anthology, p. 72–73

ASSESSMENT

✔ **Monitor Progress**

✔ **Weekly Lesson Tests, Lesson 19**
- Comprehension
- Phonics and Spelling
- Focus Skill
- Robust Vocabulary
- Grammar
- Use Reference Sources

GO online **www.harcourtschool.com/storytown**
Online Assessment
Also available on CD-ROM—Exam View®

Suggested Lesson Planner

GO online Online TE & Planning Resources

	Day 1	**Day 2**
Step 1 Whole Group		

Daily Routines
- Oral Language
- Read Aloud
- High-Frequency Words

Day 1

QUESTION OF THE DAY, p. T302
What are some famous inventions? What is one invention that you think is really important? Why?

READ ALOUD, p. T303
Transparency R97: A Glowing Idea

WORD WALL, p. T303

Day 2

QUESTION OF THE DAY, p. T314
Do you eat foods made with peanuts? Tell about what peanut foods you eat and why.

READ ALOUD, p. T315
Big Book of Rhymes and Poems, "Nuts to You and Nuts to Me"

WORD WALL, p. T315

Word Work
- phonics
- Spelling

Day 1

 phonics, p. T304
Introduce: *r*-Controlled Vowel /ir/*ear, eer*

SPELLING, p. T307
Pretest: *gear, deer, fear, year, cheer, near, hear, clear, steer, rear*

Day 2

phonics, p. T316
Introduce: *r*–Controlled Vowel /ir/*ear, eer*

SPELLING, p. T317
Word Building

Skills and Strategies
- Reading
- Fluency
- Comprehension
- Build Robust Vocabulary

Day 1

READING/COMPREHENSION, p. T308
 Introduce: Locate Information

LISTENING COMPREHENSION, p. T310
Read-Aloud: "Young Inventors"

FLUENCY, p. T310
Focus: Accuracy

BUILD ROBUST VOCABULARY, p. T311
Words from the Read-Aloud

Day 2

BUILD ROBUST VOCABULARY, p. T318
Words from the Selection
Word Detective, p. T319

READING, p. T320
"The Life of George Washington Carver"
Options for Reading

▲ Student Edition

COMPREHENSION, p. T320
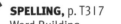 Introduce: Answer Questions

RETELLING/FLUENCY, p. T328
Accuracy

BUILD ROBUST VOCABULARY, p. T329

 Step 2 Small Groups — **Suggestions for Differentiated Instruction (See pp. T296–T297.)**

 Step 3 Whole Group

Language Arts
- Grammar **Quick Write**
- Writing

Day 1

GRAMMAR, p. T312
Introduce: Words That Compare

Daily Proofreading
Is todd the only boy in the clas
(Todd, class?)

 WRITING, p. T313
Introduce: Narrative
Writing Trait: Word Choice

Writing Prompt *Write a narrative about a day in your classroom.*

Day 2

GRAMMAR, p. T330
Review: Words That Compare

Daily Proofreading
Trisha has the small lunchbox in the clas
(smallest, class.)

 WRITING, p. T331
Review: Narrative
Writing Trait: Word Choice

Writing Prompt *Write sentences about the life of a family member or friend.*

 = Focus Skill   = Focus Strategy    = Tested Skill

phonics

Skills at a Glance

	Comprehension	**Fluency**	**Vocabulary**
• r-Controlled Vowel /ir/ear, eer • Syllable Pattern VC/V	**Focus Skill** Locate Information **Focus Strategy** Ask Questions	Accuracy	**ROBUST:** brew, snug, supplies, crop, provide, earn, committee, experiments, innovation, edible

Day 3

QUESTION OF THE DAY, p. T332
Think about something you could make with nuts. Describe how it would taste, look, and smell.

READ ALOUD, p. T333
Big Book of Rhymes and Poems, "Nuts to You and Nuts to Me"

WORD WALL, p. T333

, p. T334
Review: *r*-Controlled Vowel /ir/ear, eer

SPELLING, p. T335
State the Generalization

FLUENCY, p. T336
Accuracy:
"The Life of George Washington Carver"

COMPREHENSION, p. T337
Review: Locate Information
Paired Selection: "Nutty Facts about Peanuts"

▲ Student Edition

RESEARCH/STUDY SKILLS,
Introduce: Use Reference Sources

CONNECTIONS, p. T342

BUILD ROBUST VOCABULARY, p. T344
Review

Day 4

QUESTION OF THE DAY, p. T348
What are seeds? Tell what happens when seeds are planted in the ground.

READ ALOUD, p. T349
Big Book of Rhymes and Poems, "Tiny Seeds"

WORD WALL, p. T349

, p. T350
Introduce: Syllable Pattern VC/V

SPELLING, p. T351
Review Spelling Words

FLUENCY, p. T352
Accuracy:
"The Life of George Washington Carver"

COMPREHENSION, p. T353
Review: Locate Information

▲ Student Edition

BUILD ROBUST VOCABULARY, p. T354
Review

Day 5

QUESTION OF THE DAY, p. T358
What would happen if there were no seeds in the world?

READ ALOUD, p. T359
Big Book of Rhymes and Poems, "Tiny Seeds"

WORD WALL, p. T359

, p. T360
Review: Syllable Pattern VC/V

SPELLING, p. T361
Posttest

FLUENCY, p. T362
Accuracy:
"The Life of George Washington Carver"

COMPREHENSION, p. T363
Review: Locate Information
Read-Aloud: "Young Inventors"

▲ Student Edition

BUILD ROBUST VOCABULARY, p. T364
Cumulative Review

BELOW-LEVEL ● **ON-LEVEL** ● **ADVANCED** ● E L L

GRAMMAR, p. T346
Review: Words That Compare

Daily Proofreading
The girls's bikes were biger than the boys' bikes (girls', bigger, bikes.)

WRITING, p. T347
Review: Narrative
Writing Trait: Word Choice

Writing Prompt *Explain why young George Washington Carver was know as "the plant doctor."*

GRAMMAR, p. T356
Review: Words That Compare

Daily Proofreading
Is this the taller building in the city (tallest, city?)

WRITING, p. T357
Review: Narrative
Writing Trait: Word Choice

Writing Prompt *Write notes about what you like about your partner's biography.*

GRAMMAR, p. T366
Review: Words That Compare

Daily Proofreading
puppies are noisy than kittens (Puppies, noisier, kittens.)

WRITING, p. T367
Review: Narrative
Writing Trait: Word Choice

Writing Prompt *Write a list of ideas about a new topic of your choice for writing.*

Suggested Small-Group Planner

 45-60+ Minutes

	Day 1	Day 2
15-20+ Minutes ● **BELOW-LEVEL**	**Teacher-Directed** Leveled Reader: "Thomas Alva Edison: A Great Inventor," p. T368 Before Reading **Independent** ⭐ Listening/Speaking Center, p. T300 Extra Support Copying Masters, pp. 142, 144 ▲ Leveled Reader	**Teacher-Directed** Student Edition: "The Life of George Washington Carver," p. T320 **Independent** ⭐ Reading Center, p. T300 Extra Support Copying Masters, pp. 145–146 ▲ Student Edition
15-20+ Minutes ● **ON-LEVEL**	**Teacher-Directed** Leveled Reader: "Madam C.J. Walker: Making Dreams Happen," p. T369 Before Reading **Independent** ⭐ Reading Center, p. T300 Practice Book, pp. 142, 144 ▲ Leveled Reader	**Teacher-Directed** Student Edition: "The Life of George Washington Carver," p. T320 **Independent** ⭐ Letters and Sounds Center, p. T301 Practice Book, pp. 145–146  ▲ Student Edition
15-20+ Minutes ○ **ADVANCED**	**Teacher-Directed** Leveled Reader: "Cyrus McCormick: Friend to Farmers," p. T370 Before Reading **Independent** ⭐ Letters and Sounds Center, p. T301 Challenge Copying Masters, pp. 142, 144 ▲ Leveled Reader	**Teacher-Directed** Leveled Reader: "Cyrus McCormick: Friend to Farmers," p. T370 Read the Book **Independent** ⭐ Word Work Center, p. T301 Challenge Copying Masters, pp. 145–146 ▲ Leveled Reader

E L L English-Language Learners

In addition to the small-group instruction above, use the ELL Extra Support Kit to promote language development.

LANGUAGE DEVELOPMENT SUPPORT **Teacher-Directed** ELL TG, Day 1 **Independent** ELL Copying Masters, Lesson 19 ▲ ELL Student Handbook	**LANGUAGE DEVELOPMENT SUPPORT** **Teacher-Directed** ELL TG, Day 2 **Independent** ELL Copying Masters, Lesson 19 ▲ ELL Student Handbook

Intervention

 ▲ Strategic Intervention Resource Kit

 ▲ Strategic Intervention Interactive Reader

Strategic Intervention TG, Day 1 Strategic Intervention Practice Book, Lesson 19	Strategic Intervention TG, Day 2 Strategic Intervention Interactive Reader, Lesson 19 ▲ Strategic Intervention Interactive Reader

MONITOR PROGRESS

Small-Group Instruction

Comprehension	**Phonics**	**Comprehension**	**Fluency**	**Robust Vocabulary**	**Language Arts Checkpoint**
Focus Skill Locate Information pp. S42–S43	*r*-Controlled Vowel /ir/*ear*, *eer* pp. S38–39	Use Reference Sources p. S44–S45	Accuracy pp. S40–S41	*brew, snug, supplies, crop, provide, earn, committees, experiments, innovation, edible* pp. S46–S47	**Grammar:** Words that Compare **Writing:** Narrative pp. S48–S49

Day 3

Teacher-Directed
Leveled Reader:
"Thomas Alva Edison:
A Great Inventor," p. T368
Read the Book

Independent
⭐ Word Work Center, p. T301
Extra Support Copying Masters, p. 147

▲ Leveled Reader

Teacher-Directed
Leveled Reader:
"Madam C.J. Walker: Making
Dreams Happen," p. T369
Read the Book

Independent
⭐ Word Work Center, p. T301
Practice Book, p. 147

▲ Leveled Reader

Teacher-Directed
Leveled Reader:
"Cyrus McCormick: Friend to
Farmers," p. T370
Think Critically

Independent
⭐ Listening/Speaking Center,
p. T300
Challenge Copying Masters, p. 147

▲ Leveled Reader

LANGUAGE DEVELOPMENT SUPPORT

Teacher-Directed
Leveled Reader: "Peanuts," p. T371
Before Reading; Read the Book
ELL TG, Day 3

Independent
ELL Copying Masters, Lesson 19

▲ Leveled Reader

Strategic Intervention TG, Day 3
Strategic Intervention Interactive
Reader, Lesson 19
Strategic Intervention Practice
Book, Lesson 19

▲ Strategic Intervention Interactive Reader

Day 4

Teacher-Directed
Leveled Reader:
"Thomas Alva Edison:
A Great Inventor," p. T368
Reread for Fluency

Independent
⭐ Letters and Sounds Center,
p. T301

▲ Leveled Reader

Teacher-Directed
Leveled Reader:
"Madam C.J. Walker: Making
Dreams Happen," p. T369
Reread for Fluency

Independent
⭐ Word Work Center, p. T301

▲ Leveled Reader

Teacher-Directed
Leveled Reader:
"Cyrus McCormick: Friend to
Farmers," p. T370
Reread for Fluency

Independent
⭐ Writing Center, p. T301
Self-Selected Reading:
Classroom Library Collection

▲ Leveled Reader

LANGUAGE DEVELOPMENT SUPPORT

Teacher-Directed
Leveled Reader: "Peanuts," p. T371
Reread for Fluency
ELL TG, Day 4

Independent
ELL Copying Masters, Lesson 19

▲ Leveled Reader

Strategic Intervention TG, Day 4
Strategic Intervention Interactive
Reader, Lesson 19

▲ Strategic Intervention Interactive Reader

Day 5

Teacher-Directed
Leveled Reader:
"Thomas Alva Edison:
A Great Inventor," p. T368
Think Critically

Independent
⭐ Writing Center, p. T301
Leveled Reader: Reread for Fluency
Extra Support Copying Masters, p. 148

▲ Leveled Reader

Teacher-Directed
Leveled Reader:
"Madam C.J. Walker:
Making Dreams Happen," p. T369
Think Critically

Independent
⭐ Listening/Speaking Center,
p. T300
Leveled Reader: Reread for Fluency
Practice Book, p. 148

▲ Leveled Reader

Teacher-Directed
Leveled Reader:
"Cyrus McCormick: Friend to
Farmers," p. T370
Reread for Fluency

Independent
⭐ Reading Center, p. T300
Leveled Reader: Reread for Fluency
Self-Selected Reading:
Classroom Library Collection
Challenge Copying Masters, p. 148

▲ Leveled Reader

LANGUAGE DEVELOPMENT SUPPORT

Teacher-Directed
Leveled Reader: "Peanuts," p. T371
Think Critically
ELL TG, Day 5

Independent
Leveled Reader: Reread
for Fluency
ELL Copying Masters, Lesson 19

▲ Leveled Reader

Strategic Intervention TG, Day 5
Strategic Intervention Interactive
Reader, Lesson 19

▲ Strategic Intervention Interactive Reader

Leveled Readers & Leveled Practice
Reinforcing Skills and Strategies

LEVELED READERS SYSTEM

- **Leveled Readers**
- **Leveled Readers, CD**
- **Leveled Readers Teacher Guides**
  - *Comprehension*
  - *Vocabulary*
  - *Oral Reading Fluency Assessment*
- **Response Activities**
- **Leveled Readers Assessment**

See pages T368–T371 for lesson plans.

BELOW-LEVEL

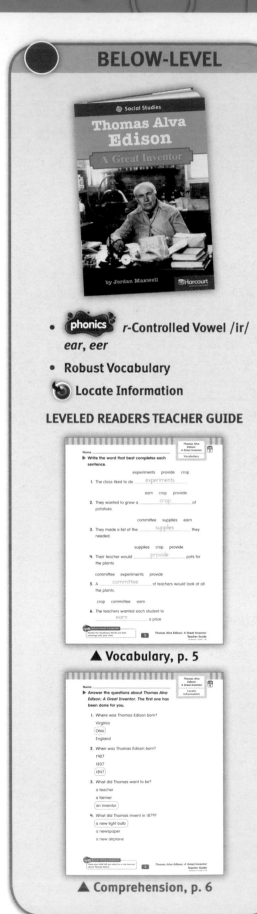

- **phonics** *r*-Controlled Vowel /ir/ *ear, eer*
- **Robust Vocabulary**
- **Locate Information**

LEVELED READERS TEACHER GUIDE

▲ Vocabulary, p. 5

▲ Comprehension, p. 6

ON-LEVEL

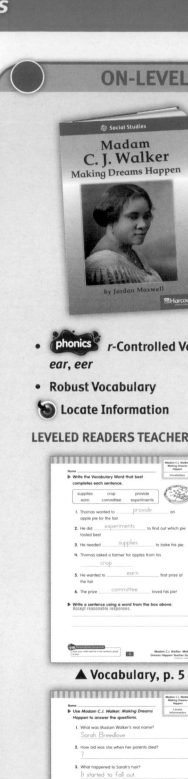

- **phonics** *r*-Controlled Vowel /ir/ *ear, eer*
- **Robust Vocabulary**
- **Locate Information**

LEVELED READERS TEACHER GUIDE

▲ Vocabulary, p. 5

▲ Comprehension, p. 6

www.harcourtschool.com/storytown

★ **Leveled Readers, Online Database**
Searchable by Genre, Skill, Vocabulary, Level, or Title
★ **Student Activities and Teacher Resources, online**

ADVANCED

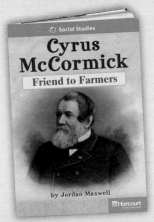

- 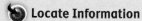 **phonics** *r*-Controlled Vowel /ir/ *ear, eer*
- **Robust Vocabulary**
- ⟳ **Locate Information**

LEVELED READERS TEACHER GUIDE

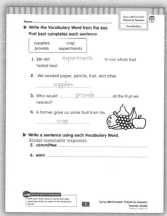

▲ **Vocabulary, p. 5**

▲ **Comprehension, p. 6**

ELL

- **Build Background**
- **Concept Vocabulary**
- **Scaffolded Language Development**

LEVELED READERS TEACHER GUIDE

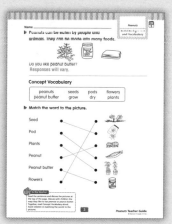

▲ **Build Background, p. 5**

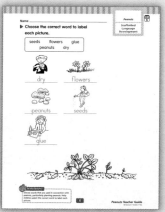

▲ **Scaffolded Language Development, p. 6**

CLASSROOM LIBRARY
for Self-Selected Reading

EASY
▲ *The Dot* by Peter H. Reynolds. **FICTION**

AVERAGE
▲ *Billy's Bucket* by Kes Gray. **FICTION**

CHALLENGE
▲ *Mae Jemison* by Thomas Streissguth. **NONFICTION**

▲ **Classroom Library Books Teacher Guide, Lesson 19**

Literacy Centers

15 Min. each

Management Support

While you provide direct instruction to individuals or small groups, other children can work on literacy center activities.

▲ Literacy Center Pocket Chart

My Activities

✓ Put a check mark next to the activities you complete.

Literacy Activities
- ☐ Listening/Speaking Read with a Recording
- ☐ Reading Read and Respond
- ☐ Writing Write a Biography
- ☐ Word Work Play "I Spy"
- ☐ Letters and Sounds Build Words

Leveled Readers
- ☐ Rereading for Fluency
- ☐ Activities (See inside back cover.)

Practice Pages
- ☐ pages 142–149

▲ Teacher Resource Book, p. 52

Homework for the Week

TEACHER RESOURCE BOOK, PAGE 22
The *Homework Copying Master* provides activities to complete for each day of the week.

GO online www.harcourtschool.com/ storytown

 LISTENING/SPEAKING

Read with a Recording

Objective
To develop fluency by listening to nonfiction selections and reading them aloud

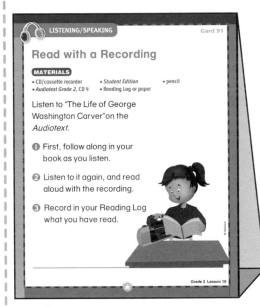

LISTENING/SPEAKING — Card 91

Read with a Recording

MATERIALS
- CD/cassette recorder
- Audiotext Grade 2, CD 4
- Student Edition
- Reading Log or paper
- pencil

Listen to "The Life of George Washington Carver" on the *Audiotext*.

❶ First, follow along in your book as you listen.

❷ Listen to it again, and read aloud with the recording.

❸ Record in your Reading Log what you have read.

Grade 2 Lesson 19

⭐ **Literacy Center Kit • Card 91**

READING

Read and Respond

Objective
To develop comprehension by rereading familiar stories and responding to them

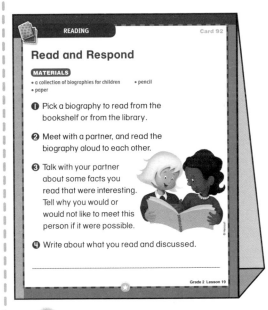

READING — Card 92

Read and Respond

MATERIALS
- a collection of biographies for children
- paper
- pencil

❶ Pick a biography to read from the bookshelf or from the library.

❷ Meet with a partner, and read the biography aloud to each other.

❸ Talk with your partner about some facts you read that were interesting. Tell why you would or would not like to meet this person if it were possible.

❹ Write about what you read and discussed.

Grade 2 Lesson 19

⭐ **Literacy Center Kit • Card 92**

WRITING

Write a Biography

Objective
To practice writing a biography of someone you know

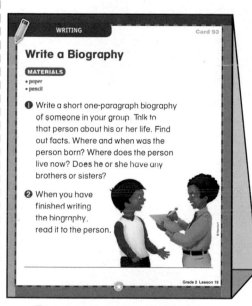

WRITING   Card 93

Write a Biography

MATERIALS
• paper
• pencil

❶ Write a short one-paragraph biography of someone in your group. Talk to that person about his or her life. Find out facts. Where and when was the person born? Where does the person live now? Does he or she have any brothers or sisters?

❷ When you have finished writing the biography, read it to the person.

Grade 2 Lesson 19

⭐ **Literacy Center Kit** • Card 93

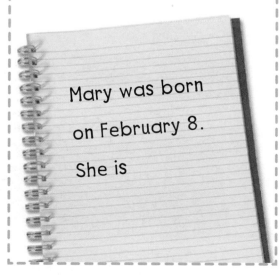

Mary was born on February 8. She is

WORD WORK

Play "I Spy"

Objective
To practice using Vocabulary Words

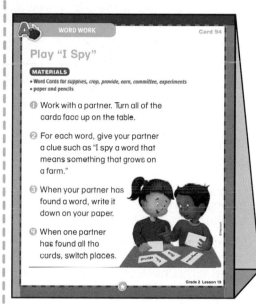

WORD WORK   Card 94

Play "I Spy"

MATERIALS
• Word Cards for *supplies, crop, provide, earn, committee, experiments*
• paper and pencils

❶ Work with a partner. Turn all of the cards face up on the table.

❷ For each word, give your partner a clue such as "I spy a word that means something that grows on a farm."

❸ When your partner has found a word, write it down on your paper.

❹ When one partner has found all the cards, switch places.

Grade 2 Lesson 19

⭐ **Literacy Center Kit** • Card 94

supplies
provide
crop
earn
committee
experiment

LETTERS AND SOUNDS

Build Words

Objective
To build words using known letter/sound correspondences

LETTERS AND SOUNDS   Card 95

Build Words

MATERIALS
• index cards with *ea, ee, r, c, d, f, h, l, m, n, p, r, s, t*
• paper and pencils

❶ Work with a partner. Use the sound and letter index cards to build words that use *ear* and *eer* for the long *e* sound in *hear* and *cheer*.

❷ Make a list of the words you build.

❸ Share your list with another set of partners and write any words you overlooked onto your list.

Grade 2 Lesson 19

⭐ **Literacy Center Kit** • Card 95

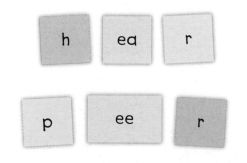

h   ea   r

p   ee   r

and Spelling

- Introduce: *r*-Controlled Vowel /ir/*ear, eer*
- Pretest

Reading/ Comprehension

 Introduce: Locate Information, *Student Edition*, pp. 118–119

- *Read-Aloud Anthology:* "Young Inventors"

Fluency

- Model Oral Fluency

Robust Vocabulary

Words from the Read-Aloud
- Introduce: *brew, snug*

Grammar

- Introduce: Words That Compare

Writing

- Narrative: Biography

Day at a Glance

Day 1

Warm-Up Routines

 Oral Language

Objective *To listen attentively and respond appropriately to oral communication*

Question of the Day

What are some famous inventions? What is one invention that you think is really important? Tell why.

Help children brainstorm inventions that they know about, such as the telephone, light bulb, and automobile. Use the following prompts:

- **Describe a fun or helpful invention that you know about.**
- **Explain how you think inventors come up with their ideas for inventions.**
- **Tell why children might be good inventors. Name some things children might invent.**

Then have children complete the following sentence frame to explain why the invention they chose is important.

The _____ is a really important invention because _____ .

Read Aloud

Objective *To listen for a purpose*

TRANSPARENCY Read aloud "A Glowing Idea" on **Transparency R97.** Use the following steps:

- **Set a purpose for listening.** Tell children to listen to find out how a young girl invented a new way to read and write in the dark.

- **Model fluent reading.** Read the article aloud. Point out that good readers go back and reread when they make a mistake.

- **Discuss the article.** Ask: **How did Becky's problem lead to a new Invention?** (Possible response: Becky thought of a clever way to solve her problem. Her idea became a new invention.)

Locate Information

A Glowing Idea

A Dark Problem

One day, ten-year-old Becky Schroeder was trying to do her homework in the car. Becky's mother had run in to the store. Because it was starting to get dark, Becky could not see the words and numbers on the paper.

A New Idea

Becky started to think about things that glowed in the dark. Some toys glowed in the dark. What if paper could glow in the dark, too?

The next day Becky and her father bought special paint that glowed in the dark. Becky painted pieces of paper and turned out the lights. It took a lot of tries, but finally it worked. The paper glowed. Becky could read and write on it in the dark!

A Big Success

Becky's invention was called the Glo-sheet. Soon people all over wanted to buy Glo-sheets. Becky and her father started a company to sell Glo-sheets. It was a huge success, all because of one glowing idea by a young girl!

Grade 2, Lesson 19   R97   Comprehension

Transparency R97

Word Wall

Objective *To read high-frequency words*

REVIEW HIGH-FREQUENCY WORDS Point to the following words at random: *already, different, everything, idea, imagine,* and *through* as well as other previously learned high-frequency words. Ask children to read and then spell each word. Go through the words several times. Have them arrange the words in alphabetical order.

already	different	everything
idea	imagine	through

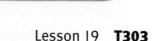

r-Controlled Vowel /ir/ear, eer

phonics *and Spelling*

Objectives

- *To recognize and blend the r-controlled vowel /ir/ear, eer*
- *To read words with /ir/ear, eer and other known letter-sounds*
- *To use /ir/ear, eer and other known letter-sounds to spell words*

Skill Trace

 Tested r-Controlled Vowel /ir/*ear, eer*

Introduce	T304–T307
Reteach	S38–S39
Review	T316–T317, T334–T335, T424
Test	Theme 4
Maintain	Theme 6, T360

 Refer to *Sounds of Letters CD* Track 16 for pronunciation of /ir/.

"Research Says"

Spelling and Reading Acquisition "Spelling instruction was found to improve children's ability to learn to read a set of similarly spelled words."

—Ehri & Wilce (1987)

Connect Letters to Sounds

WARM UP WITH PHONEMIC AWARENESS Say the words *hear* and *cheer*. Have children say the words. Say: **The words *hear* and *cheer* end with the /ir/ sound**. Then say the words *fear* and *steer*, and have children repeat. Say: **The words *fear* and *steer* also end with the /ir/ sound**. Have children say /ir/ several times.

Routine Card 1 **CONNECT LETTERS AND SOUNDS** Display the *Sound/Spelling Card* for /ir/*ear* and *eer*. Point to the letters *ear* and review their letter/sound correspondence. Say: **The letters *ear* can stand for the /ir/ sound, the sound at the end of *hear***. Touch the letters several times, and have children say /ir/ each time. Follow a similar procedure for /ir/*eer*.

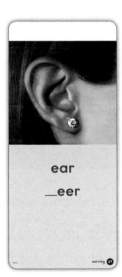

ear

_eer

earring

▲ **Sound/Spelling Card**

5-DAY PHONICS	
DAY 1	Introduce /ir/*ear*, *eer*
DAY 2	Word Building with /ir/*ear*, *eer*
DAY 3	Word Building with /ir/*ear*, *eer*
DAY 4	VC/V; Review /ir/*ear*, *eer*
DAY 5	VC/V; Review /ir/*ear*, *eer*

Work with Patterns

REINFORCE /ir/*ear*, *eer* Write the following words on the board. Point out that each word has the letters *ear*. Read each word, and then have children read it with you.

eardrum	dear
earring	tear
earsplitting	dreary

REINFORCE /ir/*eer* Repeat the procedure with the following words that have the letters *eer*.

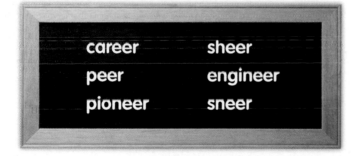

career	sheer
peer	engineer
pioneer	sneer

r-Controlled Vowel /ir/ear, eer
phonics *and Spelling*

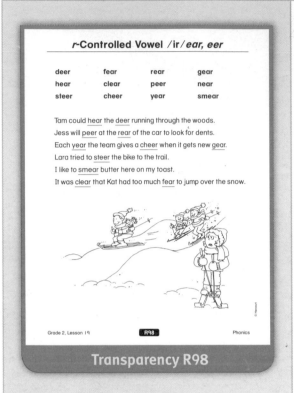

r-Controlled Vowel /ir/ear, eer

deer	fear	rear	gear
hear	clear	peer	near
steer	cheer	year	smear

Tam could hear the deer running through the woods.
Jess will peer at the rear of the car to look for dents.
Each year the team gives a cheer when it gets new gear.
Lara tried to steer the bike to the trail.
I like to smear butter here on my toast.
It was clear that Kat had too much fear to jump over the snow.

Grade 2, Lesson 19   R98   Phonics

Transparency R98

Reading Words

GUIDED PRACTICE   Display **Transparency R98** or write the words and sentences on the board. Point to the word *deer*. Read the word, and then have children read it with you.

INDEPENDENT PRACTICE   Point to the remaining words in the top portion and have children read them. Then have children read aloud the sentences and identify words with /ir/*ear* or *eer*.

Decodable Books

Additional Decoding Practice

- **Phonics**
  r-Controlled Vowel /ir/*ear, eer*
- **Decodable Words**
- **High-Frequency Words**
  See the list in *Decodable Book 16*

  See also *Decodable Books*, online (Take-Home Version).

▲ **Decodable Book 16 "Cheers and Tears"**

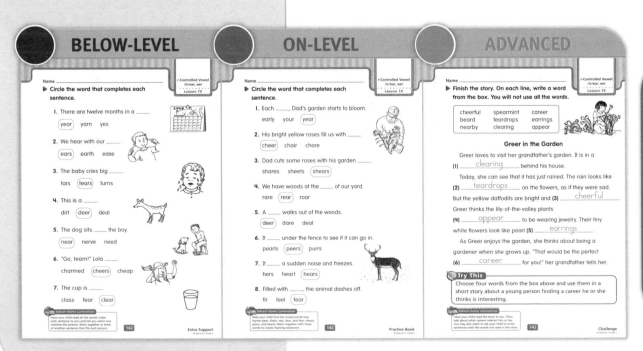

BELOW-LEVEL

▲ Extra Support, p. 142

ON-LEVEL

▲ Practice Book, p. 142

ADVANCED

▲ Challenge, p. 142

E L L

- Group children according to academic levels, and assign one of the pages on the left.

- Clarify any unfamiliar concepts as necessary. See *ELL Teacher Guide* Lesson 19 for support in scaffolding instruction.

5-DAY SPELLING

DAY 1	Pretest
DAY 2	Word Building
DAY 3	State the Generalization
DAY 4	Review
DAY 5	Posttest

Introduce Spelling Words

PRETEST   Say the first word and read the dictation sentence. Repeat the word as children write it. Write the word on the board and have children check their spelling. Tell them to circle the word if they spelled it correctly or write it correctly if they did not. Repeat for words 2–10.

Words with /ir/*ear, eer*

1. gear	I put the camping **gear** in the van.
2. deer	Maya saw a **deer** eating berries.
3. fear	Jena has a **fear** of high places.
4. year	Next **year** I will be in third grade!
5. cheer	The people at the game started to **cheer**.
6. near	Tina's house was not **near** the school.
7. hear	Luka did not **hear** the doorbell ring.
8. clear	I can revise my draft to make my writing **clear**.
9. steer	Mom turned the wheel to **steer** the car.
10. rear	The trunk is in the **rear** of the car.

ADVANCED

Challenge Words   Use the challenge words in these dictation sentences.

11. appear	I saw a rainbow **appear** after a storm.
12. pioneer	I wish I had been a **pioneer** living out west.
13. volunteer	Amir likes to **volunteer** to help animals.
14. earrings	Dad gave me **earrings** for my birthday.
15. nearby	The post office is **nearby**.

Spelling Words

1. gear	6. near
2. deer	7. hear
3. fear	8. clear
4. year*	9. steer
5. cheer	10. rear

Challenge Words

11. appear	14. earrings
12. pioneer	15. nearby
13. volunteer	

* Word from "The Life of George Washington Carver"

▲ Practice Book, p. 143

Locate Information
Comprehension

Objective

- *To use titles, tables of contents, and headings to locate information in nonfiction text*

Daily Comprehension
Locate Information

DAY 1:	Introduce Locate Information *Student Edition*
DAY 2:	Review Locate Information *Student Edition*
DAY 3:	Review Locate Information *Student Edition*
DAY 4:	Review Locate Information *Transparency*
DAY 5:	Review Locate Information *Read-Aloud Anthology*

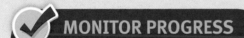

MONITOR PROGRESS

Locate Information

IF children have trouble using titles and headings to locate information in nonfiction text,	**THEN** use a different nonfiction book or article with headings to review how to use titles and headings to find information.

Small-Group Instruction, pp. S42–S43:

- ⬤ **BELOW-LEVEL:** Reteach
- ⬤ **ON-LEVEL:** Reinforce
- ⬤ **ADVANCED:** Extend

Teach/Model

REVIEW LOCATING INFORMATION   Have children read *Student Edition* page 118. Model how to locate information in nonfiction text.

> **Think Aloud**   I can quickly find information I need by looking at the chapter titles. I know that a book with the title *The Life of Dr. Martin Luther King, Jr.*, will be about Dr. Martin Luther King, Jr. The chapter with the title "The Early Years" tells me I'll find information about Dr. King's childhood, because of the words *early years*.

Practice/Apply

GUIDED PRACTICE   Draw a chart like the one on *Student Edition* page 119. Then read with children the title and table of contents for a book about Abraham Lincoln. Guide them to complete the chart for Chapter 2: Midwest Lawyer by looking at key words in the chapter title.

Chapter Title	Information
Log Cabin Boy	Tells about Abraham Lincoln's childhood
Midwest Lawyer	Tells about the middle part of Lincoln's life, when he was a lawyer in the Midwest

 **INDEPENDENT PRACTICE**   Have children explain what information they would find in Chapter 3. (information about Abraham Lincoln as President) Write their responses in the chart.

E L L

Use Pictures to Help Locate Information   If children are having trouble using key words in headings, find an article or nonfiction selection with headings and photographs or illustrations. Point to the images in each section and guide children to understand how the pictures can also be clues to the kinds of information in each section.

Focus Skill

Locate Information

You can use a **table of contents** at the beginning of a book to help you find information. Many tables of contents list **chapters** in a book and the page number on which each chapter begins. The title of the chapter gives you a clue about what you will read in that chapter.

The Life of Dr. Martin Luther King, Jr.
Table of Contents

118

Read the table of contents below. Tell about the information that might be found in the second chapter.

The Life of Abraham Lincoln
Table of Contents

Chapter Title	Information
Log Cabin Boy	Tells about Abraham Lincoln's childhood
Midwest Lawyer	
President Lincoln	

Try This!

Look back at the table of contents. What information will you find in Chapter 3?

GO online   www.harcourtschool.com/storytown

119

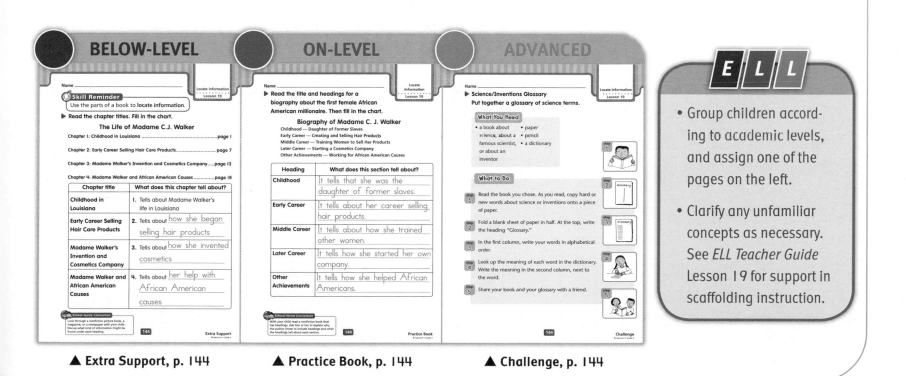

▲ **Extra Support, p. 144**   ▲ **Practice Book, p. 144**   ▲ **Challenge, p. 144**

ELL

- Group children according to academic levels, and assign one of the pages on the left.

- Clarify any unfamiliar concepts as necessary. See *ELL Teacher Guide* Lesson 19 for support in scaffolding instruction.

Listening Comprehension
Read Aloud

Objectives
- *To set a purpose for listening*
- *To listen to a biography to get information and for enjoyment*

Build Fluency

Focus: Accuracy Tell children that good readers try to read every word correctly, including the words in the title and headings in a nonfiction selection. If they make a mistake, they go back and reread so that the heading or sentence makes sense.

E L L

Clarify Vocabulary Show children photographs from magazines or websites to clarify unknown vocabulary such as *Popsicle* and *earmuffs*. For example, if children do not know what an earmuff is, show a picture of someone wearing earmuffs. Point to the earmuffs and say **These are earmuffs. They keep ears warm when it is cold.**

Before Reading

CONNECT TO PRIOR KNOWLEDGE Tell children that they will be listening to an expository nonfiction selection about young people who were inventors. Explain that one person invented the Popsicle and the other person invented earmuffs. Discuss what children know about Popsicles and earmuffs.

▲ **Read-Aloud Anthology, "Young Inventors," p. 72**

Routine Card 2 **GENRE STUDY: EXPOSITORY NONFICTION** Tell children that expository nonfiction explains true information. It tells the events in time order and often uses headings.

Think Aloud **The title tells me this is about young inventors. So, it will probably tell about more than one inventor. The headings show that one of the inventors is named Frank Epperson and the other person is named Chester Greenwood.**

 REVIEW LOCATE INFORMATION Remind children that the headings in an expository nonfiction selection tells what each section is about. Read the title and the headings to children. Suggest that children listen for key words that will help them know what the whole selection is about and what each part is about. Read the selection "Young Inventors" to children.

After Reading

RESPOND Have children explain how Frank Epperson and Chester Greenwood came to think of their inventions. Place their answers in webs on the board.

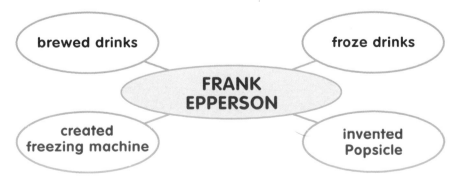

Build Robust Vocabulary

Words from the Read-Aloud

Teach/Model

 Routine Card 3

INTRODUCE ROBUST VOCABULARY Use *Routine Card 3* to introduce the words.

❶ Put the word in **selection context**.

❷ Display Transparency R102 and read the word and the **Student-Friendly Explanation**.

❸ Have children **say the word** with you.

❹ Use the word in other contexts, and have children **interact with the word's meaning**.

❺ Remove the transparency. Say the Student-Friendly Explanation again, and ask children to **name the word** that goes with it.

❶ **Selection Context:** Frank Epperson liked to **brew** his own special drinks.

❹ **Interact with Word Meaning:** I like to brew iced tea in a big glass jar in the summer. Can you say that you brew iced tea when you buy it already made at the store? Why or why not?

❶ **Selection Context:** Chester Greenwood's earmuffs had a hinge for a **snug** fit.

❹ **Interact with Word Meaning:** I have a pair of shoes that are a snug fit on my feet. If you had a pair of pants that were a snug fit on you, would they be loose and baggy, or would they fit you close and a little tight? Explain.

Practice/Apply

GUIDED PRACTICE Have children name things that can have a *snug* fit.

Objective

• *To develop robust vocabulary through context clues*

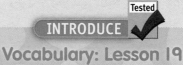 **Tested**

INTRODUCE ✓

Vocabulary: Lesson 19

brew	snug

▼ **Student-Friendly Explanations**

Student-Friendly Explanations

brew	When you brew a drink such as iced tea, you make it yourself by pouring very hot water over the tea and then cooling it.
snug	If a piece of clothing has a snug fit, it fits close to you.
innovation	When someone thinks of a new idea or product that solves a problem, the new idea or product is an innovation.
edible	If something is edible, you can eat it.

Grade 2, Lesson 19　　R102　　Vocabulary

Transparency R102

Grammar *Quick Write*

Words That Compare

5-DAY GRAMMAR	
DAY 1	Introduce Words That Compare
DAY 2	Identify Words That Compare
DAY 3	Use Words That Compare in Sentences
DAY 4	Apply to Writing
DAY 5	Weekly Review

Objectives

- *To recognize and use words that compare*
- *To use the endings -er and -est to write words that compare*

Daily Proofreading

Is todd the only boy in the clas

(Todd, class?)

Writing Trait

Strengthening Conventions

Usage Use this short lesson with children's own writing to build a foundation for revising/editing longer connected text on Day 5.

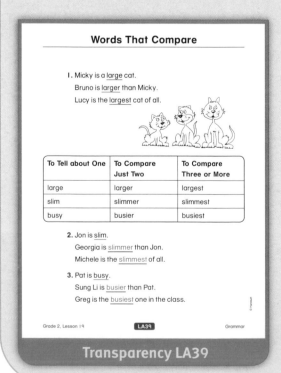

Transparency LA39

Teach/Model

INTRODUCE WORDS THAT COMPARE Explain that some adjectives compare two or more persons, places, or things. Write the following on the board: **Winter is *cold*. Winter is *colder* than fall. Winter is the *coldest* season of all!**

Have children read aloud the sentences. Explain that when two things are compared and *than* is used, such as in sentence 2, *-er* is added to the adjective. When more than two things are compared, such as in sentence 3, *-est* is added.

Write these words on the board, and explain the following:

- For adjectives that end in *e*, drop the *e* and then add *–er* or *–est*.

wide   **wid*er***   **wid*est***

- For a one-syllable adjective that has a short vowel and a consonant at the end, double the last letter and then add *–er* or *–est*.

wet   **wett*er***   **wett*est***

- For adjectives that end in a consonant and *y*, change the *y* to *i* and then add *–er* or *–est*.

lucky   **lucki*er***   **lucki*est***

Guided Practice

COMPLETE SENTENCES Display **Transparency LA39**. Read the first three sentences with children. Point out the underlined words. Explain why *large* has the *–er* or *–est* ending. Read the words in the chart. Complete the remaining items together.

Practice/Apply

WRITE SENTENCES Have children write three sentences using one of the adjectives *quick*, *quicker*, or *quickest* in each sentence. Have partners check for correct spelling and usage.

Writing
Narrative: Biography

5-DAY WRITING	
DAY 1	Introduce
DAY 2	Prewrite
DAY 3	Draft
DAY 4	Revise
DAY 5	Revise

Teach/Model

INTRODUCE NARRATIVE: BIOGRAPHY Display **Transparency LA40,** and explain that it is a narrative written by a child about her mother's life. Explain that a narrative about someone else's life is called a **biography**. Read aloud the biography, and develop a list of characteristics.

Narrative: Biography

- A narrative tells a story about a real person, event, or thing.
- A biography is a narrative about a real person's life other than you.
- A biography tells events in time order.
- A biography has facts about the person's life.

WRITING TRAIT **WORD CHOICE** Discuss how the writer uses both the words *mother* and *Mom* to help readers understand it is her mother that she is writing about.

Guided Practice

DRAFT A SHORT BIOGRAPHY Model writing a biographical paragraph about a child in your classroom. Ask a volunteer to name a few details about his or her life. Begin with a sentence such as "Jena Cheng was born in Dallas, Texas, in 2002." Point out that biographical details should be in time order.

Practice/Apply

WRITE A BEGINNING SENTENCE Have children interview a partner and start writing a biography. Have each child write a beginning sentence for the biography that tells who the person is and where the person was born. They can take turns reading their sentences to each other. Have them save the sentences for use on Days 2–5.

Objectives

- *To identify the elements of a biographical narrative*
- *To write notes about another person's life*
- *To write the first sentence of a biographical paragraph*

Writing Prompt

Write a Narrative Have children write a narrative about a day in your classroom.

Student Model: Narrative: Biography

The Life of Mom
by Karla Ramirez

Early Life in Seattle

My mother was born in Seattle, Washington, in 1975. Mom lived there until she finished kindergarten. Then her family moved to Chicago.

Mom Meets Dad in College

Mom lived in Chicago until she went to college in Boston. That is where she met my dad. Mom says Dad was shy when he first talked to her. But she liked him right away.

Back to Seattle!

Mom and Dad got married after college. Mom got a job as a teacher. Guess where it was? In Seattle! So, she and Dad moved to Seattle. That is where I was born. We still live in Seattle, and Mom teaches third grade.

Grade 2, Lesson 19   **LA40**   Writing

Transparency LA40

Day at a Glance

Day 2

 **and Spelling**

- Review: *r*-Controlled Vowel /ir/*ear, eer*
- Build Words

Robust Vocabulary

Words from the Selection

- Introduce: *supplies, crop, provide, earn, committee, experiments*

Comprehension

 Answer Questions

 Locate Information

Reading

- "The Life of George Washington Carver," *Student Edition,* pp. 122–135

 **Read!**

Fluency

- Accuracy

Robust Vocabulary

Words About the Selection

- Introduce: *innovation, edible*

Grammar **Quick Write**

- Review: Words That Compare

Writing

- Narrative: Biography

Warm-Up Routines

 Oral Language

Objective *To listen attentively and respond appropriately to oral communication*

Question of the Day

Do you eat foods made with peanuts? Tell about what peanut foods you eat and why.

Help children think about the different kinds of foods that use peanuts. Use the following prompts:

- **Name sandwiches that are made with a peanut product and other ingredients.**

- **What are some desserts or candies that are made with peanuts?**

Then have children complete the following sentence frame.

I _____ eat foods made with peanuts because _____.

Read Aloud

Objective *To listen for a purpose*

BIG BOOK OF RHYMES AND POEMS Display the poem "Nuts to You and Nuts to Me!" on page 35 and read aloud the title. Ask children to listen closely to hear the different kinds of nuts that the speaker lists. Then track the print as you read the poem aloud. Invite children to tell how they think the speaker feels about nuts.

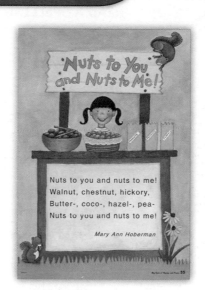

▲ **Big Book of Rhymes and Poems, p. 35**

Word Wall

Objective *To read high-frequency words*

REVIEW HIGH-FREQUENCY WORDS Point to the following words on the Word Wall: *already, different, everything, idea, imagine,* and *through* as well as other previously learned high-frequency words. Ask children to read each word aloud in unison, spell it, and read it again. Then point to words at random. For each word, have children read it, spell it, and read it again.

| already | different | everything |
| idea | imagine | through |

r-Controlled Vowel /ir/ ear, eer

 phonics *and Spelling*

Objectives

- *To blend sounds into words*
- *To spell three-, four-, five-, and six-letter words with r-Controlled vowel /ir/*

Skill Trace

Tested *r-Controlled Vowel /ir/ ear, eer*

Introduce	T304–T307
Reteach	S38–S39
Review	**T316–T317, T334–T335, T424**
Test	Theme 4
Maintain	Theme 6, T360

Spelling Words

1.	gear	6.	near
2.	deer	7.	hear
3.	fear	8.	clear
4.	year*	9.	steer
5.	cheer	10.	rear

Challenge Words

11.	appear	14.	earrings
12.	pioneer	15.	nearby
13.	volunteer		

* Word from "The Life of George Washington Carver"

Word Building

READ A SPELLING WORD Write the word *gear* on the board. Ask children to identify the letters that stand for the /ir/ sound. Have children read the word.

BUILD SPELLING WORDS Ask children which letter you should change to make *gear* become *near*. (Change *g* to *n*.) Write the word *near* on the board. Point to the word, and have children read it. Continue building spelling words in this manner. Say:

- **Which letter do I have to change to make the word *hear*, as in the sentence *I hear music*?** (Change *n* to *h*.)

- **Which letters do I have to change to make the word *clear*?** (Change *h* to *cl*.)

- **Which letters do I have to change to make the word *cheer*?** (Change *lea* to *hee*.)

- **Which letters do I have to change to make the word *deer*, as in the sentence *The deer is in the woods*?** (Change *ch* to *d*.)

gear
near
hear
clear
cheer
deer

Continue building the remaining spelling words in this manner.

BELOW-LEVEL	ADVANCED
Sort the Words Write all the spelling words on the board. Create a two-column chart with the headings *ear* and *eer*. Guide children to read each word aloud and tell you which column it should be written in.	**Homophones** Write *dear* and *deer* on the board. Point out that these two words are homophones: words that sound the same, but have different spellings and meanings. Have children think of other homophones.

5-DAY PHONICS/SPELLING

DAY 1	Pretest
DAY 2	Word Building
DAY 3	State the Generalization
DAY 4	Review
DAY 5	Posttest

Read Words in Context

APPLY PHONICS Write the following sentences on the board or on chart paper. Have children read each sentence silently. Then track the print as children read the sentence aloud.

Dad got me new football <u>gear</u>.

The team gave a big <u>cheer</u>.

My house is <u>near</u> the lake.

I got to <u>steer</u> the wagon.

After the rain, the sky was <u>clear</u>.

 WRITE Dictate several spelling words. Have children write the words in their notebooks or on a dry-erase board.

phonics Resources

Phonics Practice Book, pp. 115–120

MONITOR PROGRESS

r-Controlled Vowel /ir/ear, eer

IF children have difficulty building and reading words with the r-controlled vowel /ir/,

THEN write ear and eer on index cards and the first letters of words on other index cards. Use the cards to help children read ear, tear, dear, deer, and cheer.

Small-Group Instruction, pp. S38–S39:

● **BELOW-LEVEL:** Reteach
● **ON-LEVEL:** Reinforce
● **ADVANCED:** Extend

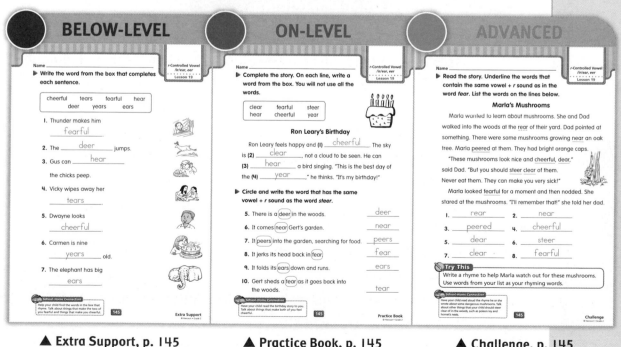

▲ Extra Support, p. 145   ▲ Practice Book, p. 145   ▲ Challenge, p. 145

ELL

• Group children according to academic levels, and assign one of the pages on the left.

• Clarify any unfamiliar concepts as necessary. See *ELL Teacher Guide* Lesson 19 for support in scaffolding instruction.

Build Robust Vocabulary

Words from the Selection

Objective

• *To build robust vocabulary*

Tested

INTRODUCE ✓

Vocabulary: Lesson 19

supplies	earn
crop	committee
provide	experiments

▼ **Student-Friendly Explanations**

Student-Friendly Explanations	
supplies	Supplies are the materials and equipment needed to do a job.
crop	A large planting of one kind of plant is a crop.
provide	When you provide something, you give it to someone.
earn	When you earn, you get money or some other kind of reward for doing something.
committee	When you are on a committee, you work with a group of people on a project or for a special reason.
experiments	Experiments are tests to try out an idea or to find out if something is true.

Grade 2, Lesson 19   **R103**   Vocabulary

Transparency R103

Word Detective

Find Words Tell children to share with a partner the Vocabulary Words they saw or heard. HOMEWORK/INDEPENDENT PRACTICE

Teach/Model

 Routine Card **4**

INTRODUCE ROBUST VOCABULARY Introduce the words using the following steps.

❶ Display Transparency R103 and read the word and the **Student-Friendly Explanation**.
❷ Have children **say the word** with you.
❸ Have children **interact with the word's meaning** by asking them the appropriate question below.

• What kind of **supplies** would you take on a camping trip?

• Name some **crops** that end up in your local grocery store.

• Name some ways you could **provide** help to your family.

• What are some ways you could **earn** money to buy things?

• How might a **committee** of people make a decision?

• How could you do **experiments** with a recipe?

Develop Deeper Meaning

EXPAND WORD MEANINGS: PAGES 120–121 Have children read the passage. Then read the passage aloud, pausing at the end of page 120 to ask children questions 1–3. Read page 121 and then discuss children's answers to questions 4–6.

1. Why would peanut plants be an important **crop**?

2. How do some states **provide** peanuts to the rest of the country?

3. What **supplies** would you need to make a peanut butter and jelly sandwich?

4. What might scientists find when they perform peanut **experiments**?

5. What would people on a **committee** need to know to decide which peanuts taste the best?

6. Other than farmers, who else might **earn** money from peanuts?

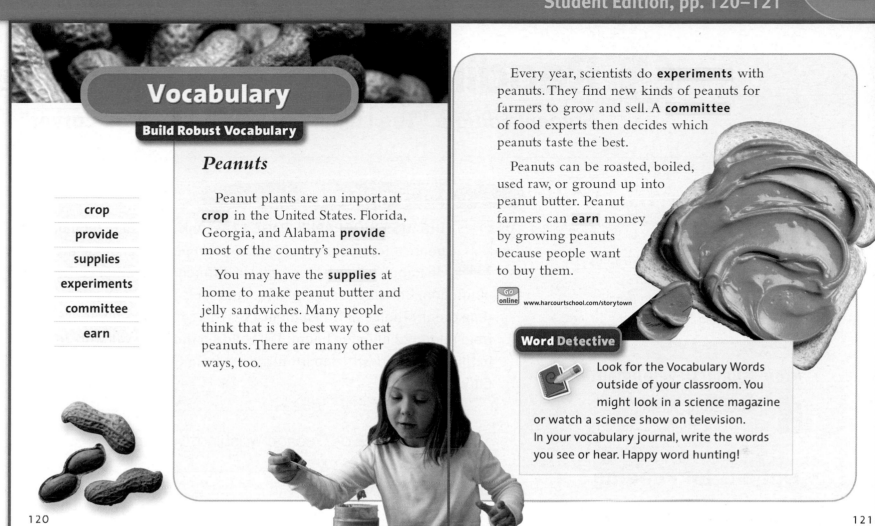

Vocabulary

Build Robust Vocabulary

crop

provide

supplies

experiments

committee

earn

Peanuts

Peanut plants are an important **crop** in the United States. Florida, Georgia, and Alabama **provide** most of the country's peanuts.

You may have the **supplies** at home to make peanut butter and jelly sandwiches. Many people think that is the best way to eat peanuts. There are many other ways, too.

Every year, scientists do **experiments** with peanuts. They find new kinds of peanuts for farmers to grow and sell. A **committee** of food experts then decides which peanuts taste the best.

Peanuts can be roasted, boiled, used raw, or ground up into peanut butter. Peanut farmers can **earn** money by growing peanuts because people want to buy them.

GO online www.harcourtschool.com/storytown

Word Detective

Look for the Vocabulary Words outside of your classroom. You might look in a science magazine or watch a science show on television. In your vocabulary journal, write the words you see or hear. Happy word hunting!

120

121

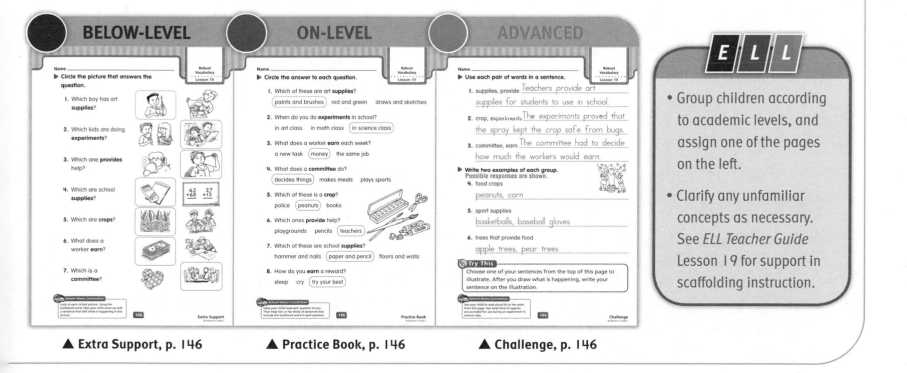

▲ Extra Support, p. 146   ▲ Practice Book, p. 146   ▲ Challenge, p. 146

E L L

- Group children according to academic levels, and assign one of the pages on the left.

- Clarify any unfamiliar concepts as necessary. See *ELL Teacher Guide* Lesson 19 for support in scaffolding instruction.

Reading

Student Edition: **"The Life of George Washington Carver"**

Objectives

- *To understand characteristics of a biography*
- *To answer questions as a strategy to monitor comprehension*
- *To apply word knowledge to the reading of a text*

Professional Development

 Podcasting: Answer Questions, Grades 2–6

Options for Reading

● BELOW-LEVEL

Preview Have children preview the selection by looking at the photographs. Guide them to predict what the selection will be about. Read each page, and have children read it after you.

● ON-LEVEL

Monitor Comprehension Have children read the selection. Ask the Monitor Comprehension questions as you go. Then lead them in retelling the selection.

● ADVANCED

Independent Reading Have children read each page silently, looking up each time they finish a page. Ask the Monitor Comprehension questions when they finish.

Genre Study

 DISCUSS BIOGRAPHY: PAGE 122 Ask children to read the genre information on *Student Edition* page 122. Guide them to distinguish how a biography is different from other varieties of nonfiction. (It tells the story of a real person's life with events told in time order.) Then use **Transparency GO7** or copy the graphic organizer from page 122 onto the board. Tell children that they will work together to fill in the chart with important events from George Washington Carver's life.

```
┌─────────────────────────────────────────┐
│   The Life of George Washington Carver   │
└─────────────────────────────────────────┘
                    ↓
┌─────────────────────────────────────────┐
│                 Heading                  │
│                  Detail                  │
└─────────────────────────────────────────┘
                    ↓
┌─────────────────────────────────────────┐
│                 Heading                  │
│                  Detail                  │
└─────────────────────────────────────────┘
                    ↓
┌─────────────────────────────────────────┐
│                 Heading                  │
│                  Detail                  │
└─────────────────────────────────────────┘
```

Comprehension Strategy

 ANSWER QUESTIONS: PAGE 122 Have children read the Comprehension Strategy information on page 122. Explain that good readers learn how to answer questions about what they are reading. Tell children that the answers to some questions are found by looking back in the selection. Other questions may require them to think about the information in the selection and then use their own knowledge to come up with an answer. Remind them that when they need to locate information for an answer quickly, they can look for key words in the headings. Explain that they might need to put different details together to answer a question.

THE LIFE OF

George Washington Carver

Genre Study

A **biography** is the story of a person's life. Look for

- events in time order.
- headings that tell what each section is about.

Comprehension Strategy

 Answer questions by looking back at the information you read in the selection.

BY JOLI K. STEVENS

George Washington Carver

122

123

Build Background

DISCUSS SCIENTISTS AND INVENTORS   Tell children that they are going to read about the life of George Washington Carver. Point out that Carver was a scientist and inventor who lived more than one hundred years ago. Invite volunteers to tell you what they know about scientists and inventors.

Routine Card 6

SET A PURPOSE AND PREDICT   Tell children that they will read this selection to get information about George Washington Carver.

- Have children read the title and headings.

- Review the photographs with children. Ask: **What do you think George Washington Carver was famous for?**

- List their predictions on the board.

- Have children read the biography to learn why George Washington Carver was an important scientist and inventor.

TECHNOLOGY

 eBook   "The Life of George Washington Carver" is available in an eBook.

 Audiotext   "The Life of George Washington Carver" is available on *Audiotext Grade 2, CD 4* for subsequent readings.

A long time ago, people didn't eat peanuts. Peanuts were used only to feed animals. A man named George Washington Carver changed that. This is his story.

Childhood

1 George Washington Carver was born around 1864 in Missouri. George and his brother, James, were raised by Moses and Susan Carver. The Carvers did not have children of their own. The boys called the Carvers Uncle Moses and Aunt Susan.

The Moses Carver House near Diamond Grove, Newton County, Missouri

George Washington Carver as a young boy

George was often sick as a child. Instead of doing farm work, he helped in the house. **2** George had his own garden. He liked to care for sick plants and make them healthy. People began to call George "the plant doctor." **3**

124

125

Monitor Comprehension

PAGES 124–125 Say: **The heading is "Childhood." Read to find out what George Washington Carver's childhood was like.**

1 NOTE DETAILS **Where and when was George Washington Carver born?** (in Missouri around 1864)

2 DRAW CONCLUSIONS **Why did George Washington Carver help around the house instead of on the farm? Read the part of the page that tells you so.** (Possible response: George was often sick. I know that farm work is hard and difficult to do if you're not strong.)

3 MAKE PREDICTIONS **George Washington Carver loved plants as a child. What kinds of jobs that involve plants might he choose when he grows up? Explain.** (Possible response: Since George loved plants and was good at taking care of them, he might work with plants when he grows up.)

Apply
Comprehension Strategies

Focus Strategy

Answer Questions Remind children that good readers answer questions by looking back at information in the selection. Explain that some answers may be "right there" in the text, while other answers come from what readers already know.

Think Aloud I want to answer the question, "Where and when was George Washington Carver born?" So I look back in the selection for the answer. The heading "Childhood" is a good clue that the information will be in this part, and it is. George Washington Carver was born in Missouri around 1864. The answer is right there.

George liked to learn about the world around him. Aunt Susan taught him to read and write, but he wanted to know more. He was always asking questions. He wanted to go to school, but the closest school for African American children was many miles away.

School Days

When George was about 12, he set off for Lincoln School, 8 miles away. He learned all that school could teach him. Then he knew he must find a new school to be able to keep learning.

George was about 16 when he moved to Fort Scott, Kansas. From then on, he moved from place to place to earn money for school by doing odd jobs. He had to pay for his books and school supplies himself. In one town, he found that another person named George Carver was living there. So he added a *W* to his own name. "It is for Washington," he told his friends. George Washington Carver became his new name. **2**

Lincoln School was a one-room schoolhouse like this one.

126   127

Monitor Comprehension

PAGES 126–127   Say: **The picture on pages 126–127 looks like a school. The heading on page 127 is "School Days." So this part must have to do with George's life in school. Read to find out.**

1 **NOTE DETAILS**   Why did George have to leave his first school? (He had learned everything there was to learn at that school.)

2 **MAKE INFERENCES**   How do you think 16-year-old George Washington Carver may have felt about leaving home to look for a new school so he could keep learning? Why do you think this? (Possible response: George liked to learn, so he must have felt excited at the possibility of finding a new school. But, he also must have been sad to leave his home.)

BELOW-LEVEL

Inflected Endings   Point to the words *learn*, *learned*, and *learning* on page 126, and in the first paragraph on page 127. Read *learn* aloud. Then point to *learned* and ask children to identify what ending has been added to learn. *(-ed)* Have children read the word with you. Repeat the procedure with *learning*. Discuss why the word *learn* might be important in a section called "School Days." Then have children follow along as you read the paragraph aloud. Tell children to notice how the word *learn* changes throughout the paragraph.

Not many African Americans went to college in the 1890s. George Washington Carver had to save money for college until he was almost 30 years old. He finally entered Simpson College, in Iowa, where he studied art. Later he went to Iowa State College to study science. He was asked to become a teacher there. **1**

Teacher and Scientist **3**

The president of Tuskegee Institute, Booker T. Washington, soon heard about George Washington Carver. He asked him to teach at Tuskegee, in Alabama. Tuskegee had poor land and poor farmers all around it. George Washington Carver saw that he could help. He got to work right away. **2**

George Washington Carver's graduation photo from Iowa State College in 1894

George Washington Carver belonged to this group, the Welch Eclectic Society, while he was a student at Iowa State College

The teacher and his students in a science class at the Tuskegee Institute

128

129

Monitor Comprehension

PAGES 128–129 Have children describe what they see. Say: **The heading on page 128 is "Teacher and Scientist." Read to find out how George Washington Carver became a teacher and a scientist.**

1 NOTE DETAILS/SEQUENCE **Where did George Washington Carver first become a teacher?** (Iowa State College)

2 DRAW CONCLUSIONS **Why do you think Booker T. Washington wanted George Washington Carver to come to the Tuskegee Institute in Alabama?** (Possible responses: There were very few African American teachers; Perhaps he thought George could help the farmers grow better crops.)

3 *Focus Skill* LOCATE INFORMATION **Why would you turn to this page to answer a question about how George Washington Carver became a teacher?** (The heading "Teacher and Scientist" is a clue that the information would be in this section.)

ELL

Word Meanings Use the photograph on page 129 to clarify the meanings of *teacher* and *scientist*. Point to George Washington Carver and explain that, like you, he is helping younger people learn. Ask children to describe the place where George Washington Carver is teaching. Lead them to understand that he is in a laboratory helping students do a science experiment. Point to the picture and identify *teacher*, *students*, *experiment*, and science *supplies*. Have children repeat the words as you point to the images in the photograph and say them. Then ask children to point to the photograph and repeat the words.

George Washington Carver's students are examining mustard plants.

A mounted peanut plant collected by George Washington Carver.

George Washington Carver taught his students that changing crops in a field help the plants grow better.

A painting of George Washington Carver caring for lilies, by Betsy Graves Reyneau, 1942

He started with the soil. He saw that too many farmers were planting cotton. Planting the same crop every year had made the soil poor.

George Washington Carver studied other crops to see what would grow well and provide food and money for the farmers. He told the farmers to plant peanuts, cowpeas, and sweet potatoes. Those crops would put good things back into the soil. He said that the soil would be better if many things were planted. The farmers didn't want to plant new things. They were afraid that no one would buy them. **① ② ③**

130

131

Monitor Comprehension

PAGES 130–131 Say: **There are photographs of George Washington Carver and other people looking at plants. Read to find out if he helps the farmers.**

① **CONFIRM PREDICTIONS** **Was your prediction accurate about what George Washington Carver might do when he grew up? Why or why not?** (Possible response: Yes. I thought he would work with plants somehow.)

② **NOTE DETAILS** **Why were the farmers afraid to grow peanuts and sweet potatoes?** (They were afraid people would not buy those crops.)

③ **EXPRESS PERSONAL OPINIONS** **Do you think it was a good or bad idea for George Washington Carver to have the farmers do something they were afraid of? Explain.** (Possible response: Good, because he was smart and probably knew something that would help the farmers.)

SCIENCE

SUPPORTING STANDARDS

Plants and Their Environments Point out that George Washington Carver knew that cotton made the soil poor, which means that over time, the soil would not have enough food, or nutrients, for the plants. Explain that nutrients in the soil are just one thing from the environment that plants need to grow. Ask children to name two other things plants need to grow (light, water) and where these things come from (the sun, rain).

George Washington Carver at work

George Washington Carver discovered that the boll weevil, an insect that eats cotton, would not eat peanuts or sweet potatoes. He found nearly 300 ways to use peanuts. They could be used to make peanut butter, flour, cheese, candy, shampoo, glue, ink, soap, and coffee. He also found more than 100 ways to use sweet potatoes. Soon the farmers started planting these crops. **2**

1

George Washington Carver's typewriter

Plant materials had to be studied closely.

People wanted to pay George Washington Carver a lot of money to come and work for them. He always said no. Money was not important to him. He decided to use his savings to help people continue his work even after he died. He also started a museum that held many of the things he had made in his lab. He won many awards for his work. He was even asked to speak to a committee of the United States Congress about peanuts and sweet potatoes. **3**

132

133

Monitor Comprehension

PAGES 132–133 Say: **George Washington Carver was always studying something. Read to see if what he learned helped persuade the farmers to plant other crops.**

1 NOTE DETAILS **What were some uses for peanuts that George Washington Carver discovered?** (They could be used to make flour, cheese, candy, ice cream, butter, shampoo, glue, ink, soap, and coffee.)

2 MAKE INFERENCES **How do you think George Washington Carver discovered the uses for peanuts and sweet potatoes?** (Possible response: George Washington Carver was a scientist who knew about plants. He probably did experiments with the plants to figure out their uses.)

3 DRAW CONCLUSIONS **How do you know that George Washington Carver's ideas worked?** (Possible response: People wanted him to work for them. He was asked to speak to Congress about his ideas.)

Use Multiple Strategies

Ask Questions Say: Asking questions about a biography helps me think about what I read. I ask myself, "Why did George Washington Carver think planting peanuts and sweet potatoes was so important?" Then I look through the last few pages to see if I can find the answer. I see that these crops help put good things back into the soil. Also, they would not be eaten by boll weevils. Finally, George Washington Carver found many uses for these crops, so the farmers could sell them. This explains why George Washington Carver wanted them to grow these crops.

George Washington Carver died on January 5, 1943, when he was almost 80 years old. He was buried at Tuskegee Institute.

In 1946, the United States Congress named January 5 George Washington Carver Day. He once said, "Know science and science shall set you free, because science is truth." The truth is that George Washington Carver helped make the world a better place through his experiments and teaching.

George Washington Carver in 1915, when he was director of the Agriculture Department of the Tuskegee Institute

This bronze sculpture honors the famous scientist and teacher

134

Think Critically

1. Under which heading can you find information about the schools George Washington Carver attended? **LOCATE INFORMATION**

2. Why did some people call George Washington Carver "the plant doctor"? **IMPORTANT DETAILS**

3. What tells you that he was a good student? **MAKE INFERENCES**

4. Why was it important to farmers that George Washington Carver found many ways to use peanuts? **DRAW CONCLUSIONS**

5. **WRITE** Why does an inventor like George Washington Carver need to be creative? Use details from the selection to support your answer. **SHORT RESPONSE**

135

Think Critically

Respond to the Literature

1. "School Days" **LOCATE INFORMATION**

2. because he had a garden and would care for sick plants **IMPORTANT DETAILS**

3. Possible response: George Washington Carver liked to learn. He liked to ask questions. He learned all there was to learn at Lincoln School. **MAKE INFERENCES**

4. Possible response: With more uses for peanuts, the farmers could sell more crops and earn more money. **DRAW CONCLUSIONS**

5. **WRITE** Possible response: Inventors need to be creative to think of new ideas. For example, George Washington Carver thought of hundreds of different uses for peanuts and sweet potatoes. **SHORT RESPONSE**

ANALYZE AUTHOR'S PURPOSE

Author's Purpose Remind children that authors have a purpose, or a reason, for writing. After children have finished reading "The Life of George Washington Carver," ask:

Why did the author write "The Life of George Washington Carver"?

- to convince readers that peanuts and sweet potatoes are better to eat than other crops

or

- to inform readers about the life of a famous scientist and the important contributions he made

Check Comprehension
Summarizing

Objectives

- *To practice summarizing a biography*
- *To read accurately in a manner that sounds like natural speech*

RETELLING RUBRIC

4	Uses details to clearly summarize the selection
3	Uses some details to summarize the selection
2	Summarizes the selection with some inaccuracies
1	Is unable to summarize the selection

Professional Development

 Podcasting: Auditory Modeling

BELOW-LEVEL

Fluency Practice For fluency practice, have children read *Decodable Book 16,* the appropriate *Leveled Reader* (pp. T368–T371), or Story 19 in the *Strategic Intervention Interactive Reader.*

Summarize

  LOCATE INFORMATION Have children name a good way to locate information in this selection. (read the headings)

REVISIT THE GRAPHIC ORGANIZER Display completed **Transparency GO7.** Have children use the completed chart to summarize George Washington Carver's life.

STORY RETELLING CARDS The cards for the selection can be used for summarizing or to help complete the graphic organizer.

▲ Story Retelling Cards 1–6, "The Life of George Washington Carver"

 # Fluency
Accuracy

Teach/Model

 **READING WITH ACCURACY** Explain that good readers make sure they read words accurately and that they correct themselves if they make a mistake. Read the section "School Days" aloud. Model rereading when you make a mistake.

Practice/Apply

ECHO-READ Read aloud the rest of the selection modeling accuracy. Have children echo-read with you.
Routine Card 8

Build Robust Vocabulary

Words About the Selection

Teach/Model

Routine Card 3

INTRODUCE ROBUST VOCABULARY Use *Routine Card 3* to introduce the words.

❶ Put the word in **selection context**.

❷ Display Transparency R102 and read the word and the **Student-Friendly Explanation**.

❸ Have children **say the word** with you.

❹ Use the word in other contexts, and have children **interact with the word's meaning**.

❺ Remove the transparency. Say the Student-Friendly Explanation again, and ask children to **name the word** that goes with it.

❶ **Selection Context:** Using peanuts to make shampoo was an **innovation** of George Washington Carver's.

❹ **Interact with Word Meaning:** Which is an example of an innovation—wheels on a car or wings on a car? Why?

❶ **Selection Context:** Peanuts and sweet potatoes are **edible**.

❹ **Interact with Word Meaning:** What is an example of something that is edible—a large pizza or a large T-shirt? Why?

Practice/Apply

GUIDED PRACTICE Ask children to do the following:

• Think of an *innovation* that would help people in your school. Draw a picture of it and explain it to a classmate.

• Write a list of five *edible* things you might find in a market. Then write another list of five things in the market that are not edible. Use pictures if you do not know the names of some of the things. Explain your lists to a partner.

Objective

• *To develop robust vocabulary through discussing a literature selection*

Tested

INTRODUCE ✓

Vocabulary: Lesson 19

innovation	edible

▼ **Student-Friendly Explanations**

Student-Friendly Explanations

brew	When you brew a drink such as iced tea, you make it yourself by pouring very hot water over the tea and then cooling it.
snug	If a piece of clothing has a snug fit, it fits close to you.
innovation	When someone thinks of a new idea or product that solves a problem, the new idea or product is an innovation.
edible	If something is edible, you can eat it.

Grade 2, Lesson 19   R102   Vocabulary

Transparency R102

Grammar  Quick Write

Words That Compare

5-DAY GRAMMAR	
DAY 1	Introduce Words That Compare
DAY 2	Identify Words That Compare
DAY 3	Use Words That Compare in Sentences
DAY 4	Apply to Writing
DAY 5	Weekly Review

Objective

- *To recognize and write words that compare in sentences*

Daily Proofreading

Trisha has the small lunchbox in the clas

(smallest, class.)

Writing Trait

Strengthening Conventions

Adjectives Use this short lesson with children's own writing to build a foundation for revising/editing longer connected text on Day 5. See also *Writer's companion*, Lesson 19.

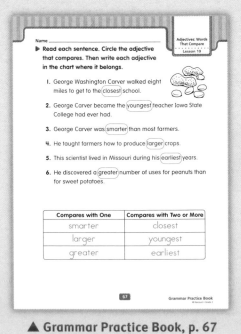

▲ Grammar Practice Book, p. 67

Review

WRITE WORDS THAT COMPARE Remind children that words with the ending -*er* compare two things, and that words with the ending -*est* compare more than two things. Write these sentences on the board.

- **Mika came home <u>late</u> than Sarah.**
- **A sweet potato is <u>big</u> than a peanut.**
- **He is the <u>busy</u> teacher in the school.**

Read aloud each sentence. Ask how many people or things are being compared. Then rewrite each sentence using the correct form of the word. (later, bigger, busiest) Remind children:

- For adjectives that end in *e*, drop the *e* and add –*er* or –*est*.
- For adjectives that end in a short vowel and a consonant, double the last letter and add –*er* or –*est*.
- For adjectives that end in a consonant and *y*, change the *y* to *i* and add –*er* or –*est*.

Guided Practice

MODEL USING WORDS THAT COMPARE Write these sentences on the board. Model how to rewrite the first sentence with the correct word that compares. Ask children to tell you how to rewrite the second sentence.

- **George was the sicker of all the children.** (sickest)
- **Growing crops was roughest in the 1900s than today.** (rougher)

Practice/Apply

WRITE SENTENCES Have children write sentences using the rules for adjectives that compare. Have partners switch papers to check for correct usage.

Writing
Narrative: Biography

5-DAY WRITING

DAY 1	Introduce
DAY 2	Prewrite
DAY 3	Draft
DAY 4	Revise
DAY 5	Revise

Prewrite

ORGANIZE YOUR NOTES   Have children look at the notes and sentences they wrote about their partner's life on Day 1 (page T313). Ask them to think of more information about their partner's life that they would want to include in their biography.

WORD CHOICE   Tell children to choose words that will help their audience know about the person they are describing. Encourage them to generate a list of descriptive words they can use to express feelings about the person.

MODEL PREWRITING   Copy on the board the chart below. Fill in the headings. Explain that a biography answers the questions *Who? What? Where?* and *When?* about a person's life. Tell children that a chart is a good way to organize the answers to these questions. Point out that it can help them put events in correct time order and identify headings for the parts of their biography. Model how to complete this chart as if children were writing a biography about you.

Who	What	Where and When
Mrs. Garcia	was born	in Texas in 1973
her mother and father	were also teachers	in Maryland and Texas
Mrs. Garcia	went to school	in Ohio

Practice/Apply

GUIDED PRACTICE   Ask children to create a similar chart to note the details they have learned about their partner. Have volunteers share their completed charts with the class.

INDEPENDENT PRACTICE   Have children use their completed charts to write headings for two parts of the biography. Have children save their notes, charts, and headings for use on Days 3–5.

Objectives

- *To develop ideas for writing about another person's life*
- *To use a graphic organizer for prewriting*

Writing Prompt

Independent Writing   Have children write three or four sentences about the life of one of their family members or friends.

Dictate Sentences   Pair children with a classmate whose first language is English. Have partners work together to complete the chart. Have children use the completed charts to dictate a sentence about their biography subject to their partner.

Day at a Glance

Day 3

phonics and Spelling

- Review: *r*-Controlled Vowel /ir/*ear*, *eer*

Fluency

- Accuracy
- "The Life of George Washington Carver," *Student Edition*, pp. 122–135

Comprehension

 Review: Locate Information

- Research/Study Skill: Review—Use Reference Sources

Reading

- "Nutty Facts About Peanuts," *Student Edition*, pp. 136–137

Robust Vocabulary

- Review: *brew, snug, supplies, crop, provide, earn, committee, experiments, innovation, edible*

Grammar

- Review: Words That Compare

Writing

- Narrative: Biography

Warm-Up Routines

Oral Language

Objective *To listen attentively and respond appropriately to oral communication*

> ### Question of the Day
> Think about something you could make with nuts. Describe how it would taste, look, and smell.

Help children think about different kinds of nuts. Ask:

- **What are some kinds of nuts people eat?**
- **How do the different kinds of nuts taste?**

Then have children complete the following sentences.

I would make _____ with nuts.

It would taste _____.

Read Aloud

Objective *To identify rhythm in poetry*

BIG BOOK OF RHYMES AND POEMS Display "Nuts to You and Nuts to Me!" on page 35 and ask children what they remember about the poem. Read aloud the middle two lines, emphasizing the rhythm of the words. Discuss how rhythm was created by the different nut names. Ask children if this wordplay makes the poem fun to listen to. Discuss. Then reread the poem, encouraging children to read along with you.

▲ **Big Book of Rhymes and Poems, p. 35**

Word Wall

Objective *To read high-frequency words*

REVIEW HIGH-FREQUENCY WORDS Review the following words on the Word Wall: *already, different, everything, idea, imagine,* and *through* as well as other previously learned high-frequency words. Point to each card and have children spell and read the word while they clap to the beat. Then invite volunteers to point to the cards as the class reviews the words several times.

already	different	everything
idea	imagine	through

r-Controlled Vowel /ir/ ear, eer and Spelling

5-DAY PHONICS	
DAY 1	Introduce /ir/*ear, eer*
DAY 2	Word Building with /ir/*ear, eer*
DAY 3	Word Building with /ir/*ear, eer*
DAY 4	VC/V; Review /ir/*ear, eer*
DAY 5	VC/V; Review /ir/*ear, eer*

Objectives

- *To use common spelling patterns to build and read words*
- *To read and write common word families*
- *To recognize spelling patterns*

Skill Trace

 Tested *r*-**Controlled Vowel /ir/*ear, eer***

Introduce	T304–T307
Reteach	S38–S39
Review	T316–T317, T334–T335, T424
Test	Theme 4
Maintain	Theme 6, T360

r-Controlled Vowel /ir/*ear, eer*

The deer walked by the garden.
Marco did not fear the thunder.
The letter started "Dear Sam."
The coach gave a cheer for his team.
The sad girl had a tear in her eye.
Mom had to steer the car around the other cars.
Are the rules about using the rear door of the classroom clear?

Grade 2, Lesson 19   R99   Phonics

Transparency R99

Work with Patterns

INTRODUCE PHONOGRAMS   Write the following phonograms at the top of a two-column chart.

-ear	-eer

Tell children that these are the endings of some words. Slide your hand under the letters as you read each phonogram. Repeat, having children read the phonograms with you.

BUILD AND READ WORDS   Write the phonograms *-ear* and *-eer* again in the appropriate columns. Then write the letter *d* in front of both phonograms. Guide children to read each word: /d/-*ear, dear*; /d/-*eer, deer*.

Have children name other words with the /ir/ sound that end with *-ear* or *-eer*. Have them tell which letter or letters to add to build each word, and write it on the board in the appropriate column. Have children read each column of words. Then point to words at random and have children read them.

Read Words in Context

READ SENTENCES   Display **Transparency R99** or write the sentences on the board or on chart paper. Have children choral-read the sentences as you track the print. Then ask volunteers to read each sentence aloud and to underline words with /ir/. Invite volunteers to add the words *fear, cheer, tear, steer, rear,* and *clear* to the appropriate column of phonograms.

5-DAY SPELLING

DAY 1	Pretest
DAY 2	Word Building
DAY 3	**State the Generalization**
DAY 4	Review
DAY 5	Posttest

Review Spelling Words

STATE THE GENERALIZATION FOR /ir/ear, eer List spelling words 1–10 on chart paper or on the board. Circle the words with /ir/ spelled *ear*, and have children read them. Ask: **What is the same in each word?** (Each word has the /ir/ sound and the letters *ear*.) Repeat the procedure for /ir/ spelled *eer*, using a different colored chalk or marker to circle the words.

WRITE Have children make a two-column chart with the headings *ear* and *eer* in their notebooks. Have them write the spelling words in the appropriate column. Remind children to use their best handwriting and to use the chart to check their spelling.

ear	eer
gear fear	deer cheer

Handwriting

FIRM PRESSURE Remind children to press firmly as they write. Remind them that pressing too hard will make their hands tired and that pressing too lightly will make the words hard to see.

Decodable Books

Additional Decoding Practice

• **Phonics**
 r-Controlled Vowel /ir/*ear, eer*
• **Decodable Words**
• **High-Frequency Words**
 See the list in *Decodable Book 16*.
 See also *Decodable Books*, online (Take-Home Version).

▲ Decodable Book 16
"A Year at the Leary Place"

Spelling Words

1.	gear	6.	near
2.	deer	7.	hear
3.	fear	8.	clear
4.	year*	9.	steer
5.	cheer	10.	rear

Challenge Words

11.	appear	14.	earrings
12.	pioneer	15.	nearby
13.	volunteer		

* Word from "The Life of George Washington Carver"

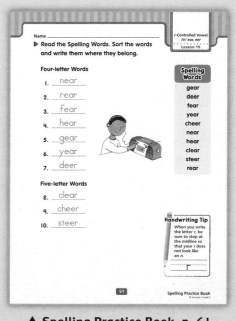

▲ Spelling Practice Book, p. 61

Fluency
Accuracy

Objective

- *To read accurately and fluently in a manner that sounds like natural speech*

 ### BELOW-LEVEL

Fluency Practice   Have children reread *Decodable Book 16*, Story 19 in the *Strategic Intervention Interactive Reader*, or the appropriate *Leveled Reader* (pp. T368–T371). Have them practice reading the text several times.

Additional Related Reading

- *From Peanut to Peanut Butter* by Robin Nelson. Lerner, 2003. **EASY**

- *The Living Earth* by Eleonore Schmid. North-South, 2000. **AVERAGE**

- *The Life and Times of the Peanut* by Charles Micucci. Houghton Mifflin, 2000. **CHALLENGE**

Review

DIBELS
Oral Reading Fluency
ORF

MODEL READING WITH ACCURACY   Remind children that good readers make sure that they read every word correctly. Tell children to:

▲ **Student Edition, pp. 122–135**

- read slowly enough to pronounce each word correctly.

- think about the meanings of the words they read.

> **Think Aloud**   **I'm going to read aloud the first pages of "The Life of George Washington Carver." I'll read slowly so that I don't make a mistake, but not so slowly that it sounds uninteresting or makes no sense. If I make a mistake, I can easily go right back and quickly reread correctly.**

Practice/Apply

Routine Card 9

GUIDED PRACTICE   Read pages 124–125 aloud. Then have children practice reading the same two pages several times with a partner. Circulate among the pairs of children, correcting any mistakes you hear as children read.

INDEPENDENT PRACTICE   Have partners reread "The Life of George Washington Carver" aloud two or three times. Remind them to make sure they read each word accurately and to correct themselves if they make a mistake. Have the partner who is listening follow along in the *Student Edition* and alert the reader when he or she misreads a word.

Locate Information
Comprehension

Review

REVIEW LOCATE INFORMATION Ask children to give examples of how they can locate information quickly in a nonfiction selection or book. Remind them that they can find information by looking at tables of contents, chapter titles, and headings. Use a social studies textbook or a nonfiction trade book with chapter titles and headings to model how to locate information.

> **Think Aloud** First, I look at the table of contents. Once I find a chapter or lesson title that seems as if it will have the information I need, I turn to that page. Then, I can look at the headings. Once I find the right heading, I read through that section to find the information I need.

Practice/Apply

GUIDED PRACTICE Have children turn to the table of contents on page 4 of the *Student Edition*. Guide children to locate information in different parts of their reading book by asking questions like these: **Where would I find the page number that the fourth unit starts on?** (the table of contents) **On what page does "Mr. Putter and Tabby Write the Book" start?** (page 22) **On what page would you find a selection written by Aliki?** (page 98)

INDEPENDENT PRACTICE Have children use the *Student Edition* to locate information about George Washington Carver's work as a scientist.

- **Where in this book will I find information about George Washington Carver?** (on page 122 in the selection "The Life of George Washington Carver")

- **Turn to page 122. Scan the headings in the selection. In what part might I find information about George Washington Carver's work as a scientist?** (under the heading "Teacher and Scientist" on page 128)

Objective

- *To use titles, tables of contents, and headings to locate information in nonfiction text*

Skill Trace
 Tested Locate Information

Introduce	T224–T225
Reteach	S42–S43
Review	T253, T269, T281, T308–T309, T337, T353, T363, T416, T437
Test	Theme 4
Maintain	Theme 5, T279

Use Reference Sources

Research/Study Skill

Objective

- *To locate information using a variety of print and computer-based reference sources*

Skill Trace

Tested Use Reference Sources

Introduce	T254–T255
Reteach	S44–S45
Review	**T338–T339, T429, T438**
Test	Theme 4
Maintain	Theme 6, T273

✓ MONITOR PROGRESS

Use Reference Sources

IF children have difficulty determining which reference sources to use for different kinds of information,	**THEN** provide them with an atlas, a dictionary, a thesaurus, and an encyclopedia volume and work with them to look up different kinds of information.

Small-Group Instruction, pp. S44–S45:

- ● **BELOW-LEVEL:** Reteach
- ● **ON-LEVEL:** Reinforce
- ● **ADVANCED:** Extend

Teach/Model

REVIEW REFERENCE SOURCES Remind children that George Washington Carver was born in Missouri but also spent time in Kansas, Iowa, and Alabama. Ask children where they would find the locations of these states. (on a map of the United States) Elicit that they could find a map of the United States in an atlas. Display **Transparency R100** and review the different kinds of reference sources.

Think Aloud I think about which reference source will most likely have the information I need. If I need to find the meaning of a word, I can use a dictionary. If I want to find a synonym for that word, I can use a thesaurus.

Continue reviewing the reference sources listed on the transparency.

Guided Practice

CHOOSING REFERENCE SOURCES Guide children in choosing the appropriate reference sources. Ask: **Where would I find**

- **a chart about the weather where we live?** (in an encyclopedia or on a website)
- **information about the life of a President of the United States?** (in an encyclopedia, in a nonfiction book, or on a website)
- **a map of Mexico?** (in an atlas or on a website)
- **the meaning of the word *gentle*?** (in a dictionary)
- **a word that means the same as *gentle*?** (in a thesaurus)

Then guide children in locating information in each of the various reference sources listed on **Transparency R100**. Have them

- look for words in a dictionary and articles in an encyclopedia by using alphabetized guide words and key words.
- use key words in a search engine and URL addresses to locate web-based articles.

Practice/Apply

USING REFERENCE SOURCES   Provide copies of the various reference sources listed on **Transparency R100** and have children work with a partner to choose and list the appropriate reference sources where they located the following information:

- the meaning of the word *extraordinary*

- the birth date of Abraham Lincoln

- a synonym for the word *simple*

- a map of Canada

- an article about how to grow plants in the classroom

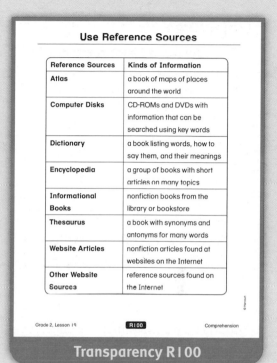

Use Reference Sources

Reference Sources	Kinds of Information
Atlas	a book of maps of places around the world
Computer Disks	CD-ROMs and DVDs with information that can be searched using key words
Dictionary	a book listing words, how to say them, and their meanings
Encyclopedia	a group of books with short articles on many topics
Informational Books	nonfiction books from the library or bookstore
Thesaurus	a book with synonyms and antonyms for many words
Website Articles	nonfiction articles found at websites on the Internet
Other Website Sources	reference sources found on the Internet

Grade 2, Lesson 19   R100   Comprehension

Transparency R100

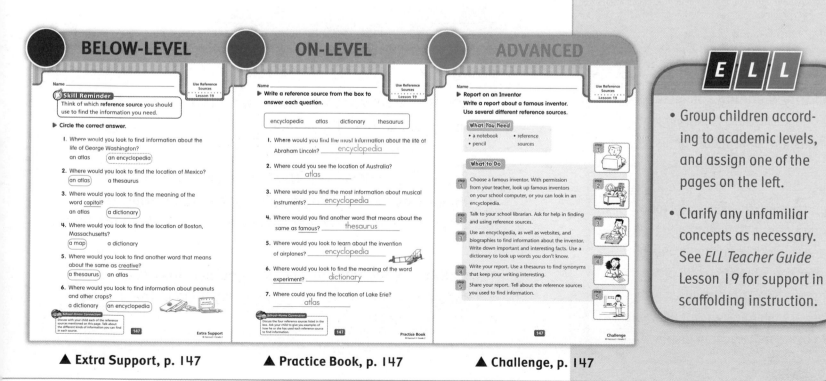

▲ Extra Support, p. 147   ▲ Practice Book, p. 147   ▲ Challenge, p. 147

ELL

- Group children according to academic levels, and assign one of the pages on the left.

- Clarify any unfamiliar concepts as necessary. See *ELL Teacher Guide* Lesson 19 for support in scaffolding instruction.

Reading
Student Edition: Paired Selection

Objectives

- *To understand characteristics of magazine articles*
- *To apply word knowledge to the reading of a text*

Writing Prompt

Reflect Work with children to use the facts from the article to write a short paragraph that answers the question *Why are peanuts so cool?* Have volunteers read their paragraphs aloud when they are done.

Clarify Meaning If possible, bring to class the following food items: an assortment of nuts, shelled peanuts, peas, and beans. Use these props to help children understand the concept of food families and to understand that peanuts are not actually nuts but members of the pea and bean family. If you have children with peanut allergies, do not allow them to be near the peanut display.

Genre Study

DISCUSS MAGAZINE ARTICLES Explain to children that "Nutty Facts About Peanuts" is an article from *Ranger Rick* magazine. Point out the magazine cover in the upper left-hand corner of page 136.

TEXT FEATURES Tell children that most magazine articles have features such as

- the title of the article.
- photographs and illustrations.
- captions—the words that tell about the pictures.
- charts, graphs, and diagrams.

USE PRIOR KNOWLEDGE/SET A PURPOSE Read aloud the title of the article. Point out that the article has different types of information about peanuts, such as a diagram and a list of fun facts. Guide children to use prior knowledge about peanuts to set a purpose for listening. Then ask volunteers to read different parts of the article aloud.

Respond to the Article

MONITOR COMPREHENSION Ask children to reread the article silently. Ask:

- **LOCATE INFORMATION** **Where would you look to find information about the number of states that have big peanut crops?** (under "Digital Peanuts")

- **PERSONAL RESPONSE** **What do you think is the most interesting or surprising fact about peanuts? Why?** (Possible response: It takes 720 peanuts to make a jar of peanut butter. That seems like a lot of peanuts!)

- **GENRE** **What helps you decide whether this article is fiction or nonfiction?** (There are many facts in the article, so it is nonfiction.)

Science

Ranger Rick

Magazine Article

Nutty Facts About Peanuts

by Gail Skroback Hennessey

Not a Nut, But a Pea

The next time you are taking a big lick of peanut butter, you can say that you are eating your vegetables. Peanuts are not really nuts but are close cousins of peas and beans.

136

Down-Under Wonder

Peanuts grow down, not up! First, a flower on a peanut plant is pollinated. Next, a tiny stem grows down toward the soil. Once it has pushed into the ground, its tip swells and grows into a pod. Usually two seeds form inside the pod. Then the pods can be dug up.

Digital Peanuts

2
The number of presidents who were peanut farmers.

6
The number of pounds of peanuts eaten by each person in the United States each year.

9
The number of states that have big peanut crops. Georgia grows the most.

300
The number of products that George Washington Carver made from the peanut plant. Some of these are shampoo, ink, plastic, and ice cream.

720
The number of peanuts needed to make a one-pound jar of peanut butter.

1,500
The number of peanut butter sandwiches the average American child has eaten by the time he or she finishes high school.

7 million
The pounds of peanut butter eaten each year by people in the United States.

137

🌐 **SOCIAL STUDIES**

SUPPORTING STANDARDS

Peanut Use in the United States   Explain that today peanuts are grown in India, China, and West Africa, as well as in parts of the United States. In the United States they are mostly grown to make peanut butter, to eat as nuts, and to use in candy and bakery products. In the southern part of the United States, the peanut plant is used as feed for cows and other livestock. After the peanuts are harvested from the plant, the rest of the plant is used as hay to feed animals. This means that peanuts are an important part of the food chain by which people in the United States get their food. Peanuts help feed the animals that give people food and milk.

 Connections

Objectives

- *To make connections between texts*
- *To make connections between texts and personal experiences*
- *To respond to text through writing*

Comparing Texts

1. Possible response: The facts showed how important peanuts are. Since George Washington Carver persuaded farmers to grow them, and he discovered so many ways to use them, he is a very important teacher and inventor. **TEXT TO TEXT**

2. Possible response: I have done an experiment to see if I could grow a plant from an avocado pit in a glass of water. **TEXT TO SELF**

3. Possible response: They want to find cures for illnesses. They want to find new sources of energy. They want to protect the environment. **TEXT TO WORLD**

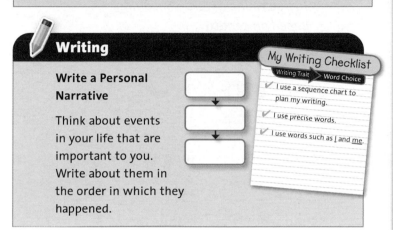

Connections

Comparing Texts

❶ How can "Nutty Facts About Peanuts" help you understand "The Life of George Washington Carver"?

❷ What kinds of experiments have you done?

❸ What kinds of problems do today's scientists want to solve?

Phonics

Write a Poem

Think of words that have the letters *ear* and *eer*. Use these words to make a rhyming poem. Then read your poem to a classmate.

I'd like to see a deer
come to me without fear.
I know I'd want to cheer
if a deer did come near.

138

Fluency Practice

Read Accurately

Choose a section of "The Life of George Washington Carver." Practice reading it aloud as a classmate follows along. Ask your classmate to point out words that you need to practice reading correctly.

Writing

Write a Personal Narrative

Think about events in your life that are important to you. Write about them in the order in which they happened.

My Writing Checklist
Writing Trait ⟩ Word Choice
✓ I use a sequence chart to plan my writing.
✓ I use precise words.
✓ I use words such as I and me.

139

PHONICS

Write a Poem Have children list words with *ear* and *eer* in two columns. After children check that their words are spelled correctly, have a volunteer read the sample poem on page 138. Have children point out the *ear* and *eer* words that rhyme. Have children use their lists as they write their poems.

I did not hear.
The deer come near.

FLUENCY

Read Accurately Pair children, and remind partners that they will take turns reading. Assign one child in each pair to read slowly and accurately the first page aloud. Remind children not to read so slowly that their reading does not sound natural. Listeners should call attention to mistakes and suggest that the reader reread these words accurately.

WRITING

Write a Personal Narrative Ask children:

• What is something that happened to you when you were younger?

• Are there any other events in your life that are important to you?

Portfolio Opportunity Children should illustrate their personal narratives and place them in their portfolios.

Build Robust Vocabulary

Objectives

- *To review robust vocabulary*
- *To determine a word's meaning based on context*

REVIEW Tested ✓

Vocabulary: Lesson 19

brew	innovation
supplies	crop
snug	edible
provide	earn
committee	experiments

Review Robust Vocabulary

USE VOCABULARY IN DIFFERENT CONTEXTS Remind children of the Student-Friendly Explanations of the Vocabulary Words introduced on Days 1 and 2. Then discuss each word, using the following prompts:

brew

- Would it make sense to say that you can brew milk? Why or why not?
- What would you need to brew a pot of tea?

supplies

- What supplies would you need to plant a garden?
- Suppose you wanted to make a card for a sick friend. What supplies would you use to decorate the card?

snug

- If you were wearing a pair of gloves in winter, would you want them to have a snug fit on your hands? Why?
- If books were too snug on a bookshelf, would it be hard to remove a book from the shelf? Explain.

provide

- If you do not provide food and water for a pet, will the pet be healthy and happy? Explain.
- What things do your family members provide you with to keep you safe, healthy, and happy?

committee

- If you were on a committee to decide where a new playground would be built, would you make the decision alone? Why?
- What kind of people might be on a committee that takes care of flowers and trees in a park? Explain.

innovation

- Would a backpack attached to a jacket be a good innovation? Why or why not?
- How might you make a new kind of pencil that would be called a great innovation?

crop

- Which of these is *not* an example of a crop: corn, peanuts, Popsicles? Why?
- Would you be more likely to find crops in a city park or on a farm? Explain.

edible

- What are some edible things you enjoy most? Why do you enjoy them?
- What are some edible things you wish you never had to have? Why don't you want them?

earn

- Tell about a time when you tried to earn money to buy something special.
- Tell how you would earn the trust of a parent, a teacher, a friend, or a pet.

experiments

- If you do experiments to see if ants like honey, what might you do?
- Describe experiments you could do to find out how people react to loud and soft sounds.

▼ Student-Friendly Explanations

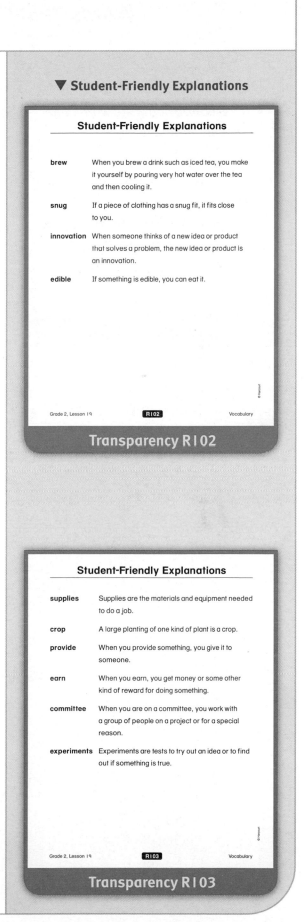

Student-Friendly Explanations

brew	When you brew a drink such as iced tea, you make it yourself by pouring very hot water over the tea and then cooling it.
snug	If a piece of clothing has a snug fit, it fits close to you.
innovation	When someone thinks of a new idea or product that solves a problem, the new idea or product is an innovation.
edible	If something is edible, you can eat it.

Grade 2, Lesson 19   R102   Vocabulary

Transparency R102

Student-Friendly Explanations

supplies	Supplies are the materials and equipment needed to do a job.
crop	A large planting of one kind of plant is a crop.
provide	When you provide something, you give it to someone.
earn	When you earn, you get money or some other kind of reward for doing something.
committee	When you are on a committee, you work with a group of people on a project or for a special reason.
experiments	Experiments are tests to try out an idea or to find out if something is true.

Grade 2, Lesson 19   R103   Vocabulary

Transparency R103

Grammar [Quick Write]

Words That Compare

5-DAY GRAMMAR

DAY 1	Introduce Words That Compare
DAY 2	Identify Words That Compare
DAY 3	**Use Words That Compare in Sentences**
DAY 4	Apply to Writing
DAY 5	Weekly Review

Objective

• *To recognize and write words that compare in sentences*

Daily Proofreading

The girls's bikes were biger than the boys' bikes

(girls', bigger, bikes.)

TECHNOLOGY

 GO online www.harcourtschool.com/storytown
Grammar Glossary

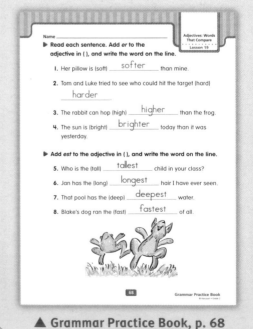

▲ Grammar Practice Book, p. 68

Review

WRITE WORDS THAT COMPARE IN SENTENCES Write these sentences on the board.

> Monte was the <u>smallest</u> of the three puppies.
> Ana was the <u>shortest</u> of the four cousins.
> Florida is much <u>hotter</u> than Alaska.
> Felix thought the plum was <u>tastier</u> than the apple.

Read aloud the first two sentences. Ask children how many things are being compared in each. (three; four) Point to the underlined words *smallest* and *shortest*, and ask children if the *-est* ending is correct in these two words. (yes, because each sentence is comparing three or more things) Repeat the procedure for the next two sentences. Ask children how the words *hot* and *tasty* changed when the *-er* ending was added. (The ending consonant *t* was doubled in *hotter*, and the *y* was changed to *i* in *tastier*.)

Practice/Apply

GUIDED PRACTICE Write the following sentences on the board. Model how to rewrite the underlined word in the first sentence. Ask volunteers to tell how to rewrite the remaining sentences.

> Today's test was the <u>hard</u> of the year. (hardest)
> I am <u>big</u> than my little brother. (bigger)
> This is the <u>sunny</u> day so far. (sunniest)
> Peanuts are <u>crunchy</u> than sweet potatoes. (crunchier)

INDEPENDENT PRACTICE Have children write sentences that include a word that compares. Have children read their completed sentences aloud.

Writing
Narrative: Biography

5-DAY WRITING	
DAY 1	Introduce
DAY 2	Prewrite
DAY 3	**Draft**
DAY 4	Revise
DAY 5	Revise

Draft a Short Biography

REVIEW A LITERATURE MODEL Have children turn to page 124 in the *Student Edition*. Read aloud the first paragraph. Point out the following:

- The first heading shows that this section is about the person's childhood.
- The first sentence tells who the biography is about.
- The first sentence tells when and where George Washington Carver was born.
- The remaining sentences give details about George Washington Carver's childhood.

DRAFT A SHORT BIOGRAPHY Have children use the two headings, their completed chart, and their notes about their partner's life to draft a short, two-paragraph biography about their partner. Point out that they can consult with their partner to refresh their memory or to add more details. Remind them to make sure events are in time order and that each section gives information that goes with its heading.

 WORD CHOICE As children write their paragraphs, encourage them to use words that describe the person whom they are writing about so that readers of their biography will clearly know what the person is like. Encourage them to also include their feelings about the subject. Tell them that they will be able to check these words and change them or add new ones when they revise and edit later.

CONFER WITH CHILDREN Meet with individual children, helping them as they write their biography. Offer encouragement for what they are doing well, and make constructive suggestions for improving any aspect of their writing, as needed.

Objectives

- *To draft a short biography*
- *To present events in correct time order*
- *To include details about the biography subject*

 Writing Prompt

Explain Have children write a sentence that explains why young George Washington Carver was known as "the plant doctor."

▲ **Writer's Companion, Lesson 19**

ADVANCED

Use Figurative Language
Encourage children to use descriptive details, such as similes, in their biography. Have them write sentences with comparisons using *like* or *as*.

Warm-Up Routines

 **and Spelling**

- Introduce: Syllable Pattern VC/V
- Review: *r*-Controlled Vowel /ir/*ear*, *eer*

Fluency

- Accuracy
- "The Life of George Washington Carver," *Student Edition*, pp. 122–135

Read!

Comprehension

Review: Locate Information

Robust Vocabulary

- Review: *brew, snug, innovation, edible, supplies, crop, provide, earn, committee, experiments*

Grammar [Quick Write]

- Review: Words That Compare

Writing ✏

- Narrative: Biography

Day at a Glance

Day 4

 Oral Language

Objective *To listen attentively and respond appropriately to oral communication*

Question of the Day

What are seeds?
Tell what happens when seeds are planted in the ground.

Use the following prompts to help children understand that plants grow from seeds. Record children's responses on the board.

- **Name some things that have seeds.**
- **Tell what happens when seeds grow.**
- **What do you do with the seeds in a piece of fruit like an orange?**
- **Have you ever planted seeds in a garden? Tell how you did it.**

Read Aloud

Objective *To listen for enjoyment*

BIG BOOK OF RHYMES AND POEMS Display the poem "Tiny Seeds" on page 36 and read the title. Tell children to listen to the poem for enjoyment. Then read the poem aloud. Explain that a cradle is a small bed for a baby. Tell children that a "cradle" for a seed would be the covering that protects the seed until it is ready to grow into a plant. Ask children to describe the different ways that tiny seeds get around "everywhere" as described in the poem. Then discuss what might happen to a seed at the end of its "winter nap."

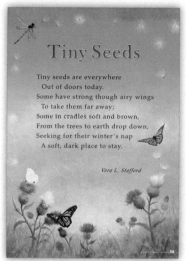

▲ **Big Book of Rhymes and Poems, p. 36**

Word Wall

Objective *To read high-frequency words*

REVIEW HIGH-FREQUENCY WORDS Point to the following words: *already, different, everything, idea, imagine,* and *through* as well as other previously learned high-frequency words. Have children read the words as a group, snapping their fingers to the syllables. Then have each child read one word aloud, continuing the rhythm. Continue until each child has had a chance to read aloud a word at least once.

already   different   everything

idea   imagine   through

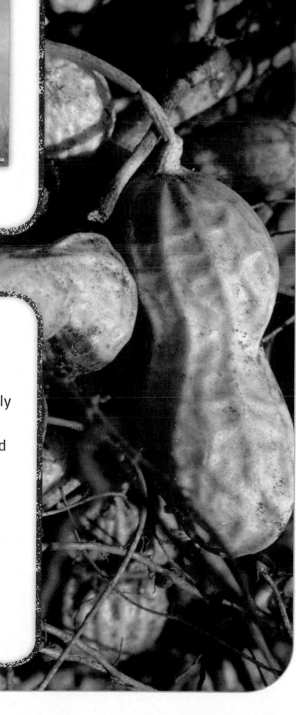

Syllable Pattern VC/V

 phonics

5-DAY PHONICS	
DAY 1	Introduce /ir/ear, eer
DAY 2	Word Building with /ir/ear, eer
DAY 3	Word Building with /ir/ear, eer
DAY 4	VC/V; Review /ir/ear, eer
DAY 5	VC/V; Review /ir/ear, eer

Objectives

- *To identify words with the syllable pattern VC/V*
- *To read words with the syllable pattern VC/V*

Skill Trace

 Tested **Syllable Pattern VC/V**

Introduce	T350
Review	T360

VC/V Syllable Pattern

The river was frozen all winter.

Dad put the cookies in the oven to bake.

Miguel could not finish all the peanuts.

Lara put her sweater in the closet.

Dad and I went to visit grandma.

Grade 2, Lesson 19   **R101**   Phonics

Transparency R101

Teach/Model

INTRODUCE SYLLABLE PATTERN VC/V   Write the word *finish* on the board and guide children to help you label the vowel/consonant/vowel pattern. Explain that in words with the VC/V pattern, the vowel sound before the break is usually short.

f i n / i s h

V C / V

MODEL DECODING VC/V WORDS   Model how to blend the syllables together to read *finish*. Cover the second syllable and have children read /fin/. Cover the first syllable and have them read /ish/. Then have them read the word—*finish*.

Distribute Syllabication Card 12 (*Teacher Resource Book* p. 92) and read it aloud. Write and demonstrate the examples on the board.

Guided Practice

IDENTIFY VC/V PATTERN   Make a chart as shown on the board. Say: *Clever* **has two syllables. The first vowel,** *e,* **has a short vowel sound, so the syllable break falls after the consonant,** *v.* **The first syllable is** *clev* **and the second syllable is** *er.* Blend and read the word. Follow a similar procedure with the other words.

Word	VC	V
clever	e v	e
lemon	em	o
cabin	ab	i

Practice/Apply

READ SENTENCES   Display **Transparency R101** or write the sentences on the board or on chart paper. Have children read the sentences aloud.

r-Controlled Vowel /ir/ ear, eer

 phonics *and Spelling*

5-DAY SPELLING

DAY 1	Pretest
DAY 2	Word Building
DAY 3	State the Generalization
DAY 4	**Review**
DAY 5	Posttest

Build Words

REVIEW THE WORDS Have children open their notebooks to the spelling words that they wrote on Day 3. Have them read the words several times and then close their notebooks.

MAP LETTERS TO SOUNDS Have children follow your directions to change one or more letters in each word to spell a spelling word. Have them write the word on a sheet of paper. Then have a volunteer change the spelling of the word on the board so that children can self-check their spelling.

- Write *deep* on the board. Ask: **Which spelling word can you make by changing the last letter?** *(deer)*

- Write *learn* on the board. Ask: **Which spelling word can you make by adding one letter to the beginning and dropping one letter at the end of the word?** *(clear)*

- Write *neat* on the board. Ask: **Which spelling word can you make by changing the last letter?** *(near)*

Follow a similar procedure for *tear (gear), star (steer), cheap (cheer), real (rear), your (year), heap (hear), spear (fear).*

CHALLENGE WORDS Write the first or second syllable of each challenge word on the board. Ask volunteers to spell each word in its entirety and write the missing letters.

BELOW-LEVEL

Focus on *r*-Controlled Vowel Write the spelling words on the board, with blanks where the letters that stand for the /ir/ sound should be. Then prompt children to complete each word.

Objective

- *To use /ir/ear and* eer *and other known letter-sounds to spell and write words*

Spelling Words

1.	gear	6.	near
2.	deer	7.	hear
3.	fear	8.	clear
4.	year*	9.	steer
5.	cheer	10.	rear

Challenge Words

11.	appear	14.	earrings
12.	pioneer	15.	nearby
13.	volunteer		

* Word from "The Life of George Washington Carver"

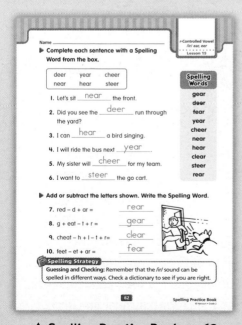

▲ Spelling Practice Book, p. 62

Fluency
Accuracy

Objective

- *To read accurately and fluently in a manner that sounds like natural speech*

✓ MONITOR PROGRESS

Fluency

IF children have difficulty reading accurately and in a manner that sounds like natural speech,	THEN have them tape-record their reading and listen to it to note places where they need to improve accuracy and work on sounding natural.

Small-Group Instruction, pp. S40–S41:

- ● **BELOW-LEVEL:** Reteach
- ● **ON-LEVEL:** Reinforce
- ● **ADVANCED:** Extend

● BELOW-LEVEL

Echo-Read   On the board, write the sentences with the list of products from the story that children might have trouble reading fluently. Read each sentence aloud and have children repeat, matching your speed, pronunciation, and phrasing. Repeat this procedure a number of times until children can read each sentence with little or no effort.

Review

 MODEL READING ACCURATELY   Read aloud page 132 of "The Life of George Washington Carver." Point out the list of items that George Washington Carver made from peanuts.

▲ Student Edition, pp. 122–135

Think Aloud   This sentence has a long list of items in it. When I read it, I read the name of each item carefully, but I don't want to stop for too long after each item. I want my reading to sound as if I'm telling someone all the different things that George Washington Carver made from peanuts. Still, I will be careful to read these words correctly since they are long words.

Practice /Apply

 GUIDED PRACTICE   Guide children to read page 132 with you, matching your expression and pronunciation.

INDEPENDENT PRACTICE   Have children read along with "The Life of George Washington Carver" on *Audiotext Grade 2,* CD 4. Have them practice reading the selection several times until they are able to read it with accuracy and in a manner that sounds like natural speech.

Locate Information
Comprehension

Review

REVIEW HOW TO LOCATE INFORMATION Ask children to explain how to locate information in a nonfiction book such as a biography. (Look at the table of contents to find chapter or lesson titles with key words that are related to the information you are looking for. Go to the chapter or lesson and look for key words in the headings.) Explain that being able to locate information quickly and easily can help children when they are doing research or looking for answers to questions.

Practice/Apply

GUIDED PRACTICE Display **Transparency R97.** Reread the biography aloud to children and ask them to identify the headings. ("A Dark Problem"; "A New Idea"; "A Big Success") Guide children to use the title and headings to locate information in the biography. Ask:

- **How would you quickly find out what the problem is?** (Look under the heading "A Dark Problem.")

- **Where would you look to find out about the new invention Becky thought of?** (Under the heading "A New Idea," because an invention is a new idea.)

- **What section is most likely to give information about whether Becky's idea was successful or not?** (The heading "A Big Success" has the key word *success,* so that section probably talks about how successful Becky's invention was.)

INDEPENDENT PRACTICE Ask children to tell you how they would find information about music in the *Student Edition.* (Use the table of contents on page 4 to find the title of the selection "Ah, Music!" Then turn to the beginning of the selection on page 98 and look for key words in the headings to find specific information.) Have children locate facts about three different musical instruments and write a sentence about each.

Objective

- *To use titles, tables of contents, and headings to locate information in nonfiction text*

Skill Trace

 Locate Information

Introduce	T224–T225
Reteach	S30–S31
Review	**T253, T269, T281, T308–T309, T337, T353, T363, T416, T437**
Test	Theme 4
Maintain	Theme 5, T279

Locate Information

A Glowing Idea

A Dark Problem

    One day, ten-year-old Becky Schroeder was trying to do her homework in the car. Becky's mother had run in to the store. Because it was starting to get dark, Becky could not see the words and numbers on the paper.

A New Idea

    Becky started to think about things that glowed in the dark. Some toys glowed in the dark. What if paper could glow in the dark, too?

    The next day Becky and her father bought special paint that glowed in the dark. Becky painted pieces of paper and turned out the lights. It took a lot of tries, but finally it worked. The paper glowed. Becky could read and write on it in the dark!

A Big Success

    Becky's invention was called the Glo-sheet. Soon people all over wanted to buy Glo-sheets. Becky and her father started a company to sell Glo-sheets. It was a huge success, all because of one glowing idea by a young girl!

Grade 2, Lesson 19   R97   Comprehension

Transparency R97

Build Robust Vocabulary

Objectives

- *To review robust vocabulary*
- *To understand vocabulary in new contexts*

REVIEW **Tested** ✓

Vocabulary: Lesson 19

brew	crop
snug	provide
innovation	earn
edible	committee
supplies	experiments

Extend Word Meanings

USE VOCABULARY IN DIFFERENT CONTEXTS   Remind children of the Student-Friendly Explanations of the Vocabulary Words. Then discuss each word in a new context.

supplies, crop   Tell children that you are going to name some farming supplies and some crops. Ask them to raise their hand if they hear the name of a farming supply. If it is a crop, they should do nothing.

water	seeds	potatoes
shovel	corn	tractor

innovation   Tell children that you will name some things. If they think it is an innovation that helps people do something, they should give the thumbs up sign. If not, they should give the thumbs down.

an apple	an elevator	a toaster
a space shuttle	an alligator	roller skates

brew   Tell children that you will ask some questions. If they think the question is about something that you brew, they should hold their hand to their mouth as if they are drinking from a glass and say "glug-glug-glug." If not, children should shake their head "no."

Should I put the sugar in your tea?

Is this meat tender?

When can I drink this coffee?

snug   Tell children that you will make some statements about how something fits. If they think it is about something that is too snug, they should say, "Too snug!" If they think it is not snug enough, they should say, "Not snug enough!"

My feet slide around in these shoes.

This hat is squeezing my head.

I can't breathe in these pants.

Word Relationships

SYNONYMS Remind children that a synonym is a word that has the same or almost the same meaning as that of another word. Write these sentences on the board, underlining the words as shown.

> My teacher was able to <u>offer</u> me art paper for the project.
>
> Did Joanna <u>make</u> enough money to buy a present for her mom?
>
> He did a science <u>test</u> to find out at what temperature water boils.
>
> The <u>group</u> met to talk about another project.
>
> The food was so burnt that it was barely <u>eatable</u>.

Ask children to read the sentences aloud and replace each underlined word with its vocabulary word synonym. (provide, earn, experiment, committee, edible) Ask children what reference source they might use to confirm the meanings of these synonyms. (a dictionary) Invite children to look up the words in a dictionary to confirm the word meanings.

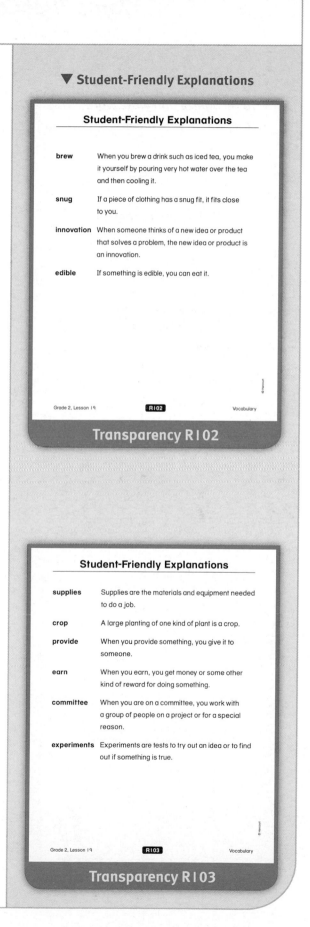

▼ **Student-Friendly Explanations**

Student-Friendly Explanations

brew	When you brew a drink such as iced tea, you make it yourself by pouring very hot water over the tea and then cooling it.
snug	If a piece of clothing has a snug fit, it fits close to you.
innovation	When someone thinks of a new idea or product that solves a problem, the new idea or product is an innovation.
edible	If something is edible, you can eat it.

Grade 2, Lesson 19   R102   Vocabulary

Transparency R102

Student-Friendly Explanations

supplies	Supplies are the materials and equipment needed to do a job.
crop	A large planting of one kind of plant is a crop.
provide	When you provide something, you give it to someone.
earn	When you earn, you get money or some other kind of reward for doing something.
committee	When you are on a committee, you work with a group of people on a project or for a special reason.
experiments	Experiments are tests to try out an idea or to find out if something is true.

Grade 2, Lesson 19   R103   Vocabulary

Transparency R103

Grammar *Quick Write*

Words That Compare

5-DAY GRAMMAR	
DAY 1	Introduce Words That Compare
DAY 2	Identify Words That Compare
DAY 3	Use Words That Compare in Sentences
DAY 4	**Apply to Writing**
DAY 5	Weekly Review

Objective

- *To recognize and write words that compare in sentences*

Daily Proofreading

Is this the taller building in the city

(tallest, city?)

Writing Trait ▶

Strengthening Conventions

Parts of Speech   Use this short lesson with children's own writing to build a foundation for revising/editing longer connected text on Day 5. See also *Writers Companion*, Lesson 19.

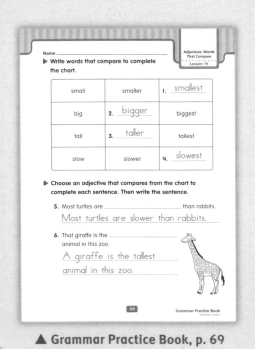

▲ Grammar Practice Book, p. 69

Review

DISCUSS WORDS THAT COMPARE   Review with children that *-er* words compare two things, and *-est* words compare three or more things. Write these sentences on the board:

It was the shorter tree in the forest.

Jared was happiest than his brother.

Kipper is a strongest horse than Chuck.

Pico the cat was quicker than a mouse.

Read the sentences aloud. Tell children that only one sentence is correct. Point to and read aloud the last sentence. Ask children how many animals are being compared. (two) Point out the word *quicker,* and confirm that it has the correct ending for comparing two things.

USE EDITOR'S MARKS   Work through the remaining sentences, correcting the words that compare as needed. Model using basic Editor's Marks to revise them.

Editor's Marks	
∧	Add
ℯ	Take out
⌐	Change
⊙	Add a period
≡	Capitalize

Practice/Apply

GUIDED PRACTICE   Write a sentence about peanuts, and include a word that compares. Elicit additional ideas from children. Write two more sentences, and model orally how to check that the correct form of the word that compares is used in each sentence.

INDEPENDENT PRACTICE   Ask children to write four sentences about plants. Tell children to use a word that compares just two things in the first two sentences, and a word that compares three or more things in the last two sentences. Have partners exchange sentences and check that the words that compare are written correctly.

Writing
Narrative: Biography

5-DAY WRITING	
DAY 1	Introduce
DAY 2	Prewrite
DAY 3	Draft
DAY 4	Revise
DAY 5	Revise

Revise Narratives

WRITE   Children will continue writing their biography. Remind them to make sure the events of the person's life are in time order. Explain that they can add paragraphs if they need to.

WORD CHOICE   Remind children to include words that will persuade readers to be interested in the subject of their biography.

REVISE   Have children read their draft to a different partner. Children should make sure that they have told events clearly and in time order. Children can look back at the charts they completed on Day 2 (T331) and at their notes to make sure they have included factual information. Children can also use their list of criteria for a biography from Day 1 (T313) to improve their writing.

Narrative: Biography

- A narrative tells a story about a real person, event, or thing.
- A biography is a narrative about a real person's life other than you.
- A biography tells events in time order.
- A biography has facts about the person's life.

Have children revise their biography. Let them work together to make sure that it clearly tells the story of the person's life, that events are in time order, and that the headings contain key words that will clearly help the reader know what each section is about. Encourage children to use Editor's Marks to revise their writing.

Editor's Marks

∧	Add
ℐ	Take out
⌁	Change
⊙	Add a period
≡	Capitalize
⬯	Check spelling

Objectives

- *To revise a draft of a short biography*
- *To include words that are appropriate for the audience and writer's purpose in a narrative*

Writing Prompt

Write Notes   Have children write a note that tells what they like about their partner's biography.

BELOW-LEVEL

Revise in Sections   Tell children that they can work on revising their biography one section at a time. For each section, they should check that the facts about the person are included in time order. Each time they have revised a section, review their work with them and provide feedback. Allow children to take a break after working on each section.

Day at a Glance

Day 5

 phonics and Spelling

- Review: Syllable Pattern VC/V
- Posttest: *r*-Controlled Vowel /ir/*ear, eer*

Fluency

- Accuracy
- "The Life of George Washington Carver," *Student Edition*, pp. 122–135

Read!

Comprehension

 Review: Locate Information

- *Read-Aloud Anthology:* "Young Inventors"

Robust Vocabulary

- Cumulative Review

Grammar *Quick Write*

- Review: Words That Compare

Writing ✏️

- Narrative: Biography

Warm-Up Routines

 Oral Language

Objective *To listen attentively and respond appropriately to oral communication*

Question of the Day

What would happen if there were no seeds in the world?

Invite children to speculate about why seeds are important to people. Use the following prompts:

- **How do you know that seeds are everywhere?**
- **How do seeds help animals and people?**
- **What are some ways that seeds are important in your life?**

Have children complete the following sentence frame to summarize their discussion.

Seeds are important because _____.

Read Aloud

Objective *To identify the use of rhyme in poetry*

BIG BOOK OF RHYMES AND POEMS Display the poem "Tiny Seeds" on page 36. Read the poem aloud, encouraging children to join in. Guide children to identify the rhyming words at the ends of lines 2 and 4 *(today, away)*. Then call on volunteers to name the rhyming words at the ends of lines 5 and 6 *(brown, down)*. Have children try to find one more word at the end of a line that rhymes with the ends of lines 2 and 4 *(stay in the last line)*. Discuss with children how the rhymes make the poem fun to read.

▲ **Big Book of Rhymes and Poems, p. 36**

Word Wall

Objective *To read high-frequency words*

REVIEW HIGH-FREQUENCY WORDS Review the following words on the Word Wall: *already, different, everything, idea, imagine,* and *through* as well as other previously learned high-frequency words. Point to one card at a time and have a volunteer read the word. Then have another child use it in a sentence. Repeat until all the words are read and used in sentences and each child has participated at least once.

already	different	everything
idea	imagine	through

Syllable Pattern VC/V  phonics

5-DAY PHONICS	
DAY 1	Introduce /ir/ear, eer
DAY 2	Word Building with /ir/ear, eer
DAY 3	Word Building with /ir/ear, eer
DAY 4	VC/V; Review /ir/ear, eer
DAY 5	VC/V; Review /ir/ear, eer

Objectives

- *To identify the syllable pattern VC/V in words*
- *To read words with the syllable pattern VC/V*

Skill Trace

 Tested Syllable Pattern VC/V

Introduce	T350
Review	**T360**

Review

READ WORDS WITH THE SYLLABLE PATTERN VC/V   Write the word *planet* on the board. Label the vowels with V and the consonant *n* with C. Point out that the word has two syllables and the first vowel has a short vowel sound. Have children join the syllables to read the word.

Practice/Apply

GUIDED PRACTICE   Write the following words on the board and have children read them: *lemon, wagon, river,* and *model*. Then make a chart as shown. Guide children in sorting the words by the short vowel sound in the first syllable. Add them to the chart.

Short *a*	Short *i*	Short *o*	Short *e*
wagon	river	model	lemon

INDEPENDENT PRACTICE   Have children think of other VC/V words and add them to the chart. Then point to words at random and have children read them.

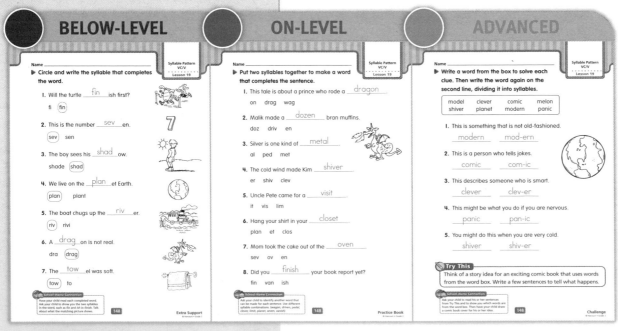

▲ **Extra Support, p. 148**   ▲ **Practice Book, p. 148**   ▲ **Challenge, p. 148**

ELL

- Group children according to academic levels, and assign one of the pages on the left.

- Clarify any unfamiliar concepts as necessary. See *ELL Teacher Guide* Lesson 19 for support in scaffolding instruction.

r-Controlled Vowel /ir/ear, eer

phonics **and Spelling**

5-DAY SPELLING

DAY 1	Pretest
DAY 2	Word Building
DAY 3	State the Generalization
DAY 4	Review
DAY 5	Posttest

Assess

POSTTEST Assess children's progress. Use the dictation sentences from Day 1.

Words with /ir/ear, eer

1. gear	I put the camping **gear** in the van.
2. deer	Maya saw a **deer** eating berries.
3. fear	Jena has a **fear** of high places.
4. year	Next **year**, I will be in third grade!
5. cheer	The people at the game started to **cheer**.
6. near	Tina's house was not **near** the school.
7. hear	Luka did not **hear** the doorbell ring.
8. clear	I can revise my draft to make my writing **clear**.
9. steer	Mom turned the wheel to **steer** the car.
10. rear	The trunk is in the **rear** of the car.

ADVANCED

Challenge Words Use the challenge words in these dictation sentences.

11. appear	I saw a rainbow **appear** after a storm.
12. pioneer	I wish I had been a **pioneer** living out west.
13. volunteer	Amir likes to **volunteer** to help animals.
14. earrings	Dad gave me **earrings** for my birthday.
15. nearby	The post office is **nearby**.

WRITING APPLICATION Have children write and illustrate a silly two-line rhyme using two or more of the spelling words.

It was odd that a pioneer gave earrings to a little deer.

Objective

• *To use r-Controlled vowel /ir/ear, eer and other known letter-sounds to spell and write words*

Spelling Words

1.	**gear**	6.	**near**
2.	**deer**	7.	**hear**
3.	**fear**	8.	**clear**
4.	**year***	9.	**steer**
5.	**cheer**	10.	**rear**

Challenge Words

11.	**appear**	14.	**earrings**
12.	**pioneer**	15.	**nearby**
13.	**volunteer**		

* Word from "The Life of George Washington Carver"

 Fluency

Objective

- *To read accurately and fluently in a manner that sounds like natural speech*

ASSESSMENT

Monitoring Progress

Periodically, take a timed sample of children's oral reading and record the number of words read correctly per minute. Children should accurately read approximately 72 words per minute in the middle of Grade 2.

Fluency Support Materials

 Fluency Builders, Grade 2, Lesson 19

 Audiotext *Student Edition* selections are available on *Audiotext Grade 2,* CD 4.

 Strategic Intervention Teacher Guide, Lesson 19

Readers' Theater

▲ **Student Edition, pp. 122–135**

 DIBELS Oral Reading Fluency **ORF**

PERFORM "THE LIFE OF GEORGE WASHINGTON CARVER" To help children improve their fluency, have them perform "The Life of George Washington Carver" as a Readers' Theater. Use the following procedures:

- Have groups of three children read the story together. Children can take turns reading each section of the selection. Have the group choose one member to read the introduction at the beginning of the selection, too.

- Listen to groups read. Provide feedback and support. Remind them that when they read, they can go back and reread words that they may have misread.

- Invite groups to read the story to classmates. Remind them to focus on reading accurately and in a way that sounds like natural speech.

E L L

Develop Vocabulary As you discuss how to read accurately, focus on multisyllabic words, such as *scientist,* that children might have trouble with. Discuss place names such as Kansas, Iowa, Alabama, and Tuskegee Institute and the names of the various products that George Washington Carver developed from peanuts and sweet potatoes. Demonstrate how to read these words.

Locate Information
Comprehension

Review

REVIEW THE SKILL Remind children that they can use parts of books and articles to quickly locate information. They can look for key words in tables of contents and in titles and headings.

SET A PURPOSE FOR LISTENING Guide children in setting a purpose for listening that includes listening to the titles and headings to compare the two young inventors, and listening to find out what kind of invention each inventor developed.

▲ **Read-Aloud Anthology, "Young Inventors," p. 72**

Practice/Apply

GUIDED PRACTICE As you read aloud "Young Inventors," record information about the two young inventors in a chart.

Frank Epperson	Chester Greenwood
• lived in San Francisco	• was 15 years old when he had his idea
• was 11 years old when he had his idea	• invented earmuffs
• Twenty years later, he took the idea and invented the Ep-sicle in 1924.	• They were called "Greenwood's Champion Ear Protectors."
• The Ep-sicle became known as the Popsicle.	• In Maine, December 21 is Chester Greenwood Day.

Then ask children which heading they would look under to find the answer to questions such as "Who invented the Ep-sicle?"

INDEPENDENT PRACTICE Ask children how they might look for information on Frank Epperson and Chester Greenwood in another book about inventions. (Possible response: Look at the table of contents. Look for key words or chapter headings such as *Frank Epperson*, *Chester Greenwood*, or *young inventors*.

Objective

• *To use titles, tables of contents, and headings to locate information in nonfiction text*

Skill Trace
 | Tested | **Locate Information**

Introduce	T224–T225
Reteach	S42–S43
Review	**T253, T269, T281, T308–T309, T337, T353, T363, T416, T437**
Test	Theme 4
Maintain	Theme 5, T279

BELOW-LEVEL

Kinesthetic Practice Provide children with a copy of a content-area textbook. Have pairs of children go on a "treasure hunt" through the book as you ask them questions such as *On what page will you find how plants grow and change?* Children then try to find the information by using parts of the book.

 Build Robust Vocabulary

Objectives

- *To review robust vocabulary*
- *To understand vocabulary in new contexts*
- *To discuss word meanings in relation to personal experience*

REVIEW Tested ✓

Vocabulary

Lesson 18	Lesson 19
attract	brew
territory	snug
volume	supplies
expression	crop
creative	provide
performance	earn
concentrate	committee
relieved	experiments
universal	innovation
audible	edible

Cumulative Review

COMPLETE A WORD CHART Using **Transparency G01**, guide children in completing two-column charts to enrich their understanding of the Vocabulary Words *edible, audible, crop, creative, brew,* and *innovation*. Ask children to name five things that are edible. Write the words in the left-hand column of the chart. Then ask children to name five things that are not edible. Write those words in the right-hand column of the chart. Once the chart for *edible/not edible* is complete, discuss why each item is where it is in the chart.

edible	not edible
carrots	books
apples	desks
bananas	car

Have children work in pairs to create and complete similar charts on separate sheets of paper for *audible/not audible, crop/not a crop, creative/not creative, brew/not brewed, innovation/not an innovation.* Children should try to name as many items for each pair of words as they can. Have partners share their completed charts with the rest of the class, explaining why each item is listed.

CONNECT TO CHILDREN'S EXPERIENCES   Discuss children's answers to the following questions.

1. **Why might an animal whose home is *snug* be very protective of its *territory*?** (Possible response: There wouldn't be room in the home for another animal because the home is so small.)

2. **What *supplies* would you need to find out which materials *attract* magnets?** (Possible response: metal objects and nonmetal objects)

3. **You were able to *earn* an A in your hardest subject. Describe the *expression* you will have when you tell your mom or dad about it.** (Possible response: I would look joyous and excited.)

4. **What might cause a member of a *committee* to speak in a very loud *volume*?** (Possible response: If he or she didn't agree with what someone else was saying; if a vote didn't turn out the way the person wanted it to.)

5. **Why would you have to *concentrate* if you were doing *experiments* or if you were involved in a *performance*?** (Possible response: You have to concentrate when doing experiments so you don't make any mistakes or don't have any accidents. You have to concentrate in a performance so you can remember what to say or do.)

6. **Have you ever been able to *provide* help to someone in school? What did you do? Was the person *relieved* to get your help?** (Possible response: I was able to provide help to a kindergartner who was learning to read. I read a Big Book with her. She was relieved when I helped her sound out some of the words.)

7. **What are some *universal* needs? Why do you think this?** (Possible response: Some universal needs are freedom, love, happiness, food, shelter, and good health. These are things everyone needs and deserves to have.)

MONITOR PROGRESS

Build Robust Vocabulary

| **IF** children have trouble understanding the meanings of the Vocabulary Words in this discussion, | **THEN** use examples from your own life to answer the questions, being sure to use the Vocabulary Words in a context that reinforces the meaning. |

Small-Group Instruction, pp. S46–S47

● **BELOW-LEVEL:** Reteach
● **ON-LEVEL:** Reinforce
● **ADVANCED:** Extend

Grammar Quick Write

Words That Compare

5-DAY GRAMMAR	
DAY 1	Introduce Words That Compare
DAY 2	Identify Words That Compare
DAY 3	Use Words That Compare in Sentences
DAY 4	Apply to Writing
DAY 5	Weekly Review

Objective

- *To recognize and write words that compare in sentences*

Daily Proofreading

puppies are noisy than kittens
(Puppies, noisier, kittens.)

 Language Arts Checkpoint

If children have difficulty with the concepts, see pages S48–S49 to reteach.

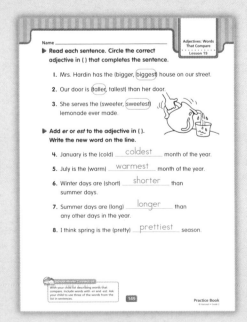

▲ **Practice Book, p. 149**

Review

REVIEW WORDS THAT COMPARE Review the following rules for words that compare. Write these rules on the board:

- Adjectives that end with *-er* describe just two things.

- Adjectives that end with *-est* describe three or more things.

- For adjectives that end in *e*, drop the *e* and then add *-er* or *-est*.

- For a one-syllable adjective that ends in a short vowel and a consonant, double the last letter and then add *-er* or *-est*.

- For adjectives that end in a consonant and *y*, change the *y* to *i* and then add *-er* or *-est*.

Practice/Apply

GUIDED PRACTICE Model revising the following sentence.

Sweet potatoes are sweet than peanuts. (sweeter)

Write the following sentences on the board. Have volunteers help you correct them.

A sweet potato is heavy than a peanut. (heavier)

An apple seed is tiniest than a peanut. (tinier)

The redwood is the taller tree in the forest. (tallest)

INDEPENDENT PRACTICE Have children write four sentences about George Washington Carver using words that compare. Have childen choose one sentence to read aloud.

Writing
Narrative: Biography

5-DAY WRITING

DAY 1	Introduce
DAY 2	Prewrite
DAY 3	Draft
DAY 4	Revise
DAY 5	Revise

Revise

REVISE BIOGRAPHIES Ask children to check that their biography tells about events in time order and that it includes interesting details about the person's life. Children should also make sure that their writing clearly tells about the subject and expresses their feelings about him or her. Then tell children to think about ways to improve their biography.

REVIEW CONVENTIONS Remind children to make sure they have capitalized proper nouns such as names of people and places. They should also check that each sentence ends with a period. Remind them also to check that their writing is clear and their handwriting is neat.

 WORD CHOICE After children revise their writing, discuss how to include words that help the reader better understand the person the writer is describing. Ask a volunteer to read aloud a biography draft, and point out examples of word choices.

NOTE: A 4-point rubric appears on page R8.

SCORING RUBRIC

	6	5	4	3	2	1
FOCUS	Completely focused, purposeful.	Focused on topic and purpose.	Generally focused on topic and purpose.	Somewhat focused on topic and purpose.	Related to topic but does not maintain focus.	Lacks focus and purpose.
ORGANIZATION	Ideas progress logically; paper conveys sense of completeness.	Organization mostly clear; paper gives sense of completeness.	Organization mostly clear, but some lapses occur; may seem unfinished.	Some sense of organization; seems unfinished.	Little sense of organization.	Little or no sense of organization.
SUPPORT	Strong, specific details; clear, exact language; freshness of expression.	Strong, specific details; clear, exact language.	Adequate support and word choice.	Limited supporting details; limited word choice.	Few supporting details; limited word choice.	Little development; limited or unclear word choice.
CONVENTIONS	Varied sentences; few, if any, errors.	Varied sentences; few errors.	Some sentence variety; few errors.	Simple sentence structures; some errors.	Simple sentence structures; many errors.	Unclear sentence structures; many errors.

REPRODUCIBLE RUBRICS for specific writing purposes and presentations are available on pages R2–R8.

Objective
• *To revise a biography*

Writing Prompt

Independent Writing Have children generate a list of ideas about a new topic of their choice for writing.

WEEKLY LESSON TEST

▲ **Weekly Lesson Tests, pp. 200–211**

• Selection Comprehension with Short Response
• Phonics and Spelling
• Focus Skill
• Use Reference Sources
• Robust Vocabulary
• Grammar
• Fluency Passage **FRESH READS**

 For prescriptions see pp. A2–A6. Also available electronically on StoryTown Online Assessment and Exam View®.

 Podcasting: Assessing Fluency

Leveled Readers

Reinforcing Skills and Strategies

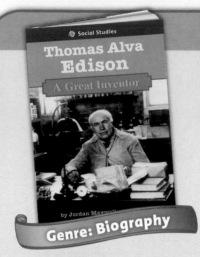

BELOW-LEVEL

Thomas Alva Edison: A Great Inventor

SUMMARY   Thomas Edison did not do well in school but showed an early interest in experimenting. He went on to invent more than one thousand products and improvements.

- **phonics** *r*-Controlled Vowel /ir/ *ear, eer*
- **Vocabulary**

 Locate Information

Focus Skill

Before Reading

BUILD BACKGROUND/SET PURPOSE   Help children understand that an inventor is someone who tries to make something new that is useful. Point to various objects, and ask why each was invented. Then guide children to preview the story and set a purpose for reading it.

Reading the Book

PAGES 4–7   **LOCATE INFORMATION**   **Why is this section called "The Early Years"?** (It tells about Edison's childhood and early life.)

PAGES 8–9   **DRAW CONCLUSIONS**   **Why did Thomas Edison leave his job as a telegraph operator?** (Possible response: Maybe he grew tired of doing the same thing and wanted to make a better telegraph.)

REREAD FOR FLUENCY   Have partners take turns reading the book one page at a time. Remind children to practice until they can read every word correctly and every sentence naturally.

Think Critically   *(See inside back cover for questions.)*

1 **NOTE DETAILS**   Edison made over one thousand inventions.

2 **SPECULATE**   Possible responses: Maybe he was bored at school or maybe he was always thinking of other things he could be doing.

3 **DESCRIBE CHARACTERS**   Possible responses: clever, hardworking

4 **LOCATE INFORMATION**   pages 3 and 11

5 **PERSONAL RESPONSE**   Answers will vary.

LEVELED READERS TEACHER GUIDE

▲ Vocabulary, p. 5

▲ Comprehension, p. 6

www.harcourtschool.com/storytown

★ **Leveled Readers Online Database**
  Searchable by Genre, Skill, Vocabulary, Level, or Title
★ **Student Activities and Teacher Resources, online**

ON-LEVEL

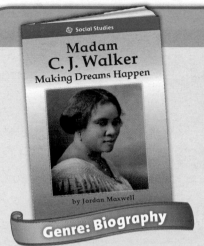

Genre: Biography

Madam C. J. Walker: Making Dreams Happen

SUMMARY   Madam C. J. Walker's invention of beauty products for African Americans eventually made her wealthy and gave others new ways to earn money.

• **phonics**   *r*-Controlled Vowel /ir/*ear, eer*
• **Vocabulary**

  Locate Information

Before Reading

BUILD BACKGROUND/SET PURPOSE   Ask children to name famous people. Choose one who could be considered inspiring, and ask for ideas about why the person is admired. Then guide children to preview the story and set a purpose for reading it.

Reading the Book

PAGES 6–7   **LOCATE INFORMATION**   **Which heading leads you to information about how Sarah suddenly had a new idea?** ("An Amazing Dream" tells about her dream about a hair mixture.)

PAGES 11–13   SUMMARIZE   How did Madam C. J. Walker become so successful and rich? (Possible responses: She figured out how to sell her products and trained others to sell them around the country. She built a factory and training school.)

REREAD FOR FLUENCY   Have partners take turns reading the book. Remind children to help each other say the words correctly.

Think Critically

(See inside back cover for questions.)

1 **NOTE DETAILS**   Her real name was Sarah Breedlove.

2 **LOCATE INFORMATION**   pages 4 and 5, "The Early Years"

3 **DESCRIBE CHARACTERS**   Possible responses: clever, hardworking

4 **CAUSE AND EFFECT**   Her hair started to fall out and she had a dream about a mixture that would make her hair grow back again.

5 **PERSONAL RESPONSE**   Answers will vary.

LEVELED READERS TEACHER GUIDE

▲ Vocabulary, p. 5

▲ Comprehension, p. 6

Leveled Readers

Reinforcing Skills and Strategies

ADVANCED

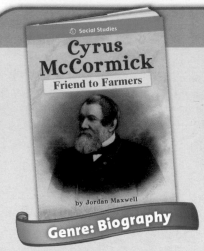
Cyrus McCormick
Friend to Farmers
by Jordan Maxwell
Genre: Biography

Cyrus McCormick: Friend to Farmers

SUMMARY Cyrus McCormick spent years inventing a machine to cut and harvest grain. His reaper would change farming throughout the world.

- **phonics** *r*-Controlled Vowel /ir/*ear, eer*
- **Vocabulary**

Focus Skill **Locate Information**

Before Reading

BUILD BACKGROUND/SET PURPOSE Ask children for examples of machines, and talk about the problems that the machines solved. Then guide children to preview the story and set a purpose for reading it.

Reading the Book

PAGES 6–10 PROBLEM/SOLUTION What problems did McCormick's reaper solve? (Possible response: People had always cut grain by hand, but that took a long time and was hard work. The reaper cut grain faster and more easily, even in wet weather.)

PAGE 10 LOCATE INFORMATION Which heading would lead you to information about why McCormick won the contest? ("Success!")

REREAD FOR FLUENCY Have partners take turns reading pages. Remind them to reread as many times as needed for an accurate reading.

Think Critically *(See inside back cover for questions.)*

1 NOTE DETAILS His first invention was a cradle for carrying grain. He invented it when he was fifteen.

2 IDENTIFY WITH CHARACTER Possible responses: disappointed, annoyed, determined to keep trying

3 LOCATE INFORMATION page 7

4 PERSONAL RESPONSE Answers will vary.

5 SUMMARIZE Cyrus's invention helped farmers harvest crops faster.

LEVELED READERS TEACHER GUIDE

Name _____
▶ Write the Vocabulary Word from the box that best completes each sentence.

| supplies | crop |
| provide | experiments |

1. We did ___experiments___ to see which fruit tasted best.

2. We needed paper, pencils, fruit, and other ___supplies___

3. Who would ___provide___ all the fruit we needed?

4. A farmer gave us some fruit from his ___crop___

▶ Write a sentence using each Vocabulary Word. Accept reasonable responses.
5. committee _____
6. earn _____

▲ Vocabulary, p. 5

Name _____
▶ Answer the questions about *Cyrus McCormick: Friend to Farmers.*

1. Where did Cyrus McCormick grow up?
   on a farm in Virginia

2. What did Cyrus invent when he was fifteen?
   a cradle for grain

3. In what year did Cyrus make a reaper to cut grain?
   1831

4. Where did Cyrus move in 1847?
   Chicago

5. When did Cyrus die?
   1884

▲ Comprehension, p. 6

 **E L L**

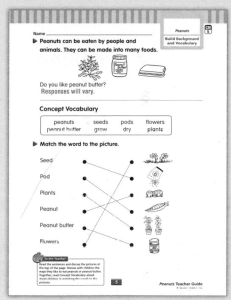

Peanuts

SUMMARY This informational book shows how peanut plants grow, how peanuts are picked and dried, and how they are used.

Genre: Nonfiction

- **Build Background**
- **Concept Vocabulary**
- **Scaffolded Language Development**

Before Reading

BUILD BACKGROUND/SET PURPOSE Ask children if they have ever seen peanuts in a shell. Where do they think the shell comes from? Then guide children to preview the story and set a purpose for reading it.

Reading the Book

PAGE 1 LOCATE INFORMATION Where is the title page, and what can you learn from it? (On the first page; the title gives the topic of the book.)

PAGES 11–14 MAIN IDEA What do all the sentences on pages 11–14 tell about? (Possible response: People can eat peanuts in different ways.)

REREAD FOR FLUENCY Have partners take turns pointing to a picture and reading the sentences that go with it. Remind children to practice until they can read all words correctly and all sentences smoothly.

Scaffolded Language Development

(See inside back cover for teacher-led activity.)

Provide additional examples and explanation as needed.

LEVELED READERS TEACHER GUIDE

▲ **Build Background and Vocabulary, p. 5**

▲ **Scaffolded Language Development, p. 6**

Lesson 20
Theme Review and Vocabulary Builder

WEEK AT A GLANCE

Phonics
REVIEW
- Digraphs /n/*kn*; /r/*wr*; /f/*gh*; *ph*
- Short Vowel /e/*ea*
- Vowel Diphthong /oi/*oi, oy*
- *r*-Controlled Vowel /ir/*ear, eer*

Spelling
REVIEW
- Words with *kn, wr, gh,* and *ph*
- Words with *ea*
- Words with *oi* and *oy*
- Words with *ear* and *eer*

Reading

READERS' THEATER
"What's My Job?" GAME SHOW

COMPREHENSION STRATEGIES

Reading Your Social Studies Book:
"North America" SOCIAL STUDIES TEXTBOOK

Fluency
REVIEW
- Intonation
- Accuracy

Comprehension
REVIEW

 Setting
Follow Directions

 Monitor Comprehension: Read Ahead

 Locate Information
Use Reference Sources

 Answer Questions

Robust Vocabulary

INTRODUCE *encountered, originated, sleuths, host, statue, risk, responds, accurately, opponent, impulsive*

Grammar [Quick Write]
REVIEW
- Adjectives
- Adjectives for Senses
- Number Words
- Words that Compare

Writing: Revise and Publish
REVIEW Writing Traits: Organization
REVIEW Writing Trait: Word Choice

Weekly Lesson Test

 = Focus Skill   = Focus Strategy   = Tested Skill

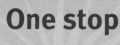

One stop
for all
your Digital *needs*

Digital
CLASSROOM

 www.harcourtschool.com/storytown
To go along with your print program

FOR THE TEACHER

Prepare   Professional Development

 Videos for Podcasting

Plan & Organize   Online TE & Planning Resources*

Teach   Transparencies

access from Online TE

Assess    Online Assessment*

with Student Tracking System and Prescriptions

FOR THE STUDENT

Read   Student eBook*

 Strategic Intervention Interactive Reader

Leveled Readers

Practice & Apply   Splash into Phonics CD-ROM

 Also available on CD-ROM

Literature Resources

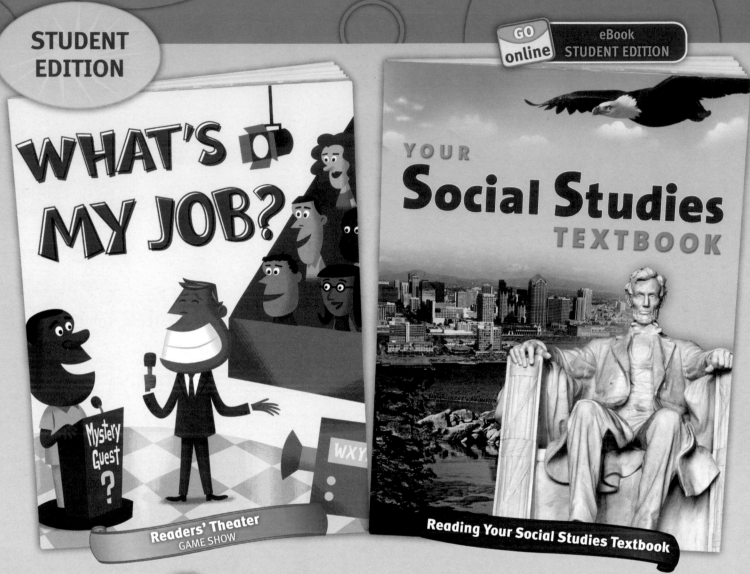

STUDENT EDITION

GO online eBook STUDENT EDITION

WHAT'S MY JOB?

Mystery Guest ?

WXY

Readers' Theater
GAME SHOW

YOUR **Social Studies** TEXTBOOK

Reading Your Social Studies Textbook

 ◀ **Audiotext** *Student Edition selections are available on Audiotext Grade 2, CD 4.*

REVIEW THEME CONCEPTS
Using Readers' Theater and a Social Studies Textbook

Paired Selections

SOCIAL STUDIES **What's My Job?, pp. 142–153**

SUMMARY Game show contestants must ask questions to guess the job of the mystery guest.

SOCIAL STUDIES **North America, pp. 154–157**

SUMMARY Children will learn which countries make up the continent of North America.

Support for Differentiated Instruction

 LEVELED READERS

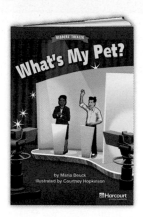 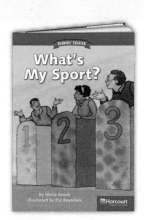  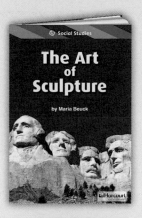

 **BELOW-LEVEL**  **ON-LEVEL**  **ADVANCED**  **E L L**

LEVELED PRACTICE

◀ **Strategic Intervention Resource Kit,** Lesson 20

◀ **Strategic Intervention Interactive Reader, Lesson 20**
Strategic Intervention Interactive Reader Online

◀ **ELL Extra Support Kit, Lesson 20**

◀ **Challenge Resource Kit, Lesson 20**

 BELOW-LEVEL
Extra Support Copying Masters, pp. 150, 152–153, 155–158, 160–161

 ON-LEVEL
Practice Book, pp. 150–161

ADVANCED
Challenge Copying Masters, pp. 150, 152–153, 155–158, 160–161

ADDITIONAL RESOURCES

artist evision

- Teacher Resource Book, pp. 53, 115, 134–139
- Spelling Practice Book, pp. 63–66
- Grammar Practice Book, pp. 71–72
- Reading Transparencies R104–R105
- Test Prep System
- ◀ **Literacy Center Kit, Cards 96–100**
- Sound/Spelling Cards
- ◀ **Fluency Builders**
- ◀ **Picture Card Collection**
- Read-Aloud Anthology, pp. 74–75

ASSESSMENT

✔ **Weekly Lesson Tests, Lesson 20**
- Comprehension   • Robust Vocabulary

✔ **Rubrics, pp. R2–R8**

 www.harcourtschool.com/ storytown
Online Assessment
Also available on CD-ROM—Exam View®

Suggested Lesson Planner

  Online TE & Planning Resources

	Day 1	**Day 2**

  **Step 1 Whole Group**

Daily Routines
- *Oral Language*
- *Read Aloud*
- *High-Frequency Words*

Day 1

QUESTION OF THE DAY, p. T384
What are some things that people can do with their pet dogs and cats?

READ ALOUD, p. T385
Big Book of Rhymes and Poems, "My Cat and I"

WORD WALL, p. T385

Day 2

QUESTION OF THE DAY, p. T402
What do the sounds you hear at school remind you of?

READ ALOUD, p. T403
Big Book of Rhymes and Poems, "The Drum"

WORD WALL, p. T403

Word Work
- phonics
- *Spelling*

Day 1

 phonics, p. T386
Review: Digraphs /n/kn; /r/wr; /f/gh, ph

SPELLING, p. T388
Pretest: *know, wrong, tough, phone, breath, health, soil, joy, deer, rear*

Day 2

phonics, p. T404
Review: Short Vowel /e/ea

SPELLING, p. T405
Word Building

Skills and Strategies
- *Reading*
- *Fluency*
- *Comprehension*
- *Build Robust Vocabulary*

Day 1

COMPREHENSION, p. T389
  Review: Setting

BUILD ROBUST VOCABULARY, p. T390
Words from the Readers' Theater

READING

READERS' THEATER
Read Aloud/Read Along: "What's My Job?," p. T392

FLUENCY, p. T392
Model Oral Fluency

BUILD ROBUST VOCABULARY, p. T399
Words About the Readers' Theater

Day 2

COMPREHENSION, p. T406
 Review: Setting
Follow Directions

READING

 **READERS' THEATER**
Read Together: "What's My Job?," p. T408

FLUENCY, p. T408
Model Oral Accuracy

BUILD ROBUST VOCABULARY, p. T409
Words from the Read-Aloud

 Read!
WHAT'S MY JOB?

▲ Student Edition

Step 2 Small Groups

Suggestions for Differentiated Instruction (See pp. T378–T379.)

 Step 3 Whole Group

Language Arts
- *Grammar* **Quick Write**
- *Writing*

Day 1

GRAMMAR, p. T400
Review: Adjectives

Daily Proofreading
where is Sams' red lunchbox? (Where, Sam's)

 WRITING, p. T401
Revise
Writing Trait: Organization

Writing Prompt *Write about which piece from Theme 4 was the most difficult to write. Tell why.*

Day 2

GRAMMAR, p. T410
Review: Adjectives for Senses

Daily Proofreading
Do we have a test on friday. (Friday?)

  WRITING, p. T411
Revise:
Writing Trait: Organization

Writing Prompt *Think about a favorite food and write a few sentences to describe what it smells like.*

 = Focus Skill   = Focus Strategy    = Tested Skill

phonics REVIEW | **Comprehension** REVIEW | **Fluency** REVIEW | **Vocabulary** INTRODUCE

Skills at a Glance

• Lessons 16–19

 Focus Skills Setting, Locate Information

 Focus Strategy Monitor Comprehension: Read Ahead, Answer Questions

• Intonation
• Accuracy

ROBUST: *encountered, originated, sleuths, host, statue, risk, responds, accurately, opponent, impulsive*

Day 3

QUESTION OF THE DAY, p. T412
Do you think that it would be fun to be part of a marching band? Why do you think so?

READ ALOUD, p. T413
Big Book of Rhymes and Poems, "Here Comes the Band"

WORD WALL, p. T413

 , p. T414
Review: : Vowel Diphthong /oi/*oi, oy*

 SPELLING, p. T415
State the Generalization

 COMPREHENSION, p. T416
 Review: Locate Information
Review: Follow Directions

FLUENCY

 READERS' THEATER
Choose Roles/Rehearse: "What's My Job?," p. T418

 BUILD ROBUST VOCABULARY, p. T419
Review

▲ Student Edition

 GRAMMAR, p. T420
Review: Number Words

Daily Proofreading
We visited dallas on thursday. (Dallas, Thursday)

 WRITING, p. T421
Publish
Writing Trait: Presentation

 *Writing Prompt* Tell why art or music is important to you.

Day 4

QUESTION OF THE DAY, p. T422
What is the most surprising thing about seeds?

READ ALOUD, p. T423
Big Book of Rhymes and Poems, "Tiny Seeds"

WORD WALL, p. T423

 , p. T424
Introduce: *r*-Controlled Vowel /ir/*ear, eer*

 SPELLING, p. T425
Review Spelling Words

READING COMPREHENSION STRATEGIES
 Review: Monitor Comprehension: Read Ahead and Answer Questions, p. T426

 COMPREHENSION, p. T429
Review: Use Reference Sources

FLUENCY READERS' THEATER
Rehearse Roles: "What's My Job?," p. T430

 BUILD ROBUST VOCABULARY, p. T431
Review

▲ Student Edition

 GRAMMAR, p. T432
Review: Words That Compare

Daily Proofreading
Would you like some berrys. (berries?)

 WRITING, p. T433
Publish
Writing Trait: Conventions

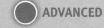 *Writing Prompt* Write about how you decided on the illustrations, photos, or items you included with your writing.

Day 5

QUESTION OF THE DAY, p. T434
What are some ways you can use a notebook?

READ ALOUD, p. T435
Big Book of Rhymes and Poems, "New Notebook"

WORD WALL, p. T435

phonics, **SPELLING,** p. T436
Posttest

COMPREHENSION, p. T437
Review: Locate Information
Review: Use Reference Sources

FLUENCY

READERS' THEATER
Perform: "What's My Job?," p. T439

▲ Student Edition

GRAMMAR, p. T440
Review: Lessons 16–19

Daily Proofreading
Dr Browns office is next door. (Dr., Brown's)

WRITING, p. T441
Present
Writing Trait: Word Choice

Writing Prompt Write about a piece of writing shared by a classmate.

● **BELOW-LEVEL** ● **ON-LEVEL** ● **ADVANCED** E L L

Suggested Small-Group Planner

 45-60+ Minutes

	Day 1	Day 2
15-20+ Minutes **BELOW-LEVEL**	**Teacher-Directed** Leveled Reader: "What's My Pet?," p. T442 Before Reading **Independent** ⭐ Listening/Speaking Center, p. T382 Extra Support Copying Masters, p. 150 ▲ Leveled Reader	**Teacher-Directed** Student Edition: "What's My Job?," p. T392 **Independent** ⭐ Reading Center, p. T382 Extra Support Copying Masters, pp. 152–153  ▲ Student Edition
15-20+ Minutes **ON-LEVEL**	**Teacher-Directed** Leveled Reader: "What's My Sport?," p. T443 Before Reading **Independent** ⭐ Reading Center, p. T382 Practice Book, p. 150 ▲ Leveled Reader	**Teacher-Directed** Student Edition: "What's My Job?," p. T392 **Independent** ⭐ Letters and Sounds Center, p. T383 Practice Book, pp. 152–153  ▲ Student Edition

15-20+ Minutes **ADVANCED**	**Teacher-Directed** Leveled Reader: "What's My Hobby?," p. T444 Before Reading
	 Independent ⭐ Letters and Sounds Center, p. T383 Challenge Copying Masters, p. 150
	  ▲ Leveled Reader
		Teacher-Directed Leveled Reader: "What's My Hobby," p. T444 Read the Book
		 Independent ⭐ Word Work Center, p. T383 Challenge Copying Masters, pp. 152–153
		  ▲ Leveled Reader

E L L

English-Language Learners

In addition to the small-group instruction above, use the ELL Extra Support Kit to promote language development.

LANGUAGE DEVELOPMENT SUPPORT

Teacher-Directed
ELL TG, Day 1

Independent
ELL Copying Masters, Lesson 20

 ▲ ELL Student Handbook

LANGUAGE DEVELOPMENT SUPPORT

Teacher-Directed
ELL TG, Day 2

Independent
ELL Copying Masters, Lesson 20

 ▲ ELL Student Handbook

Intervention

▲ Strategic Intervention Resource Kit   ▲ Strategic Intervention Interactive Reader

Strategic Intervention TG, Day 1
Strategic Intervention Practice Book, Lesson 20

Strategic Intervention TG, Day 2
Strategic Intervention Interactive Reader, Lesson 20

 ▲ Strategic Intervention Interactive Reader

Day 3

Teacher-Directed
Leveled Reader:
"What's My Pet?," p. T442
Read the Book

Independent
⭐ Word Work Center, p. T383
Extra Support Copying Masters,
pp. 155–157

▲ Leveled
Reader

Teacher-Directed
Leveled Reader:
"What's My Sport?,"
p. T443
Read the Book

Independent
⭐ Writing Center, p. T383
Practice Book, pp. 155–157

▲ Leveled
Reader

Teacher-Directed
Leveled Reader:
"What's My Hobby?," p. T444
Think Critically

Independent
⭐ Listening/Speaking Center,
p. T382
Challenge Copying Masters,
pp. 155–157

▲ Leveled
Reader

LANGUAGE DEVELOPMENT SUPPORT

Teacher-Directed
Leveled Reader: "The Art of Sculpture,"
p. T445
Before Reading; Read the Book
ELL TG, Day 3

Independent
ELL Copying Masters, Lesson 20

▲ Leveled
Reader

Strategic Intervention TG, Day 3
Strategic Intervention Interactive
Reader, Lesson 20
Strategic Intervention Practice Book,
Lesson 20

▲ Strategic Intervention
Interactive Reader

Day 4

Teacher-Directed
Leveled Reader:
"What's My Pet?,"
p. T442
Reread for Fluency

Independent
⭐ Letters and Sounds Center,
p. T383
Extra Support Copying Masters, p. 158

▲ Leveled
Reader

Teacher-Directed
Leveled Reader:
"What's My Sport?,"
p. T443
Reread for Fluency

Independent
⭐ Word Work Center, p. T383
Practice Book, p. 158

▲ Leveled
Reader

Teacher-Directed
Leveled Reader:
"What's My Hobby?," p. T444
Reread for Fluency

Independent
⭐ Writing Center, p. T383
Challenge Copying Masters, p. 158
Self-Selected Reading: Classroom
Library Collection

▲ Leveled
Reader

LANGUAGE DEVELOPMENT SUPPORT

Teacher-Directed
Leveled Reader: "The Art of Sculpture,"
p. T445
Reread for Fluency
ELL TG, Day 4

Independent
ELL Copying Masters, Lesson 20

▲ Leveled
Reader

Strategic Intervention TG, Day 4
Strategic Intervention Interactive
Reader, Lesson 20

▲ Strategic Intervention
Interactive Reader

Day 5

Teacher-Directed
Leveled Reader:
"What's My Pet?,"
p. T442
Think Critically

Independent
⭐ Writing Center, p. T383
Leveled Reader: Reread for Fluency
Extra Support Copying Masters, pp. 160–161

▲ Leveled
Reader

Teacher-Directed
Leveled Reader:
"What's My Sport?,"
p. T443
Think Critically

Independent
⭐ Listening/Speaking Center,
p. T382
Leveled Reader: Reread for Fluency
Practice Book, pp. 160–161

▲ Leveled
Reader

Teacher-Directed
Leveled Reader:
"What's My Hobby?," p. T444
Reread for Fluency

Independent
⭐ Reading Center, p. T382
Leveled Reader: Reread for Fluency
Challenge Copying Masters, pp. 160–161
Self-Selected Reading: Classroom Library Collection

▲ Leveled
Reader

LANGUAGE DEVELOPMENT SUPPORT

Teacher-Directed
Leveled Reader: "The Art of Sculpture,"
p. T445
Think Critically
ELL TG, Day 5

Independent
Leveled Reader: Reread for Fluency
ELL Copying Masters, Lesson 20

▲ Leveled
Reader

Strategic Intervention TG, Day 5
Strategic Intervention Interactive
Reader, Lesson 20

▲ Strategic Intervention
Interactive Reader

Leveled Readers & Leveled Practice
Reinforcing Skills and Strategies

LEVELED READERS SYSTEM

- **Leveled Readers**
- **Leveled Readers, CD**
- **Leveled Readers Teacher Guides**
  - *Comprehension*
  - *Vocabulary*
  - *Oral Reading Fluency Assessment*
- **Response Activities**
- **Leveled Readers Assessment**

See pages T442–T445 for lesson plans.

BELOW-LEVEL

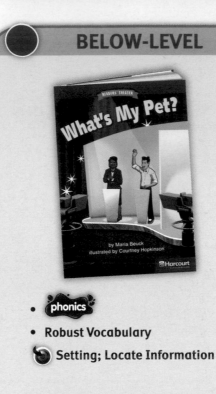

- **phonics**
- **Robust Vocabulary**
- **Setting; Locate Information**

LEVELED READERS TEACHER GUIDE

▲ Vocabulary, p. 5

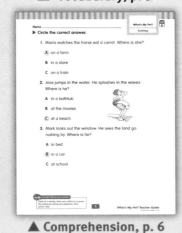

▲ Comprehension, p. 6

ON-LEVEL

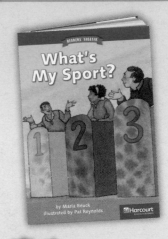

- **phonics**
- **Robust Vocabulary**
- **Setting; Locate Information**

LEVELED READERS TEACHER GUIDE

▲ Vocabulary, p. 5

▲ Comprehension, p. 6

ADVANCED

- **phonics**
- **Robust Vocabulary**
- **Setting; Locate Information**

LEVELED READERS TEACHER GUIDE

▲ Vocabulary p. 5

▲ Comprehension, p. 6

ELL

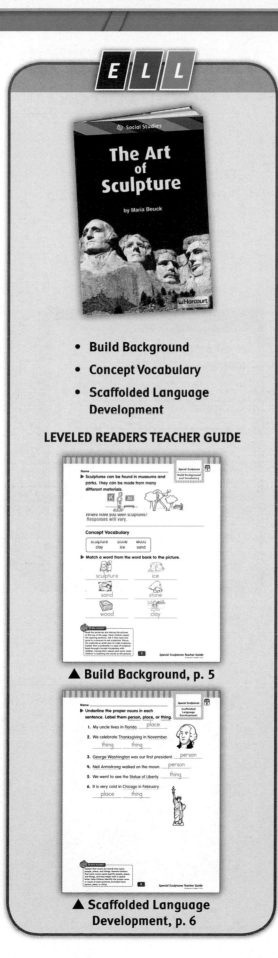

- **Build Background**
- **Concept Vocabulary**
- **Scaffolded Language Development**

LEVELED READERS TEACHER GUIDE

▲ Build Background, p. 5

▲ Scaffolded Language Development, p. 6

CLASSROOM LIBRARY

for Self-Selected Reading

EASY

▲ *The Dot* by Peter H. Reynolds.
FICTION

AVERAGE

▲ *Billy's Bucket* by Kes Gray.
FICTION

CHALLENGE

▲ *Mae Jemison* by Thomas Streissguth.
NONFICTION

▲ **Classroom Library Books Teacher Guide, Lesson 20**

Literacy Centers

15 Min. each

Management Support

While you provide direct instruction to individuals or small groups, other children can work on literacy center activities.

▲ **Literacy Center Pocket Chart**

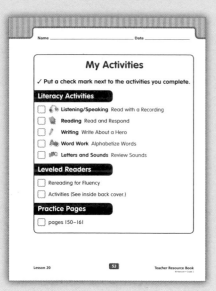

Name _____ Date _____

My Activities

✓ Put a check mark next to the activities you complete.

Literacy Activities

☐ Listening/Speaking Read with a Recording
☐ Reading Read and Respond
☐ Writing Write About a Hero
☐ Word Work Alphabetize Words
☐ Letters and Sounds Review Sounds

Leveled Readers

☐ Rereading for Fluency
☐ Activities (See inside back cover.)

Practice Pages

☐ pages 150–161

Lesson 20   53   Teacher Resource Book

▲ **Teacher Resource Book, p. 53**

 ## Homework for the Week

TEACHER RESOURCE BOOK, PAGE 23

The *Homework Copying Master* provides activities to complete for each day of the week.

 GO online www.harcourtschool.com/ storytown

LISTENING/SPEAKING

Read with a Recording

Objective
To develop fluency by listening to familiar selections and reading them aloud

---

LISTENING/SPEAKING   Card 96

Read with a Recording

MATERIALS
- CD/cassette player
- Audiotext Grade 2, CD 4
- Student Edition
- Reading Log or paper
- pencil

Listen to "What's My Job?" on the *Audiotext*.

❶ Follow along in your book while you listen.

❷ Listen to it again and read aloud with the recording. Notice the rise and fall of the reader's voice.

❸ Use your Reading Log to record what you read.

Grade 2 Lesson 20

⭐ **Literacy Center Kit • Card 96**

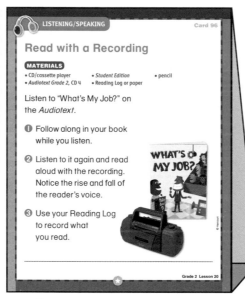

READING

Read and Respond

Objective
To develop comprehension by reading fiction selections and responding to them

---

READING   Card 97

Read and Respond

MATERIALS
- Student Edition
- Leveled Readers
- books from the classroom library
- paper
- pencil

❶ Choose a story to read from your *Student Edition* or other books. You can work alone or with a partner.

❷ After reading the story, write the title and tell what you liked about the story.

❸ Share with a partner what you wrote.

Grade 2 Lesson 20

⭐ **Literacy Center Kit • Card 97**

✏️ WRITING

Write about a Hero

Objective
To practice writing a paragraph about another person

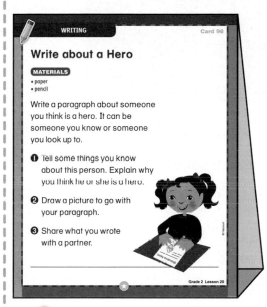

Literacy Center Kit • Card 98

🍎 WORD WORK

Alphabetize Words

Objective
To practice alphabetizing words

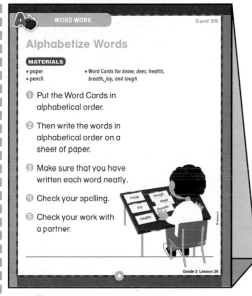

Literacy Center Kit • Card 99

ABC LETTERS AND SOUNDS

Review Sounds

Objective
To read and write words using known letter/sound correspondences

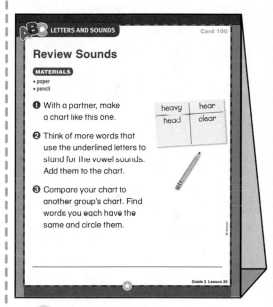

Literacy Center Kit • Card 100

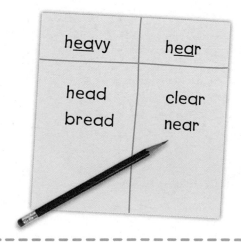

Warm-Up Routines

phonics and Spelling

- Review: Digraphs /n/*kn*; /r/*wr*; /f/*gh, ph*
- Pretest

Reading/ Comprehension

Review: Setting Monitor Comprehension

Robust Vocabulary

Words from Readers' Theater

- Introduce: *sleuths, host, statue, risk, responds, accurately*

Words About the Readers' Theater

- Introduce: *opponent, impulsive*

Fluency

READERS' THEATER

- Read Aloud/ Read Along
- "What's My Job?" *Student Edition,* pp. 142–153

Grammar `Quick Write`

- Review: Adjectives

Writing ✏

- Select a Piece and Revise

Oral Language

Objective *To listen attentively and respond appropriately to oral communication*

Question of the Day

What are some things that people can do with their pet dogs and cats?

Invite children to tell why cats and dogs make nice companions.

- **What are some games people play with their pet cats or dogs?**

- **Why do you think dogs and cats are nice to own?**

Then have children use one of the following sentence frames:

> **If I had a cat or a dog, we could _____.**

> **One thing I like about my dog/cat is _____.**

Read Aloud

Objective *To listen for a purpose*

BIG BOOK OF RHYMES AND POEMS Display the poem "My Cat and I" on page 29 and read the title aloud. Ask children to recall what the poem is about. Explain that the poet uses a number of action words in the poem, and have children listen for the action words as you read the poem aloud. Then read the poem. Ask children to name the action words they heard and act them out. (flop, jumps, kneads, rubs, purrs) Reread the poem, emphasizing the action words. Invite children to join in.

▲ **Big Book of Rhymes and Poems, p. 29**

Word Wall

Objective *To read high-frequency words*

REVIEW HIGH-FREQUENCY WORDS Review the following words on the Word Wall: *question, something, sure, enjoy, coming, idea, quite, believe, different,* and *guess*. Point to words at random and have children read them together as a group. Then ask each child to read five words that you point to in quick succession.

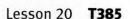

Digraphs /n/ kn; /r/ wr; /f/ gh, ph

phonics *and Spelling*

Objectives

- *To recognize the digraphs /n/kn; /r/wr; /f/gh, ph*
- *To read words with the digraphs /n/kn; /r/wr; /f/gh, ph, and other known letter-sounds*
- *To use the digraphs /n/kn; /r/wr; /f/gh, ph, and other known letter-sounds to spell words*

Skill Trace

 Tested Digraphs /n/*kn*; /r/*wr*; /f/*gh, ph*

Introduce	T30–T33
Reteach	S2–S3
Review	T42–T43, T64–T65, T386–T387
Test	Theme 4

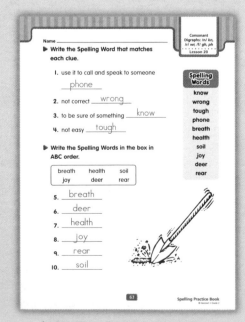

▲ Spelling Practice Book, p. 63

 Review

REVIEW PHONICS ELEMENTS Explain to children that during this week, they will review the phonics elements they learned during Theme 4. Tell them that they will focus on one phonics element each day, beginning with digraphs /n/*kn*, /r/*wr*, and /f/*gh, ph*.

WARM UP WITH PHONEMIC AWARENESS Say the words *knock* and *knight*. Have children repeat the words. Say: **The words *knock* and *knight* begin with the /n/ sound.** Repeat with the words *knee* and *knot*. Say: **The words *knee* and *knot* also begin with the /n/ sound.** Have children say /n/ several times.

Follow a similar procedure for /r/, using the words *wrist* and *wrote*, and for /f/ using the words *rough* and *phone*.

Routine Card 1 **CONNECT LETTERS AND SOUNDS** Review the letter/sound correspondences for digraphs /n/*kn*. Display the *Sound/ Spelling Cards* for *kn*. Ask children to say the sound that the letters stand for. Ask volunteers to name some words that include the /n/ sound spelled *kn*, and begin a list of the words they suggest on the chalkboard. In each word, ask children to identify the letters that stand for the /n/ sound. Follow a similar procedure for the digraphs /r/*wr*, and /f/*gh, ph*.

▲ Sound/Spelling Cards

5-DAY PHONICS

DAY 1	Review /n/*kn*, /r/*wr*, /f/*gh, ph.*
DAY 2	Review /e/*ea*
DAY 3	Review /oi/*oi, oy*
DAY 4	Review /ir/*ear, eer*
DAY 5	Cumulative Review

Practice/Apply

GUIDED PRACTICE   Using the chart you have created, ask volunteers to choose one column of words to read. Then have the group choral-read the words with each volunteer. Finally, ask volunteers to suggest sentences using one word from each column. Write their ideas on the board, underlining any words with digraphs /n/*kn*, /r/*wr*, and /f/*gh, ph.*

> **This is a <u>photo</u> of my <u>knee</u> and my <u>wrist</u>.**
>
> **Karl <u>knew</u> how to <u>write</u> a message after the <u>phone</u> call.**
>
> **Shari <u>wrote</u> a story about a <u>tough</u> <u>knight</u>.**

INDEPENDENT PRACTICE   Have children work with partners to write sentences using words with the digraphs /n/*kn*, /r/*wr*, and /f/*gh, ph.* Tell partners to exchange papers with another pair and to read aloud each other's sentences.

ADVANCED

Find Additional Words   Have partners make a list of additional words that they think might include the digraphs /n/*kn*, /r/*wr*, and /f/*gh, ph.* Then have children use a dictionary to check the spelling of the words. Have children add to their list other words with these digraphs they find in the dictionary.

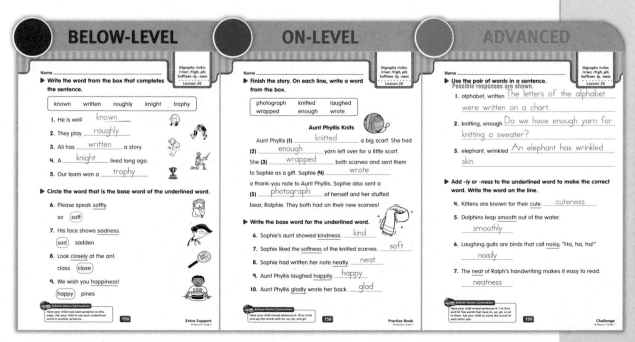

▲ Extra Support, p. 150   ▲ Practice Book, p. 150   ▲ Challenge, p. 150

ELL

• Group children according to academic levels, and assign one of the pages on the left.

• Clarify any unfamiliar concepts as necessary. See *ELL Teacher Guide* Lesson 20 for support in scaffolding instruction.

Spelling
Review

5-DAY SPELLING

DAY 1	Pretest
DAY 2	Word Building
DAY 3	State the Generalization
DAY 4	Review
DAY 5	Posttest

Objective

- *To review spelling words from previous lessons*

Spelling Words

1. **know***   6. **health**
2. **wrong***   7. **soil**
3. **tough**   8. **joy**
4. **phone**   9. **deer**
5. **breath**   10. **rear**

* Words from "What's My Job?"

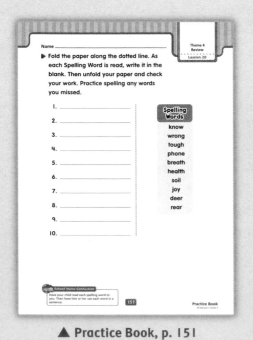

▲ Practice Book, p. 151

Reinforce the Skill

PRETEST   Say the first word and read the dictation sentence. Repeat the word as children write it. Write the word on the board and have children check their spelling. Tell them to circle the word if they spelled it correctly or write it correctly if they did not. Repeat for words 2–10.

Words with /n/*kn*, /r/*wr*, /f/*gh, ph*; /e/*ea*; /oi/*oi, oy*; /ir/*ear, eer*

1. know   I **know** the answer to that question.
2. wrong   We got lost when we took a **wrong** turn at the light.
3. tough   Gino had a **tough** time opening the package.
4. phone   You can use this **phone** to call your mother.
5. breath   Se-Jin was out of **breath** when he finished the race.
6. health   My aunt's **health** improved when she exercised.
7. soil   The **soil** in the garden was soggy after the rain.
8. joy   Watching the sunrise filled me with **joy**.
9. deer   I saw a **deer** in the meadow early this morning.
10. rear   There is another exit at the **rear** of the theater.

Setting

Comprehension: Review

Reinforce the Skill

DISCUSS SETTING   Have children reread *Student Edition* page 18. Model how to determine the setting of a story.

Think Aloud   As I begin reading a story, I look for clues that tell me about the setting. Details that tell where and when the story takes place help me picture the story in my mind.

Practice/Apply

GUIDED PRACTICE   Draw a chart like the one on *Student Edition* page 19. Then have children return to "Jamaica Louise James" on *Student Edition* pages 328–349. Guide children to use information from the story and the illustrations to tell when and where the story takes place. Add this information to the chart. Ask children to tell why the setting is important to the story. (Jamaica's big idea is to decorate the subway station.)

Story	When	Where
"Jamaica Louise James"	the present, winter	a big city, a subway station

INDEPENDENT PRACTICE   Have partners choose a fiction story from an earlier theme and create a similar chart to tell about the story's setting. Have them discuss how the story might change if it had a different setting.

Objective

• *To identify the setting of a story*

Skill Trace

Tested   **Setting**

Introduce	T34–T35
Reteach	S6–S7, S18–S19
Review	T67, T83, T95, T134–T135, T171, T187, T197, T389, T406
Test	Theme 4
Maintain	Theme 5, T87

Build Robust Vocabulary

Words from the Readers' Theater

Objective

- *To build robust vocabulary*

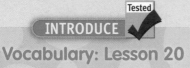

Tested ✓

INTRODUCE

Vocabulary: Lesson 20

sleuths	risk
host	responds
statue	accurately

▼ **Student-Friendly Explanations**

Student-Friendly Explanations

sleuths	Sleuths are people who try to solve crimes or mysteries.
host	The host of a program introduces the guests and talks with them.
statue	A statue is a work of art, often showing a person, that can be seen from all sides. It may be made of wood, stone, bronze, or some other hard material.
risk	If you take a risk, you take a chance of harm or a bad result.
responds	If someone responds to a question, he or she is giving an answer.
accurately	When you do something without making any mistakes, you have done it accurately.

Grade 2, Lesson 20   R105   Vocabulary

Transparency R105

Teach/Model

Routine Card 4

INTRODUCE ROBUST VOCABULARY   Introduce the words, using *Routine Card 4*.

❶ Display **Transparency R105** and have children read the word and the **Student-Friendly Explanation**.
❷ Have children **say the word** with you.
❸ Have children **interact with the word's meaning** by asking them the appropriate question below.

- If you had to solve a mystery, would you want help from fire-fighters or from **sleuths**? Why?

- Would you **risk** leaving your lunch on the bus? Why or why not?

- Would the **host** of a party refuse to answer the door? Explain.

- When someone **responds** to your question, does he or she have to say something? Tell why or why not.

- Where are some places you might see a **statue**?

- When you've done homework **accurately**, have you made mistakes? Explain.

Develop Deeper Meaning

EXPAND WORD MEANINGS   Guide children to discuss each word in a deeper context.

1. Would **sleuths** want to solve a mystery? Explain.
2. Why is it important to think about a **risk** before you take it?
3. What are some ways you might expect a **host** to act? Why?
4. What do you expect to hear when someone **responds** to you?
5. What kind of **statue** might you see in a museum?
6. If you've answered a question **accurately**, is your answer wrong? Why?

Managing Readers' Theater

"What's My Job?"

Set the Stage

OVERVIEW Use the following suggestions to help children prepare a Readers' Theater presentation of "What's My Job?" See page T439 for additional performance ideas.

MODEL FLUENT READING Model fluent, expressive reading by reading aloud the script on *Student Edition* pages 142–153 (pp. T392–T398) as children follow along. Then read the script again as children read along. Use the Monitor Comprehension questions to assess children's comprehension of the selection. Consider performance options for the end of the week. You may want to invite parents or other guests and allow children to create invitations.

READ TOGETHER Have children read the scripts on their own for the first time. Guide children to read with accuracy and appropriate intonation. Encourage them to use the fluency tips to help them read more fluently.

CHOOSE ROLES AND REHEARSE Distribute copies of the script (*Teacher Resource Book*, pp. 134–139). Assign children to groups and have them practice reading different roles aloud. After children read, assign roles or have children choose their own. Encourage children to highlight their parts and to practice reading their scripts at home.

REHEARSE Have children work in their assigned groups to read the script as many times as possible. Informally observe the groups and give feedback on children's accuracy and intonation. You may want to have children rehearse while using the backdrop for "What's My Job?" (*Teacher Resource Book*, p. 115).

PERFORM Assign each group a scene to perform. Have children stand in a row at the front of the classroom and read the script aloud. Groups who aren't performing become part of the audience. Encourage the audience to give feedback after the performances about each group's accuracy, reading rate, and expression.

Professional Development

 Podcasting: Readers' Theater

▲ Teacher Resource Book, pp 134–139

▲ Teacher Resource Book, p. 115

READERS' THEATER

Read Aloud/Read Along: "What's My Job?"

5-DAY READERS' THEATER	
DAY 1	Read Aloud/Read Along
DAY 2	Read Together
DAY 3	Choose Roles/Rehearse
DAY 4	Rehearse Roles
DAY 5	Perform

Objectives

- *To identify the genre of a selection and its distinguishing characteristics*
- *To set a purpose for listening*

TECHNOLOGY

 eBook "What's My Job?" is available in an eBook.

 Audiotext "What's My Job?" is available on *Audiotext Grade 2,* CD 4 for subsequent readings.

ELL

Leveled Parts In "What's My Job?" the part of the Mystery Guest has been specially designed for children needing ELL support. If you have more than one ELL child, you may want to have ELL children share this part.

Build Background

DISCUSS GENRE Have children turn to page 142. Explain that "What's My Job?" presents a game show in the form of a play. Explain to children that the play is a fictional story meant to be performed for an audience.

 PREVIEW READERS' THEATER WORDS Point to and read aloud the words on *Student Edition* page 142: *sleuths, host, statue, risk, responds,* and *accurately.* Have children read the words aloud with you.

Reading for Fluency

DISCUSS FLUENCY TIPS Have children read the Reading for Fluency text on *Student Edition* page 142. Remind them that these are the two fluency strategies they learned to use in Lessons 16–19. Explain that throughout the Readers' Theater they will find fluency tips that will remind them to read accurately and with appropriate intonation.

SET A PURPOSE Tell children to listen and read along as you read the selection aloud and demonstrate how to read carefully and correctly. Suggest that they listen to the way that you raise or lower your voice to make it sound natural and relaxed.

READ ALOUD/READ ALONG Have children follow along as you read the script aloud. Remind them to pay close attention to the way you raise or lower your voice, and how you correct errors as you read.

Think Aloud As I read "What's My Job?" aloud, I will read the words carefully. I'll correct myself if I make any mistakes. I will raise and lower my voice the way I would if I were talking to someone.

Read the script aloud a second time. This time, tell children to listen to what the selection tells about, because you will ask them questions.

READERS' THEATER

sleuths

host

responds

accurately

risk

statue

Reading for Fluency

When you read a script aloud,

- make your voice go up and down to help you read with expression.

- take time to read each word correctly.

WHAT'S MY JOB?

Characters

Announcer	Player 2
Host	Player 3
Player 1	Mystery Guest

Setting

The set of a television game show ①

Announcer: Good morning, everyone! Welcome to "What's My Job?"—the game show in which super sleuths use their super detective skills. Here's the host of our show, Sandy Beach, to entertain us.

Host: Good morning! Let's get started. I think most of you have already watched "What's My Job?" For those who haven't, here are the rules. ②

142

143

Monitor Comprehension

PAGES 142–143 Have children look at the illustrations. Ask them where the play might take place. Have them read to find out.

① 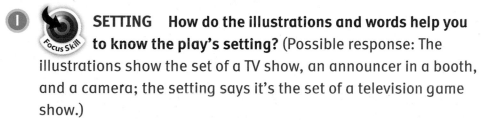 **SETTING** **How do the illustrations and words help you to know the play's setting?** (Possible response: The illustrations show the set of a TV show, an announcer in a booth, and a camera; the setting says it's the set of a television game show.)

② **MAKE PREDICTIONS** **What do you think the contestants will have to do? How do you know?** (Possible response: They will try to figure out something about the Mystery Guest, because the Announcer has said they will have to "use their super detective skills.")

 **SOCIAL STUDIES**

SUPPORTING STANDARDS

ENTERTAINMENT Ask children to identify a type of mass communication used before television. (Possible response: radio) Explain that radio game shows were popular in the United States before television. Before radio and television, people played "parlor games" in their own homes that were like game shows.

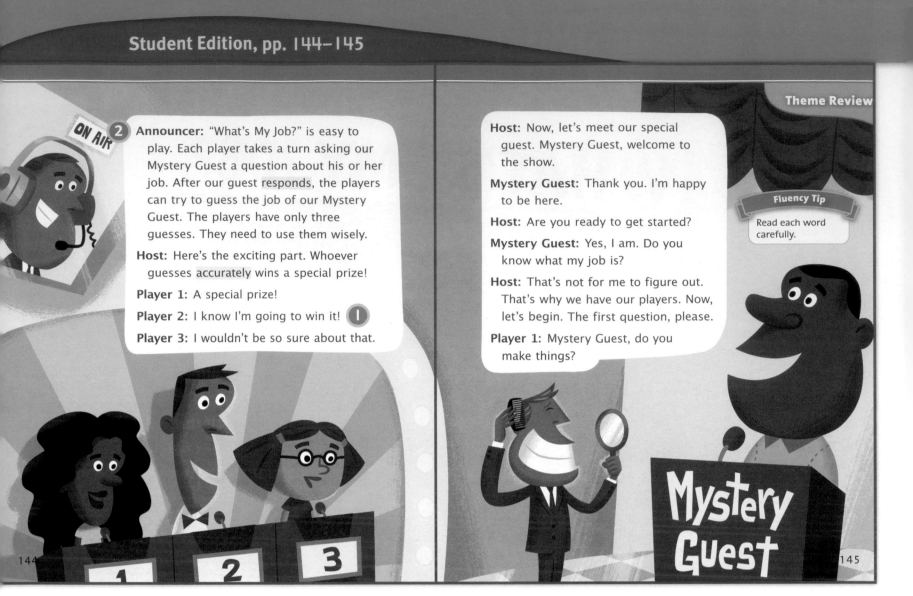

ON AIR

2 **Announcer:** "What's My Job?" is easy to play. Each player takes a turn asking our Mystery Guest a question about his or her job. After our guest responds, the players can try to guess the job of our Mystery Guest. The players have only three guesses. They need to use them wisely.

Host: Here's the exciting part. Whoever guesses accurately wins a special prize!

Player 1: A special prize!

Player 2: I know I'm going to win it! **1**

Player 3: I wouldn't be so sure about that.

Host: Now, let's meet our special guest. Mystery Guest, welcome to the show.

Mystery Guest: Thank you. I'm happy to be here.

Host: Are you ready to get started?

Mystery Guest: Yes, I am. Do you know what my job is?

Host: That's not for me to figure out. That's why we have our players. Now, let's begin. The first question, please.

Player 1: Mystery Guest, do you make things?

Fluency Tip

Read each word carefully.

Mystery Guest

144   145

Monitor Comprehension

PAGES 144–145   Have children look at the illustrations, and ask them to tell what might be happening. Have them read to find out.

1 **CHARACTER'S TRAITS**   What do you think Player 2 is like? Why do you think so? (Possible response: He seems to think he is the sure winner; he announces he will win.)

2 **LOCATE INFORMATION**   How would a person playing the part of the Announcer know which lines to read? (He or she would look for the bold-faced names, or headings, that tell which character is speaking.)

Focus Skill

Reading for Fluency

Fluency Tip   **Accuracy**   Model working to read with accuracy.

Think Aloud   I always have to pay attention to be sure that what I read makes sense. If it doesn't, I know I've probably made a mistake. For example, if I said *acting* instead of *accurately* when I was reading the Announcer's lines on page 144, I would notice my mistake and reread the entire sentence again.

Theme Review

Mystery Guest: Yes, I do.

Player 2: Oh, I know what your job is!

Host: Don't you think you should ask a question first, Player 2? ❶

Player 2: Okay. Mystery Guest, do you make something that people ride in?

Mystery Guest: No, I don't.

Player 2: Really? Well, I guess I don't know what your job is, after all.

Host: Player 3, what is your question for our Mystery Guest?

Player 3: Mystery Guest, do you make something that people enjoy by using their senses?

Mystery Guest: Yes, I do.

Host: Aha! That means seeing, feeling, smelling, hearing, and tasting. It sounds as if you do something creative. Are there any guesses from our players?

Player 2: I know! You make music. You are a musician!

Mystery Guest: No, I'm not. ❷

Fluency Tip

Player 2 is always in a hurry to answer. How should you read these lines?

146

147

Monitor Comprehension

PAGES 146–147 Ask children to look at the illustrations. Ask whether they think the players have guessed what the Mystery Guest does. Have them read to find out.

❶ **CHARACTER'S TRAITS Now what can you tell about Player 2? How do you know?** (Possible response: Player 2 does not think carefully; he just makes guesses without listening for clues.)

❷ *Focus Skill* **SETTING Have the players guessed what the Mystery Guest does? How do you know?** (Possible response: No, even though the studio sign is lit up to say "yes," the mystery guest tells them they have not guessed correctly.)

Reading for Fluency

Fluency Tip **Intonation** Explain to children why the Host's voice would sound different from the voices of other characters.

Think Aloud When people want others to pay attention to what they are saying, they may raise their voices and speak as though they are in charge. I will speak a little louder when I read the part of the Host. He is enthusiastic but wants the players to play the game correctly.

Theme Review

Fluency Tip

Reading slowly and carefully will help you read accurately.

Monitor Comprehension

PAGES 148–149   Have children look at the illustrations. Ask whether they think the players have solved the mystery yet. Have them read to find out.

① **SUMMARIZE**   **What clues do the players have about what the Mystery Guest does?** (They know he uses a hammer to make things, and that people can use their senses to enjoy the things he makes.)

② **LOCATE INFORMATION**   **If you wanted to review the information the players got from the Mystery Guest, how could you quickly locate it?** (Possible response: You could look for the boldfaced headings labeled *Mystery Guest*.)

Reading for Fluency

Fluency Tip   **Accuracy**   Point out that Player 2 seems excitable and is too quick with his answers. Explain that someone reading this part would probably have to practice beforehand to be careful to read his lines correctly.

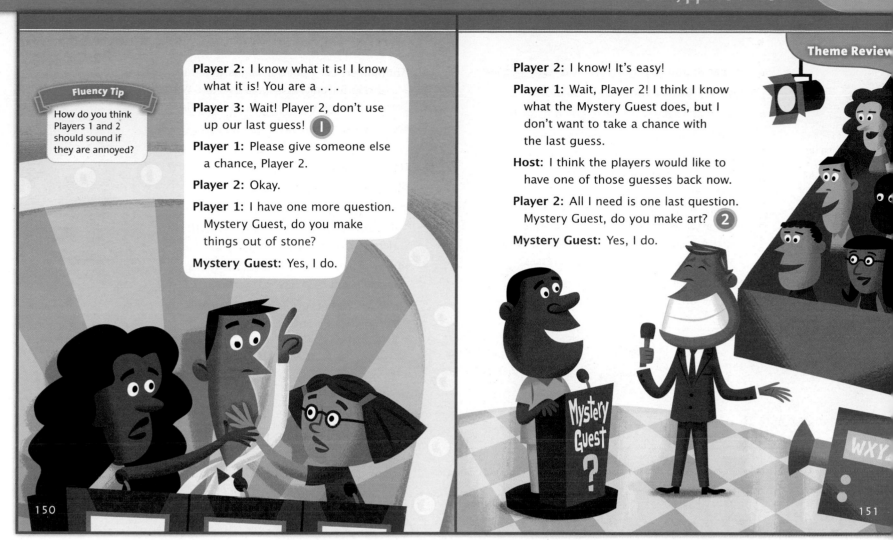

Monitor Comprehension

PAGES 150–151   Have children look at the Illustration. Ask them why the other players are covering Player 2's mouth. Have them read to find out.

1 **DRAW CONCLUSIONS**   **What would happen if the other players allowed Player 2 to say whatever he wanted to say on the game show?** (Possible response: He might yell out the wrong answer, and they would all lose the game.)

2 **MAKE INFERENCES**   **Do you think Player 2 really knew the right answer?** (Possible response: His last question was "Do you make art?" so he probably could have figured it out correctly this time.)

Reading for Fluency

Fluency Tip   **Intonation**

Remind children that an interruption cuts into what another person is saying. The word *Wait!* on page 150 should be said quickly and loudly, so that Player 3 sounds as if she is stopping Player 2 from saying the wrong thing.

Fluency Tip

Breaking the announcer's long part into shorter sections will make it easier to read.

Player 3: You're a sculptor!

Mystery Guest: Yes, I am a sculptor!

Player 2: That's what I was going to say!

Host: I'm sorry, Player 2, we can have only one winner.

Announcer: That was good detective work, Player 3. You concentrated on the clues. A sculptor uses a hammer to make a statue out of stone, and statues are art! A sculptor can sell art to people who want it for their homes or businesses.

Host: Actually, all of our players did a great job, but Player 3 earned the prize. ❶ ❷

CLAP CLAP CLAP

WINNER

152

Announcer: Let's put our hands together and clap for our Mystery Guest, too. We want to thank you for being on our show.

Mystery Guest: I really liked the show. It was a lot of fun!

Host: By the way, Player 3, do you like art?

Player 3: I sure do.

Host: That's good, because your prize is a statue made by our Mystery Guest! Here it is! Aren't you thrilled?

Player 2: I'm startled. The statue looks just like you.

Host: That's because it is me—Sandy Beach, your carefree game show host. Now that's art!

153

Monitor Comprehension

PAGES 152–153 Have children look at the announcer clapping. Do they think there is a winner? Have them read to find out.

❶ **MAIN IDEA AND DETAILS** **What information did the winner use to figure out the job of the Mystery Guest?** (Possible response: The mystery guest makes things that people enjoy with their senses. He uses a hammer and stone, so he is a sculptor.)

❷ **DRAW CONCLUSIONS** **Do you think it is better to make a quick guess when you are being a sleuth, or is it better to take your time and think about it first?** (Possible response: It is better to think first. Player 2 might have been given a chance to guess if he had not already used so many chances making quick guesses without thinking first.)

ART

SUPPORTING STANDARDS

Point out to children that Player 3 asked "Mystery Guest, do you make something that people enjoy by using their senses?" and his answer was yes. Ask students which senses can be used to enjoy a sculpture. (sight, touch) Ask them how this art form is different from poetry, a painting, or music.

Build Robust Vocabulary

Words About the Readers' Theater

Teach/Model

 Routine Card 3

INTRODUCE ROBUST VOCABULARY   Use *Routine Card 3* to introduce the words.

❶ Put the word in **selection context**.

❷ Display Transparency R104 and read the word and the **Student-Friendly Explanation**.

❸ Have children **say the word** with you.

❹ Use the word in other contexts, and have children **interact with the word's meaning**.

❺ Remove the transparency. Say the Student-Friendly Explanation again, and ask children to **name the word** that goes with it.

❶ **Selection Context:** Only one **opponent** would win the game.

❹ **Interact with Word Meaning:** Which opponent would be most likely to win a contest—one who was prepared or one who didn't really care? Explain.

❶ **Selection Context:** Player 2 was **impulsive** and didn't take time to think about his questions and answers.

❹ **Interact with Word Meaning:** Would someone who was impulsive be more likely to save his or her money or spend it? Tell why.

Practice/Apply

GUIDED PRACTICE   Ask children to do the following:

• Describe a time when you cheered for one *opponent* to win a game or a contest. Tell what the other opponent was like.

• Explain whether it is *impulsive* to study for a test, or to sing a happy song on a sunny day.

INDEPENDENT PRACTICE   Have children work with a partner to name two situations in which they would be *opponents*, and two situations in which they might be *impulsive*.

Objective

• *To develop robust vocabulary through discussing a literature selection*

Tested

INTRODUCE ✓

Vocabulary: Lesson 20

opponent   **impulsive**

▼ **Student-Friendly Explanations**

Student-Friendly Explanations

encountered	If you met someone you didn't expect to see, you encountered that person.
originated	The time when something started or began is when it originated.
opponent	When you play against someone else to win a game or contest, you are that person's opponent.
impulsive	When someone often does things without thinking, that person is impulsive.

Grade 2, Lesson 20   R104   Vocabulary

Transparency R104

Grammar

Quick Write

Review: Adjectives

5-DAY GRAMMAR	
DAY 1	Review Adjectives
DAY 2	Review Adjectives for Senses
DAY 3	Review Number Words
DAY 4	Review Words That Compare
DAY 5	Cumulative Review

Objectives

- *To identify and use adjectives*
- *To use adjectives in sentences*

Daily Proofreading

where is Sams' red lunchbox?
(Where, Sam's)

Writing Trait

Strengthening Conventions

Review Use these short daily lessons with children's own writing to continue building a foundation for revising/editing longer connected text. See also *Writer's Companion*, Lesson 20.

Reinforce the Skill

REVIEW ADJECTIVES   Review what children have learned about adjectives by using the following points:

- An adjective tells about a noun.
- Some adjectives tell about color.
- Some adjectives tell about size or shape.

Write the following nouns on the board:

balloon   cake   car

Tell children that an adjective can be added to each word to tell the color, size, or shape of the noun. Point to and read aloud *balloon*. Write *green* before *balloon*. Elicit that *green* tells the color of the balloon. Have children suggest adjectives that tell the size, shape, or color for the remaining words.

Practice/Apply

GUIDED PRACTICE   Write the following incomplete sentences on the board. Ask children to help you add adjectives to tell about the color, size, or shape of the underlined nouns.

My <u>backpack</u> is _____.
Please bring me a _____ <u>box</u>.
I saw a _____ <u>nest</u> in the tree.

INDEND PRACTICE   Display two items, such as a flower in a vase and a book. Have children write two sentences about each item to tell about its shape, color, or size. Have partners read each other's sentences and underline the adjectives.

The flower is <u>purple</u>.
The flower has <u>big</u> petals.

Writing

Select a Piece and Revise

5-DAY WRITING	
DAY 1	Select a Piece and Revise
DAY 2	Revise
DAY 3	Publish
DAY 4	Publish
DAY 5	Present

Revise

SELECT WRITING Tell children to select one of the writing pieces they started earlier in this theme, such as the how-to paragraph or the poem. Tell them to reread it and think about what they could do to improve it. Explain that they will revise the piece of writing that they select, and will decide on a way to publish their writing to share it with others.

Point out that when children reread their writing from earlier in the theme they may notice parts that could be clearer, or places where they could have used more colorful adjectives.

WRITING TRAIT **ORGANIZATION** Tell children to check the organization of the piece they select to revise. Students should ask themselves if the order makes sense and if the details tie together in an order that flows.

ADD DESCRIPTIVE WORDS Remind children that reviewing and revising using descriptive words can help improve their writing. Write this sentence on the board: *We painted my room red.* Discuss how revising the sentence to *We painted my room a bright fire-engine red* helps give a better idea of the color. Encourage children to use a thesaurus or dictionary to find more possibilities.

GRAMMAR–WRITING CONNECTION Remind children to check that they use adjectives that describe color, size, and shape correctly, and that they are satisfied with other adjectives they have included.

Objective

• *To revise a piece of writing*

Writing Prompt

Independent Writing Have children write a notebook entry telling which piece from Theme 4 was the most difficult or tricky to write, and explain why.

Discuss Revisions Encourage children to tell or point out changes they might like to make, and help children note their ideas. If needed, ask questions about the piece to help generate ideas for revision. Work with children to identify words and phrases they can use as they revise.

Day at a Glance

Day 2

 phonics and Spelling
- Review: Short Vowel /e/*ea*

Comprehension

 Focus Skill
- Review: Setting
- Review: Antonyms

Fluency

READERS' THEATER

- Read Together: "What's My Job?"
Student Edition
pp. 142–153

Read!

Robust Vocabulary

- *Read-Aloud Anthology:* "Mount Rushmore"
- *Words from the Read-Aloud*
Introduce: *encountered, originated*

Grammar [Quick Write]

- Review: Adjectives for Senses

Writing

- Revise

Warm-Up Routines

 Oral Language

Objective *To listen attentively and respond appropriately to oral communication*

> ### Question of the Day
> **What do the sounds you hear at school remind you of?**

Invite children to discuss the sounds they hear at school and tell how they are like music. Use the following prompts:

- **What sounds at school have a special beat? How does that beat sound?**

- **When I hear the sound of many feet going down the stairs, it reminds me of drum beats. What other sounds at school remind you of music?**

Have children complete the following sentence frames.

> **One sound I hear at school is _____.**
>
> **It reminds me of _____.**

Read Aloud

Objective *To listen for a purpose*

BIG BOOK OF RHYMES AND POEMS Display the poem "The Drum" on page 31 and read aloud the title. Remind children that they read this poem earlier in the theme. Tell children to listen for what the speaker says as you read the poem aloud. Then read the poem. Discuss what the speaker might mean by "I'm gonna beat out my own rhythm." Choral-read the first three lines of the poem, and have children read the final two lines using their own rhythm.

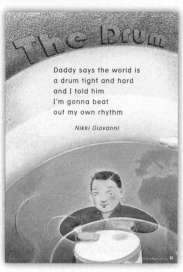

The Drum

Daddy says the world is
a drum tight and hard
and I told him
I'm gonna beat
out my own rhythm

Nikki Giovanni

▲ Big Book of Rhymes and Poems, p. 31

Word Wall

Objective *To read high-frequency words*

REVIEW HIGH-FREQUENCY WORDS Review the following words on the Word Wall: *question, something, sure, enjoy, coming, idea, quite, believe, different,* and *guess.* Point to the words at random. For each word, have children read it, spell it, and finally read it again. Then point to a word, call on a child to use it in a sentence, and then read the word together again.

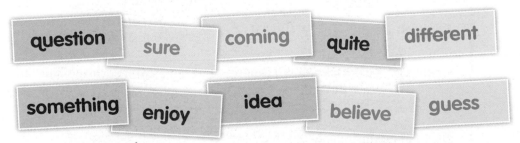

question   sure   coming   quite   different

something   enjoy   idea   believe   guess

Short Vowel /e/ ea
phonics *and Spelling*

Objectives

- *To recognize the short vowel /e/ sound of* ea
- *To read words with /e/ea and other known letter-sounds*
- *To use /e/ea and other known letter-sounds to spell words*

Spelling Words

1. **know***	6. **health**
2. **wrong***	7. **soil**
3. **tough**	8. **joy**
4. **phone**	9. **deer**
5. **breath**	10. **rear**

* Words from "What's My Job?"

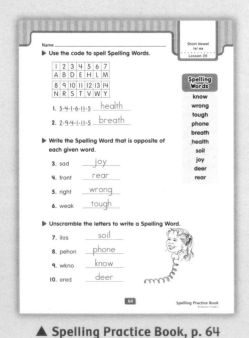

▲ Spelling Practice Book, p. 64

Review

READ A SPELLING WORD Write the word *health* on the board. Ask children to identify the vowel pair in the word. Remind children that *ea* can stand for the /e/ sound. Then read the word—*health*. Have children read the word. Discuss that *ea* can also stand for the /ē/ sound in *read,* and that good readers think about which sound makes sense in the sentence they are reading.

BUILD SPELLING WORDS Have children follow your directions to change one or more letters in each of the following words to make a spelling word. Have them write the word on a sheet of paper or in their notebooks. Then have a volunteer change the spelling of the word on the board so that children can self-check their spelling.

- Write *head* on the board. Ask: **Which spelling word can you make by changing the last letter?** *(health)*

- Write *path* on the board. Ask: **Which spelling word can you make by changing the first letter?** *(breath)*

Follow a similar procedure with the words *knot (know), bone (phone), steer (deer), wrote (wrong), toy (joy), near (rear), enough (tough), boil (soil).*

BELOW-LEVEL	ADVANCED
Spelling Game List the spelling words on the board. Then say: **I'm looking for a word with the /e/ sound that names something I take many times a day. (breath)** Ask similar question for the other words, focusing on targeted phonic elements.	**Write Rhymes** Have children think of and write a word that rhymes with each spelling word. Have partners exchange lists and write the spelling word that matches each rhyming word.

5-DAY PHONICS
DAY 1 Review /n/kn, /r/wr, /f/gh, ph
DAY 2 Review /e/ea
DAY 3 Review /oi/oi, oy
DAY 4 Review /ir/ear, eer
DAY 5 Cumulative Review

Read Words in Context

APPLY PHONICS Write the following sentences on the board or on chart paper. Have children read each sentence silently. Then track the print as children read the sentence aloud.

> I took a deep <u>breath</u> and jumped into the pool.
>
> Eating fruits and vegetables is good for your <u>health</u>.
>
> You should water the plant when the <u>soil</u> feels dry.
>
> Cindy ran to the kitchen to answer the <u>phone</u>.
>
> I got one answer <u>wrong</u> on the test.

WRITE Write the spelling words on the board or on chart paper. On their own, have children write the words in alphabetical order. Have partners check each other's work.

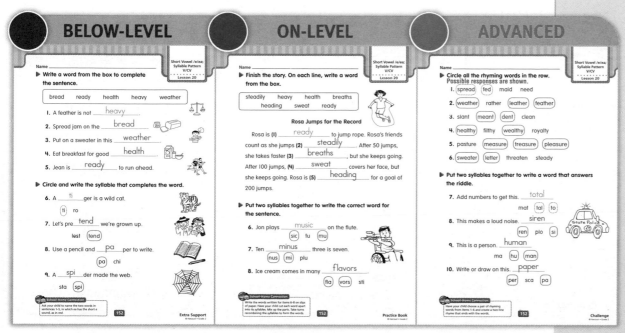

BELOW-LEVEL

▲ Extra Support, p. 152

ON-LEVEL

▲ Practice Book, p. 152

ADVANCED

▲ Challenge, p. 152

ELL

- Group children according to academic levels, and assign one of the pages on the left.

- Clarify any unfamiliar concepts as necessary. See *ELL Teacher Guide* Lesson 20 for support in scaffolding instruction.

Setting
Comprehension: Review

Objectives
- *To identify the setting of a story*
- *To analyze setting elements*

Skill Trace
Setting

Introduce	T34–T35
Reteach	S18–S19
Review	T67, T83, T95, T134–T135 T171, T187, T197, T389, T406
Test	Theme 4
Maintain	Theme 5, T87

Review

DISCUSS SETTING Have children turn to *Student Edition* page 54. Remind children of how to identify the setting of a story.

Think Aloud **As I read a story, I notice clues that tell me about the time of day, the season, and where the main character is. Sometimes the setting will change during a story. Noticing the setting and how it changes helps me understand the story.**

Practice/Apply

GUIDED PRACTICE Draw a chart like the one on *Student Edition* page 55. Return to "Mr. Putter and Tabby Write the Book," *Student Edition* pages 22–43, and guide children to add details about the setting to the chart.

INDEPENDENT PRACTICE Have children complete the chart to show how the setting of the story changes.

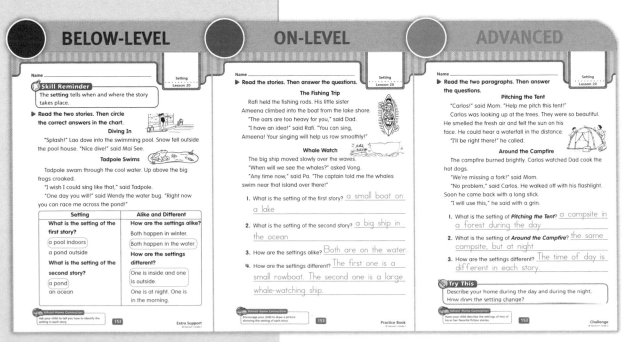

▲ **Extra Support, p. 153**   ▲ **Practice Book, p. 153**   ▲ **Challenge, p. 153**

- Group children according to academic levels, and assign one of the pages on the left.

- Clarify any unfamiliar concepts as necessary. See *ELL Teacher Guide* Lesson 20 for support in scaffolding instruction.

Follow Directions

Comprehension: Review

5-DAY PHONICS	
DAY 1	Introduce /o/o
DAY 2	Word Building with /o/o
DAY 3	Word Building with /o/o and /i/i
DAY 4	Inflections -ed, -ing; Review /o/o
DAY 5	Inflections -ed, -ing; Review /o/o

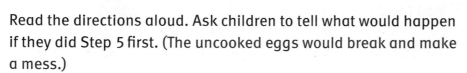
Reinforce the Skill

EXPLAIN FOLLOW DIRECTIONS   Discuss reading and following directions with children. Elicit that directions provide information about how to do or make something. Model how to follow written directions:

> **Think Aloud**   I know that if I want to follow directions, I have to read the directions carefully and then follow the steps in the correct order.

Practice/Apply

GUIDED PRACTICE   Remind children that in "Mr. Putter and Tabby Write the Book," Mr. Putter made boiled eggs. Write the following steps on the board or on chart paper.

1. Place eggs in a pan. Fill the pan with enough water to cover the eggs.

2. Place the pan on the stove. Bring the water to a boil.

3. When the water boils, lower the heat. Cook for 15 minutes.

4. Take the pan off the stove. Run cold water over the eggs for a minute so they don't overcook.

5. Roll the eggs between your hands to crack and remove the shells.

Read the directions aloud. Ask children to tell what would happen if they did Step 5 first. (The uncooked eggs would break and make a mess.)

INDEPENDENT PRACTICE   Have partners work together to write a set of directions that tell how to sharpen a pencil or how to put word cards in alphabetical order. Then have them exchange their directions with another pair and discuss how to follow the steps.

Objectives

- *To identify the purpose of reading, such as to follow directions*
- *To follow written directions*

Skill Trace
Tested Follow Directions

Introduce	T68–T69
Reteach	S12–S13, S24–S25
Review	**T172–T173, T407, T417**
Test	Theme 4
Maintain	Theme 6, T87

READERS' THEATER

Read Together: "What's My Job?"

5-DAY READERS' THEATER	
DAY 1	Read Aloud/Read Along
DAY 2	Read Together
DAY 3	Choose Roles/Rehearse
DAY 4	Rehearse Roles
DAY 5	Perform

Objective

- *To practice reading fluently and accurately with appropriate intonation*

Fluency Support Materials

Fluency Builders, Grade 2, Lesson 20

Audiotext "What's My Job?" is available on *Audiotext Grade 2*, CD 4.

What's My Job?

Characters

Announcer	Player 1	Player 3
Host	Player 2	Mystery Guest

Announcer: Good morning, everyone! Welcome to "What's My Job?"—the game show in which super sleuths use their super detective skills. Here's the host of our show, Sandy Beach, to entertain us.

Host: Good morning! Let's get started. I think most of you have already watched "What's My Job?" For those who haven't, here are the rules.

Announcer: "What's My Job?" is easy to play. Each player takes a turn asking our Mystery Guest a question about his or her job. After our guest responds, the players can try to guess the job of our Mystery Guest. The players have only three guesses. They need to use them wisely.

Host: Here's the exciting part. Whoever guesses accurately wins a special prize!

Player 1: A special prize!

Player 2: I know I'm going to win it!

Lesson 20: What's My Job? 124 Teacher Resource Book

▲ **Teacher Resource Book, pp. 134–139**

Preview

GENRE Have children open their books to page 142–153, or distribute photocopies of the script from *Teacher Resource Book* pages 134–139. Help children recall that "What's My Job?" is a play script about a game show. Remind them that a play is a story that is written to be performed. Explain that this particular play will be read aloud only, but that the characters' feelings can be understood by how children use intonation and expression to read the lines.

Focus on Fluency

DISCUSS INTONATION AND ACCURACY Remind children that in this theme they learned that good readers read carefully to say each word as written, and they correct themselves if they make a mistake. Point out that they should also raise or lower their voice to make a point or to show how a character is feeling.

Read Together

ORAL READING Have children take turns reading different parts in the Readers' Theater script. Point out that parts will be assigned later. Explain that in this first reading, they should concentrate on reading accurately and using intonation to help them read more fluently. Then have small groups of children begin reading the script aloud. Tell children that when they make mistakes, they should stop, correct their mistakes, and continue reading.

Visit the different groups, listening to children read. Offer encouragement, and model fluent reading as children need it.

Think Aloud I can tell that the Host has an outgoing personality, and that his job is to keep the show going smoothly. I will raise my voice when I read his lines to get the attention of the listeners.

Build Robust Vocabulary
Words from the Read-Aloud

Teach/Model

 Routine Card 3

INTRODUCE ROBUST VOCABULARY Use *Routine Card 3* to introduce the last two words.

Read-Aloud Anthology, ▶ **"Mount Rushmore," p. 74**

❶ Put the word in **selection context**.

❷ Display Transparency R104 and say the word and the **Student-Friendly Explanation**.

❸ Have children **say the word** with you.

❹ Use the word in other contexts, and have children **interact with the word's meaning**.

❺ Remove the transparency. Say the Student-Friendly Explanation again, and ask children to **name the word** that goes with it.

❶ **Selection Context:** Gutzon Borglum **encountered** problems when he was working on creating Mount Rushmore.

❹ **Interact with Word Meaning:** What are some things you might do if you encountered problems while doing some homework?

❶ **Selection Context:** Work on the memorial at Mount Rushmore **originated** in 1927.

❹ **Interact with Word Meaning:** If you knew that work on a new school originated a year ago, would you know when it was completed? Why?

Practice/Apply

GUIDED PRACTICE Ask children to tell a partner about when his or her time in school *originated* and describe a time when he or she *encountered* a problem in school.

INDEPENDENT PRACTICE Have children write a sentence that tells of a problem they *encountered* in first grade.

Objective

• *To develop robust vocabulary through discussing a literature selection*

INTRODUCE ✓ **Tested**

Vocabulary: Lesson 20

encountered   **originated**

▼ **Student-Friendly Explanations**

Student-Friendly Explanations

encountered	If you met someone you didn't expect to see, you encountered that person.
originated	The time when something started or began is when it originated.
opponent	When you play against someone else to win a game or contest, you are that person's opponent.
impulsive	When someone often does things without thinking, that person is impulsive.

Grade 2, Lesson 20 ▫ R104 ▫ Vocabulary

Transparency R104

Grammar [Quick Write]

Review: Adjectives for Senses

5-DAY GRAMMAR	
DAY 1	Review Adjectives
DAY 2	Review Adjectives for Senses
DAY 3	Review Number Words
DAY 4	Review Words That Compare
DAY 5	Cumulative Review

Objectives

- *To recognize that adjectives for senses describe how something looks, smells, tastes, sounds, or feels*
- *To write using adjectives for senses*

Daily Proofreading

Do we have a test on friday.

(Friday?)

Writing Trait

Strengthening Conventions

Review Use these short daily lessons with children's own writing to continue building a foundation for revising/editing longer connected text.

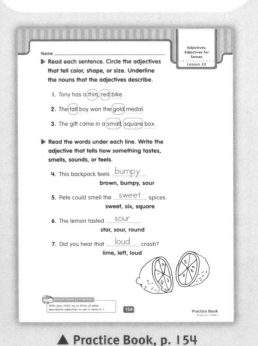

▲ Practice Book, p. 154

Reinforce the Skill

REVIEW ADJECTIVES FOR SENSES Review the following points with children:

- Adjectives for senses are words that describe how something looks, smells, tastes, sounds, or feels.
- Adjectives for senses can come before or after the word they describe.
- Adjectives for senses make writing more colorful and fun to read.

Brainstorm a list of adjectives for each of the senses. Ask volunteers to dictate sentences that include at least one of the adjectives from the list. Write children's sentences on the board, underlining the sensory adjectives.

Practice/Apply

GUIDED PRACTICE Model revising the following sentence to include one or more sensory adjectives.

Kevin wanted a glass of lemonade. (Kevin wanted an icy glass of sweet lemonade.)

Write the following sentences on the board. Ask volunteers to help you add sensory adjectives to each one.

The puppy barked.

Mrs. Brown brought us some muffins.

Kelly sat down in the chair.

 INDEPENDENT PRACTICE Have children write sentences using sensory adjectives. Have volunteers read aloud their sentences.

Writing
Revise

5-DAY WRITING
DAY 1 Select a Piece and Revise
DAY 2 Revise
DAY 3 Publish
DAY 4 Publish
DAY 5 Present

Revise

REVISE Explain to children that good writers want to be satisfied with their work and may revise their writing several times before they feel that their work is at its best. Point out that by having a friend or an adult read through a draft, a writer may get suggestions or ideas that he or she might not have thought of or considered.

Think Aloud I like to have a friend read my writing when I am revising. I like to hear what he or she likes about my work, and it really helps to get ideas about how I could make my writing even better.

Have children work with a partner to read each other's work as they continue to revise their drafts. Encourage readers to be clear about parts they enjoy or admire, and to provide clear, positive suggestions to help improve the piece.

WRITING TRAIT **ORGANIZATION** Have children check that their ideas flow smoothly in an order that makes sense. Suggest that they check that each idea is closely conected to the main topic of their writing. Point out that they should omit any unrelated ideas.

GRAMMAR–WRITING CONNECTION Remind children to check that they have included strong adjectives. Remind children to use Editor's Marks to indicate changes they want or need to make.

CONFER WITH CHILDREN Meet with individual children, helping them as they revise their writing. Ask children to tell what changes their partner suggested, and how they plan to address them. Offer encouragement for what they are doing well, and make constructive suggestions for improving an aspect of the writing, as needed.

Editor's Marks	
∧	Add
ℐ	Take out
⋀	Change
⊙	Add a period
≡	Capitalize
◯	Check spelling

Objectives

- *To progress through the stages of the writing process*
- *To revise a self-selected piece of assigned writing*

Writing Prompt

Use Sense of Smell Have children think about a favorite food and write a few sentences to describe what it smells like.

▲ **Writer's Companion, Lesson 20**

Day at a Glance

Day 3

phonics and Spelling

- Review: Vowel Diphthong /oi/*oi*, *oy*

Comprehension

- Review: Locate Information
- Review: Follow Directions

Fluency

READERS' THEATER

- Choose Roles/Rehearse: "What's My Job?" *Student Edition*, pp. 142–153

Read!

Robust Vocabulary

- Review: *sleuths, host, statue, risk, responds, accurately*

Grammar *Quick Write*

- Review: Number Words

Writing ✏️

- Publish

Warm-Up Routines

⏱ Oral Language

Objective *To listen attentively and respond appropriately to oral communication*

Question of the Day

Do you think it would be fun to be part of a marching band?

Why do you think so?

Invite children to speculate about what it would be like to be in a marching band.

- **What instruments would be easy to march with? Which ones might be difficult to march with?**

- **Would you like to march past the people watching the parade? Why or why not?**

Write children's ideas on the board.

Read Aloud

Objective *To read a poem aloud using appropriate volume and expression*

BIG BOOK OF RHYMES AND POEMS
Display the poem "Here Comes the Band" on page 33. Review the onomatopoetic words used in the poem and the sounds they make. Divide children into four groups, and assign each group an instrument named in the poem. Practice a choral reading of the poem. When you get to each instrument, have just the members of that group say the sound and pantomime playing the instrument.

▲ Big Book of Rhymes and Poems, p. 33

Word Wall

Objective *To read high-frequency words*

REVIEW HIGH-FREQUENCY WORDS Review the following words on the Word Wall: *question, something, sure, enjoy, coming, idea, quite, believe, different,* and *guess.* Then divide the class into two groups. Have the members of each group go through the words in order several times. Taking turns, each child should read one word at a time.

Vowel Diphthong /oi/ *oi*, *oy*

 phonics *and Spelling*

5-DAY PHONICS	
DAY 1	Review /n/*kn*, /r/*wr*, /f/*gh*, *ph*
DAY 2	Review /e/ *ea*
DAY 3	Review /oi/*oi*, *oy*
DAY 4	Review /ir/*ear*, *eer*
DAY 5	Cumulative Review

Objectives

- *To recognize and blend the vowel diphthong /oi/*oi*, *oy**
- *To read words with /oi/*oi*, *oy* and other known letter sounds*
- *To use /oi/*oi*, *oy* and other known letter sounds to spell words*

Skill Trace

 Tested **Vowel Diphthong /oi/*oi*, *oy***

Introduce	T220–T223
Reteach	S26–S27
Review	T232–T233, T250–T251, T414
Test	Theme 4

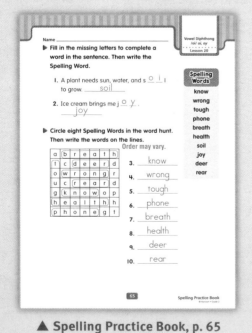

▲ Spelling Practice Book, p. 65

Review

Routine Card 1

CONNECT LETTERS AND SOUNDS   Remind children that they have learned that the letters *oi* and *oy* can stand for the /oi/ sound. Display the *Sound/Spelling Card* for /oi/*oi*, *oy*. Point to *oi* and review the letter/sound correspondence. Say: **The letters *oi* can stand for the /oi/ sound, the sound in *coin*.** Touch *oi* several times, and have children say /oi/ each time. Repeat with *oy*. Say: **The letters *oy* can also stand for the /oi/ sound, the sound in *toy*.** Touch *oy* several times, and have children say /oi/ each time.

▲ Sound/Spelling Card

Read Words in Context

APPLY PHONICS   Write the following sentences on the board or on chart paper. Have children read each sentence silently. Then track the print as children read the sentences aloud.

> I'm glad you could <u>join</u> us to <u>enjoy</u> the art show at the museum.
>
> Please <u>point</u> out the <u>oil</u> painting you liked of a <u>boy</u> and a pony.
>
> It's very <u>noisy</u> in here today!
>
> Let's use quiet <u>voices</u> so we don't <u>annoy</u> others.

5-DAY SPELLING

DAY 1	Pretest
DAY 2	Word Building
DAY 3	**State the Generalization**
DAY 4	Review
DAY 5	Posttest

Review Spelling Words

STATE THE GENERALIZATION FOR /oi/oi, oy List spelling words 1–10 on chart paper or on the board. Circle the word *soil* and ask children to read it. Ask a volunteer to identify the letters that stand for the /oi/ sound and underline them. Then repeat the process with the word *joy*. Follow a similar procedure to identify the letters that stand for the following phonic elements:

- digraphs /n/*kn*; /r/*wr*; /f/*gh, ph*
- short vowel /e/*ea*
- *r*-controlled vowel /ir/*ear, eer*

WRITE Have children write the spelling words in their notebooks. Remind them to use their best handwriting and to use the chart to check their spelling.

Handwriting

LETTER SIZES Remind children to make sure that they have used appropriate sizes for tall and short letters.

Spelling Words

1.	**know***	6.	**health**
2.	**wrong***	7.	**soil**
3.	**tough**	8.	**joy**
4.	**phone**	9.	**deer**
5.	**breath**	10.	**rear**

* Words from "What's My Job?"

BELOW-LEVEL

Work with a Partner Have partners write each spelling word on an index card. Have one child choose a card and say the word. Next their partner spells the word while the first child checks the spelling. Then have them switch roles.

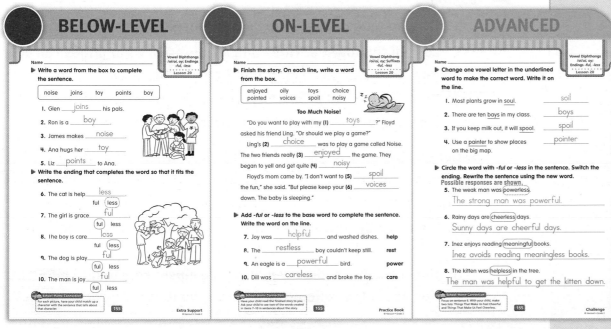

▲ **Extra Support, p. 155**   ▲ **Practice Book, p. 155**   ▲ **Challenge, p. 155**

E L L

- Group children according to academic levels, and assign one of the pages on the left.

- Clarify any unfamiliar concepts as necessary. See *ELL Teacher Guide* Lesson 20 for support in scaffolding instruction.

Locate Information
Comprehension: Review

Objective

- *To use the parts of a book to locate information*

Skill Trace

 Tested **Locate Information**

Introduce	T224–T225
Reteach	S30–S31, S42–S43
Review	**T253, T269, T281, T308–T309, T337, T353, T363, T416, T437**
Test	Theme 4
Maintain	Theme 5, T279

Reinforce the Skill

DISCUSS LOCATE INFORMATION Remind children that they can use different parts of a book to help them locate information. Discuss these parts of a book, using the *Student Edition*:

- A **Table of Contents** tells on which page each selection begins.

- An **index** is a list of subjects, arranged in alphabetical order, with page numbers. Have children locate the Index of Titles and Authors on pages 498–499.

- **Headings** tell what a section of a selection will be about. Have children turn to "The Life of George Washington Carver" on pages 122–135, and point out the headings.

- Words in a **glossary** or **dictionary** are arranged in alphabetical order, with guide words at the top of each page. Have children locate the Glossary which begins on page 486.

Practice/Apply

GUIDED PRACTICE To practice locating information in different parts of a book, ask the following questions about the *Student Edition*:

1. **On what page does "Annie's Gifts" begin?** (page 58)

2. **Look at the Index of Titles and Authors. On what pages can you find "Sarah Enters a Painting"?** (page 88)

3. **What are the guide words on the page where you can find the meaning of the word *expression*?** (*except* and *fragrant*)

INDEPENDENT PRACTICE Have children return to "The Life of George Washington Carver" on pages 122–135 and write answers to the following questions:

4. **What are the headings in this selection?** (*Childhood, School Days, Teacher and Scientist*)

5. **Under which heading would you be most likely to find information about the college at which Carver taught?** (*Teacher and Scientist*)

Follow Directions
Comprehension: Review

Reinforce the Skill

REVIEW FOLLOW DIRECTIONS Remind children that they need to follow directions when they play a new game, go to a new place, or make something. Elicit and review things good readers should do to follow directions. (Read all the directions first; look for steps or words that tell about order, read directions again.)

GUIDED PRACTICE Place a number of red and blue crayons on a table. Assign an even number of volunteers to a red team and a blue team. Write the following directions on the board or on chart paper.

1. Go to the table and take one crayon that is not the color of your team.

2. Exchange crayons with someone on the other team.

Read the directions. Have teams follow them. At the end, each child should have a crayon that matches his or her team's color.

INDEPENDENT PRACTICE Have children write a sentence to explain what might happen if they did not follow Step 1 correctly. (They would have the wrong color crayon.)

Objectives

- To identify the purpose for reading, such as to follow directions
- To follow written two-step directions

Skill Trace
Tested Follow Directions

Introduce	T68–T69
Reteach	S12–S13, S24–S25
Review	**T172–T173, T407, T417**
Test	Theme 4
Maintain	Theme 6, T87

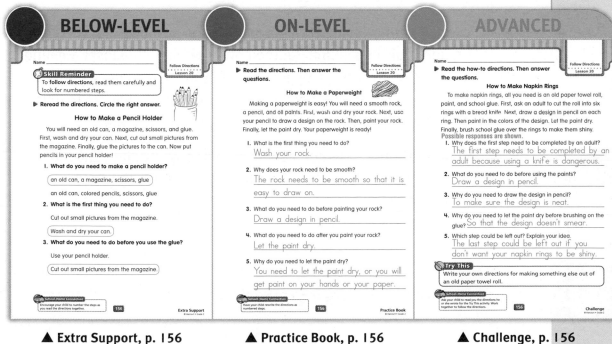

▲ Extra Support, p. 156   ▲ Practice Book, p. 156   ▲ Challenge, p. 156

ELL

- Group children according to academic levels, and assign one of the pages on the left.
- Clarify any unfamiliar concepts as necessary. See *ELL Teacher Guide* Lesson 20 for support in scaffolding instruction.

READERS' THEATER

Choose Roles: "What's My Job?"

5-DAY READERS' THEATER	
DAY 1	Read Aloud/Read Along
DAY 2	Read Together
DAY 3	**Choose Roles/Rehearse**
DAY 4	Rehearse Roles
DAY 5	Perform

Objective

- *To practice reading accurately with appropriate intonation*

Fluency Support Materials

Fluency Builders, Grade 2, Lesson 20

 Audiotext "What's My Job?" is available on *Audiotext Grade 2,* CD 4.

Choosing Roles You may wish to assign children needing language development support to the role of the Mystery Guest. Children who need less support may choose their own roles.

Focus on Fluency

READ ACCURATELY WITH INTONATION Remind children that when they read aloud, they should use a tone of voice that reflects the speaker's feelings. Explain that they should raise or lower their voice as they would if they were speaking to a friend. Remind them to read words carefully, so that what the character is saying makes sense.

Practice Reading

CHOOSE/ASSIGN ROLES Distribute copies of the script to the children if you have not already done so. Based on your observations on Day 2, assign or have children choose roles. Although the play is just one extended scene, you may wish to divide it into sections and split the roles among children so that everyone has a part. After you assign roles, encourage children to highlight the parts they will read aloud.

PRACTICE AND REHEARSE You may wish to have children involved in "scenes" sit together in groups. Read through the text one or two times. Have listeners follow along. Allow children time to become familiar with their lines. You may find it helpful to group children as though they were on the set of a game show.

Provide feedback to individuals and groups by modeling, encouraging, and praising children for their efforts and enthusiasm. Remind children to correct themselves when they make a mistake and to practice using appropriate intonation. Encourage children to give positive feedback to each other as they read their parts.

Monitor children's engagement with their own reading. Encourage them to note text they read fluently, as well as text they need to practice more.

Build Robust Vocabulary

Review

Reinforce Word Meanings

USE VOCABULARY IN DIFFERENT CONTEXTS   Remind children of the Student-Friendly Explanations. Discuss each word in a new context.

sleuths

- What skills do sleuths need?

host

- Tell about someone who was a host at a school show or concert.

statue

- How do you think an artist might make a statue?

risk

- When is it a risk to cross a street?

responds

- What happens when someone responds to an invitation?

accurately

- Does it matter if you don't do your homework accurately? Why?

Objectives

- *To review robust vocabulary*
- *To figure out a word's meaning based on its context*

REVIEW ✓ Tested

Vocabulary

sleuths	risk
host	responds
statue	accurately

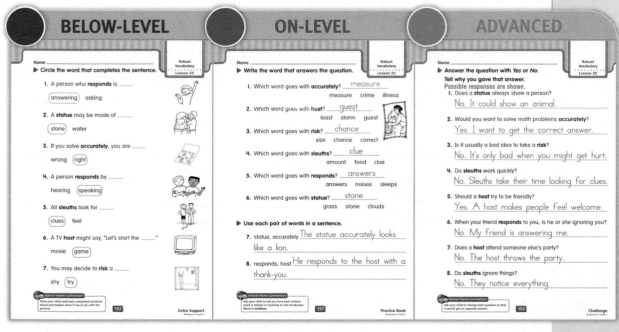

▲ **Extra Support, p. 157**   ▲ **Practice Book, p. 157**   ▲ **Challenge, p. 157**

E L L

- Group children according to academic levels, and assign one of the pages on the left.

- Clarify any unfamiliar concepts as necessary. See *ELL Teacher Guide* Lesson 20 for support in scaffolding instruction.

Grammar *Quick Write*

Review: Number Words

5-DAY GRAMMAR	
DAY 1	Review Adjectives
DAY 2	Review Adjectives for Senses
DAY 3	Review Number Words
DAY 4	Review Words That Compare
DAY 5	Cumulative Review

Objectives

- *To identify exact and inexact number words*
- *To use exact and inexact number words in writing*

Daily Proofreading

We visited dallas on thursday.

(Dallas, Thursday)

Writing Trait

Strengthening Conventions

Review Use these short daily lessons with children's own writing to continue building a foundation for revising/editing longer connected text. See also *Writer's Companion*, Lesson 20.

Reinforce the Skill

REVIEW NUMBER WORDS Remind children that number words tell how many. Write the following number words on the board: *some, eight, few, twenty*. Then create a chart like the following and work together to sort the words. Write the words in the chart.

Exact Number Words	Inexact Number Words
eight	some
twenty	few

Ask children to name some other words that tell about numbers, and add them to the chart.

Practice/Apply

GUIDED PRACTICE Write the following sentences on the board:

Our dog had six puppies.

Two of them are black and white.

Five of the puppies have spots.

Three of them are sleeping now.

Ask children to identify the number words in each sentence. Then ask children to revise the last three sentences and replace the exact number words with inexact words. (Possible responses: *Some, Most, A few*)

INDEPENDENT PRACTICE Display a picture of a group of one type of animal. Have children use number words to write three sentences about the animals in the picture. Have children underline the number words they use in each sentence.

Writing
Publish

5-DAY WRITING

DAY 1	Select a Piece and Revise
DAY 2	Revise
DAY 3	**Publish**
DAY 4	Publish
DAY 5	Present

Publish

CHOOSE A PUBLISHING IDEA   Explain to children that they may choose a publishing idea that works well for the kind of writing they have selected. You may wish to suggest the following option.

- **Create a Writing Mobile:**   Have children tape or glue their writing to a piece of cardboard or card stock. They can then make illustrations, use photos, or collect a couple of small items that can be hung at the bottom of the writing. Children will need to punch holes at the bottom of the cardboard and a hole at the top of each item to hang. They can use short pieces of ribbon, string, or yarn to tie the items and hang them from the cardboard.

WRITING TRAIT **PRESENTATION**   Point out that children should proofread their final draft carefully to be sure that there are no new errors. Tell children that any drawing or designs that are part of their publishing idea should be neat and clear.

PREPARE FINAL WRITING   Once children have chosen their publishing idea, they may either write on paper in their best handwriting or use available technology to type and print their writing.

Objectives

- *To progress through the stages of the writing process*
- *To publish a self-selected piece of assigned writing*

Writing Prompt

Independent Writing   Have children write to tell why art or music is important to them.

DAILY ROUTINES

Day at a Glance

Day 4

 phonics and Spelling

- *r*-Controlled Vowel /ir/*ear*, *eer*

COMPREHENSION STRATEGIES

Focus Strategy Review: Read Ahead, Answer Questions

- Reading Your Social Studies Book: "North America," *Student Edition* pp. 154–157

Comprehension/ Reading

- Review: Use Reference Sources

Fluency

READERS' THEATER

- Rehearse Roles: "What's My Job?" *Student Edition*, pp. 142–153

Robust Vocabulary

- Review: *sleuths, host, statue, risk, responds, accurately, opponent, impulsive, encountered, originated*

Grammar [Quick Write]

- Review: Words that Compare

Writing

- Publish

Warm-Up Routines

 ## Oral Language

Objective *To listen attentively and respond appropriately to oral communication*

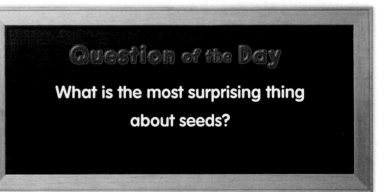

Question of the Day

What is the most surprising thing about seeds?

Brainstorm a list of facts and ideas about seeds. Use the following prompts as needed.

- **What does a seed need to grow into a plant?**

- **Does a plant ever grow in a surprising place? Give an example.**

Have children use a sentence frame to tell something surprising about seeds.

> **I think the most surprising thing about seeds is _____.**

Read Aloud

Objective *To listen for a purpose*

BIG BOOK OF RHYMES AND POEMS Display the poem "Tiny Seeds" on page 36 and read the title. Remind children of their discussion of surprising things about seeds, and ask them to think about what surprising things they hear about seeds as they listen to the poem. Then read the poem aloud. Use images from the poem to discuss the poet's ideas about seeds. Ask questions like the following: **Do you think the poet was ever surprised by seeds? What part of the poem do you think shows her surprise?** (Possible response: Some have strong though airy wings/To take them far away;)

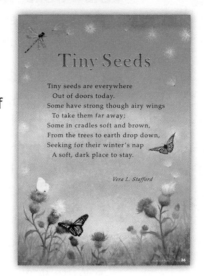

Tiny Seeds

Tiny seeds are everywhere
Out of doors today.
Some have strong though airy wings
To take them far away;
Some in cradles soft and brown,
From the trees to earth drop down,
Seeking for their winter's nap
A soft, dark place to stay.

Vera L. Stafford

▲ Big Book of Rhymes and Poems, p. 36

Word Wall

Objective *To read high-frequency words*

REVIEW HIGH-FREQUENCY WORDS Review the following words on the Word Wall: *question, something, sure, enjoy, coming, idea, quite, believe, different,* and *guess.* Have one child choose a card, read the word, and spell it. Repeat the procedure until each child has read and spelled at least two words.

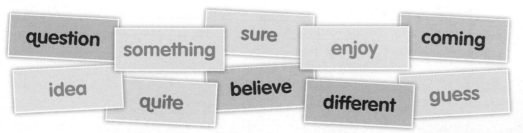

r-Controlled Vowel /ir/ ear, eer

phonics and Spelling

Objectives

- *To recognize and blend the sound /ir/ear and eer*
- *To read words with /ir/ear, eer, and other known letter-sounds*
- *To use /ir/ear, eer, and other known letter-sounds to spell words*

Spelling Words

1. **know***	6. **health**
2. **wrong***	7. **soil**
3. **tough**	8. **joy**
4. **phone**	9. **deer**
5. **breath**	10. **rear**

* Words from "What's My Job?"

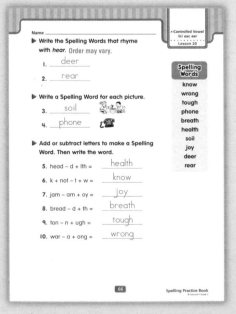

▲ **Spelling Practice Book, p. 66**

Review

READ A WORD Write the word *near* on the board. Ask children to identify the letters that stand for the /ir/ sound. Remind them that the letters *ear* and *eer* can both stand for the /ir/ sound.

BUILD SPELLING WORDS Have children follow your directions to change one or more letters in each of the following words to spell a spelling word. Have them write the word on a sheet of paper or in their notebooks. Then have a volunteer change the spelling of the word on the board so that children can self-check their spelling.

- Write *cheer* on the board. Ask: **Which spelling word can you make by changing the first two letters?** (deer)

- Write *hear* on the board. Ask: **Which spelling word can you make by changing the first letter?** (rear)

deer
rear

Use a similar procedure for the rest of the spelling words: *bread (breath), strong (wrong), boy (joy), heal (health), knit (know), rough (tough), tone (phone), coil (soil).*

BELOW-LEVEL

Identify and Spell Words List the spelling words on the board. Say: **I'm thinking of a word that names an animal that lives in the woods.** Have children identify the word *(deer)* and spell it. Continue in this manner for all of the spelling words. Then erase the words. Say each word and have children spell it.

ADVANCED

Play a Game Have children work in pairs. Have one child give a clue that tells about the meaning of a spelling word. Have their partner guess the word and spell it. Then have children switch roles.

Day 4

5-DAY PHONICS
DAY 1	Review /n/kn, /r/wr, /f/gh, ph.
DAY 2	Review /e/ea
DAY 3	Review /oi/oi, oy
DAY 4	Review /ir/ear, eer
DAY 5	Cumulative Review

Read Words in Context

APPLY PHONICS Write the following sentences on the board or on chart paper. Have children read each sentence silently. Then track the print as children read the sentence aloud.

> Marlon stopped running to catch his <u>breath</u>.
>
> Mom had a <u>tough</u> day at work.
>
> Taking walks is good for my <u>health</u>.
>
> I am waiting for a <u>phone</u> call from my cousin.
>
> Lin and Karin found seats in the <u>rear</u> of the bus.
>
> I dialed the <u>wrong</u> number when I called Grandma.

 WRITE Have children use each spelling word to write a question.

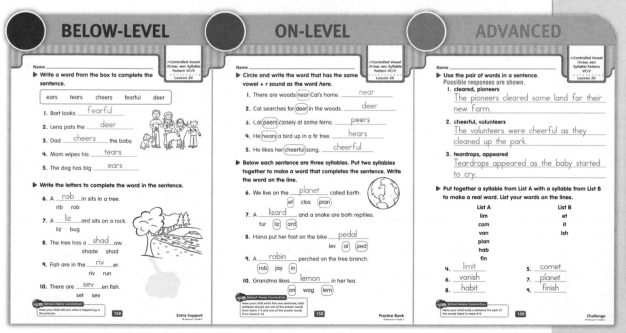

▲ **Extra Support, p. 158**   ▲ **Practice Book, p. 158**   ▲ **Challenge, p. 158**

E L L

- Group children according to academic levels, and assign one of the pages on the left.

- Clarify any unfamiliar concepts as necessary. See *ELL Teacher Guide* Lesson 20 for support in scaffolding instruction.

Comprehension Strategies
Review

Objectives

- *To apply reading strategies to content-area reading*
- *To analyze features of textbooks*

Reading Your Social Studies Book

PREVIEW PAGES 154–157 Have children scan the pages. Tell them that these pages tell about ways to better understand social studies textbooks. Explain that pages 154–155 tell about features that are often found in them, as well as comprehension strategies that can be used to help read these types of pages.

SET A PURPOSE Tell children that as they read these pages, they should look for ideas they can use the next time they read from their social studies textbooks. Then have them read the first two paragraphs under the heading Reading Your Social Studies Book.

DISCUSS TEXT FEATURES Point out and explain the following features often found in social studies textbooks, as shown on page 155:

- **Titles** These tell what each lesson will focus on.

- **Vocabulary Words** New vocabulary words are often in dark print and highlighted.

- **Maps** Maps usually have a title and labels to give information about the places in the lesson.

Review the Focus Strategies

DISCUSS COMPREHENSION STRATEGIES Have children read and discuss the information on reading ahead and answering questions.

- **Reading Ahead** may give readers information to help them understand something that is confusing.

- **Answering Questions** about a selection helps a reader find the answer "right there" in the text. For other questions, readers might need to think about what they know and put it together with information from the text.

APPLY TO READING SOCIAL STUDIES TEXTBOOKS Have children use the comprehension strategies as they read pages 156–157.

BELOW-LEVEL

Preview the Selection Explain that previewing a selection helps readers prepare for what they will be reading. Guide children to preview the text. Point out that while the title gives a general idea of what the chapter will be about, children can also find information about the main ideas in the chapter from the side column on the left-hand page.

Lesson 20

COMPREHENSION STRATEGIES
Review

Reading Your Social Studies Book

Bridge to Content-Area Reading Social studies books have special features that help you read for information. Some of these are titles, special vocabulary, and maps.

Read the notes on page 155. How can the features help you read?

Review the Focus Strategies

You can also use the strategies you learned in this theme to help you read.

Monitor Comprehension—Read Ahead
If something you are reading does not make sense, read ahead to gather more information.

Answer Questions
Use information from what you read to answer questions. Look back in the text to check your answers.

Use comprehension strategies as you read "North America" on pages 156–157.

154

Theme Review

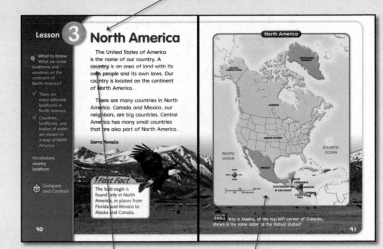

TITLE
The title tells what the lesson will be about.

VOCABULARY
New vocabulary words are in dark print. The meaning of the word is explained in the sentence. Vocabulary words are also in the glossary in the back of your social studies book.

MAP
Maps give you information about the places in the lesson. Use the compass rose to find north, south, east, and west.

155

Social Studies Textbook Features

Point out the features of social studies textbooks noted on page 155.

Chapter Titles Point to *Lesson 3,* and explain that the title is in larger print and located close to the lesson number.

Vocabulary Words highlighted or in dark print help the reader notice the word and locate the word later when it is time to review.

Maps Sometimes maps use colors to show how things are alike and different.

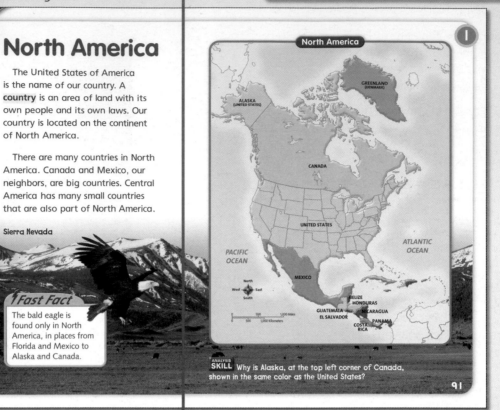

Apply the Strategies Read these pages from a social studies book. As you read, stop and think about how you are using comprehension strategies.

Stop and Think

How could reading ahead help you answer the question at the bottom of the page?

Lesson 3

North America

What to Know
What are some landforms and countries on the continent of North America?

✓ There are many different landforms in North America.

✓ Countries, landforms, and bodies of water are shown on a map of North America.

Vocabulary
country
landform

Compare and Contrast

The United States of America is the name of our country. A **country** is an area of land with its own people and its own laws. Our country is located on the continent of North America.

There are many countries in North America. Canada and Mexico, our neighbors, are big countries. Central America has many small countries that are also part of North America.

Sierra Nevada

Fast Fact
The bald eagle is found only in North America, in places from Florida and Mexico to Alaska and Canada.

North America

GREENLAND (DENMARK)
ALASKA (UNITED STATES)
CANADA
UNITED STATES
PACIFIC OCEAN
ATLANTIC OCEAN
MEXICO
BELIZE
GUATEMALA
HONDURAS
EL SALVADOR
NICARAGUA
COSTA RICA
PANAMA

ANALYSIS SKILL Why is Alaska, at the top left corner of Canada, shown in the same color as the United States?

90

91

156

157

Monitor Comprehension

PAGES 156–157 Have children use comprehension strategies as they read pages 156–157.

① **LOCATE INFORMATION** **After scanning the pages, what features tell you quickly what these two pages are about?** (The lesson title and the map title tell me that this information is about North America only.)

② **LOCATE INFORMATION** **What feature within the body of the text will give me the definitions of new social studies vocabulary?** (Vocabulary in dark or highlighted print is usually defined in the sentence in which it appears or in the glossary at the back.)

Stop and Think

Apply Comprehension Strategies

Read Ahead Model how reading ahead can help answer questions.

Think Aloud I scanned the map, but reading ahead and thinking about the question at the end helped me really think about how Alaska is part of the United States.

Answer Questions Point out that to answer the question under the map, readers need to combine information from the map and what they read in the text.

Use Reference Sources
Comprehension: Review

Reinforce the Skill

EXPLAIN REFERENCE SOURCES Tell children that good readers use reference sources to help them find information. Display an example of a dictionary, a thesaurus, an encyclopedia, and an atlas. Ask:

- **What information would I find in a dictionary?** (the meanings and spellings of words)

- **Why might I use a thesaurus?** (to find words that have about the same meaning as another word)

- **Why might I use an encyclopedia?** (to find information on a particular topic)

- **What information would I find in an atlas?** (maps and information about places in the world)

Practice/Apply

GUIDED PRACTICE Guide children to determine which reference source to use to answer the following questions Say: **Where would I find**

- **information about the history of California?** (encyclopedia)

- **a map of the state of California?** (atlas, encyclopedia)

- **the meaning of the word** *permanent*? (dictionary)

- **a word that means the same as** *permanent*? (thesaurus)

INDEPENDENT PRACTICE Provide copies of each reference source, and have children use them to locate the following information:

- a word that means almost the same as the word *playful*

- a map of Texas

- the meaning of the word *flawless*

- where Benjamin Franklin was born

Have children write down the information they found and the reference source they used. Then have pairs share their findings.

Objectives

- *To understand the purposes of various reference sources*
- *To identify which reference source to use to accomplish a task*
- *To practice using a dictionary, thesaurus, encyclopedia, and atlas*

Skill Trace

 Use Reference Sources

Introduce	T254–T255
Reteach	S32–S33, S44–S45
Review	**T338–T339, T429, T438**
Test	Theme 4
Maintain	Theme 6, T273

READERS' THEATER

5-DAY READERS' THEATER

DAY 1	Read Aloud/Read Along
DAY 2	Read Together
DAY 3	Choose Roles/Rehearse
DAY 4	**Rehearse Roles**
DAY 5	Perform

Rehearse Roles: "What's My Job?"

Objective

• *To read fluently and accurately with appropriate intonation*

Fluency Support Materials

Fluency Builders, Grade 2, Lesson 20

 Audiotext "What's My Job?" is available on *Audiotext Grade 2,* CD 4.

"Research Says"

Repeated Reading "Reading rate increased significantly from one to three readings, an occurrence that brought instructional-level readers to near mastery-level performance."
—Rasinki, et al.
(1994)

▲ **Teacher Resource Book, pp. 134–139**

Focus on Fluency

READING ACCURATELY WITH INTONATION Have children continue to rehearse reading their parts aloud fluently. Explain to children that since they are going to perform the Readers' Theater tomorrow, they should imagine that they have their audience before them when they rehearse. Remind children to use appropriate intonation as they read and to correct themselves if they make a mistake. Encourage them to read clearly and loudly enough so that everyone in the audience can hear them.

Think Aloud **When I am reading the part of the Announcer, I want to use a friendly tone of voice that explains what is going on. I want to raise my voice to offer encouragement and read carefully so that everyone understands the show's rules.**

Practice Reading

REHEARSE ROLES Have the class read through the script, following their assigned parts. Encourage listeners to offer constructive criticism, focusing on positive aspects of the reading as well as areas for improvement.

Monitor children's reading and model reading particular lines if children are having difficulties. If you copied pages 134–139 in the *Teacher Resource Book* so children have individual scripts, you may want to encourage them to mark those words or sections that they want to improve.

You may wish to prepare a simple set and props for various roles, such as desks for the players. Children may wear nametags that tell their roles. Provide time for groups to practice the switching of roles.

Have children practice one more time for their last rehearsal, as if their audience is listening to them read. You may wish to use the backdrop on page 115 of the *Teacher Resource Book.*

Build Robust Vocabulary

Review

Reinforce Word Meanings

USE VOCABULARY IN DIFFERENT CONTEXTS   Remind children of the meanings of the words. Then discuss each word in a new context.

sleuths, statue, opponent   Tell children that they must be sleuths and figure out how a statue and an opponent might be alike. After you read a description, the sleuths should say, "That's a statue!" "That's an opponent!" or "That could be both."

> **could be wearing a costume**
>
> **could challenge you to a race**

accurately   Tell children if what you name is something they think they could do accurately on the first try, they should raise their hand. If not, they should do nothing.

> write your name with your eyes closed
>
> spell *encyclopedia*

risk   Tell children if they feel what you name is something they should not risk, they should say, "Don't risk it!" If they feel otherwise, they should say, "I'd risk it."

> **reading a scary story**   **trying a new kind of food**

impulsive   Tell children if they think what you name sounds like an impulsive act, they should hold up their hand to say *Stop*. If not, they should wave their hand *Go*.

> go grocery shopping with a friend
>
> decide to fly to Japan today

encountered   Ask children to nod their heads if they think what you name is something that most people will have encountered by the time they are old. If not, they should shake their heads.

> **many birthday cakes**   **winning a billion dollars**

host   Ask children to stand and smile charmingly if you name a place that might have a host.

> a library   a restaurant

Objectives
- *To review robust vocabulary*
- *To figure out a word's meaning based on its context*

REVIEW | Tested

Vocabulary

sleuths	accurately
host	encountered
statue	originated
risk	opponent
responds	impulsive

Grammar
Quick Write

Review: Words That Compare

5-DAY GRAMMAR	
DAY 1	Review Adjectives
DAY 2	Review Adjectives for Senses
DAY 3	Review Number Words
DAY 4	**Review Words That Compare**
DAY 5	Cumulative Review

Objective

• *To recognize and write words that compare in sentences*

Daily Proofreading

Would you like some berrys.

(berries?)

Writing Trait

Strengthening Conventions

Review   Use these short daily lessons with children's own writing to continue building a foundation for revising/editing longer connected text. See also *Writer's Companion*, Lesson 20.

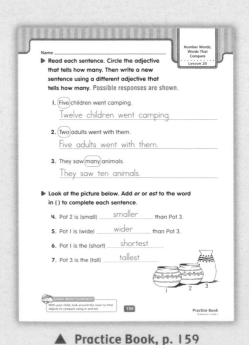

▲ Practice Book, p. 159

Reinforce the Skill

REVIEW WORDS THAT COMPARE   Review the following rules for words that compare.

• Adjectives that end with *-er* compare just two things.

• Adjectives that end with *-est* compare three or more things.

Then write the following sentences on the board. Have children tell which sentence correctly uses a word that compares, and which does not. Have a volunteer revise the incorrect sentence.

Keira can run faster than her older brother.

This is the riper banana in the bunch. (ripest)

Practice/Apply

GUIDED PRACTICE   Write the following sentences on the board. Have volunteers help you correct them by using in each sentence the correct word that compares.

The kitten has softest fur than its mother. (softer)

The whale is the larger of all the mammals. (largest)

I made a wish on the brighter star in the sky.
   (brightest)

Cereal is crunchiest than oatmeal. (crunchier)

INDEPENDENT PRACTICE   Display three items that are the same color, such as a banana, a yellow pencil, and a yellow marker. Write two sentences like the following on the board:

The marker is bigger than the pencil.

The banana is the biggest item in the group.

Allow children to examine the items. Then have children write a sentence that compares two of the things, and a sentence that compares the three things. Have volunteers share their sentences with the class.

Writing
Publish

5-DAY WRITING

DAY 1	Select a Piece and Revise
DAY 2	Revise
DAY 3	Publish
DAY 4	Publish
DAY 5	Present

Publish

 MODEL FINAL PROOFREADING Tell children that they should review their writing by proofreading it one last time. Explain that while they may think that there are no errors in their work, good writers want to be sure that their work is as correct as it can be.

Think Aloud **I like to read my writing one last time to make sure that I have not made any errors. When I do this, I read to make sure that I've checked punctuation and spelling, and that I haven't left out any words. I might find that I've written the same word twice!**

Have children proofread their written piece. Show children how to use correction fluid, pens, or tape to make any final corrections.

Handwriting

NEATNESS COUNTS Remind children to use their best handwriting for any information that they add to their revised piece. Point out that hard-to-read writing can cause readers to become confused or distracted.

WRITING TRAIT **CONVENTIONS** Have children review their writing one last time and ask themselves the following questions:

- Have I included my name? A title (if wanted)?

- Have I checked spelling? Capital letters? Commas and end marks?

- Is my handwriting as neat as it can be?

Allow children time to complete a final check of their work.

Objectives

- *To progress through the stages of the writing process*
- *To publish a self-selected piece of assigned writing*

Writing Prompt

Independent Writing Have children write to tell about how they decided on the illustrations, photos, or items they included with their writing.

Adopt a Pet! *by Lin*

My favorite place is our town animal shelter. It's a friendly place where you can come to adopt an animal that needs a good home. There are frisky kittens and playful puppies. There are also adult dogs and cats that need a new place to live. I like to volunteer at the shelter because there's nothing better than a wet lick on the face from a furry friend!

 Find a New Friend!

TECHNOLOGY

GO online Children can use a word-processing program to produce and design their final piece of writing.

Warm-Up Routines

DAILY ROUTINES

Day at a Glance

Day 5

 phonics and Spelling

- Lessons 16–19 Review
- Postest

Comprehension

 Review: Locate Information and Use Reference Sources

Fluency

READERS' THEATER

- Intonation
- Perform: "What's My Job?"
  Student Edition, pp. 142–153

Read!

Grammar [Quick Write]

- Lesson 16–19 Review

Writing

- Present

 Oral Language

Objective *To listen attentively and respond appropriately to oral communication*

Question of the Day

What are some ways you can use a notebook?

Use the following prompts to have children brainstorm different ways that people can use notebooks.

- **What are some ways you use a notebook at school? At home?**
- **What are some jobs that people might use a notebook for?**
- **Why might it help to record your ideas in a notebook?**

Have children complete the following sentence frame to tell about their ideas.

I could use a notebook to _____.

Read Aloud

Objective *To listen for enjoyment*

BIG BOOK OF RHYMES AND POEMS Display
the poem "New Notebook" on page 32 and
read the title. Ask children to recall how the
poet uses words to create pictures to describe
what a new notebook looks like. Then read
the poem aloud. Explain that poets sometimes choose to use words with similar vowel
sounds that make the poem interesting to
read and listen to. Read the poem again,
emphasizing the repeated long *i* and
long *o* sounds. Help children identify the
words with these sounds. (lines, fine, like;
notebook, snowy, strokes, crows)

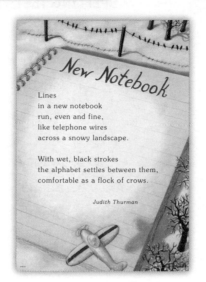

New Notebook

Lines
in a new notebook
run, even and fine,
like telephone wires
across a snowy landscape.

With wet, black strokes
the alphabet settles between them,
comfortable as a flock of crows.

Judith Thurman

▲ **Big Book of Rhymes
and Poems, p. 32**

Word Wall

Objective *To read high-frequency words*

REVIEW HIGH-FREQUENCY WORDS Review the following words on the
Word Wall: *question, something, sure, enjoy, coming, idea, quite, believe,
different,* and *guess*. Point to a word and ask children to read the word. Go
through the words several times.

question   something   sure   enjoy   coming

idea   quite   believe   different   guess

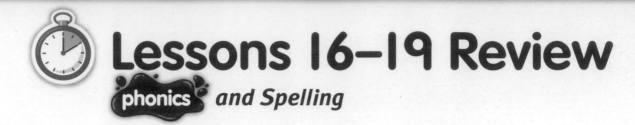

Lessons 16–19 Review
phonics *and Spelling*

Objective

• *To review spelling words*

Spelling Words

1. **know***	6. **health**
2. **wrong***	7. **soil**
3. **tough**	8. **joy**
4. **phone**	9. **deer**
5. **breath**	10. **rear**

* Words from "What's My Job?"

Assess

SPELLING TEST   Assess children's progress using the dictation sentences.

Words with /n/*kn*, /r/*wr*, /f/*gh, ph*; /e/*ea*; /oi/*oi, oy*; or /ir/*ear, eer*

1.	know	I **know** the answer to that question.
2.	wrong	We got lost when we took a **wrong** turn at the light.
3.	tough	Gino had a **tough** time opening the package.
4.	phone	You can use this **phone** to call your mother.
5.	breath	Se-Jin was out of **breath** when he finished the race.
6.	health	My aunt's **health** improved when she exercised.
7.	soil	The **soil** in the garden was soggy after the rain.
8.	joy	Watching the sunrise filled me with **joy**.
9.	deer	I saw a **deer** in the meadow early this morning.
10.	rear	There is another exit at the **rear** of the theater.

Locate Information
Comprehension: Review

Reinforce the Skill

REVIEW LOCATING INFORMATION   Remind children that most nonfiction books are organized so that readers can find information. Have children use their *Student Edition* to locate and discuss the table of contents, the index, and the glossary.

Practice/Apply

GUIDED PRACTICE   Use children's science or social studies textbook to practice locating information. Guide children to locate the table of contents, chapter titles and headings, the index, the glossary, and guide words. Then choose and name a chapter from the book. Ask the following questions:

- **How could I find out which page this chapter begins on?** (Use the table of contents.) **What is the first page of this chapter?**

- **What are the headings in this chapter?**

INDEPENDENT PRACTICE   Identify vocabulary from the chapter. Have children locate the terms in the glossary and write the guide words from the corresponding glossary pages. Have partners compare their findings.

Objective

- *To use the parts of a book to locate information*

Skill Trace

 Locate Information

Introduce	T224–T225
Reteach	S30–S31, S42–S43
Review	**T253, T269, T281, T308–T309, T337, T353, T363, T416, T437**
Test	Theme 4
Maintain	Theme 5, T279

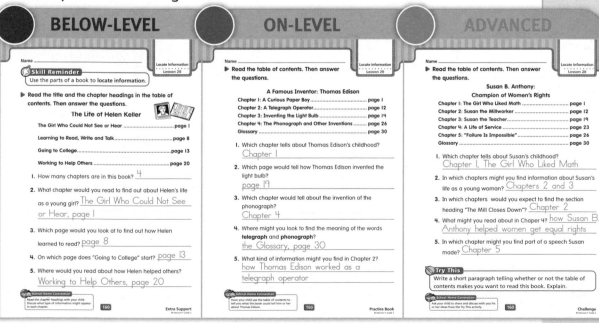

▲ Extra Support, p. 160   ▲ Practice Book, p. 160   ▲ Challenge, p. 160

E L L

- Group children according to academic levels, and assign one of the pages on the left.

- Clarify any unfamiliar concepts as necessary. See *ELL Teacher Guide* Lesson 20 for support in scaffolding instruction.

Use Reference Sources
Research/Study Skill

Objectives

- *To understand the purposes of various reference sources*
- *To identify which reference source to use to accomplish a task*
- *To practice using a dictionary, thesaurus, encyclopedia, and atlas*

Skill Trace

 Tested **Use Reference Sources**

Introduce	T254–T255
Reteach	S32–S33, S44–S45
Review	**T338–T339, T429, T438**
Test	Theme 4
Maintain	Theme 6, T273

Reinforce the Skill

REVIEW REFERENCE SOURCES   Display a dictionary, a thesaurus, an atlas, and an encyclopedia. Complete this chart with children:

Reference Source	We use it to find:
dictionary	the meanings and spellings of words
thesaurus	synonyms for words
atlas	maps and information about places
encyclopedia	information on a particular topic

Practice/Apply

GUIDED PRACTICE   Brainstorm a list of topics, words, and places that children would like to learn more about. Then use the sources to find information to answer their questions.

INDEPENDENT PRACTICE   Have partners work together to find information for other ideas from the list.

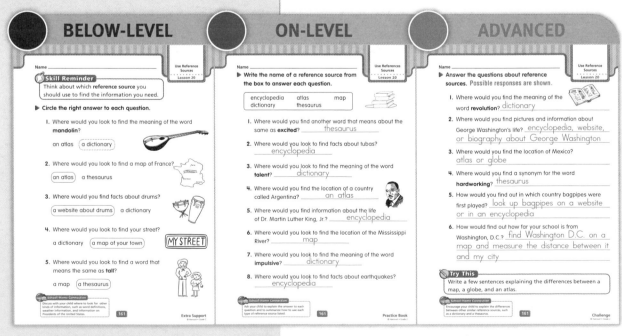

▲ **BELOW-LEVEL**   ▲ **ON-LEVEL**   ▲ **ADVANCED**

▲ Extra Support, p. 161   ▲ Practice Book, p. 161   ▲ Challenge, p. 161

ELL

- Group children according to academic levels, and assign one of the pages on the left.

- Clarify any unfamiliar concepts as necessary. See *ELL Teacher Guide* Lesson 20 for support in scaffolding instruction.

READERS' THEATER

Perform: "What's My Job?"

5-DAY READERS' THEATER

DAY 1	Read Aloud/Read Along
DAY 2	Read Together
DAY 3	Choose/Rehearse Roles
DAY 4	Rehearse Roles
DAY 5	Perform

Performance Ideas

PRESENTATION STRATEGIES   Help children warm up for the performance as if the show were about to be televised. Remind groups to enter and exit smoothly and quietly. Explain that the entire cast should take a bow at the end. Explain that while members are not reading, they should become part of the audience and listen attentively and quietly. You may want to project the backdrop for "What's My Job?" against a board or screen.

Focus on Fluency

READING ACCURATELY WITH INTONATION   Remind children to use the fluency tips they've been practicing all this week.

- Raise or lower your voice as you do when speaking to a friend.

- Read carefully, and correct yourself if you make a mistake.

Perform

SPEAKING AND LISTENING   Before children perform Readers' Theater, review good rules for reading and being part of an audience.

- I look up occasionally at the audience as I read.

- I read clearly and with feeling.

- I listen quietly and politely as others read.

RUBRIC   See the rubric for presentations on page R5.

EVALUATE   Invite children or others in the audience to comment positively about how the readers read.

Objectives

- *To evaluate oral reading for fluency*
- *To speak in complete sentences*

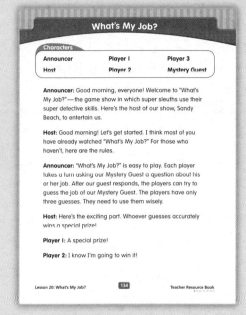

▲ Teacher Resource Book, pp. 134–139

▲ Teacher Resource Book, p. 115

Grammar Quick Write

Review: Lessons 16–19

5-DAY GRAMMAR	
DAY 1	Review Adjectives
DAY 2	Review Adjectives for Senses
DAY 3	Review Number Words
DAY 4	Review Words That Compare
DAY 5	Cumulative Review

Objectives

- To identify and use adjectives
- To use exact and inexact number words correctly
- To recognize and write words that compare in sentences

Daily Proofreading

dr Browns office is next door.

(Dr., Brown's)

Writing Trait →

Strengthening Conventions

Review Use these short daily lessons with children's own writing to continue building a foundation for revising/editing longer connected text. See also *Writer's Companion*, Lesson 20.

Reinforce the Skills

MIXED REVIEW Discuss with children the following points:

- Adjectives tell about a noun. Some adjectives describe shape, color, and size.

- Adjectives for senses describe how something looks, smells, tastes, sounds, or feels. An adjective for senses can come before or after the word it describes.

- Number words tell how many. They may be exact, such as *three, fourteen,* or *hundred*. They may be inexact, such as *few, some,* and *many*.

- Adjectives that end with *-er* compare just two things.

- Adjectives that end with *-est* compare three or more things.

Practice/Apply

GUIDED PRACTICE Write the following sentences on the board. Guide children to identify adjectives that tell about shape, color, and size, sense adjectives, number words, and adjectives that end with *-er* and *-est*.

> The round yellow sun shone on a summer day.
>
> Angie told Kenny that today would be much hotter than yesterday.
>
> Kenny ordered creamy peach and added a few walnuts.
>
> Angie chose the biggest peppermint shake on the menu.

INDEPENDENT PRACTICE Have partners work together to write sentences about things in their school or classroom. Their sentences should include at least one example of an adjective that tells about size, shape, or color.

Writing

Present

5-DAY WRITING	
DAY 1	Select a Piece and Revise
DAY 2	Revise
DAY 3	Publish
DAY 4	Publish
DAY 5	Present

Share

CELEBRATE WRITING Provide an opportunity for children to share their published pieces of writing. Encourage children to read aloud to the group, using the fluency skills they have practiced.

WORD CHOICE Take this opportunity to praise examples of good word choice and use of appropriate wording for audience and purpose, particularly for those children who exhibited significant effort to improve their writing in this area.

LISTENING AND SPEAKING SKILLS Remind children that when they are reading aloud, they should

- speak clearly and at an appropriate pace.
- use appropriate intonation.

Remind listeners that they should

- listen critically and responsively.
- ask for clarification as needed

NOTE: A 4-point rubric appears on page R8.

SCORING RUBRIC

	6	5	4	3	2	1
FOCUS	Completely focused, purposeful.	Focused on topic and purpose.	Generally focused on topic and purpose.	Somewhat focused on topic and purpose.	Related to topic but does not maintain focus.	Lacks focus and purpose.
ORGANIZATION	Ideas progress logically; paper conveys sense of completeness.	Organization mostly clear; paper gives sense of completeness.	Organization mostly clear, but some lapses occur; may seem unfinished.	Some sense of organization; seems unfinished.	Little sense of organization.	Little or no sense of organization.
SUPPORT	Strong, specific details; clear, exact language; freshness of expression.	Strong, specific details; clear, exact language.	Adequate support and word choice.	Limited supporting details; limited word choice.	Few supporting details; limited word choice.	Little development; limited or unclear word choice.
CONVENTIONS	Varied sentences; few, if any, errors.	Varied sentences; few errors.	Some sentence variety; few errors.	Simple sentence structures; some errors.	Simple sentence structures; many errors.	Unclear sentence structures; many errors.

REPRODUCIBLE STUDENT RUBRICS for specific writing purposes and presentations are available on pages R2–R8.

Objectives

- *To publish and share writing*
- *To listen attentively to oral presentations*
- *To speak clearly using an appropriate pace and phrasing*

Writing Prompt

Reflect Have children write about something they learned from a classmate's presentation.

WEEKLY LESSON TEST

▲ **Weekly Lesson Tests, pp. 212–216**

- Selection Comprehension with Short Response
- Robust Vocabulary

 For prescriptions, see pp. A2–A6. Also available electronically on StoryTown Online Assessment and Exam View®.

 Podcasting: Assessing Fluency

Leveled Readers

Reinforcing Skills and Strategies

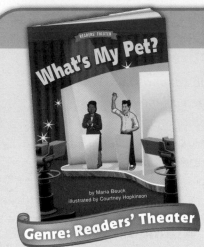

BELOW-LEVEL

What's My Pet?

SUMMARY Contestants on a game show try to guess what kind of pet the Mystery Guest has.

- **phonics** Lessons 16–19 **Review**
- **Vocabulary**
  - **Focus Skill** **Setting; Locate Information**

Before Reading

BUILD BACKGROUND/SET PURPOSE Ask children what they think might happen on a game show called "What's My Pet?" Guide them to preview the play and to set a purpose for reading it.

Reading the Book

PAGES 4–14 **SETTING** **How is the setting of the play similar to the one in "What's My Job?"** (Both have lights, an audience, and a stage set.)

PAGES 4–14 **LOCATE INFORMATION** **How would an actor reading the part of the Host find his lines?** (He would look for the heading *Host* on each page.)

REREAD FOR FLUENCY Have partners or small groups read pages 11–14. Remind them to read each word carefully and to think about whether they should raise or lower their voice.

Think Critically *(See inside back cover for questions.)*

1. **SETTING** The play's setting was a television game show set.

2. **LOCATE INFORMATION** You find out what the prize was on page 14.

3. **NOTE DETAILS** The Mystery Guest's pet was a mouse.

4. **MAKE INFERENCES** Possible response: Player 2 was going to guess a bird, because he asked if the pet had feathers.

5. **PERSONAL RESPONSE** Answers will vary.

LEVELED READERS TEACHER GUIDE

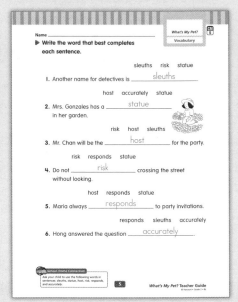

▲ Vocabulary, p. 5

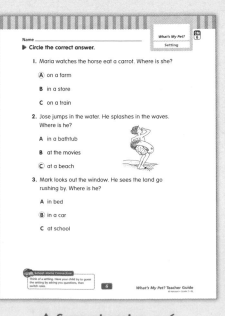

▲ Comprehension, p. 6

ON-LEVEL

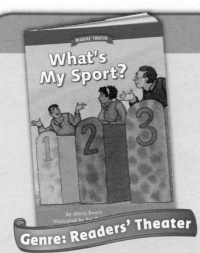

Genre: Readers' Theater

What's My Sport?

SUMMARY Contestants on a game show try to guess the sport the Mystery Guest plays.

- **phonics** **Lessons 16–19** Review
- **Lesson Vocabulary**

 Setting; Locate Information

Before Reading

BUILD BACKGROUND/SET PURPOSE Ask children what they think about game shows. Guide them to preview the play and set a purpose for reading it.

Reading the Book

PAGES 4–14 🌀 **SETTING** How is the setting of the play similar to the one in "What's My Job?" How is it different? (Both have lights, an audience, and a stage set. In "What's My Job?" the Mystery Guest is seen. Here, he or she is behind a screen.)

PAGES 12–14 🌀 **LOCATE INFORMATION** If you had a book on winter sports, where might you look to see if it included snowboarding? (the table of contents or the index)

REREAD FOR FLUENCY Have partners or small groups decide on roles and read pages 8–14 together. Remind children to raise or lower their voices when it makes sense to do so.

Think Critically

(See inside back cover for questions.)

1. 🌀 **SETTING** The play's setting is a television game show set.

2. 🌀 **LOCATE INFORMATION** page 12

3. **CONTEXT CLUES** Possible responses: Things were getting exciting. The players were nervous. Player 3 might be knocked out of the game.

4. **TEXT STRUCTURE AND FORMAT** The book has a list of characters.

5. **PERSONAL RESPONSE** Answers will vary.

LEVELED READERS TEACHER GUIDE

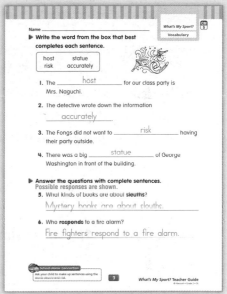

▲ Vocabulary, p. 5

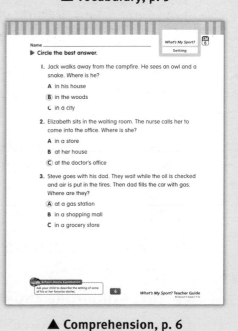

▲ Comprehension, p. 6

Leveled Readers

Reinforcing Skills and Strategies

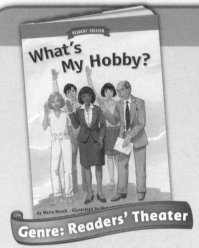

ADVANCED

What's My Hobby?

SUMMARY   Contestants on a game show try to guess the Mystery Guest's hobby.

 **Genre: Readers' Theater**

 phonics   Lessons 16–19 Review
- **Lesson Vocabulary**
- **Setting; Locate Information** *Focus Skill*

Before Reading

BUILD BACKGROUND/SET PURPOSE   Ask children to tell why contestants on game shows need to be good listeners. Guide them to preview the play and set a purpose for reading it.

Reading the Book

PAGES 4–14   **SETTING**   How is the setting of the play similar to the one in "What's My Job?" How is it different? (Both have lights, an audience, and a stage set. In "What's My Job?" the Mystery Guest is seen. Here, she is behind a screen.)

PAGE 12   **LOCATE INFORMATION**   If you had a book about photography, where might you look to see if it tells about the history of photography? (the table of contents, the index)

REREAD FOR FLUENCY   Have partners take turns reading pages 10–14. Suggest that they alternate roles on each page. Remind children to adjust their intonation as needed and to read the words carefully and naturally.

Think Critically   *(See inside back cover for questions.)*

1. **SETTING**   The play's setting is a television game show set.
2. **LOCATE INFORMATION**   page 12
3. **INTERPRET CHARACTER'S EMOTIONS**   Possible responses: annoyed, frustrated, impatient
4. **TEXT STRUCTURE AND FORMAT**   The book has a list of characters.
5. **PERSONAL RESPONSE**   Answers will vary.

LEVELED READERS TEACHER GUIDE

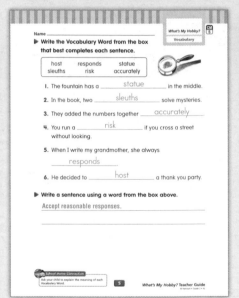

▲ Vocabulary, p. 5

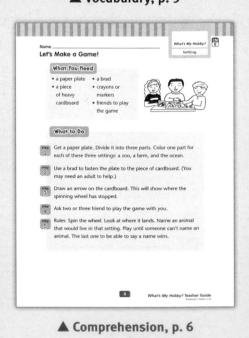

▲ Comprehension, p. 6

www.harcourtschool.com/storytown

★ **Leveled Readers Online Database**
Searchable by Genre, Skill, Vocabulary, Level, or Title
★ **Student Activities and Teacher Resources, online**

ELL

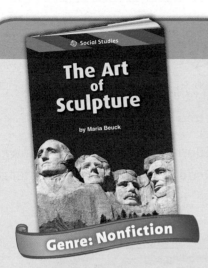

Genre: Nonfiction

The Art of Sculpture

SUMMARY   Artists can create sculptures using many different kinds of materials.

- Build Background
- Concept Vocabulary
- Scaffolded Language Development

Before Reading

BUILD BACKGROUND/SET PURPOSE   Ask children to tell about or sketch an image of a sculpture they have seen. Guide them to preview the book and set a purpose for reading it.

Reading the Book

PAGES 4–14   **SETTING**   What are some settings where you might see sculptures? (Possible responses: a park, a garden, an island, a city street, a beach)

PAGE 9   **LOCATE INFORMATION**   If you were looking at a book about the artwork of Native Americans, where might you look to see if it included totem poles? (the table of contents, the index)

REREAD FOR FLUENCY   Have partners take turns reading the book a page at a time. Remind children to read carefully and to raise their voice slightly when they want to make a special point.

Scaffolded Language Development

(See inside back cover for teacher-led activity.)

Provide additional examples and explanation as needed.

LEVELED READERS TEACHER GUIDE

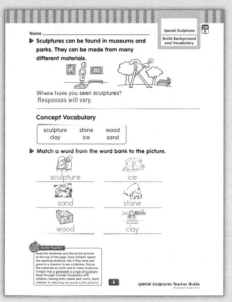

▲ Build Background and
Vocabulary, p. 5

▲ Scaffolded Language
Development, p. 6

Theme Wrap-up and Review

Discuss the Literature

Use the questions below to guide children in making connections across the texts in this theme.

- **In what way do the selections in this theme tell about using imagination and creativity?** (Possible response: All of the selections tell about subjects that are creative or that take imagination.)

- **Why was "The Life of George Washington Carver" included in this theme?** (Possible response: George Washington Carver had to use his imagination and be creative to find so many uses for peanuts.)

- **Which selection from the theme shows the best use of imagination and creativity?** (Responses will vary but should include information from the selection that was chosen.)

Return to the Theme Connections

Complete a graphic organizer to show information compiled from the selections children have read in this theme.

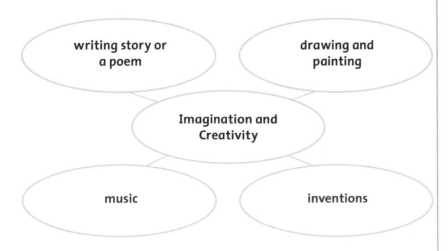

Response Option

REFLECT Have children reflect on and write about using their imagination and creativity.

SELF-ASSESSMENT Children can reflect on their own progress using the My Reading Log blackline master on *Teacher Resource Book*, p. 64.

▲ Teacher Resource Book, p. 64

LITERATURE CRITIQUE CIRCLES Have children meet in small groups to discuss and reflect on the literature in this theme. Encourage children to share their likes and dislikes about the following:

- genres
- subjects/topics
- illustrations or photographs

Remind children to support their opinions with text-based reasons and details.

Children may also like to use this time to recommend to classmates any books they read and enjoyed during independent reading. Have them list promising titles for future reading.

Musical Creations

PRESENT BAND PERFORMANCES Group members may present their instruments to an audience before performing their song together. Encourage them to demonstrate what they have learned in a creative way.

PRESENTATION IDEA Suggest that children play the roles of a conductor and the instruments themselves to demonstrate how each instrument makes its sounds.

- **Tell group members to decide** who will take the part of the conductor and what the conductor will say to introduce each instrument, including his or her own.

- **Explain that each instrument should give its name** and tell how it works with a brief demonstration. As children prepare their explanations, remind them to use the pronouns *I*, *me*, and *mine* as if their instrument is talking.

To evaluate children's work, you may wish to use the Rubric for Presentations on page R5.

School-Home Connection

Theme Project Presentations You may want to invite family members to see the completed instruments and children's presentations. Guide children in writing an invitation for the event that includes the appropriate date, time, and location.

Monitor Progress
at the end of Theme 4

THEME 4 TEST After instruction for Theme 4, assess student progress in the following areas:

- Comprehension of grade-level text
- Phonics
- Robust Vocabulary
- Grammar
- Writing to a prompt
- Fluency*

(*Note on Fluency: Assessment can be staggered to make sure all students can be individually assessed.)

 Podcasting: Assessing Fluency

GO online ONLINE ASSESSMENT

- ✔ Theme 4 Test
- ✔ Weekly Lesson Tests
- ✔ Student Profile System to track student growth
- ✔ Prescriptions for Reteaching

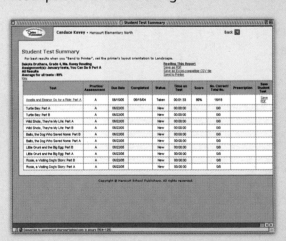

GO online www.harcourtschool.com/storytown

MONITOR PROGRESS

Use Data to Inform Instruction for Theme 4

IF performance was	THEN, in addition to core instruction, use these resources:
● **BELOW-LEVEL: Reteach**	• Below-Level Leveled Readers • Leveled Readers System • Extra Support Copying Masters • Strategic Intervention Resource Kit • Intervention Station, Primary
● **ON-LEVEL: Reinforce**	• On-Level Leveled Readers • Leveled Readers System • Practice Book
● **ADVANCED: Extend**	• Above-Level Leveled Readers • Leveled Readers System • Challenge Copying Masters • Challenge Resource Kit

SMALL-GROUP INSTRUCTION

Phonics

Objective

To practice and apply knowledge of the digraphs /n/kn, /r/wr, and /f/gh, ph

Decodable Book 13

"The Gentle Knight," "Fun with Tricky Knots," "Wrap It Up!," "The Twice-Wrapped Gifts," "Dolphins," and "A Fun Day for Phil" ▶

 MONITOR PROGRESS

Phonics After small-group instruction, are children able to read words with /n/*kn,* /r/*wr,* and /f/*gh, ph*?

If not, provide additional small-group practice with the sounds. See the *Strategic Intervention Resource Kit* for additional support.

Strategic ▶ Intervention Resource Kit

 BELOW-LEVEL **RETEACH**

Connect Letters and Sounds

Routine Card 1 Use *Routine Card 1* and the *Sound/Spelling Card* to review the letter/sound correspondence /n/*kn*. Write the words *knot, know, knock,* and *knife* on the board. Read the words aloud, emphasizing the initial consonant sound /n/. Underline the *kn* digraph in each one, reminding children that the letters *kn* together can spell the /n/ sound and helping them see that the *k* is silent. Follow a similar procedure for /r/*wr,* and /f/*gh, ph* using these words: *wrong, wreck, wrap, wrist; graph, phone, photo, phrase; tough, laugh, rough, enough.* Then have children read aloud *Decodable Book 13.* Pause at the end of each page to review any word that children struggled to read.

 ON-LEVEL **REINFORCE**

Word Building

Display the following words in dark type and read them with children: **snack** (knack), **trap** (wrap), **grape** (graph), and **touch** (tough). For each word, have children tell you which letter to change to spell the word in parentheses. Write this word as children dictate, and have them read it with you. Then write the following sentences for children to read:

Phil has a knack for making a graph.

It is tough to wrap this big gift.

Direct children to read *Decodable Book 13* aloud. Ask questions about the story to make sure that children understood what they read.

Write in Code

Display this key: *kn = n, wr = r, gh = f, ph = f.* Have children each write a short message that contains several words with *f, n,* and *r* in them. (If necessary, brainstorm some possible words as a group, listing the words on the board.) Then direct children to replace each *f* in their message with *ph* or *gh*, each *n* with *kn*, and each *r* with *wr*. After they have neatly copied their "coded" messages, have them exchange papers with a partner and use the code to figure out one another's messages.

> It's ghukn to wride phast ikn the wraikn.
>
> It's fun to ride fast in the rain.

Fluency

Objective
To read accurately and fluently with intonation that sounds like natural speech

Use Punctuation Marks Point out the periods, question marks, and exclamation points in the appropriate *Leveled Reader*. Model how your voice changes as you read a statement, a question, and an exclamation. Have children imitate your intonation. Then have them echo-read as you read the book with them.

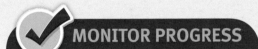 **MONITOR PROGRESS**

Fluency After small-group instruction, are children able to read accurately, with intonation that sounds like natural speech?

If not, provide additional small-group practice. See the *Strategic Intervention Resource Kit* for additional support.

Strategic ▶ Intervention Resource Kit

BELOW-LEVEL · RETEACH

Model Fluent Reading

Routine Card 10 Remind children that good readers raise and lower their voices to make their reading sound like natural speech, as if they were talking rather than reading. Tell children that there are two things they can do to help them do this: (I) They can pay attention to punctuation marks, which tell them when to pause and how to use their voices. (2) They can look for important, or key, words in a sentence, raising their voices when they get to these words to highlight them for the listener. Distribute copies of *A New Painting* to children. Read the book aloud to them, modeling how to use natural-sounding intonation. As you read, note how you use question marks and exclamation points to know how your voice should change. Also note from time to time how you raised your voice to highlight key words. In these instances, have children echo-read the sentences with you, imitating your intonation. Finally, have them read the book with a partner; remind them to monitor each other's reading, offering corrections as they listen.

● ON-LEVEL REINFORCE

Echo-Reading

Routine Card 8 Distribute *The Best Birthday* to children, and explain that they will practice reading aloud with appropriate intonation, so that they sound like they are talking naturally rather than reading. Read each page aloud to children, modeling how you use punctuation marks as cues to pausing and adjusting intonation, and how you raise your voice to highlight key words in a sentence. Have children read aloud after you, imitating your intonation. After reading the book through in this manner, have children practice reading it with a partner. Monitor their reading, providing feedback about their intonation and the accuracy of their reading.

● ADVANCED EXTEND

Partner Reading

Routine Card 10 Ask a volunteer to explain how a reader's voice changes when reading aloud a statement, a question, or an exclamation. Remind children that they should also remember to pause at the end of sentences, and to look for key words to highlight in a sentence by raising their voices on these words. Distribute *First Prize* to children, and tell them that they will be practicing reading aloud with natural-sounding intonation that sounds like they are talking to a friend rather than reading. Group children in pairs, having one child read the book aloud while the other listens. After the first child is done, direct the listener to offer constructive feedback about reading with natural-sounding intonation. Then have children switch roles and repeat the procedure.

LEVELED READERS

● **BELOW-LEVEL**

▲ A New Painting

● **ON-LEVEL**

▲ The Best Birthday

● **ADVANCED**

▲ First Prize

Comprehension
Setting

Objective
To identify the setting of a story

Clarify Meaning   Use the setting children are in to clarify the two aspects of setting:

Where are we? in the classroom

When is it? today (Use the calendar and clock to identify the exact day, date, and time.)

Comprehension   After small-group instruction, are children able to identify the setting in a story?

If not, provide additional small-group practice with the skill. See the *Strategic Intervention Resource Kit* for additional support.

Strategic ▶
Intervention
Resource Kit

BELOW-LEVEL   RETEACH

Guided Review

Have children turn to page 18 in the *Student Edition*. Read aloud the text and go over the chart to review setting for children. Then read aloud "Mia's Snowman" on page 19. Prompt children to identify both elements in the setting by asking them to find words that tell *when* the story takes place and then to find words that tell *where* the story takes place. Guide them by using prompts such as these:

Look at the first paragraph. Where is Mia?

Read the second paragraph. What day is it? What season is it?

Use that information to complete the chart on page 19. Revisit stories that children have read in their *Student Editions*, using the art and story openers to determine the settings. Guide children using prompts similar to the ones above.

Setting	
When	Where

Identify and Discuss Setting

Remind children that the setting is where and when a story takes place. Have children revisit the stories they have read in the *Student Edition*, using the art and story openers to identify the various settings, prompting them by asking

Where does this story take place?

When does this story take place?

Then ask children to name some favorite stories, to discuss what happens in them, and to determine their settings.

 ADVANCED **EXTEND**

Identify and Discuss Setting

Have a volunteer explain what the setting of a story is, making sure both *where* and *when* are included. Ask each child to name a favorite story and identify its setting. Then have the group brainstorm other interesting places where a story could take place. List them on the board. Now have them think of different times when a story might take place, such as today or last week, a particular season or year, some time in the past, or some time in the future. Suggest that children note down in their notebooks any setting that interests them; they might want to use it sometime in a story that they write.

> Setting Idea:
> A rain forest on Venus in the future.

Comprehension
Follow Directions

Objective
To identify the purpose of reading directions and to follow written two-step directions

Clarify Meaning Use numbers to help children understand common clue words. Write the following on the board:

First = 1

Next = 2

Last = 3

Use the listed words as you give children simple 3-step directions. Have children hold up one finger when you say the word *first,* two fingers when you say the word *next,* and three fingers when you say *last.*

 MONITOR PROGRESS

Comprehension After small-group instruction, are children able to identify the purpose of reading directions and then read and follow those directions?

If not, provide additional small-group practice with the skill. See the *Strategic Intervention Resource Kit* for additional support.

Strategic ▶ Intervention Resource Kit

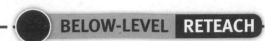
BELOW-LEVEL RETEACH

Guided Review
Remind children that they have to read and follow directions all the time, such as when they take a test or learn a new game. Go over the important things to look for when reading directions:

> **Read the title or heading, so you know what the directions are for.**
>
> **Look through the directions once to see what you need to do.**
>
> **Look at any pictures that may help you understand a step.**
>
> **Reread, looking for numbered steps and clue words.**

List some common clue words for children (such as *first, next, then, finally, before, after,* and *while*). Write simple numbered directions on the board with the title "How to Get Ready for a Fire Drill." Include some clue words. Read the directions with children. Ask them what these directions are for; how many steps there are; what they need to do first, next, and so forth. Afterward, have them go back and identify any clue words used.

Follow Directions

Remind children of important things to look for when reading directions. Display a set of directions (with a title, numbered steps, and some clue words) to make a simple drawing. Go over the directions with children, discussing the title, the general idea of the directions, and any clue words that appear. After children complete their drawings, compare them and discuss any problems children had following the directions.

Create and Follow Directions

Have children brainstorm times when they have had to follow written directions. Have children note important elements of directions, such as the title, numbered steps, any pictures, and any clue words contained in the steps. Brainstorm clue words that directions might contain. Then have children think of what the class does during a Fire Drill. Ask them to work together to create a set of directions, complete with a title, at least one picture, and numbered steps that include some clue words. Go over the completed directions together, making any necessary changes, and have children create a final copy that can be posted in the classroom.

WHAT TO DO IN A FIRE DRILL
1. First, stop what you are doing and stop talking.
2. Line up quietly at the front of the room.
3. Follow the teacher out of the classroom.

Robust Vocabulary

Objective
To review robust vocabulary

REVIEW ✓ Tested
Build Robust Vocabulary

disturb	**enchanting**
underneath	**instead**
procrastinate	**thrilled**
diversion	**review**
cozy	**celebrate**

✓ MONITOR PROGRESS

Robust Vocabulary After small-group instruction, are children able to use and understand the Vocabulary Words?

If not, provide additional small-group practice with the words. See the *Strategic Intervention Resource Kit* for additional support.

Strategic ▶ Intervention Resource Kit

BELOW-LEVEL   RETEACH

Reintroduce the Words

Routine Card 3 Use *Routine Card 3* and **Transparencies R81 and R82** to reintroduce all ten words. Review the Student-Friendly Explanations until children are familiar with the words. Then ask questions such as the following to check understanding. Be sure children explain their answers.

disturb	If you disturb your friends, do you bother them or leave them alone?
underneath	Which of these is underneath you—the sky or the ground?
procrastinate	If you procrastinate on a job, do you get it done early or late?
diversion	Which of these is a diversion if you're cleaning your room—a pile of books falls over or you find and reread a comic book that you like.
cozy	Which of these is a cozy place—a busy street or a comfortable chair?
enchanting	Would an enchanting place be wonderful or scary?
instead	If you went hiking instead of biking, did you do one or two things?
thrilled	If you were thrilled when you went on an amusement park ride, would you really want to go again or would you *never* want to go again?
review	What does a book review do—tell everything that happens in a book or tell why one reader liked or didn't like the book?
celebrate	Which of these would you celebrate—you just won a race or you just lost a race?

ON-LEVEL REINFORCE

Apply Word Knowledge

Display the Vocabulary Words and review the Student-Friendly Explanations. Then use each of the following synonyms in a sentence, and have children name the Vocabulary Word that can replace the synonymous word or phrase: **magical** (enchanting), **comfortable** (cozy), **have a party for** (celebrate), **excited** (thrilled), **opinion** (review), **below** (underneath), **choose something different** (instead), **bother** (disturb), **put off doing** (procrastinate), and **amusement** (diversion). After identifying the correct Vocabulary synonym, have children brainstorm a sentence for each Vocabulary Word.

ADVANCED EXTEND

Create Word Associations

Display the ten Vocabulary Words for children, ask volunteers to read them, and briefly discuss what each one means. Then ask children to think of pairs of Vocabulary Words that could go together; for example, *thrilled* and *celebrate* could go together because you would be thrilled if people wanted to celebrate your birthday. Tell children that they can use a Vocabulary Word more than once and that they should be prepared to explain why they put two particular Vocabulary Words together. When children are ready, have them share and explain their word associations.

E L L

Clarify Meaning Use smiling and frowning faces to help children grasp the positive or negative emotional aspects of these Vocabulary Words: **disturb, cozy, enchanting, thrilled,** and **celebrate**. Have children repeat each word after you and mimic the face you make.

Student-Friendly Explanations

disturb	If you disturb someone, you make a noise that bothers him or her.
underneath	If something is underneath you, it is below you.
procrastinate	If you procrastinate, you delay or avoid doing something you need to do.
diversion	A diversion is something that takes you away from what you are doing or thinking about.

Grade 2, Lesson 16   R81   Vocabulary

Transparencies R81, R82

Grammar and Writing
Language Arts Checkpoint

Objectives

- *To recognize that adjectives describe nouns*
- *To write a how-to paragraph*

Adjectives

1. Justin looked at the _____ kitten. (Accept reasonable responses.)
2. The kitten's <u>fur</u> was _____.
3. The kitten played with _____ yarn.
4. Justin put the kitten on a _____ pillow.
5. The kitten napped on a _____ couch.
6. The _____ birds flew away from the kitten.
7. The kitten looked at the _____ cat.
8. The kitten chased the _____ boy.

Grade 2, Lesson 16   LA31   Grammar

Transparency LA31

BELOW-LEVEL **RETEACH**

Review Adjectives

Remind children that an adjective is a describing word that tells about a noun. Write the following phrases on the board, circle each adjective (*round, green,* or *big*), and ask what it tells about the pillow:

- **the round pillow** (shape)
- **the green pillow** (color)
- **the big pillow** (size)

Display **Transparency LA31**, which children have seen before. Guide them in completing each sentence with an adjective that tells something about the underlined noun.

REVIEW HOW-TO PARAGRAPH   Remind children that a how-to paragraph tells how to make or do something. Use the following directions to review the features of this kind of paragraph: the title, the materials needed, the steps to follow, and the sentences written as commands.

Read the how-to paragraph to children. Discuss what would happen if the sentences were written out of order. Guide children to find clue words that tell them when to do something. (*First, Then, Now*)

MAKE NICE ICE CUBES

You'll need:
  ice cube tray
  small pieces of fruit
  water or fruit juice

First, drop fruit pieces into each section of the ice cube tray. Then fill the tray with water or juice. Put it in the freezer until it's frozen. Now you can add your fruity ice cubes to cold drinks for a tasty treat!

ON-LEVEL REINFORCE

Connect Grammar and Writing

Remind children that the sentences in a how-to paragraph, which are usually commands, have to be very clear—they may include an adjective to better describe how to do something. Display the following directions:

EVERYDAY ART

Materials: red, green, blue, and white paper; a pencil; small objects to trace; scissors; markers; paste or glue

Gather three objects from your desk. Trace around one on the red paper, another on the green paper, and the third on the blue paper. Cut each one out, and decorate it with markers. Paste the three shapes in a design on the white paper.

Use these directions to review features of a how-to paragraph: title, materials, steps in order, sentences as commands. Guide children to locate any adjectives and to explain what they tell about the nouns they modify.

Adjective Placement   Children may be used to having the noun come before the adjective in their native language. On the board, write the following equation: *adjective + noun*. Provide two lists: adjectives and nouns the adjectives can modify. Guide children to use the equation to help them put words from each list together to form a phrase that you then use in an oral sentence.

Treasure Hunt Directions

Tell children that to review how-to paragraphs they are each going to hide something in the room for the rest of the group to find. Then they will have to write careful directions that tell what to do to find the object, beginning with the starting point. Provide this model:

Start at the door. Take three big steps forward. Turn right. Take four more steps. Reach for something red. Inside is the treasure!

Give partners an object about the same size to hide. When they are all ready, have pairs exchange directions and see if they can find the hidden objects. Then have children identify any adjectives in the directions, explaining what they tell about the nouns they modify.

Phonics

Objective

To practice and apply knowledge of the short vowel /e/ea

Decodable Book 14

"Get Ready, Get Fit, Go!," "Monkey and the Wealthy Cat" ▶

✓ MONITOR PROGRESS

Phonics After small-group instruction, are children able to read words with /e/*ea*?

If not, provide additional small-group practice with the sound. See the *Strategic Intervention Resource Kit* for additional support.

Strategic ▶ Intervention Resource Kit

Connect Letters and Sounds

Routine Card 1 Use *Routine Card 1* and the *Sound/Spelling Card* to review the letter/sound correspondence for the short vowel /e/*ea*. Write the words *head, breath, sweat,* and *meant* on the board. Read the words aloud, and have children tell you what vowel sound they hear in the middle of each word. (/e/) Point out that the vowel letters *ea* together can stand for short *e*. Now display and say these words: *seat, deal, mean,* and *steam*. Remind children that *ea* can stand for the long *e* sound as well as for the short *e* sound. Then have children read aloud *Decodable Book 14*. Pause at the end of each page to review any word that children struggled to read.

Word Building

Display the following words in dark type and read them with children: **reads** (ready), **sweet** (sweat), **herd** (head), deed (dead), and **throats** (threats). For each word, have children tell you which letter to change to spell the word in parentheses. Write this word as children dictate, and have them read it with you. Then write the following sentences for children to read:

> Are you ready to cut off the dead leaves?
>
> My head is covered with sweat.
>
> It is not good to use threats to teach your dog.

Direct children to read *Decodable Book 14* aloud. Ask questions about the story to make sure that children understood what they read.

Write *ea*-Heavy Sentences

Begin with the spelling words for this lesson, and have children brainstorm other words in which *ea* stands for short *e,* listing their ideas on the board. (You may want to give them hints for words such as *breakfast, feather, weather, leather, sweater, instead, dead, spread, threat, healthy,* and *wealth.*) Then list words from Lesson 4 in which *ea* stands for long *e,* and follow a similar procedure, prompting as needed for words such as *beach, bead, cream, dream, neat, leaf, meat, pea, steam, teach,* and *wheat.* Now have children see how many *ea* words they can combine In a phrase. You might start with two-word phrases—such as *heavy cream, steady weather,* and *team sweater*—and then work up to three-word phrases, such as *heavy leather bead* and *healthy wheat bread.* Invite children to plck one or two of these phrases to illustrate.

Fluency

Objective
To read accurately and fluently with intonation that sounds like natural speech

Practice Pitch   Children may use different intonations in their first language. Give them a few chances to imitate you as you read the appropriate *Leveled Reader* sentence by sentence. Suggest they think of each sentence as a kind of song. Use finger pointing up and down to signal pitch changes.

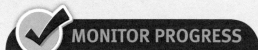 **MONITOR PROGRESS**

Fluency   After small-group instruction, are children able to read their *Leveled Reader* smoothly, with appropriate intonation that matches the mood?

If not, provide additional small-group practice. See the *Strategic Intervention Resource Kit* for additional support.

Strategic ▶
Intervention
Resource Kit

BELOW-LEVEL   RETEACH

Model Fluent Reading

Routine Card 10   Remind children that good readers read aloud with feeling, changing their tone or pitch to match the meaning of certain words, phrases, or punctuation. Point out that one way to make reading aloud interesting to listen to is to think about the mood of the story. Is something scary happening? Something silly? Does a character feel sad, happy, excited, or bored? Explain that a low voice goes with a serious, scary, or sad mood. A higher voice goes with a light, silly, or excited mood. Guide them to say the following phrase with the appropriate intonation changes: *I'm reading in an excited way, a silly way, and a scared way.* Discuss how their voices changed. Then distribute copies of *Hannah's Dance*. Read the book aloud, modeling using intonation to match mood. Point out a few dramatic sentences to children, and have them echo-read these sentences with you. Then have them read the book with a partner. Remind partners to monitor one another's reading and to offer corrections and suggestions as they listen.

Echo-Reading

Routine Card 8

Distribute *Joshua and the Tigers* to children, and explain that they will practice reading this book aloud using intonation (raising and lowering their voices) that matches the mood of the text. Before you read each page aloud to children, briefly discuss what mood you are planning to convey. Then model using intonation to convey mood, and have children read aloud after you, imitating your intonation. After reading the book through in this manner, have children practice reading it with a partner. Listen as partners read and monitor one another, adding your feedback about how well they are using intonation to convey mood and feeling.

ON-LEVEL REINFORCE

ADVANCED EXTEND

Partner Reading

Routine Card 10

Have children brainstorm different kinds of moods that a story can have (*e.g.*, funny, serious, sad, happy, scary). Point out that when good readers read aloud, they match their voices to the mood of the story. Distribute *Hunter's Secret* to children, and tell them that they will be practicing using intonation, raising and lowering their voices, to help them read more fluently and in a way that is more dramatic. Group children in pairs, having one child listen while the other reads the book aloud. After the reader is done, have the listener give constructive feedback about the accuracy and smoothness of the reading, as well as about appropriate intonation that matches the mood. Then have children switch roles and repeat the process.

LEVELED READERS

● **BELOW-LEVEL**

▲ Hannah's Dance

● **ON-LEVEL**

▲ Joshua and the Tigers

● **ADVANCED**

▲ Hunter's Secret

Comprehension
Setting

Focus Skill

Objective

To understand the importance of setting to the story and to compare settings

Clarify Meaning   Help children understand comparisons. Use two classroom objects (such as a pencil and a pen). As children name similarities, say, *"Yes, they are alike. They both __."* For differences, say, *"Yes, they are different. A pencil __, but a pen __.".*

✓ MONITOR PROGRESS

Comprehension   After small-group instruction, are children able to identify the setting of a story and understand its importance to the story?

If not, provide additional small-group practice with the skill. See the *Strategic Intervention Resource Kit* for additional support.

Strategic ▶
Intervention
Resource Kit

- - - BELOW-LEVEL   RETEACH - - -

Guided Review

Have children turn to page 54 in the *Student Edition*. Read aloud the text and review what the setting is and why it is important. Then read aloud the prompt on page 55 and go over the chart. Determine whether the chart listings tell about ways in which the two story settings are alike or ways in which they are different. Reproduce the chart on the board, and work with children to complete it, comparing the settings of "Frog and Toad All Year" and "Mr. Putter and Tabby Write the Book" (using the information from the bottom row of the chart on *Student Edition* page 55).

Pick two stories with easily contrasting settings that children have already read in their *Student Editions*, such as "The Great Ball Game" and "Click, Clack Moo: Cows That Type." Guide children to contrast how these two settings differ, drawing on the chart format used earlier.

Setting	
When	Where

Identify and Discuss Setting

Remind children that the setting is where and when a story takes place. Have children revisit some stories they have read in the *Student Edition*, using the art and story openers to identify the settings and then to compare them. Use "Click, Clack, Moo: Cows That Type" to discuss the importance of the setting to a story:

Could this story take place in the city? Why not?

Have children name favorite stories and determine their settings. Discuss why the setting is important. For example, a story set in the past cannot have modern machines; it will be hot and damp in a story set in a rainforest.

ADVANCED EXTEND

Change Settings

Ask a volunteer to tell what the setting in a story is. Have children name favorite stories and determine their settings. Note these on the board. Then tell children that they are going to explore how important the setting is to a story. Ask each child to pick one of the listed stories and change one part of the setting. For example, if the story takes place in the country, they might move it to the city or to the desert or to the shore. If a story takes place in the present, they might move it back many years into the past or move it ahead many years into the future. Have children think how this would change what happens in their favorite story and then write four things that would change. Ask each child to identify what change he or she made and then to read aloud the sentences that tell some of the things that would change. Sum up by having children discuss how the setting is important to a story.

Comprehension
Follow Directions

Objective
To identify the purpose of reading directions and to follow written two-step directions

Act Out Meaning   Read aloud each step in a set of directions for a common classroom procedure (such as the one used in Reteach), and help children show what they are to do for that step. Perform each step with the children as you read it in the directions, emphasizing the order words and step numbers. After you are done, prompt children to repeat the directions by prompting them with order words such as:

What do you do First? Next? Last?

Comprehension   After small-group instruction, are children able to identify the purpose of reading directions and then read and follow those directions?

If not, provide additional small-group practice with the skill. See the *Strategic Intervention Resource Kit* for additional support.

**Strategic ▶
Intervention
Resource Kit**

 BELOW-LEVEL   RETEACH

Guided Review
Have children recall times when they have had to read and follow directions, such as when they take a test or learn a new game. Go over the important things to look for when reading directions:

Read the title or heading, so you know what the directions are for.

Look through the directions once to see what you need to do.

Look at any pictures that may help you understand a step.

Reread, looking for numbered steps and clue words.

Work together to brainstorm some common clue words (such as *first, next, then, finally, before, after,* and *while*). Using some of these clue words, write simple directions on the board for a common classroom procedure. Read the directions with children. Ask them what these directions are for; how many steps there are; what they need to do first, next, and so forth. Afterward, have them go back and identify any clue words used.

ON-LEVEL   REINFORCE

Follow a Recipe

Recall with children that when they read directions, they should look at the title or heading to determine what the directions are about; look through the directions and any pictures to get an idea of what to do; and then reread carefully, using clue words like *first* and *after* as well as numbered steps to help them follow the directions correctly. Display a simple recipe. Go over these directions with children, discussing the title, the purpose of the directions, and any clue words that appear. Then depending on your classroom resources, have children follow the recipe to make a given dish or read each step to children and have them pantomime what they would do.

Fruit Salad

2 apples
2 oranges
bunch of grapes
cherries
2 bananas

ADVANCED   EXTEND

Create and Follow Directions

Have children brainstorm classroom procedures that they have to follow during the school week. Have them select one of these procedures and work together to create a set of directions for their classmates. Remind them that their directions should have a title, pictures if needed, and numbered steps that may include clue words. Go over the directions with children, making any necessary changes, and then have children create a final copy that can be posted in the classroom.

FREE READING TIME

1. First, take out your free reading book. Or get a new book from one of the book bins.

2. Then, find a quiet place to read.

3. Read quietly until it's time to get ready for lunch.

Robust Vocabulary

Objective
To review robust vocabulary

REVIEW
Build Robust Vocabulary

journeyed	sipped
frail	entertain
horrendous	except
melodious	carefree
stomped	screeching

MONITOR PROGRESS

Robust Vocabulary After small-group instruction, are children able to use and understand the Vocabulary Words?

If not, provide additional small-group practice with the words. See the *Strategic Intervention Resource Kit* for additional support.

Strategic ▶
Intervention
Resource Kit

BELOW-LEVEL RETEACH

Reintroduce the Words

Routine Card 3 Use *Routine Card 3* and **Transparencies R88 and R89** to reintroduce all ten words. Review the Student-Friendly Explanations until children are familiar with the words; then ask questions such as the following to check understanding. Be sure children explain their answers.

journeyed	If you journeyed to Africa, did you write a letter or make a trip?
frail	Which person is frail—someone who's been sick or someone who's been exercising?
horrendous	If you had a horrendous time at a party, would you be sad or happy?
melodious	Which of these makes melodious sounds—thunder, a fog horn, a singer, or an alarm?
stomped	If you stomped around, would you be quiet or noisy?
sipped	Which one gets sipped—hot soup, a ham sandwich, or ice cream?
entertain	If you entertain people, are they amused or angry?
except	If you like all vegetables except carrots, do you like carrots most of all or least of all?
carefree	Is a carefree person relaxed or nervous?
screeching	Is a screeching sound pleasant to hear or unpleasant to hear?

ON-LEVEL REINFORCE

Apply Word Knowledge

Display the Vocabulary Words for children and review the Student-Friendly Explanation for each one. Tell them that you will use each word in a sentence. They should tell you whether your sentence is true or false. For example, *Mack did a horrendous job cleaning up, so he was very proud.* (false) *Because the tea was hot, Myra sipped it.* (true) *Ping likes green, so he has baseball caps in every color except green.* (false) If a sentence is determined to be false, ask children to explain why it isn't true.

ADVANCED EXTEND

Assign Value

Explain that words can have positive associations by giving us feelings of joy, pleasure, strength, and goodness. Give children some examples (*smile, wonderful, sunshine, gift, dance*). Words with negative associations bring up feelings of sadness, pain, anger, fear, evil, and weakness (*mistake, stumble, sobbing, illness, fight*). Words that are neutral don't have positive or negative associations all by themselves (*basket, walk, this, hat, you*). List *positive* on the board beside a smiling face, *negative* beside a face with a down-turned mouth, and *neutral* beside a face with a straight mouth. Display the Vocabulary Words. For each one, have children discuss and decide as a group whether the word has a positive, a negative, or a neutral association. Make sure the group's discussion about each word includes reasons for the final decision.

Clarify Meaning   Use sound effects to convey to children the difference between a **carefree melodious** sound (perhaps light music) and a **horrendous screeching** sound (make a noise that makes children want to cover their ears).

Student-Friendly Explanations

journeyed	If you have traveled on a long trip, you have journeyed.
frail	When you feel very weak, you are frail.
horrendous	When you see or hear something horrible or frightening, it is horrendous.
melodious	If you hear musical sounds that are pleasant to listen to, you are hearing something melodious.

Grade 2, Lesson 17   **R88**   Vocabulary

Transparencies R88, R89

Grammar and Writing
Language Arts Checkpoint

Objectives
- *To identify and use sense adjectives*
- *To write a description*

Sense Adjectives

1. Cam climbed onto the <u>noisy</u> train. (noun: train)
2. The train car felt <u>hot</u> and <u>stuffy</u>. (noun: car)
3. Cam sat on a <u>soft</u>, <u>bouncy</u> seat. (noun: seat)
4. A conductor with a <u>blue</u> hat punched Cam's ticket. (noun: hat)
5. The hole puncher made a <u>sharp</u>, <u>snapping</u> sound. (noun: sound)
6. Cam tore open a <u>shiny</u> bag of popcorn. (noun: bag)
7. The train suddenly blew its very <u>loud</u> whistle. (noun: whistle)
8. A <u>small</u> child next to Cam let out a cry. (noun: child)
9. Cam shared his <u>salty</u> popcorn with the child. (noun: popcorn)
10. The child wiped off his <u>wet</u> cheeks and smiled. (noun: cheeks)

Grade 2, Lesson 17 · LA35 · Grammar

Transparency LA35

BELOW-LEVEL **RETEACH**

Review Sense Adjectives

Remind children that adjectives are words that tell about nouns. Point out that some adjectives tell how something looks, smells, tastes, sounds, or feels. List and read aloud the phrases below. For each one, have children identify which word is the adjective and which is the noun. Then guide them to link the adjective to the sense of sight, smell, taste, sound, or touch.

> red truck
> noisy game
> fuzzy blanket
> smoky fireplace
> sweet honey

Display **Transparency LA35**, reminding children that they have seen it before. Guide them in identifying the adjectives and the nouns they modify. Then have them identify which sense is attached to each adjective.

REVIEW DESCRIPTIONS   Remind children that a description tells what something is like. Display and use the paragraph below to review these key elements of a descriptive paragraph: *The first sentence tells what will be described. Each sentence gives details that create a picture. Sense adjectives are used throughout. The paragraph has a beginning, a middle, and an end.*

> **I love to eat an orange. I like its bright color and its round shape. I like to peel its tough skin. As the peel comes off, there's a spray that's like a mist. The mist smells sweet. Then I take a bite. There's nothing better than the juicy taste of an orange!**

After reading the paragraph to children and using it to review descriptive elements, guide children to find the various sensory adjectives, to locate the nouns they modify, and to identify what senses are appealed to. Then work with children to write a new paragraph about another favorite food.

ON-LEVEL REINFORCE

Connect Grammar and Writing

Remind children that paragraphs that describe something always contain adjectives. The adjectives might tell what it looks like, smells like, sounds like, tastes like, or feels like. Display this opening sentence for a descriptive paragraph:

Breakfast is my favorite meal.

Have children brainstorm what kinds of foods are good to eat for breakfast, what kind of smells these foods have, what they taste and feel like, and what kind of noises people make when eating them. List these ideas on the board. Work with children to complete the descriptive paragraph, using as many different kinds of sensory words as possible. When the paragraph is complete, review it with children to be sure it makes sense. Discuss the various adjectives used and the senses they appeal to.

Provide Visual Support Using the phrases in the Reteach activity, underline the adjective in each phrase and point to the relevant sensory organ: eye (sight), nose (smell), mouth (taste), ear (sound), or hand (touch). Have children imitate your gesture as they say each phrase with you.

ADVANCED EXTEND

Describe a Memory

Ask children to think back to when they were younger, not yet in school. Have them think of a particular scene from long ago and create a descriptive paragraph entitled "I Remember." Remind them that the first sentence in their description should identify the scene, so the reader knows what is being described. Encourage them to use as many of their senses to describe the scene as possible. Once their drafts are complete, have them edit and revise using Editor's Marks. Then ask them to share their finished draft with the rest of the group.

Phonics

Objective
To practice and apply knowledge of the vowel diphthong /oi/oi, oy

Decodable Book 15

"The Best Toy" and "Coins, Coins, Coins" ▶

 MONITOR PROGRESS

Phonics   After small-group instruction, are children able to read words with /oi/*oi* and *oy*?

If not, provide additional small-group practice with the sound. See the *Strategic Intervention Resource Kit* for additional support.

Strategic ▶ Intervention Resource Kit

 **BELOW-LEVEL   RETEACH**

Connect Letters and Sounds

Routine Card 1   Use *Routine Card 1* and the *Sound/Spelling Card* to review the vowel diphthong /oi/*oi, oy*. Write the words *join, boil,* and *point* on the board. Say the words, and ask children what vowel sound they hear in the middle of these words. (/oi/) Explain that in these words, the vowel letters *oi* together make one sound and that this sound is /oi/. Follow a similar procedure for *oy* using the words *boy, joy,* and *toy*. Guide children in reading the words and identifying the letters that stand for the /oi/ sound. Then have children read aloud *Decodable Book 15*. Pause at the end of each page to review any word that children struggled to read.

 ON-LEVEL   REINFORCE

Word Building

Write the letters *oi* and *oy* on the board. Add letters to build the words *join, coin, coil, boil, boy, joy,* and *toy* one at a time, asking children to name the letter that must be changed to create the new word (or letters, when going from *boil* to *boy*). Have children read each new word as it is built. Then write the following sentences for children to read:

The boy was filled with joy to get a coin and a toy.

Roy will join me and boil the moist coil.

Now have children read aloud the stories in *Decodable Book 15*. Afterward, ask questions about each story to make sure that children understood what they read.

Write Rhyming Sentences

Display the phonograms -*oy* and -*oil*. Have children brainstorm words that end with these letters (*boy, joy, toy, coy, Roy, enjoy; boil, broil, coil, foil, oil, soil, toil*), listing their words on the board or on chart paper. Ask children to create rhyming sentences, choosing from the words on display. When children are ready, invite them to share their rhyming sentences with the group.

I got some soil.
I wrapped it in foil.

I met a new boy.
His name is Roy.

Fluency

Objective
To read accurately and fluently with intonation that sounds like natural speech

Word Identification Explain that children should look at a sentence to make sure they know all the words before reading it aloud. Go sentence by sentence through an appropriate *Leveled Reader*. Identify and sound out any unfamiliar words before you read a sentence aloud and have children echo-read it.

 **MONITOR PROGRESS**

Fluency After small-group instruction, are children able to read text with fluency and accuracy?

If not, provide additional small-group practice. See the *Strategic Intervention Resource Kit* for additional support.

Strategic ▶
Intervention
Resource Kit

 **BELOW-LEVEL** **RETEACH**

Model Fluent Reading

Routine Card **10** Remind children that good readers make sure they read each word correctly. Explain two things that will help children do this:

Read slowly, so you have enough time to pronounce each word correctly.

Go back and reread if you make a mistake.

Distribute copies of *Music Is About Sounds* to children. Read the book aloud to them, modeling fluency by occasionally slowing up to read a longer, more complex sentence at a slower pace. Afterward, draw children's attention to what you have just done. Have children echo-read the page with you, matching your speed. Then have them read the book with a partner. Give them feedback about how natural-sounding their voices are, but also listen for and correct any inaccuracies.

ON-LEVEL REINFORCE

Echo-Reading

Routine Card 8 Remind children that good readers read in a natural-sounding way, as if talking to a friend, but sometimes slow down for a longer sentence, to make sure they read each word correctly. Distribute *Playing in an Orchestra* to children, and explain that they will practice reading aloud accurately in a natural-sounding voice. Read each page aloud, occasionally slowing to read a complex sentence. Have children read aloud after you, matching your pace. After reading the book through in this way, have children practice reading with partners. Remind listeners to monitor their partner's reading, alerting the reader when a mistake has been made.

ADVANCED EXTEND

Partner Reading

Routine Card 10 Help children recall that they can slow down their reading to make sure they read a complicated sentence aloud with accuracy. Remind them to go back and reread a sentence if they make a mistake. Distribute *Music for Everyone* to children, and tell them that they will be practicing reading the text with accuracy. Remind them, however, that they should always try to read aloud in a natural-sounding voice, as if talking to a friend, even when they slow down to read more carefully. Group children in pairs, having one child read the book aloud while the other listens. If the second child hears a mistake, he or she should stop the reader so that the mistake can be corrected. When the first child is done reading the book, have the listener offer constructive feedback about how natural-sounding the reading sounded and how accurately the book was read. Then have children switch roles and repeat the reading aloud.

LEVELED READERS

BELOW-LEVEL

▲ Music Is About Sounds

ON-LEVEL

▲ Playing in an Orchestra

ADVANCED

▲ Music for Everyone

Comprehension

Locate Information

Objective
To identify the setting of a story

Alphabetical Order Children who haven't yet mastered the alphabet should have access to an alphabet display, which they can use while using a glossary or index. Work with them to alphabetize some words to the first, and second letters.

 MONITOR PROGRESS

Comprehension After small-group instruction, are children able to use the parts of a book to locate information?

If not, provide additional small-group practice with the skill. See the *Strategic Intervention Resource Kit* for additional support.

Strategic ▶
Intervention
Resource Kit

● - - - **BELOW-LEVEL** **RETEACH** - - - - ●

Guided Review
Remind children that nonfiction books are organized so that readers can find information more easily. Point out that good readers know how to use the parts of a book to find the information they want. Use children's science or social studies textbook to review the parts of a book:

The Table of Contents: Ask children on which page different chapters begin. Have children turn to those pages to verify the listings.

Chapter Titles, Headings: Have children use a chapter title to figure out what information will be in that chapter. Do the same with a heading.

Glossary, Guide Words: Have children look for certain words in the glossary, helping them use the guide words to determine if a word is on a particular page.

Index: Have children tell you whether a book contains information on a topic that isn't and one that is in the index. For a given entry, have children check the pages listed to find information on that topic.

Use Parts of a Book

Use children's science or social studies textbooks to review these parts of a book: table of contents, chapter titles, headings, glossary and guide words, and index. Discuss the purpose of each. Give children prompts such as these to practice using the parts of a book:

Find out whether this book has information about (topic in book).

On which page does Chapter 3 begin? What is the title of this chapter? What is it probably about? Find a heading in the chapter. What information do you think you'll find in this section?

What does (term in Glossary) mean? How did you find this word?

Do a Book Walkthrough

Ask children to take out their science or social studies textbooks. Remind them that nonfiction books are organized so that readers can find information more easily. Now have children walk you through the textbook, stopping and pointing out book parts that they can use to find information in the textbook. For each part, they should "teach" you the purpose of this part and show you how to use it.

Research/Study Skill

Use Reference Sources

Objective

To use reference sources such as a dictionary, a thesaurus, an encyclopedia, and an atlas

Clarify Meaning   Help children distinguish between a *dictionary* and a *thesaurus*, which may seem almost identical to them. Show children how the same word (such as *terrify* or *gallop*) appears in each one, helping children see the difference between meanings and synonyms. Use several examples.

 MONITOR PROGRESS

Comprehension   After small-group instruction, are children able to identify the purpose of a dictionary, a thesaurus, an encyclopedia, and an atlas?

If not, provide additional small-group practice with the skill. See the *Strategic Intervention Resource Kit* for additional support.

Strategic ▶ Intervention Resource Kit

· · · · · · · · · · · · BELOW-LEVEL RETEACH · · · · · · · · · · · ·

Guided Review

Remind children that good readers know how to use different reference sources to find particular information. Create a chart like the one below to review several kinds of reference sources:

WHAT	WHEN
Dictionary	You want to find out what a word means and how to spell it.
Thesaurus	You want to find words that have about the same meaning.
Encyclopedia	You want to find information on a topic.
Atlas	You want to find maps of a state, country, or part of the world, as well as other information about these places.

Now prompt children to decide which reference source to use in a given situation. For example, *What reference source would you use if you want to find out about Japan? If you want to see where Japan is? If you want to find out the meaning of the word* sushi, *a kind of Japanese food?*

● ON-LEVEL REINFORCE

Identify and Distinguish Reference Sources

Display a dictionary; a thesaurus; an encyclopedia volume, CD, or DVD; and an atlas. Review the purposes of each one with children. Then give them various research "assignments," such as the ones below, and have them tell you which reference sources they would use and why.

You want to find out which is bigger—South America or Africa.

You want to find a more interesting word than *scared* to use in a poem.

You want to find out different meanings for the word *bay*.

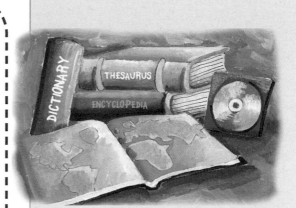

● ADVANCED EXTEND ✎

Create Research Questions

Display a dictionary, thesaurus, atlas, and an encyclopedia volume, CD, or DVD. Have children identify each one and discuss its purpose. Then have children work with a partner to think of when they might want to use each of these reference sources. In particular, they should think of two questions that could be answered by using each reference source. Afterward, have the group compare their questions and pick one or two to follow through on with each reference source, seeing if they can find the information they need to answer the question in the one you have on display.

Atlas

1. Is there land at the South Pole?

2. How many oceans are there?

Robust Vocabulary

Objective
To review robust vocabulary

REVIEW

Build Robust Vocabulary

attract	expression
territory	creative
universal	performance
audible	concentrate
volume	relieved

MONITOR PROGRESS

Robust Vocabulary After small-group instruction, are children able to use and understand the Vocabulary Words?

If not, provide additional small-group practice with the words. See the *Strategic Intervention Resource Kit* for additional support.

**Strategic ▶
Intervention
Resource Kit**

BELOW-LEVEL RETEACH

Reintroduce the Words

Routine Card 3

Use *Routine Card 3* and **Transparencies R95 and R96** to reintroduce the words to children. Review the Student-Friendly Explanations until they are familiar with the words. Check understanding with prompts like the following, having children explain their answer each time.

attract	If certain smells attract flies, are they smells flies dislike or like?
territory	Is a lion's territory where it lives or what it eats?
universal	If an idea is universal, is it something everyone believes in or something that only a few people believe in?
audible	Which of these is audible—sunlight or thunder?
volume	Is the volume of a sound how high or low it is or how soft or loud?
expression	If you play music with expression, do you play it with feeling or do you play it perfectly, with no mistakes?
creative	Which of these is a creative act—cleaning your room, making a peanut-butter sandwich, or drawing a picture?
performance	Which of these is a performance—getting ready to go to school or singing a song in front of the class?
concentrate	If you concentrate, do you think hard or do you relax?
relieved	Which of these would make you feel relieved—studying to take a test or finding out you got a good mark on a test?

● ON-LEVEL REINFORCE

Show and Tell

Review the Student-Friendly Explanation for each Vocabulary Word. Then use prompts that involve children telling examples or showing examples for each Vocabulary Word. For example:

Name something creative that you like to do.

Name a time when you had to concentrate.

Show me some expressions and tell me what they mean.

Show me how you would look if you were relieved.

Make sure all children respond to the prompts.

● ADVANCED EXTEND ✏

Write About a Picture

Display and discuss the meanings of the Vocabulary Words, consulting the Student-Friendly Explanations if needed. Then display a photograph of a performance, such as a dance performance, rock or orchestral concert, or a play. Have children discuss what it would be like if they went to see this performance. What would they do, see, hear, and feel? Then have them work together to write several sentences that tell about this picture. Explain that they must use all the Vocabulary Words in these sentences. Be prepared to help them if they have trouble using a particular word, such as *universal*. (They might say something about how everyone loves going to a live performance. It's a *universal* feeling.)

> At first the music wasn't very audible. We had to concentrate to hear the words. But then the band turned up the volume.

Clarify Meaning   Use pictures from books or magazines that each show a **creative performance**. Point out people's facial **expressions**, looking for ones that you can use to illustrate **concentrate** and **relieved**. Use musical performances to illustrate audible and volume.

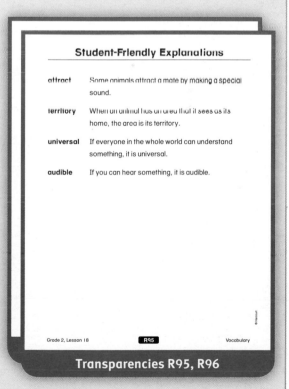

Student-Friendly Explanations

attract	Some animals attract a mate by making a special sound.
territory	When an animal has an area that it sees as its home, the area is its territory.
universal	If everyone in the whole world can understand something, it is universal.
audible	If you can hear something, it is audible.

Grade 2, Lesson 18   **R95**   Vocabulary

Transparencies R95, R96

Grammar and Writing
Language Arts Checkpoint

Objectives
- *To recognize number words*
- *To write a poem*

BELOW-LEVEL **RETEACH**

Review Number Words

Remind children that adjectives tell more about nouns; sometimes they tell "how many." Point out that these number words may tell exactly how many or only about how many. Display the following examples, read them aloud, and contrast them for children:

- Exactly how many: two cats, ten books, twenty-five blocks

- About how many: a few cats, some books, many blocks

Display number words that don't give exact amounts: *few, some, many, most, several, all*. Name a classroom item and have children come up with a sentence that starts with *I see*, adds a number word, and ends with the item. For example, *I see five windows. I see some paper.* Write each sentence on the board. Then have children identify the number word and tell whether it tells the exact amount or just tells about how much.

REVIEW WRITING A POEM   Revisit a couple of poems in the *Student Edition*, one of which uses a rhyme scheme and both of which contain sensory words. Use these sentences to point out features in the poems:

- A poem has a title.

- A poem uses words in a creative way and may use rhyming words.

- A poem uses colorful words and details to help the reader see, hear, or feel what the writer is telling about.

If there are any number words, point them out as well. Pick one place and have children brainstorm what they could tell about it that would help readers see, hear, feel, smell, or taste what it was like. Then work together to compose the poem.

ON-LEVEL REINFORCE

Connect Grammar and Writing

Remind children that a poem uses words in a creative way. It may include rhyming words and usually includes sensory words that tell what the special thing looks, smells, sounds, tastes, or feels like. Explain that when a writer tells what something looks like, number words may be used. Have children point out the exact number word and the inexact number word in this sentence: *Some children sat at the table, but one child sat alone.* Work together with children to write a poem about something that is outside the classroom or school. Brainstorm phrases that describe things they can see (including exact and inexact number words), hear, touch, and smell. Guide them to put these phrases together to create a poem. When complete, display the poem in the classroom.

ADVANCED EXTEND

Create a Number Poem

Have children give you examples of exact and inexact number words. Remind them that a poem uses words in a creative way, and that a poem uses colorful words and details to help the reader see, hear, or feel what the writer is telling about. Tell children you want them to work with a partner to create a poem that tells about being some place where they can see different-sized groups, such as animals at a zoo, items on shelves in a store, or transportation on a busy street. Direct children to pick a place, brainstorm what they would see (including exact and inexact number words), hear, smell, and touch or feel. Then have them use these phrases to create a poem, reminding them to add a title that tells what their poem is about. When pairs are ready, invite them to share their poems with the group or class.

Numbers Adjectives, including numerical ones, may change in children's home language to match the gender and number of the noun that it modifies. Have children count crayons and chairs and other classroom objects (one crayon, two crayons, three crayons) so they can see that the numbers never change.

Phonics

Objective
To practice and apply knowledge of the r-*Controlled vowel /ir/ear, eer*

Decodable Book 16

"Cheers and Tears" and "A Year at the Leary Place" ▶

MONITOR PROGRESS

Phonics After small-group instruction, are children able to read words with /ir/*ear, eer*?

If not, provide additional small-group practice with the sound. See the *Strategic Intervention Resource Kit* for additional support.

Strategic ▶ Intervention Resource Kit

BELOW-LEVEL RETEACH

Connect Letters and Sounds

Routine Card 1

Use *Routine Card 1* and the *Sound/Spelling Card* to review the r-Controlled vowel /ir/*ear, eer*. Display the words *hear, near,* and *year*. Have children listen as you pronounce these words and tell you what sound all of them share. (/ir/) Then have them tell you what letters they all share (*ear*). Point out that here the letters *e-a-r* make one sound and that they can stand for the /ir/ sound. Follow a similar procedure for *eer*, using *deer, steer,* and *cheer*. Then have children read aloud *Decodable Book 16*. Pause at the end of each page to review any word that children struggled to read.

ON-LEVEL REINFORCE

Word Building

Display the following words in dark type and read them with children: **neat** (near), **far** (fear), **heard** (hear), **steel** (steer), **yearn** (year), and **peek** (peer). For each word, have children tell you whether to add a letter, subtract a letter, or change a letter to spell the word in parentheses. Write this word as children dictate, and have them read it with you. Then write the following sentences for children to read:

> I fear the steer that is near my home.

> We hear and peer at birds all year long.

Direct children to read *Decodable Book 16* aloud. Ask questions about the story to make sure that children understood what they read.

ADVANCED EXTEND

Word Sorts

Give children this array of words: *card, dear, earth, herd, steer, heard, deer, yarn, year, jerk.* First have children sort these words by vowel sounds (3 groups). Then have them sort the /ûr/ and /ir/ groups by spellings (2 subgroups: *er* and *ear; eer* and *ear*). Then have them look across their sorts for words that sound the same but are spelled differently (*herd* and *heard; deer* and *dear*). Now direct children to add at least one word to each of their word groups.

Fluency

Objective

To read accurately and fluently with intonation that sounds like natural speech

Increasing Speed Tell children that they should practice sentences in the appropriate *Leveled Reader* that cause them problems. They should start at a speed slow enough to pronounce all the words, then repeat the sentence until they can say it at a slow but natural-sounding speed.

Fluency After small-group instruction, are children able to read text with accuracy while maintaining a speed that sounds like natural speech?

If not, provide additional small-group practice. See the *Strategic Intervention Resource Kit* for additional support.

Strategic ▶ Intervention Resource Kit

Model Fluent Reading

Routine Card 10 Remind children that good readers make sure their reading is accurate by reading slowly enough to pronounce each word correctly. Point out, however, that they don't want to read aloud so slowly that their listeners get bored. Distribute copies of *Thomas Alva Edison: A Great Inventor* to children. Model reading the first page too quickly, stumbling over a word or two. Then reread the page with exaggerated slowness. Finally, read it with accuracy and at a reasonably slow speed. Ask children to tell you which version worked best. Have children echo-read the page with you, matching your speed. Read the rest of the book aloud to children. Occasionally slow down slightly for a longer or more complex sentence, and have children echo-read this sentence with you, again matching your speed. Now direct them to read the book with a partner. Listen to their readings, providing feedback on their speed but also drawing attention to any inaccuracies.

ON-LEVEL REINFORCE

Echo-Reading

Routine Card 8 Remind children that good readers sometimes slow down for a complicated sentence to read each word correctly, but they do so without slowing down so much that their reading sounds odd. Distribute *Madam C.J. Walker: Making Dreams Happen*, and read the opening to model the difference between reading slowly and reading too slowly. Ask children which version sounded odd. Now read each page aloud, occasionally slowing down slightly to read a complicated sentence. Have children read aloud after you, matching your change of pace. Afterward, have them practice reading with partners. Remind listeners to monitor their partner's reading, alerting the reader when a mistake has been made, while you provide feedback on their speed.

ADVANCED EXTEND

Partner Reading

Routine Card 10 Remind children that fluent readers will slow down from time to time as they read, to make sure they pronounce every word accurately. Distribute *Cyrus McCormick: Friend to Farmers* to children, and tell them that they will be practicing reading the text at a speed that sounds natural, even when they have to slow down to make sure they read accurately. Group children in pairs, having one child read the book aloud while the other listens. If the second child hears a mistake, he or she should stop the reader so that the mistake can be corrected. The listener should also draw attention to any sentence that is read too slowly. The reader should attempt this sentence again, trying to increase the speed slightly while maintaining accuracy. Then have children switch roles and repeat the process of reading aloud.

LEVELED READERS

● BELOW-LEVEL

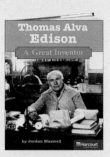

▲ **Thomas Alva Edison: A Great Inventor**

● ON-LEVEL

▲ **Madame C.J. Walker: Making Dreams Happen**

● ADVANCED

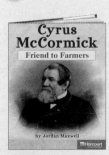

▲ **Cyrus McCormick: Friend to Farmers**

Comprehension
Locate Information

Objective
To use titles and headings to locate information in a nonfiction story

Clarify Meaning Help children understand the headings. Link *early years* to the time when children are in elementary, middle, and high school. Link *middle years* to when a person is a parent, raising children. Link *later years* to when a person is a grandparent.

MONITOR PROGRESS

Comprehension After small-group instruction, are children able to use titles and headings to locate information in a nonfiction text?

If not, provide additional small-group practice with the skill. See the *Strategic Intervention Resource Kit* for additional support.

Strategic ▶
Intervention
Resource Kit

Guided Review

Have children turn to page 118 in the *Student Edition*. Read aloud the paragraph on this page to review how to use headings. Guide children through the chart on this page, reading aloud the text and using the artwork for support. Then work together to complete the chart on the next page.

Use titles and headings in children's science or social studies textbooks to provide practice in looking for key words and thinking about what kind of information might be found under each one. First, display or draw attention to a title or heading. Then point to each word in the title or heading and ask, **Is this word important?** Once key words have been determined, ask, **What does (key words) make you think of?** List some of children's ideas, discuss them, and have children decide what kind of information will be found under this title or heading. You may want to read aloud some of the text to validate children's predictions.

Chapter Title	Information

Use Titles and Headings

Remind children that titles and headings can help them locate information in a nonfiction text. Look through classroom copies of children's magazines or nonfiction books with the group. Stop and discuss the various titles and headings that you come across. Have children tell you which words in the title or heading are important and then predict what the text will be about. You may want to read a bit of the text to validate children's predictions.

Evaluate Titles and Headings

Remind children that good readers use titles and headings to help them locate information in a nonfiction text. Give pairs of children a nonfiction book that contains chapter titles and headings. Direct each pair to look at each chapter head and decide what they expect the chapter to be about, jotting down their prediction. Then have them begin reading, following a similar procedure with each heading. Afterward, they should decide if the chapter titles and headings did a good job of getting the reader ready for what the text would be about. Have them present their book to the group, explaining why they think the book did a good job with titles and headings or did not do a good job.

Research/Study Skill
Use Reference Sources

Objective

To understand when and how to use a dictionary, a thesaurus, an encyclopedia, and an atlas

Alphabetical Order   Give children practice looking up entries in a dictionary and an encyclopedia. Give them entry words that involve alphabetizing to the first and second letter. Be sure they have an alphabet chart for easy reference.

Comprehension   After small-group instruction, do children know when and how to use a dictionary, a thesaurus, an encyclopedia, and an atlas?

If not, provide additional small-group practice with the skill. See the *Strategic Intervention Resource Kit* for additional support.

Strategic ▶
Intervention
Resource Kit

Guided Review

Display examples of a dictionary, a thesaurus, an encyclopedia volume, and an atlas. Remind children of the kinds of information they can find in each. Point out the various entries in the dictionary, thesaurus, and encyclopedia as you elicit that the information (words, topics) is arranged in alphabetical order. Prompt children to decide which reference source to use in a given situation, displaying these prompts:

Which would you use if you wanted to see where Hudson Bay is?

Which would you use if you wanted to find out about (a topic that can be found in your encyclopedia)?

Which would you use if you wanted to know other meanings for the word *bay*?

Which would you use if you wanted to know another word that you could use instead of the word (entry in your thesaurus)?

Help children use the reference sources to find the answers.

Compare Sources

Display and review the uses of a dictionary, a thesaurus, an encyclopedia volume, and an atlas. Then have children watch as you go online and use a search engine to locate web-based reference materials. Have children discuss how these materials are different from their print counterparts. Then have them look up information in online and print reference sources. Which do they think are easier to use? Faster to use? More complete?

Treasure Hunt

Display a dictionary, a volume of an encyclopedia, a thesaurus, and an atlas. Pair up children and give them each a list of ten things to find in the displayed reference sources, making sure the answers can be readily found and that all the reference sources will be used. Direct partners to locate the information and record the information they found. Have each pair read their answers aloud, asking other pairs to tell whether they agree or disagree with the answers and tell why.

1. Find out what the word *flabbergasted* means.

2. Find out the name of the biggest island in the Hawaiian Islands.

3. Find out what a kangaroo eats.

Robust Vocabulary

Objective
To review robust vocabulary

Tested

REVIEW ✓

Build Robust Vocabulary

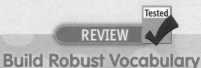

brew	**crop**
snug	**provide**
innovation	**earn**
edible	**committee**
supplies	**experiments**

✓ MONITOR PROGRESS

Robust Vocabulary After small-group instruction, are children able to use and understand the Vocabulary Words?

If not, provide additional small-group practice with the words. See the *Strategic Intervention Resource Kit* for additional support.

Strategic ▶
Intervention
Resource Kit

◖ BELOW-LEVEL RETEACH ◗

Reintroduce the Words

Routine Card 3

Use *Routine Card 3* and **Transparencies R102 and R103** to reintroduce all ten words to children. Review the Student-Friendly Explanations until the words are familiar; then ask questions such as the following to check understanding. Be sure children explain their answer.

brew — Which person brews iced tea? Tim buys a bottle of iced tea in the store. Kim makes iced tea at home, using tea bags and water.

snug — Which of these is snug: a sweater that's too small for you or a sweater that's too big for you?

innovation — Is an innovation something new or something old?

edible — Which of these is edible: a shoe, an apple, or a rock?

supplies — Which of these are pet supplies: puppies or puppy food?

crop — Is a farm crop something a farmer grows or something a farmer buys?

provide — If you are supposed to provide hot dogs at a class picnic, do you bring enough hot dogs for yourself or enough for everyone in your class?

earn — Which of these could a child do to earn money: go to a bank or do some work for a neighbor?

committee — Which of these things might a committee do: decide where to have a town art show or paint a picture for the town art show?

experiments — Which one does experiments: a librarian or a scientist?

ON-LEVEL **REINFORCE**

Word Associations

Review the Student-Friendly Explanation for each word, and use it in a sentence for children. Display the words. Prompt word associations by asking, for example, *Which word goes with dessert?* Children should respond with a word and an explanation; in this case, *edible*, since you eat a dessert and desserts aren't crops. Other possible associations to use include *tea* (brew), *farmer* (crop), *tight* (snug), *group* (committee), *tests* (experiments), *money* (earn), *gear* (supplies), *give* (provide), and *new* (innovation). For each word, you might have children suggest other possible word associations.

Visual Support   When you go over the Student-Friendly Explanations, use props, show magazine or textbook pictures, or do pantomime for *snug,* (art) *supplies, crop, committee, experiments,* and *edible.*

ADVANCED **EXTEND**

Is/Is Not Examples

Display the Vocabulary Words, and review the Student-Friendly Explanations. For each word, offer an explanatory sentence that either is or is not an example of the word. Children should identify the example by saying *is* or *is not*, and then offering an explanation for their response. Possible sentences to use:

*One way to **brew** tea is to buy it in a store.* (is not)

*One kind of **crop** is corn.* (is)

*One thing a **committee** does is to make decisions.* (is)

*One thing that is **snug** is a big robe.* (is not)

*One thing that is **edible** is a rock.* (is not)

*Pens and pencils are school **supplies**.* (is)

*One place where **experiments** are done is in science class.* (is)

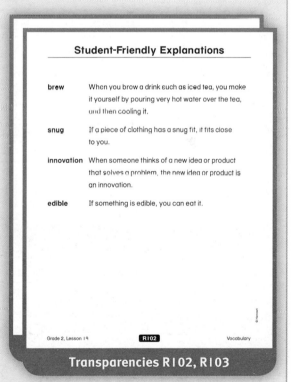

Transparencies R102, R103

Grammar and Writing
Language Arts Checkpoint

Objectives

- *To recognize and use -er and -est words that compare*
- *To write a biographical narrative*

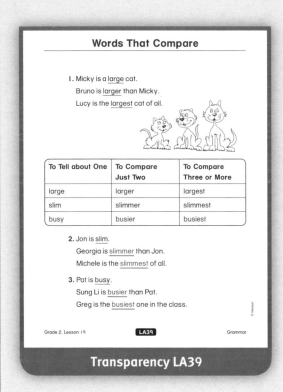

Words That Compare

1. Micky is a large cat.
   Bruno is larger than Micky.
   Lucy is the largest cat of all.

To Tell about One	To Compare Just Two	To Compare Three or More
large	larger	largest
slim	slimmer	slimmest
busy	busier	busiest

2. Jon is slim.
   Georgia is slimmer than Jon.
   Michele is the slimmest of all.

3. Pat is busy.
   Sung Li is busier than Pat.
   Greg is the busiest one in the class.

Grade 2, Lesson 19   LA39   Grammar

Transparency LA39

BELOW-LEVEL RETEACH

Review Words That Compare

Display three different colored pencils of different lengths. Write these sentences on the board: *The red pencil is short. The blue pencil is shorter than the red one. The green pencil is the shortest of all.* Read the sentences with children, and circle the adjectives. Underline the comparative endings as you make these points:

When you compare just two things, you can use an adjective that ends with -*er*.

When you compare three or more things, you can use an adjective that ends with -*est*.

Display **Transparency LA39,** reminding children that they have seen it before. Review the chart with them, and guide them in reading and filling in the sentences with the correct form of the underlined adjective. Have children create new sentences by replacing *slim* with *small* in number 2 and *busy* with *funny* in number 3.

REVIEW WRITING A BIOGRAPHICAL NARRATIVE   Remind children that a narrative is a story about a person, animal, event, or thing. Then review features of a biographical narrative:

It tells about the life of a real person by giving facts and details.

It usually tells events in time order.

Have children revisit "The Life of George Washington Carver," beginning on page 122 in the *Student Edition*, to find some facts that the author included. Then have children brainstorm people they would like to write about. Pick one that all children know, and make a list of the kinds of facts they could include in a biographical narrative about this person, such as where and when the person was born, schooling, and accomplishments, etc.

ON-LEVEL REINFORCE

Connect Grammar and Writing

Remind children that a biographical narrative is a story about a real person that includes facts about the person's life. Writers of biographies may compare one person to other people. Remind children that when they compare two things, they can use an adjective that ends with *-er*; when they compare three or more things, they can use an adjective that ends with *-est*. Display these sentences from a biography about a make-believe athlete who wins races: *Tino was always fast. He ran faster than his friends. He was the fastest runner in his high school.* Read and discuss the sentences with children. Then have them think about someone they would like to write a biographical narrative about. How could they compare this person to other people, using adjectives that end with *-er* and *-est*? (If necessary, provide the comparative forms of *tall, funny, big, hard, smart, kind,* and *happy* to give children ideas for their comparisons.)

Biographical Sketch

Have children discuss what goes into a biographical narrative. Ask them to think about someone in their family that they would like to write a short biography of (about a page in length). Have them begin by listing some things that make this person special, and by comparing this person to other people in the family. Remind children that when they make comparisons, they can use adjectives that end with *-er* and *-est*. Have children draft their biographical sketch, and share it with the group. After getting feedback, they may elect to revise, proofread, and publish their biographical sketch. At this point, you might have them share the finished biography with the whole class.

Comparative Endings Children's home language may not involve adding endings to form comparatives. Provide equivalents for adjectives under discussion, using equations like these:

colder = more cold

coldest = most cold

Teacher's Notes

Assessment

Good assessments tell you what your students need to learn to meet grade-level standards.

It's not just about scoring the students—or the teacher, for that matter. It's about helping teachers **know what to teach and how much.**

Reading education is a **growing science.** We know more about how children learn to read than we did in the past. This **knowledge gives us the power** to use assessment to inform instruction. Assessment exposes the missing skills so that teachers can fill in the gaps.

Good assessment is part of instruction.

Think about it: if you are testing what you are teaching, then the test is another **practice and application** opportunity for children. In addition, when tests focus on the skills that are essential to better reading, testing informs teachers about which students need more instruction in those essential skills.

What is the best kind of assessment to use?

Using more than one kind of assessment will give you the clearest picture of your students' progress. **Multiple measures** are the key to a well-rounded view.

First, consider the assessments that are already **mandated** for you: your school, your district, and your state will, of course, tell you which tests you must use, and when. In addition to these, you should use **curriculum-based assessments** to monitor your students' progress in *StoryTown*.

The following curriculum-based assessments are built into *StoryTown*.

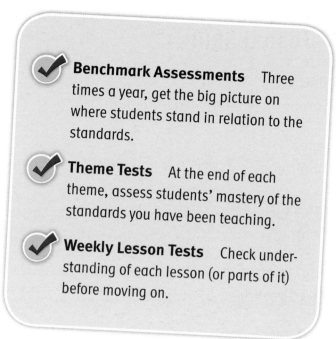

Benchmark Assessments Three times a year, get the big picture on where students stand in relation to the standards.

Theme Tests At the end of each theme, assess students' mastery of the standards you have been teaching.

Weekly Lesson Tests Check understanding of each lesson (or parts of it) before moving on.

On a daily basis, point-of-use **Monitor Progress** notes help you check understanding and reteach or extend instruction. Additional checklists and rubrics are provided to help you monitor students' comprehension, writing, listening, and speaking.

The *Benchmark Assessments,* the *Theme Tests,* and the *Weekly Lesson Tests* are all available online. Students can take the tests on the computer, or you can use pencil-and-paper and enter the scores into the database later. Either way, *StoryTown Online Assessment* will help you track students' progress and share their growth with administrators and families.

 StoryTown Online Assessment

Using Assessment to Inform Instruction

Specific prescriptions based on Harcourt Reading Assessments.

✔ **Tested Skills** **Prescriptions**

Phonics

Digraphs /n/*kn,* /r/*wr,* /f/*gh, ph*......................................Reteach, pp. S2–S3

Fluency

Intonation..Reteach, pp. S4–S5

Focus Skill

Setting...Reteach, pp. S6–S7

Comprehension

Follow Directions..Reteach, pp. S8–S9

Robust Vocabulary

Lesson 16..Reteach, pp. S10–S11

Grammar/Writing

Adjectives..Reteach, pp. S12–S13

Lesson 17 Weekly Test

✔ Tested Skills

Prescriptions

Phonics
Short Vowels /e/ *ea* .... Reteach, pp. S14–S15

Fluency
Intonation... Reteach, pp. S16–S17

Focus Skill
Setting... Reteach, pp. S18–S19

Comprehension
Follow Directions.. Reteach, pp. S20–S21

Robust Vocabulary
Lesson 17.. Reteach, pp. S22–S23

Grammar/Writing
Adjectives for Senses .... Reteach, pp. S24–S25

Weekly Test

✔ Tested Skills   Prescriptions

Phonics

Vowel Diphthong /oi/*oi, oy*.............................Reteach, pp. S26–S27

Fluency

Accuracy..Reteach, pp. S28–S29

Focus Skill

Locate Information.......................................Reteach, pp. S30–S31

Reference Skills

Use Reference Sources.................................Reteach, pp. S32–S33

Robust Vocabulary

Lesson 18 ....Reteach, pp. S34–S35

Grammar/Writing

Number Words ....Reteach, pp. S36–S37

Weekly Tests

✔ Lesson 19 Tested Skills   Prescriptions

Phonics
r-Controlled Vowel /ir/ear, eer .... Reteach, pp. S38–S39

Fluency
Accuracy .... Reteach, pp. S40–S41

Focus Skill
Locate Information .... Reteach, pp. S42–S43

Reference Skills
Use Reference Sources .... Reteach, pp. S44–S45

Robust Vocabulary
Lesson 19 .... Reteach, pp. S46–S47

Grammar/Writing
Words That Compare .... Reteach, pp. S48–S49

✔ Lesson 20 Tested Skills

Selection Comprehension
"What's My Job?" .... Monitor Comprehension,
                                                             pp. T393–T398

Robust Vocabulary
Lesson 20 .... Build Robust Vocabulary,
                                                             pp. T399, T409, T419, T431

Theme 4 Test

✔ Tested Skills

Tested Skills	Prescriptions
Phonics	Reteach, pp. S2–S3, S14–S15, S26–S27, S38–S39
Focus Skill	Reteach, pp. S6–S7, S18–S19, S30–S31, S42–S43
Comprehension	Reteach, pp. S8–S9, S20–S21, S32–S33, S44–S45
Robust Vocabulary	Reteach, pp. S10–S11, S22–S23, S34–S35, S46–S47
Grammar/Writing	Reteach, pp. S12–S13, S24–S25, S36–S37, S48–S49
Fluency	Reteach, pp. S4–S5, S16–S17, S28–S29, S40–S41

BELOW-LEVEL RETEACH
- Below-Level Leveled Readers
- Leveled Readers System
- Extra Support Copying Masters
- Strategic Intervention Resource Kit
- Intervention Station, Primary

ON-LEVEL REINFORCE
- On-Level Leveled Readers
- Leveled Readers System
- Practice Book

ADVANCED EXTEND
- Advanced Leveled Readers
- Leveled Readers System
- Challenge Copying Masters
- Challenge Resource Kit

To determine whether students need even more support, use your district-approved diagnostic and screening assessments.

ADDITIONAL RESOURCES

Using Rubrics

A **rubric** *is a tool a teacher can use to score a student's work.*

A **rubric** *lists the criteria for evaluating the work, and it describes different levels of success in meeting those criteria.*

Rubrics *are useful assessment tools for teachers, but they can be just as useful for students. They explain expectations, and can be powerful teaching tools.*

RUBRIC Rubrics for Retelling and Summarizing

- There are separate rubrics for fiction and nonfiction. Before students begin their retellings or summaries, ask them which rubric should be used. Then point out the criteria and discuss each one.

- Have students focus on the criteria for excellence listed on the rubric so that they have specific goals to aim for.

RUBRIC Rubrics for Presentations

- Before students give a presentation, discuss the criteria listed on the rubric. Help them focus on the criteria for excellence listed on the rubric so that they have specific goals to aim for.

- Discuss the criteria for listening with students who will be in the audience. Point out the criteria for excellence listed on the rubric so that they have specific goals to aim for.

RUBRIC Rubrics for Short- and Extended-Responses

- Before students begin a short- or extended-response, discuss the criteria for excellence listed on the rubrics so that they have specific goals to aim for.

- Tell students that the short-response task should take about five to ten minutes to complete, and the extended-response should take much longer to complete.

RUBRIC Rubric for Writing

- When you introduce students to a new kind of writing through a writing model, discuss the criteria listed on the rubric, and ask students to decide how well the model meets each criterion.

- Before students attempt a new kind of writing, have them focus on the criteria for excellence listed on the rubric so that they have specific goals to aim for.

- During both the drafting and revising stages, remind students to check their writing against the rubric to keep their focus and to determine if there are any aspects of their writing they can improve.

- Students can use the rubrics to score their own writing. They can keep the marked rubric in their portfolios with the piece of writing it refers to. The marked rubrics will help students see their progress through the school year. In conferences with students and family members, you can refer to the rubrics to point out both strengths and weaknesses.

Score of 4

The student:

- names and describes the main and supporting characters and tells their actions
- tells about the setting, including both time and place
- retells the plot in detail
- describes the problems and solutions in the story
- uses phrases, language, vocabulary, or sentence structure from the story
- accurately defines the theme or meaning of the story
- provides extensions of the story such as making connections to other texts, relating experiences, making inferences and/or making generalizations
- discriminates between reality and fantasy, fact and fiction
- requires little or no prompting

Score of 3

The student:

- names and describes the main characters
- tells about the setting
- retells most of the plot accurately with some details
- describes some of the problems and solutions in the story
- uses some phrases, language, or vocabulary from the story
- relates some aspects of the theme or meaning of the story
- provides some extensions of the story such as making connections to other texts or relating relevant experiences
- discriminates between reality and fantasy, fact and fiction
- may require some prompting

Score of 2

The student:

- tells some details about the story elements, including characters, setting, and plot, with some omissions or errors
- cannot correctly identify problems or corresponding solutions in the story
- uses very little language and vocabulary from story
- shows minimal understanding of the theme or meaning
- provides minimal extensions of the story
- confuses reality and fantasy, fact and fiction
- requires some prompting to retell the story

Score of 1

The student:

- tells few if any details about the story elements, possibly with errors
- has little or no awareness of the theme of the story
- provides no extensions of the story
- confuses reality and fantasy, and fact and fiction
- unable to retell the story without prompting

Score of 4

The student:
- provides a summarizing statement
- relates the main idea and important supporting details
- creates a focused, coherent, logical, and organized structure; stays on topic; and relates important points to the text
- understands relationships in the text such as recognizing cause and effect relationships, chronological order, or comparing and contrasting information
- uses phrases, language, or vocabulary from the text
- clearly identifies the conclusion
- identifies the author's purpose for creating the text
- provides extensions of the text such as making connections to other texts, relating relevant experiences, making inferences and/or making generalizations
- requires little or no prompting

Score of 3

The student:
- tells the topic of the text
- relates the main idea and relevant details
- creates a coherent structure and stays on topic
- mostly understands relationships in the text such as recognizing cause and effect relationships, chronological order, or comparing and contrasting information
- uses some language, or vocabulary from the text
- tells the conclusion or point of the text
- identifies the author's purpose
- provides some extensions of the text such as making connections to other texts or relating relevant experiences
- may require some prompting

Score of 2

The student:
- minimally relates the topic of the text
- shows minimal understanding of main idea and omits many important details
- provides some structure; might stray from topic
- understands few, if any, relationships in the text or recognizes chronological order
- uses little or no language and vocabulary from the text
- does not fully understand conclusion or point of the text
- shows some awareness of author's purpose
- provides few, if any, extensions of the text
- requires some prompting to retell the story

Score of 1

The student:
- shows little or no understanding of main idea and omits important details
- provides a poorly organized or unclear structure
- does not understand relationships in or of the text
- does not understand conclusion of the text
- provides no extensions of the text
- is unable to retell the story without prompting

Scoring RUBRIC for Presentations

Score	SPEAKING	VISUALS	MARKERS	WORD PROCESSING	HANDWRITING
6	The speaker uses very effective pacing, volume, intonation, and expression.	The writer uses visuals such as illustrations and props. The text and visuals clearly relate.	The title, side heads, page numbers, and bullets are used very well. They make it easy for the reader to find information in the text.	Fonts and sizes are used very well, which helps the reader enjoy reading the text.	The slant of the letters is consistent throughout. The letters are clearly formed, spaced equally, and easy to read.
5	The speaker uses effective pacing, volume, intonation, and expression consistently.	The writer uses visuals well. The text and visuals relate to each other.	The title, side heads, page numbers, and bullets are used very well. They help the reader find most information.	Fonts and sizes are used well.	The slant of the letters is almost the same throughout. The letters are clearly formed. Spacing is nearly equal.
4	The speaker uses effective pacing, volume, intonation, and expression fairly consistently.	The writer uses visuals fairly well.	The title, side heads, page numbers, and bullets are used fairly well. They usually help the reader find information.	Fonts and sizes are used fairly well, but could be improved upon.	The slant and form of the letters is usually consistent. The spacing between words is usually equal.
3	The speaker uses effective pacing, volume, intonation, and expression, but not consistently.	The writer uses visuals with the text, but the reader may not understand how they are related.	The writer uses a title, page numbers, or bullets. Improvement is needed.	Fonts and sizes are used well in some places, but make the paper look cluttered in others.	The handwriting is readable. There are some inconsistencies in shape, form, slant, and spacing.
2	The speaker needs to work on pacing, volume, intonation, and expression.	The writer tries to use visuals with the text, but the reader is confused by them.	The writer uses very few markers. This makes it hard for the reader to find and understand the information in the text.	Fonts and sizes are not used well. The paper looks cluttered.	The handwriting is somewhat readable. There are many inconsistencies in shape, form, slant, and spacing.
1	The speaker's techniques are unclear or distracting to the listener.	The visuals do not make sense with the text.	There are no markers such as title, page numbers, bullets, or side heads.	The writer has used too many different fonts and sizes. It is very distracting to the reader.	The letters are not shaped, formed, slanted, or spaced correctly. The paper is very difficult to read.

Scoring RUBRIC for Short and Extended Responses

	Score of 4	Score of 3	Score of 2	Score of 1	Score of 0
EXTENDED-RESPONSE	The response indicates that the student has a thorough understanding of the reading concept embodied in the task. The student has provided a response that is accurate, complete, and fulfills all the requirements of the task. Necessary support and/or examples are included, and the information is clearly text-based.	The response indicates that the student has an understanding of the reading concept embodied in the task. The student has provided a response that is accurate and fulfills all the requirements of the task, but the required support and/or details are not complete or clearly text-based.	The response indicates that the student has a partial understanding of the reading concept embodied in the task. The student has provided a response that includes information that is essentially correct and text-based, but the information is too general or too simplistic. Some of the support and/or examples and requirements of the task may be incomplete or omitted.	The response indicates that the student has very limited understanding of the reading concept embodied in the task. The response is incomplete, may exhibit many flaws, and may not address all requirements of the task.	The response indicates that the student does not demonstrate an understanding of the reading concept embodied in the task. The student has provided a response that is inaccurate; the response has an insufficient amount of information to determine the student's understanding of the task; or the student has failed to respond to the task.
SHORT-RESPONSE			The response indicates that the student has a complete understanding of the reading concept embodied in the task. The student has provided a response that is accurate, complete, and fulfills all the requirements of the task. Necessary support and/or examples are included, and the information given is clearly text-based.	The response indicates that the student has a partial understanding of the reading concept embodied in the task. The student has provided a response that includes information that is essentially correct and text-based, but the information is too general or too simplistic. Some of the support and/or examples may be incomplete or omitted.	The response indicates that the student does not demonstrate an understanding of the reading concept embodied in the task. The response is inaccurate; the response has an insufficient amount of information to determine the student's understanding of the task; or the student has failed to respond to the task.

	Score of 6	Score of 5	Score of 4	Score of 3	Score of 2	Score of 1
FOCUS	The writing is narrowly focused on the main topic and subtopics, and has a clearly defined purpose.	The writing is focused on the topic and purpose.	The writing is generally focused on the topic and purpose with occasional drifts.	The writing is somewhat focused on the topic and purpose with off-topic sentences common.	The writing is related to the topic but does not have a clear focus.	The writing is not focused on the topic and/or purpose.
ORGANIZATION	The ideas in the paper are well-organized and presented in logical order. The paper seems complete to the reader.	The organization of the paper is mostly clear. The paper seems complete.	The organization is mostly clear, but the paper may seem unfinished.	The paper is somewhat organized, but seems unfinished.	There is little organization to the paper.	There is no organization to the paper.
SUPPORT	The writing has strong, specific details. The word choices are clear and fresh.	The writing has strong, specific details and clear word choices.	The writing has supporting details and some variety in word choice.	The writing has few supporting details. It needs more variety in word choice.	The writing uses few supporting details and very little variety in word choice.	There are few or no supporting details. The word choices are unclear, misused, or confusing.
CONVENTIONS	The writer uses a variety of sentences. There are few or no errors in grammar, spelling, punctuation, and capitalization.	The writer uses a variety of sentences. There are a few errors in grammar, spelling, punctuation, and capitalization.	The writer uses some variety in sentences. There are quite a few errors in grammar, spelling, punctuation, and capitalization.	The writer uses simple sentences. There are often errors in grammar, spelling, punctuation, and capitalization.	The writer uses unclear sentences. There are many errors in grammar, spelling, punctuation, and capitalization.	The writer uses awkward sentences. There are numerous errors in grammar, spelling, punctuation, and capitalization.

Scoring RUBRIC for Writing

	Score of 4	Score of 3	Score of 2	Score of 1
IDEAS	The paper is clear and focused. It is engaging and includes enriching details.	The paper is generally clear and includes supporting details, with minor focusing problems.	The paper is somewhat clear but the writer does not effectively use supporting details.	The paper has no clear central theme. The details are either missing or sketchy.
ORGANIZATION	The ideas are well organized and in a logical order.	The ideas are generally well organized and in a logical order.	The ideas are somewhat organized.	The ideas are not well organized and there is no logical order.
VOICE	The writer consistently uses creative ideas and expressions.	The writer's ideas and expressions are generally creative.	The writer's ideas and expressions are somewhat creative.	The writer lacks creativity in ideas and expressions.
WORD CHOICE	The writing uses vivid verbs, specific nouns, and colorful adjectives well. The writing is very detailed.	The writing may use some vivid verbs, specific nouns, and colorful adjectives. The writing is detailed.	The writing may use few interesting words. The writing is only somewhat detailed.	The writing lacks interesting word choice. The writing also lacks detail.
SENTENCE FLUENCY	The writing flows smoothly. The writer uses transitions, and a variety of sentences.	The writing flows generally well. The writer uses some variety in sentences.	The writing flows somewhat. The writer does not use much variety in his or her sentence structure.	The writing does not flow. The writer uses little or no variety in sentences, and some sentences are unclear.
CONVENTIONS	The writer uses standard writing conventions well, with few or no errors.	The writer uses most standard writing conventions well, but makes some errors.	The writer uses some writing conventions well, but makes distracting errors.	The writer makes continuous errors with most writing conventions, making text difficult to read.

© Harcourt

Additional Reading

BLAST OFF! This list is a compilation of the additional theme- and topic-related books cited in the lesson plans. You may wish to use this list to provide students with opportunities **to read at least thirty minutes a day** outside of class.

Theme 4 | DREAM BIG

Aylmore, Angela.
Plucking (Making Music). Steck-Vaughn, 2006. Let's make music! Readers are encouraged to make music creatively in this vibrant book that explores various instruments and how to play them. **EASY**

Boonyadhistarn, Thiranut.
Origami: The Fun and Funky Art of Paper Folding. Capstone, 2006. A do-it-yourself crafts book for children and pre-teens on origami. **CHALLENGE**

Brown, Marc.
Arthur Writes a Story. Little, Brown, 1998. Arthur has to write a story as a homework assignment and keeps changing his idea of what to write as he talks to his friends. *Children's Choice.* **AVERAGE**

Cox, Judy.
My Family Plays Music. Holiday House, 2003. A musical family with talents for playing a variety of instruments enjoys getting together to celebrate. *Children's Choice.* **AVERAGE**

Ehrhardt, Karen.
This Jazz Man. Harcourt, 2006. Presents an introduction to jazz music and nine well-known jazz musicians, set to the rhythm of the traditional song, "This Old Man." Includes brief facts about each musician. **CHALLENGE**

Grejniec, Michael.
What Do You Like? North-South, 1995. Some children learn that they can like the same things and still be different. **EASY**

Jango-Cohen, Judith.
Mount Rushmore. Lerner, 2003. Describes the meaning, history, and creation of the stone monument to four American presidents carved into Mount Rushmore, South Dakota. **AVERAGE**

Leedy, Loreen.
Look at My Book: How Kids Can Write & Illustrate Terrific Books. Holiday House, 2005. Proves ideas and simple directions for writing, illustrating, designing, and binding books. *Award-Winning Author.* **CHALLENGE**

McCloskey, Robert.
Lentil. Puffin, 1978. In this classic story, a boy named Lentil brings his entire community together by joyfully playing his harmonica. *Award-Winning Author/Illustrator.* **CHALLENGE**

Micucci, Charles.
The Life and Times of the Peanut. Houghton Mifflin, 2000. Examines the history and statistics of peanuts, their agriculture, and influence. *Award-Winning Author.* **CHALLENGE**

Nelson, Robin.
From Peanut to Peanut Butter. Lerner, 2003. Briefly introduces the process by which peanuts are made into peanut butter. *Award-Winning Author.* **EASY**

Rotner, Shelley and Kelly, Sheila, ED.D.
What Can You Do?: A Book About Discovering What You Do Well. Millbrook, 2001. Explores different talents that make children unique—from skiing to spelling. *Award-Winning Authors.* **AVERAGE**

Schmid, Eleonore.
The Living Earth. North-South, 2000. Students learn how fragile the Earth's ecosystem is, and how important it is to nourish soil for harvests. *Award-Winning Author.* **AVERAGE**

Steinberg, Laya.
Thesaurus Rex. Barefoot, 2003. Thesaurus Rex, a loveable dinosaur, introduces children to synonyms in this rhyming text that takes him throughout his day. **EASY**

Thomas, Isabel.
Sculpting (Action Art). Heinemann, 2005. Introduces readers to sculpting techniques, sculpting materials, and sculpting processes. **EASY**

Lesson Vocabulary

Theme 4

The following Robust Vocabulary Words are introduced in Lessons 16–20.

Lesson 16	Lesson 17	Lesson 18	Lesson 19	Lesson 20
celebrate	carefree	attract	brew	accurately
cozy	entertain	audible	committee	encountered
disturb	except	concentrate	crop	host
diversion	frail	creative	earn	impulsive
enchanting	horrendous	expression	edible	opponent
instead	journeyed	performance	experiments	originated
procrastinate	melodious	relieved	innovation	sleuths
review	screeching	territory	provide	statue
thrilled	sipped	universal	snug	responds
underneath	stomped	volume	supplies	risk

Cumulative Vocabulary

The following words appear in the *Student Edition* selections in Grade 2.

absolutely*
absurd*
accent*
accolade*
accomplish
accurately
ached*
acquired*
admit
adorable*
adorn*
affinity*
agile*
allowance*
alternatives*
announcement*
anonymous*
area
archaic*
aspire*
assistance*
assortment*
assumed^
attached*
attack
attempt*
attend
attract*
audible*
award
barely
bargain
beautifying*
belongings*

beneath*
bewildered*
beyond
bizarre*
blended
blockades*
boost
brew*
brisk*
budge
bulk*
career*
carefree
carefully
celebrate
challenge*
chilly*
circling*
clambered*
clumsy*
clutched*
collection
comfortable
committee
common
competitive*
compromise*
concentrate
consider*
correspond*
cozy
cradled
crave*
create

creative
crop
crowd (v.)
crumpled
dangerous*
dappled*
defeated*
delay
delivered
deny*
depend*
described*
diligent*
disability*
disappear
discovery
distance
distraught*
distrust*
disturb*
diversion*
drench*
durable*
earn
edge*
edible*
efficient*
enchanting
encountered*
entertain
enthusiast*
entire
entranced*
evasive*

except
exchanged
excitable*
executive*
experiments
expression
extinct*
extinguish*
extravaganza*
extremely
fantastic
feasible
fellow*
feud*
filthy*
fleeing*
flitted*
flutters*
fragrant
frail*
frisky*
gently
gobbled*
grand
grunted
habitat*
halfheartedly*
hazard*
heed*
hesitate*
hilarious
historical
horrendous*
host

housed*
identify*
ignore*
immense*
impatiently*
impressive
improve*
improvise*
impulsive*
industrious*
inexplicable*
innovation*
instantly*
instead
insult (v.)*
itinerary*
journeyed*
jubilant*
juggling*
kin*
last (v.)
leisurely*
literature
location*
lock*
majestic
master (v.)*
melodious*
minor*
misplaced*
mull*
native*
negotiate*
neighborly*

nominate*
noticed
official*
opinionated*
opponent*
original*
originated*
paced*
passion*
patience*
pattern
peered
penalty*
performance
personalities
pleaded
pledge*
plentiful*
position*
positive*
preference*
previous*
principles*
priorities*
procrastinate*
proficient*
provide
prying*
race*
raggedy
ramble*
rare
rattling*
recently*

recreation*
refuse*
relieved
renowned*
replied
report
request*
responds
responsibility*
review
rickety*
risk
role*
romp*
rosy*
route*
satisfied*
scampering
screeching
sealed
selected*
semblance*
separated
serious
serve
settled
sipped
sleuths
smothered
snug*
soaked*
spare
specially*
spectator*

spoiled
squatted*
startle*
statue
stomped
struggle*
strutted*
style*
superior*
supplies
swirling*
technique*
tedious*
territory*
thickens*
thrifty*
thrilled
traction*
trance*
trooped (v.)*
underestimate*
underneath*
universal*
unselfish*
upbeat
ventured*
volume
wilting*
witness*
witty
worthwhile*
zoom*

High-Frequency Words

above
accept
ago
already
believe
bicycle
board
bought
brother
brought
care

caught
cheer
children
clear
coming
cook
covered
curve
different
draw
early

ears
eight
enjoy
enough
especially
everything
exercise
expensive
fair
father
favorite

finally
guess
half
hundred
idea
imagine
impossible
interesting
knee
laughed
learn

lose
million
minute
picture
police
popular
prove
question
quite
shoes
short

sign
sometimes
special
straight
sugar
sure
sweat
though
through
thumb
touch

tough
understand
wash
wear
woman
woods
world
worry
year
young

* Listening and Speaking Vocabulary

Handwriting

Individual students have various levels of handwriting skills, but they all have the desire to communicate effectively. To write correctly, they must be familiar with concepts of

- size (tall, short)
- open and closed
- capital and lowercase letters
- manuscript vs. cursive letters
- letter and word spacing
- punctuation

To assess students' handwriting skills, review samples of their written work. Note whether they use correct letter formation and appropriate size and spacing. Note whether students follow the conventions of print, such as correct capitalization and punctuation. Encourage students to edit and proofread their work and to use editing marks. When writing messages, notes, and letters, or when publishing their writing, students should leave adequate margins and indent new paragraphs to help make their work more readable for their audience.

Stroke and Letter Formation

Most manuscript letters are formed with a continuous stroke, so students do not often pick up their pencils when writing a single letter. When students begin to use cursive handwriting, they will have to lift their pencils from the paper less frequently and will be able to write more fluently. Models for Harcourt and D'Nealian handwriting are provided on pages R14–R17.

Position for Writing

Establishing the correct posture, pen or pencil grip, and paper position for writing will help prevent handwriting problems.

Posture Students should sit with both feet on the floor and with hips to the back of the chair. They can lean forward slightly but should not slouch. The writing surface should be smooth and flat and at a height that allows the upper arms to be perpendicular to the surface and the elbows to be under the shoulders.

Writing Instrument An adult-sized number-two lead pencil is a satisfactory writing tool for most students. As students become proficient in the use of cursive handwriting, have them use pens for writing final drafts. Use your judgment in determining what type of instrument is most suitable.

Paper Position and Pencil Grip The paper is slanted along the line of the student's writing arm, and the student uses his or her nonwriting hand to hold the paper in place. The student holds the pencil or pen slightly above the paint line—about one inch from the lead tip.

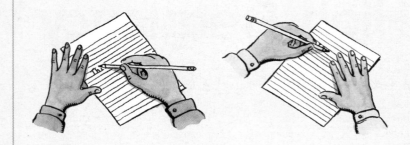

Meeting the Needs of All Learners

The best instruction builds on what students already know and can do. Given the wide range in students' handwriting abilities, a variety of approaches may be needed.

Extra Support For students who need more practice keeping their handwriting legible, one of the most important understandings is that legible writing is important for clear communication. Provide as many opportunities for classroom writing as possible. For example, students can

- **Make a class directory listing the names of their classmates.**
- **Draw and label graphic organizers, pictures, and maps.**
- **Contribute entries weekly to their vocabulary journals.**
- **Write and post messages about class assignments or group activities.**
- **Record observations during activities.**

ELL English-Language Learners can participate in meaningful print experiences. They can

- **Write signs, labels for centers, and other messages.**
- **Label graphic organizers and drawings.**
- **Contribute in group writing activities.**
- **Write independently in journals.**

You may also want to have students practice handwriting skills in their first language.

Challenge To ensure continued rapid advancement of students who come to second grade writing fluently, provide

- **A wide range of writing assignments.**
- **Opportunities for independent writing on self-selected and assigned topics.**

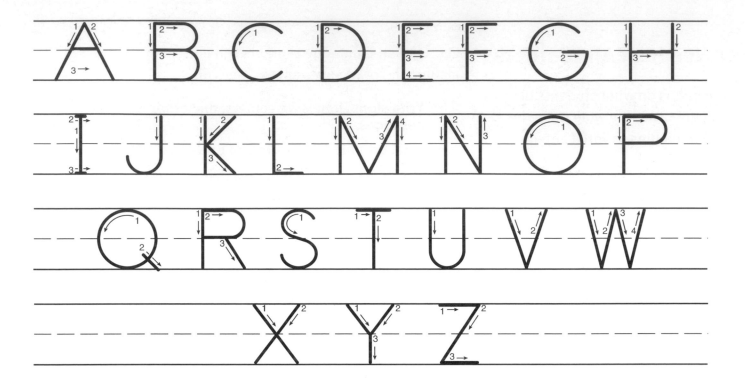

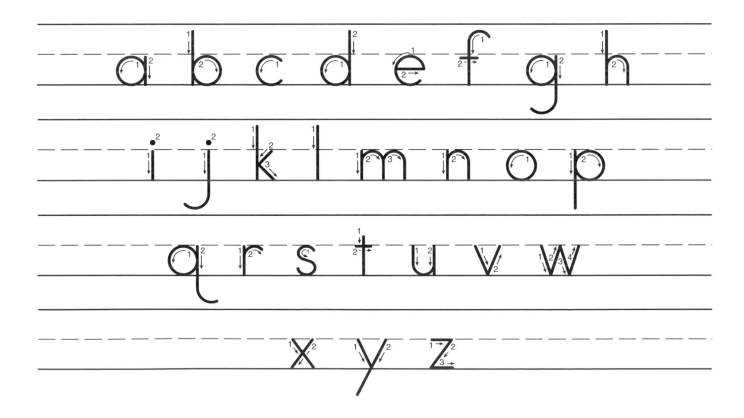

Handwriting Cursive Alphabet

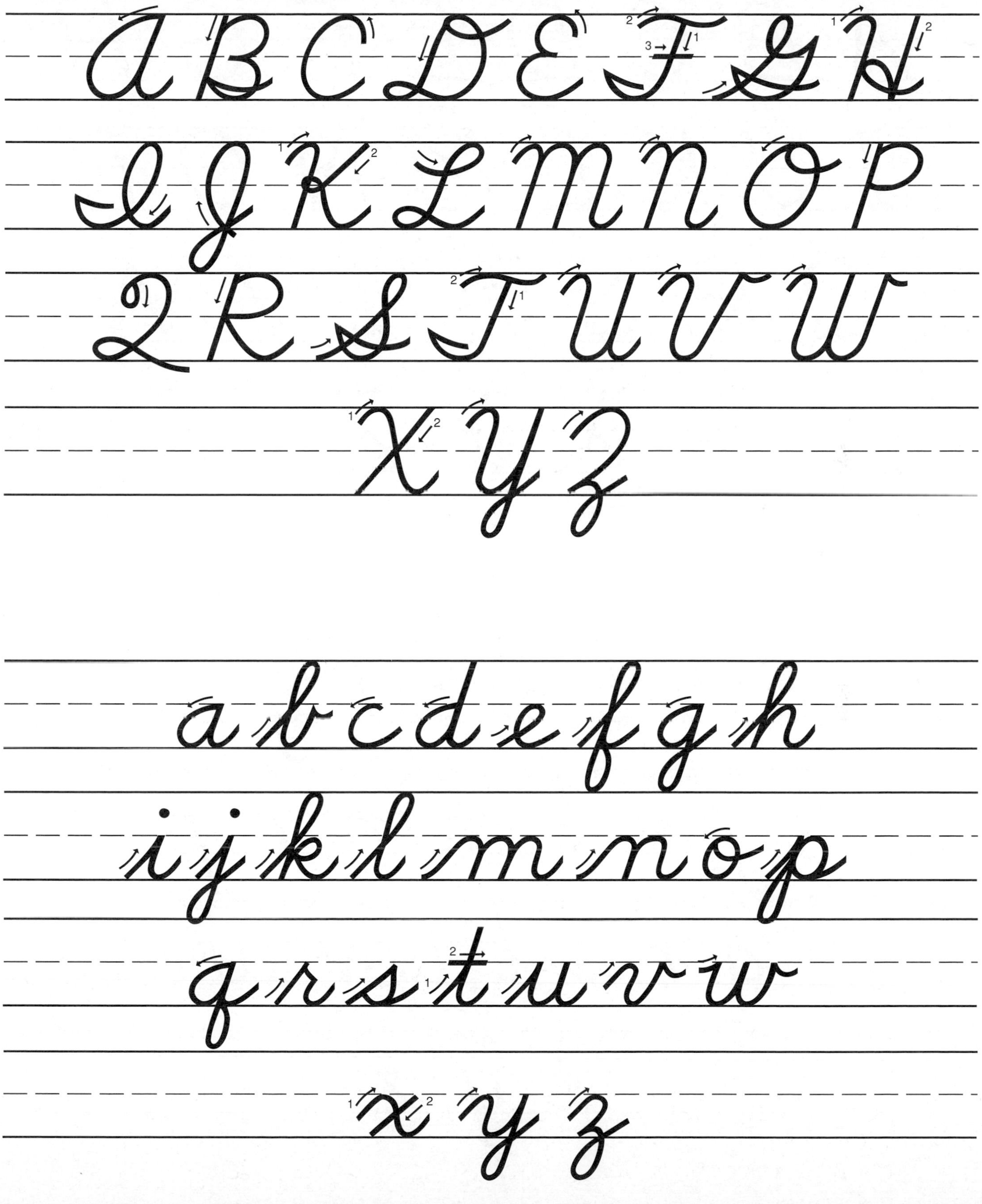
A B C D E F G H
I J K L M N O P
Q R S T U V W
X Y Z
a b c d e f g h
i j k l m n o p
q r s t u v w
x y z

D'Nealian Handwriting Manuscript Alphabet

A B C D E F G H

I J K L M N O P

Q R S T U V W

X Y Z

a b c d e f g h

i j k l m n o p

q r s t u v w

x y z

D'Nealian Handwriting Cursive Alphabet

A B C D E F G H

I J K L M N O P

Q R S T U V W

X Y Z

a b c d e f g h

i j k l m n o p

q r s t u v w

x y z

Introducing the Glossary

MODEL USING THE GLOSSARY Explain to children that a glossary often is included in a book so that readers can find the meanings of words used in the book.

- Read aloud the introductory page.

- Model looking up one or more words.

- Point out how you rely on **alphabetical order** and the **guide words** at the top of the Glossary pages to locate the **entry word**.

As children look over the Glossary, point out that illustrations accompany some of the Student-Friendly Explanations.

Encourage children to look up several words in the Glossary, identifying the correct page and the guide words. Then have them explain how using alphabetical order and the guide words at the top of each page helped them locate the words.

Tell children to use the Glossary to confirm the pronunciation of Vocabulary Words during reading and to help them better understand the meanings of unfamiliar words.

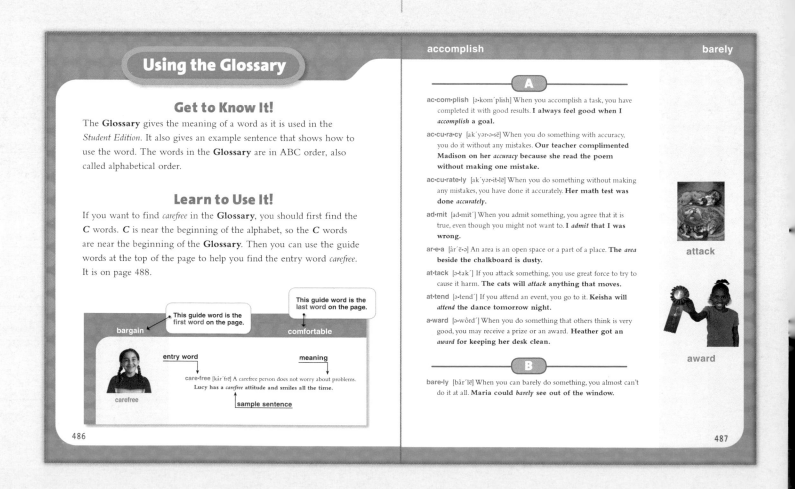

Using the Glossary

Get to Know It!

The **Glossary** gives the meaning of a word as it is used in the *Student Edition*. It also gives an example sentence that shows how to use the word. The words in the **Glossary** are in ABC order, also called alphabetical order.

Learn to Use It!

If you want to find *carefree* in the **Glossary**, you should first find the *C* words. *C* is near the beginning of the alphabet, so the *C* words are near the beginning of the **Glossary**. Then you can use the guide words at the top of the page to help you find the entry word *carefree*. It is on page 488.

This guide word is the first word on the page.

This guide word is the last word on the page.

bargain   comfortable

entry word   meaning

care·free [kâr´frē] A carefree person does not worry about problems. **Lucy has a** *carefree* **attitude and smiles all the time.**

carefree

sample sentence

486

accomplish   barely

A

ac·com·plish [ə·kom´plish] When you accomplish a task, you have completed it with good results. **I always feel good when I** *accomplish* **a goal.**

ac·cu·ra·cy [ak´yər·ə·sē] When you do something with accuracy, you do it without any mistakes. **Our teacher complimented Madison on her** *accuracy* **because she read the poem without making one mistake.**

ac·cu·rate·ly [ak´yər·it·lē] When you do something without making any mistakes, you have done it accurately. **Her math test was done** *accurately*.

ad·mit [ad·mit´] When you admit something, you agree that it is true, even though you might not want to. **I** *admit* **that I was wrong.**

ar·e·a [âr´ē·ə] An area is an open space or a part of a place. **The** *area* **beside the chalkboard is dusty.**

at·tack [ə·tak´] If you attack something, you use great force to try to cause it harm. **The cats will** *attack* **anything that moves.**

at·tend [ə·tend´] If you attend an event, you go to it. **Keisha will** *attend* **the dance tomorrow night.**

a·ward [ə·wôrd´] When you do something that others think is very good, you may receive a prize or an award. **Heather got an** *award* **for keeping her desk clean.**

attack

award

B

bare·ly [bâr´lē] When you can barely do something, you almost can't do it at all. **Maria could** *barely* **see out of the window.**

487

bar·gain [bär´gən] If you didn't have to pay much to buy something good, you got a bargain. **The pencil was a *bargain* at only five cents.**

be·yond [bi·yond´] Something that is beyond something else is farther away. *Beyond* the fence was a field with cows.

blend·ed [blend´əd] When things are blended, they are mixed together so that you can't tell there are separate parts. **Melissa *blended* yellow and blue to make green.**

boost [boost] If you give someone a boost, you help lift him or her up to reach something. **He will need a *boost* to reach the water fountain.**

budge [buj] If you budge something, you move it just a little. **I can't seem to *budge* this heavy box.**

---C---

care·free [kâr´frē] A carefree person does not worry about problems. **Lucy has a *carefree* attitude and smiles all the time.**

care·ful·ly [kâr´fəl·lē] When you do something carefully, you pay close attention to what you are doing so that you don't make a mistake. **Grandma unwraps presents *carefully* so that she doesn't rip the paper.**

cel·e·brate [sel´ə·brāt] If you are happy about something, you may have a party to celebrate. **He likes to *celebrate* his birthday with friends.**

col·lec·tion [kə·lek´shən] When you have a collection, you have a group of things that are kept together. **Jane has a large doll *collection*.**

com·fort·a·ble [kum´fər·tə·bəl] When you are comfortable, you feel good just as you are. **I feel *comfortable* wearing this soft jacket.**

carefree

celebrate

488

com·mit·tee [kə·mit´ē] When you are on a committee, you work with a group of people on a project or for a special reason. **A *committee* will decide who wins the art contest.**

com·mon [kom´ən] If something is common, there is a lot of it or it happens often. **It is *common* to see crabs running on the beach.**

con·cen·trate [kon´sən·trāt] When you concentrate, you put all of your attention on one thing. **You must *concentrate* to solve the puzzle.**

co·zy [kō´zē] If a place is cozy, it makes you feel warm, happy, and comfortable. **The kitten curls up in its *cozy* little cat bed.**

cra·dled [krād´(ə)ld] If you cradle something, you hold it closely as if you were taking care of it. **Laura *cradled* her guinea pig.**

cre·ate [krē·āt´] When you create, you use your imagination to make something new. **He can *create* such funny stories.**

cre·a·tive [krē·ā´tiv] If you are creative, you use new or different ideas to make or do something. **Dawn is very *creative* in the way she uses colors in her art.**

crop [krop] A large planting of one kind of plant is a crop. **We grew a large *crop* of pumpkins this year.**

crowd [kroud] When people or animals gather in large numbers, they crowd together. **The children began to *crowd* around the artist as he painted a picture.**

crum·pled [krum´pəld] If you crumple something, you gently crush it or bunch it up. **The writer *crumpled* his story and threw it in the trash.**

cradled

creative

crop

489

---D---

de·lay [di·lā´] If you delay something, you keep it from happening as soon as it should. **Line up quickly so that we will not *delay* our lunch.**

de·liv·ered [di·liv´ərd] If you deliver something, you take it from one place and bring it to another. **They *delivered* the pizza so quickly!**

dis·ap·pear [dis·ə·pir´] When something disappears, you can't see it anymore. **Watch the bubbles *disappear* in the air!**

dis·cov·er·y [dis·kuv´ər·ē] When you learn something or find something for the first time, you make a discovery. **A way to keep people from getting colds would be an important *discovery*.**

dis·tance [dis´təns] Distance is how far away something is. **The park was at a great *distance* from Li's house.**

---E---

earn [ûrn] When you earn, you get money or some other kind of reward for doing something. **Jimmy will rake leaves to *earn* money for a new baseball mitt.**

en·chant·ing [in·chant´ing] If you think someone or something is enchanting, you think that person or thing is likeable and enjoyable. **The princess was *enchanting* when she smiled.**

en·ter·tain [en·tər·tān´] When you entertain an audience, you do something, such as acting or singing, that you think people will enjoy. **We like to *entertain* our friends with puppet shows.**

en·tire [in·tīr´] An entire thing is all of that thing. **Pedro's *entire* room was clean.**

delivered

entertain

490

ex·cept [ik·sept´] When you talk about every thing except one, you mean all but that one. **Every grade *except* kindergarten can take part in the spelling bee.**

ex·changed [iks·chānjd´] When you exchanged things, you gave something to someone and you got something else in return. **She *exchanged* phone numbers with Sandy so that they could call each other after school.**

ex·per·i·ments [ik·sper´ə·mənts] Experiments are tests to try out an idea or to find out if something is true. **Paul's *experiments* proved that cats do not enjoy baths but do enjoy toys.**

ex·pres·sion [ik·spresh´ən] If you use expression when you speak, you use your voice, your face, or your body to add meaning to what you say. Reading aloud with expression is using your voice to match the action of the story and the characters' feelings. **The *expression* in the storyteller's face and voice made it clear that the character was delighted.**

ex·treme·ly [ik·strēm´lē] Something that is extremely a certain way is very much that way. **The line for the movie was *extremely* long and moved slowly.**

---F---

fan·tas·tic [fan·tas´tik] If something is fantastic, it is wonderful. **The field trip to the zoo was *fantastic*!**

fea·si·ble [fē´zə·bəl] If something is feasible, it can be done. **It is *feasible* that we can get there on time if we hurry.**

fic·tion [fik´shən] Fiction is writing that tells a story with characters, setting, and plot. **Jarod knew that the book was *fiction* because one of the characters was a talking dog.**

fra·grant [frā´grənt] Something that is fragrant has a pleasing, sweet smell. **I can smell the *fragrant* flowers outside the window.**

expression

fragrant

491

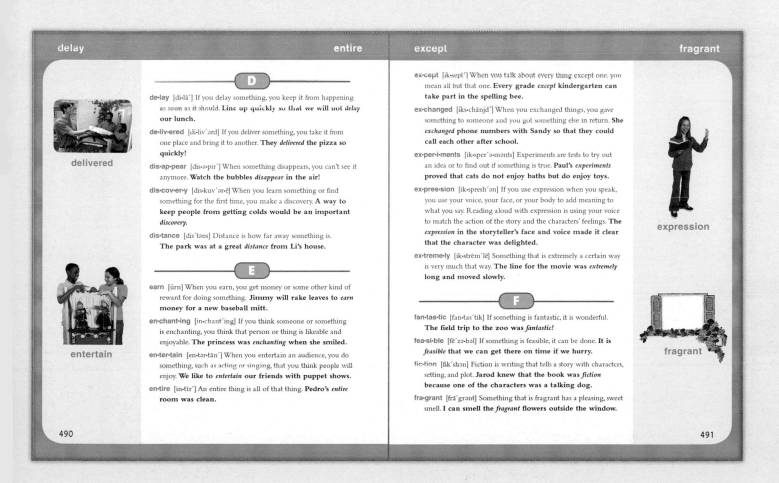

G

gen·re [zhän′rə] Genre is writing style. **Bobby likes detective stories, so he reads books in the mystery *genre*.**

gen·tly [jen′tlē] If you do something gently, you do it in a way that is careful and kind. **Sal petted the newborn colt very *gently*.**

grand [grand] If something is grand, it is important and wonderful. **We saw a *grand* parade on the Fourth of July.**

grunt·ed [grunt′əd] If you grunted, you made a small, deep sound in your throat. **The strong man *grunted* when he lifted the weights.**

grand

H

hi·lar·i·ous [hi·lâr′ē·əs] When you think something is hilarious, you think it is very, very funny. **It was *hilarious* when the giraffe stuck out its tongue!**

his·tor·i·cal [his·tôr′ə·kəl] Something that is historical is part of history. **There were many *historical* items in the museum.**

host [hōst] The host of a program introduces the guests and talks with them. **Ms. Miller will be the *host* for our guest speakers.**

hilarious

I

im·pres·sive [im·pres′iv] When you think something is impressive, you think it is very, very good. **Lisa's speech was *impressive*.**

in·stead [in·sted′] When you do one thing instead of a second thing, you do it in place of the second thing. **Use a pen, *instead* of a pencil, to write the letter.**

492

in·to·na·tion [in′tō·nā′shən] Intonation is the rise and fall of your voice as you read aloud. **The *intonation* of her voice changed when she read the adventure story.**

L

last [last] Something that will last will be able to be used for a long time. **The new steel bridge will *last* a very long time.**

lit·er·a·ture [lit′ər·ə·chər] Stories and poems are kinds of literature. **That poem is my favorite piece of *literature*.**

M

ma·jes·tic [mə·jes′tik] If something is majestic, it seems as important and grand as a king or a queen. **The *majestic* mountain had a cap of white snow.**

majestic

N

non·fic·tion [non′fik′shən] Nonfiction is writing that gives information about a topic. **Juan wanted to learn about dinosaurs, so he checked out a *nonfiction* book.**

no·ticed [nō′tist] If you noticed something, you observed it carefully. **All of us *noticed* how well the music teacher sang.**

P

pat·tern [pat′ərn] When you see a design in something, you are seeing a pattern. **The lighthouse had a *pattern* of stripes.**

peer [pir] If you peer, you look closely at something. **The principal would *peer* through the door to see why we were noisy.** *Another meaning*—A person who is equal to you in age or can do something as well as you is your peer. **Jill was placed on a soccer team with her *peers* from the second grade.**

pattern

493

per·form·ance [pər·fôr′məns] When you sing, dance, or act in front of an audience, you are giving a performance. **Jenny's dance *performance* was very good.**

per·son·al·i·ties [pûr′sən·al′ə·tēz] People's personalities are made up of all the ways they act, think, and feel that make them special. **All of the performers had such friendly *personalities*!**

phras·ing [frāz′ing] Phrasing is grouping words that go together when you read aloud. **When Elsa learned to use *phrasing*, she was able to read smoothly.**

plead·ed [plēd′əd] If you plead, you beg someone for something. **Frank's cousin *pleaded* to be allowed to go with us.**

pro·vide [prə·vīd′] When you provide something, you give it to someone. **Please *provide* me with an address so I can mail the letter.**

punc·tu·a·tion [pungk·chōō·ā′shən] Punctuation marks are used in sentences to show meaning to the reader. **Some *punctuation* marks, such as periods, go at the end of a sentence.**

performance

R

rag·ged·y [rag′id·ē] When something is raggedy, it looks rough and torn at the edges, like a rag. **Our clothes looked *raggedy* after we had been camping for two weeks.**

rare [râr] If something is rare, it is not found or seen very often. **I found a *rare* Spanish coin at the beach.** *Another meaning*—If you like meat that has not been cooked very long, you like it rare. **My uncle orders steak cooked *rare*, but I like mine well done.**

rare

read·ing rate [rē′ding rāt] Your reading rate is the speed at which you can read correctly and also understand what you are reading. **As Josh read more books, his *reading rate* became faster.**

494

re·lieved [ri·lēvd′] If you are relieved, you feel happy because some kind of worry is gone. **I was *relieved* to find my books where I had left them.**

re·plied [ri·plīd′] When you answered someone's question, you replied. **John always *replied* politely to his uncle.**

re·port [ri·pôrt′] When you make a report, you tell what you have learned or found out. **Tim's *report* was about bears.**

re·sponds [ri·spondz′] If someone responds to a question, he or she is giving an answer. **Celeste *responds* often to questions in class.**

responds

re·view [ri·vyōō′] If you say or write what you think about a play, a book, or a movie, you are giving a review. **The *review* in the newspaper said that this movie was very good.**

risk [risk] If you take a risk, you take a chance of harm or a bad result. **You take a *risk* of falling if you run in the rain.**

S

scam·per·ing [skam′pər·ing] If you were scampering, you were running in a playful way. **It's fun to watch the kittens *scampering* and playing in the backyard.**

scampering

screech·ing [skrēch′ing] If you hear a screeching noise, you hear a loud, high sound that can hurt your ears. **The roller coaster made a *screeching* sound when it went around the curve.**

seal [sēl] If you seal something, you close it up tightly. *Seal* **the box before you mail it.** *Another meaning*—A seal is an animal with fins that spends time both in the water and on land. **A *seal* can swim in the water better than it can walk on land.**

screeching

sep·a·rat·ed [sep′ə·rāt·əd] If you separated things, you sorted them into groups. **Tasha *separated* the red blocks from the blue blocks.**

495

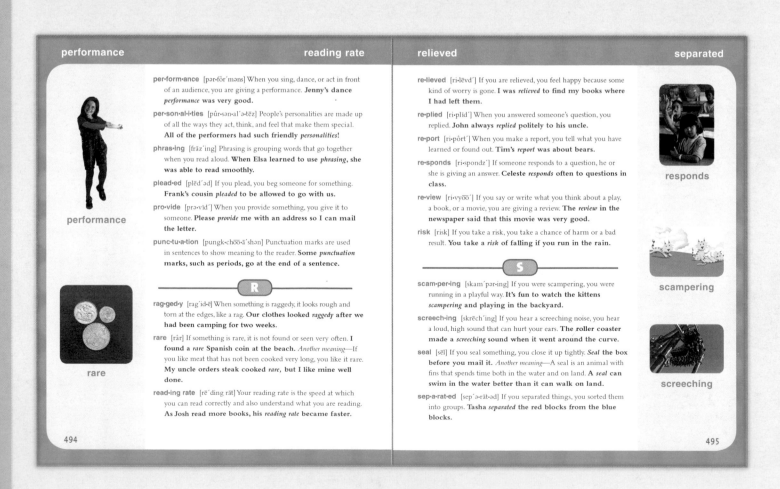

serve

statue

se·ri·ous [sir´ē·əs] When something is serious, it is important and not at all funny. **A fire alarm is a *serious* matter.**

serve [sûrve] When you serve people, you bring them food and drinks. ***Serve* breakfast to your mother.**

set·tled [set´əld] If something settled, it moved slowly until it came to rest. **The soil *settled* to the bottom of the pail of water.**

sipped [sipt] If you sipped, you took a very small drink of something. **Rachel *sipped* the soda slowly so that she would not get hiccups.**

sleuths [slōōths] Sleuths are people who try to solve crimes or mysteries. **Detectives are *sleuths* who work to solve crimes.**

smoth·ered [smuth´ərd] If you smother something, you cover it completely so that it has no air. **We *smothered* the campfire with sand to put out the flames.**

spare [spâr] If you have spare time, money, or space, you have extra that you do not need. **Do you have some *spare* paper that I could use?**

spoiled [spoild] If you spoiled something, you damaged or ruined it. **The painting was *spoiled* when Adam folded it while it was still wet.**

stat·ue [stach´ōō] A statue is a work of art, often showing a person, that can be seen from all sides. It may be made of wood, stone, bronze, or some other hard material. **I saw a *statue* of Abraham Lincoln.**

stomped [stompt] If you stomped, you use your feet to make heavy, pounding steps. **Stan *stomped* his feet on the mat to get the dirt off his shoes.**

supplies

upbeat

sup·plies [sə·plīz´] Supplies are the materials and equipment needed to do a job. **Bring *supplies* such as glue and ribbon for the project.**

syl·la·ble [sil´ə·bəl] A syllable is the smallest part of a word that includes a vowel sound. ***Picnic* is a word that includes two *syllables*.**

 T

thrilled [thrild] If something thrilled you, it made you feel excited and happy. **I was *thrilled* to jump into the swimming pool on such a hot day!**

 U

up·beat [up´bēt] If you are upbeat, you are cheerful. **No matter what happens, Rob is always *upbeat* about it.**

 V

vol·ume [vol´yōōm] When you change the volume on a TV or a radio, you change how loud or soft the sound is. **The *volume* of the radio was too low for me to hear.**

 W

wit·ty [wit´ē] If you are witty, you say things in a clever and funny way. **My uncle is *witty* and tells good jokes.**

Index of Titles and Authors

Page numbers in green refer to biographical information.

Professional Bibliography

Armbruster, B.B., Anderson, T.H., & Ostertag, J.
(1987). Does text structure/summarization instruction facilitate learning from expository text? *Reading Research Quarterly,* 22 (3), 331–346.

Ball, E. & Blachman, B.
(1991). Does phoneme awareness training in kindergarten make a difference in early word recognition and developmental spelling? *Reading Research Quarterly,* 26 (1), 49–66.

Baumann, J.F. & Bergeron, B.S.
(1993). Story map instruction using children's literature: effects on first graders' comprehension of central narrative elements. *Journal of Reading Behavior,* 25 (4), 407–437.

Baumann, J.F., Seifert-Kessell, N., & Jones, L.A.
(1992). Effect of think-aloud instruction on elementary students' comprehension monitoring abilities. *Journal of Reading Behavior,* 24 (2), 143–172.

Beck, I.L., Perfetti, C.A., & McKeown, M.G.
(1982). Effects of long-term vocabulary instruction on lexical access and reading comprehension. *Journal of Educational Psychology,* 74 (4), 506–521.

Bereiter, C. & Bird, M.
(1985). Use of thinking aloud in identification and teaching of reading comprehension strategies. *Cognition and Instruction,* 2, 131–156.

Blachman, B.
(2000). Phonological awareness. In M. Kamil, P. Mosenthal, P.D. Pearson, & R. Barr (Eds.), *Handbook of Reading Research,* (Vol. 3). Mahwah, NJ: Erlbaum.

Blachman, B., Ball, E.W., Black, R.S., & Tangel, D.M.
(1994). Kindergarten teachers develop phoneme awareness in low-income, inner-city classrooms: Does it make a difference? *Reading and Writing: An Interdisciplinary Journal,* 6 (1), 1–18.

Brown, I.S. & Felton, R.H.
(1990). Effects of instruction on beginning reading skills in children at risk for reading disability. *Reading and Writing: An Interdisciplinary Journal,* 2 (3), 223–241.

Chall, J.
(1996). *Learning to read: The great debate* (revised, with a new foreword). New York: McGraw-Hill.

Dowhower, S.L.
(1987). Effects of repeated reading on second-grade transitional readers' fluency and comprehension. *Reading Research Quarterly,* 22 (4), 389–406.

Ehri, L. & Wilce, L.
(1987). Does learning to spell help beginners learn to read words? *Reading Research Quarterly,* 22 (1), 48–65.

Fletcher, J.M. & Lyon, G.R.
(1998) Reading: A research-based approach. In Evers, W.M. (Ed.) *What's Gone Wrong in America's Classroom*, Palo Alto, CA: Hoover Institution Press, Stanford University.

Foorman, B., Francis, D., Fletcher, J., Schatschneider, C., & Mehta, P.
(1998). The role of instruction in learning to read: Preventing reading failure in at-risk children. *Journal of Educational Psychology,* 90 (1), 37–55.

Fukkink, R.G. & de Glopper, K.
(1998). Effects of instruction in deriving word meaning from context: A meta-analysis. *Review of Educational Research,* 68 (4), 450–469.

Gipe, J.P. & Arnold, R.D.
(1979). Teaching vocabulary through familiar associations and contexts. *Journal of Reading Behavior,* 11 (3), 281–285.

Griffith, P.L., Klesius, J.P., & Kromrey, J.D.
(1992). The effect of phonemic awareness on the literacy development of first grade children in a traditional or a whole language classroom. *Journal of Research in Childhood Education,* 6 (2), 85–92.

Juel, C.
(1988). Learning to read and write: A longitudinal study of fifty-four children from first through fourth grades. *Journal of Educational Psychology,* 80, 437–447.

Lundberg, I., Frost, J., & Petersen, O.
(1988). Effects of an extensive program for stimulating phonological awareness in preschool children. *Reading Research Quarterly,* 23 (3), 263–284.

McKeown, M.G., Beck, I.L., Omanson, R.C., & Pople, M.T.
(1985). Some effects of the nature and frequency of vocabulary instruction on the knowledge and use of words. *Reading Research Quarterly,* 20 (5), 522–535.

Nagy, W.E. & Scott, J.A.
(2000). Vocabulary processes. In M. Kamil, P. Mosenthal, P.D. Pearson, & R. Barr (Eds.), *Handbook of Reading Research,* (Vol. 3) Mahwah, NJ: Erlbaum.

National Reading Panel
(2000). *Teaching Children to Read.* National Institute of Child Health and Human Development, National Institutes of Health, Washington, D.C.

O'Connor, R., Jenkins, J.R., & Slocum, T.A.
(1995). Transfer among phonological tasks in kindergarten: Essential instructional content. *Journal of Educational Psychology,* 87 (2), 202–217.

O'Shea, L.J., Sindelar, P.T., & O'Shea, D.J.
(1985). The effects of repeated readings and attentional cues on reading fluency and comprehension. *Journal of Reading Behavior,* 17 (2), 129–142.

Paris, S.G., Cross, D.R., & Lipson, M.Y.
(1984). Informed strategies for learning: A program to improve children's reading awareness and comprehension. *Journal of Educational Psychology,* 76 (6), 1239–1252.

Payne, B.D. & Manning, B.H.
(1992). Basal reader instruction: Effects of comprehension monitoring training on reading comprehension, strategy use and attitude. *Reading Research and Instruction,* 32 (1), 29–38.

Rasinski, T.V., Padak, N., Linek, W., & Sturtevant, E.
(1994). Effects of fluency development on urban second-grade readers. *Journal of Educational Research,* 87 (3), 158–165.

Rinehart, S.D., Stahl, S.A., & Erickson, L.G.
(1986). Some effects of summarization training on reading and studying. *Reading Research Quarterly,* 21 (4), 422–438.

Robbins, C. & Ehri, L.C.
(1994). Reading storybooks to kindergartners helps them learn new vocabulary words. *Journal of Educational Psychology,* 86 (1), 54–64.

Rosenshine, B. & Meister, C.
(1994). Reciprocal teaching: A review of research. *Review of Educational Research,* 64 (4), 479–530.

Rosenshine, B., Meister, C., & Chapman, S.
(1996). Teaching students to generate questions: A review of the intervention studies. *Review of Educational Research,* 66 (2), 181–221.

Sénéchal, M.
(1997). The differential effect of storybook reading on preschoolers' acquisition of expressive and receptive vocabulary. *Journal of Child Language,* 24 (1), 123–138.

Shany, M.T. & Biemiller, A.
(1995) Assisted reading practice: Effects on performance for poor readers in grades 3 and 4. *Reading Research Quarterly,* 30 (3), 382–395.

Sindelar, P.T., Monda, L.E., & O'Shea, L.J.
(1990). Effects of repeated readings on instructional- and mastery-level readers. *Journal of Educational Research,* 83 (4), 220–226.

Snow, C.E., Burns, S.M., & Griffin, P.
(1998). *Preventing Reading Difficulties in Young Children.* Washington, D.C.: National Academy Press.

Stahl, S.A. & Fairbanks, M.M.
(1986). The effects of vocabulary instruction: A model-based meta-analysis. *Review of Educational Research,* 56 (1), 72–110.

Stanovich, K.E.
(1986) Matthew effects in reading: Some consequences of individual differences in the acquisition of literacy. *Reading Research Quarterly,* 21 (4), 360–406.

Torgesen, J., Morgan, S., & Davis, C.
(1992). Effects of two types of phonological awareness training on word learning in kindergarten children. *Journal of Educational Psychology,* 84 (3), 364–370.

Torgesen, J., Wagner, R., Rashotte, C., Rose, E., Lindamood, P., Conway, T., & Garvan, C.
(1999). Preventing reading failure in young children with phonological processing disabilities: Group and individual responses to instruction. *Journal of Educational Psychology,* 91(4), 579–593.

Vellutino, F.R. & Scanlon, D.M.
(1987). Phonological coding, phonological awareness, and reading ability: Evidence from a longitudinal and experimental study. *Merrill-Palmer Quarterly,* 33 (3), 321–363.

White, T.G., Graves, M.F., & Slater, W.H.
(1990). Growth of reading vocabulary in diverse elementary schools: Decoding and word meaning. *Journal of Educational Psychology,* 82 (2), 281–290.

Wixson, K.K.
(1986). Vocabulary instruction and children's comprehension of basal stories. *Reading Research Quarterly,* 21 (3), 317–329.

Program Reviewers & Advisors

Elizabeth A. Adkins,
Teacher
Ford Middle School
Brook Park, Ohio

Jean Bell,
Principal
Littleton Elementary School
Avondale, Arizona

Emily Brown,
Teacher
Orange Center Elementary School
Orlando, Florida

Stephen Bundy,
Teacher
Ventura Elementary School
Kissimmee, Florida

Helen Comba,
Language Arts Supervisor K-5
Southern Boulevard School
Chatham, New Jersey

Marsha Creese,
Reading/Language Arts Consultant
Marlborough Elementary School
Marlborough, Connecticut

Wyndy M. Crozier,
Teacher
Mary Bryant Elementary School
Tampa, Florida

Shirley Eyler,
Principal
Martin Luther King School
Piscataway, New Jersey

Sandy Hoffman,
Teacher
Heights Elementary School
Fort Myers, Florida

Amy Martin,
Reading Coach
Kingswood Elementary School
Wickenburg, Arizona

Rachel A. Musser,
Reading Coach
Chumuckla Elementary School
Jay, Florida

Dr. Carol Newton,
Director of Elementary Curriculum
Millard Public Schools
Omaha, Nebraska

Alda P. Pill,
Teacher
Mandarin Oaks Elementary School
Jacksonville, Florida

Dr. Elizabeth V. Primas,
Director
Office of Curriculum and Instruction
Washington, District of Columbia

Candice Ross,
Staff Development Teacher
A. Mario Loiderman Middle School
Silver Spring, Maryland

Sharon Sailor,
Teacher
Conrad Fischer Elementary School
Elmhurst, Illinois

Lucia Schneck,
Supervisor/Language Arts, Literacy
Irvington Board of Education
Irvington, New Jersey

RuthAnn Shauf,
District Resource Teacher
Hillsborough County Public Schools
Tampa, Florida

Jolene Topping,
Teacher
Palmetto Ridge High School
Bonita Springs, Florida

Betty Tubon,
Bilingual Teacher
New Field Primary School
Chicago, Illinois

Janet White,
Assistant Principal
MacFarlane Park Elementary School
Tampa, Florida

KINDERGARTEN REVIEWERS

Denise Bir,
Teacher
Destin Elementary School
Destin, Florida

Linda H. Butler,
Reading First State Director
Office of Academic Services
Washington, District of Columbia

Julie Elvers,
Teacher
Aldrich Elementary School
Omaha, Nebraska

Rosalyn Glavin,
Principal
Walter White Elementary School
River Rouge, Michigan

Jo Anne M. Kershaw,
Language Arts Program Leader,
K-5
Longhill Administration Building
Trumbull, Connecticut

Beverly Kibbe,
Teacher
Cherry Brook Elementary School
Canton, Connecticut

Bonnie B. Macintosh,
Teacher
Glenallan Elementary School
Silver Spring, Maryland

Laurin MacLeish,
Teacher
Orange Center Elementary School
Orlando, Florida

Mindy Steighner,
Teacher
Randall Elementary School
Waukesha, Wisconsin

Paula Stutzman,
Teacher
Seven Springs Elementary School
New Port Richey, Florida

Martha Tully,
Teacher
Fleming Island Elementary School
Orange Park, Florida

EDITORIAL ADVISORS

Sharon J. Coburn,
National Reading Consultant

Hector J. Ramirez,
National Reading Consultant

Dr. Nancy I. Updegraff,
National Reading Consultant

Scope and Sequence

	Gr K	Gr 1	Gr 2	Gr 3	Gr 4	Gr 5	Gr 6
Reading							
Concepts About Print							
Understand that print provides information	▨						
Understand how print is organized and read	▨						
Know left-to-right and top-to-bottom directionality	▨						
Distinguish letters from words	▨						
Recognize name	▨						
Name and match all uppercase and lowercase letter forms	▨						
Understand the concept of word and construct meaning from shared text, illustrations, graphics, and charts	▨						
Identify letters, words, and sentences	▨						
Recognize that sentences in print are made up of words	▨						
Identify the front cover, back cover, title page, title, and author of a book	▨	▨	▨				
Match oral words to printed words	▨	▨					
Phonemic Awareness							
Understand that spoken words and syllables are made up of sequence of sounds	▨						
Count and track sounds in a syllable, syllables in words, and words in sentences	•						
Know the sounds of letters	•	▨					
Track and represent the number, sameness, difference, and order of two or more isolated phonemes	•						
Match, identify, distinguish, and segment sounds in initial, final, and medial position in single-syllable spoken words	•						
Blend sounds (onset-rimes/phonemes) to make words or syllables	•						
Track and represent changes in syllables and words as target sound is added, substituted, omitted, shifted, or repeated	•						
Distinguish long- and short-vowel sounds in orally stated words	▨						
Identify and produce rhyming words	•						
Decoding: Phonic Analysis							
Understand and apply the alphabetic principle	▨	▨					
Consonants; single, blends, digraphs in initial, final, medial positions	•	•	•	•			
Vowels: short, long, digraphs, r-controlled, variant, schwa	•	•	•	•			
Match all consonant and short-vowel sounds to appropriate letters	•	•					
Understand that as letters in words change, so do the sounds	•	•					
Blend vowel-consonant sounds orally to make words or syllables	•	•					
Blend sounds from letters and letter patterns into recognizable words	•						
Decoding: Structural Analysis							
Inflectional endings, with and without spelling changes: plurals, verb tenses, possessives, comparatives-superlatives		•	•	•			
Contractions, abbreviations, and compound words		•	•	•			
Prefixes, suffixes, derivations, and root words			•	•	•	•	•
Greek and Latin roots					•	•	•
Letter, spelling, and syllable patterns		▨	▨	▨	▨	▨	▨
Phonograms/word families/onset-rimes		▨	▨	▨	▨	▨	▨
Syllable rules and patterns		▨	▨	▨	▨	▨	▨
Decoding: Strategies							
Visual cues: sound/symbol relationships, letter patterns, and spelling patterns	▨	•					
Structural cues: compound words, contractions, inflectional endings, prefixes, suffixes, Greek and Latin roots, root words, spelling patterns, and word families		•					
Cross check visual and structural cues to confirm meaning							

Key:

Shaded area - Explicit Instruction/Modeling/Practice and Application

• *Tested—Assessment Resources: Weekly Lesson Tests, Theme Tests, Benchmark Assessments*

	Gr K	Gr 1	Gr 2	Gr 3	Gr 4	Gr 5	Gr 6
Word Recognition							
One-syllable and high-frequency words	•	•	•				
Common, irregular sight words	•	•	•				
Common abbreviations			•				
Lesson vocabulary		•	•	•	•	•	•
Fluency							
Read aloud in a manner that sounds like natural speech							
Read aloud accurately and with appropriate intonation and expression		•	•	•	•	•	•
Read aloud narrative and expository text with appropriate pacing, intonation, and expression			•	•	•	•	•
Read aloud prose and poetry with rhythm and pace, appropriate intonation, and vocal patterns			•	•	•	•	•
Vocabulary and Concept Development							
Academic language							
Classify-categorize		•					
Antonyms			•	•	•	•	
Synonyms			•	•	•	•	
Homographs				•			
Homophones				•			
Multiple-meaning words			•		•	•	•
Figurative and idiomatic language					•		•
Context/context clues			•	•	•	•	•
Content-area words							
Dictionary, glossary, thesaurus			•	•	•		
Foreign words							•
Connotation-denotation							
Word origins (acronyms, clipped and coined words, regional variations, etymologies, jargon, slang)							
Analogies							
Word structure clues to determine meaning			•	•	•		•
Inflected nouns and verbs, comparatives-superlatives, possessives, compound words, prefixes, suffixes, root words			•	•	•	•	•
Greek and Latin roots, prefixes, suffixes, derivations, and root words					•	•	•
Develop vocabulary							
Listen to and discuss text read aloud							
Read independently							
Use reference books							
Comprehension and Analysis of Text							
Ask/answer questions							
Author's purpose		•	•	•	•	•	
Author's perspective					•	•	
Propaganda/bias							
Background knowledge: prior knowledge and experiences							
Cause-effect		•	•	•	•	•	
Compare-contrast		•	•	•	•	•	•
Details		•	•	•	•	•	•
Directions: one-, two-, multi-step			•	•	•		•
Draw conclusions	•	•			•	•	•
Fact-fiction				•	•	•	

Key:

Shaded area - Explicit Instruction/Modeling/Practice and Application

• *Tested—Assessment Resources: Weekly Lesson Tests, Theme Tests, Benchmark Assessments*

	Gr K	Gr 1	Gr 2	Gr 3	Gr 4	Gr 5	Gr 6
Fact-opinion					•	•	
Higher order thinking							
Analyze, critique and evaluate, synthesize, and visualize text and information							
Interpret information from graphic aids			•	•		•	
Locate information			•		•		
Book parts				•	•		
Text features				•	•		
Alphabetical order		•			•		
Main idea: stated/unstated		•			•	•	•
Main idea and supporting details	•	•	•	•	•	•	•
Make generalizations						•	
Make inferences			•	•	•		•
Make judgments						•	•
Make predictions/predict outcomes	•	•	•	•	•		
Monitor comprehension							
Adjust reading rate, create mental images, reread, read ahead, set/adjust purpose, self-question, summarize/paraphrase, use graphic aids, text features, and text adjuncts					•		
Organize information							
Alphabetical order							
Numerical systems/outlines							
Graphic organizers							
Paraphrase/restate facts and details					•	•	
Preview							
Purpose for reading							
Referents							
Retell stories and ideas			•	•			
Sequence		•		•	•	•	•
Summarize			•	•	•	•	•
Text structure							
Narrative text			•	•	•	•	
Informational text (compare and contrast, cause and effect, sequence/chronological order, proposition and support, problem and solution)			•	•	•	•	•

Study Skills

	Gr K	Gr 1	Gr 2	Gr 3	Gr 4	Gr 5	Gr 6
Follow and give directions			•	•	•		•
Apply plans and strategies: KWL, question-answer relationships, skim and scan, note taking, outline, questioning the author, reciprocal teaching							•
Practice test-taking strategies							

Research and Information

	Gr K	Gr 1	Gr 2	Gr 3	Gr 4	Gr 5	Gr 6
Use resources and references			•		•	•	•
Understand the purpose, structure, and organization of various reference materials							
Title page, table of contents, chapter titles, chapter headings, index, glossary, guide words, citations, end notes, bibliography			•	•	•		
Picture dictionary, software, dictionary, thesaurus, atlas, globe, encyclopedia, telephone directory, on-line information, card catalog, electronic search engines and data bases, almanac, newspaper, journals, periodicals				•	•	•	•
Charts, maps, diagrams, time lines, schedules, calendar, graphs, photos			•		•	•	•
Choose reference materials appropriate to research purpose					•	•	•

Viewing/Media

	Gr K	Gr 1	Gr 2	Gr 3	Gr 4	Gr 5	Gr 6
Interpret information from visuals (graphics, media, including illustrations, tables, maps, charts, graphs, diagrams, time lines)			•	•			•

Key:

Shaded area - Explicit Instruction/Modeling/Practice and Application

    • *Tested—Assessment Resources: Weekly Lesson Tests, Theme Tests, Benchmark Assessments*

	Gr K	Gr 1	Gr 2	Gr 3	Gr 4	Gr 5	Gr 6
Analyze the ways visuals, graphics, and media represent, contribute to, and support meaning of text			░	░	░	░	•
Select, organize, and produce visuals to complement and extend meaning		░	░	░	░	░	░
Use technology or appropriate media to communicate information and ideas		░	░	░	░	░	░
Use technology or appropriate media to compare ideas, information, and viewpoints			░	░	░	░	░
Compare, contrast, and evaluate print and broadcast media				░	░	░	░
Distinguish between fact and opinion					░	░	░
Evaluate the role of media					░	░	░
Analyze media as sources for information, entertainment, persuasion, interpretation of events, and transmission of culture					░	░	░
Identify persuasive and propaganda techniques used in television and identify false and misleading information						░	░
Summarize main concept and list supporting details and identify biases, stereotypes, and persuasive techniques in a nonprint message						░	░
Support opinions with detailed evidence and with visual or media displays that use appropriate technology					░	░	░

Literary Response and Analysis

Genre Characteristics

	Gr K	Gr 1	Gr 2	Gr 3	Gr 4	Gr 5	Gr 6
Know a variety of literary genres and their basic characteristics	░	░	•	•			
Distinguish between fantasy and realistic text	░	░	░	░			
Distinguish between informational and persuasive texts					░	░	░
Understand the distinguishing features of literary and nonfiction texts: everyday print materials, poetry, drama, fantasies, fables, myths, legends, and fairy tales	░	░	•	•			
Explain the appropriateness of the literary forms chosen by an author for a specific purpose					░	░	░

Literary Elements

Plot/Plot Development

	Gr K	Gr 1	Gr 2	Gr 3	Gr 4	Gr 5	Gr 6
Important events	░	•	•	•			
Beginning, middle, ending of story	•	•	•	•			
Problem/solution		•	•	•	░	░	•
Conflict					•	•	•
Conflict and resolution/causes and effects					•	•	•
Compare and contrast			•	•	•	•	

Character

	Gr K	Gr 1	Gr 2	Gr 3	Gr 4	Gr 5	Gr 6
Identify	•	•	•				
Identify, describe, compare and contrast			•	•	•		
Relate characters and events			░	░	░	░	•
Traits, actions, motives				•	•	•	•
Cause for character's actions					•	•	
Character's qualities and effect on plot					•	•	•

Setting

	Gr K	Gr 1	Gr 2	Gr 3	Gr 4	Gr 5	Gr 6
Identify and describe	•	•	•	•			
Compare and contrast			•	•	░	░	•
Relate to problem/resolution					░	░	•

Theme

	Gr K	Gr 1	Gr 2	Gr 3	Gr 4	Gr 5	Gr 6
Theme/essential message		░	░		•	•	•
Universal themes					░	░	•

Mood/Tone

	Gr K	Gr 1	Gr 2	Gr 3	Gr 4	Gr 5	Gr 6
Identify						░	•
Compare and contrast						░	░

Key:

Shaded area - Explicit Instruction/Modeling/Practice and Application

   • *Tested—Assessment Resources: Weekly Lesson Tests, Theme Tests, Benchmark Assessments*

Literary Devices/Author's Craft	Gr K	Gr 1	Gr 2	Gr 3	Gr 4	Gr 5	Gr 6
Rhythm, rhyme, pattern, and repetition							•
Alliteration, onomatopoeia, assonance, imagery						•	•
Figurative language (similes, metaphors, idioms, personification, hyperbole)				•	•	•	•
Characterization/character development				•	•	•	•
Dialogue							
Narrator/narration							
Point of view (first-person, third-person, omniscient)						•	•
Informal language (idioms, slang, jargon, dialect)							

Response to Text

	Gr K	Gr 1	Gr 2	Gr 3	Gr 4	Gr 5	Gr 6
Relate characters and events to own life							
Read to perform a task or learn a new task							
Recollect, talk, and write about books read							
Describe the roles and contributions of authors and illustrators							
Generate alternative endings and identify the reason and impact of the alternatives							
Compare and contrast versions of the same stories that reflect different cultures							
Make connections between information in texts and stories and historical events							
Form ideas about what has been read and use specific information from the text to support these ideas							
Know that the attitudes and values that exist in a time period or culture affect stories and informational articles written during that time period							

Self-Selected Reading

	Gr K	Gr 1	Gr 2	Gr 3	Gr 4	Gr 5	Gr 6
Select material to read for pleasure							
Read a variety of self-selected and assigned literary and informational texts							
Use knowledge of authors' styles, themes, and genres to choose own reading							
Read literature by authors from various cultural and historical backgrounds							

Cultural Awareness

	Gr K	Gr 1	Gr 2	Gr 3	Gr 4	Gr 5	Gr 6
Connect information and events in texts to life and life to text experiences							
Compare language, oral traditions, and literature that reflect customs, regions, and cultures							
Identify how language reflects regions and cultures							
View concepts and issues from diverse perspectives							
Recognize the universality of literary themes across cultures and language							

Writing

Writing Strategies

	Gr K	Gr 1	Gr 2	Gr 3	Gr 4	Gr 5	Gr 6
Writing process: prewriting, drafting, revising, proofreading, publishing							
Collaborative, shared, timed writing, writing to prompts		•	•	•	•	•	•
Evaluate own and others' writing							
Proofread writing to correct convention errors in mechanics, usage, and punctuation, using handbooks and references as appropriate				•	•	•	•

Organization and Focus

	Gr K	Gr 1	Gr 2	Gr 3	Gr 4	Gr 5	Gr 6
Use models and traditional structures for writing							
Select a focus, structure, and viewpoint							
Address purpose, audience, length, and format requirements							
Write single- and multiple-paragraph compositions				•	•	•	•

Revision Skills

	Gr K	Gr 1	Gr 2	Gr 3	Gr 4	Gr 5	Gr 6
Correct sentence fragments and run-ons							
Vary sentence structure, word order, and sentence length							
Combine sentences							

Key:

Shaded area - Explicit Instruction/Modeling/Practice and Application

   • *Tested—Assessment Resources: Weekly Lesson Tests, Theme Tests, Benchmark Assessments*

	Gr K	Gr 1	Gr 2	Gr 3	Gr 4	Gr 5	Gr 6
Improve coherence, unity, consistency, and progression of ideas							
Add, delete, consolidate, clarify, rearrange text							
Choose appropriate and effective words: exact/precise words, vivid words, trite/overused words							
Elaborate: details, examples, dialogue, quotations							
Revise using a rubric							

Penmanship/Handwriting

	Gr K	Gr 1	Gr 2	Gr 3	Gr 4	Gr 5	Gr 6
Write uppercase and lowercase letters							
Write legibly, using appropriate word and letter spacing							
Write legibly, using spacing, margins, and indention							

Writing Applications

	Gr K	Gr 1	Gr 2	Gr 3	Gr 4	Gr 5	Gr 6
Narrative writing (stories, paragraphs, personal narratives, journal, plays, poetry)		•	•	•	•	•	•
Descriptive writing (titles, captions, ads, posters, paragraphs, stories, poems)		•	•				
Expository writing (comparison-contrast, explanation, directions, speech, how-to article, friendly/business letter, news story, essay, report, invitation)					•	•	•
Persuasive writing (paragraph, essay, letter, ad, poster)					•	•	•
Cross-curricular writing (paragraph, report, poster, list, chart)							
Everyday writing (journal, message, forms, notes, summary, label, caption)							

Written and Oral English Language Conventions

Sentence Structure

	Gr K	Gr 1	Gr 2	Gr 3	Gr 4	Gr 5	Gr 6
Types (declarative, interrogative, exclamatory, imperative, interjection)		•	•		•	•	•
Structure (simple, compound, complex, compound-complex)		•	•	•	•	•	•
Parts (subjects/predicates: complete, simple, compound; clauses: independent, dependent, subordinate; phrase)		•	•	•	•	•	•
Direct/indirect object						•	•
Word order		•					

Grammar

	Gr K	Gr 1	Gr 2	Gr 3	Gr 4	Gr 5	Gr 6
Nouns (singular, plural, common, proper, possessive, collective, abstract, concrete, abbreviations, appositives)		•	•	•	•	•	•
Verbs (action, helping, linking, transitive, intransitive, regular, irregular; subject-verb agreement)		•	•	•	•	•	•
Verb tenses (present, past, future; present, past, and future perfect)		•	•	•	•	•	•
Participles; infinitives						•	•
Adjectives (common, proper; articles; comparative, superlative)		•	•	•	•	•	•
Adverbs (place, time, manner, degree)				•	•	•	•
Pronouns (subject, object, possessive, reflexive, demonstrative, antecedents)		•	•	•	•	•	•
Prepositions; prepositional phrases					•	•	•
Conjunctions					•	•	•
Abbreviations, contractions			•	•	•	•	•

Punctuation

	Gr K	Gr 1	Gr 2	Gr 3	Gr 4	Gr 5	Gr 6
Period, exclamation point, or question mark at end of sentences		•	•	•	•	•	•
Comma							
Greeting and closure of a letter						•	•
Dates, locations, and addresses						•	•
For items in a series					•	•	•
Direct quotations					•	•	•
Link two clauses with a conjunction in compound sentences					•	•	•
Quotation Marks							
Dialogue, exact words of a speaker				•	•	•	•
Titles of books, stories, poems, magazines					•	•	•

Key:

Shaded area - Explicit Instruction/Modeling/Practice and Application

- *Tested—Assessment Resources: Weekly Lesson Tests, Theme Tests, Benchmark Assessments*

	Gr K	Gr 1	Gr 2	Gr 3	Gr 4	Gr 5	Gr 6
Parentheses/dash/hyphen						•	•
Apostrophes in possessive case of nouns and in contractions		•	•	•	•	•	•
Underlining or italics to identify title of documents					•	•	•
Colon							
Separate hours and minutes						•	•
Introduce a list						•	•
After the salutation in business letters						•	•
Semicolons to connect dependent clauses							

Capitalization

	Gr K	Gr 1	Gr 2	Gr 3	Gr 4	Gr 5	Gr 6
First word of a sentence, names of people, and the pronoun *I*		•	•	•	•	•	•
Proper nouns, words at the beginning of sentences and greetings, months and days of the week, and titles and initials of people		•	•	•	•	•	•
Geographical names, holidays, historical periods, and special events			•	•			•
Names of magazines, newspapers, works of art, musical compositions, organizations, and the first word in quotations when appropriate						•	•
Use conventions of punctuation and capitalization			•	•	•	•	•

Spelling

	Gr K	Gr 1	Gr 2	Gr 3	Gr 4	Gr 5	Gr 6
Spell independently by using pre-phonetic knowledge, sounds of the alphabet, and knowledge of letter names							
Use spelling approximations and some conventional spelling							
Common, phonetically regular words		•	•	•	•	•	•
Frequently used, irregular words		•	•	•	•	•	•
One-syllable words with consonant blends			•	•	•	•	•
Contractions, compounds, orthographic patterns, and common homophones				•	•	•	•
Greek and Latin roots, inflections, suffixes, prefixes, and syllable constructions				•	•	•	•
Use a variety of strategies and resources to spell words							

Listening and Speaking

Listening Skills and Strategies

	Gr K	Gr 1	Gr 2	Gr 3	Gr 4	Gr 5	Gr 6
Listen to a variety of oral presentations such as stories, poems, skits, songs, personal accounts, or informational speeches							
Listen attentively to the speaker (make eye contact and demonstrate appropriate body language)							
Listen for a purpose							
Follow oral directions (one-, two-, three-, and multi-step)							
For specific information							
For enjoyment							
To distinguish between the speaker's opinions and verifiable facts							
To actively participate in class discussions							
To expand and enhance personal interest and personal preferences							
To identify, analyze, and critique persuasive techniques							
To identify logical fallacies used in oral presentations and media messages							
To make inferences or draw conclusions							
To interpret a speaker's verbal and nonverbal messages, purposes, and perspectives							
To identify the tone, mood, and emotion							
To analyze the use of rhetorical devices for intent and effect							
To evaluate classroom presentations							
To respond to a variety of media and speakers							
To paraphrase/summarize directions and information							
For language reflecting regions and cultures							

Key:

Shaded area - Explicit Instruction/Modeling/Practice and Application

- *Tested—Assessment Resources: Weekly Lesson Tests, Theme Tests, Benchmark Assessments*

	Gr K	Gr 1	Gr 2	Gr 3	Gr 4	Gr 5	Gr 6
To recognize emotional and logical arguments						▓	
To identify the musical elements of language			▓	▓			
Listen critically to relate the speaker's verbal communication to the nonverbal message					▓		

Speaking Skills and Strategies

	Gr K	Gr 1	Gr 2	Gr 3	Gr 4	Gr 5	Gr 6
Speak clearly and audibly and use appropriate volume and pace in different settings	▓	▓	▓	▓	▓	▓	▓
Use formal and informal English appropriately	▓	▓	▓	▓	▓	▓	▓
Follow rules of conversation	▓	▓	▓	▓	▓	▓	▓
Stay on the topic when speaking		▓	▓	▓	▓	▓	▓
Use descriptive words		▓	▓	▓	▓	▓	▓
Recount experiences in a logical sequence		▓	▓	▓	▓	▓	▓
Clarify and support spoken ideas with evidence and examples			▓	▓		▓	▓
Use eye contact, appropriate gestures, and props to enhance oral presentations and engage the audience			▓	▓	▓	▓	▓
Give and follow two-, three-, and four-step directions		▓	▓	▓	▓	▓	▓
Recite poems, rhymes, songs, stories, soliloquies, or dramatic dialogues	▓	▓	▓	▓	▓	▓	▓
Plan and present dramatic interpretations with clear diction, pitch, tempo, and tone			▓	▓	▓	▓	▓
Organize presentations to maintain a clear focus			▓	▓	▓	▓	▓
Use language appropriate to situation, purpose, and audience			▓	▓	▓	▓	▓

Make/deliver

	Gr K	Gr 1	Gr 2	Gr 3	Gr 4	Gr 5	Gr 6
Oral narrative, descriptive, informational, and persuasive presentations			▓	▓	▓	▓	▓
Oral summaries of articles and books			▓	▓	▓	▓	▓
Oral responses to literature			▓	▓	▓	▓	▓
Presentations on problems and solutions			▓	▓	▓	▓	▓
Presentation or speech for specific occasions, audiences, and purposes			▓			▓	▓
Vary language according to situation, audience, and purpose			▓	▓	▓	▓	▓
Select a focus, organizational structure, and point of view for an oral presentation						▓	▓
Participate in classroom activities and discussions	▓	▓	▓	▓	▓	▓	▓

Key:

Shaded area - Explicit Instruction/Modeling/Practice and Application

- Tested— Assessment Resources: Weekly Lesson Tests, Theme Tests, Benchmark Assessments

Index

Abbreviations
See **Decoding/Word Work,**
abbreviations; **Grammar,**
abbreviations
Academic Language
See **Vocabulary**
Academic Vocabulary
See **Student Edition,** Glossary;
Vocabulary
Accelerated Reader, 2-1: T18, T116,
T200, T280; **2-2:** T18, T116, T202,
T286; **2-3:** T18, T114, T282; **2-4:**
T18, T118, T208, T292; **2-5:** T18,
T120, T208, T300; **2-6:** T18, T120,
T204, T294
Accuracy
See **Fluency,** accuracy
Acknowledgments, 2-1: R86; **2-2:** R86;
2-3: R50; **2-4:** R86; **2-5:** R86; **2-6:**
R86
Activity Cards
See **Literacy Centers**
Adjectives
See **Grammar,** adjectives
Adjust Reading Rate
See **Fluency,** reading rate
Advanced Learners, Activities for
See **Differentiated Instruction,**
Advanced Learners, notes for
Advanced Readers
See **Leveled Readers,** Advanced
Readers
Affixes
See **Decoding/Word Work,** inflections,
prefixes, suffixes; **Vocabulary,**
prefixes, suffixes, roots
Alliteration
See **Comprehension Skills,** figurative/
poetic language, alliteration

Alphabetical Order
See **Comprehension Skills,**
alphabetical order
Answer Questions
See **Focus Strategies,** answer
questions
Antonyms
See **Vocabulary,** antonyms
Art
See **Content-Area Reading,** art;
Cross-Curricular Connections,
art; fine art
Articles
See **Genre,** magazine article
Ask Questions
See **Focus Strategies,** ask questions
Assessment, 2-1: A1–A6; **2-2:** A1–A6;
2-3: A1–A6; **2-4:** A1–A6; **2-5:**
A1–A6; **2-6:** A1–A6
See also **Monitor Progress; Rubrics**
Benchmark Assessments, **2-1:** T436;
2-2: T448; **2-3:** T436; **2-4:** T448;
2-5: T456; **2-6:** T458
decoding assessment, **2-1:** T43, T97,
T141, T193, T225, T273, T305,
T355; **2-2:** T43, T97, T141, T227,
T311; **2-3:** T43, T95, T139, T189,
T221, T275, T307, T357; **2-4:**
T43, T143, T233, T285, T317,
T367; **2-5:** T43, T145, T233,
T325; **2-6:** T43, T145, T229, T319
Oral Reading Fluency Assessment,
2-1: T60, T69, T83, T93, T154,
T163, T179, T189, T236, T245,
T259, T269, T318, T327, T341,
T351; **2-2:** T58, T83, T93, T156,
T181, T191, T242, T251, T265,
T275, T328, T353, T363; **2-3:**
T67, T81, T91, T152, T161, T175,
T185, T261, T271, T343, T353;
2-4: T82, T94, T162, T186, T196,
T244, T268, T280, T328, T352,
T362; **2-5:** T60, T84, T96, T162,
T186, T196, T252, T276, T288,

T336, T360, T370; **2-6:** T60, T84,
T96, T182, T192, T270, T282,
T362, T372
Portfolio Opportunity, **2-1:** T73, T111,
T113, T169, T249, T331; **2-2:** T73,
T111, T113, T171, T255, T343;
2-3: T71, T109, T111, T165, T251,
T333; **2-4:** T73, T113, T115, T177,
T259, T343; **2-5:** T115, T117,
T265, T349; **2-6:** T115, T117,
T171, T259, T351
prescriptions, **2-1:** T97, T193, T273,
T355, A2–A6; **2-2:** T97, T195,
T279, T367, A2–A6; **2-3:** T95,
T189, T275, T357, A2–A6; **2-4:**
T99, T201, T285, T367, A2–A6;
2-5: T101, T201, T293, T375,
A2–A6; **2-6:** T101, T197, T287,
T377, A2–A6
Self-Assessment, **2-1:** T110–T111,
T434; **2-2:** T110–T111; **2-3:**
T108–T109, T434; **2-4:** T112–
T113, T446; **2-5:** T114–T115,
T454; **2-6:** T114–T115, T456
Spelling Posttest, **2-1:** T91, T187,
T267, T349, T424; **2-2:** T91,
T189, T273, T361, T436; **2-3:**
T89, T183, T269, T351, T424;
2-4: T93, T195, T279, T361, T436;
2-5: T95, T195, T287, T369, T444;
2-6: T95, T191, T281, T371, T446
Spelling Pretest, **2-1:** T33, T131,
T215, T295, T376; **2-2:** T33,
T131, T217, T301, T388; **2-3:**
T33, T129, T211, T297, T378; **2-4:**
T33, T133, T223, T307, T388;
2-5: T33, T135, T223, T315, T396;
2-6: T33, T135, T219, T309, T398
StoryTown Online Assessment, **2-1:**
T7, T436; **2-2:** T7, T448;
2-3: T7, T436; **2-4:** T7, T448; **2-5:**
T7, T456; **2-6:** T7, T458

Commas

See **Fluency,** punctuation; **Writing,** forms, friendly letter

Common Errors

See **Grammar**

Communication Skills

See **Speaking and Listening**

Compare and Contrast

See **Comprehension Skills,** compare and contrast

Comparing Texts

See **Student Edition,** comparing texts;

Comparisons, Make

See **Comprehension Skills,** comparisons, make

Compound Words

See **Decoding/Word Work,** compound words

Comprehension Skills

See also **Focus Skills**

alphabetical order, **2-5:** T185; **2-6:** T273

author's craft/important details, **2-1:** T234

author's craft/language use, **2-2:** T252, T316; **2-3:** T236, T313, T319; **2-4:** T57, T150, T152, T153, T154, T156, T157, T160, T161, T242; **2-5:** T153; **2-6:** T151, T328, T335

author's purpose

See **Focus Skills**

author's viewpoint **2-3:** T146

cause and effect

See **Focus Skills**

characters

See **Focus Skills**

characters' emotions, **2-1:** T57, T149, T195, T231, T274, T275; **2-2:** T146, T196, T235, T280, T281, T370; **2-3:** T52, T55, T277, T278; **2-4:** T54, T56, T150, T154, T156, T161, T203, T204; **2-5:** T52, T157; **2-6:** T50, T103, T379, T404

characters, identify with, **2-1:** T100; **2-2:** T99, T198, T282, T319, T369; **2-3:** T57, T96, T97; **2-4:** T101, T158, T370; **2-6:** T380

characters' motivations, **2-1:** T50, T148; **2-2:** T55, T282, T369; **2-3:** T50; **2-4:** T157; **2-5:** T332

characters' traits, **2-1:** T150, T232; **2-2:** T56, T100, T368; **2-3:** T48, T232, T430, T431; **2-4:** T53, T55, T394, T395; **2-6:** T102

classify/categorize, **2-1:** T313

compare and contrast, **2-1:** T51, T100, T317, T385; **2-2:** T71, T320; **2-3:** T98, T145, T150, T163, T192, T359, T384; **2-4:** T149, T202, T204, T205; **2-5:** T70–T71, T136, T152, T160, T172–T173, T197, T240, T244; **2-6:** T70, T154, T237, T245, T328

comparisons, make, **2-1:** T98, T277, T310; **2-2:** T52, T54, T282, T320, T370; **2-3:** T190, T226, T312, T313, T314, T315; **2-4:** T187; **2-5:** T334; **2-6:** T359, T368, T369, T379

conclusions, draw, **2-1:** T58, T98, T99, T151, T152, T197, T231, T234, T311, T313, T356, T357, T382, T383; **2-2:** T48, T147, T237, T240, T281, T322, T326, T371, T394; **2-3:** T49, T50, T56, T96, T97, T98, T99, T144, T226, T229, T235, T317, T386; **2-4:** T50, T57, T100, T101, T102, T149, T150, T151, T160, T161, T202, T203, T243, T287, T322, T324, T326, T327, T368, T397, T398; **2-5:** T51, T55, T59, T157, T161, T238, T243, T245, T246, T247, T248, T251, T331, T403; **2-6:** T48, T58, T104, T157, T200, T201, T243, T324, T336, T407

connections, make, **2-5:** T332

details, important, **2-1:** T58, T233, T317; **2-2:** T56, T146, T147, T149, T152, T154, T169, T323, T326; **2-3:** T57, T151, T319; **2-4:** T57, T287, T327; **2-5:** T59, T161, T251, T335; **2-6:** T58, T157, T243, T245, T336

details, note, **2-1:** T48, T49, T51, T52, T53, T54, T55, T56, T57, T71, T98, T146, T147, T152, T165, T166, T167, T194, T196, T230, T275, T276, T310, T311, T312, T314, T315, T356, T357, T358; **2-2:** T48, T49, T50, T51, T98, T99, T100, T196, T198, T238, T280, T281, T324, T370, T393, T442, T443, T444; **2-3:** T48, T49, T52, T53, T96, T97, T98, T144, T145, T147, T150, T190, T192, T228, T233, T276, T278, T312, T313, T314, T316, T317, T318, T358, T359, T360, T383, T385, T430, T431, T432; **2-4:** T49, T51, T53, T100, T148, T149, T151, T152, T202, T203, T204, T238, T286, T287, T288, T322, T323, T324, T325, T326, T368, T369, T370; **2-5:** T48, T50, T52, T54, T56, T58, T73, T238, T242, T245, T330, T333, T401; **2-6:** T48, T49, T53, T55, T56, T70, T102, T103, T150, T153, T155, T198, T199, T200, T237, T240, T241, T244, T289, T290, T324, T325, T326, T329, T331, T332, T333, T335, T378, T452

fact and opinion, **2-1:** T356, T358; **2-6:** T289, T290

fantasy/realistic text, **2-2:** T232, T239, T280

fiction and nonfiction

See **Focus Skills**

figurative/poetic language, **2-2:** T317; **2-4:** T36, T50, T149, T153, T154,

T156, T193; **2-5:** T55, T174, T175; **2-6:** T138, T189

alliteration, **2-1:** T323; **2-4:** T174; **2-5:** T367; **2-6:** T53, T179

metaphor, **2-2:** T153, T261

onomatopoeia, **2-4:** T226, T229, T247, T249, T263

repetition, **2-2:** T333; **2-3:** T63, T137, T391; **2-4:** T256; **2-5:** T93; **2-6:** T65, T163, T179, T227, T267

rhyme, **2-1:** T304; **2-2:** T226, T247, T309, T310; **2-3:** T87, T181, T243, T249, T267, T349, T401; **2-4:** T63, T79, T157, T174, T229, T231, T256, T263, T277, T359; **2-5:** T65, T133, T138, T167, T193, T232, T257, T341; **2-6:** T65, T143, T144, T171, T181, T251, T259

rhythm, **2-1:** T347; **2-2:** T63; **2-3:** T243; **2-4:** T157, T167, T174, T256, T275, T333; **2-5:** T93, T167, T193, T273, T285; **2-6:** T93, T151, T256

follow directions, **2-4:** T68–T69, T172–T173; **2-6:** T81, T87, T89

generalize, **2-1:** T357; **2-5:** T158; **2-6:** T288

genre, **2-1:** T71, T247, T329; **2-2:** T169, T341; **2-3:** T69, T249; **2-4:** T70, T174, T256, T340; **2-5:** T73, T151, T154, T174, T262, T346; **2-6:** T70, T169, T348

graphic aids

See **Focus Skills**

inferences, make

See **Focus Skills**

judgments, make, **2-1:** T310; **2-2:** T321, T324; **2-3:** T228; **2-4:** T153; **2-5:** T159, T404; **2-6:** T153, T234

locate information

See **Focus Skills**

main idea, **2-1:** T234; **2-2:** T283, T317; **2-3:** T51, T149; **2-4:** T270, T286, T289, T371; **2-5:** T249, T262; **2-6:** T63, T105, T238, T242, T289, T290, T291, T378, T381

main idea and details

See **Focus Skills**

metacognitive, **2-6:** T453, T454

personal opinions, express, **2-1:** T99, T100, T234, T357, T358; **2-2:** T50, T51, T101, T154, T235, T237, T282, T321, T370, T396; **2-3:** T55, T146, T316, T358, T359, T384; **2-4:** T49, T51, T100, T101, T102, T160, T325; **2-5:** T50, T150, T155, T160, T246; **2-6:** T151, T153, T155, T156, T241, T244; T289

personal response, **2-1:** T71, T98, T167, T194, T195, T196, T247, T274, T275, T276, T329, T356; **2-2:** T71, T98, T99, T100, T196, T197, T198, T280, T281, T282, T341, T398; **2-3:** T69, T96, T98, T163, T249, T276, T277, T278, T331, T431; **2-4:** T70, T174, T202, T203, T204, T256, T287, T340, T368, T369, T370; **2-5:** T73, T174, T262, T346, T406; **2-6:** T70, T102, T103, T104, T169, T198, T199, T200, T256, T288, T290, T348, T378, T379, T380, T452, T453, T454

plot, **2-2:** T218–T219, T252, T266, T276, T280, T281, T282, T302–T303, T338–T339, T354, T364, T368, T369, T370, T371, T416, T428, T437, T442, T443, T444, T445; **2-4:** T85; **2-5:** T34–T35, T36, T49, T53, T57, T60, T69, T75, T85, T97, T102, T103, T104, T105, T136–T137, T138, T148, T151, T153, T156, T159, T161,

T162, T171, T187, T197, T202, T203, T204, T205, T436; **2-6:** T86

predictions, make and confirm

See **Focus Skills**

prior knowledge, **2-1:** T36, T71, T99, T134, T165, T218, T247, T298, T315, T329; **2-2:** T29, T36, T46, T48, T50, T127, T134, T144, T146, T151, T169, T220, T304, T341; **2-3:** T36, T69, T132, T147, T163, T214, T300; **2-4:** T36, T70, T136, T226, T237, T240, T256, T310, T321, T340; **2-5:** T36, T56, T72, T86, T138, T152, T174, T226, T237, T262, T318, T329, T346; **2-6:** T36, T47, T70, T138, T168, T222, T233, T255, T256, T271, T283, T312, T348

problem/solution, **2-1:** T195, T356; **2-2:** T148, T198, T368; **2-3:** T98, T277; **2-4:** T100, T103, T158, T370; **2-5:** T136, T138, T148, T150, T151, T156, T158, T160, T162, T171, T187, T197; **2-6:** T56, T103, T104

reference sources, use, **2-1:** T12; **2-4:** T12, T254–T255, T338–T339; **2-6:** T12, T152, T273

sequence, **2-1:** T99, T149, T151, T165, T166, T194, T312; **2-2:** T153, T237; **2-3:** T96, T97, T359; **2-4:** T50, T52, T100, T101, T287, T324; **2-5:** T226, T241, T242, T245, T246; **2-6:** T56, T104, T242, T332, T334, T357, T379, T453

setting

See **Focus Skills**

speculate, **2-1:** T196, T314, T316, T357; **2-2:** T152, T197, T235, T240, T325; **2-3:** T147, T148, T191, T192, T227; **2-4:** T241, T248, T368; **2-5:** T48, T54, T59;

review, **2-2:** T188, T350, T360

consonant plus *-le*

> *See* **Decoding/Word Work,**
>> multisyllabic words, syllable
>> pattern C-*le*

consonants

> /s/*c;* /j/*g, dge,* **2-3:** T205, T251,
> T276, T277, T278, T279
>> reintroduce, **2-3:** T208–T211
>> review, **2-3:** T220–221,
>>> T244–T245, T259, T269,
>>> T402–T403

contractions, **2-1:** T53

> reintroduce, **2-5:** T358
> review, **2-5:** T368
> *See also* **Grammar,** contractions

CVC, **2-1:** T31, T80, T90, T129; **2-4:**
T305

CVCe, **2-1:** T209, T212–T215, T224–
T225, T242–243, T249, T256,
T257, T266, T267, T371, T402

digraphs

> /ch/*ch, tch;* /sh/*sh;* /th/*th,* **2-3:** T27,
> T71, T96, T97, T98, T373
>> reintroduce, **2-3:** T30–T33
>> review, **2-3:** T42–T43, T64–
>>> T65, T79, T89, T376
> /n/*kn;* /r/*wr;* /f/*gh, ph,* **2-4:** T27,
> T73, T100, T101, T102, T383
>> reintroduce, **2-4:** T30–T33
>> review, **2-4:** T42–T43, T64–
>>> T65, T81, T93, T386–T387

diphthongs

> *See* **Decoding/Word Work,** vowel
> diphthongs

inflections

> *-ed, -es* (*y* to *i*)
>> introduce, **2-3:** T172
>> review, **2-3:** T182
> *-ed, -ing* (double final consonant)
>> introduce, **2-3:** T258
>> review, **2-3:** T268
> *-ed, -ing* (drop final *e*)
>> introduce, **2-2:** T80

review, **2-2:** T90; **2-4:** T323

> *-ed, -ing* (no spelling change)
>> introduce, **2-1:** T338
>> review, **2-1:** T348
> *-er, -est*
>> introduce, **2-6:** T360
>> review, **2-6:** T370
> *-es* (*f* to *v*)
>> introduce, **2-6:** T180
>> review, **2-6:** T190
> *-s, -es*
>> introduce, **2-1:** 176
>> review, **2-1:** T186

long vowels

> /ā/*a-e;* /ī/*i-e;* /ō/*o-e;* /(y) o͞o/*u-e,*
> **2-1:** T209, T249, T274, T275,
> T276, T277, T371
>> reintroduce, **2-1:** T212–T215
>> review, **2-1:** T224–T225,
>>> T242–243, T257, T267,
>>> T402
> /ā/*ai, ay,* **2-2:** T125, T171, T383
>> reintroduce, **2-2:** T128–T131
>> review, **2-2:** T140–T141,
>>> T162–T163, T179, T189,
>>> T404
> /ā/*ea, ei(gh), ey,* **2-6:** T303, T351
>> reintroduce, **2-6:** T306–T309
>> review, **2-6:** T318–T319,
>>> T344–T345, T361, T371,
>>> T434
> /ē/*ee, ea,* **2-1:** T289, T331, T356,
> T357, T358, T359, T371
>> reintroduce, **2-1:** T292–T295
>> review, **2-1:** T304–T305,
>>> T324–T325, T339, T349,
>>> T412
> /ē/*ey, y,* **2-3:** T123; **2-4:** T131
>> reintroduce, **2-3:** T126–T129
>> review, **2-3:** T138–T139,
>>> T158–T159, T165, T183,
>>> T392–T393
> /ī/*ie, igh,* **2-2:** T27, T73, T383
>> reintroduce, **2-2:** T30–T33

review, **2-2:** T42–T43, T64–
T65, T81, T91, T386–T387

> /ō/*oa, ow,* **2-2:** T295, T343, T383
>> reintroduce, **2-2:** T298–T301
>> review, **2-2:** T310–T311,
>>> T334–T335, T351, T361,
>>> T424

multisyllabic words

> CVC pattern in longer words, **2-6:**
> T360
>> introduce, **2-1:** T80
>> review, **2-1:** T90; **2-4:** T305
> CVCe pattern in longer words
>> introduce, **2-1:** T256
>> review, **2-1:** T266
> syllable pattern C-*le*
>> introduce, **2-2:** T262
>> review, **2-2:** T272
> syllable pattern VCCV
>> introduce, **2-3:** T78
>> review, **2-3:** T88, T340, T350
> syllable pattern V/CV
>> introduce, **2-4:** T184
>> review, **2-4:** T194; **2-5:** T184,
>>> T194
> syllable pattern VC/V
>> introduce, **2-4:** T350
>> review, **2-4:** T360; **2-5:** T184,
>>> T194

nonsense words, **2-1:** T80, T176,
T256, T338; **2-2:** T178, T262,
T350; **2-3:** T78, T340; **2-5:** T274;
2-6: T82

open syllables, **2-3:** T123, T126–
T129, T138–T139, T158–T159,
T165, T183, T373, T392–T393;
2-4: T184, T194; **2-5:** T184, T194

phonograms, **2-1:** T66, T73, T160,
T224, T242, T249, T324; **2-2:**
T64, T162, T248, T334; **2-3:** T64,
T244, T326; **2-4:** T64, T168,
T250, T334; **2-5:** T66, T168,
T258, T342; **2-6:** T66, T164,
T252, T344

T300, T303, T311, T313, T360; **2-3:** T32, T35, T43, T45, T88, T128, T131, T139, T141, T182, T210, T213, T221, T223, T268, T296, T299, T307, T309, T350, T377, T380, T393, T394, T395, T413, T425; **2-4:** T32, T35, T43, T45, T69, T92, T132, T135, T143, T145, T173, T194, T222, T225, T233, T235, T255, T278, T306, T309, T317, T319, T339, T360, T387, T405, T406, T415, T417, T419, T425, T437, T438; **2-5:** T32, T35, T43, T45, T71, T94, T134, T137, T145, T147, T173, T194, T222, T225, T233, T235, T269, T286, T314, T317, T325, T327, T353, T368, T395, T413, T414, T423, T425, T427, T433, T445, T446; **2-6:** T32, T35, T43, T45, T77, T94, T134, T137, T145, T147, T175, T190, T218, T221, T229, T231, T263, T280, T308, T311, T319, T321, T355, T370, T397, T415, T416, T425, T427, T429, T435, T447, T448

Challenge Resource Kit, **2-1:** T5, T19, T117, T201, T281, T363; **2-2:** T5, T19, T117, T203, T287, T375; **2-3:** T5, T19, T115, T197, T283, T365; **2-4:** T5, T19, T119, T209, T293, T375; **2-5:** T5, T19, T121, T209, T301, T383; **2-6:** T5, T19, T121, T205, T295, T385

Challenge Teacher Guide, **2-1:** T5; **2-2:** T5; **2-3:** T5; **2-4:** T5; **2-5:** T5; **2-6:** T5

ELL Copying Masters, **2-1:** T5, T19, T117, T201, T281, T363; **2-2:** T5, T19, T117, T203, T287, T375; **2-3:** T5, T19, T115, T197, T283, T365; **2-4:** T5, T19, T119, T209, T293, T375; **2-5:** T5, T19, T121, T209,

T301, T383; **2-6:** T5, T19, T121, T205, T295, T385

ELL Extra Support Kit, **2-1:** T5, T19, T117, T201, T281, T363; **2-2:** T5, T19, T117, T203, T287, T375; **2-3:** T5, T19, T115, T197, T283, T365; **2-4:** T5, T19, T119, T209, T293, T375; **2-5:** T5, T19, T121, T209, T301, T383; **2-6:** T5, T19, T121, T205, T295, T385

ELL-Level Readers, **2-1:** T101, T197, T277, T359, T433; **2-2:** T101, T199, T283, T371, T445; **2-3:** T99, T193, T279, T361, T433; **2-4:** T103, T205, T289, T371, T445; **2-5:** T105, T205, T297, T379, T453; **2-6:** T105, T201, T291, T381, T455

ELL Teacher Guide, **2-1:** T32, T35, T43, T45, T90, T130, T133, T141, T143, T186, T214, T217, T225, T227, T266, T294, T297, T305, T306, T307, T348, T375, T395, T403, T413, T425; **2-2:** T32, T35, T43, T45, T130, T133, T141, T142, T143, T188, T216, T219, T227, T228, T229, T272, T300, T303, T311, T313, T360; **2-3:** T32, T35, T43, T45, T88, T128, T131, T139, T182, T210, T213, T222, T223, T268, T296, T299, T307, T309, T350, T380, T393, T394, T395, T403, T413, T425; **2-4:** T32, T35, T43, T45, T69, T92, T132, T135, T143, T145, T173, T194, T222, T225, T233, T235, T255, T278, T306, T309, T317, T319, T339, T360, T387, T405, T406, T415, T419, T425, T437, T438; **2-5:** T32, T35, T43, T45, T71, T94, T134, T137, T145, T147, T173, T194, T222, T225, T233, T235, T269, T286, T314, T317, T325, T327, T353, T368,

T395, T413, T414, T423, T425, T427, T433, T445, T446; **2-6:** T32, T35, T43, T45, T77, T94, T134, T137, T145, T147, T175, T190, T218, T221, T229, T231, T263, T280, T308, T311, T319, T321, T355, T370, T415, T416, T425, T427, T429, T435, T447, T448

English-Language Learners, notes for, **2-1:** T13, T31, T32, T34, T35, T36, T43, T44, T45, T49, T52, T56, T62, T63, T68, T75, T87, T90, T93, T94, T105, T109, T129, T130, T132, T133, T134, T141, T142, T143, T147, T154, T156, T162, T171, T186, T189, T214, T217, T218, T225, T226, T227, T232, T239, T244, T266, T269, T270, T293, T296, T298, T306, T311, T320, T321, T326, T333, T345, T351, T352, T375, T380, T389, T394, T395, T403, T406, T413, T425; **2-2:** T13, T32, T35, T36, T43, T44, T45, T49, T53, T61, T71, T105, T109, T129, T130, T133, T134, T141, T142, T143, T147, T150, T164, T181, T185, T188, T191, T216, T219, T220, T227, T228, T229, T234, T235, T250, T257, T259, T272, T275, T299, T300, T302, T303, T304, T311, T312, T313, T320, T328, T330, T331, T336, T339, T347, T360, T363, T387, T390, T401, T405, T406, T407, T415, T418, T425, T437; **2-3:** T13, T31, T32, T35, T36, T43, T44, T45, T49, T51, T61, T66, T73, T85, T88, T91, T92, T103, T107, T127, T128, T131, T132, T139, T140, T141, T146, T160, T167, T182, T185, T186, T210, T212, T213, T214, T221, T222, T223, T227,

Digital Classroom
See **Technology,** technology resources

Digraphs
See **Decoding/Word Work,** digraphs

Diphthongs
See **Decoding/Word Work,** vowel diphthongs

Draft
See **Reading-Writing Connection,** process writing, draft; **Writing,** process writing, draft

Drama
See **Genre,** play; **Readers' Theater**

Draw Conclusions
See **Comprehension Skills,** conclusions, draw

eBook
See **Technology,** technology resources

Echo-Read
See **Fluency,** echo-read

T307, T309, T350, T380, T393, T394, T395, T403, T413, T425; **2-4:** T32, T35, T43, T45, T69, T92, T132, T135, T143, T145, T173, T194, T222, T225, T233, T235, T255, T278, T306, T309, T317, T319, T339, T360, T387, T405, T406, T415, T419, T425, T437, T438; **2-5:** T32, T35, T43, T45, T71, T94, T134, T137, T145, T147, T173, T194, T222, T225, T233, T235, T269, T286, T314, T317, T325, T327, T353, T368, T395, T413, T414, T423, T425, T427, T433, T445, T446; **2-6:** T32, T35, T43, T45, T77, T94, T134, T137, T145, T147, T175, T190, T218, T221, T229, T231, T263, T280, T308, T311, T319, T321, T355, T370, T415, T416, T425, T427, T429, T435, T447, T448

Enrichment
    See **Differentiated Instruction,** Advanced Learners, notes for

ePlanner
    See **Technology,** technology resources, ePlanner

Etymologies
    See **Vocabulary**

Evaluate Writing
    See **Reading-Writing Connection,** writing, evaluate/publish; **Writing,** process writing, evaluate

Everyday Print Materials
    See **Genre,** functional text

Exclamatory Sentences
    See **Grammar,** commands and exclamations

Expository Texts
    See **Genre,** nonfiction

Expository Writing
    See **Writing,** forms, paragraph that explains

Expression
    See **Fluency,** expression

Extra Support Copying Masters
    See **Differentiated Instruction,** Extra Support Copying Masters

Fable
    See **Genre,** fable

Fact and Opinion
    See **Comprehension Skills,** fact and opinion

Family Involvement
    See **Teacher Resource Book,** School-Home Connections

Fantasy
    See **Genre,** fantasy

Fantasy/Realistic Text
    See **Comprehension Skills,** fantasy/realistic text

Fiction
    See **Focus Skills,** fiction and nonfiction; **Genre,** fiction

Fiction and Nonfiction
    See **Focus Skills,** fiction and nonfiction

Fine Art
    See **Cross-Curricular Connections,** art; fine art

Flexible Grouping
    See **Lesson Planner,** 5-Day Small-Group Planner

Fluency
    See also **Assessment,** Oral Reading Fluency Assessment; **Literacy Centers,** Listening and Speaking Center; **Monitor Progress,** fluency accuracy, **2-1:** T29, T36, T60, T69, T83, T93, T98, T99, T100, T101, T127, T134, T154, T163, T179, T189, T194, T195, T196, T197, T298, T379, T380, T383,

T386, T396, T406, T418, T427; **2-3:** T381; **2-4:** T219, T226, T244, T252, T259, T268, T280, T286, T287, T288, T289, T303, T310, T328, T336, T343, T352, T362, T368, T369, T370, T371, T394, T396, T408, T418, T430, T439; **2-5:** T96, T186, T370

Additional Related Reading, **2-1:** T69, T163, T327, R9; **2-2:** T67, T165, T251, T337, R9; **2-3:** T67, T161, T247, T329, R9; **2-4:** T66, T170, T252, T336, R9; **2-5:** T68, T170, T260, T344, R9; **2-6:** T68, T166, T254, T346, R9

choral-read, **2-1:** T98, T101, T197, T274, T277, T294, T340, T347, T359; **2-2:** T181, T242, T392; **2-3:** T64, T158, T261; **2-4:** T82, T162, T256; **2-5:** T252, T276, T336; **2-6:** T84, T169, T182, T362

echo-read, **2-1:** T60, T83, T236, T341; **2-2:** T58, T83, T156, T265, T328; **2-3:** T142, T152, T261, T320; **2-4:** T58, T82, T186, T244, T268, T280, T328, T352; **2-5:** T60, T84, T162, T360; **2-6:** T60, T84, T158, T182, T232, T246, T256, T270, T279, T338, T362

expression, **2-2:** T242, T251, T255, T265, T275, T304, T328, T337, T353, T363; **2-3:** T71, T191, T277, T360, T381, T396, T418, T430; **2-4:** T73, T391, T392; **2-5:** T29, T36, T60, T68, T75, T84, T96, T131, T138, T162, T170, T177, T186, T403, T406, T416, T426, T438, T447

intonation, **2-2:** T36, T58, T67, T83, T134, T156, T165, T181,

T191, T394, T397, T398, T408, T418, T430, T439; **2-3:** T71, T191, T204, T277, T360, T381; **2-4:** T29, T36, T58, T66, T82, T94, T100, T101, T102, T103, T129, T136, T162, T170, T177, T186, T196, T202, T203, T204, T205, T391, T392, T395, T397, T408, T418, T430, T439; **2-5:** T153

pace, **2-1:** T211, T218, T236, T245, T259, T269, T274, T275, T276, T277, T291, T318, T327, T331, T341, T351, T356, T357, T358, T359, T380, T382, T384, T396, T406, T418, T427; **2-3:** T381; **2-5:** T311, T318, T336, T344, T349, T360, T370, T402, T404, T416, T426, T438, T447

partner-read, **2-1:** T73, T100, T154, T169, T179, T196, T259, T275, T276, T318, T327, T331, T356, T357, T358; **2-2:** T73, T171, T343, T353; **2-3:** T238, T247, T251, T261, T333; **2-4:** T66, T73, T101, T102, T103, T170, T177, T202, T203, T204, T205, T252, T259, T286, T287, T289, T336, T343, T368, T369, T370, T371; **2-5:** T68, T75, T170, T260, T344, T349; **2-6:** T68, T102, T104, T105, T166, T171, T198, T199, T201, T254, T259, T288, T289, T290, T291, T346, T351, T381, T452, T453, T454, T455

phrasing, **2-3:** T207, T214, T238, T247, T251, T261, T271, T276, T279, T293, T300, T320, T329, T343, T353,

T358, T359, T361, T382, T386, T396, T406, T418, T427, T430, T432, T433; **2-5:** T288; **2-6:** T215, T246, T254, T259, T270, T282, T288, T290, T291, T312, T338, T346, T362, T372, T378, T379, T381, T402, T404, T406, T407, T418, T428, T440, T449, T452, T453, T454, T455

prosody, **2-2:** T36, T58, T67, T83, T134, T156, T165, T181, T191, T394, T397, T398, T408, T418, T430, T439; **2-3:** T204, T381; **2-4:** T29, T36, T58, T66, T82, T94, T100, T101, T102, T103, T129, T136, T162, T170, T177, T186, T196, T202, T203, T204, T205, T391, T392, T395, T397, T408, T418, T430, T439; **2-5:** T153

punctuation, **2-3:** T29, T36, T58, T81, T91, T97, T98, T99, T122, T125, T132, T152, T161, T175, T185, T190, T192, T193, T372, T383, T385, T396, T406, T418, T427, T430, T432, T433; **2-4:** T66, T82, T196; **2-5:** T84; **2-6:** T29, T36, T60, T68, T73, T84, T96, T102, T103, T104, T105, T131, T138, T158, T166, T171, T182, T192, T198, T199, T201, T222, T270, T282, T305, T312, T346, T351, T362, T402, T405, T418, T428, T440, T449, T452, T453, T454, T455

Readers' Theater, **2-1:** T93, T99, T189, T269, T351, T379–T386, T396, T406, T418, T427; **2-2:** T93, T191, T275, T363, T391– T398, T408, T418, T430,

T439; **2-3:** T91, T185, T271, T278, T353, T381–T386, T396, T406, T418, T427; **2-4:** T94, T196, T280, T288, T362, T391–T398, T408; **2-5:** T96, T177, T196, T288, T370, T399–T406, T416, T426, T438, T447; **2-6:** T73, T96, T103, T192, T282, T372, T378, T379, T380, T401–T408, T418, T428, T440, T449

reading rate, **2-1:** T211, T218, T236, T245, T259, T269, T274, T275, T276, T277, T291, T318, T327, T331, T341, T351, T356, T357, T358, T359, T380, T382, T384, T396, T406, T418, T427; **2-3:** T381; **2-5:** T260, T311, T318, T336, T344, T349, T360, T370, T402, T404, T416, T426, T438, T447

repeated reading, **2-1:** T98, T99, T100, T101, T194, T195, T196, T197, T274, T275, T276, T277, T356, T357, T358, T359, T418; **2-2:** T98, T99, T100, T101, T196, T197, T198, T199, T280, T281, T282, T283, T368, T369, T370, T371, T430, T442, T443, T444, T445; **2-3:** T96, T97, T98, T99, T190, T191, T192, T193, T276, T277, T278, T279, T358, T359, T360, T361; **2-4:** T100, T101, T102, T103, T162, T202, T203, T204, T205, T286, T287, T288, T289, T368, T369, T370, T371, T442, T443, T444, T445; **2-5:** T102, T103, T104, T105, T202, T203, T204, T205, T294, T295, T296, T297, T376,

T398, T420; **2-2:** T60, T76, T86,
T158, T174, T184, T244, T258,
T268, T330, T346, T356; **2-3:**
T60, T74, T84, T154, T168, T178,
T188, T240, T254, T264, T322,
T336, T346, T356, T398, T420;
2-4: T60, T76, T88, T164, T180,
T190, T246, T262, T274, T330,
T346, T356; **2-5:** T62, T78, T90,
T164, T180, T190, T254, T270,
T282, T338, T354, T364; **2-6:**
T62, T78, T90, T160, T176, T186,
T248, T264, T276, T340, T356,
T366, T420

Grammar-Writing Connection
See **Writing,** Grammar-Writing
Connection

Graphic Organizers
See also **Focus Strategies,** use graphic
organizers; **Teacher Resource
Book,** graphic organizers;
Transparencies, graphic
organizers
cause-and-effect diagram, **2-6:** T35,
T46, T50, T57, T60, T69, T73,
T97, T136, T148, T151, T154,
T158, T167, T171, T193
charts, **2-1:** T46, T50, T54, T57, T60,
T90, T92, T94, T134, T144, T154,
T157, T188, T190, T208, T216,
T217, T228, T239, T246, T249,
T266, T268, T270, T298, T321,
T331, T348, T350, T352, T353,
T377, T426; **2-2:** T34, T35, T46,
T68, T70, T132, T133, T144,
T146, T151, T159, T162, T166,
T190, T192, T193, T248, T272,
T274, T276, T277, T320, T334,
T343, T360, T362, T364; **2-3:**
T36, T46, T61, T88, T90, T92,
T142, T155, T182, T184, T212,
T213, T268, T270, T272, T273,
T310, T316, T320, T323, T350,
T352, T354, T373, T379, T394,

T404, T425, T426; **2-4:** T34, T46,
T64, T67, T73, T84, T92, T95,
T96, T110, T134, T142, T165,
T168, T171, T184, T197, T236,
T244, T247, T250, T270, T271,
T278, T281, T282, T308, T331,
T334, T335, T350, T360, T363,
T364, T420, T438; **2-5:** T66, T70,
T71, T87, T94, T168, T173, T177,
T194, T198, T236, T252, T255,
T258, T265, T274, T278, T286,
T289, T290, T324, T345, T349,
T368, T371; **2-6:** T50, T66, T73,
T94, T109, T136, T148, T151,
T154, T164, T167, T171, T176,
T185, T190, T193, T194, T195,
T221, T222, T232, T233, T236,
T249, T252, T255, T259, T273,
T275, T283, T310, T344, T347,
T351, T370, T373, T399, T416,
T426, T447
diagram, **2-6:** T241
graph, **2-2:** T12
sequence chart, **2-2:** T105; **2-4:** T61,
T320, T328; **2-5:** T138, T241,
T328, T336, T349; **2-6:** T161
story map, **2-1:** T105; **2-2:** T61, T218,
T220, T230, T232, T236, T239,
T242, T245, T255, T276, T302,
T303, T304, T314, T316, T325,
T328, T416, T426; **2-3:** T50,
T224, T241; **2-4:** T46, T51, T85,
T107, T111, T146, T158; **2-5:** T34,
T46, T49, T50, T57, T60, T69,
T97, T148, T150, T156, T162,
T165, T197, T397; **2-6:** T322,
T324, T331, T338, T341, T351
Venn diagram, **2-4:** T149; **2-5:** T339,
T415; **2-6:** T226,
word web, **2-1:** T95, T191; **2-2:** T75;
2-3: T93, T187, T355; **2-4:** T198,
T226, T310; **2-5:** T109, T372; **2-6:**
T98, T284, T374

Graphs
See **Focus Skills,** graphic aids;
Graphic Organizers

Handwriting, 2-1: T67, T161, T243,
T325, T349, T403, T421, R12–
R17; **2-2:** T65, T163, T249, T335,
T415, T421, T433, R12–R17; **2-3:**
T65, T245, T327, T403, T409,
T421, R12–R17; **2-4:** T65, T169,
T251, T335, T415, T433, R12–
R17; **2-5:** T67, T101, T169, T259,
T343, T423, T441, R12–R17; **2-6:**
T67, T165, T253, T287, T345,
T425, T443, R12–R17

High-Frequency Words, 2-1: T27, T29,
T41, T44–T45, T65, T68, T79,
T82, T89, T92, T98, T99, T100,
T101, T125, T127, T139, T142–
T143, T159, T162, T175, T178,
T185, T188, T194, T195, T196,
T197, T209, T211, T223, T226–
T227, T241, T244, T255, T258,
T265, T268, T274, T275, T276,
T277, T289, T291, T303, T306–
T307, T323, T326, T337, T340,
T347, T350, T356, T357, T358,
T359, T371, T373, T378, T380,
T391, T395, T401, T405, T411,
T417, T423, T426, T430, T431,
T432, T433; **2-2:** T27, T29, T41,
T44–T45, T63, T66, T79, T82,
T89, T92, T98, T99, T100, T101,
T125, T127, T139, T142–T143,
T161, T164, T177, T180, T187,
T190, T196, T197, T198, T199,
T211, T213, T225, T228–T229,
T247, T250, T261, T264, T271,
T274, T280, T281, T282, T283,
T295, T297, T309, T312–T313,
T333, T336, T349, T352, T359,

Questions
 See **Focus Strategies,** answer questions; ask questions; **Grammar**

Quotation Marks
 See **Grammar,** punctuation; **Writing,** forms, story: dialogue; traits, conventions

r-**Controlled Vowels**
 See **Decoding/Word Work,** *r*-Controlled vowels

Reaching All Learners
 See **Differentiated Instruction**

Read Ahead
 See **Focus Strategies,** read ahead

Read Aloud

2-2: T97, T111, T113, T195, T279, T367, T441, R8; **2-3:** T95, T189, T275, T357, T429, R8; **2-4:** T99, T113, T115, T201, T285, T367, T441, R8; **2-5:** T101, T115, T117, T201, T293, T375, T449, R8; **2-6:** T101, T115, T117, T197, T287, T377, T451, R8

short response, **2-1:** R6; **2-2:** R6; **2-3:** R6; **2-4:** R6; **2-5:** R6; **2-6:** R6

6-point rubric, **2-1:** T97, T111, T113, T193, T273, T355, T429, R7; **2-2:** T97, T111, T113, T195, T279, T367, T441, R7; **2-3:** T189, T275, T357, T429, R7; **2-4:** T99, T113, T115, T201, T285, T367, T441, R7; **2-5:** T101, T115, T117, T201, T293, T375, T449, R7; **2-6:** T101, T115, T117, T197, T287, T377, T451, R7

Scaffolded Language Development
See **Differentiated Instruction,** Scaffolded Language Development

School-Home Connection, 2-1: T13, T435; **2-2:** T13, T447; **2-3:** T13, T435; **2-4:** T13, T447; **2-5:** T13, T455; **2-6:** T13, T457

See also **Teacher Resource Book,** School-Home Connections

Science
See **Content-Area Reading,** science; **Cross-Curricular Connections,** science

Scope and Sequence, 2-1: R26–R33; **2-2:** R26–R33; **2-3:** R26–R33; **2-4:** R26–R33; **2-5:** R26–R33; **2-6:** R26–R33

Second-Language Support
See **English-Language Learners**

Selecting Topics
See **Writing,** process writing, prewrite

Self-Assessment
See **Assessment,** Self-Assessment

Self-Selected Reading
See **Classroom Library Collection**

Sentence Fluency
See **Writing,** traits, sentence fluency

Sentence Structure
See **Grammar,** sentences; **Writing,** forms, sentences

Sentence Variety
See **Writing,** traits, sentence fluency

Sentences
See **Grammar,** sentences

Sequence
See **Comprehension Skills,** sequence

Setting
See **Comprehension Skills,** setting; **Focus Skills,** setting

Short Response
See **Rubrics,** writing, short response

Short Vowels
See **Decoding/Word Work,** short vowels

Sight Words
See **High-Frequency Words**

Singular Possessive Nouns
See **Grammar,** singular possessive nouns

Six Traits of Writing
See **Writing,** traits

Small-Group Instruction
See **Differentiated Instruction,** Small-Group Instruction

Small-Group Planner
See **Lesson Planner,** 5-Day Small-Group Planner

Social Studies
See **Content-Area Reading,** social studies; **Cross-Curricular Connections,** social studies

Software
See **Technology,** technology resources

Sound/Spelling Cards, 2-1: T30, T128, T212, T292, T374, T402; **2-2:** T30, T128, T214, T298, T386, T414; **2-3:** T30, T126, T208, T294, T376, T402; **2-4:** T30, T130, T220, T304, T386, T414; **2-5:** T30, T132, T220, T312, T394, T422; **2-6:** T30, T132, T216, T306, T396, T424

Speaking and Listening
See also **Vocabulary,** robust vocabulary

audience, **2-1:** T418, T427; **2-2:** T430, T439; **2-3:** T418, T427; **2-4:** T430, T439; **2-5:** T438, T447; **2-6:** T440, T449

comprehension/focus skills, **2-1:** T94, T190, T270, T352; **2-2:** T94, T192, T276, T364; **2-3:** T92, T186, T272, T354; **2-4:** T95, T197, T281, T363; **2-5:** T97, T197, T289, T371; **2-6:** T97, T193, T283, T373

oral language, **2-1:** T13, T14–T15, T28, T40, T64, T78, T88, T126, T138, T158, T174, T184, T210, T222, T240, T254, T264, T290, T302, T322, T336, T346, T372, T390, T400, T410, T422, T435; **2-2:** T13, T14–T15, T28, T40, T62, T78, T88, T126, T138, T160, T176, T186, T212, T224, T246, T260, T270, T296, T308, T332, T348, T358, T384, T402, T412, T422, T434, T447; **2-3:** T13, T14–T15, T28, T40, T62, T76, T86, T124, T136, T156, T170, T180, T206, T218, T256, T266, T292, T304, T324, T338, T348, T374, T390, T400, T410, T422, T435; **2-4:** T13, T14–T15, T28, T40, T62, T78, T90, T128, T140, T166, T182, T192, T218, T230, T248, T264, T276, T302, T314, T332, T348, T358, T384, T402, T412, T422, T434,

T447; **2-5:** T13, T14–T15, T28, T40, T64, T80, T92, T130, T142, T166, T182, T192, T218, T230, T256, T272, T284, T310, T322, T340, T356, T366, T392, T410, T420, T430, T442, T455; **2-6:** T13, T14–T15, T28, T40, T64, T80, T92, T130, T142, T162, T178, T188, T214, T226, T250, T266, T278, T304, T316, T342, T358, T368, T394, T412, T422, T432, T444, T457

read aloud, **2-1:** T29, T36, T41, T65, T69, T79, T83, T89, T93, T127, T134, T139, T159, T163, T175, T179, T185, T189, T211, T218, T223, T241, T245, T255, T259, T265, T291, T298, T303, T323, T327, T337, T341, T347, T373, T379, T380–T386, T391, T396, T401, T406, T411, T418, T423, T427; **2-2:** T29, T36, T41, T83, T127, T134, T139, T161, T165, T177, T181, T187, T191, T213, T220, T225, T247, T251, T261, T265, T271, T275, T297, T304, T309, T333, T337, T349, T353, T359, T363, T385, T391, T392–T398, T403, T408, T413, T418, T423, T430, T435, T439; **2-3:** T26, T29, T36, T41, T63, T77, T81, T87, T122, T125, T132, T137, T157, T171, T175, T181, T207, T214, T219, T243, T257, T261, T267, T293, T300, T305, T325, T339, T343, T349, T375, T381, T382–T386, T391, T396, T401, T406, T411, T418, T423, T427; **2-4:** T29, T36, T41, T63, T66, T79, T82, T91, T94, T129, T136, T141, T167, T170, T183, T186, T193, T196, T219, T226, T231, T249, T252, T265, T268, T277, T280, T303, T310, T315, T333, T336, T349,

T352, T359, T362, T385, T391, T392–T398, T403, T408, T413, T418, T423, T430, T435, T439; **2-5:** T29, T36, T41, T65, T68, T81, T84, T93, T96, T131, T138, T143, T167, T170, T183, T186, T193, T196, T219, T226, T231, T257, T260, T273, T276, T285, T288, T311, T318, T323, T341, T344, T357, T360, T367, T370, T393, T399, T400–T406, T411, T416, T421, T426, T431, T438, T443, T447; **2-6:** T29, T36, T41, T65, T81, T84, T93, T96, T131, T138, T143, T163, T166, T179, T182, T189, T192, T215, T222, T227, T251, T254, T267, T270, T279, T282, T305, T312, T317, T343, T346, T359, T362, T369, T372, T395, T401, T402–T408, T413, T418, T423, T428, T433, T440, T445, T449

Speculate

See **Comprehension Skills,** speculate

Spelling

See also **Assessment,** Spelling Posttest; Spelling Pretest

consonants /s/*c* or /j/*g, dge,* words with, **2-3:** T211, T220–T221, T245, T259, T269, T378, T402–T403, T424

digraphs /ch/*ch, tch;* /sh/*sh;* /th/*th,* words with, **2-3:** T33, T42–T43, T65, T79, T89, T378, T424

digraphs /n/*kn;* /r/*wr;* /f/*gh, ph,* words with, **2-4:** T33, T42–T43, T65, T81, T93, T388, T436

diphthong /oi/*oi, oy,* words with, **2-4:** T223, T232–T233, T251, T267, T279, T414, T436

diphthong /ou/*ou, ow,* words with, **2-5:** T33, T42–T43, T67, T83, T95, T396

long vowels /ā/*a-e,* /ī/*i-e,* /ō/*o-e,* /(y)o͞o/*u-e,* words with, **2-1:** T215, T224–T225, T243, T257, T267, T403, T424

long vowel /ā/*ai, ay,* words with, **2-2:** T131, T140–T141, T163, T179, T189, T405, T436

long vowel /ē/*ea, ei(gh), ey,* words with, **2-6:** T309, T318–T319, T345, T361, T371, T435, T446

long vowels /ē/*ee, ea,* words with, **2-1:** T295, T304–T305, T325, T339, T348, T412, T413, T424

long vowel /ē/*ey, y,* words with, **2-3:** T129, T138–139, T159, T173, T183, T378, T392–T393, T424

long vowel /ī/*ie, igh,* words with, **2-2:** T33, T42–T43, T65, T81, T91, T388, T436

long vowel /ō/*oa, ow,* words with, **2-2:** T301, T310–T311, T335, T351, T361, T425, T436

notebook, **2-1:** T43, T67, T141, T161, T225, T243, T305, T325, T393, T403; **2-2:** T43, T65, T141, T163, T227, T249, T311, T335, T415; **2-3:** T43, T65, T139, T159, T221, T245, T307, T327, T393, T403; **2-4:** T43, T65, T143, T169, T233, T251, T317, T335, T415; **2-5:** T43, T67, T145, T169, T233, T259, T325, T343, T423; **2-6:** T43, T67, T145, T165, T181, T229, T253, T319, T345, T425

palindromes, **2-1:** T42

r-Controlled Vowel, /âr/*air, are,* words with, **2-5:** T315, T324–T325, T343, T359, T369, T433

r-Controlled Vowel, /är/*ar,* words with, **2-2:** T217, T226–T227, T249, T263, T273, T415, T436

r-Controlled Vowel, /ir/*ear, eer,* words with, **2-4:** T307, T316–T317, T335, T351, T361, T424, T436

T412, T417, T419, T423, T424, T426; **2-4:** T29, T33, T37, T41, T42, T44, T59, T63, T65, T74, T79, T81, T86, T93, T129, T133, T137, T141, T142, T144, T163, T167, T169, T178, T179, T183, T185, T188, T189, T193, T195, T198, T219, T223, T227, T231, T232, T234, T245, T249, T251, T260, T265, T267, T272, T277, T279, T282, T303, T307, T311, T315, T316, T318, T329, T333, T335, T344, T345, T349, T351, T354, T355, T359, T361, T364, T385, T388, T399, T403, T404, T409, T413, T415, T419, T423, T424, T431, T435, T436; **2-5:** T29, T33, T37, T41, T42, T44, T61, T65, T67, T76, T81, T83, T88, T93, T95, T98, T131, T135, T139, T143, T144, T146, T163, T167, T179, T183, T185, T188, T193, T195, T198, T219, T223, T227, T231, T232, T234, T253, T257, T259, T266, T273, T275, T280, T285, T287, T290, T311, T315, T319, T323, T324, T326, T337, T341, T343, T350, T357, T359, T362, T367, T369, T372, T393, T396, T398, T407, T411, T412, T417, T421, T423, T427, T431, T432, T439, T443, T444; **2-6:** T29, T33, T37, T41, T42, T44, T61, T65, T67, T74, T81, T83, T88, T93, T95, T98, T131, T135, T139, T143, T144, T146, T159, T163, T165, T172, T179, T181, T184, T189, T191, T194, T215, T219, T223, T227, T228, T230, T247, T251, T253, T260, T267, T269, T274, T279, T281, T284, T305, T309, T313, T317, T318, T320, T339, T343, T345, T352, T359, T361, T364, T369, T371, T374,

T395, T398, T400, T409, T413, T414, T419, T423, T425, T429, T433, T434, T441, T445, T446

Word Order, 2-1: T62, T86, T96; **2-4:** T60

Word-Processing Skills
 See **Technology,** technology skills, word-processing skills

Word Recognition
 See **Decoding/Word Work; High-Frequency Words; Word Wall**

Word Sort, 2-1: T92, T188, T268, T348, T350, T426; **2-2:** T92, T190, T274, T362, T438; **2-3:** T88, T90, T184, T270, T326, T327, T350, T352, T426; **2-4:** T64, T73, T92, T232, T250, T278, T282, T316, T364; **2-5:** T42, T94, T144, T185, T194, T198, T290; **2-6:** T66, T94, T185, T190, T194, T195, T252, T259, T275, T280, T344, T370

Words to Know
 See **High-Frequency Words**

Word Wall, 2-1: T29, T41, T65, T79, T89, T127, T139, T159, T175, T185, T211, T223, T241, T255, T265, T291, T303, T323, T337, T347, T373, T391, T401, T411, T423; **2-2:** T29, T41, T63, T79, T89, T127, T139, T161, T177, T187, T213, T225, T247, T261, T271, T297, T309, T333, T349, T359, T385, T403, T413, T423, T435; **2-3:** T29, T41, T63, T77, T87, T125, T137, T157, T171, T181, T207, T219, T243, T257, T267, T293, T305, T325, T339, T349, T375, T391, T401, T411, T423; **2-4:** T29, T41, T63, T79, T91, T129, T141, T167, T183, T193, T219, T231, T249, T265, T277, T303, T315, T333, T349, T359, T385, T403, T413, T423, T435; **2-5:** T29, T41, T65, T81, T93, T131, T143, T167, T183,

T193, T219, T231, T257, T273, T285, T311, T323, T341, T357, T367, T393, T411, T421, T431, T443; **2-6:** T29, T41, T65, T81, T93, T131, T143, T163, T179, T189, T215, T227, T251, T267, T279, T305, T317, T343, T359, T369, T395, T413, T423, T433, T445

 See also **High-Frequency Words**

Word Web
 See **Graphic Organizers,** word web; **Vocabulary,** word web

Word Work, 2-1: T27, T30–T33, T42–T45, T66–T68, T80–T82, T90–T92, T125, T128–T131, T140–T143, T160–T162, T176–T178, T186–T188, T209, T212–T215, T224–T227, T242–T244, T256–T258, T266–T268, T289, T292–T295, T304–T307, T324–T326, T338–T340, T348–T350, T371, T374–T376, T378, T392–T393, T395, T402–T403, T405, T412–T413, T417, T424, T426; **2-2:** T27, T30–T33, T42–T45, T64–T66, T80–T82, T90–T92, T125, T128–T131, T140–T143, T162–T164, T178–T180, T188–T190, T211, T214–T217, T226–T227, T248–T250, T262, T272–T274, T295, T298–T301, T310–T312, T334–T336, T350–T352, T360–T362, T383, T386–T388, T390, T404–T405, T407, T414–415, T417, T424–T425, T429, T436, T438; **2-3:** T27, T30–T33, T42–T45, T64–T66, T78–T80, T88–T90, T123, T126–T129, T138–T141, T158–T160, T172–T174, T182–T184, T205, T208–T211, T220–T221, T268–T270, T291, T294–T296, T306, T326–T328, T340–T341, T350–T352, T373, T376–T378, T380, T392–T393, T395, T402–T403, T405, T412–

publish, **2-1:** T97, T111, T409;
  2-2: T111, T421, T433; **2-3:**
  T109, T409, T429; **2-4:** T113,
  T421, T433; **2-5:** T115, T429;
  2-6: T115, T431, T443
purposes for writing, **2-1:** T104, T112;
  2-2: T104, T112; **2-3:** T102,
  T103, T104–105, T106, T110; **2-4:**
  T106, T114; **2-5:** T108, T116; **2-6:**
  T39, T63, T79, T91, T108, T116
rubrics, **2-1:** T97, T111, T193, T273,
  T355, T429, R6–R8; **2-2:** T97,
  T111, T195, T279, T441, R6–R8;
  2-3: T95, T109, T189, T275, T357,
  T429, R6–R8; **2-4:** T99, T113,
  T201, T285, T367, T441, R6–R8;
  2-5: T101, T115, T201, T293,
  T375, T449, R6–R8; **2-6:** T101,
  T115, T197, T287, T377, T451,
  R6–R8
self-selected writing, **2-1:** T97, T389;
  2-2: T367, T401; **2-3:** T389; **2-4:**
  T401; **2-5:** T409; **2-6:** T411
short response
  See **Writing,** forms, response to
    literature
Student-Writing Models, **2-1:** T106–
  T107; **2-2:** T106–T107; **2-3:**
  T104–T105; **2-4:** T108–T109; **2-5:**
  T110–T111; **2-6:** T110–T111
timed writing, **2-1:** T112–T113; **2-1:**
  T112–T113; **2-3:** T110–T111; **2-4:**
  T114–T115; **2-5:** T116–T117; **2-6:**
  T116–T117
traits
  conventions, **2-1:** T110, T421,
    T429; **2-2:** T110, T433, T441;
    2-3: T107, T108, T217, T241,
    T255, T265, T275, T303,
    T323, T337, T347, T357,
    T421, T429; **2-4:** T112, T433;
    2-5: T114, T201, T441; **2-6:**
    T114, T225, T249, T265, T277,

T287, T315, T341, T357,
    T367, T377, T443, T451
  ideas/focus, **2-1:** T39, T63, T77,
    T87, T108, T137, T157, T173,
    T183, T193, T389, T399; **2-2:**
    T108; **2-3:** T106, T389, T399;
    2-4: T110; **2-5:** T112; **2-6:**
    T39, T63, T79, T91, T101,
    T112, T113, T141, T161, T177,
    T187, T197, T411, T421
  organization, **2-1:** T108, T109,
    T221, T239, T253, T263,
    T273, T301, T321, T335,
    T355; **2-3:** T107; **2-4:** T39,
    T61, T77, T89, T99, T110,
    T111, T139, T165, T181, T191,
    T201, T411; **2-5:** T113; **2-6:**
    T112, T113
  presentation, **2-1:** T111, T409,
    T435; **2-2:** T111, T421, T447;
    2-3: T109, T435; **2-4:** T113,
    T447; **2-5:** T115, T429, T455;
    2-6: T115, T431
  sentence fluency, **2-2:** T109, T110,
    T223, T245, T259, T269, T279,
    T307, T331, T347, T357, T367;
    2-5: T39, T63, T79, T91, T101,
    T113, T165, T181, T191, T201,
    T419, T449
    See also **Writing,** forms,
      friendly letter
  voice, **2-2:** T39; **2-3:** T106, T108
  word choice, **2-2:** T61, T77, T97,
    T108, T109, T137, T159,
    T175, T185, T195; **2-4:** T111,
    T112, T229, T247, T263, T275,
    T285, T313, T331, T347,
    T357, T367, T411; **2-5:** T112,
    T114, T229, T255, T271, T283,
    T293, T321, T339, T355,
    T365, T375, T409
    See also **Writing,** dialogue
Writing on Demand, **2-1:** T112–T113;
  2-2: T112–T113; **2-3:** T110–T111;

2-4: T114–T115; **2-5:** T116–T117;
  2-6: T116–T117
writing prompts, **2-1:** T39, T63, T77,
  T87, T97, T137, T157, T173,
  T183, T193, T221, T239, T253,
  T263, T273, T301, T321, T335,
  T345, T355, T389, T399, T409,
  T421; **2-2:** T39, T61, T77, T87,
  T97, T137, T159, T175, T185,
  T195, T223, T245, T259, T269,
  T279, T307, T331, T347, T357,
  T367, T401, T411, T421, T433;
  2-3: T39, T61, T75, T85, T95,
  T135, T155, T169, T179, T189,
  T217, T241, T255, T265, T275,
  T303, T323, T337, T347, T357,
  T389, T399, T421; **2-4:** T39,
  T61, T77, T89, T99, T139, T165,
  T174, T181, T191, T201, T229,
  T247, T263, T275, T285, T313,
  T331, T340, T347, T357, T367,
  T401, T411, T421, T433; **2-5:**
  T39, T63, T79, T91, T101, T141,
  T165, T181, T191, T201, T229,
  T255, T262, T271, T283, T293,
  T321, T339, T346, T365, T409,
  T419, T429, T441; **2-6:** T39, T63,
  T70, T79, T91, T101, T141, T161,
  T177, T187, T197, T225, T249,
  T256, T265, T277, T287, T315,
  T341, T348, T357, T367, T377,
  T421, T443
writing strategies, **2-1:** T39, T63,
  T108, T137, T157, T221, T239,
  T301, T321; **2-2:** T39, T61, T108,
  T137, T159, T223, T245, T307,
  T331; **2-3:** T39, T61, T106, T135,
  T155, T217, T241, T303, T323;
  2-4: T39, T61, T110, T139, T165,
  T229, T247, T313, T331; **2-5:**
  T39, T63, T112, T141, T165,
  T229, T255, T321, T339; **2-6:**
  T39, T63, T112, T141, T161,
  T225, T249, T315, T341

Acknowledgments

For permission to reprint copyrighted material, grateful acknowledgment is made to the following sources:

Robin Bernard: "Brush Dance" by Robin Bernard. Text copyright © 2004 by Robin Bernard.

Georges Borchardt, Inc., on behalf of the Estate of John Gardner: "Always Be Kind to Animals" and "The Lizard" from *A Child's Bestiary* by John Gardner. Text copyright © 1977 by Boskydell Artists, Ltd.

Boyds Mills Press, Inc.: "Bumblebees" from *Lemonade Sun and Other Summer Poems* by Rebecca Kai Dotlich. Text copyright © 1998 by Rebecca Kai Dotlich. Published by Wordsong, an imprint of Boyds Mills Press.

Curtis Brown, Ltd.: "My Name" from *Kim's Place and Other Poems* by Lee Bennett Hopkins. Text copyright © 1974 by Lee Bennett Hopkins. Published by Henry Holt and Company. "Night Game" from *Sports! Sports! Sports!* by Lee Bennett Hopkins. Text copyright © 1999 by Lee Bennett Hopkins. Published by HarperCollins Publishers. "Quiet Morning" by Karen Winnick from *Climb Into My Lap*, selected by Lee Bennett Hopkins. Text copyright © 1998 by Karen Winnick. Published by Simon & Schuster, Inc.

Sandra Gilbert Brüg: "Soccer Feet" by Sandra Gilbert Brüg.

Estate of William Rossa Cole: "Here Comes the Band" by William Cole.

Trustees of Mrs. F. C. Cornford Will Trust: "Dogs" from *Collected Poems* by Frances Cornford. Published by Cresset Press, 1954.

The Cricket Magazine Group, a division of Carus Publishing Company: "Bat Habits" by Mary Ann Coleman and Oliver M. Coleman, Jr. from *Click* Magazine, April 2004. Text © 2004 by Mary Ann Coleman.

Farrar, Straus and Giroux, LLC: "the drum" from *Spin a Soft Black Song, Revised Edition* by Nikki Giovanni. Text copyright © 1971, 1985 by Nikki Giovanni. "sun" from *All the Small Poems and Fourteen More* by Valerie Worth. Text copyright © 1987, 1994 by Valerie Worth.

Betsy Franco: "At the Bike Rack" by Betsy Franco. Text copyright © 2004 by Betsy Franco.

Emily George: "Aliona Says" by Emily George from *Pocket Poems*, selected by Bobbi Katz. Text copyright © 2004 by Emily George.

Harcourt, Inc.: "Nuts to You and Nuts to Me" from *The Llama Who Had No Pajama: 100 Favorite Poems* by Mary Ann Hoberman. Text copyright © 1974 by Mary Ann Hoberman.

HarperCollins Publishers: "Play" from *Country Pie* by Frank Asch. Text copyright © 1979 by Frank Asch. "Benita Beane" from *Something BIG Has Been Here* by Jack Prelutsky. Text copyright © 1990 by Jack Prelutsky.

Florence Parry Heide: "Rocks" by Florence Parry Heide. Text copyright © 1969 by Florence Parry Heide.

Henry Holt and Company, LLC: "Keepsakes" from *Is Somewhere Always Far Away?* by Leland B. Jacobs. Text © 1967 by Leland B. Jacobs; text © 1995 by Allen D. Jacobs.

Judith Infante: "The Poet Pencil" by Jesús Carlos Soto Morfín, translated by Judith Infante from *The Tree Is Older Than You Are*, selected by Naomi Shihab Nye. Text copyright © by Jesús Carlos Soto Morfín; English translation copyright © by Judith Infante.

Bobbi Katz: From "Did You Ever Think?" by Bobbi Katz. Text copyright © 1981, renewed 1996 by Bobbi Katz. "When You Can Read" from *Could We Be Friends? Poems for Pals* by Bobbi Katz. Text copyright © 1994 by Bobbi Katz. Published by Mondo Publishing, 1997.

Little, Brown and Co. Inc.: "Far Away" from *One at a Time* by David McCord. Text copyright © 1965, 1966 by David McCord.

Gina Maccoby Literary Agency: "Bookworm" by Mary Ann Hoberman. Text copyright © 1975 by Mary Ann Hoberman.

Marian Reiner: "Macaw" from *I Never Told and Other Poems* by Myra Cohn Livingston. Text copyright © 1992 by Myra Cohn Livingston. "Night Creature" from *Little Raccoon and Poems from the Woods* by Lilian Moore. Text copyright © 1975 by Lilian Moore.

Marian Reiner, on behalf of the Boulder Public Library Foundation, Inc.: "My Cat and I" from *Out in the Dark and Daylight* by Aileen Fisher. Text copyright © 1980 by Aileen Fisher.

Marian Reiner, on behalf of Constance Levy: "Cowscape" from *A Crack in the Clouds and Other Poems* by Constance Levy. Text copyright © 1998 by Constance Kling Levy. "Hide-and-Seek" from *A Tree Place and Other Poems* by Constance Levy. Text copyright © 1994 by Constance Kling Levy.

Marian Reiner, on behalf of Judith Thurman: "New Notebook" from *Flashlight and Other Poems* by Judith Thurman. Text copyright © 1976 by Judith Thurman.

Joanne M. Roberts: "My Snake" by Jo Roberts. Text copyright © 2004 by Jo Roberts.

Scholastic Inc.: "The Swarm of Bees" by Elsa Gorham Baker, "Sharing the Swing" by Alice Crowell Hoffman, "My Bike" by Bobbe Indgin, and "Tiny Seeds" by Vera L. Stafford from *Poetry Place Anthology*. Text copyright © 1983 by Edgell Communications, Inc. Published by Scholastic Teaching Resources.

Tiger Tales, an imprint of ME Media LLC, Wilton, CT: "Chimpanzee" from *Rumble in the Jungle* by Giles Andreae. Text © 1996 by Giles Andreae.

S©ott Treimel NY: "First Snow" and "Grown-ups" from *Seasons: A Book of Poems* by Charlotte Zolotow. Text copyright © 2002 by Charlotte Zolotow. "People" from *All That Sunlight* by Charlotte Zolotow. Text copyright © 1967, text copyright renewed © 1995 by Charlotte Zolotow. Published by HarperCollins Publishers.

Photo Credits

Teacher's Notes

Teacher's Notes

Teacher's Notes

Teacher's Notes